P9-CDH-318

Wissenschaftliche Untersuchungen
zum Neuen Testament · 2. Reihe

Herausgegeben von
Martin Hengel und Otfried Hofius

68

Personal Speech-Ethics
in the Epistle of James

by

William R. Baker

Bob,
I thought you might like to see this
actually completed. Thanks for you
friendship and support.
Bill

J.C.B. Mohr (Paul Siebeck) Tübingen

Die Deutsche Bibliothek – CIP-Einheitsaufnahme

Baker, William R.:
Personal speech ethics in the epistle of James / by William R. Baker.
– Tübingen: Mohr, 1995
   (Wissenschaftliche Untersuchungen zum Neuen Testament: Reihe 2; 68)
   ISBN 3-16-145958-X
NE: Wissenschaftliche Untersuchungen zum Neuen Testament / 02

The book was typeset by Sam Boyd Enterprise in Singapore, printed by Gulde-Druck in Tübingen on acid-free paper from Papierfabrik Niefern and bound by Heinr. Koch in Tübingen.

Printed in Germany.

ISSN 0340-9570

To the memory of my father

Enned R. Baker

Though he died in 1973,
he had so much to do with the completion of this thesis.

Preface

The term "personal speech-ethics" sounds foreign to contemporary man. Not only is the term unfamiliar, but the concern which it describes is far removed from what people today associate with their endeavor to be ethical. Time and again during my course of study, upon announcing the title of my thesis I have been met with looks of bewilderment from academics and non-academics alike. I doubt this would have happened in the ancient Mediterranean world. People in that time understood that morality in speaking is intrisic to the fabric of society, essential for friendship, vital for learning, and, indeed, plays a part in most beneficial aspects of human existence.

Any work of this kind puts the author in debt to many people, not only for academic assistance but also for practical help and for personal support and friendship.

In the first category, I would like to thank Professor Robin S. Barbour, Professor I. Howard Marshall, and Dr. Ruth Edwards of the Department of New Testament Exegesis in the Divinity Faculty at King's College, University of Aberdeen.

In the second category, I would like to thank Teresa Clark, the Divinity secretary, and also the library personnel at the now closed King's College Library, especially the always cheerful and efficient Jennifer at the information desk.

In the third category, I would like to thank my mother, friends at the Christian Church of Hoffman Estates (Illinois), friends at Bridge of Don Baptist Church (Aberdeen), and these in the Aberdeen postgraduate community: Rolando and Aida Aranzamendez, Doug and Donna Barranger, Hans and Susan Bayer, Barry and Kathy Blackburn, Craig and Fran Blomberg, Gary and Carol Burge, Danny and Linda Clymer, Dean Fleming, Conrad and Shanesse Gempf, Russ and Linda Glessner, Skip and Micky Heard, Pi Shün and Yun Li Kang, Henry and Lois Lazenby, Bob and Marilyn Lowery, Mike and Krystal Nola, Eckart and Barbara Schnabel, Gary and Karen Shogren, and Phil and Anne Towner. Finally, I would like to thank my wife, Joni, whose help is of all three types mentioned above and much, much more.

Finally, I would like to thank St. Louis Christian College for granting me time to work on the revision of this thesis for publication and to Martin Hengel and Georg Siebeck at J. C. B. Mohr for their interest in having this thesis published and in their patient assistance.

My hope is that this monograph will not only benefit the reader academically but also motivate the reader — as the author of James and the authors of the ancient Mediterranean literature were trying to do for their readers — to speak truly, with integrity, with grace, with benefit to others, and with all honesty to God.

November 1994   William R. Baker

Table of Contents

Preface   v

Abbreviations   xiii

General Introduction   1

Specialised Introduction   6

    Epistle of James   6
    Wisdom   7
    Paraenesis   12
    Theology and Ethics   15
    Use in Moral Instruction   21

Part I.

The Rudiments of Speech-Ethics

Chapter 1: Background   23

    Near Eastern Wisdom Literature   23
        Controlled Speech   23
        Listening, Words, and Deeds   25
        The Power of Words   26
    Old Testament   27
        Controlled Speech   27
        Listening, Words, and Deeds   33
        The Power of Words   38
    Apocrypha and Pseudepigrapha   43
        Controlled Speech   43
        Listening   46
        Words and Deeds   47
        The Power of Words   48
    Qumranic Literature   49
        Controlled Speech   49
        Listening   52
        Words and Deeds   53
        The Power of Words   54
    Rabbinic Literature   55
        Controlled Speech   55
        Listening   58
        Words and Deeds   58
        The Power of Words   59

Graeco-Roman Literature 60
    Controlled Speech 60
    Listening 64
    Words and Deeds 66
    The Power of Words 67
Philonic Literature 69
    Controlled Speech 69
    Listening 71
    Words and Deeds 72
    The Power of Words 74
New Testament 75
    Controlled Speech 75
    Listening 79
    Words and Deeds 80
    The Power of Words 81

Chapter 2: Epistle of James 84

Exegesis 84
    James 1:19–27 84
    James 1:19 84
    James 1:20 88
    James 1:21 89
    James 1:22 92
    James 1:23–24 93
    James 1:25 94
    James 1:26 96
    James 1:27 97
Analysis 99
    Controlled Speech 99
    Listening 100
    Words and Deeds 101
    The Power of Words 102

Part II.

The Evil of the Tongue

Chapter 3: Background 105

Near Eastern Wisdom Literature 105
Old Testament 105
Apocrypha and Pseudepigrapha 111
Qumranic Literature 113
Rabbinic Literature 115
Graeco-Roman Literature 117
Philonic Literature 120
New Testament 121

Chapter 4: Epistle of James 123

Exegesis 123
    James 3:1—12 123
    James 3:1 123
    James 3:2 124
    James 3:3—4 124
    James 3:5 125
    James 3:6 126
    James 3:7—8 128
    James 3:9 130
    James 3:10—12 131
    James 4:1—2b 135
Analysis 136

Part III.
Speech in Inter-Human Relationships

Chapter 5: Background 139

Near Eastern Wisdom Literature 139
Old Testament 140
    Gossip 141
    Slander 142
    Mockery 143
    Cursing 144
    Hot-tempered Speech 145
    Flattery and Deceit 145
    Tactlessness 146
    Perjury 146
    Partiality 147
    Reproof 148
Apocrypha and Pseudepigrapha 149
Qumranic Literature 152
Rabbinic Literature 154
Graeco-Roman Literature 159
Philonic Literature 168
New Testament 170

Chapter 6: Epistle of James 175

Exegesis 175
    James 3:18 175
    James 4:1—2b 177
    James 4:11—12 178
    James 5:9 180
Analysis 181

Part IV.

Speech in Human-Devine Relationships

Chapter 7: Background 187

   Near Eastern Wisdom Literature 187
   Old Testament 188
      Praise 189
      Prayer 190
      Blasphemy 193
   Apocrypha and Pseudepigrapha 196
   Qumranic Literature 199
   Rabbinic Literature 204
   Graeco-Roman Literature 211
   Philonic Literature 214
   New Testament 218

Chapter 8: Epistle of James 222

   Exegesis 222
      James 4:2c−10 222
      James 4:2c−3 222
      James 4:4 223
      James 4:5−6 225
      James 4:7−10 229
      James 4:13−17 231
      James 4:14 232
      James 4:15 233
      James 4:16 233
      James 4:17 234
      James 5:13−18 235
      James 5:13 235
      James 5:14 236
      James 5:15 238
      James 5:16a 239
      James 5:16b−18 240
      James 1:5−8 241
      James 1:5 241
      James 1:6 241
      James 1:7−8 242
   Analysis 243
      Praise 243
      Prayer 244
      Blasphemy 247

Part V.

The Relationship of Speech to Truth

Chapter 9: Background 249

Near Eastern Wisdom Literature 249
Old Testament 251
   The Value of True Speech 251
   God is True 252
   The Lying and Deception of Men 253
   Vows and Oaths 255
Apocrypha and Pseudepigrapha 257
Qumranic Literature 260
Rabbinic Literature 263
Graeco-Roman Literature 267
Philonic Literature 271
New Testament 274

Chapter 10: Epistle of James 278

Exegesis 278
   James 5:12 278
Analysis 281

Conclusion 283

Bibliography 291

Indexes 311

Abbreviations

Not included in the list below are standard abbreviations for Jewish, Greek, and Christian writings for which the reader may consult N.G.L. Hammond and H.H. Scullard, eds. *The Oxford Classical Dictionary* (Oxford: Clarendon, 1970); H.G. Liddell and R. Scott, *A Greek-English Lexicon* (Oxford: Clarendon, 1968, ninth ed.); or G. Kittel, ed., *Theological Dictionary of the New Testament*, G.W. Bromiley, trans. (Grand Rapids, Eerdmans, 1964–1976).

AB	Anchor Bible
AEL	Lichtheim, Miriam. *Ancient Egyptian Literature.* 2 vols. London: University of California, vol. 1:1973, vol. 2:1976.
Ag.Soph.	Isocrates, *Against the Sophists*
AJT	*American Journal of Theology*
And.	Euripedes, *Andromache*
ANET	*Ancient Near Eastern Texts.* Edited by J.B. Pritchard. Princeton: Princeton University, 1969.
ANRW	Aufstieg und Neidergang der römischen Welt. Edited by H. Temporini. Berlin: de Gruyter, 1972–.
Antid.	Isocrates, *Antidosis*
APOT	*Apocrypha and Pseudepigrapha of the Old Testament.* Edited by R.H. Charles, Oxford: Clarendon, 1913.
Areo.	Isocrates, *Areopagiticus*
ARN	Aboth de Rabbi Nathan (Version A; Goldin)
ARNB	Aboth de Rabbi Nathan (Version B; Saldarini)
AsSeign	*Assemblees du Seigneur*
ATR	*Anglican Theological Review*
Bacc.	Euripides, *Bacchae*
BASOR	*Bulletin of the American Schools of Oriental Research*
BDB	*A Hebrew and English Lexicon of the Old Testament.* Edited by Francis Brown, S.R. Driver, and Charles A. Briggs. Oxford: Clarendon, 1906.
BEThL	Bibliotheca Ephemeridum Theologicarum Loveniensium
BETS	*Bulletin of the Evangelical Theological Society*
BNTC	Black's New Testament Commentaries
BSac	*Bibliotheca Sacra*
BT	*The Babylonian Talmud.* Edited by I. Epstein. 35 vols. London: Soncino, 1935–1952.
BTr	*Bible Translator*
BTB	*Biblical Theological Bulletin*
BVC	*Bible et vie chretienne*
BWL	*Babylonian Wisdom Literature.* Edited by W.G. Lambert. Oxford: Clarendon, 1960.
CBQ	*Catholic Biblical Quarterly*
ChQR	*Church Quarterly Review*
Const.	Seneca, *De Constantia,* in *Moral Essays*
CurTM	*Currents in Theology and Mission*
DBM	*Deltion Biblikon Meleton*
De aud.	Plutarch, *De recta ratione audiendi,* in *Moralia*
De educ.	Plutarch, *De liberis educandis,* in *Moralia*
De gar.	Plutarch, *De garrulitate,* in *Moralia*

De ira	Plutarch, *De cohibenda ira*, in *Moralia*
De recta	Plutarch, *De recta ratione audiendi*, in *Moralia*
De vit.	Plutarch, *De vituoso pudore*, in *Moralia*
DSSE	*The Dead Sea Scrolls in English*. Edited by Geza Vermes. Harmondsworth: Penguin, 1975.
DTT	*Dansk teologisk tidsskrift*
EM	Seneca, *Epistulae Morales*
ErfTS	*Erfurter theologische Studien*
EQ	*Evangelical Quarterly*
ET	*Expository Times*
Exp	*Expositor*
Frag.	Plutarch, *Fragments*, in *Moralia*
GOTR	*Greek Orthodox Theological Review*
HTR	*Harvard Theological Review*
HUCA	*Hebrew Union College Annual*
ICC	International Critical Commentary
IllBD	*Illustrated Dictionary of the Bible*. Edited by J.D. Douglas and N. Hillyer. 3 vols. Leicester: Inter-Varsity, 1980.
Int	*Interpretation*
IntBD	*Interpreter's Dictionary of the Bible*. Edited by G.A. Buttrick. New York: Abingdon, 1962.
ISBE	*International Standard* Bible Encyclopedia. Edited by James Orr, Grand Rapids: Eerdmans, 1930.
JAAR	*Journal of the American Academy of Religion*
JAOS	*Journal of the American Oriental Society*
JB	Jerusalem Bible
JBL	*Journal of Biblical Literature*
JETS	*Journal of the Evangelical Theological Society*
JQR	*Jewish Quarterly Review*
JR	*Journal of Religion*
JSHRZ	Jüdische Schriften aus hellenistisch-römischer Zeit
JSJ	*Journal for the Study of Judaism*
JSS	*Journal of Semitic Studies*
JTS	*Journal of Theological Studies*
KB-H	*A Concise Hebrew and Aramaic Lexicon of the Old Testament*. Edited by William L. Holladay. Based on the lexical work of Ludwig Koehler and Walter Baumgartner. Grand Rapids: Eerdmans, 1971.
KJV	King James Version
LAE	*The Literature of Ancient Egypt*. Edited by William Kelly Simpson. London: Yale University, 1973.
LB	Living Bible
LCL	Loeb Classical Library
LingBib	*Linguistica Biblica*
LS-J	Liddell, H.G., and Scott, R. *A Greek-English Lexicon*. Edited by Henry Stuart Jones and Roderick McKenzie. Ninth ed. Oxford: Clarendon, 1940 (with 1968 Supplement).
ME	Seneca, *Moral Essays*
MR	*Midrash Rabbah*. Edited by H. Freedman and M. Simon. 5 vols. London: Soncino, 1977.
NAB	New American Bible
NASB	New American Standard Bible
NCBC	New Century Bible Commentary
NEB	New English Bible
NFE	*Nova Fragmenta Euripidea*. Edited by Colin Austin. Berlin, 1968.
Nic.	Isocrates, Nicocles
NICNT	New International Commentary on the New Testament
NICOT	New International Commentary on the Old Testament
NIDNTT	*New International Dictionary of New Testament Theology*. 3 vols. Edited by Colin Brown. Grand Rapids: Zondervan, 1975–78.

NIGNTC	New International Greek New Testament Commentary
NIV	New International Version
NovT	*Nowum Testamentum*
OCD	*Oxford Classical Dictionary.* Edited by N.G.L. Hammond and H.H. Scullard. Oxford: Clarendon, 1970.
OTL	Old Testament Library
OTP	*Old Testament Pseudepigrapha.* Edited by James H. Charlesworth. 2 vols. Garden City, NY: Doubleday, 1983, 1985.
Pan.	Pesikta de Rab Kahana
PesK.	Pesikta Rabbati
Pes.Rab.	Pesiqta Rabbati
QE	Philo, *Quaestiones et Solutiones in Exodum*
QG	Philo, *Quaestiones et Solutiones in Genesin*
Quint.Frat.	Cicero, *Epistulae ad Quintum Fratrem*
Quo.adul.	Plutarch, *Quomodo adulator ab amico*, in *Moralia*
Quo.poetas	Plutarch, *Quomodo adulescens poetas audire debeat*, in *Moralia*
RA	*A Rabbinic Anthology.* Edited by C.G. Montefiore and H. Loewe. New York: Schocken, 1974.
RevB	*Review Biblique*
RevExp	*Review and Expositor*
RHR	*Revew de l'historie des religions*
RQ	*Revue de Qumran*
RSV	Revised Standard Version
RTP	*Revue de theologie et de philosphie*
SAIW	*Studies in Ancient Israelite Wisdom.* Edited by James L. Crsnshaw. New York: KTAV, 1976.
SBL	Society of Biblical Literature
SE	*Studia Evangelica*
SemBib	*Semiotique et Bible* [Lyon]
SJT	*Scottish Journal of Theology*
SNTU	*Studien zum New Testament und seiner Umwelt*
SPAW	*Sitzungsberichte der preussischen Akademie der Wissenschaft*
S.S.R.	Songs of Solomon Rabbah
ST	*Studia Theologica*
Stob.	Stobaeus, Joannis. *Anthology.* Edited by Curtinus Wachsmuth and Otto Hense. 5 vols. Berlin: Weidmannas, 1884ff.
StudPhil	*Studia Philonica*
SVOTA	*The Septuagintal Version of the Old Testament and Apocrypha.* London: Bagster, n.d.
TB	Tyndale Bulletin
TDNT	*Theological Dictionary of the New Testament.* Edited by G. Kittel. 10 vols. Translated by G.W. Bromiley. Grand Rapids: Eerdmans, 1964–76.
TDOT	*Theological Dictionary of the Old Testament.* Edited by G.J. Botterweck and Helmer Ringgren. Translated by G.W. Bromiley. Grand Rapids: Eerdmans, 1974–.
TEV	Today's English Version
TGL	*Theologie und Glaube*
ThV	*Theologische Versuch*
TLZ	*Theologische Literaturzeitung*
TNTC	Tyndale New Testament Commentaries
To Dem.	Isocrates, *To Demonicus*
To Nic.	Isocrates, *To Nicocles*
TOTC	Tyndale Old Testament Commentaries
TU	*Texte und Untersuchungen zur Geschichte der altchristlichen Literatur*
TWBB	*A Theological Word Book of the Bible.* Edited by Alan Richardson. London: SCM, 1957.
UBS[3]	*The Greek New Testament.*Third Edition. London: United Bible Societies, 1976.
Vit.	Seneca, *De vita Beata*

VT	*Vetus Testamentum*
WIANE	*Wisdom in Israel and in the Ancient Near East.* Edited by Martin Noth and D. Winton Thomas. (Fest. H.H. Rowley.) Supplements to *VT*, vol. 3. Leiden: E.J. Brill, 1955.
Works	Hesiod, *Works and Days*
WuA	*Wort und Antwort*
ZAW	*Zeitschrift für die alttestamentliche Wissenschaft*
ZKT	*Zeitschrift für katholische Theologie*
ZNW	*Zeitschrift für die neutestamentliche Wissenschaft*
ZPEB	*Zondervan Pictorial Encyclopedia of the Bible.* 5 vols. Edited by Merrill C. Tenney. Grand Rapids: Zondervan, 1975.

General Introduction

Critical research into the Epistle of James can be characterised as both sparse and narrow. It is sparse in that so little has been done, as fewer than twenty theses have been written in Great Britain and North America since 1900; it is narrow in that the vast majority of these concentrate on topics of an introductory nature. This estimation of the situation is only reinforced by a survey of scholarly articles and monographs that have been published. Geyser's criticism (p. 25) of the situation is well-deserved when he says regarding James that "N.T. scholarship in our century does not seem to have progressed much beyond the times of Luther and even those of Eusebius. In dispute are still authorship, object, and character of this letter."

Admittedly, introductory topics such as the issues of authorship, date, place of writing, recipients, composition, and nature of the writing are all extremely difficult matters for this particular New Testament book and deserve the careful attention they have received. The complex nature of these issues with respect to the Epistle of James is revealed by the fact that there is very little scholarly consensus on any of them[1]. However, the concentration on introductory matters hardly excuses the virtual ignoring of matters which relate to the content and actual thought of James[2].

One of the earliest attempts to tackle an aspect of James' thought in a thesis was in 1968 when Roy Bowen Ward wrote on "The Communal Concern of the Epistle of James," focusing on James 2:1—13. In 1973, Francis Xavier Kelly dealt with "Poor and Rich in the Epistle of James." For the most part, Kelly attempted to overturn the identification between being poor and being Christian made by Dibelius (pp. 39—45). In doing this, he examined in varying detail James 1:9—12; 2:1—9; 4:13—5:13. In 1974, Peter H. Davids completed his study of "Themes in the Epistle of James

---

1 Wessell, 42–43, in his 1953 thesis makes the assessment that "although over a century and a quarter of criticism has probed the problems of the Epistle, no general agreement has been reached, either with regard to authenticity or the closely related subject of authorship." In his 1969 article, Polhill, 369, proclaims, "Today one who surveys the current literature on James is faced with a perplexing number of differing positions." A similar comment can be found in Cranfield, 185.

2 Ladd, 588, makes the objective appraisal that "there is a dismaying lack of good studies in the thought of James."

that are Judaistic in Character." This thesis examined the three major themes of testing, origin of sin, and poverty-piety as well as the minor theme of wisdom. These themes involved Davids with James 1:5—8, 13—15, 17—18; 2:1—13; 3:13—18; 4:1—10, 13—17; 5:1—6. In that he attempted to demonstrate James' use and adaptation of ideas contained in Jewish background literature, his work included a much greater mass of background study than the works of those before him.

Most recently, three theses have appeared which deal with matters of content in the Epistle of James. In 1981, yet another thesis on "Poor and Rich in the Epistle of James: A socio-Historical and Exegetical Study" was completed. This was by Pedrito Uriah Maynard-Reid and dealt with 1:9—11; 2:19; 4:13—17; 5:1—6. A year later Charlie William Boggan finished his examination of "Wealth in the Epistle of James," which explored the same section of James as did Maynard-Reid. Also in 1982, Cain Hope Felder wrote on "Wisdom, Law, and Social Concern in the Epistle of James," which involved him with 1:19—27; 2:1—13; 4:1—10, 11—12; 5:1—6.

It is the objective of this thesis to contribute to these recent efforts to explore various themes in James by examining in detail a conceptual theme that is prominent in James but which has not previously been developed in scholarly research. It is hoped, too, to articulate a theme which lies embedded in portions of James which, for the most part, have been passed over in the research mentioned above.

The theme of personal speech-ethics suits the above objectives in an ideal fashion. It is a primary concern in the Epistle of James, involving 1:5—8, 19—27; 3:1—12, 18; 4:1—17; 5:9, 12—18 and arising more obliquely at numerous other points in the writing. It is also a theme that has aroused scant notice, much less detailed exploration.

The term "personal speech-ethics" is my own attempt to capture the idea of ethics or morality as applied to interpersonal communication. Simply put, it is the rights and wrongs of utterance. It involves when to speak, how to speak, and to whom to speak, as well as when, how, and to whom not to speak. It includes to a certain extent the process of human speech and its relationship to thoughts and actions. Only to a very limited extent does formal speaking relate to it.

Personal speech-ethics, or simply speech-ethics as it will be referred to in the thesis, is not a unified concept that can be identified with any particular word found in the New Testament or in ancient literature. But the conglomerate of concerns I have associated with speech-ethics exudes from the Epistle of James more than anywhere else in the New Testament. It is also prevalent in ancient Mediterranean literature. Corresponding to its treatment in James, a fivefold division to the examination of speech-ethics is suggested. These divisions are: the rudiments of speech-ethics

(1:19—27), the evil of the tongue (3:1—12; 4:1—2b), speech in inter-human relationships (3:18; 4:1—2b, 11—12; 5:9), speech in human-divine relationships (4:2c—10, 13—17; 5:13—18; 1:5—8, and the relationship of speech to truth (5:12). These five divisions will comprise the major sections of this thesis.

The great concern for speech-ethics which characterises the people of the ancient Mediterranean world goes hand in hand with the predomi- nance of the spoken word as their primary means of communication. For them, it is the spoken word which carries authority and conveys meaning in ways far superior to the written word which is viewed as more easily misunderstood or falsified (Ong, 115). Oral communication is an event as important to a person's ethical behaviour as deeds — and in some ways more important — since it is in speech that a person most directly conveys his interior thought, motivation, and desires (Ong, 111, 138). Of course, these latter observations are as true for contemporary man as for ancient man. Modern sociological studies refer to speech as action and as objectification of selfhood[3]. The difference is that the written word has superseded the oral in so many ways for contemporary man any idea of ethics in speech is viewed as having only minimal importance[4].

In the ancient Mediterranean world, however, the situation was quite the opposite. Speech-ethics was a major concern which was unrestricted by cultural differences. Often preserved in proverbial sayings which could easily transcend cultures, this concern can be found in the Old Testament as well as in the later types of Jewish literature: Apocrypha and Pseud- epigrapha, Qumranic, and Rabbinic. It can be found in the earliest Graeco-Roman literature. It can be found in Egyptian and Babylonian wisdom literature, some documents of which are among the oldest known to man. It can also be found in Philo and in the New Testament.

The breadth and depth of concern for speech-ethics in ancient Mediterran- ean literature has not been documented before any more than such concern has been developed as a theme in James. An attempt to do this comprises a secondary objective for this thesis. This "background" to the study of speech-ethics in James will be separated into the same divisions that are found in James. Let the reader be forewarned, however, that even a survey of the ideas relating to speech-ethics which are found in the literature of the ancient Mediterranean world makes for substantial sections of background in this thesis. A wealth of material exists, and it is in part this very fact which needs to be conveyed. It is also desired to

---

3 Berger and Luckmann, 50–53, 173–174; Sleeper, 447.
4 Bok, xix, 289, makes the telling point about the lack of concern by contemporary man for speech–ethics when she notes the complete absence of any reference to or an article on lying or deception in the eight volume *Encyclopedia of Philoso- phy* (edited by Paul Edwards). The same is the case for truthfulness, trust and veracity.

provide fair and accurate representation of the ideas on speech-ethics that
were entertained by the ancients. Sometimes only quotation can convey
the ideas adequately.

If the five background sections which pertain to each kind of background literature were read together, they would constitute a thorough
survey of speech-ethics for that particular kind of literature. As it is,
however, the primary objective of examining the background literature is
to demonstrate the breadth of support it provides the Epistle of James and
its ideas about speech-ethics, both assumed and articulated. With this in
mind, the thesis is constructed in such a way as to maximise this
realization. Examination of each aspect of speech-ethics as found in James
is arranged so that it immediately follows the relevant background
literature. The Rudiments of Speech-Ethics, for instance, is one section
comprised of a background survey and then exegesis of the passage of
primary importance in the Epistle of James. The exegesis is followed by
an analysis based on the exegesis but which also draws upon the other
relevant but more minor comments in James. This will enable comparison
between James and the background literature to take place in the thesis
conclusion.

The goal of examining background literature is to compile, as much as
is reasonably possible, all the available ideas which could have been
known by the author of the Epistle of James and which could have
influenced his thoughts and assumptions regarding speech-ethics[5].

The discovery of literal borrowing by the author of James does not fall
within the scope of this thesis[6]. The goal to discover and evaluate ideas
which the epistle shares with the background literature is broader than this.

Of the theses which have been devoted to issues of thought in the
Epistle of James, this thesis identifies most closely with that of Davids. He
notes the need to show the development of ideas in the traditions from
which James draws in order to determine not only which tradition
influenced the author most on a particular thought but also to determine
the author's own contribution as a "theologian," or original thinker, and
how he adapted ideas for his own purposes[7]. This Davids seeks to do with
regard to certain Jewish traditions in James and for the most part proves
successful.

---

5   Occasionally, I may refer to the author as James. In doing this, I merely state his
    designation in the first verse. Little consensus exists on the author's identity. For the
    sake of the thesis, any time between A.D. 40–100 is a dependable working theory.
6   Besides, Perdue, 241–242, in commenting on the lines of research which have pre-
    dominated the study of James, notes that investigation into parallels to James' teaching
    has become an increasingly stagnant endeavour.
7   Davids, "Themes," 2a–3a. Such an approach to James undercuts the views of Martin
    Dibelius on the nature of James.

With the topic of speech-ethics, it cannot be assumed that the background is restricted to Judaism. Thus, unlike his thesis, a survey of Graeco-Roman literature is included. The inclusion of Near Eastern Wisdom Literature reflects the deeply rooted nature of the concern for speech-ethics in the ancient oriental culture. The wider scope of background material covered also allows the thesis more ably to fulfill the call made by C. Freeman Sleeper ("Bultmann," 56) for New Testament ethical studies which, "explore the extent to which early Christians shared the perspectives of their own time."

Despite the indebtedness to Davids, this thesis takes exception to his conclusion which distances James from the line of wisdom tradition ("Themes," 445, 498). Such a conclusion may be warranted based on the themes Davids examines, but it comes into serious question when a topic like speech-ethics is approached.

In summary, this thesis seeks to demonstrate that: 1) speech-ethics is a major concern in the Epistle of James, 2) this concern reflects the breadth and depth of concern for speech-ethics in the ancient Mediterranean world, 3) the basic aspects and the majority of ideas expressed or assumed about speech-ethics in James are shared by and supported in the literature which represents the varying cultures and times of this world, 4) some of the ideas in the Epistle of James are the distinctive and Christian thoughts of the author.

Specialized Introduction:
Speech-Ethics and Wisdom in James

Epistle of James

Speech-ethics is a major concern in the Epistle of James. Although the persistent ethical character of James is undisputed[1], the dominance of speech-ethics rarely is noted[2].

James' ethical character is evidenced by the striking statistic that the 108 verses of James contain 54 imperatives[3]. The unnoticed fact is that 23 of these 54 imperatives are concerned directly with matters pertaining to speech-ethics, and 6 more are concerned indirectly[4]. Impressive enough as this is, the proportion of imperatives concerned with speech-ethics increases significantly when it is realized that fully 11 of the 54 imperatives in James have purely rhetorical functions, and 3 more are contained within an illustration[5]. This reduces the number of imperatives

---

1 The opening statement by Schrage, *Ethik*, 266, is characteristic: "Keine andere Schrift des Neuen Testaments ist so sehr von ethischen Fragen beherrscht wie der Jakobusbrief." See similar statements in Laws, "Ethics," 299; Schawe, 132; Maston, 23.

2 Commendable exceptions are: in the realm of commentaries, Laws, 26–27, and Cadoux, 48–53; in ethics, Schrage, *Ethik*, 277, and Schnackenburg, 359; and in theology, Guthrie, 929. As an introductory monograph, Rendall, 47–52, devotes a great deal of space to the significance of speech–ethics to James.

3 The figure does not include the imperative future indicative in 2:8 (ἀγαπήσεις), the imperative infinitive in 4:15 (ἀντὶ τοῦ λέγειν), and the imperative participle in 5:1 (ὀλολύζοντες). A sense of imperative is implied in the following verses: 1:21, 26, 27(2); 2:14–26; 3:1–12, 18; 4:11, 16; 5:9, 14, 20.

4 The 23 directly pertaining to speech–ethics are: 1:5 (αἰτείτω); 1:6 (αἰτείτω); 1:9 (καυχάσθω); 1:13 (λεγέτω); 1:19 (ἔστω); 2:1 (ἔχετε); 2:12 (λαλεῖτε, ποιεῖτε); 3:1 (γίνεσθε); 3:14 (κατακαυχᾶσθε, ψεύδεσθε); 4:9 (κλαύσατε); 4:11 (καταλαλεῖτε); 5:1 (κλαύσατε); 5:9 (στενάζετε); 5:12 (ὀμνύετε, ἤτω); 5:13 (προσευχέσθω, ψαλλέτω); 5:14 (προσκαλεσάσθω, προσευξάσθωσαν); 5:16 (ἐξομολογεῖσθε, εὔχεσθε). The 6 indirectly pertaining to speech–ethics are: 1:6 (πλανᾶσθε); 1:21 (δέξασθε); 4:9 (πενθήσατε); 5:7 (μακροθυμήσατε); 5:8 (μακροθυμήσατε, στηρίξατε). Further, of the 13 implied commands and 3 non–imperative mood commands, 7 have to do with speech–ethics (1:26; 3:1–12; 4:15; 5:1, 9, 20). If these were to be included in the overall figure of the proportional number of commands pertaining to speech–ethics, it would be 36 of 70.

5 Those functioning rhetorically are: 1:16 (πλανᾶσθε); 1:19 (ἴστε, possibly indicative), 2:5 (ἀκούσατε); 2:24 (ὁρᾶτε); 3:4 (ἰδού); 4:11 (ἄγε νῦν); 5:1 (ἄγε νῦν); 5:4, 11, 17 (ἰδού); 5:20 (γινώσκετε). The three imperatives which function within an illustration are in 2:3 (κάθου, στῆθι, κάθου).

calling for a response from the reader to only 40. Further, of the remaining 11 imperatives, the 8 concentrated in 4:7—10 are concerned with repentance and not with ethics as such[6]. Thus, it may be observed that of the 32 imperatives in James which deal with ethics, 29 are concerned with speech-ethics.

The significance of speech-ethics to James is further illustrated by the work of two German scholars. Both considered James' concern for speech to be the cohesive principle binding the entire writing together and attempted to demonstrate this in schematic outlines. Ernst Pfeiffer, in 1850, based his efforts on the tripartite aphoristic statement in 1:19, "Let everyone be quick to hear, slow to speak, and slow to anger." He viewed the first part as being elaborated in 1:20—2:28, the second, in 3:1—12, and the third in 3:13—4:13. James 1:1—18, he viewed as introductory, and 4:14—5:20, he viewed as simply various admonitions. Some years later, 1904, H. J. Cladder proposed a symmetrical arrangement of James, which he saw as being comparable to Hebrew poetry, with 1:19—27 comprising the focal point[7].

The importance of these proposals does not so much lie in whether they reflect with exact precision the logical arrangement of the author but in the fact that they demonstrate the visibility of James' concern for speech-ethics to those with a discerning eye. There is no intention here to pin James' concern for speech-ethics to an outline or to make yet another claim for the thematic center of the writing.

Wisdom

Concern for speech-ethics is found primarily in wisdom literature. Hebrew wisdom, concentrated in Proverbs, Job, Ecclesiastes, Wisdom of Solomon, and Sirach, abounds with proverbial sayings about good and bad speech. Egyptian and Babylonian wisdom literature, predating and paralleling the Hebrew, set the tone for wisdom literature throughout the ancient Mediterranean world[8]. Egyptian diplomatic corps collected wisdom sayings

---

6 These are: ὑποτάγητε, ἀντίστητε, ἐγγίσατε, καθαρίσατε, ἁγνίσατε, ταλαιπωρήσατε, μετατραπήτω, ταπεινώθητε. The three that remain are in 1:4 (ἐχέτω); 1:7 (οἰέσθω); 3:13 (δειξάτω).

7 Cladder anticipated the more recent proposals which have come from P. Davids, 22–27, who depends so closely on Francis. It is ironic, though, that Cladder's proposals are based on Hebrew poetry, whereas Francis' and Davids' are based upon Hellenistic letter form.

8 Many scholars write of the influence of Egyptian and Babylonian wisdom: Crenshaw, 213; R. Scott, lii; Bryce, 210; R. Williams, 231; R. Scott, *Way*, 45; Muilenberg, 99;

from other cultures. They also shared their own. Speech-ethics is part of all this.

Most speech-ethics is associated with wisdom literature but not exclusively. Qumranic literature, which shuns wisdom sayings in favor of legal and prophetic material, still contains advice about speech[9]. Likewise, Graeco-Roman literature, which develops well beyond the collection proverbs by Hesiod and Theognis, contains insights about speech-ethics in its essays, speeches, plays, and poems. Rabbinic literature carries on not only the tradition of the law but wisdom as well. Pirke Aboth and the 630 sayings attributed to "the sages" demonstrates this. Philo's chief aim is to procure wisdom. However, he attempts to achieve this, not by collecting maxims and proverbs but by exploring the inner recesses of the Jewish Pentateuch by means of allegory[10]. Philo's unique blend of Hebrew and Greek thought maintains concern for speech-ethics. In the New Testament, the gospels, but especially Q, depicts Jesus as excelling in the wisdom tradition [11]. Paul identifies Jesus with wisdom and characterizes the preaching about the crucified Christ as the wisdom of God[12]. Not surprisingly, concern about speech-ethics continues to be expressed by New Testament writers, as well.

More than any other single New Testament book, James carries on in the tradition of wisdom[13], so normally associated with concern for

Rankin, 7; Rylaarsdam 1–17; H. Robinson, 235–238; Porteous, 153; von Rad, *Theology*, 1:429; Gressmann, "Lehre;" Gressmann, *Israel's*; Kevin, 126–127.

9 Explanations for this vary. Worrell, 406, suggests that the Qumran community avoided wisdom because their arch rivals, the Pharisees, had appropriated it. Hengel, 2:145, n. 716, postulates that Qumran found wisdom inadequate and preferred revealed knowledge.

10 *Vita* 78. See also Winston, 4–6; Dillon, 142–143; Sandmel, 17—28.

11 Mt. 11:16–19 (Lk. 7:31—35); Mt. 11:25–27 (Lk. 10:21–23); Mt. 23:34–36 (Lk. 11:49–51); Mt. 23:37–39 (Lk. 13:34–35); Mt. 12:42 (Lk. 11:31). See also Beardslee, 34—35; Beardslee, *Synoptic*, 234–238; Suggs, 5—20; Küchler, 583–584; Christ, 74–75; 93, 129–132, 153–154; Feuillet; J. M. Robinson; and Koester.

12 1 Cor. 1 and 2. Controversy surrounds what precise relationship Paul has in mind and what exactly Paul has in mind by wisdom. Reese, "Christ," synthesises the arguments offered for Paul's identification of Christ with pre–existent wisdom. The chief proponent of this view is Feuillet, *Christ*. See also Küchler, 583–584; Dunn, 163–212; Kim, 124–125, 258; and Dillistone. Van Roon, Horsley, and B. Pearson, argue against Feuillet.

13 Baasland; Halson; Obermüller, 235; Luck, "Jakobusbrief," and "Weisheit;" MacGorman. Ropes, 16–20, protests at classifying James wisdom literature but readily points out that the author made heavy use of wisdom literature. P. Davids, 24, considers the view that James is wisdom literature to be old–fashioned and in "Themes," 445, discounts any direct dependence on wisdom literature. Davids' view is heavily undermined by Hoppe, 32–43, 147, who finds James' background in Jewish widsom literature to be the key to understanding James' theology. Whether or not James has "all" the traits of wisdom literature is not the point. It has plenty to be considered to be following in the line of wisdom tradition like no other New Testament book.

speech-ethics. Aphorisms are fondly employed, often as confirmatory conclusions of discourse units (1:27; 2:13; 3:18; 4:17). Practical admonitions which can be applied by the individual to a wide range of circumstances are prevalent (for instance, 1:5,22; 2:12; 4:11). The writing, at least on the surface, is carefree and unordered.

James has the cross-cultural characteristic of wisdom literature. Much of its subject matter and many of its views are paralleled in traditional Jewish and Graeco-Roman wisdom literature with which the author must have been quite familiar[14]. Holding a predominant place in his catalogue of wisdom must have been the teachings of Jesus to which numerous parallels may be drawn[15].

The author considers himself to be a teacher (3:1). This he displays by the manner in which he presents his ideas, earmarked by Obermüller as "so pedantische"[16]. Also, much of his instruction rests upon "horizontal" authority [17], i.e. his own keen observations and also notions drawn from wisdom tradition and other sources (including Scripture) which he assumes his readers accept. Finally, in his own peculiar way James, like Sirach, appears to make the place of law in ethics dependent upon wisdom (Hoppe, 99; Schnabel). At the very least, he blurs the long-held distinction between wisdom and law (Schnackenburg, 352).

The idea of wisdom occupies a significant place in James, indicated by its appearance in the opening paragraph (1:2—8) and the concentrated attention given to it later in the writing (3:13—18)[18]. The author apparently

---

14 Dibelius, 26–27, notes numerous parallels in Sir., Wis., T.12 Patr., Philo, and recognizes Hellenistic influence. See also Ropes, 18–20, Mayor, cxvi–cxxvii; Hoppe, 32–43, 147.

15 Deppe finds over 175 different allusions from Jesus tradition claimed by 53 scholars since the beginning of critical scholarship. Some of the most heavily supported dependencies on Jesus tradition are: 4:11–12 to Mt. 7:1 (Lk. 6:25); 3:12 to Mt. 7:16–18 (Lk. 6:44–45); 5:2 to Mt. 6:19–20 (Lk. 6:37; 12:33); and 5:12 to Mt. 5:33–37. P. Davids, 49, finds fundamental similarities with Luke in vocabulary, eschatology, and social outlook. The substantial listings of synoptic parallels in Mayor, lxxv–lxxxviii, Davies, *Setting*, 402–404, and Mussner, 47–54, for the most part have been incorporated into the chart in P. Davids, 47–48. Relevant studies in this area include: Schawe, 134–136; Wanke; Lohse; Shepherd; Dillman; P. Davids, "Jesus".

16 Obermüller, 235, pictures James enumerating his points with "die fünf Finger," as a Rabbi doing a Christian Halacha on wisdom. Wanke considers James primary New Testament evidence concerning the early Christian teaching office.

17 As contrasted with the prophetic writing, which may be viewed as vertical because it comes directly from God and concerns the covenant, wisdom writing is characterised as horizontal. Concerned primarily with the individual and his personal success in living, wisdom is pragmatic teaching drawn from time-tested experience. The prophet speaks a "Thus says the Lord;" the wise man speaks in proverbs, riddles, parables, and illustrations. See R. Scott, *Way*, 100–135; Lindblom, 197; Ranston, 22–25; Rylaarsdam, 52, 99–118; Rankin, 3–4; Kent, 24–26; Würthwein, 122; Gemser, "Structure," 208–219; Zimmerli, "Struktur;" von Rad, *Theology*, 1:434; Kent and Burrows, 13.

18 Felder, 29–65,165, attempts to establish wisdom, along with law, as "leitmotivs" in James.

assumes that the readers know what he means by σοφία for he employs
the term four times — and σοφός one time — without any definition
(Cantinat, 38). However, his usage of the terms does provide enough
information to sketch what some of the contours of wisdom were for him.

First, wisdom in James is not purely an ideological concept. It is joined
intricately to practical expression. To the theoretical question in 3:13 about
who is or should be considered σοφὸς καὶ ἐπιστήμων comes the didactic
admonition in reply that such a person's actions should prove whether or
not this is an accurate description of him. If his actions are characterized
by good behaviour, then he has demonstrated that they are directed by
wisdom. As continued in 3:14, if his actions are engendered from a heart
filled with bitter jealousy and selfish desire, and yet such a person claims
to be wise, he is labelled arrogant and a liar. The crucial test, though, is in
his deeds. In taking this line, James is thoroughy consistent with his earlier
insistence in 2:14—26 that actions have an irrevocable place alongside faith in a proper scheme of justification.

Secondly, James separates wisdom into categories of true and false, as
Calmet also recognizes. The so-called wisdom claimed by the person whose
actions are motivated by jealousy and ambition does not "come down
from above." In fact, it is specified in 3:15 to be earthly, natural, and even
demonic. The arrogant liar may call it wisdom, but it is not. This is
proven by the chaos it causes. On the other hand, true wisdom is from
above and is evidenced by positive, identifiable traits. These traits, listed in
3:17, include being peaceable, gentle, compliant, full of mercy and good
fruits, impartial, and non-hypocritical.

Thirdly, James considers wisdom to be important for harmonious
communal and personal relationships[19]. False wisdom motivated by ambition and jealousy, as stated in 3:16, produces disorder. It also produces the
communal strife detailed in 4:1—2. In contrast, the person who is truly
wise brings about peace because his character traits are beneficial in
community life.

Fourthly, James considers wisdom to be a critical requirement for
Christians to reach full maturity in their faith[20]. The failure of the author
to connect 1:4 and 1:5 with nothing more than the catch words λειπόμενοι
and λείπεται makes it difficult for the relationship between wisdom and
maturity to be spelled out much more specifically[21]. Yet, certainly the

---

19 Kirk, 27; Ward; Felder.
20 "Full maturity" is an attempt to capture the sense of τέλειοι καὶ ὁλόκληροι in 1:4. P.
    Davids, "Themes," 337–338, rightly points out that the words function as a hendiadys.
    DuPlessis, 234–235 considers a number of qualities to be included, such as persistency,
    deeds, dynamism, progression, and wholeness and completeness of character. See also P.
    Davids, 70.
21 But see Hoppe, 18–43; P. Davids, "Themes," 308–359; and Luck, "Weisheit."

author perceives wisdom (in the sense with which he gives the term shape in 3:13—18) to bring a person from endurance to perfection in the progressive sequence he constructs.

Fifthly, wisdom in James is thought to be a primary gift from God. It is "from above" as 3:15, 17 speaks of it. The Christian who sincerely prays for it will receive it (1:5—6). Although not specified, it must be foremost in the author's mind in 1:17 (P. Davids, 88, and Schnackenburg, 352) when he says that "every perfect gift is from above, coming down from the Father." The notion of δώρημα and δόσις links with τοῦ διδόντος and δοθήσεται in 1:5, and τέλειον links with 1:4. Also ἄνωθεν links with 3:15, 17.

The association of wisdom with being the good and perfect gift from God, the strikingly close relationship between wisdom and the Spirit in intertestamental literature and in certain places in Pauline literature, and the parallels between Jas. 3:13—18 and Gal. 5:22—6:8, have encouraged some scholars such as Kirk and P. Davids (pp. 54—56) to conclude that the function of wisdom in James is interchangeable with that of the Holy Spirit elsewhere in the New Testament. Dillman (p. 176) draws away from such a broad claim and specifies that wisdom in James should be associated with the fruit of the Spirit. Although not directly intended, substantial support for these views is supplied by Hoppe. He (pp. 50—51) not only views wisdom as the perfect gift from God (1:17), but he also associates it with the word of truth (1:18) and thereby with salvation (1:21) and justification (3:18). Wisdom, along with faith, is seen as the pervasive theological undergirding of the entire epistle (pp. 16—17). It is the power which enables a person to be reborn and to reach his full potential as a Christian within the will of God (pp. 70—71).

The parallels in Hoppe's description to the Holy Spirit are striking. However, to say that James intends the reader to identify wisdom with the Spirit as Kirk and P. Davids both imply would be to assume too much and to overreach the evidence. We do not know what the readers of James know of the Spirit nor has anyone suggested a reason why the author would wish to substitute wisdom for the function of the Spirit, even though it is true that James makes no reference to the Spirit[22]. In light of Hoppe's work, however, it does seem reasonable to say that wisdom in James has functions that are parallel to what we know of the Spirit elsewhere in the New Testament.

James, then, should be placed within the sphere of wisdom and wisdom literature, even though it is also observed that the author adds his own distinctive Christian outlook to current concepts of wisdom.

---

22 The only use of τὸ πνεῦμα is in 4:5 and not even Kirk or P. Davids believe the Holy Spirit is in mind.

James does exhibit some characteristics that do not fall within the sphere of wisdom. These resemble prophetic tradition[23]. The manifold imperatives produce a tone that is reminiscent of prophetic authority, as Mussner (p. 33) notes. The castigation of the rich (1:9—11; 2:6; 5:1—6) is unparalleled in severity outside the Old Testament prophets (Lillie, *Studies,* 93—95; Schrage, *Ethik,* 278—279). The nearness of eschatological judgment results in a prophetic urgency for changes in attitudes and in conduct to occur (5:2, 9). The idealism so characteristic of prophetic demands is integral to the ethical perspective of James (1:4, 17, 25; 2:23; 3:2)[24]. Further, this idealism is motivated much more by theocentric (and even Christocentric) concerns than by anthropocentric concerns. Finally, although James appears unordered as a whole, and indeed eludes attempts to be satisfactorily represented in an outline, extremely close-knit, well-ordered reasoning occurs within certain discourse units, especially 2:1—13 and 2:14—26.

In light of these prophetic qualities in James, the writing is best viewed as a unique blend of wisdom and prophetic tradition[25].

Paraenesis

The term "paraenesis" was virtually unknown in New Testament circles before Dibelius. However, the weight of his evidence in applying the term to James has influenced all study of James since it was first proposed in his 1921 commentary. Very little discussion of James takes place today without a presumption of its paraenetic character.

As Dibelius (p. 3) defines it, paraenesis refers to "a text which strings together admonitions of general ethical content." Paraenesis is characterized by an eclecticism which draws heavily from older traditional wisdom materials, a lack of continuity in thought which is superficially linked together by catchwords, an unsystematic repetition of identical motifs, and a content which is so general in nature that it cannot be applied to one particular set of circumstances even though it consists of admonitions which appear to be directed to a particular audience (pp. 2—11).

From Dibelius' point of view, the nature of paraenesis itself disallows the author from having, or at least conveying, any unified purpose, any

---

23 Dillman, 286; Mussner, 24; Guthrie, 928; Obermüller, 234–235.
24 Zmijewski; Blondel, 146–148; Hoppe, 18–43; Mussner, 59; Lohse, 21–22; DuPlessis, 233–240.
25 Obermüller, 234-235, believes that that James intends to transform prophecy into wisdom.

goals, or any motivations for writing, excludes him from projecting any theology, and severely restricts him from any originality (pp. 2—11, 21—22). Any attempt to examine themes of a theological or an ethical nature in James, thus, is seriously called into question by Dibelius' view if they are adopted in full.

The introduction of the term paraenesis seems to be a suitable identification of a literary form common to wisdom literature. Dibelius' keen applicaiton of the term to James in particular is beneficial in many ways. However, a number of questionable points should keep one from accepting his view wholeheartedly.

First, it is questionable whether the whole of James should be branded paraenesis as Dibelius desires. He himself (p. 5) recognizes the three central sections of James to be treatises (2:1—12, 14—16; 3:1—12) "where the structure and lines of thought were apparently shaped by the author himself." Dibelius himself suggests that within these sections, if anywhere, the author's purpose is to be found. However, he fails to apply this insight to a discussion of purpose. He also misses the fact that it is within such "treatises" that the examination of theology should be possible, which Hoppe has demonstrated[26]. Further, Dibelius' motivation is called into question when he attempts to re-label these treatises "expanded paraenesis" (p. 3).

Secondly, Dibelius' suggestion that paraenetic material is incapable of conveying anything of the author's personal views is questionable. Dibelius himself (p. 5) points out — but again fails to apply — the fact that the author's choice of traditional material as well as his arrangement of it is significant in this respect. Mussner (p. 24) astutely observes that a single theological principle could well determine the author's choice of otherwise widely diverse paraenetic material[27]. Hoppe (p. 16) believes the order in which the author arranges the material could also be controlled by a theological point of view[28]. Moreover, the author's goals and purposes could be contained in these aspects of writing.

Perdue (p. 243) points out that the general applicability of paraenesis (by which Dibelius separates the reader from the author) pertains to the individual precepts themselves and not to whole paraenetic texts which do have recognizable social settings. He (p. 246) adds that paraenesis can often

---

26 Hoppe differs slightly from Dibelius in determining 3:13–18 rather than 3:1–12 as one of three main teaching treatises. Zmijewski examines 2:14–26, 3:13–18, and 1:16–25 to determine James' theological center to be Christian perfection.

27 See also Blondel, 141; and Luck.

28 He demonstrates that both the sections of "die Spruchparänese" and "die theologisch lehrhafte Auseinandersetzung" (2:1–13,14–26; 3:13–18) exhibit a unified theological point of view from which they derive.

involve a close, intensely personal relationship between the teacher (author) and his student (readers).

Many scholars disagree with Dibelius at this point because they detect in James something more than a collection of traditional material. Although their approaches differ, they all spot a persuasive quality about the writing. Ropes (pp. 6—18) liken it to a public tract and labels the entire work diatribe. Wuellner (p. 42), approaching James from the perspective of discourse analysis methods, discovers a passionate desire in the author to win his readers over to his point of view. Wuellner (p. 32) also speaks of it as a public tract. Other scholars identify this persuasive quality as homiletic or sermonic[29]. Schrage (*Ethik*, 267) depicts this quality as an "eindringliche Ruf." Blondel (p. 141) finds in James' paraenesis "un sens nettement missionarie" and proceeds to detail its theological themes.

Thus, paraenesis can convey information about the author's personal views, his theology, and his motivations for writing. The information may need to be inferred, but nevertheless it is there to be found[30].

Thirdly, Dibelius' assumption that lack of continuity is a prime characteristic of paraenesis is to be questioned. With this, he attempts to drive immovable wedges between James' basic units of thought. All bear equal weight; none is subordinate to another; no logical relationship is intended.

Dibelius has a point here. The logical progression of thought in James is certainly not that of a tightly argued essay with overt signposts. The pitfalls in attempting to outline James are notorious and usually include little more than broad topics[31]. Usually when subordination is attempted, some aspects of James are slighted or forced[32].

---

29 Wessel, 78–91; P. Davids, 23; Agourides, 67; Amphoux, 56; Forbes.

30 J. Williams', 68–69, assessment of the general characteristics of gnomic wisdom contrasts sharply with Dibelius' view of paraenesis. He considers it to have both poetic and philosophical qualities.

31 See Blondel, 142; Cantinat, 36; Songer, 383–384; Jones; Farrar, 2:23.

32 P. Davids, 28, who adapts the form–critical work of Francis, really forces 1:22–25 when he labels it "Obedience requires generosity" and when he labels 3:1–12 as having something to do with anger because it is supposed to mirror 1:19–21. Adamson, 44–45, whose outline, consisting of such headings as "Some Christian Advice" (3:2–18 and "Conclusion" (5:1–18) hardly lives up to his proclaimed objective on p. 1 to vindicate James' structure. The extensively detailed outline by Hiebert, 48–53, forces the testing theme into all the larger unit headings. On the opposite extreme, the simple "concentric structure" proposed by Reese, which resembles Davids' approach, lacks detailed support. The nearly scientific analysis by Fry results in an incredible uniformity in setting off the writing into three main sections (1:2–11; 1:12–5:6; 5:7–20), but each one labelled "Testing and Endurance". Finally, the attempts to search for an external source to unlock the mystery of James' structure point up the desparate lengths to which some will go. D. Beck looks to Qumran and 1QS. Blenker looks to Job (LXX). Gertner looks to Ps. 12:1–5 (Hos. 10). Meyer looks to T.12 Patr.

The fact that an overall cohesion is not easily observable does not mean that the author had no plan or purpose for putting the ideas together[33]. Neither should it imply that he intends no cohesion between units of thought[34]. Simply, the author's plan, therefore the relationships between all the units, has not been fully discovered. In some cases the author may intend the catchword links to be more than superficial word-play. If, as Perdue (pp. 244—245, 249) suggests, the first intended readers of James had heard most of the instruction previously and the writing was to serve as a reminder, then presumably they could readily understand the progression of thought throughout, even if we cannot.

James may not explain its cohesion also because the author intends for multiple layers of meaning to be discerned. Overly precise language might narrow the wide public in view. James may be compared to a circuit board with a few simple lights and buttons on the front but with a maze of connecting wires under the surface. Thus, many different themes in James, theological, ethical and otherwise, which may not be overtly obvious may be legitimately open for discovery and development.

Finally, Perdue's more recent work does not mention lack of continuity as a characteristic of paraenesis, as opposed to Dibelius' earlier assertion.

Many fruitful results have come from Dibelius' connection of paraenesis with James. He was wrong, however, to push a number of his observations to the extreme, such as treating the whole of the writing as paraenesis, thinking of paraenesis as blocking communication of the author's own views, and presuming the lack of continuity in James to be completely impenetrable[35]. Thus, study of ethical and theological themes such as speech-ethics in James is a legitimate enterprise[36]. So too the general ethical and theological perspective of the writing may be explored.

Theology and Ethics

Some critics question the Christian nature of James and dub its ethics sub-Christian[37]. The first is based upon the compatibility of the writing to

---

33 Whybray, "Proverbs," criticizes McKane for separating proverbs from their contexts for analysis and proceeds to demonstrate that the arrangement of proverbs is significant in reflecting cohesive theological themes.

34 Despite the failure of any one outline to portray James convincingly, relationships between numerous parts have been established. See Mussner and Hoppe.

35 As P. Davids, 25, rightly evaluates, Dibelius stops at the form critical level of analysis and ignores redactional analysis.

36 As P. Davids, "Perspective," 97, says, "The age of the string-of-pearls conception of the letter is past, and its essential theological unity is ready for exploration."

37 Furnish, *Love*, 177, says, "There is little in James that is either specifically or

Jewish literature and the lack of explicit Christian theology, notably
Christology, in undergirding the seemingly random ethical admonitions.
The second is based upon the perception that James fails to elevate the
love command to the supreme position in its ethics. The following
discussion of the general characteristics of James' ethics will show these
views to be unwarranted and demonstrate James' ethics to be compatible
with its placement in the New Testament canon.

In James, theological ideas are interwoven with the ethical. However,
the desire to solicit behavioural changes is the uppermost concern. James
usually begins a topic of concern with an imperative. This is then followed
by the indicative which supplies motivational support[38]. The sustained
theological argument about faith and works (2:14—26) occurs out of the
author's need to give theological support for the primary concern of
motivating readers to be actively doing the word of God (1:19—27).

Two more compact examples of this are in James 5:8 and 5:9. In 5:8, the
admonition to be patient is followed by assurance of the imminent coming
of the Lord. In 5:9, the admonition not to complain about one another is
followed by the warning that judgment will be soon[39]. In these instances,
as in many others James, the author presumes that the readers are fully
acquainted with and accept the theological ideas which are raised. The
theological ideas normally are tailored to suit the numerous admonitions
which occur. They cannot be expected to explore exhaustively the
theological subject. Making theology support ethics in this way does not
make James less Christian just because Paul's method for the most part is
the reverse.

Many theological ideas familiar to the New Testament do appear in
James. Concerning God[40], James refers to his unity and uniqueness (2:19),
his total separation from evil and his absolute goodness (1:12—13, 17), his
role as Creator (1:17—18), his sovereignty (1:18; 5:13—15), his responsiveness

---

distinctly Christian, whether in respect of the content of the admonitions or their
grounding." See also Houlden, 67, 106; J. Sanders, *Ethics*, 115–128; R. White, 204–209;
and Via. The seed of distrust about James' Christian nature goes back to Spitta and
also Massebieau who proposed that the addition of "Christ" to 1:1 and 2:1 was just
cosmetic in order to make an originally Jewish writing Christian. This view, adapted
by Meyer a bit later, deservedly has received heavy criticism and the penetrating
Christian nature vindicated by Dibelius, 22–25; Ropes, 32–33; Polhill, 373–374;
Agourides, 70–71; Noack; Henderlite, 469–472; Braumann; and Hoppe.

38 Green, 316–334, finds this pattern to predominate in 1 Peter, as well. He also noted
that it can be seen in Paul (Rom. 13:1; 14:3; 1 Cor. 10:7–10; Phil. 2:14, 15), although Paul
prefers to begin with the theological indicative. Further, Green suggests that this
pattern finds its root in the ethical portions of Jewish literature.

39 Further instances of this imperative/indicative pattern are in 1:2–3, 4, 5, 6, 7, 9–11,
13–15, 19–20, 22–27; 2:1–11, 12–13; 3:1–12; 4:11–12; 5:1–6.

40 See Mussner, 97–98; P. Davids, 40–41, and Obermüller, 236.

to sincere prayer (1:5—6; 4:2—3; 5:17—18), his demand for repentance in men (4:7—10), his opposition to "the world" (4:4), and his sympathy for the poor and wrath toward the arrogant rich (1:9, 11, 27; 2:5; 5:1—5).

The fact that direct reference to Christ is made only twice has misled some to think there are no Christological ideas in James. However, as many as six references to him as "Lord" (1:1; 2:1; 5:7, 8, 14, 15), two to him as "Judges" (4:12; 5:9), and two to his "Name" (2:7; 5:14) more than make up for this[41]. James refers to his deity[42], his imminent return, his role as eschatological judge, the power of his name in healing, and the utterance of his name in Christian baptism. From the significant role that Jesus' teaching appears to have throughout James, one must also acknowledge the presumption of Jesus' authority for the author as well as for the readers[43]. The lack of reference to Jesus' death and resurrection and the failure to use these as motivational support for ethics may be explained by the dwelling of the author on pre-Easter Jesus tradition (Schawe, 135).

With regard to ideas about salvation, corresponding to the well-known stress given to the importance of Christian faith being practiced (1:22—25; 2:14—26), James emphasizes a person's dependence upon God. Sincere repentance from sin and turning away from the "world" are essential for acceptance by God (4:4—10)[44]. God's word of truth gives men birth (1:18). Reception of his implanted word enables the word to be done obediently (1:21). Tapping into his wisdom "from above" facilitates a person to attain the full potential of his faith (3:13—18).

Although it has been suggested that James elevates works above faith for justification (Schrage, *Ethik*, 269), this is true only rhetorically. In 2:14 —26, James is doing verbal battle with those whom he believes have wrongly separated works from their proper place alongside faith in an acceptable scheme of justification. He pictures faith as the junior partner "working together with works" in 2:22, merely as an attempt to redress the imbalance others have caused. In artificially separating faith from works in order to discuss faith, a distinction has been made which James thinks is misleading. Faith and works are inseparable in the real life of the maturing Christian.

---

41 See Mussner, "Christologie." The article also appears as a supplement to the third and fourth editions of his commentary, pp. 250–254. See also Braumann, P. Davids, 39–41; Obermüller, 236–237. Obermüller goes as far as to call the traits listed in 3:17 descriptions of Jesus!

42 The τῆς δόξης of 2:1 is sometimes viewed this way. Hiebert, 161, also notes the relevancy of 2:7 and the mention of blaspheming Jesus' name as an indication of his deity.

43 Mussner, "Christologie," 115, considers the influence of Jesus' tradition in James to be a formidable witness of "indirect Christology." See also Cranfield, 184–184.

44 Stevens, 282–283; and P. Davids, "Themes," 360–396.

Concerning eschatology, James' presumption of the Lord's imminent return (5:7) and his eschatological judgment (5:9) have been noted already as significant motivational factors in James' ethics[45].

Like other New Testament books, despite the dominant concern for ethical behaviour, James lays out no ethical system. While James pays respect to Old Testament laws, particularly the Ten Commandments (2:11), it appears to distance itself from the cultic aspects of the law and stress the moral[46]. If anything occupies the center of James' ethics, it is the command to love one's neighbor. James 2:8, describes Lev. 19:18 (LXX) the "royal law[47]". Partiality, thereby, is branded as sinful on the basis that it constitutes a violation of loving one's neighbor. Stumbling on the one point, partiality, makes one guilty of violating the whole, the law of love. Similarly, James 4:11—12 argues forcibly that speaking against one another violates the royal law of loving one's neighbor. Also implied in the discussion about works in 2:14—26 is that these are to be works based on love (Lohse, 3; Schawe, 136—137).

L. Johnson finds five more passages which may well be thought by the author of James to be further sub-violations of the law of love. Johnson's claim is that 2:1, 8, 9; 4:11; 5:4, 9, 12, 20 are violations of specific commandments found in Lev. 19:12—18[48]. Designating the law as "royal" indicates the superior rank of the law to the author (Mussner, 126), its connection to the Kingdom of God (Schrage, 272), and its well-known association with the ethical teaching of Jesus[49]. It is fair, then, to consider the law of love to be the primary ethical principle in James[50].

---

45 See Schrage, *Ethik*, 270; P. Davids, 38–39; Mussner, 207–210.

46 Schrage, *Ethik*, 273–274; P. Davids, 47–48; Felder, "Partiality," 63.

47 Cranfield, 192; Mitton, 88; Ropes, 199; Dibelius, 142, prefer to read the idea of "whole law" from 2:10 into this verse because otherwise νόμος is being misused in referring to a single command for which ἐντολή is the proper word choice. However, νόμος can be used to refer to a single precept (Rom. 7:2) as Laws, 107 points out. James 2:10–11 introduces and illustrates an accepted principle of law which the author desires to apply to partiality and the law of love. To act with partiality breaks the law of love. In James 2:8, the "love command" is not viewed as one command among many but as the command that encompasses all commands, as Jesus suggests in Matthew. See Laws, 114; Seitz, 476; Mussner, 250; P. Davids, 114; Reicke, 29; Davies, *Setting*, 405; Schnackenburg, 351.

48 Lev. 19:12/Jas. 5:12; Lev. 19:13/Jas. 5:4; Lev. 19:15/Jas. 2:1, 9; Lev. 19:16/Jas. 4:11; Lev. 19:17b/Jas. 5:20; Lev. 19:18a/Jas. 5:9; Lev. 19:18b/Jas. 2:8. Although the love command appears to be nothing other than one more article in a series of precepts, James may view it as the substratum for the others because: 1) it is last in the series, 2) it is the only positively stated precept in the series, 3) it is spotlighted by Jesus in early Christian tradition.

49 Davies, *Setting*, 405, says, "The royal law is the law of the Messiah here summed up in terms of *agape*." See also Mussner, 250; P. Davids, 114; Hoppe, 89; Laws, 110.

50 It does not provide the interpretative key to the entirety of James (Schrage, *Ethik*, 273; Laws, 299) as Mussner supposes, but it is the basis of the ethical teaching.

Redesignated the "law of freedom[51]" in 2:12, James says the royal law of love is the yardstick for divine judgment of all human behaviour. This may not seem freeing. However, the freeing aspect lies in its capacity to lift the burden of the many restrictive laws imposed externally upon a person. The all-encompassing rule of loving one's neighbor exercised internally and freely replaces these (Schrage, *Ethik*, 273). Yet, the power to apply neighbor love to situations in life does not reside within the person alone or even in the royal law itself[52].

Tracing the antecedents of the "law of freedom" in James indicates this. The "perfect law of liberty" appears in 1:25 as a redesignation of the "implanted word" (which is to be humbly accepted) in 1:21, which in turn is called earlier the "word of truth" (by which God brings men forth) in 1:18. The original antecedent of the "word of truth" can be traced through the "good and perfect gift" (which comes from above) to "wisdom" (for which one is encouraged to ask God in order to be complete) in 1:5, which further connects to the "wisdom which comes from above" in 3:17. This brings one to 3:13 and the necessary relationship made between good deeds and true, godly wisdom[53]. From these connections, the following points can be drawn regarding James' ethics and freedom.

First, the association of the royal law with freedom has to do even more with a person's spirituality than with his moral behaviour. Accepting the gospel of Jesus Christ frees his outward behaviour[54]. Spiritual freedom leads to freedom in the moral realm and rescues a person from repressive bondage to law[55]. Knowing that he is accepted by God frees a person to love his fellow man. Scholars agree that "word of truth," "implanted word," and "perfect law of truth" refer in some respect to the gospel.

Secondly, James understands such normally divergent entities as gospel and law[56], salvation and ethics, wisdom and love, all to be components of a single conglomerate. Living by the law of freedom connects with having

---

51   The origin of the term, which appears twice in James (1:25; 2:12) is a genuine puzzle. As Ammassari, 24, says, "Nobody either in the Bible or in Judaism had ever given this epithet of liberty to the law." Ammassari thinks it derives from the Messianic faith of the author of James. See also Stauffer, who is countered by Nötscher, "'Gesetz,'" and Eckert.

52   Via, 262, says that James' understanding of the law is really "non-legal," allows "contextual freedom," and provides a means to "break through legalism."

53   The relationship between this maze of terms can be seen more fully in Hoppe. See also Schnackenburg, 350–353, and Zmijewski, 76.

54   Henderlite, 470; Schrage, *Ethik*, 270.

55   Ward, 127–132, concludes that "implanted word" (James 1:21) attempts to express inwardness as it relates to the law. Many Old Testament passages contain the notion that doing the law comes about only as a result of its being in the heart (e.g. Deut. 30:14).

56   Schrage, *Ethik*, 267; Goppelt, 2:203; Cranfield, 188; Reicke, 23.

faith in Jesus Christ. Good behaviour and justification (grace) are classed together (Lohse, 21—22, and Via, 262). Loving one's neighbor is part of God's wisdom.

Thirdly, the ultimate purpose is to enable the individual to achieve complete maturity — spiritually, morally, socially — within the will of God[57]. Wisdom, from which all the antecedents flow, is suggested in 1:5 to be the key to perfection.

Fourthly, James' perception of law focuses away from Jewish or even Old Testament law. The law as the author understands it is different in content and in kind. It is law as Jesus has newly re-constituted it[58], encapsulated in love of neighbor and operated by internal, spiritual means.

Numerous concepts have been presented as unifying the divergent ethical themes which constitute the Epistle of James. Among these are: testing[59], patience and steadfastness (Stevens, 277; Fry, 430), wisdom (White, 1:208; Hoppe, 18—43), a practical realisation of faith (Schrage, *Ethik*, 266; Blondel, 141; Maston, 23), whole-heartedness (Henderlite, 464; Mayor, cvii), piety/anti-secularism (K. Weiss), piety/poverty (Dibelius, 47—50), suffering (P. Davids, "Perspective," 97), perfection[60], and anti-doublemindedness[61], Each one has its merits, and any choice that is made must be held tenously because of the nature of the writing.

The suggestion with the most merit, though, is perfection, or complete maturity because it can accommodate most easily all the other themes. Also, the matter of perfection arises early in the writing (1:4) and is tied tightly to wisdom which was just discussed as critical to the royal law of love. The term "perfect" reappears twice in chapter one (1:17, 25) and again in 2:22 and 3:2. Perfection in terms of maturity is a desirable ethical goal for James. Finally, perfection is a theme which is able to incorporate 5:19—20 with ease. Most other suggestions ignore or deal awkwardly with this closing concern of James. However, within a perfection theme, it can be seen that the person who strays from faith is at the opposite pole from

---

57 In this, James contributes to the distinctiveness of Christian ethics from that of Jews and Greeks. See Osborn, vii.

58 See Davies, *Setting*, 402–404; P. Davids, 117–118; Laws, 114; Hort, 56; Dibelius, 120, 146.

59 Hiebert, "Themes;" P. Davids, "Themes," 310; Cranfield, 186; Fry, 430.

60 Zmijewski, 50–78; Hoppe, 18–43; Blondel, 146–148; Lohse, 21–22. Mussner, 58–59, after stating that he wishes to seek "keine gedankliche Einheit des Briefes," mentions "vollkommenen Christen zu machen" as one of four themes put forward as holding the letter together.

61 Laws, "Ethics," and commentary, 29–32. Her view hangs on the use of δίψυχος in 1:8 and 4:8. She thinks that an emphasis on imitating "the singleness of God" in James complements the attack on doubleness. The biggest difficulty with her view, as she candidly admits (p. 304), is the lack of explicit mention in James of imitating God. See also Vlachos. On the origin of δίψυχος, see Seitz, "Antecedents;" Wolverton; Seitz, "Afterthoughts;" S. Marshall.

complete maturity whereas the one who has the insight, fortitude, and concern to bring such a one back to faith exemplifies complete maturity.

James notably lacks any direct appeal to the importance of imitating Christ for Christian ethical behaviour. Nevertheless, it does appeal to Abraham, Job, Elijah, and even Rahab as worthy models[62]. The accent on a stricter standard of judgment for teachers may reveal an understanding of their role in the Christian community not only as imparters of Christian knowledge but also as models of Christian behaviour, at least in their speech. In that the author includes himself as a teacher, he also probably views his own life as an example.

Use in Moral Instruction

The extensive concern for ethics in the Epistle of James in comparison with the rest of the New Testament has made it a favourite source for Christians seeking ethical guidance. How early and widespread this would have occurred is difficult to say given the relatively late universal recognition of the writing's canonical status[63]. However, it surely had impact on the churches to which it was originally sent.

James transmits the wisdom of various cultures and past generations (Dibelius, 4—5). James' contribution to future generations is that it condenses this ethical wisdom and re-packages it for the Christian community. The catchwords which are used extensively in James to link units of thought make handy memory devices for the passing on of its ethical wisdom orally from person to person, church to church, and even generation to generation.

James has had an important role in the research which has taken place on New Testament catechetical teaching, this centering primarily on 1 Peter[64]. As Selwyn (p. 459) acknowledges, the catechetical status of a particular text is difficult to prove. Nevertheless, substantial evidence exists that new Christians were presented a commonly agreed set of instructions near their baptism to help them in doctrine and ethics. The development of such teaching seems a reasonable necessity, as Wessel (p. 61) acknowledges as the church moved away from its Jewish roots.

James may reflect such accepted initiatory teaching in places (Mussner, "Tauflehrer," Braumann). However, Boismard's claim for a liturgical

---

62 P. Davids, "Tradition," 113–126. Perdue, 246, suggests that role models are common in paraenesis.

63 See P. Davids, 7–9; Dibelius, 51–56; Mayor, lxvi–lxxxiv.

64 See Carrington and Selwyn, 364–466. Selwyn recognizes James 1:18, 21, 27; 2:8; 4:5–7, 8, 11 as relevant.

function for James 1:12, 17—21, 26—27; 4:6—10 is too specific for the evidence and wrenches a formality from James which conflicts with its very
nature[65]. Likewise, Halson's (pp. 312—313) declaration that James consists
entirely of a collection of catechetical material emanating from a "school"
of catechists who were aligned with wisdom tradition overreaches the
available evidence.

Perdue's research into the social functions of paraenesis bears more
appealing fruit. He (p. 252) discovers that "paraenetic instruction is
designed to aid in the process of recreating the moral character of an
individual so that he may become capable of living a new life in
accordance with the group's or role's behaviour patterns." Thus, paraenesis
often conveys the wisdom of an experienced group member — a teacher
— to the immature, perhaps young, novice who requires ideological and
ethical re-orientation (p. 250). If provides the individual with a new
framework by which he can interpret the world outside the group and
find his new social role within it now that he is a member (p. 253).

Perdue's application of these features of paraenesis to James is insightful. By advancing beyond concentration on a few possible catechetical
passages and focusing upon the paraenetic nature of the writing and what
that may well mean for its social function, he provides an illuminating
perspective from which to understand the important role James may have
played in early Christian moral education.

---

65 See the detailed critique of Boismard's theory by Mounce, 217–242.

Part I

The Rudiments of Speech-Ethics

Chapter 1: Background

Near Eastern Wisdom Literature

The central value of the counselor to his ruler lies in his ability to speak well. The priority of speaking well is stipulated by Ptah-Hotep (*ANET*, 412), who says, "Teach him first about speaking. Then he may set an example for the children of officials."

The principle way of becoming a skilled speaker is to study the writings of wise predecessors, according to Ani (*AEL*, 2:140). Yet, the true secret of good speech is considered to be an unknown entity since even the untrained can have it while the trained struggle to develop it according to Ptah-Hotep (*ANET*, 412).

However, speech is much more than just the ability to articulate words that are convincing. It also requires a certain amount of reasoned knowledge and the ability to listen and understand others. Combining the two is no simple task, as Ptah-Hotep (*LAE*, 168) attests, saying, "Speech is more difficult than any craft."

Controlled Speech

Control is the way the advisor advances the principle of order. The following quotations from various Near Eastern primary sources establish the importance of control[1]:

> Let your mouth be controlled and your speech guarded:
> Therein is a man's wealth — let your lips be very precious.

> Beware of careless talk; guard your lips.

> Exert yourself to restrain your speech.

> Control your mouth; so will your counsel be [heard] among the magistrates . . . Be patient when you speak, and you will say distinguished things; then will the magistrates who shall hear say: 'How good is his utterance!'

---

1 The quotations are from the following sources, in order of their appearance: Counsels of Wisdom, 26–30, 131, 134 (*BWL*, 101); Ptah–Hotep (*LAE*, 175); Amen–em–Opet (*LAE*, 245–246); Ahiqar 7:96–99 (*ANET*, 428).

Something else of value in the heart of God is to
   stop and think before speaking.
Do not get into a quarrel with the argumentative man
   nor incite him with words; . . .
Sleep on it before speaking
   for a storm come forth like fire in hay is
   the hot–heated man in his appointed time.
May you be restrained before him.

My son, chatter not overmuch so that you speak out every word that comes to your
mind . . . More than all watchfulness, watch your mouth.

According to these admonitions, controlled speech depends upon self-imposed restraint. Such restraint can be taught to another by discipline (Ptah-Hotep, *LAE*, 164) and by example (Ptah-Hotep, *LAE*, 174).

Controlled speech is expected especially at times when it is the most difficult to maintain, as in times of anger. As Amen-em-Opet (*LAE*, 251) observes, "When a man's heart is upset, words travel faster than wind and rain." The ideal response to a situation of anger is not considered to be mere silence but rather an even-tempered reply. Ptah-Hotep (*LAE*, 168) says, "Do not keep silence, but beware lest you offend or answer a word with anger." It is further suggested that a controlled response be cultivated by first turning away from the source of irritation before returning with a response (Ptah-Hotep, *LAE*, 168–169).

Under normal circumstances, the person who is silent typifies the best speech habits. This most extreme form of control, it is thought, will bring him happiness and fulfillment in life. The following quotations from the literature speak of this[2]:

Do not talk a lot. Be silent, and you will he happy.

Fill yourself with silence, you will find life
   and your body shall flourish upon earth.

. . . the submissive man prospers, the moderate man is praised, the tent is open for the
silent man, and the place of the contended man is wide.

Such absolute control is rare. Thus, a person who is able to be silent will be admired (Ptah-Hotep, *LAE*, 163). His perpetuation of *maat* in society stands out, according to Amen-em-Opet (*LAE*, 246).

The silent man will be of special value to the ruler who uses him as counsel. His silence will serve to accent the weight of his words when he speaks. He will provide enormous aid to the king's efforts to bring about order in society. Ptah-Hotep (*LAE*, 168) exhorts, "Speak only when you can clarify the issue."

---

2 In order, Ani (*ANET*, 420); Amen–em–Opet, (*LAE*, 247); Kagemni (*LAE*, 177).

Silence is actually a valuable skill in argumentation. The advice for the counselor to the king in Ptah-Hotep (*LAE*, 161) speaks of the value of silence in three crucial situations. When arguing with a person of superior authority (also Ani, *AEL*, 2:143), the advice is:

> Bend down your arms and bow your back; if you disagree with him he will not side with you. You should make little of the evil speaking by not opposing him in his arguments; it means he will be dubbed an ignoramus when your self-control has matched his prolixity.

If one is arguing against an equal, Ptah-Hotep suggests silence again:

> Let your virtue be manifest against him in silence when he is speaking ill; great will be the talk on the part of the hearers, and your name will be fair in opinion of the magistrates.

When disputing with a person of inferior position and skill, Ptah-Hotep advises restraint, saying, "Do not be aggressive against him in proportion as he is humble."

When a person does speak, he is advised to say things that will be beneficial and to suppress anything that would be harmful. The advice in Ani (*AEL*, 2:143) for dealing with an angry person is: "Speak sweetly when he speaks sourly." More generally, Amen-em-Opet (*LAE*, 250) says, "Set a good report on your tongue while the bad thing is covered up inside you." Likewise, Ani (*ANET*, 420) makes a similar point.

The Counsels of Wisdom (*BWL*, 105) says:

> . . . speak what is of good report.
> . . . speak well of people . . .
> [utter] what is decent.

The way to accomplish these positive responses to situations in life is suggested by Amen-em-Opet (*LAE*, 258):

> Be strong in your heart; make your mind firm[3];
>   do not steer with your tongue.
> The tongue of a man is the steering oar of a boat;
>   and the Lord of All is its pilot.

Listening, Words, and Deeds

Ptah-Hotep (*ANET*, 414) says, "[When] hearing is good, speaking is good."

From a pragmatic point of view, patient listening is a good idea. Not only might one learn something from someone else, but he also earns the right to be heard by others when he speaks according to Ptah-Hotep (*LAE*, 175).

---

3 A similar sentiment is expressed earlier in Amen-em-Opet (*LAE*, 252). There it is said: "Do not separate your mind from your tongue."

Listening, however, is not merely waiting one's turn to speak. It involves careful internalisation of what one is hearing or reading. Anyone who neglects to do this with regard to the wisdom of those who have gone before him is doomed to failure. Therefore, Amen-em-Opet (*LAE*, 244) says:

> Give your ears and hear what is said,
>> Give your mind over to their interpretation:
> It is profitable to put them in your heart,
>> But woe to him that neglects them!
> Let them rest in the shrine of your insides
>> That they may act as a lock in your heart;
> Now when there comes a storm of words,
>> They will be a mooring post on your tongue.

One of the purposes of such internalisation is so that the listener may be able to understand fully what the other person said, scrutinising it before be responds. Then when his turn comes to speak he will be accurate and penetrating (Ptah-Hotep, *LAE*, 165, 175).

A good speaker conducts himself in a war that demonstrates obedient response to what he hears (Ptah-Hotep, *LAE*, 165).

A long passage in Ptah-Hotep (*LAE*, 173) carefully interweaves the three notions of hearing, internalising, and obedient doing:

> Hearing is good and speaking is good, but he who hears is a possessor of benefits. Hearing is good for the hearer, and better is hearing than anything, for fair love comes [thus] into being. How good it is that a son should accept what his father says. Old age comes about for him by means of it. He who hears is one whom God loves, but one who does not hear is one whom God detests. It is the heart which educates its owner in hearing or in not hearing, for the life, prosperity, and health of a man depend upon his heart; it is the hearer who hears what is said, and he who acts according to what is said, is one who loves hearing. How good it is that a son should obey his father, and joyful is he to whom this is said.

The Power of Words

The importance of using words economically is evident from what has already been said. Underlying this basic principle of speech-ethics in Near Eastern Wisdom Literature is a mystical concept about words[4]. A word once spoken is considered to be eternal. It cannot be reclaimed or reversed by its speaker. It persists in perpetuity as an entity in itself, lost to the speaker's control forever. Understandably, such beliefs solicit great care in speaking. Ptah-Hotep (*ANET*, 414) says:

---

4 Regarding Mesopotamian religions, Jacobsen, 15, says, "The creative power of the word underlies all Mesopotamian religious literature. It may be assumed to have been most clearly and strongly felt in earliest time, and it probably varied with use in rituals, for instruction, or for entertainment."

Every word is carried on, without perishing in this land forever. It makes for expressing well the speech of the very officials. It is what teaches a man to speak to the future so that it may hear it . . .

Ahiqar (*ANET*, 428) says:

For a word is a bird: once it is released no man can recapture it. First count the secrets of your mouth; then bring out your words by number.

The Counsels of Wisdom (*BWL*, 105) succinctly says, "For what you say in a moment will follow you afterwards."

Not only are uttered words independent and eternal, but they also carry immense power and influence. Ahiqar (*ANET*, 428) reckons this is especially true for a king. The more important a person is the more influential are his words. Ahiqar (*ANET*, 429) thinks the mouth of the person who is successful is an instrument of the gods.

Old Testament

Controlled Speech

Controlled speech is the trademark of the wise man. Prov. 17:27 says: "A man of knowledge uses words with restraint."

By contrast, one of the trademarks of a wicked man is his loose mouth given free rein for evil (Ps. 50:19)[5], belching forth uncontrolled and unrestrained (Ps. 59:7). Regardless of his apparent success or failure in the present life, such a person will eventually meet his Waterloo in God's rebuke (Ps. 50:21). Furthermore, Proverbs considers it a reliable principle that such a one will come to ruin in this life as well (Ps. 13:3).

A person who lacks self-control is defenseless against the influence of evil in his life (Prov. 25:28) and is bound to come to ruin, according to the Hebrew concept of God, for evil always loses sooner or later. The righteous person, however, will pray daily for God's help to control his tongue as modelled by Ps. 141:3, which says:

Set a guard over my mouth, O Lord,
    keep watch over the door of my lips.

He also has the further example to follow of Ps. 39:1 in which the writer resolves to guard his mouth "as with a muzzle[6]."

---

5 Both Weiser, 398, and A. Anderson, 388, support the rendering of שלחת as "giving free rein" in Ps. 50:19. The rendering "let loose" is in NASB and is supported by Briggs, 1:420.

6 In this instance, the Psalmist resolved not to utter his complaint to God in the hearing of his enemies for fear of giving his enemies false impressions about God. See A. Anderson, 1:309; Weiser, 328; Briggs, 1:345. See also Ps. 17:3.

28 *Chapter 1*

From this general concern for control stems further advice in the Old Testament about temper, verbosity, simplicity, silence and gracious speech.

Moments of anger are probably the most difficult times to control one's speech. Yet the position of the Old Testament is unequivocal. Speech must be controlled on these occasions. Prov. 29:11 is representative of Old Testament thought when it says:

> A fool gives vent to his anger,
> but a wise man keeps himself under control[7].

The concern for controlling displays of anger is not merely abstract, either. It is rooted in the knowledge that hot-tempered speech will invariably be sinful. It will stir up dissension and lead to further quarrelling[8].

The Old Testament is concerned about the maintenance of peace and harmony in a community (Prov. 17:1), and thus speaks favourably of the patient, even-tempered man because he calms quarrels and promotes peace (Prov. 15:1). Such a man nobly represents the very manner of God who, as Ps. 145:8 says, is "gracious and compassionate, slow to anger and rich in love."

The Old Testament concern for controlled speech extends beyond special situations like those of anger to a desire that speech be controlled as a general characteristic of one's daily life. Verbosity is the characteristic of a fool (Eccl. 10:14; Prov. 10:8, 10).

The chatterer's downfall is the result of generations of observation. Verbosity makes a person ripe for sin every time he opens his mouth (Prov. 10:19). Its root cause is vanity, and its assured result, progressive ignorance (Prov. 18:2). Not only that, there is the practical result: verbosity is a hindrance to meaningful communication[9]. As Eccl. 6:11 says,

> The more the words,
> the less the meaning,
> and how does that profit anyone?

Just as the Old Testament is opposed to verbosity, so is it also opposed to obscure, intellectual profundity. Difficult truths are understood best when explained simply and succinctly. This is conveyed in Prov. 18:4, which say:

> The word of a man's mouth are deep waters,
> but the fountain of wisdom is a babbling brook.

---

7 The foolishness of uncontrolled temper is also spoken of in Prov. 14:17, 29; 20:3; 29:20; Eccl. 7:9. The wisdom of a controlled temper is espoused in Prov. 10:10; 12:16; 16:32; 17:27; 20:11.
8 Prov. 15:18; 20:3; 29:21; Ps. 37:7–9.
9 It is not without reason that Job and his "friends" accuse each other of verbosity. See Job 15:2; 16:3; 18:2; 19:2.

The words for "deep waters" (מַיִם עֲמֻקִּים), as in Prov. 20:5, are best taken negatively, conveying the idea of unfathomable obscurity, while the words for "babbling brook" (נַחַל נֹבֵעַ) are best taken positively, conveying the idea of easy-to-see simplicity[10]. The idea is that while the common man wrongly thinks he is being wise when he uses obscure language, the truly wise man knows that true wisdom is characterised by simplicity.

God's concern for this principle of control is evidenced not only in his preference for using thick-tongued Moses over silver-tongued Aaron (Ex. 4:10—17) but also in his own effort to avoid language that is difficult for his people to understand[11].

Intrinsic to the Old Testament concept of controlled speech is the conviction that absolute control, or silence, is essential at times, and that certain situations call just as much for being quiet as other situations appropriately demand speaking out. As Eccl. 3:7b observes, "[There is] a time to be silent and a time to speak."

The ability to know when to be silent and the ability to harness one's tongue at such times is one of the supreme marks of a wise man. As Prov. 17:28 says,

> Even a fool is thought wise if he keeps silent
> and discerning if he holds his tongue.

Such controlled demeanor is not only smart[12] in terms of minimising the utterance of foolish and harmful statements that will later be regretted, but it also displays an admirable attitude of personal humility as well as a respect for others and a genuine interest in their opinions. Job claims that he was a recipient of respect for such a manner of life when he reminisces in Job 29:8—10, 21:

---

10 There is a fairly even division among commentators over whether מַיִם עֲמֻקִּים should be taken positively or negatively and over whether the two clauses in the proverb are antithetical or climactic. McKane, 513, and Toy, 384, opt for a rendering as follows: "The words of a man's mouth are deep waters, a bubbling brook, a spring of wisdom." The difficulty with this is the clearly negative use of עָמֹק elsewhere in the Old Testament in the sense of "unintelligible" (Isa. 33:19, Ezek. 3:5) in relationship to speech and "impenetrable" (Ps. 64:7) and "mysterious" (Job 11:8; Ps. 92:6) elsewhere. Toy's complaint that "a fountain is not a brook" in criticising the translation of "the fountain of wisdom is a babbling brook" is out of order. The language is clearly figurative and need not be pushed to such literalness. Although the absence of any conjunction allows the possibility of a climactic sense to the proverb, I take it to be antithetical along with R. Scott, 114, and Gemser, *Salamos*, 75.

11 Deut. 30:11—14. Although many of his acts are beyond human comprehension (Ps. 131:1; Prov. 30:18), in this case at least, he has made a deliberate effort to make his word simple and easy to understand. This leaves the people no legitimate excuse for failure to obey.

12 Prov. 12:23a calls the man who keeps his knowledge to himself עָרוּם, meaning "shrewd," "clever" or in contemporary vernacular, "smart." As Prov. 12:23b and 29:20 point out, the fool conducts himself in the opposite manner.

The young men saw me and stepped aside
    and the old men rose to their feet;
The chief men refrained from speaking
    and covered their mouths with their hands;
The voices of the nobles were hushed,
    and their tongues stuck to the roof of their mouths.

Men listened to me expectantly,
    waiting in silence for my counsel.

Elihu, in Job 32:4—10, claims that he has remained silent out of respect for the others who are older and presumably wiser, even though he has obviously been disappointed by their speeches. It may be that his virtuous waiting, in contrast to Job and the others, is intended to indicate that his speech truly represents God (Job 32:7—8, 18; 33:4).

Elsewhere in the Old Testament, particularly in the Psalms and Lamentations, the importance of waiting patiently and silently before the Lord is emphasised. Ps. 37:7 says, "Be still before the Lord and wait patiently for him[13]." Lam. 3:25—26 says,

The Lord is good to those who wait for Him,
To the person who seeks Him.
It is good that he waits silently.
For the salvation of the Lord.

Waiting exhibits a conscious attitude of respect and dependence upon God as well as a confident expectancy that he will eventually explain confusing events in life satisfactorily. David, to whom most of the Psalms which voice or recommend this attitude are attributed, is possibly the best Old Testament example of this[14]. In contrast, Job is an example of one who willfully did not keep his mouth shut during a most crucial test of his character and loyalty to God. Self-righteously, he proclaims:

Therefore I will not keep silent.
I will speak out of the anguish of my spirit.
I will complain in the bitterness of my soul[15].

---

13 "Be still" is the Qal imperative of דום which as a noun means "silence." It is used in the context of waiting for God also in Ps. 62:1 and in Lam. 3:26. In the former, the idea of waiting must be assumed for no word for it appears in the Hebrew. Other references to waiting for the Lord are found in Ps. 37:34; 40:1; 52:9; 62:1; 69:4; 119:114; 130:5. The word used most for waiting in these references is קוה which implies a sense of expectation and eagerness. The other word used occasionally is יחל which usually emphasises the temporal and the virtues of endurance and patience, i.e., Job 6:11.

14 See Ps. 38:12 in particular but also Ps. 40:1; 52:9; 62:1.

15 Job 7:11. It is arguable that while Job did not sin by cursing God he did fall far short of God's expectations for him by "multiplying his words against God" as Elihu accuses (34:37; 35:16). It is of no little significance that God begins his speech (38:2) with the uncontested accusation: "Who is this that darkens my counsel with words without knowledge?" Of importance, too, is that Job finally submits to God's accusation and determines to "say no more" (40:4–5) and, indeed, retracts his words

As a people, Israel is also accused of foolishly casting aside this important attitude of silent dependence before God (Ps. 106:13). In forecasting the destruction of Jerusalem, Isaiah (29:3—4) envisages the people being forced into the humble position of dependence by God himself.

The desired result of the concern in the Old Testament for keeping speech under control is that a person's speech be habitually gracious, perceptive, appropriate to the situation, and at all cost, genuinely beneficial to those listening. As Prov. 10:32a says, "The lips of the righteous know what is fitting[16]."

The righteous man will consciously use his speech to promote goodwill, to benefit society in every situation he encounters. Not only will he find personal satisfaction in such apt and timely speaking (Prov. 15:23; 25:11) but he will also likely gain the favour of his king (Prov. 22:11) and society. There is good reason for this. As Prov. 16:21 observes:

Pleasant words are a honeycomb,
Sweet to the soul and healing to the bones.

Words of kindness are genuinely therapeutic to individuals and to society. It may be a paradox that gentle words are powerful enough to "turn away wrath" (Prov. 15:1) or to "break a bone" (Prov. 25:15). However, words, spoken graciously do exhibit a kind of power on society that is undeniably effective. Keen instruction presented pleasantly is devoured by those listening like a child craving candy[17]. Job (29:22—23) attests that people will drink in gentle words "as the spring rain." In his closing message, Moses resolves that his speech be gentle and gracious in order that it might effectively proclaim the Lord's message. Deut. 32:2—3a says:

Let my teaching drop as the rain,
My speech distill as dew,
As the droplets in the fresh grass
And as the showers in the herb.
For I proclaim the name of the Lord;

---

and repents (42:3–6) before God in his final speech. See Pope 348; Driver and Gray, 347–348; Kissane, 292, for help on integrating these verses into the context of Job. What I have deduced so far suggests further that Job's ideal response to his dilemma was to be quiet and bear his misery without complaint, demonstrating every confidence in God's justice and sovereignty, patiently waiting for God to eventually make the situation understandable. Indeed, he should have followed the advice he gave to his friends in 13:5, "If only you would be altogether silent! For you, that would be wisdom."

16 The word translated "fitting" is a participial form of רצה, which contains the implication of being pleasant by saying something favourable or helpful. See Prov. 10:11; 14:35; Deut. 33;16. See also McKane, 424, for an explanation of Prov. 10:32 in this sense.

17 Prov. 16:21, says, "Pleasant words promote instruction." The root of the word for pleasant, מתק, literally means "sweet." Compare Prov. 16:24.

The ability to produce speech that is gracious is rated highly by the Old Testament, as we have seen[18]. But, how is this accomplished?

The key is one's heart[19]. As Prov. 16:23a says, "A wise man's heart guides his mouth." Prov. 23:15—16 zeros in on the heart as the key to appropriate speech when it says:

> My son, if your heart is wise,
>   then my heart will be glad.
>   My inmost being will rejoice
> When your lips speak what is right[20].

Gracious speech is produced when the inner man determines what the outer man says[21]. Speech which is unguided by man's inner resources of thought and determination is incapable of being gracious or beneficial to others because it is by definition uncontrolled. As Prov. 21:29 says, "An upright man gives thought to his ways[22]."

Elihu (Job 33:3) is confident that his speech is appropriate and beneficial because he knows his heart is "upright," and he has put careful thought into what he is about to say after waiting patiently. David's speech is described by Saul's servant as "prudent." He is a person who demonstrates the internal characteristics of wisdom by the way he speaks[23]. Prov. 16:21 says, "The wise in heart are called discerning [prudent]."

A foolish or ungracious heart cannot produce truly gracious speech. Care must be taken not to confuse fluency with gracious speech. Someone

---

18 Von Rad, *Theology*, 1:431, evaluates Israel's concern for gracious speech as greater than that of her Babylonian and Egyptian neighbors.

19 Vriezen, 328, makes the keen observation that "in the teaching of the Old Testament . . . man's disposition, the heart, is again and again considered to be of decisive importance for man's activity." See Prov. 4:23 and Isa. 29:1. See also Prov. 10:8; 16:1; 22:11; Ps. 17:3, where the heart and speech are associated.

20 Notice the a–b–b–a sentence arrangement here. The word for "right," ישׁר, refers to what is true and fitting. The significance of this verse is that it emphasises that "right speech" means there is no discrepancy between speech and intent. See McKane, 387.

21 The thought processes are an intricate part of the functioning of the inner man, the heart. Sorg says that "the heart is the seat of understanding and of knowledge, of rational forces and powers." As Blocher, 23, perceptively asks, "If the heart both thinks and wills, and is man's religious organ, how could thought function independently?" See also Blackman and Baumgärtel, 606–607. Important scriptural references which link the heart with thinking are, among others: Gen. 6:5; Deut. 4:39; Isa. 10:7; Prov. 4:23; 15:28.

22 See also Prov. 5:6; 14:8, 15.

23 The word "prudent" (בין in the Niphal) is also paralleled with "wise" in Isa. 29:14 and Hos. 14:9. It is the same word used in Prov. 14:8. Perhaps it can be said that a person whose speech is "wise in heart" characteristically thinks before he speaks. See Müller, 372, for a discussion of the relationship between "wisdom" and "heart" in the Old Testament. There he refers to more passages which use the phrase "wise in heart" (Job 9:4; 37:24; Prov. 10:8).

can be quick with the tongue or good with words but not be described as a gracious, perceptive, or beneficial speaker. God did not choose Aaron to confront Pharaoh but rather Moses. His preference to use the simple speech of Moses was because Moses' heart, his inner resources, were right for the job. Even when he conceded to work through the naturally fluent speech of Aaron, he still worked through Moses' heart, not Aaron's[24].

The heart is the place in which God desires to work, where his word is heard (Baumgärtel, 612). Very few in the Old Testament are noted for having their God-guided heart control their speech so that it can be described as habitually gracious. Along with Moses and David, there is Joseph, Solomon, and Daniel[25]. Of course, the prophets must be seen in this light to some extent as well. God himself is a gracious speaker in that when he speaks to man in the Old Testament his speech is always perceptive, appropriate to the situation, and intentionally beneficial to mankind[26].

Listening, Words, and Deeds

Just as central to the concern for speech-ethics in the Old Testament as controlled speech is listening. In fact, the two share a dynamic relationship toward the common end of bringing about speech that is gracious. Listening is the key activity of the heart which makes it wise.

The reader of Proverbs is pommelled with commands to listen and pay attention to the forthcoming words of advice[27]. Proverbs also concerns itself most with listening to the advice of others.

A connection between listening and gracious speaking is made by Prov. 5:1—2:

My son, pay attention to my wisdom;
  listen well to my words of insight
That you may maintain discretion
  and your lips may preserve knowledge[28].

---

24 See Ex. 4:10–17. Samson spoke in clever riddles (Judg. 14:14, 18; 15:16), but he was foolish.

25 Both Joseph (Gen. 41:33) and Solomon (1 Ki. 3:12) are described as "prudent" (נבון) as is David. Daniel is indirectly (Dan. 1:4) depicted as being "endowed with understanding and discerning [בין] knowledge." Later on (1:30), he is specifically called wise and understanding. Significantly, both Joseph and Daniel are depicted as invaluable counselors to their respective kings. R. Scott, *Way*, 87–89, includes a discussion of the importance of Joseph as a wisdom figure.

26 Job 9:4 describes God as "wise in heart."

27 Among other references, see Prov. 1:8; 2:1–2; 4:1, 10; 5:1, 7; 6:20; 7:1–3, 24; 8:6, 33; 16:20; 19:20, 27; 22:17–18; 23:12, 22.

28 Two different words for listening are paralleled here: קשב ("pay attention") and אזנך חט (literally, "stretch out," "incline your ear"). There is some discussion about the text in 5:2 by R.Scott, 54, and Toy, 101–102.

A connection between listening and the heart is made by Prov. 4:20—21 (cf. Prov. 7:24; 23:12):

> My son, pay attention to what I say,
>   listen closely to my words.
> Do not let them out of your sight,
>   keep them within your heart.

The heart is envisaged as a guarded storage place for wisdom (Prov. 4:23). Yet, these pearls of wisdom are expected to be polished and "ready on your lips," according to Prov. 22:17—18.

Memorisation of wise sayings (such as those in Proverbs) is at least partially what is in mind in these last three quotations[29]. Rote memorisation of words is not all that is meant since elsewhere in Proverbs it is words bound in the heart that are spoken of as having real influence in a person's life (Prov. 4:22—23; 6:20—24; 7:1—4).

Proverbs contains an abundance of references connecting listening to the development of wisdom in man. Prov. 19:20 (cf. Prov. 12:15; 13:1, 10) is a good representative of many passages when it says:

> Listen to advice and accept instruction,
>   and in the end you will be wise.

For the truly wise man, this receptivity to advice and instruction even extends to rebuke and correction[30].

The person who does not listen to instruction from others is considered to be arrogant, empty of knowledge, and sure to demonstrate the folly of his ways when he attempts to speak[31]. In contrast, the person who listens is certain to be blessed in all that he says and does[32].

A good Old Testament example of one who astutely listened and benefited from the wisdom of another is Moses. In Ex. 18:24, it is said that Moses listened to his father-in-law Jethro and wisely carried out his suggestion of apportioning out the responsibilities of judging the people. In contrast, Pharaoh is described in Ex. 8:15 as "not listening to Moses and Aaron."

Another example is Job who describes himself (29:31) as one to whom others respectfully listened. Joseph, David, Solomon, and Daniel are not only depicted as being listened to because of their wisdom but also because of being good listeners themselves[33].

---

29 See McKane, 375; Barclay, 40–41.
30 Prov. 10:8; 13:13; 15:31; 25:12.
31 Prov. 10:8; 12:15; 13:1, 13; 18:13; 19:27.
32 Prov. 1:33; 4:23; 8:33; 16:20; 19:20.
33 The idea of attentiveness is contained within the intention of בין ("prudent"), a word by which all four are described.

The emphasis on learning from the wisdom of parents and sages[34] is grounded not only in sociology but also in theology. This wisdom is born out of the practical observation and experience of the working order of the universe created by God. It is indirect, horizontal wisdom from and about him[35]. This connection between wisdom and the knowledge of God is established in Prov. 2:1—6, when Wisdom says:

> My son, if you accept my word
>   and store up my command within you,
> turning your ear to wisdom
>   and applying your heart to understanding,
> and if you look for it as for silver
>   and search for it as for hidden treasure,
> then you will understand the fear of the Lord
>   and find the knowledge of God.

As far as Proverbs is concerned, then, listening to the wisdom of men ultimately is listening to God. This perspective only heightens the importance of listening, with the goal of obtaining a wise heart which can habitually produce controlled and gracious speech.

However, as important as it is to listen to people, who sometimes and only indirectly utter the wisdom of God, so much more important is it to listen to the very words of God himself spoken directly to men. Proverbs does not concern itself with this important implication outside of one possible verse[36]. However, this lack is more than adequately balanced by the rest of the Old Testament[37]. Listening to God is one of the central imperatives for the Hebrew individual and for his nation. There is good reason for this, as Ps. 119:130 observes:

> The unfolding of Thy words gives light,
> It gives understanding to the simple.

---

34 Prov. 1:8; 4:20; 6:20; 23:22; Job 8:8—10.

35 Similar to Israel's way of seeing God in the wisdom which has been passed down through generations, is her way of seeing the passing down of her history as the recording of the activity of God. See Deut. 32:7; Ps. 44:1—4; 78:4.

36 Prov. 16:20 says, "He who gives attention to the word shall find good, and blessed is he who trusts in the Lord". McKane, 498, by suggesting three possible understandings of this verse, leaves open the possibility which is put forward by Toy, 329. Toy proposes that "the word" here refers to the word of the Lord as represented by legal and prophetic documents as well as the wisdom of wise men. If a chiasm is intended here, the credibility of this proposal is strengthened further.

37 Muilenburg, "Ethics," 528, speaking about Israel, says: "Thus it was possible to describe her entire tradition in the speaking–hearing relationship. In crucial moments of history, words were spoken which concerned the interior meaning of her existence and destiny. At Sinai the confrontation was with the words of God: God spoke all these words. The prophets were his instruments to speak his words. In the cult the priests preserved, transmitted, and implemented into reality the words which had been spoken. Priests, prophets, and lawgiver were one in the common cry, 'Hear, O Israel,' " Brockington, 232, even suggests that the name "Yahweh" is an imperfect tense Hebrew word meaning "to speak."

God's word, whether it be in the form of written law, prophetic speakers, history, or a word to an individual, is perceptive and can adequately can counsel and explanation to any situation, great or small, national or private. One who listens to God's word, storing it continually in his heart, will have the vital key to speak graciously (Ps. 37:30—31)[38].

Memorisation of the law is a necessary step toward filling the heart with it, but this is only the beginning of what should be a perpetual process requiring a person to always be listening and ever-expecting enlightenment from God[39]. It requires giving God complete and undivided attention (Ps. 86:11).

Samuel is a good example of one who gave God full attention in his heart his whole life. He is memorable for his attentiveness to God's voice as a boy serving Eli in the temple (1 Sam. 3). He also initiated the line of Old Testament prophets whose job was to listen attentively to God's word in order to deliver it clearly to their nation and to the world.

Balaam is memorable for faithfully hearing and delivering God's word under stressful circumstances (Num. 23—24). To have done otherwise would have been to speak presumptuously and to have violated God's explicit word as enunciated in Deut. 18:20—22.

Moses, David, Joseph, and Daniel are noteworthy for their attentiveness to God's word which not only produced gracious speech in their lives as already noted but which also produced God's word itself on occasion.

In sharp contrast to these men who nobly model the dynamic relationship between gracious speech and listening to God are those wicked men of Israel spoken in Ps. 50:16—19 to whom God says, "You . . . cast my words behind you." Zech. 7:11—12 describes the nation of Israel herself as refusing to listen to God and bearing the consequences.

The words of the Lord to his chosen nation are from beginning to end wrapped in the imperative to pay attention and listen to him[40]. If they would only listen, God continually guarantees that they would receive his manifold blessing[41]. But, from the day he brought them out of Egypt until the last days of exile, the people of Israel are best characterised as a nation "not listening." As Jer. 7:24—27 describes them:

> But they did not listen or pay attention; instead, they followed the stubborn inclination of their evil hearts. They went backward not forward. From the time your forefathers left Egypt until now, day after day, again and again I sent you my servants the

---

38 See also Ps. 40:8; 119:11; Deut. 6:6; 11:8; 30:14; Isa. 51:7; Jer. 31:33.
39 See Ps. 119:114, 147—148; 130:5; Prov. 16:20.
40 The cry "Hear, O Israel" resounds throughout the Old Testament from the first commandment to the last prophet. See Deut. 5:1; 6:3—4; 9:1; 20:3; 1 Sam. 12:14—15; Amos 3:1; 4:1; 5:1; Mic. 1:2; 3:1, 7; Mal. 2:2. Note also comments by Muilenburg, "Ethics," 528.
41 Deut. 11:13; 15:5; 30:8; 32:2.

prophets. But they did not listen to me or pay attention. They were stiff–necked and did more evil than their forefathers. When you tell them all this, they will not answer[42].

Jeremiah goes further in this passage (7:28) to speak of Israel as "the nation that has not obeyed the Lord their God or responded to correction" and to conclude from this that "truth has perished and has been cut off from their mouth." Two important truths for understanding Old Testament speech-ethics may be drawn from this.

First, proper listening implies obedience. Hearing and doing are inviolably connected[43]. If one has truly heard God's word, he will incorporate it into his life. Conversely, if one does not do God's word, he has not really heard it[44].

Secondly, there is a link between listening to God, obedience, and speech. True and gracious speech simply is not possible for a person who is not habitually listenting to God and obeying his word. Indeed, ungracious speech is a sure indicator of that person's disobedience and resistance to God's voice in his heart.

Notably, Jer. 31:31—34 anticipates a day when the whole process toward Israel's obedience to God will be radically simplified. The mighty gulf between God's will and his people's obedience will be eliminated. People will no longer have to listen! The biggest hindrance to Israel's obedience will be dropped from the process. All the wisdom of God will be placed within the heart of each person in such a way that what God wants will be done without fault.

However, until that day[45], the person who desires to obey God must commit himself to listening to his word. His every word and every deed will emerge out of a wise heart that consistently listens for God's word wherever it may be found. In fact, he will have come full circle when he realises that in order for the process to begin his speech must be under control. As Ps. 32:9 enigmatically warns:

42 Such pessimism regarding Israel's attentiveness to God's word is reiterated in Ps. 8:11–13; Jer. 11:8; 18:18; 44:17; Ezek. 20:8; Zech. 7:11–14; Mal. 2:2. One cannot get away from the fact that Israel is called to "an oral engagement, to participate in the responsibility of the give–and–take of words," as Muilenburg, 29, puts it.

43 On numerous occasions, Israel promises to do what the Lord says (Ex. 19:8; 24:3, 7; Deut. 5:27; Josh. 24:24). Moses listened and did what his father–in–law said (Ex. 18:24). David charges Solomon to walk in God's ways (1 Ki. 2:2–4). The characters in Job are quick to admonish one another to "hear it and apply it to yourself" (Job 5:27; 21:2; 33:2, 31, 33; 34:2, 16).

44 As Prov. 20:11 astutely observes, "Even a child is known by his actions; whether his conduct is pure and right." Josiah (2 Ki. 22:11) is a good example of an individual who responded immediately and properly upon hearing God's word. See also Isa. 29:13–14 and Neh. 8:9.

45 Both Harrison, 140, and Nicholson, 70, speak of it being "inaugurated" in the coming of Jesus.

Do not be as the horse or as the mule which have no understanding;
Whose trappings include bit and bridle to hold them in check,
Otherwise they will not come near you[46].

The Power of Words

Words have power[47]. Controlled speech is an effort to minimise the
negative and destructive power of words; gracious speech is an attempt to
maximise the positive and beneficial power of words. Job is a good
example of one who experienced both the hurt of words (19:1) and the joy
of helping others with words (4:3).

One of the most significant statements about the power of words is
found in Prov. 18:20—21 (cf. Prov. 12:14), which says:

From the fruit of his mouth a man's stomach is filled;
   with the harvest of his lips he is satisfied.
The tongue has the power of life and death
   and those who love it will eat its fruit[48].

This verse admonishes people to be aware of the power of the tongue
and to be mature enough to accept the consequences of it (for good or
bad). This should provide motivation to harness speech for good.

Many suggest that the Old Testament is consistent with other literature
of the ancient Near East in considering the awesome power of words to
be inherent in words themselves. Once words leave the speaker's mouth,
they have a life and power which is separate and independent from him,
even being capable of generating their own effect after lying dormant for
a long period[49]. Support for this view is advocated on the basis of three
principal arguments. However, close scrutiny reveals serious inadequacies

---

46 The point of these words which are attributed to God appears to be that God is
    capable of restraining man's speech in order to enable proper communication between
    man and himself to take place. However, God would greatly prefer it if man would
    keep his mouth under control on his own and obey him willingly. See Weiser,
    286–287. Dahood, 1:196, argues poignantly that מֶתֶג means "muzzle" rather than
    simply bridle here. He does this on the basis of 2 Ki. 19:28 where the object depicted
    prevents the animal from biting or raising its voice. In this light, the choice of "bit
    and bridle" by NASB is appropriate.
47 Such recognition is inherent in a number of references cited above in the section on
    controlled speech. See especially Prov. 11:11; 15:1–4; 16:24; 25:15. Vriezen, 253, observes:
    "To an even greater degree than the modern Westerner, the Oriental of ancient times
    was impressed by the importance of the word; he would never have called the word
    'nur Schall und Rauch' (mere sound and fury); to his mind it is something laden with
    power."
48 McKane takes fruit strictly as "good fruit." The fact that Hos. 10:13 uses "fruit" to
    depict "lies" considerably weakens his case. J. Williams, "Power," 54–55, in using this
    proverb as an example of ambiguous proverbs, thinks that this proverb is purposely
    ambiguous on the point of whether the fruit is good or evil.
49 Among many others espousing this view is Eichrodt, 1:69–70, 173. On p. 69, he says
    that words "virtually have a life of their own; they are like independent beings

which undermine this axiom in many Old Testament theologies and commentaries[50].

First, by drawing from the fact that דכר can refer to a word or a thing, it is typical to glean the principle that the Hebrew, like his neighbors in the Near East, was "unable to differentiate between word and object, idea and actuality [51]." This principle is also commonly derived from the supposed etymological background of דכר as "back" or "background." Both these uses of דכר are discredited by Barr, *The Semantics of Biblical Language*. Using precisely these two uses of דכר as examples, Barr dislodges the legitimacy of using etymology in the place of actual word usage. He specifically discredits the practice of combining the "alternate" meanings of "words" and "thing" into a composite meaning[52]. He makes the telling observation (p. 133) that the meaning "thing" or "matter" for דכר is derived from "word," the primary meaning, and not the other way around. Therefore, דכר means "things" only as an outgrowth of "word[53]."

Secondly, von Rad appeals to the example of people's names having inherent power in the Old Testament times[54]. In a less celebrated work, Barr, "Names," carefully dismantles this view. Barr's argument is threefold: 1) an examination of names in the Old Testament reveals that the only names with power are names of powerful people or names of gods; 2) not all Old Testament names can be translated into meaningful phrases and on the occasions when this is done, it is precisely because the meaning of the name itself is obscure or because the historical situation is significant; 3) of the names which clearly have intelligible meaning in the Old Testament, most do not make assertions about the name-bearer at all but about God[55]. Von Rad does not expand on how a person's name might have power apart from him nor does he give any examples of the independent power of names.

---

waiting their opportunity to invade reality. And even when this is denied them they remain dangerous for a long time, like a long-forgotten mine in the sea, or a grenade in a ploughed field." See also von Rad, *Theology*, 2:18–85, and Jacob, 127, among others.

50 Thiselton, "Words" challenges this popular view.

51 Von Rad, *Theology*, 2:81; Muilenburg, "Ethics," 528; Brockington; Procksch. Thiselton, "Words," 289, details Old Testament theologians who use this argument.

52 Barr, 129–140. He discusses the general confusion over that fact that "dibber" (speak) and "debir" (back room) have no etymological relationship whatsoever. See also KB–H and also Schmidt.

53 When the word is translated "thing," it usually refers to something someone said or did, or to a general incident that occurred. The references to an actual physical object are extremely rare and usually somewhat obscure as in Ex. 9:4 (but see Barr's comments on this, p. 137).

54 Von Rad, *Theology*, 2:83, says "Even in everyday life, however, certain words were thought of as having power inherent in them, as for example peoples' names."

55 Barr, "Names," 19–20. Within the article, he also deals masterfully and in great detail with the incident involving Nabel (1 Sam. 25:25), i.e. "as he is, so is he called."

The third and by far the most potent argument evoked by those who view words as having independent power is based upon incidents and statements in the Old Testament which involve blessings and/or cursings. However, the following examination of key passages will demonstrate this approach to be inadequate as well.

It is claimed that David's dying charge for Solomon to have Shimei killed (1 Ki. 2:8) is based on his fear that Shimei's curse of him (2 Sam. 16:7—8), if not quashed, will live on to harm Solomon[56]. Yet, surely, Shimei's curse was deactivated when he begged forgiveness for it (2 Sam. 19:16—23). Shimei's death was required by Ex. 22:28 anyway. The only reason why it was not carried out by David was because he originally thought Shimei might be cursing him on God's behalf (2 Sam. 16:10). When he realised the curse was not from God, due to the fact that he re-entered Jerusalem to reclaim his throne (2 Sam. 19:16—23), out of mercy he vowed not to inflict the required punishment. Therefore, the request for Shimei's death is based on justice or perhaps even on personal revenge, but it is not based on fear of the curse[57].

It is also claimed that David's request for a blessing from the Gibeonites (2 Sam. 21:1—6) and the quick utterance of a blessing by Micah's mother after cursing "the thief" who turned out to be her son (Judg. 17:1—4) are both efforts to disarm the unleashed power of a curse by a blessing[58]. Although it is true that the blessings are intended to counteract curses in these incidents, it is also evident that God is the power behind both the curses and the blessings, not the words themselves. The effectiveness of the Gibeonite curse is rooted in God. So also is its revelation to David as well as the urgency to rectify the sin committed against them (21:1)[59]. The appeal of Micah's mother is to the Lord (17:2—3)[60].

It is claimed that the reasoning behind the forbidding of curses against the deaf (Lev. 19:14) lies in the unrelenting power of the words even against those who cannot hear them[61]. However, Brichto demonstrates that קלל in this verse refers to insults and abusive language which might cause

---

56 Eichrodt, 2:70; Gray, *Kings*, 103; Montgomery, 90; Blank, 93.
57 Hertzberg, 345–346, 366, and Mauchline, 291–292. Brichto, 140, 193–194, suggests that the word in 2 Sam. 16:7 and 1 Ki. 2:8 does not really even mean "curse" as such but rather "denounce," or "rail at."
58 Eichrodt, 2:70; Gray, *Kings*, 263; Cundall, 183; Moore, *Judges*, 373, Blank, 94.
59 Mauchline, 300–301, and Hertzberg, 382, make plausible attempts to locate the actual incident (1 Chron. 22:6–23; Josh. 9:3–15, respectively). Both suggest that it is the resulting slaughter of Saul's household by David that is part of the reasoning behind Shimei's curse of David.
60 See Scharbert. The appeal to the Lord may be only superficial and "vain" in this incident and be intended to illustrate how far away the people were from God and their need for a king, i.e. Judg. 17:6.
61 Blank, 94; Porter, 154; Noth, 141; Snaith, 130; Motyer, 1:349.

the victim embarrassment or hurt. His detailed word study eliminates the legitimacy of appealing to word-power to explain this verse.

In 1 Sam. 14:24—28[62], Saul makes a general curse which Jonathan does not hear and unwittingly disobeys. Saul also makes a separate, specific curse on Jonathan himself. Neither of these two curses come to pass. In conjunction with this, Num. 5:16—28, a text used by some to support the word-power theory (Gray, 363), actually undermines it. It is true that the woman is required to drink the curse, but more importantly it is not effective unless she is guilty[63]. God is the power behind the curse in this text. Similarly, his desire to bless Jonathan (1 Sam. 14:6—15) stands above Saul's curses on him (Scharbert, 265, and Hertzberg, 114). As Prov. 26:2 confirms, "Like a fluttering sparrow or a darting swallow, an undeserved curse does not come to rest."

God's control of cursings and blessings is brought home memorably by the incident with Balaam (Num. 22:6—24:25). As a prophet of Yahweh, he was physically unable to pronounce a curse upon Israel when it was the Lord's will that they be blessed (Mowvley, 75). The fulfillment of a blessing or a curse, then, is the prerogative of God alone and is not any way dependent upon the power of words that might be uttered.

It is this truth which best explains the curious incident when Isaac — seemingly by mistake — blesses Jacob instead of Esau (Gen. 27:33—37)[64]. The reason why Isaac does not revoke the blessing is not because he could not but because he believed the successful trickery by Rebekah and Jacob was somehow providential. In other words, if God was behind it all, then it would be fruitless to attempt to change it[65].

God alone is the source of power behind blessings and cursings in the Old Testament[66]. There is no need to draw from situations involving cursings and blessings in the Old Testament the idea that words are thought to have a magical power. Further, even if there was a convincing

---

62 Harrelson cites this passage as evidencing traces of the magical power of words in the Old Testament. See also Eichrodt, 2:370.

63 Scharbert, 265, 412, 417. Contrast, Blank, 89.

64 A similar situation is when Jacob crosses his hands when blessing Joseph's sons (Gen. 48:14). Harrelson suggests this as evidence supporting a magical view of words in the Old Testament. Moore, *Judges*, 374, suggests the same about Gen. 27:33–37.

65 Mowvley, 76. Murtonen, 161, suggests also that Jacob's ability to deceive confirmed to Isaac that Jacob possessed the necessary enterprising nature to use the blessing profitably.

66 This is confirmed by the careful studies of Murtonen, Mowvley, and Brichto. It should be noted here that Brichto, 212–215, offers evidence to discredit the suggestion by Blank, 77, that the passive structure of curses without a subject is evidence for the independent power of words. In fact, Brichto thinks it is nothing more than a stylistic accident which assumes God as subject. See also Mowinckel, 2:45–46.

case regarding cursings and blessings, it would only show that some words under special circumstance are thought to have "quasi-material" power[67]. This would hardly justify formulating a general principle about a view of all words[68].

After concentrating so heavily on the power of words, it might be good to be reminded of their limitations recognized in Proverbs and perceptively noted by Kidner (p. 47). First, he notes that words are no substitute for deeds; for example, they cannot replace honest work (Prov. 14:23). Secondly, they cannot alter facts (Prov. 26:23, 26), Thirdly, words alone cannot compel response (Prov. 29:19); for instance, the effectiveness of a verbal rebuke depends upon the wisdom of the one who receives it (Prov. 27:10).

To these three can be added a fourth limitation having to do with the authority of the speaker[69]. Note for example Prov. 16:14, which says, "A king's wrath is a messenger of death," and Eccl. 8:4, which says, "Since a king's word is supreme, who can say to him 'what are you doing?' " However, the power of a king's word is rooted in the special, divine authority he has received from God[70]. Thus, he is also warned to be more careful lest he abuse his power by uttering words which "betray justice" or "contain lies" (Prov. 16:10; 17:7). The words of some people, then, are more powerful than the words of others, and, conversely, some are less powerful.

Finally, it must be recognized that the power of anyone's words, from that of king to that of the humblest slave, is ultimately limited in proportion to the proximity of his words to God's will at the time and under the circumstances in which they are spoken. This seems to be the best understanding of the thought behind Prov. 16:1, which says:

> To man belong the plans of the heart,
>   but from the Lord comes the reply of the tongue.

On the other hand, as Prov. 22:12 indicates, God stands as guardian over knowledge and "frustrates the words of trusted advisors and takes away the discernment of elders." Thus, "There is no wisdom, no insight, no plan that can succeed against God[71]." If a person desires his speech to be powerful, then, he is directed to build up his heart in the wisdom and knowledge of God.

---

67 Eichrodt, 1:173, uses "quasi-material" with respect to words.
68 Thiselton, "Words," 296, suggests that even in such a case, J. L. Austins' suggestions about "performative utterances" offers a far more plausible explanation for the effect of curses and blessing in the Old Testament than the suggestion of independent or magical power. See Austin, 154–158, and Austin, *Papers*, 233–252.
69 See Thiselton, "Words," 292, and Muilenburg, "Ethics," 528.
70 Eccl. 8:2; Prov. 16:10; 1 Sam. 8–10.
71 Prov. 21:30. See also Ps. 119:43.

Apocrypha and Pseudepigrapha

Controlled Speech

The advice about speech-ethics in the Apocrypha and Pseudepigrapha, as in the Old Testament, centers around the concern for control. Sir. 28:24—25 candidly advises:

> As you enclose your vineyard with a thorn hedge
> and lock up your silver and gold,
> so also put a crossbar and a balance on your words
> and a door and a bolt on your mouth[72].

The person who succeeds in doing this is considered a wise man; the person who cannot is considered a chattering fool, according to Sir. 21:25. The controlled words of the wise man will be sought for counsel by the local assembly; the uncontrolled chatter of the fool is considered a cumbersome burden to the community (Sir. 21:16—17), while the carefully measured words of the wise man inspire admiration and confidence (Sir. 20:21). For this reason, the king especially is advised in Aristeas 215 to "govern your words."

Anger, as in the Old Testament, never justifies the use of uncontrolled speech. When angered, a person is advised to hold back his words until he has calmed (Sir. 1:22—23). A person who is unable to control the venting of his anger is duly warned that he is physically shortening his own life (Sir. 30:24; 6:2—4) and one day, as 2 Enoch (A) 44:3 says, "The Lord's great anger will cut him down." T. Dan testifies that anger blinds one to the truth and takes control of both body and soul[73]. The control of anger, however, can be accomplished, according to 4 Macc. 2:11—23, by allowing the "Reason" which God gave man to reign over his passions to remain in control. The speaker in Ps.Sol. 16:10—11 takes a more direct approach and calls upon God himself to aid him in controlling his "anger and unreasoning." As in the Old Testament, God is viewed as the model of control in this realm for, as Wis. 15:1 says, he is "slow to anger[74]."

---

72 It is fairly common to rearrange these verses by placing vs. 25b after 24a and 25a after 24b as is done by Ziegler, Sauer, and *APOT*, 1:410. Although this may be warranted with regard to form, there is no textual basis for it. Thus, it seems preferable to go along with Rahlfs, who leaves the text alone. The word translated "crossbar" (ζυγόν) refers to "the yoke or crossbar by which two horses, mules, or oxen were put to the plough or carriage" (LS–J).

73 T.Dan 1:8; 2:1–4:7; 6:8. Also, T.Jud. 16:3.

74 The word used is μακρόθυμος, which is sometimes rendered "long-suffering" or "patient." However, it is translated "slow to anger" in Wis. 15:1 by Winston, *Wisdom*, 281, as well as by NAB. As Winston notes, it would appear to be based upon Ex. 34:6. Also, Aristeas 253.

Verbosity again is the habit of a fool; the wise man is notable for how few words he used (Sir. 20:4, 7,12; 21:20). The young man who wishes to advance in society is stringently advised concerning his speech by Sir. 32:7—8:

> Speak, if you are young when the need arises,
> but twice at the most, and only when asked.
> Be brief, say much in few words;
> be like a man who knows but all the same keeps silent.

Silence, as indicated above, has its proper place as a severe but often necessary form of control. There are times to speak out and times to be silent, and it is the supreme mark of the wise man not only to know the difference but to do what is required in the situation at hand (Sir. 4:23; 20:1, 18—19, 30). This falls partly under the realm of social etiquette for which Sirach shows deep concern[75]. There are those, of course, who are totally unconcerned about social etiquette, whose speech is best classified as filthy and boorish[76]. Sirach sternly warns against becoming accustomed to speaking this way because such speech is sinful and merits death. Sirach is also concerned about wasting words and the effort to produce them in hopeless situations[77].

Silence is generally considered to be an honourable trait [2 Enoch (B) 43:2; Sir. 26:14]. In T.Jos., for example, it is considered to be a sign of Joseph's respect for his brothers (and father) and of his own virtuous forbearance of suffering that he remained in silent before the Ishmaelite slave-traders about his true lineage[78].

However, mere silence can indicate many things, as Sir. 20:4a, 5—6a observes:

> One man is silent and is thought wise, . . .
> One man is silent because he has nothing to say;
>   another is silent, biding his time.
> A wise man is silent until the right time comes.

The wise man knows, particularly in situations of confrontation, that a period of silence will better enable him "to hold fast the will of God and to cast away the will of Satan" (T.Naph. 3:1) when he does reply. It will also enable him to "ascertain the facts before speaking," as Sir. 18:19 advises[79]. If he has no knowledge of the matter, his best choice, however,

---

75 Sir. 11:8; 21:24; 31:12—32:13.
76 Sir. 23:15. This is a concern not found in the Old Testament.
77 Sir. 21:14—15; 22:12. Sir. 37:11 lists nine types of people to avoid speaking with on certain topics.
78 T.Jos. 10:6—11:4; 14:2; 15:1-7; 17:1. Hollander, 69—72, contends that being silent is one of the central characteristics of Joseph's attitude in this story which is generalised as forbearance of endurance in the paraenetic passages following this story (17:1-8).
79 Ziegler, Rahlfs, Sauer, NAB, and NEB, against *APOT*, 1:380, prefer the textual reading

will be to remain silent. As Sir. 5:11—13 (cf. Sir. 11:8) says:

> Be quick to hear,
>   but patiently slow to answer.
> If you have the knowledge,
>   answer your neighbor.
> If not,
>   put your hand over your mouth.

Although proper silence is important, it must not be used as an excuse for a person to shirk his responsibility to share his counsel on behalf of his community[80]. There are times when he must speak. When he does so, his speech must be positive, uplifting, and genuinely beneficial to the situation at hand and to the society in which he lives. Such "gracious speech," rates high among society's values. It is the crowning glory of a woman's beauty; it is a blessing in the life of any man[81]. As Sir. 40:21 evaluates it:

> The flute and the harp offer sweet melody,
>   but better than either is a voice that is gracious[82].

Of course, the value of gracious speech in society is that it promotes friendship and affableness among people (Sir. 6:5). Indeed, truly gracious speech can work to break down long-standing social barriers and substantially sweeten any act of charity (Sir. 4:8; 18:14—16). Its power is sometimes seen in its well-ordered eloquence, but its effectiveness is always determined by the power of God (Aristeas 266).

As in the Old Testament, it is a person's heart which is the key to gracious speech. This is because it is the inner man, the heart and mind, which determines what the outer man, the mouth and lips, will say. As Sir. 21:26 (also 21:17) puts it:

> The heart of the fool is in his mouth,
>   but the mouth of the wise man is in his heart.

Thus, the person who desires to speak graciously must work at making his heart gracious. This can only be accomplished by opening his heart to God's influence, to his law and to his wisdom (Sir. 2:15—17; 4:11—17). Even when this is accomplished, he will have to be on constant guard so that

---

from the Greek manuscripts over the Syriac. Sirach shows a particular concern that a person's speech be well—informed. See Sir. 11:7; 33:4. Note also such advice to the kind in Aristeas 255, 256, 266.

80 Sir. 4:23, 27—28; 20:30—31; 37:22, 25.

81 Sir. 36:22—23; 2 Enoch (B) 42:13. In Sir. 36:22—23, a textual variant account for a difference in renderings. Rahlfs, Ziegler, and NEB have "mercy and gentleness are in her tongue." *APOT*, 1:433 and NAB have "her speech is kindly [soothing]"

82 The Greek word ἡδεῖα means "pleasant" with regard to taste or just in a general sense. The rendering "kind" or "true" used in most translations seems to be based upon the Hebrew word underlying it which is ברה (from ברר). See Vattioni, 217.

his heart and his words are kept synchronised (Sir. 5:10; 1:24—26). It is
notable that when Sir. 22:27 asks, "Who will set a guard over my mouth
and upon my lips an effective seal?" the inquirer proceeds to bid God to
"apply a rod of correction over my heart," (Sir. 23:2). The control of the
tongue by the heart requires mastery of the heart by God.

A number of people, both men and women, are distinguished as
gracious speakers in the Apocrypha and Pseudepigrapha. Among the men
are "the Lawgiver" (Moses), Onias, Eleazer, the Elect one, and the
Septuagint translators[83]. The most notable woman in this regard is Judith
(Judith 8:28—29; 11:20—23). Esther is depicted as requesting such speech
from God, and the presumption is that she received it for her task (Add.
Esth. C:24).

Listening

As in the Old Testament, listening is important to speech-ethics in the
Apocrypha and Pseudepigrapha because it is by this means that the heart
is thought to obtain the wisdom with which to produce graciously
controlled speech. As Sir. 3:28 (cf. 1 Enoch 94:5) says:

> The wise heart understands proverbs,
>   and the ear that listens to wisdom rejoices.

The person who is truly wise will not only gather wisdom, but he will
share it with others, even adding his own fresh insight to it (Sir. 21:25).

But to whom could a person listen for this wisdom? This is something
that he must consider with great care. As Sir. 37:8 warns, "Be on the alert
when one proffers advice." However, he will be safe if he makes an effort
to associate with those who are wise because they will pass on the
wisdom accumulated over the ages[84].

Of course, this includes listening to those wise men who put the
tradition down in written form, like Ben Sira[85]. A person should also listen
to his parents, especially his father[86]. He will do well, too, to meditate on
wisdom and the law[87]. Above all, he must listen to God, praying for truth

---

83 In order, see Aristeas 139; 2 Macc. 15:12; 4 Macc. 5:35–6:1; I Enoch 51:3; Aristeas 200,
    294.
84 Sir. 6:34–35; 8:8–9; 9:14–16; 37:12. 1 Macc. 2:65.
85 Sir. 16:22–23; 50:27–29. See also Wis. 6:25.
86 Sir. 3:1–15; 7:27–28; 30:1–3. Although Sirach is adamant that the mother should receive
    equal respect and honour from her children, when it comes to commenting
    specifically on the matter of instruction, only the father is mentioned (30:1–3). This
    may indicate a lowering of position in this regard for the mother in light of the
    specific mention of her instructing her children in Prov. 6:20–22, of which Ben Sira
    must have been aware.
87 Sir. 14:20–15:10; 6:36–37; 37:12; 9:15.

and opening his heart to God's leading[88]. God is the source of wisdom and knowledge (Sir. 17:5—6). As Wis. 7:15 puts it: "He is the guide of wisdom and the director of the wise[89]". When a situation presses for decision, he will be there enabling a person to sift through his accumulation of wisdom and respond with the most gracious answer. And so, in Aristeas 239 (cf. Sir. 8:9), when the king asks how he is to become motivated to listen, the sage replies,

> By remembering that all knowledge is useful, because it enables you by the help of God in a time of emergency to select some of the things which you have learned and apply them to the crisis which confronts you.

Words and Deeds

There is a relationship drawn between words and deeds in the Apocrypha and Pseudepigrapha. The relationship is first seen in the realm of obedience. True obedience occurs only when a person has been affected in both word and deed by the requests or demands of another. Thus, children are instructed to honour their fathers "in word and deed," in Sir. 3:8. Samuel must be classed as obedient to God because both in his words and his deeds he was responsive to God's word (Sir. 46:13—15). Thus, it can be seen that in the realm of obedience, words and deeds must operate in tandem.

The relationship of words and deeds is evident in another way. In this sense, a person's deeds are seen to be responsive to his words. Sir. 36:16 says,

> Speech is the origin of every deed;
> intention precedes every action.

Thus, Sir. 4:29 links together the traits of careless speech and careless words in the same person. Although this observation is generally true, discrepancies occur regularly in human nature. For instance, Solomon is depicted in Sir. 47:13—24 as having his speech and actions out of synchronisation: his words were wise, but his actions were foolish. This type of discrepancy, however, never occurs in God's character. In 2 Enoch (B) 33:4, he says, "My word is deed." Thus, his words are always objectified by action. In the case of Samuel's obedience to his work, it might be said that Samuel's deeds objectified God's words.

---

88 Sir. 37:15; 39:6—8. Sib.Orac. 3:584—586; 3 Bar. 1:6—7.

89 The word for "director" is διορθωτής. It may be rendered in a negative sense as a corrector of mistakes (Winston, *Wisdom*, 172; NEB; *APOT*, 1:546) or in a positive sense as a director who set one straight from the beginning (NAB). The latter sense seems more in line with the preceding line which refers to God as a guide (ὁδηγός).

Both of these relationships between words and deeds, of course, are entirely dependent upon directions from the heart. Obedience in either word or deed is determined first by the internal obedience of the heart[90]. So too, with reference to the objectification of words in actions, it must be remembered that the words themselves, which are the origin of actions, originate in the heart. Thus, there is a great deal of concern in this literature that a person, "Walk in singleness of heart!" as T.Iss. 4:1 puts it[91].

Two goals of speech-ethics can be observed here: 1) to coordinate obedience to various authorities (parents, God, etc.) between speech and actions, 2) to seek to solidify what one says into actions.

The Power of Words

As in the Old Testament, it is understood in the Apocrypha and Pseudepigrapha that words have power in society. Sir. 37:17—18 says:

> The root of the heart's deliberations
>   produces four branches:
> good and evil, life and death;
>   and the tongue is the absolute master over them all.

Some people can raise their position in society by their ability to produce wise words (Sir. 20:26); the words of others, like those of parents and kings (Sir. 3:9; Aristeas 253), are deemed powerful already because of their positions of authority over others in society. So too, the words of some people, like those of Judas Maccabeus, are naturally inspiring (2 Macc. 15:17), while the words of others, like those of Nebuchadnezzar as depicted by Judith 1—2, despite being uttered by a person in authority, are so weak that they can only be made effective by the use of armed force. However, words issuing from the human tongue can destroy cities, overthrow dynasties, smash bones, and bring down the strongest of men (Sir. 28:14—18).

As powerful as words are, like the Old Testament, the writers of the Apocrypha and Pseudepigrapha never conceive of words as independent from the speaker or their power as independent of the speaker's authority. The power in blessing and cursing resides in God[92]. For that matter, the success of any word is considered to be in the hands of God "for both we and our words are in his hands," says Wis. 7:16. Aristeas 201 explains that

---

90 2 Bar. 46:5. See also Sir. 2:15; 4 Ezra 3:20—28.
91 Doubleness of anything is heavily opposed in this literature. Double sight, double hearing, double tongue, and double heart are all spoken of in negative terms. See T.Ben. 6:5–7; 1 Enoch 91:4; Sir. 1:25; 28:13.
92 Sir. 3:1–2, 9. Sir. 21:27 warns an ungodly man not to curse his adversary in order that he not bring the curse upon himself. God has *a priori* determined not to honour the curse uttered by a man whose life is lived in total disregard for God.

"since the universe is managed by providence, and since we rightly perceive that man is the creation of God, it follows that all power and beauty of speech comes from God." Thus, Aristeas 18 concludes that

> when men from pure motives plan some action in the interest of righteousness and the performance of noble deeds, Almighty god brings their efforts and purpose to a successful issue.

Thus, the power of God is the source for the powerful words of men like Joshua, Elijah, and Elisha (Sir. 46:4—5; 48:3—6, 12—16). On the other hand, people can be counselled not to fear the words of a sinful man because his words are void of God's power (1 Macc. 2:62; Sir. 21:27). Only God's words are powerful enough to create the world and never fail in their purpose[93]. So, if a person wants his words to be powerful, he must attempt to speak what God wants said by placing himself under God's control. This is just what Wis. 5:15 depicts Solomon doing:

> God grant that I speak in accord with his mind,
> and conceive thoughts worthy of his gifts[94].

Qumranic Literature

Controlled Speech

The Essenes were noted for the strict control they maintained in their speech. Josephus records that before their morning prayers, "they utter not one word concerning routine matters" and that "no shouting or disturbance ever defiles the house; they allow each to speak in turn[95]." He describes them as "just managers of their wrath" and as "controllers of their angers" [*BJ*. II,8:6(#135)]. And before their meals, he registers with admiration, they take their seats "in silence" [*BJ*. II, 8:5(#130, 133)].

The Dead Sea Scrolls confirm this concern for controlled speech in the community life of Qumran. It is particularly evident in their numerous rules designed to regulate the interchange of speech. A great deal of their penal code (1QS 6:24—7:25) is taken up with violations regarding speech[96]. Formal punishment was to be meted out for such things as disrespectful

---

93 Sir. 42:15; 43:17; Wis. 9:1; Sib.Orac. 3:20–27, all speak of God creating the universe by his word. Sib.Orac. 3:572–573; 698–701, speak of the persistence of God's will.
94 Adapted from Winston, *Wisdom*, 172.
95 *BJ*. II,8:5(#128, 132). See Thackery for the Greek and English of this whenever it is cited.
96 Some violations like blasphemy, lying, gossip, and slander will be considered in later sections.

speech, impatient speech, a display of anger[97], utterance of a foolish
word [98], interruption of another, and even for silly laughter. On the
Sabbath, CD 10:18—20 emphasises that there was to be no discussion on
matters of profit or wealth, no talk of work to be done on the next day,
nor any foolish or idle word spoken. Even when a member of the
community was formally reproving another for violation of community
rules such as these, 1QS 5:25—6:1 says this was to be done lovingly, without
anger or disrespect.

Control of one's speech appears to be especially important in the
community assemblies which were held to provide opportunity for open
inquiry into the law or community problems. At these occasions, the
procedures for speaking were regulated with notorious strictness so that
order was guaranteed. Speaking out of turn or out of place with respect to
one's rank was a cardinal error, as was interruption of another speaker.
Also, questions addressed to the council were to be stated in conformity to
a prescribed style. The question itself could not be asked until the council
had given the questioner approval.

When a person at Qumran did open his mouth to speak, if he was truly
committed to the purposes of the community, his words would be positive
and uplifting to the hearer. When interpreting Scripture, care was to be
taken that this be done in a manner appropriate to the situation[99]. As 1QS
10:26 says, it should be "full of loving charity towards the disheartened
and an encouragement to those whose hearts are troubled." When faced
with arrogance, the response should be born out of a contrite spirit (1QS
11:1).

Qumranic literature betrays a clear awareness, following on from the
Old Testament, that truly beneficial or gracious speech is directly
dependent upon the quality of a person's heart. Thus, the truly committed
covenanter vowed (1QS 10:21—22, 24):

> I will not keep Belial in my heart,
>   nor will folly be heard in my mouth.
> On my mouth shall not be found
>   criminal deceit and falsity and lies . . .
> I will cause empty words to cease from my lips;
>   pollution and crookedness from the knowledge in my heart.

In contrast to the person who allowed his heart and, thus, his speech to be
controlled by the forces of evil, the words which the covenanter produced

---

97 It is angry speech directed at a priest that is specifically restricted here in 1QS 7:2,
   but see also 1QS 5:25 and CD 9:6–8.
98 1QS 7:9. The word נבל is found together with ריק, meaning "vain," "empty," or
   "reckless" in CD 10:18 with reference to types of speech prohibited on the Sabbath.
   For ריק, see also 1QS 10:24.
99 1QS 1:9; 1QS 10:25.

were to be "the fruit of holiness." (1QS 10:22) They were to be the result of his inner sanctity and allegiance to God and the forces of righteousness. The Teacher of Righteousness shows that he knew well this truth when he says in 1QH 10:7,

> What can I say unless you open my mouth;
> and how can I answer unless you enlighten me?

Qumranic literature includes some rather unique notions concerning the community's approach to speech-ethics that are worthy of note. The first has to do with wrath. Although anger was not to be displayed toward a fellow community member nor toward a repentant outsider, the truly committed member of the community (1QS 10:19—20) was not to allow his wrath to diminish against "the men of falsehood," nor was he to show any compassion toward any "who depart from the Way."

The second and third notions have to do with silence. Although this trait does not receive special attention as a positive characteristic of an individual's speech-ethics, it does receive such attention as a negative one. In a terribly legalistic interpretation of Lev. 19:17, CD 9:6—8 says that if a person "remains silent towards his comrade from one day to another and then later speaks to him in the heat of his anger, it is an action punishable by death[100]." The man here is condemned as much for his silence as for his anger in that he has failed to reprove his comrade when he could have done so civilly in accordance with the principle of law from Leviticus.

The third notion also has to do with silence being viewed negatively, this time as an act of betrayal. In 1QpHab 5:9—12, it is said that when the Teacher of Righteousness was being chastised by the Man of Lies, the other council members remained silent. They would not stand as witnesses of the truth.

The fourth notion has to do with control. Much of the knowledge revealed to the Qumran covenanters was considered mysterious and secret. Therefore, the truly committed community member who had been given this knowledge was to be extremely careful with whom he shared it. He was (1QS 10:24—25) to "impart/conceal knowledge with discretion" and "prudently hedge it within a firm bound." This was done in order "to preserve faith and strong judgment in accordance with the justice of God."

---

100   See also 1QS 5:25—6:1.

Listening

The idea of listening to men is never considered in Qumranic literature[101]. This is not particularly surprising because if this "prophetic" community had listened to the wisdom of men, it would never have been established. The Qumran community stood as a visible protest against those who had their ears filled with the knowledge of men but who refused to listen to the all-encompassing wisdom of God. To them, this was the only issue worth discussing with regard to listening.

In Qumranic literature, God stands supreme as the dispenser of all wisdom[102]. It is he alone who pours out understanding and who sheds forth the light of knowledge into a person's heart[103], who indeed, "illumines one's face" (1QH 4:27; 1QS 2:2—4). Only in God's truth does a person's soul find satisfaction (1QS 10:30—31). In order to receive this knowledge from God, the committed covenanter will meditate on His truth all day long (1QH 10:20) by studying the Scriptures, particularly the Law and the Prophets (1QS 6:6; 8:9). He will also "heed the voice" of and "lend his ears" to the Teacher of Righteousness and "not dispute the precepts of righteousness when hearing them" [CD(B) 2(20):28, 33]. This man, the originator of the community, appears to be the only mere man the community is expected to heed (1QH 17:26—28), but this is because he peculiarly "speaks from the mouth of God[104]." As 1QH 2:17—19 seems to convey, it is he "whose mouth you [God] have confirmed, and into whose heart you have put teaching and understanding that he may open a fountain of knowledge to all men of insight." It is he into whose heart God engraved the law (1QH 4:10).

Unfortunately, not everyone listens to God's voice, and Qumranic literature is acutely aware of this. There is the stinging reminder in CD 3:7—12 that the people of Israel in the past were stubborn in their hearts and would not heed God and thus were punished. 4QpHos 2:5 remembers that they ignored their prophets and listened instead to those that led them astray. So too, in their own day, the Qumran community thought that there were many who "are not firm in God's truth," who "seek God with stubbornness of heart," and "who do not listen to His voice[105]. The result is

---

101 The Temple Scroll (11QTemple 64:2–6), however, does reiterate the importance of a son heeding the discipline of his father and mother. See Maier.

102 1QS 4:3, 18; 10:12; 11:6; 1QH 1:7, 14, 29; 9:17, 23.

103 1QH 7:26; 10:4; 12:11–13; 14:8; 1QS 1:21; 2:2; 11:3, 15, 18.

104 1QpHab 2:1 speaks of him this way in contrast to the Man of Lies, who is considered to be the high priest at Jerusalem. The most likely candidates for this post appear to be Simon or Jonathan Maccabeus. See Vermes, 150–152.

105 1QH 4:14–15. Note the more generalised condemnation of these types of people in 1QH 15:18–19.

that these false teachers (presently leading the people of Israel in Jerusalem) speak to the people "with barbarian lips and in a foreign tongue," betray the will of God, and lead the people who listen to them astray. As far as the Qumran community is concerned, nothing else could result since God wisely keeps true understanding hidden from those whose hearts have been given over to the forces of evil (1QH 4:14; 5:26). Punishment will certainly be the lot for such men (1QH 4:16—17). In contrast, the Qumran community stands as representative of those who cling in steadfast obedience to the commandments of God[106] and who diligently heed one (the Teacher of Righteousness) who resolutely instructs them in the knowledge of God.

Words and Deeds

The Qumran community believed that in every righteous word and action a person was totally dependent upon God. In 1QH 12:34[107], the speaker says:

> And how shall I speak unless you [God] open my mouth;
>   how understand unless you teach me?
> How shall I seek you unless you uncover my heart,
>   and how follow the way this is straight
>   unless you guide me?

It is their view that God, in fact, knows what a person is intending to say before he says it (1QH 1:23; 1QH 1:27—29).

Although it is understood that many people attempt to resist subordinating themselves to God by aligning themselves instead with Belial and the forces of evil, those in the Qumran community determined that they would "not take a single step away from God's words . . . nor depart from his true ordinances, straying neither to the right nor to the left[108]." They were resolved that no temptation by the forces of evil would cause them to turn their backs on God and his will (1QS 1:16—17). This would be a community of people who "practice truth, righteousness, and justice on the earth" and who "walk no more in the stubbornness of a guilty heart[109]." Like no group of people had ever done before, they would give real meaning to the concept of obedience. They truly saw themselves as

---

106 CD 3:13–20. Unlike evil men, they do not "rebel against god's commands" nor "alter his words," as 1QH 14:14–15 puts it. It is an important characteristic of the Qumran community that they "cling" (Hiphyl of חזק) to God's commandments. See 1QS 5:1, 3; 1QSb 1:2; 1QH 4:39; 15:11; 16:7; 18:9.
107 See also 1QS 3:6–12; 11:2–9, 17; 1QH 2:23; 4:31–32; 7:6–12; 10:7; 15:12; 17:26.
108 1QS 1:14–15. See also 1QS 9:25.
109 1QS 1:5. See also 1QS 5:3, 25; 8:2. The Qumran covenanters considered themselves to be a community of truth (1QS 2:24, 26), a company of God's truth (1QM 13:12), and witnesses of the truth (1QS 8:6).

God's people. The expectation they had of their priests is a good example
of all this. The blessing pronounced upon them in 1QSb 3:27 holds out to
them the ideal to be so holy and righteous in their words and in their
deeds that their lives provide the standard for the judgment of leaders and
nobles of the nations.

The Power of Words

Qumranic literature is aware that words can be powerful. This is
particularly true in the person of the Teacher of Righteousness. The power
of his words is considered to be totally dependent upon God (1QH 4:27, 25).
In experiencing God's power in his words, he knows them to be unstop-
pable, especially in efforts to encourage and support those who are being
buffeted by those who oppose God. In 1QH 8:16, 35—36, he says:

> And you, O my God, have put into my mouth
> as it were autumn rain for all . . .
> and a spring of living waters which shall not run dry; . . .
> But you have made the tongue in my mouth to grow without going back,
> and there was no one to silence it.
> For the tongue of the disciples was given to me
> to restore the spirit of them that stagger
> and to sustain the weary with the word[110].

By God's power, his words have proved potent against the rebellious (1QH
2:8) and devastating to those who would attempt to speak for the forces of
evil[111].

The only other person who is described as wielding such devastating
power in his words is the "Prince of the Congregation[112]," whose blessing
includes the proscription (1QSb 5:23—25) to "strike the people down by the
might of your mouth" and to "slay the ungodly by the breath of your lips."

Of course, God's own words, as an extension of his sovereignty, are
viewed as all-powerful in Qumranic literature. His word established the
world order (1QS 10:1—8). Any who despise His word are destined for
destruction[113]. God's word, when spoken, is permanent. He will never turn

---

110   The translation here follows substantially Dupont–Sommer. Because of 8:16, I agree
      with him against *DSSE*, Mansoor, and Holm–Nielson that 8:35–36 reflects a state of
      despair and failure for the psalmist (the Teacher).

111   1QH 7:10–12; 8:36. Compare also 1QH 7:29 and 12:31, which speak of no one being able
      to answer a reproof from God.

112   Dupont–Sommer, 112, n. 2, identifies this person as the supreme temporal leader of
      the community and equates him with the Messiah of Israel. He is differentiated by
      Dupont–Sommer, 113, n. 1, from the Teacher of Righteousness who was the first, or
      priestly Messiah.

113   1QS 5:14. See also 1QS 4:17. Every effort was made in their community not to defile
      themselves by transgressing even one word from God. See 1QS 1:14; 5:14; 8:21.

back his word[114], and certainly no mere man can change any of them and get away with it (1QH 15:14).

As in the Old Testament, swearing, cursing, and blessing are considered to be under God's jurisdiction, and there is no consideration at all for the possibility that such words (or any words for that matter) have power apart from him[115].

Rabbinic Literature

Controlled Speech

Much of the concern about speech-ethics in Rabbinic literature, as has been the case in all the Jewish literature, unites around the concept of control [116]. Aboth 1:11 focuses on the special need for wise men to be careful in what they say and teach or else to reap dire consequences and set in motion harmful repercussions. It says:

> You sages, watch your words lest you incur the penalty of exile and be exiled to a place of evil water, and the disciples who come after you to drink thereof and die — and thus the Heavenly Name be profaned[117].

Elsewhere, Aboth counsels a judge to "be guarded in your speech," and Aboth 1:5 admonishes men who wish to be wise not to talk "too much with women[118], and lists "putting a fence around one's words" as one of the 48 requirements for acquiring Torah (Aboth 6:6). ARN 1 (p. 7) exhorts

---

114 1QH 13:18,19. Dupont-Sommer is wrong to translate the critical sentence here as, "Thy word will not turn back." The subject is clearly God and should be rendered, "you will not take back your word." *DSSE*, Lohse, *Qumran*, Mansoor, and Holm–Nielson all agree.

115 1Q22 1:10 (The Words of Moses) which is inspired by the farewell speech in Deut., a phrase occurs which depicts "the curses" as highly animated. However, there is no doubt, as in Deut., that God is considered to be the power behind the ability to search and destroy transgressors of his covenant.

116 Neusner, 225–230, 240, asserts that control, or self–control, is the key component of all Rabbinic ethics.

117 Aboth 4:16 calls a teaching error a "sin of presumption." There is some difference of opinion as to what "evil waters" (מים הרעים) refers to in Aboth 1:11. ARNB 22 (p. 140) says that it refers to heathen nations. Saldarini, 355, cites Albeck, 355, who thinks that it refers to wrong opinions and notes that in Aboth 1:4 learning is compared with drinking.

118 It goes on to say, "Whoever talks too much with a woman brings evil upon himself, neglects the study of the Torah, and in the end will inherit Gehinnom." However, ARN 15 (p. 110) understands the verse to refer to the potentiality of confidences shared even with one's wife becoming, as it were, slander and gossip via the wife's chatter with other wives. ARN 7 (p. 48) suggests only that the wife will think badly of the man after hearing the confidential information from her husband. Another opinion in ARNB 15 (p. 110) is concerned about the eventual seduction and ruin of the wise man who converses with a woman.

in general that "a man should be patient and not short-tempered in his speech." Outside of Aboth, Ber. 17a records that when Mar the son of Rabina concluded his prayers, he added: "My God, keep my tongue from evil and my lips from speaking guile[119]."

It is recognized within Rabbinic literature, as in other Jewish literature, that the control of anger is among the most strategic spheres of speech control. A person is completely devoid of wisdom when displaying angry speech[120]. Thus, Aboth 2:15 speaks straightforwardly, saying, "Do not be easily moved to anger[121]." To be so is to be counted among the wicked, while to be slow to anger is to be numbered among the righteous (Aboth 5:14). The latter person, quite admirably, is in control of his evil impulses (Aboth 4:1). He is loved by God and endowed with his wisdom (Pes. 113b; GenR. 19:1). In contrast, the former person, being saddled with a quick temper which is stoked by human wisdom and fired by the Tempter, thoroughly disqualifies himself from ever teaching and has apportioned himself a life that is aptly described as "not life[122]."

There are times when proper control of speech calls for absolute silence, and the ability to be so is much lauded in Rabbinic literature. Aboth 1:17 records Simeon, the son of Gamaliel, saying, "All my days I have grown up among the wise, and I have found nothing of better use than silence[123]." ARN 22 (p. 100) makes a logical deduction from this statement and adds: "If silence is becoming for the wise, how much more for the foolish[124]." Joshua ben Levi is said to have expressed a similar sentiment: "A word is worth a *sela'*, silence two *sela's*[125]." Silence is specifically advocated by the rabbis for dealing with an angry friend or with one who is in mourning[126], it is acclaimed in those who have been insulted or cursed[127], and it is

---

119 Moore, 2:195, notes that this request also comes at the close of the daily common prayer (Tefillah) and results from turning the injunction from God in Ps. 34:13 into a prayer. See Singer, 58. See also GenR. 81:2; DeutR. 1:9.

120 Pes. 66b. Sifre, Num., 60a, having in mind Lev. 10:16; Num. 20:10; 31:14, uses Moses as an example of this.

121 ARN 15 (p. 78) comments that this verse teaches that a person should be patient like Hillel and not short-tempered like Shammai. It then preceeds to relate a number of stories which mostly depict the patience of Hillel (all of ch. 15).

122 GenR. 19:1; Shab. 105b; Aboth 2:6; Pes. 113b; Urbach, 474.

123 This saying can also be found in LevR. 16:5; EcclR. 5:5 attributed to different rabbis.

124 This saying is also found in Pes. 99a. See also Aboth 3:17 which speaks of silence being a fence around wisdom.

125 LevR. 16:5. In Meg. 18a, this same saying is attributed to Rabbi Dimi. In Hul. 89a, in answering the question of what a man should be pursuing in the world, Rabbi Isaac responds that "he should be silent."

126 Aboth 4:23; EcclR. 3:7. With regard to the person in mourning, Hertz, 63, mentions that according to Jewish custom consoling with the mourner is not to begin until after the burial.

127 On insult, see Shab. 88b and Esther's "ban of silence" in EstherR. 6:12. On curse, see Mid.Ps. 86:1.

prescribed as a form of prayer and an attitude of worship highly valued by God (Ber. 24b; Meg. 18a; Mid.Ps. 19:1).

Despite the general tendency to extol silence in Rabbinic literature, there are some instances in which silence is seen as sinister and is roundly condemned: for instance, when a witness withholds his evidence or when a person fails to protest what he knows to be unjust retribution[128].

When a person does speak, Rabbinic literature offers the usual advice. Brevity and simplicity are recommended[129]. Verbosity is viewed as a sure forerunner to sin by Simeon the son of Gamaliel[130]. The following passage from Aboth 5:10 (also ARN 10, p. 55) speaks of the importance of proper etiquette, patience, poignancy, clarity, and honesty:

> A wise man does not speak ahead of him who is greater than he is in wisdom and does not interrupt the speech of his associate. He is not hasty to answer. He questions according to the subject matter and answers to the point. He speaks about the first thing first and the last thing last. Regarding that which he does not know, he says, 'I do not know.' He acknowledges the truth. The reverse of this is to be found in the boor.

To this portrait of the controlled speaker, Yoma 86a adds the quality of being congenial[131]. Ta'an. 4a, likewise, asserts that a man should train himself to be gentle[132]. The key to such "gracious speech," as has been seen elsewhere, is the heart. In commenting on Aboth 3:6, ARNB 32 (p. 187) adds these words of Rabbi Nehunya ben Hakana:

> He who gives his heart over to words of Torah is relieved of words of folly. But he who gives his heart to words of folly will be deprived of words of Torah[133].

Thus, a person must endeavor to fill his heart with the wisdom God has supplied him in the Torah if he wishes to speak wisely and graciously. GenR. 67:3 even suggests that it is possible for the especially blessed person to have his mouth directly "overpowered" by God.

---

128 On failing to testify, see San. 4:5; Pes. 113b. For further comment, see Moore, 2:181, where he cites Sifra 89a. On failing to protest, see the incident involving Doeg, Saul, the priests of Nob, and Abner, in which Abner is condemned along with the others because, "Though he had opportunity, he did not protest the ensuing tragedy." This is commented upon in LevR. 26:2; NumR. 19:2; Mid.Ps. 12:2.

129 Aboth 1:15; 2:5. See also the pertinent comment on Aboth 1:1 from the Commentary of Rabbi Menahem ben Solomon Hameiri which is cited by Goldin, Talmud, 45–46. L. Jacobs, 235, also quotes some relevant comments by Maimonides from *Hilkhot Deot* 2:4–5, which says: "A man should train himself to speak only when it is absolutely necessary . . . A man should see to it that what he says has much content but little quantity. Where quantity exceeds the context it is folly."

130 Aboth 1:17. ARN 12 (p. 71) speaks of saying much (and doing little) as characteristic of the wicked.

131 See also Ket. 17a; Aboth 1:15; S.S.R. 4:11.

132 See also Ta'an. 20a' Shab. 30b; LevR. 33:1.

133 Aboth 2:13 depicts a "good heart" helping a man maintain the "good way." See also Aboth 3:10; 6:6; EcclR. 1:16; GenR. 73:12.

Listening

A rash person is described as one who gives his mouth priority over his ears (Shab. 88a). In contrast, the wise man will control his mouth and give precedent to listening. To whom should one listen?

First, Aboth advocates listening to the wise; "Let your house be a meeting house for the wise; sit amidst the dust of their feet; and thirstily drink in their words[134]." It speaks favourable of learning from the elderly as opposed to learning from the group (Aboth 4:6).

Secondly, Aboth advocates listening to Torah: "Be diligent in the study of the Torah[135]!" In Aboth 6:9, the words of Prov. 6:27, originally given in the context of urging a child to listen to the teaching of its father and mother, are taken over to apply to listening to Torah.

A person learns Torah from the wise men. In Aboth 4:18, Rabbi Nehorai says, "Bring yourself to a home of the Torah . . . for there your associates will help you learn it." By learning Torah from them, a person is listening to God.

Words and Deeds

Aboth 1:15 (also ARN 12, p. 71) enjoins, "Say little and do much." This statement is consistent with the emphasis on deeds throughout Rabbinic literature [136]. The concern is not simply for random, meaningless deeds, however. Rather, it is for deeds which reflect obedience to God's will. Aboth 2:4 says, "Do his will as if it were your will. . .[137]." God's will, of course, is in the Torah, and thus, obedient action requires diligent study to learn the Torah[138]. The point of this study of Torah is action[139]. Thus, there is no point to studying and learning the Torah if one intends to be disobedient to it (LevR 35:7). Controlled speech enables a person to learn from God through study of the Torah. It is an obedient deed itself since both oral and written Torah encourage it.

It is possible for a person to do or say better than he knows, assuming he has a basic knowledge of Torah[140]. But he can also know better than

---

134 See also ARN 6 (p. 40); Aboth 2:15; 6:6.
135 Nothing should distract. See Aboth 3:9, 14; ARN 21 (p. 98).
136 Aboth 1:17; 3:19; ARN 24 (pp. 103–105); ARNB 44 (p. 275).
137 On the importance of obedience to precepts, see Aboth 2:1; ARNB 32 (p. 191); Urbach, 389.
138 Sifre Deut. §41. 79a–79b (*RA*, p. 186); Sifra 111b (*RA*, p. 187). On the importance of diligent study, see ARN 24 (pp. 103–105); 28 (p. 117); ARNB 31 (p. 184).
139 Aboth 4:6; 5:17; 6:6; NumR. 14:10; Sifra 110c; Mekilta (Lauterbach, 2:182); Yoma 86a; ARN 24 (p. 104).
140 Aboth 3:12; Sifre Deut. §79, 91a; DeutR. 11:6; Tanna de Be Eliyyahre (Friedmann, p. 31) as quoted in *RA*, p. 177.

what he does or says. In this light, the rabbis think God does take into account a person's intentions[141]. However, they also speak of God hating him "who speaks one thing with his mouth and another thing in his heart[142]." In contrast, the goal for a person should be to fill his heart with Torah which will help him to control his deeds and his intentions so they correspond more and more to one another and to God's will[143]. In this respect, a person's speech, as part of his deeds, should correspond with the knowledge of the Torah he is accumulating within. But his speech and deeds should also bear some correspondence to one another, as does God's: "The mere speech of the Holy One, blessed be He, is equivalent to action" (GenR. 44:22).

The Power of Words

Divine speech is so powerful and dynamic that most people would equate it with action (LevR. 1:11; ExR. 4:3). Belief in the power of God's word in Rabbinic literature is most commonly expressed by reference to the power of the Torah or the words of Torah. For the rabbis, these are the words of God. The words of Torah are so much related to the power of God that even a sincere discussion of them is thought to be accompanied by his presence (Aboth 3:3—4:7).

Aboth 2:8 (also ARNB 31, p.184)) says, "He who has acquired for himself words of Torah has acquired for himself life in the world to come. An understanding of the words of Torah gives power to live in this world, too (Aboth 6:7). For one thing, it helps keep him from sinning by giving him counsel (Aboth 6:1). For another, the words of Torah are thought of as a medicine which, when stored in the chambers of the heart, is strong enough to overpower a person's natural inclination to be evil[144]. The words of Torah, however, not only have the power of life for living but also the power of death. In Shab. 88b (cf. Yoma 72b), it is said:

'Just as a prince has the power of life and death, so has the Torah.' This is as the Raba has said, 'For those who turn to the right in it, it is a drug of life; for those who turn to the left, it is a drug of death.'

The power of men's words is dependent on God's power. This can be seen especially in the matter of cursing. To be effective at all, the curse must include the Name of God or an acceptable substitute (Sheb. 4:3; 36a; Ket. 72a). Yet, even with that condition satisfied, there is the recognition

---

141 Sifre Deut. §32, 73a–73b; §117, 98b; Mid.Ps. 30:2, 4.
142 Pes. 113b; B.Metzia 49a; Mid.Ps. 12:1.
143 GenR. 67:8; Aboth 2:13; 3:10; ARNB 32 (p. 187).
144 Sifre Deut. §45, 82b (*RA*, p. 125); Mid.Prov. 24:31 (48b).

that God has the right to overrule any curse — even if it is warranted[145]. It is also presumed that the success of any curse is powered by God[146].

Rabbinic literature does, however, record stories which reflect the superstitious and magical ideas which had gathered around popular belief in the power of God's name[147]. In this case, the power of God is believed to be encased in the name itself and released upon the correct utterance of it by someone in a charm, incantation, or curse[148]. The power of the Name is, then, quite separate from God's will and even man's will if he is careless in his use of it[149].

Such practices and beliefs are recognized by some rabbis as diversions from the written Torah. In San. 10:1, Rabbi Akiba condemns the use of charms for healing the sick, and, elsewhere, Abba Saul condemns the pronunciation of the Name[150]. Suppression of the pronouncing of God's name, which led to the use of numerous legally bona fide substitutes, may have been an attempt to counter the magical misuse of God's name by Jews and by pagans. The secrecy surrounding the Name in reality led to an increased belief in its power for those who knew the correct letters and pronunciation[151]. The existence of such belief in the power inherent in God's name can be viewed as further evidence, however perverted, for the recognition that the people were utterly dependent upon God, if only upon his name, for truly powerful speech and were convicted about the unreproachable power of his speech.

Graeco-Roman Literature

Controlled Speech

Given the central importance of self-control to Greek ethics in general, it should come as no surprise to find this characteristic dominating the

---

145 Ket. 56a; ExR. 4:3; NumR. 20:19; RuthR. 1:13.
146 San. 113a. Thus, the power in the blessing or the curse of an ordinary person should not be underestimated (Meg. 15a, 28a).
147 Urbach, 124–134; Moore, 1:425–428.
148 See ExR. 1:30 and LevR. 32:4, both of which speaks of Moses slaying the Egyptian by using the Name of God. God's name is said to have been written on Moses' rod (DeutR. 3:8). Seamen are said to have calmed rough seas with clubs engraved with "I am that I am, Yah, the Lord of hosts." (B.Bathra 73a)
149 J. Yoma 40d; EcclR. 3:11; Tos.Mak. 5:10.
150 See also ARN 12 (p. 71). In San. 82b, cursing by enchantment is considered to be analogous to blasphemy.
151 See Moore, 1:425–428, and Urbach, 130. Discussion of some of the common substitute names for God can be found in L.Jacobs, 136–146; Moore, 1:429–432; Kohler, 58–62.

concern for speech-ethics in particular[152]. As Diog.L. 8:20 tells it, Pythagoras was respected because "he was never known to overeat, to behave loosely, or to be drunk." This highly esteemed characteristic of self-control carried over into his speech, as well[153]. Diog.L. in 1:105 also transmits the following saying which he attributes to Anacharsis, the renowned sixth century B.C. Scythian prince: "Bridle speech, gluttony, and sensuality."

The figurative association of speech-control with the restraining action of bridling or reining a horse is common and figures in the writing of Euripides (*Bacc.* 386—389) but probably receives the most notable expression by Plato in *Laws* 701c:

> What again is our object all of this? Evidently, I must, every time, rein in [ἀναλαμβάνω] my discourse like a horse, and not let it run away with me as though it had no bridle in its mouth.

A close connection is made in Graeco-Roman literature between controlling speech, or bridling the tongue, and controlling the mind or the thoughts. This appears as early as Theognis, which in line 365 says, "Restrain your mind [νόος]; let mildness ever wait on your tongue," and which in line 759 says, "May Apollo set straight both our tongue and our mind." This association is carried on by Isocrates who heartily advises Democles in *To Dem.* 41: "Always when you are about to say anything, first weigh it in your mind, for with many the tongue outruns the thought," and by Plutarch, who in his commentary on Hesiod's *Works* declares in effect that a person's judgment should be master over his tongue[154]. Plutarch (*Mor.* 15:#89) further believes that nature provides its own demonstration that the tongue should be controlled — and this by the reason — because it has put "a fence of teeth in front of the tongue" and placed "the brain above it."

Plutarch in his *De gar.* is really only representative of the undercurrent of abhorrence present in Graeco-Roman literature for the non-stop talker. Plutarch believes that idle speech or chatter has absolutely no redeeming social qualities, that it is harmful and dangerous, that chatterers themselves are understandably despised by their fellows, and that they completely

---

152 A good example of a passage in which a writer moves from a general discussion of self–control to speech control is in Cic., *Fin.* 2:46–47.

153 It is said that he restrained from laughter, giving insults, and telling vulgar tales. Plutarch, likewise, speaks admiringly of Cato the Younger in *Lives*, Cato the Younger 1:5, and of Zeno, in *Mor.* 6:505d, the latter for biting off his tongue under torture to tell secrets.

154 Plut., *Mor.* 15:#89. See also Plut., *Mor.* 6:514e, where the advocates reflection before speaking, and 6:510a, where he speaks of reason being the proper barrier to talkativeness.

destroy the otherwise pleasant quality of speech by using it in such enormous   quantities[155]. So, Plutarch writes his treatise in order to cure those who have this despicable affliction of talkativeness (Plut., *Mor*. 6:510d—514c). Menander had articulated many years earlier this insight: "The one who has no wisdom but who chatters much on every point exhibits his character in his words[156]."

Plutarch is not just aroused to condemn those who speak too often but also those who are verbose, especially in formal oration. In a rather catty comment in *Mor*. 1:41d, he says, "It seems to have been Melanthius, who being asked about Diogenes' tragedy, said he could not get sight of it there were so many words in the way." Applaudingly, he records:

> Ephisophon, who bragged that he could speak the whole day long on any topic whatsoever, they [the Spartans] expelled from the country saying that the good orator must keep his discourse equal to the subject at hand[157].

Aristophanes has Euripides say:

> I know the man, I've scanned him through and through, a savage–creating, stubborn–putting fellow, uncurbed, unfettered, uncontrolled of speech, unperiphrastic, bombasiloquent[158].

Plutarch, again, as many others in Graeco-Roman literature, sings the virtues of outright silence. He reckons silence to be something profound, awesome, mysterious, and even in a sense holy (Plut., *Mor*. 6:515a). This is because of its unsurpassed power over the spoken word. In *Mor*. 6:505f, he says:

> No spoken word, it is true has ever done such service as in many instances words unspoken . . . Hence, I think, we have men as teachers, but in keeping silence we have gods.

He says more on this matter in *Mor*. 1:10f:

> For timely silence is a wise thing and better than any speech . . . For again, nobody was ever sorry because he kept silent, but hundreds because they talked[159].

He contends in *Mor*. 6:506c that a first-rate education should teach a person to be silent first and then to speak.

---

155 See Plut., *Mor*. 6:504c–f. Theog. 295–298 also speaks of the burden the chatterer is to society and of everyone's hate for him.
156 Men. 682k. Similar ideas are present in Theog. 611–614, 1167–1168. Hasty speech, in view of Cleobulus (Diog.L. 1:88) is a sign of madness.
157 Plut., *Mor*. 3:239d. See also *Mor*. 3:208c; 6:510e.
158 Aristoph., *Frogs* 2:373. The last word in the quotation is from the triple compound κομποφακελορρήμων which combines the ideas of pomp (κόμπος), bundle (φάκελος), and words (ῥῆμα). The word previous to it, ἀπεριλάλητον, means the person is not to be out–talked.
159 See also Plut., *Mor*. 6:515a; Isoc., *To Dem*. 41. Plutarch notes that geese, in fear of the eagles, put stones in their mouths to inhibit their gaggling when they crossed Mt. Taurus. (*Mor*. 6:510a; 12:967b).

So, silence is a mark of the wise, talkativeness the mark of a fool. But a wise man cannot always be silent, or he will be thought ignorant after a time, as Theophrastus implied (Diog.L. 5:40), and he certainly does not want the fool to dominate conversation with his inane chatter, a concern that Theognis deliberates (Theog. 95—298, 625—626). Epictetus recognizes these things and gives the more realistic advice in *Ench*. 33:2: "And be silent for the most part, or else make only the most necessary remarks, and express these in few words[160]."

The mark of the truly wise man, then, is being a master at knowing when to speak and what to say at the most appropriate moment[161]. This should be done simply, lucidly, concisely, with distinction, and in faultless Greek, as so aptly summarised by Zeno[163]. When he speaks, his speech will always be courteous, cordial, tactful, pleasant, and beneficial[163]. This gracious quality in speech will mark the wise man's conversation with his friends but also with those who are offensive. In a classic example of Stoic thinking, Epictetus treats this topic in *Ench*. 42. He says:

> When someone treats you badly or speaks badly of you, remember that he acts or speaks because he thinks it is incumbent upon him. That being the case, it is impossible for him to follow what appears good to you, but what appears good to himself, whence, it follows that, if he get a wrong view of things, that man that suffers is the man that has been deceived . . . If, therefore, you start from this point of view, you will be gentle with the man who reviles you. For you should say on each occasion, 'He thought about it that way.'

The ability to speak appropriately and graciously is thought to come from a person's faculty of reason. Plutarch speaks of it as "judgment" (κρίσις) in *Mor*. 15:#89.

Epictetus, in II,23:1—47, speaks of it as ἡ προαιρετική, which refers to a person's pre-disposition toward certain choices. In his view, this "moral purpose," as it is sometimes translated, will bring the best results if one is converted to the peculiar and superior outlook on moral reality which Stoicism teaches. Dio Chrysostom, in 32:12—16, speaks of God's role in this procedure, and this is something Epictetus would probably be reluctant to deny[164]. However, he would endorse the idea only in the peculiar Stoic sense in which "myself" is never clearly separated from God. Thus,

---

160 Isoc., *To Dem*. 41, allows only two occasions for speech: ". . . when the subject is one which you know thoroughly and when you are compelled to speak."
161 For example, see Plut., *Mor*. 6:504c; 15:#89; Epict. II,23:15; IV,12:17; Isoc., *To Dem*. 31; *To Nic*. 33.
162 Diog.L. 7:59. On simplicity of speech, see also Cic., *Fin*. 2:46; Eur., *Pheonissae* 469.
163 See Xen., *Mem*. III,11:10; Isoc., *To Dem*. 20, 23; *To Nic*. 34; Cic., *Fin*. 2:47; Epict. II,10:9; *Ench*. 45; Plut., *Mor*. 1:10a; 6:461e, 464c; Theog. 365—366.
164 See Epict. II,8:11–14, 17:22–25; III,24:95; IV,7:20, 12:7–18.

appropriate speech ultimately defers to a person's mind and its ability to grasp and apply a philosophical outlook, in this case, Stoicism.

Drunkenness is not to be allowed because it induces a person to lose control of himself and his speech (Plut., *Mor.* 6:503a; Theog. 480—496). Seneca [*De ira* (*ME*) III,6:3] considers anger a similar problem. Cicero shows how extensively anger is treated by Graeco-Roman writers when he remarks that anger was something there was no need for him to discuss because of the "repeated utterances of the greatest philosophers" on the matter[165]. Yet, two of the major essays on anger were still to come! These were Seneca's *De ira* and Plutarch's *De cohibenda ira*, both of which are extensive examinations into the harmfulness, causes, and cures of an angry disposition and outbursts of temper[166]. Restraint of the tongue is viewed as a key factor which the easily angered man must seek to develop in order to cure his angry outbursts which are so harmful and later regretted[167].

Listening

One of the characteristics of non-stop talkers which most irritates Plutarch is that such people simply do not listen *De gar.* (*Mor.* 6:502c). He continues in 502d;

> Indeed, one might think that the babbler's ears have no passage bored through to the soul, but only to the tongue. Consequently, while others retain what is said, in non-stop talkers it goes straight through in a flux; they then go around like empty containers, void of wisdom, but full of noise.

In *Mor.* 1:39b, Plutarch notes that "it is a common saying that nature has given each of us two ears and one tongue because we ought to do less talking than listening." He makes this appeal to nature in order to demonstrate the validity of his view that a sound education should entail children learning "to hear much and speak little."

Dio Chrysostom (32:2), in the introduction of his speech to the people of Alexandria, makes a similar though more situational appeal. If his audience could just be "slow to speak and self-restrained enough to keep

---

165 Cic., *Quint. Frat.* I,1:37. Stob. II,20:1–69, supplies an excellent anthology to what Cicero may refer. In addition, see Theog. 365–366; Arist., *EN* II,5:3 (1106a2); II,9:2 (1109a28–29); IV,5:8 (1126a14); and also Diog.L. 8:20, remarking on Pythagoras; notability for freedom from anger.

166 Epictetus, too, speaks extensively on anger in I,18:1–23, 26:7, 28:1–33.

167 Plut., *Mor.* 6:454f, 455b; Sen., *De ira* (*ME*) III,1:1, 5:1–2. The connection between the controlled tongue and anger is implied in Plut., *Mor.* 1:7e, when among his list of the goals of education, Plutarch includes "to hold the tongue in check, to conquer anger, to control the hands." Diog.L. 8:22–23 ascribes a similar grouping of ideas to Pythagoras. Lucian, in the second century A.D., in *Demonax* 51, adds listening to the relationship.

silent" for awhile in order to listen to him, he suggests that their thoughts just might be the wiser the next time they open their mouths to speak.

Plutarch cautions those who listen to professional orators like Dio Chrysostom not to be convinced naively by a speaker's flashy style or by his reputation. Rather, one should listen critically to the subject matter before being persuaded of anything[168]. However, he would applaud the basic point that disciplined listening is essential to the development of vital, worthwhile speech. But he would even go further and connect listening to personal, moral conduct. In *Mor.* 1:48d, he says, "Right listening is the beginning of right living[169]."

Since listening has such profound consequences, deciding to whom one will listen in life is critical. Plutarch, in *Mor.* 2:145e, advises a former student, Eurydice, to listen to and "to be conversant with the sayings of the wise and good" and to always have these "at the tip of your tongue." He also recommends knowing the great and wise poets of the past, although he cautions against taking too literally the negative ethical models which are sometimes present in their writings[170]. One should diligently listen to his own teachers, but Plutarch advises listening with courtesy to every speaker, although this should always be done critically[171]. One should listen obediently to one's parents[172]. Isocrates, in *To Dem.* 14 even formulates golden rule-like advice on this subject: "Conduct yourself toward your parents as you would have your children conduct themselves toward you."

Epictetus desires that people should listen to God. He means this, of course, in a Stoic sense which ultimately directs a person to himself[173].

Seneca, in *ME* VII, 27:7—8, advises his readers to listen attentively to those who speak and promote virtue as they would the gods or the priests of the gods. They ought to be silent just as they would during a sacrifice that they "may listen with attentive ear and hushed voice." Maintaining the

---

168 Plut., *Mor.* 1:41a–42c. See also Sen., *EM* 108:7–11, 38; Thuc. III,38; Isoc., *To Nic.* 39; Dio Chrys. 33:4–5.

169 See also Plut., *Mor.* 1:38c; Sen., *EM* 108:35; Plato, *Laws* 688d.

170 Plut., *Mor.* (*Quo. poetas*) 1:14e–37b. Isoc., *To Nic.* 42–43, comments specifically on the value of Hesiod, Theognis, and Phocylides.

171 Plut., *Mor.* 1:31f, 38c, 39c, 40b. See also *Lives*, Cato the Younger 1:5. The excellent student is encouraged to formulate critical questions as he listens. On this, also see Plato, *Rep.* 534e.

172 See Plut., *Mor.* 1:7e; 3:237d; Epict. I,12:19–35; Xen., *Mem.* II,2:1–14; Plato, *Laws* 701b. See Dover, 273–275, who in his comments on this matter notes the importance of Aiskhines 1:24; Aniphon 4,a.6; Men., fr. 600; Antiphanes, fr. 262; Dem. 24:60,102; and others.

173 See also Epict. III,24:95, 111, 114; IV,12:7–18; Sen., *ME* VII,15:7.

comparison, he says that they even should reverence the writings of those who promote virtue as sacred[174].

Words and Deeds

Listening in Graeco-Roman literature, especially with regard to God and parents, includes obedience. The words of these specially authoritative persons are to be converted as rapidly as possible into deeds by the listener (Seneca, *EM* 108:36—37).

The association of words and deeds in Graeco-Roman literature is almost automatic when a writer is dealing with ethics[175]. This accentuates a number of different points, the first of which is that the words of others are to become the listener's deeds.

Secondly, the association of words and deeds emphasises that a person's deeds should be consistent with his own words. A father's deeds should be consistent with his words if he intends to rebuke his son for wrong behaviour[176]. A philosopher ought to be able to demonstrate the rightness of his view by his own conduct or else be quiet altogether[177]. A man who acts like a slave is not free no matter what he might say (Theog. 979—982). A person should combine cordial address with a courteous manner (Epict. IV,1:146—155). Plato, in *Rep.* 383a, presents God as the archetype of consistency "in word and deed."

Thirdly, the association between words and deeds emphasises that a person must strive to be virtuous in both his words and his deeds. In this case, these are dual aspects of a person's ethical goodness, but there is no particular emphasis on consistency. As early as Homer's *Iliad*, one finds Phoenix saying to Achilles: "Therefore he [Peleus] has sent me to teach you all these things, to be both a speaker of words and a doer of deeds[178]." Plato (*Prot.* 326b) speaks of musical education making a person to be "better equipped for both speech and action." Xenophon and Theognis believe that the gods know "our words and our deeds" and think that this should prevent us "from doing and saying" what they would disapprove[179]. Cicero (*Fin.* 2:47) advocates people to enshrine "moral beauty in word and in deed."

---

174 In this passage, he goes on (27:8) to advise his audience to listen closely to anyone who displays signs of speaking for a god.

175 Plato, *Laws* 717d; Epict., *Ench.* 42; Plut., *Mor.* 1:14a, are good examples of this.

176 Men. 662k; Isoc., *To Nic.* 38; Plut., *Mor.* 1:14a.

177 Sen. *EM* 108:38–39; Epict., *Ench.* 46,52. Seneca, in *ME* VII,17–30, very astutely attempts to turn back the view of many that all philosophers fail to practice what they preach.

178 Hom., *Il.* 9:435–443. F. Beck, 60, reckons that this reference to words and deeds indicates these to be priorities in education as early as epic times.

179 Theog. 1179–1180; Xen., *Mem.* I,1:19; Sen. *ME* VII,20:5; Isoc., *To Nic.* 34.

Fourthly, words are thought to be the best gauge of a person's character, which stands behind and enlightens his "ways," or deeds. This view is best expressed by Plutarch, in *Mor*. 1:33f, in which he quotes a line and then comments:

> 'It is character that persuades and not the speech.' No rather it is both character and speech, or character by means of speech, just as a horseman uses a bridle, or a helmsman uses a rudder, since virtue has no instrument so humane or so much like itself as speech.

This view of Plutarch's surfaces in at least two other places in his writings. In *Mor*. 1:10a, he quotes Democritus as saying that "a word is a deed's shadow," and in *Mor*. 6:464d, he associates together "evil words and offensive actions."

This high view of speech is not novel to Plutarch. Indeed, Isocrates proferred a similar view much earlier. In *To Nic*. 8, he says, "Discourse which is true and lawful is just the outward image of a good and faithful soul." His words will not come from "the edge of the lips," as Seneca puts it in *EM* 10:3—4, but rather his "utterances come from a solid foundation." They will be consistent with his character. However, he must beware of those of unvirtuous character who seek to hide their true character behind smooth words. As Men. 767k (also 821k) expresses it, "I hate a bad man saying what is good." Professionally trained orators are the most notable examples of those who juggle words to deceive in this way[180].

Finally, Isocrates actually goes further than Plutarch. He places speech even above the thoughts. In *To Nic*. 9, he says, "In all our actions as well as our thoughts speech is our guide."

The Power of Words

Earlier it was noted that Plutarch and others in Graeco-Roman literature consider judicious silence to be more powerful than speech[181]. In this view, what is primarily in mind is the superior ability of silence to procure beneficial results in various situations. Plutarch cites an example in *Mor*. 6:506e. However, Plutarch would by no means deny that spoken words are powerful. In his view, this power is more often harmful and destructive than beneficial. He is all too aware, as he says in *Mor*. 1:10f, "of countless men who have fallen into the greatest misfortunes through intemperate speech[182]." The superiority of silence over spoken words, in Plutarch's view (*Mor*. 1:10f), is inherent in the fact that "the unspoken word can easily be uttered later, but the spoken word cannot possibly be recalled."

---

180 See Sen., *EM* 108:38; Isoc., *To Nic*. 1–2; Aristoph., *Frogs* 813–829; Plut., *Mor*. 1:41c–42c.
181 In *EM* 38:1–2, Seneca speaks of the power of minimal, low–toned words.
182 Plut., *Mor*. 1:11a–c; 6:505b–d cites numerous examples.

Elsewhere in Graeco-Roman literature, there is general acknowledgment that words are powerful and that the power can be beneficial when used appropriately. Menander, in 560k, says:

> The spoken word is man's physician in grief. For this alone has soothing claims for the soul. And the wisest men of times long ago call this a dainty drug.

The figure of a drug is popular among Graeco-Roman writers to describe speech[183]. Gorgias uses it but incorporates the positive and negative potential of drugs to "bring to an end either the disease or the life[184]." He goes on to speak of words having the capability to bring about grief or pleasure or even fear. Harmfully persuasive words, as he extends the metaphor, can even "drug or bewitch the soul." Such vivid awareness of the evil potential of words, however, did nothing to diminish Gorgias' zeal to teach people how to excel in oratorical and persuasive skills. The ability to disseminate the power to "persuade the mass of the people" proved an irresistible lure to him (Plato, *Gorgias* 452d).

Gorgias was one of the first and certainly the most candid among Greek writers to recognize the power of the words of well-trained speakers. The art of oratory and knowledge of rhetoric eventually became nearly synonymous with Graeco-Roman education and culture. It is not surprising, then, that the power of words in the literature usually has to do with the persuasive skills of public oratory[185]. Although Isocrates (*To Nic.* 1—10) acknowledges that skilled orators can — and many do (Plato, *Phaedrus* 261b) — "deceive by their speech and put their eloquence to unjust uses," he defends the value of eloquence to society by pointing out that it is the power that brings about most of man's blessings in life. It sets man apart from the wild beast; it enables man to establish cities, laws, and the arts; in fact it is the power behind all societal institutions and enables people to live together, learn, confute the bad, and exonerate the good. That kind of beneficial power ought not to be censored and discarded because some men abuse it, he argues. Indeed, it is an historical fact that Isocrates' arguments in defense of teaching oratory and rhetoric were persuasive and eventually won the day in Graeco-Roman culture.

Epictetus and Plutarch both would want to deny that the persuasive power of words comes simply from a speaker's mechanical skill in contriving and delivering them. Truly powerful speech comes from the speaker's conviction about what he is saying, notes Epictetus (III,16:7—10). Plutarch, as we have already seen, thinks that a person's character must

---

183 See also Plut., *Mor.* 1:73; 6:502b.
184 Gorgias, *Econium on Helen* 14; Diels, 2:292–293; Freeman, *Ancilla*, 131.
185 In addition to the references cited in the discussion, see Ovid, *Ex Ponto* I,2:113–123; Dio Chrys. 33:1, 45.

have something to do with it (Plut., *Mor*. 1:33f). Dio Chrysostom, who himself was a speaker of note and certainly aware of the power of speech, believes that God is involved in the success of a speaker's words, especially if they are thought to be wise, appropriate, needed, and beneficial with respect to the audience[186].

The power of words in Graeco-Roman literature is tied to the power of the speaker or, in the case of Dio Chrysostom, to the providence of God. It is not seen as something inherent in the words themselves[187]. Plutarch, in *Mor*. 6:507a—b, refers to "the poet" (Homer) as saying that "words" are "winged." Whatever Homer may have meant[188], Plutarch at any rate uses the ideas merely as an image to convey the irretrievability of spoken words and the dissemination of loose talk by some people. Plato, in *Laws* 717d, warns children who would speak disrespectfully of their parents because for such "light and winged words there is a most heavy penalty — for over such matters Nemesis, messenger of Justice is appointed to keep watch." This refers to loose, uncontrolled reproach of parents by children which a god overhears. The words do not act on the parents apart from the children's intention. Hesiod speaks of talk being like a god in *Works* 760—764, but in this he is simply characterising the ability of gossip to pass seemingly forever from one person to the next. Isocrates, in *To Philip* 104, speaks of the power of the words "freedom" to break up empires, but this is not separate from the willingness of people to believe in the concept.

Philonic Literature

Controlled Speech

The control of speech is viewed by Philo as a primary aspect of self-restraint (*Spec*. 2:195; *Congr*. 80). He is well aware that the unbridled

---

186 Dio Chyrs. 32:12–13; Xen., *Eq*. 8:13.
187 Mundle, "Curse," speaks of the "intrinsic power" of the spoken word in classical thought, but he does not list any primary source references for this statement.
188 The words ἔπεα πτερόεντα are apparently a common formula for referring to speech in Homer. Neither the examination of the formula by Calhoun nor by J. Thomson give any thought to demonstrating primitive beliefs in the intrinsic power of words. Thomson holds that the metaphor is derived from archery and thus refers to "feathered words" which indicate their ability to fly straight and be easily comprehended. Calhorn finds the formula is associated with emotional reactions in tense situations. This can be delight as well as anger or fear. In his view, the formula, then, refers to words which are spoken quickly, with animation, or some physical symptom of emotion. With this latter suggestion, one might compare Dio Chrysostom's description of a brand of oratorical power in 33:4–5.

tongue is dangerous, "bringing chaos and confusion into everything[189]."
Thus, it is his view that the purpose of lips is to control, regulate, and at
times inhibit speech which flows from the mouth and the tongue even as a
dam controls a mighty river or as a fence or hedge restricts movement
through the countryside (*Congr.* 33; *Som.* 2:262). He speaks with deep
admiration for Zeno because he had the fortitude to bite off his own
tongue while under torture rather than reveal secrets (*Prob.* 108; *Det.*
175—176).

In Philo, speech control is most often spoken of in terms of silence.
This is a positive that in both the foolish and the wise. In *Det.* 102 (also
Her. 14), he says that "those who have truly learned to speak have also
learned to be silent." Silence can be used for harm just as much as speech.
As he says in *Spec.* 4:90, "Some desire to keep unspoken what should be
told or to keep what should be silent left unsaid, and avenging justice
attends on utterance in the one case and silence in the opposite[190]. The true
objective is to keep silent at the right time as well as to speak at the right
time. For instance, praise of God as a first-fruit offering of the mind is
appropriate when one has been blessed (*Som.* 2:267—273).

Silence should be used as an aid to maximise the effectiveness of
beneficial speech. In *Conf.* 37, he says that "silence is actually a power,
sister to the power of speech, husbanding the fitting words until the
perfect moment for utterance arrives." Both powers are envisaged by
Philo as dispensed ultimately by God (*Conf.* 39). However, conscience is
spoken of as a further aid to keeping the tongue in check (*Det.* 23).

Appropriate speech admits of infinite variation according to the timing
but also according to the person(s) addressed and the subject matter
(*Post.* 108—111). Appropriate speech also assumes an air of gentleness and
kindliness about it[191].

To Philo, as noted in *Det.* 40, the mind is "the fountain of words."
From it flow the thoughts which form the basis of speech. In some sense,
thoughts and speech are mutually dependent, the thoughts supplying
substance and truthfulness and speech supplying expression and clarity[192].
But thoughts are considered the primary donor by Philo[193]. Also, it is the
mind through which God has ready access to speech (*Mig.* 80—81). A
person should make his mind a fit place from which God can direct his
thoughts. This task will of necessity set him on the path toward procuring

---

189 *Abr.* 21; 29; also *Leg.* 162; *Spec.* 2:7; *Mos.* 2:198.
190 Philo speaks of Flaccus, prefect of Alexandria, as eventually negative in his speech in
     this way (*Flacc.* 51) but as originally positive in the opposite way (*Flacc.* 2).
191 *Abr.* 208; *Sob.* 52; *Mut.* 39; *Her.* 127.
192 *Mig.* 79–81; *Mos.* 2:127–129; *Som.* 2:260; *Det.* 126–129.
193 *Det.* 40,127–129; *Mut.* 240–242; *Spec.* 1:259.

wisdom and virtue which — not without God's aid — will positively affect his speech as well as his actions (Horsley, "Wisdom"). Rather than perpetuating mere silence, this course will certify him when he speaks to do so for God even as Moses did and to do so with appropriate timing and gentleness but also with force and conviction[194]. In *Her.* 14, Philo says:

> . . . those should keep silent who have nothing worth hearing to say, and those should speak who have put their faith in the God–sent love of wisdom, and not only speak with ordinary gentleness but shout with a louder cry.

Display of anger is not considered appropriate speech by Philo. It is harmful and a product of the irrational, the passions[195]. It is the sworn enemy of clarity and truthfulness (*L.A.* 3:123—124). Thus, Philo offers various pieces of advice for controlling anger (*Agr.* 17; *Mig.* 210; *L.A.* 3:124). These mostly amount to giving reason sway over the passions. Moses is held up as the model of one who learned to control his anger (*L.A.* 3:131). Angry display is also related by Philo to drunkenness (*Virt.* 162; *Som.* 2:165, 192—193).

Listening

According to Philo, one of the purposes of ears is to filter through incoming speech to the benefit of the soul (*Spec.* 1:342—343). What is heard is to be instructive, disciplinary, and maturing. This necessarily rules out listening to the wordy, sophistic controversies of professional orators which are gauged to entertain and concentrate on trivialities[196]. Those who engage in such practices cannot be "properly held either to speak or to hear," says Philo in *Som.* 2:264. This also rules out listening to idle and slanderous gossip "in meddlesome curiosity," as mentioned in *Abr.* 21.

The kind of instruction Philo does advocate listening to — and this with keen attention — is exemplified in the manner and subject matter of the Theraputae's senior teacher (*Vita* 31, 75—82). Shying away from clever rhetoric and with quiet composure, this model teacher delivers a thoughtfully wise lesson. He discusses questions which arise from Scripture or something related that listeners may raise. He spins out the inner meaning of Scripture by allegory with calm repetition in order to allow these living truths to imprint themselves firmly upon the thoughts in the rational souls of his hearers.

The audiences among the Theraputae likewise are presented as worthy models of listening. This is because they do so with quiet attentiveness,

---

194 *Her.* 15–16; *Mig.* 80–81; *Leg.* 245.
195 *Mig.* 210; *L.A.* 3:147. Philo holds that Joseph was sold into slavery because of the wrath of his brothers. See *Jos.* 173.
196 *Som.* 2:264. Philo holds nothing but disdain for "word–mongers," as he calls them in *Congr.* 53. See also *Som.* 1:105–108; *Congr.* 51–53; *Post.* 101; *Vita* 31, 75.

showing their occasional approval only by facial expressions and nods[197].
They exemplify what Philo speaks of in *Her.* 11—12 as those who are
"silent with the tongue and hear with the ears," who are "silent and hear
with the soul also." In order to hear with the soul a person must cast away
all distracting thoughts from his mind and concentrate on listening to the
speaker. This kind of concentration is important especially when a person
wishes to listen to God because his voice is only "visible to the soul," as
Philo puts it in *Mig.* 52, and not to the ears.

Philo's stress on listening to God and obeying his commandments
cannot be overemphasised (*L.A.* 3:54; *Som.* 2:261—267). He heaps praises on
Abraham for this (*Abr.* 60—67). In *Dec.* 37—39, he maintains that the Ten
Commandments are addressed as to an individual in order to make "the
hearer more ready to obey." Listening to God is much more than
following his written/spoken commandments. It involves listening internally to the voice of the Divine Logos within, responding more and more
to it and eventually turning one's whole life — from the inside out — over
to God's will (*Abr.* 60—61).

Philo also stresses listening to parents in the sense of respecting them.
Parents are spoken of as God's servants in *Dec.* 119—120 and "he who
dishonours the servant dishonours the Lord." Without noting disapproval,
Philo goes on to transmit the view of "some bolder spirits" who "say that
a father and mother are in fact gods revealed to sight who copy the
Uncreated in His work as the Framer of life."

Words and Deeds

It is critical to Philo that people follow God's injunctions to them
obediently. Regardless as to whether these be realised naturally or from
Scripture, the objective is to translate God's words into action (*Mig.* 129).
Words and deeds together represent a person's life in obedient service to
God (*Spec.* 1:317; *Mig.* 128).

The ability to translate his own words into action is considered one of
the primary properties of God. He accomplishes this so swiftly that it is
probably a more accurate description to say as Philo does that "whatever
God says is not words but deeds[198]. "Bringing words into harmony with
deeds and deeds with words," is projected as a fitting goal for people in
Spec. 2:52—53. People's lives should not only mirror God's injunctions,
then, but their words and deeds should reflect each other.

---

197 Ibid. Also *Fug.* 122 and *Spec.* 2:62.
198 *Dec.* 47. See also *Sac.* 65–66; *Cher.* 77.

But Philo even goes beyond this. He is most adamant in calling for the harmonisation of words and deeds with the thoughts, as well. In *Praem.* 81 (cf. *Mos.* 2:138—141), it says:

> For if our words correspond with our thoughts and intentions and our actions with our words and the three mutually follow one another, bound together with indissoluble bonds of harmony, happiness prevails, and happiness is wisdom pure of all falsehood.

Elsewhere, in *Virt.* 184, Philo says that a person who maintains such harmony "will be well-pleasing to God, thus becoming at once God-loving and God-beloved."

Although such harmonisation is Philo's abiding desire for people, he knows it is difficult to achieve in reality. This becomes clear in *Mut.* 240—244, where he involves the three elements of thoughts, words, and deeds in a discussion about transgressions under the law and a person's obligations and ability to control himself at three graduated levels. Philo considers it best for a person to control himself at the level of the thoughts, although he admits that "a man's thoughts are sometimes not due to himself but come from outside his will." Second best is to control at the level of speech. This a person should be able to do for speech is wholly voluntary. This also means the person is fully culpable for any offence or transgressions he may utter, even if such things are judged with a certain leniency by the law of Moses. The area of deeds is considered the absolute line of defence. Control here must be unwavering. The implication of all this, especially in light of what has been observed elsewhere in Philo, is that control at the level of thoughts is only possible with God's help and if God's will (through the Divine Logos) is the dominant "outside" influences. Then, words and deeds will fall into line with the God-controlled thoughts.

With thoughts representing the inner aspect of man, Philo is fond of using words and deeds together to represent the outward, observable manifestation of a person's life. For instance, in referring to the patriarchs, Philo speaks of "that excellence of words and deeds which adorned their lives[199]." To him, a person is known for what he is by his words and deeds. Shallow talk indicates a shallow and closed mind (*Prob.* 11; *Post.* 108). Vile speech is the sign of a bad man[200]. Lack of responsible action invalidates so-called "wisdom" being spouted[201]. He is certainly aware that some are quite good at hiding their true intentions by deceitful speech as well as overshadowing their lack of deeds by clever oratory (*Mut.* 195—199). These

---

199 *Abr.* 37. See further: *Flacc.* 40; *Prob.* 2; *Mos.* 2:66; *Som.* 2:83; *Virt.* 190; *Praem.* 107. Discussion of speech and/or action as external manifestations of inner disposition can be found in *Mos.* 2:127–130; *Spec.* 4:69; *Praem.* 82; *Det.* 126–128.
200 *Prob.* 99, 155; *Post.* 55; *Conf.* 48; *Abr.* 20–24.
201 *Congr.* 46, 53; *Som.* 1:105–108; *Det.* 43–44; *Mos.* 2:212; *Post.* 101; *Mut.* 193.

things are despised and are to be rejected outright in favour of harmonisation of one's life.

The Power of Words

In *Her.* 4 Philo speaks of silence enabling wise thoughts to be formulated
and flow to the mouth, ready for utterance. Silence thus increases the
power of words.

Philo recognizes that speech has the power to do much good. He speaks
of song and speech in *Spec.* 1:343 as "medications, giving health, and
preserving life." He goes on further to articulate the benefitical power of
speech, saying that it:

> checks and hampers impulses to vice and effects the cure of those in whom foolish
> and distressful thoughts have gained the mastery. It deals more gently with the docile,
> more drastically with the rebellious, and thus becomes the source of the greatest
> possible benefits[202].

Philo also recognizes the power of speech to do harm *(Det.* 174).

According to Philo, one of the keys to being able to speak powerfully,
especially in public oratory is an intimate understanding of what one
wishes to say *(Det.* 131; *Mig.* 79—80). But given an awareness of what he
says elsewhere about the thoughts being God's avenue to a person's speech,
we know that he envisages God as the sharpener of the thoughts and the
primary key to the production of truly powerful speech *(Dec.* 13). Philo
perceives God to be the source behind the power that eventuated in
Moses' speech *(Mig.* 80—81; *Her.* 14—17). The same is held to be the case
for Joseph whose life as a statesman is epitomised in the statement that he
was "unsurpassed in comeliness, wisdom and power of language[203]."

Philo does not view speech or the power involved in it as in any way
independent of the speaker, except as God may be the ultimate power
guiding his thoughts. Philo does describe speech in one place, *Mut.* 247, as
"light and winged by nature," but as he himself explains he means that
speech is like an arrow in its swiftness to reach its target and in its
irretrievability.

---

202 In *Som.* 1:102–104, Philo argues that the power of speech is one of the best gifts God
has given man because it is: 1) a weapon of defence, 2) a covering for shame, 3) an
adornment of life.
203 *Jos.* 268. See also *Jos.* 42, 269. In *Jos.* 117, after Joseph's interpretation of his dreams,
the king is given to say to Joseph, "I think that God is with the words you speak."

New Testament

Controlled Speech

In the New Testament, general admonitions for the control of speech are not prominent. Much more prominent is dispraise of numerous specific categories of speech, such as the angry outburst[204] and others which are unsettling to interpersonal relationships (to be dealt with in Part III).

More than equalising the deficiency of general admonitions on this topic in the New Testament are the telling words assigned to Jesus which appear in Mt. 12:36—37:

> But I tell you that for each careless word they speak men shall give an account for it on the day of judgment. For by your words you will be vindicated and by your words you will be condemned.

The first sentence, perhaps with a bit of dramatic hyperbole, describes the consequences of uttering useless, non-beneficial words (ἀργόν)[205]. The position of πᾶν ῥῆμα as well as the protuberance and singular tense of περὶ αὐτοῦ emphasise that it is each careless word that is in question. As in a courtroom, people are pictured being compelled to muster a defense before God for each and every errant word which has escaped their control during the course of their lives. With proverbial, self-justifying flair[206], the second sentence offers reasons for such a strict judgment of words being appropriate. It presumes an acceptance of the view that a person's speech is directly related to the disposition of his inner nature, as is propounded in Mt. 12:33—35 (Lk. 6:43—45). There it is expressed that good speech is an accurate gauge of a good heart (and thus of a genuinely good person with respect to God and men), as is evil speech of an evil heart. Thus, a person's words will vindicate (δικαιωθήσῃ) his good nature, but on the other hand his words, if evil, will also condemn (καταδικασθήσῃ) him[207].

Another general admonition for speech control is found in 1 Pet. 3:10, in

---

204   Gal. 5:20; 1 Cor. 13:5; 2 Cor. 12:20; Eph. 4:31; Col. 3:8; Tit. 1:7.

205   The Greek word ἀργός can refer to those who are unemployed (Mt. 20:3, 6) and by inference can mean "lazy" (1 Tim. 5:13). Here, it seems to convey the idea of useless words that are of no benefit to anyone.

206   The proverbial nature of this verse is commonly noted. See Hill, 219; Allen, 138; McNeile, 181.

207   There is some question about the contextual relationship between Mt. 12:32—33 and Mt. 12:36—38. The former condemns uttering blasphemous words against the Holy Spirit. Presumably, such words are deliberate. The latter condemns the unintentional verbal slip, that is if ἀργός is taken as "careless." Hendrickson, 531, takes vs. 36 as a general rule which incorporates what goes before, i.e. if every careless word is condemned, then certainly deliberate words are included. This seems plausible enough. Perhaps, even simpler is to take ἀργός more in the sense of "useless" or "non-beneficial."

which Peter appropriates into his own catalogue of ethical advice words from Ps. 34:12—13 (LXX). True and abiding life for the Christian in the present as well as the future eschatological hope[208] is contingent upon controlling the tongue, restraining it, stopping it (παύω) from its propensity to speak evil.

Silence in itself is not commended as a wisdom virtue in the New Testament. This is not to say that it does not have a place of importance in the events and teachings recorded therein. It appears that Jesus almost routinely charged those he healed, the demoniacs he exorcised, and even the disciples he taught to remain silent about who he was[209]. Mt. 12:16—21 says that this was in order to fulfill the words of Isa. 42:1—4. But it also probably had something to do with preventing the premature release of the full revelation that Jesus was the Christ which might have been a hindrance to the overall effect and purpose of his ministry. The tradition concerning Jesus' silence at his trial appears conspiciously in each of the Synoptic Gospels and probably is the basis of the encouragement in 1 Pet. 2:18—25 for all Christians to bear patiently all suffering for Christ's sake in silence. Both 1 Thes. 4:11 and 1 Tim. 2:2 recommend the quiet life to Christian as a way to affect their culture significantly on behalf of Christ. It appears that the same evangelistic motivation lies behind the advice given to slaves in Tit. 2:9 not to talk back to their master, to Christian wives in 1 Pet. 3:1—6 to be specially submissive to their non-Christian husbands, to those with ecstatic utterances in 1 Cor. 14:30—37 to be silent when necessary for order to be maintained in worship, and even to women to be silent in 1 Cor. 14:34—35 and to be restricted in their teaching in 1 Tim. 2:12—15[210].

How can the solid substratum of support for the ethical value of silence be explained in light of the gaping absence of any general recommendations for silence? An answer may be suggested by considering this situation in light of the foundational position occupied by evangelism in the New Testament writings. Open verbal acknowledgment of Christ before men coupled with fearlessly bold preaching of the gospel is at the heart of Christianity[211], is indispensable for its advancement, and is

---

208 It is generally acknowledged that Peter has highlighted the eschatological dimension which was lacking in the original emphases of the psalm. See Selwyn, 190; J. Kelly, 138; Best, 131.

209 Mk. 1:25, 34 (Lk. 4:35, 41); Mt. 8:4 (Mk. 1:44—45; Lk. 5:14); Mt. 12:16—21 (Mk. 3:11—12); Mt. 16:20 (Mk. 8:30; Lk. 9:21); Mk. 9:9—10 (Mt. 17:9; Lk. 9:31).

210 Both of these references come in the context of concern for what non-Christians think (1 Cor. 14:20—25; 1 Tim. 2:3—4), although admittedly there appear to be theological and/or traditional reasons for supporting the comments about women's silence in each reference as well.

211 For instances, see Mt. 10:32 (Lk. 12:8—9); Acts 9:27; 13:46; 14:3; 18:9; 19:8; 26:26; 28:31; Rom. 10:14—18; Phil. 1:14—18. With regard to the importance of boldness, two excellent studies

fundamental for those who by faith enter into it. Would a New Testament writer want to risk giving the impression — even with regard to a value as highly esteemed as silence — that sharing the gospel message with someone is ever to be restricted? Thus, silence in the New Testament never stands as an ethical value in its own right but is only urged as an aid in promoting the gospel with regard to non-adherents. The ultimate goal of such silence is to provide favourable conditions for sharing the gospel message.

When conversing with his non-Christian neighbors about routine matters — but especially about Christ — Col. 4:5—6 strongly emphasises that the Christian's attitude and manner are to be gracious.

The apologetic direction of the conversations in view is evident from τὸν καιρὸν ἐξαγοραζόμενοι and ἀποκρίνεσθαι. Nevertheless, the actual statement which presses for gracious speech, in view of the πάντοτε, would appear to cover a wider area and include general conversation.

Further demand for graciousness applied strictly in defence of the Christian faith is made in 1 Pet. 3:16 and in 2 Tim. 2:25. In both of these, the word which conveys the concept of graciousness in the course of speaking is πραΰτης, which accepts the importance of a gentle, courteous demeanor. A synonym, ἐπεικής, is used in 1 Tim. 3:3 to characterise qualified church leaders and in Phil. 4:5 and Tit. 3:2 to describe an attitude to which all Christians should aspire. It emphasises a patient, yielding, even forgiving spirit (which may imply the withholding of unnecessarily harsh speech) to another who is perhaps deserving of it.

In Col. 4:6, the dative of χάρις is used which, in addition to referring to speech that is generally beneficial to the outsider, may include grace imparted by the sharing of the gospel message (Lohse, *Colossians*, 168). In this sense, the reference to conversation being seasoned with salt (ἅλατι ἠρτυμένος) may include the notion of the preserving effects of the gospel as well as the importance of careful, thoughtful preparation in order to make the suggestion as appealing as possible to the non-Christian[212].

In Eph. 4:25—32, the case for giving χάρις its full theological weight appears to be even stronger[213]. It is the direct object of the verb δῷ which has as its indirect object τοῖς ἀκούουσιν. Also, the encouragement to

---

of the Christian use and ultimate takeover of the Greek word παρρησία come from Marrow and van Unnik.

212 Nauck based on Rabbinic background material, relates the use of salt here to wisdom.

213 Barth, 520, after presenting the possibility that "Eph. 4:29 may charge the saints to converse with their fellow men in such a way that their words become a vehicle and demonstration of the very grace of God," concludes that among the remarkable things about this verse is that "it attributes to speech above all (and, perhaps, exclusively) the power to communicate God's grace."

beneficial speech is made clear quite apart from χάριν by ἀγαθὸς πρὸς οἰκοδομήν earlier in the sentence.

Since τοῦ πλησίου αὐτοῦ in 4:25 is followed by ὅτι ἐσμὲν ἀλλήλων μέλη the phrase εἴ τις ἀγαθὸς πρὸς οἰκοδομήν in 4:29 must apply primarily to conversation within the Christian community, although certainly not excluding wider public contacts (Barth, 520; Mitton, *Eph-sians*, 167—168). Elsewhere in the New Testament "edification" appears as a major working principle for life within the Christian community[214].

As in Jewish literature, Mt. 12:34 (Lk. 6:45) indicates that the ability to produce gracious speech is contingent upon an individual's heart, wherein his goodness is stored[215]. But this is not the end of the matter in the New Testament. Gracious speech which in any way imparts God's grace is considered dependent upon the active presence of the Holy Spirit within the individual. In Lk. 4:22, the description of Jesus' speech as "words of grace" appears to be related to his citation of Isa. 61:1: "The Spirit of the Lord is upon me." It certainly refers at least to the fact that what he said on that occasion carried the unmistakable mark of divine power[216]. In Eph. 4:29—31, the notion that the Spirit is grieved when his desire for the individual to speak edifying words which impart grace is thwarted by the believer's unwholesome speech must be included in any attempt to understand within its context the concern about grieving the Holy Spirit[217].

Further, in 1 Cor. 2:12—13, Paul says:

> Now we have not received the spirit of the world but the Spirit who is from God so that we should know the things given to us by God which we also speak, not in words taught by human wisdom but rather in those taught by the Spirit, expressing the spiritual with the spiritual[218].

By this means, Paul concludes in vs. 16 that "we have the mind of Christ." In addition, all three Synoptic Gospels record Jesus' promise to his disciples that when they are under severe trial for the sake of the gospel the Holy Spirit will lead their mouths to say what the situation demands[219]. Finally, 1

---

214 See Rom. 14:19; 15:2; 1 Cor. 14:12, 26; 2 Cor. 12:19; 13:10. All these references presume an internal Christian context. The only one of these references which does not have the Christian community exclusively in view is Rom. 15:2, which, like Eph. 4:29, applies the principle of edification to one's neighbor but within the wider context appears to have the Christian community also in mind (14:19; 15:5).

215 See also Rom. 10:10 on the direct relationship between the heart and the mouth.

216 See Acts 14:3; 20:24, 32, plus I. Marshall, *Luke*, 186.

217 See Mitton, *Ephesians*, 170; J. A. Robinson, 113; Abbott, 143—144.

218 See also 1 Cor. 1:5 where a person's speech is thought to be enriched by the gospel and 1 Cor. 12:3 where it is expressed that no one can say that Jesus is Lord apart from the influence of the Holy Spirit. Compare also Mt. 16:17 where Jesus identifies Peter's confession of his Lordship as only being possible through divine influence.

219 See Mt. 10:17—21 (Mk. 13:11; Lk. 21:14—15) but also Acts 4:8; 7:55—56; 9:17—28, which attempt to demonstrate the fulfillment of this promise.

Pet. 4:11 indicates that all Christians who speak under even wider circumstances are to consider themselves to be delivering the very words of God (Selwyn, 219; J. Kelly, 180; Best, 160).

Listening

Although the New Testament endorses the important concept of drawing upon "whatever is true" (Phil. 4:8—9), the distinctive accent is decidedly upon listening to Jesus Christ, the wisdom of God 1 Cor. 1:32, "in whom are hidden all the treasures of wisdom and knowledge" (Col. 2:3).

If the number of occurrences in the Gospels and Revelation are any indication, Jesus must have challenged his audiences often with the resounding plea: "He who has ears, let him hear[220]." It was critical that they listen and listen well to what he said because it was from God, and it was a matter of life and death [221].

The same austere attitude toward listening passes on to those whom Jesus sends out to speak for him. This is observed at the commission of the Seventy to preach about the coming of the Kingdom of God, (Lk. 10:16; Mt. 10:24; Jn. 5:23). Earlier in the context it is said that the fate for any city which rejects Jesus' messengers will be worse than that of Sodom and Gomorrah (Lk. 10:12; Mt. 10:15).

The discernment to listen to and truly hear Jesus and his message, most notably in Johannine literature (Jn. 5:24; for instance), is made the infallible rod for separating men into the godly and the ungodly, the saved and the unsaved. Jesus comes from God and delivers his words. Therefore, those who do not listen to Jesus are not of God (Jn. 8:47). This extends to those entrusted with Jesus' message. Thus, 1 Jn. 4:6 can say, "Whoever knows God, listens to us." But Acts 4:12 also says, "There is salvation in no one else." Thus, those like Mary who sit at Jesus' feet and listen to his teaching are heartily commended in the Gospels as are those groups of people as in Ephesus who listened and responded to the message of truth, to the gospel of their salvation[222]. Accordingly, those like some of the Pharisees who refuse to listen, and even more, who dare to scoff at Jesus and his message are categorically condemned as being aligned with the devil[223].

The New Testament writers, seemingly reflecting the attitude of Jesus, treat the Jewish Scriptures with the greatest respect, placing them on a par

---

220   Mt. 11:15; 13:43; 25:29; Mk. 4:23; 7:16; Lk. 8:8; 14:35; Rev. 2:7, 11, 17, 28; 3:6, 13, 22; 12:9. See also I. Marshall, *Luke*, 320.
221   Jn. 5:24; 7:16–18; 8:26, 51–52; 10:27–28; 12:49; 14:10, 31; 17:6–8.
222   Lk. 10:38–42 and Eph. 1:13; Acts 28:26–28; Rom. 10:18–21.
223   Jn. 8:43–45; 1 Jn. 2:20–25; Mt. 11:21–23; Lk. 10:13–14; 16:14–15.

with the very words of God (θεόπνευστος)[224]. In 2 Tim. 3:15—16, they are
spoken of as inspired by God and recommended heartily as a most
valuable source of wisdom and instruction. However, the passage also
places their value within the delimiting perspective of the overwhelming
significance of Jesus Christ. They are valuable because they "are able to
give you the wisdom that leads to salvation through faith which is Christ
Jesus[225]." Similarly, Jn. 5:24 indicates that however much Scripture may
speak of eternal life, it is only attainable through Jesus Christ. Thus,
listening to the words of Scripture is deemed worthwhile for the Christian
but never apart from listening to the words of Jesus and his message of
salvation. Both Jewish Scripture and Jesus' words are from God, but the
latter takes precedence over the former.

Words and Deeds

As with listening, Jesus dominates the New Testament treatment of the
relationship between words and deeds, particularly with respect to
obedience. His words must be heard, but the wise man will act upon them
as well (Mt. 7:21; Lk. 6:47). The passage goes on to imply that the person
who obeys Jesus' teaching will stand secure against the trying onslaughts
in life as well as make it through divine judgment (Hill, 153; I. Marshall,
Luke, 275). Similarly, the Parable of the Sower asserts that the one who
truly hears Christ's message of the Kingdom will be able to retain it
against all the evil pressures of the world and will produce much fruit
from it[226]. The Gospels also give weight to the value of being obedient to
the word of God[227]. Jesus is cited as the supreme example of this in Heb.
5:7—9.

In Johannine literature, keeping Christ's commandments is presented as
the flawless evidence of a person's love for him; the failure to do so is
seen as evidence of a person's hate[228]. Obeying the commandments of God
also receives due emphasis, particularly in 1 John (2:17; 3:22; 5:2—4), but
this is not seen necessarily as something separate. This is because one of
the commandments of God, as stated in 1 Jn. 3:22, is thought to be "to
believe in the name of His Son Jesus Christ[229].

---

224 See, for instance, Mt. 15:3–9 (Mk. 7:9–13); Lk. 24:44; Mt. 5:18 (Lk. 16:17), keeping in
     mind also the numerous quotations of the Old Testament which appear on Jesus' lips
     in the Gospel accounts and upon which the other New Testament books rely.
225 Compare also Jesus' post–resurrection effort to enlighten his disciples concerning his
     place in the Scriptures, noted in Lk. 24:44.
226 Mt. 13:18–23 (Mk. 4:13–20; Lk. 8:11–15). In Jn. 15:5, the point is made that it is Christ
     who enables fruit to be produced.
227 Lk. 11:28; Mk. 3:35 (Mt. 12:50; Lk. 8:21); Mt. 4:4; 5:19; 15:1–9 (Mk. 7:1–13).
228 Jn. 14:15, 21, 23–24; 15:9–17; 1 Jn. 2:3–5; 3:21–24.
229 On the interconnection between Christ's teaching and doing God's will, see Jn. 7:16–18.

In Pauline literature, particularly in 2 Thes. 1:7—9, the idea of disobedience to the gospel of Jesus being associated with not knowing God is spoken of as grounds for eternal destruction (cf. 2 Cor. 10:5; 1 Pet. 4:17). In Rom. 2:12, Paul also speaks of the positive benefit of hearing and doing the Law of God. However, Paul ranks his own ethical instruction highly as well, as 1 Thes. 3:14 and 2 Cor. 2:9 make clear. In Phil. 4:8—9, the idea is widened even further so that what he requires to be put into practice includes "whatever you have learned or received or heard from me, or seen in me." In general principle, 1 Cor. 10:31 makes the point that whatever one does is to be done to the glory of Christ (cf. Mt. 5:10). On a different track, Paul's writings and those influenced by him accent the importance of Christians obeying their parents as well as the importance of Christians obeying their church leaders[230].

There are a few glimmerings in the New Testament of other concepts associated with words and deeds found in the literature previously examined. First, words and deeds are used together to embody the observable manifestations of a person's behaviour (Acts 1:1; 7:23). Secondly, consistency between a person's words and his deeds is deemed something for which to seek. The Pharisees, for example, are condemned by Jesus in Mt. 23:3 because their deeds do not measure up to their speech (cf. Mk. 12:40; Lk. 20:47). Thirdly, words and deeds are considered sufficient guides to a person's character. As Mt. 12:33 (cf. Lk. 6:43—45) says, "A tree is known by its fruit." Of course, elsewhere in the New Testament, it is acknowledged that there are those who are able to deceive with their smooth talk or sophisticated rhetoric, and such are warned against[231]. However, Tit. 1:16 declares confidence that their deeds in that case will eventually find them out. On the other hand, true wisdom from God, says Mt. 11:19 (Lk. 6:35) is vindicated (ἐδικαιώθη) by her deeds.

Finally, 1 Jn. 3:17—18 relays the fresh notion that in certain situations, words — however good — are insufficient and even hypocritical. If a person is truly motivated by the love of God and he has the means, he must aid the person in desperate need of material goods. Words will not do.

The Power of Words

Once again, Jesus must comprise the hub of discussion. His words above all others in the New Testament are notable for their power. With simple

---

230 Rom. 1:30; Col. 3:20; Eph. 6:1–2; 1 Tim. 3:4; Tit. 1:6; Heb. 13:12.
231 Paul is anxious to disassociate himself from those who peddle (καπηλεύοντες) the word of God (2 Cor. 2:17) and those who attempt to flatter with their speech (1 Thes.

words like "Be clean!" (καθαρίσθητι), "Go!" (ὑπάγετε), and "Arise!"
(ἐγέρθητι), he is depicted as healing lepers, casting out demons, and raising
the dead[232]. With other words, he heals the paralytic, the sightless, and the
speechless [233]. The sea and wind calm to his rebuke[234]. His words are
authoritative, eliciting eager commitment to his call by some[235], but even
those who remain uncommitted appear to recognize the authority inherent
in his teaching[236]. That he himself considered his words eternally valid and
durable is apparent when he is recorded as saying, "Heaven and earth will
pass away, but my words will not pass away[237].

In the Gospels, the power of Jesus' words is tied inextricably to the
authority he has received from God as God's son, the Messiah[238]. The
display of his power is at least one way in which the Gospel writers
attempt to demonstrate Jesus' divinity. His word is equivalent to that of
God's in power as well as in authority.

In contrast, any word-power that his disciples might display comes not
from themselves but from Jesus and his authority[239]. Indeed, an important
underlying principle in the Gospels is that the power to accomplish the
seemingly miraculous with — such as casting out demons and moving
mountains — is correlative to dedicated belief in Jesus[240]. This principle
applies to speaking effectively for Christ in tense situations as well (Lk.
21:14—15). Other passages which refer to this principle (Mt. 24:19—20; Mk.
13:11), state that it is the Holy Spirit who will actually perform this
function on his behalf. In Acts, the Spirit is credited as the source of the
bold and effective speaking done by Jesus' followers[241].

2:3–5). He warns Christians against such people in Col. 2:4, 8; Eph. 4:14; 5:6; Rom.
16:17–18. See also 2 Tim. 3:13; Jude 16.
232 On the leper, see Mt. 8:3 (Mk. 1:41; Lk. 5:13). On casting demons out, see Mt. 8:32 (Mk.
5:13; Lk. 8:32); Mk. 1:23–28 (Lk. 4:33–37). Mt. 8:16–17 comments that Jesus "cast out
spirits with a word." On raisings from the dead, see Lk. 7:14; Mt. 9:18–26 (Mk. 5:28–34;
Lk. 8:49–56); Jn. 12:38–43.
233 Mt. 9:1–8 (Mk. 2:1–12; Lk. 17:26); Mt. 20:29–34 (Mk. 10:46–52; Lk. 18:35–43); Jn. 5:1–14;
Mk. 7:34.
234 Mt. 8:23–27 (Mk. 4:35–41; Lk. 8:22–25).
235 Mt. 9:9 (Mk. 2:13–14; Lk. 5:27–28); Mt. 4:18–22 (Mk. 1:16–20).
236 Mt. 7:28–29 (Mk. 1:21–22; Lk. 4:31–32).
237 Mt. 24:36 (Mk. 12:33; Lk. 21:23); Jn. 6:62. See Lindars, 274; Barret, 251, Brown, 1:300;
Hill, 323.
238 For example, see Mt. 8:29 (Mk. 5:7; Lk. 8:28); Mk. 1:24 (Lk. 4:34); Lk. 4:41.
239 Mt. 10:16 (Mk. 3:13; 6:7; Lk. 9:1); Lk. 10:17–20. This is painfully obvious when the
disciples fail in their own efforts to cast out the demon in Mt. 17:14–21 (Mk. 9:14–29;
Lk. 9:37–43).
240 Mk. 16:17; Jn. 15:7; 16; Mt. 21:20–22 (Mk. 11:20–25). See also the miracles in Acts which
are done mostly in the name of Jesus.
241 See, for example Acts 1:8; 2:1–37; 4:5–12, 31–35; 6:3, 6; 8:6; 13:52; 14:3. See also Marrow
and van Unnik.

Throughout the rest of the New Testament, the power of Christ and of the Spirit is integrally related to the preaching of the gospel. Paul appears to attempt to depict this dynamic as it works within him in Col. 1:28–29. In 1 Thes. 1:5, Paul speaks more specifically of the Holy Spirit and associates it both with power and personal conviction. The gospel is not considered just a matter of words, however true and important. It is dynamic and grows in believers, sometimes effecting miraculous change in them as 1 Pet. 1:23 emphasises[242]. After quoting Isa. 40:6, it concludes, "And this was the word which was preached to you." Thus, the gospel of Jesus Christ delivered by Spirit-empowered speakers bears all the dynamic qualities of God himself.

---

242 Whether or not one insists that the seed is not to be equated with the word of God as is the case with Selwyn, 151–152, and Best, 94–95 (J. Kelly, 80, takes the opposite stance), the relevant point is that both are described effectively as eternally living. Even more important is that the gospel is identified firmly with this dynamic word of God.

Chapter 2: Epistle of James

James 1:19

By combining the vocative ἀδελφοί μου ἀγαπητοί with the imperative ἴστε, James signals a shift of focus from what procedes. The vocative ἀδελφοί is employed this way at least nine other times in the epistle, in 1:2, 16; 2:1, 5, 14; 3:1; 4:11; 5:7, 12. It is usually accompanied by μου, but not always (4:11; 5:7). The other times, in 2:5 and most relevantly in 1:16, ἀγαπητοί adjoins. Although there is little argument against the rightful claim of ἴστε to be the correct textual reading[1], the question of whether to take it as imperative or indicative continues to divide opinion. The case for the indicative (Mayor, 65) consists of the point that the other two New Testament uses of ἴστε (Eph. 5:5; Heb. 12:17) are indicative (although Eph. 5:5 is disputable) and the point that the indicative allows the difficult δέ which follows ἔστω to be taken in its most usual adversative sense, marking as insufficient mere knowledge of what is said in 1:18 (Hiebert, 123; Reicke, 19—20). However, the fact that James usually associates the vocative ἀδελφοί with imperatives[2] and uses οἴδατε in 4:4 as indicative (ἴστε being used to differentiate according to Hort, 35) weighs heavily in favour of ἴστε being imperative. In this sense, then, it calls attention to the importance of the aphoristic admonition which follows Laws, 80; Mussner, 99).

The admonition has universal scope as πᾶς ἄνθρωπος indicates and is to receive constant application as the present imperative ἔστω presumes. The use of πάντες alone would have been sufficient, indeed, the normal way to refer to humanity in general. However, the addition of ἄνθρωπος reflects the Semitic background of the author (P. Davids, 92) and also arises naturally after the creation context of 1:18 (Hort, 35). These factors further emphasise the importance of the admonition.

The introductory δέ has proven difficult to explain. If it retains its adversative sense, it is hard to find anything in the previous context with which it stands in contrast (unless one takes the ἴστε as indicative as do

---

1 Adamson, 78, makes an attempt but is countered very capably by P. Davids, 91.

2 The only exceptions out of 15 uses are the association with questions in 2:14 and 3:12 and the association with a declarative sentence in 3:10. See P. Davids, 91.

Hiebert and Reicke). P. Davids (91), following Dibelius (p. 109), suggests that the δέ was an original part of the context from which the cited proverb came. However, it is difficult to believe that the source of the proverb was so revered that James dared not alter even a δέ. Rather, as a proverb, it would by its very nature be susceptible to alteration and improvement by popular usage. This would apply to smoothing it out for various contextual uses. James frequently uses particles to connect proverbial-like statements to the context (2:13; 3:18; 4:17). Nowhere else does anyone suggest that the particle is part of the original proverb, even in 3:18, where δέ appears.

With regard to the use of δέ itself, it is a favourite for James (37 times), and he knows its full range of meaning. It is used in a continuative sense seven times (1:15, 22; 2:2, 3, 16, 23, 25; 3:18)[3] and even as an intensifier at least once (1:13). It appears in 1:9 where there is no necessity for any particle to be used. Further, with no apparent change of meaning, in 2:23 δέ is substituted for καί when quoting Gen. 15:6 (LXX). If he can alter a passage he considers Scripture in a situation like this, it seems unlikely he would be timid about altering a proverb to suit his context. This instance also demonstrates that he views δέ and καί as interchangeable and that he prefers δέ.

Thus, the δέ which introduces the admonition in 1:19 is best viewed as James' own choice and not as attached to the original context of a proverb. It should be read in a continuation sense (Amphous, 93—94; Mussner, 99), or else it should be seen as a stylistic feature.

Both the style and the content of the tripartite phrase ταχὺς εἰς τὸ ἀκοῦσαι, βραδὺς εἰς τὸ λαλῆσαι, βραδὺς εἰς ὀργήν indicate its proverbial nature. The catchy, punctuated phrasing, parallel in style yet contrasting in choice of words, reveals that it has been most carefully crafted for essay memorisation and transmitted through popular ethical thought (Dibelius, 111).

The origin of the tripartite proverb remains unknown. There are some close parallels in terms of thought and style in both Jewish and Graeco-Roman literature. Sir. 5:11, commonly cited as the closest parallel (Ropes, 169), involves the first two members of the proverb and is sometimes translated similarly (NAB). However, it actually uses only one parallel word (ταχύς)[4]. Indeed, Ward (pp. 180—181) observes that Sir. 5:11 makes a decidedly different emphasis. The admonition to answer deliberately is conditioned in Sir. 5:12 on a person having knowledge or understanding. In James, it is absolute. A closer parallel comes from Plut., *Mor.* 1:39b, who

---

3 Amphoux, "coordonnant," 95–96.
4 It reads: γίνου ταχὺς ἐν ἀκροάσει σου καὶ ἐν μακροθυμίᾳ φθέγγου ἀπόκρισιν.

relates that a quality education includes teaching the students πολλὰ μὲν ἀκούειν μὴ πολλὰ δὲ λέγειν⁵. At least the thought is stated in more absolute terms and is conveyed by infinitives. Earlier, Plut., *Mor.* 1:10b, lists τὸ τὴν γλῶτταν κατέχειν, τὸ τῆς ὀργῆς ὑπεράνω γίγνεσθαι as necessary "rules of conduct." Dio Chrysostom, 32:2, reveres people who are βραδὺ μὲν φθεγγομένους. Aboth 5:14 speaks of a person being "hard to anger" (כוח לכעס) or "easy to anger" (קשה לכעוס). The contrasting adverbs quick (מהר) and slow (קשה) are employed in Aboth 5:15 in combination with a preposition and infinitive (לשמוע) with regard to a person's ability to learn⁶.

Plenty of ideas were available from which the proverb could have been constructed. But the fact is that no one source contains all three parts in one statement. Therefore, it is possible that the "proverb" was coined by the author of James himself for his own purposes inside or outside of this writing.

The proverbial tripartite phrase is important to the author. Not only does it head this section and is it accented by the opening ἴστε, it also provides the structure for the section⁷. Verses 20—21 expand on the third member of the phrase, verses 22—25 on the first, and verse 26 on the second, with verse 27 providing a summary conclusion. The author does nothing in his elaboration on the parts of the phrase to enlighten the reader about the meaning of the proverb itself or about the relationship between the three parts.

As Dibelius (p. 111) notes, the claim of the tripartite saying lies in its Greek formulation regardless of the origin of the ideas. The duplication of the εἰς τό plus aorist active infinitive contrasted by the adverbial antonyms in the first two members results in a melodious ring which is heightened by the identical number of syllables used for each word. The repetition of εἰς from the first two parts and of βραδύς from the second successfully ties the third to the other two despite the change from the infinitive to the noun and the dropping of the article. The variance from the first two parts is due probably to the nature of the word ὀργή. The verb form is deponent and averse to active endings⁸. The variance plus its position does give the impression that the third member is being ac-

---

5   See also the very similar but later admonition from Lucian, *Demonax* 51, which says: ὀλίγα μὲν λαλῶν, πολλὰ δὲ ἀκούων.

6   See also Ovid, *Ex Ponto* 1:2 for the use of quick and slow with an infinitive in Latin (*ad poenas princeps, ad praemia velox*).

7   Via, 263, and Dibelius, 108. E. Pfeiffer considers it the key to the structure of the entire epistle.

8   The word ὀργίζομαι is not used as an infinitive in the New Testament and is only rarely used so the LXX. The two uses as an aorist infinitive are in 4 Ki. 19:28 and Ps. 123 (124):3 and are in the passive, ὀργισθῆναι. In both cases, these are articular infinitives.

centuated as the result of observing the other two cautions. In this sense, the three members are a progression. Being quick to hear will result in being slow to speak which will result in being slow to anger. They may be applied practically to a particular instance, or they can be viewed as an overall challenge to improve one's general character.

The use of εἰς τό plus the infinitive in the tripartite phrase makes it a reasonable assumption that the proverb, at least in this form, is contemporary since this type of construction is rare in Classical Greek but on the increase in Hellenistic Greek of the New Testament period (Turner, 142; Robertson, *Grammar* 1069). Robertson (*Grammar*, 1071), in discussing εἰς τό, notes that there is not much different in sence from ἐπὶ τῷ or πρὸς τό with the infinitive. James' joining of the εἰς τό phrases with the adverbs ταχύς and βραδύς produces a movement image. A person should approach the opportunity to speak with caution. He should be reticent to approach angry speech at all, especially if he abides by the first two dicta.

The general nature of the proverb allows a broad scope of application. If the context which precedes and which follows is scanned, it becomes apparent that James finds spiritual application in the proverb which builds upon the general social application[9]. Readiness to hear God and his word of truth and obediently to translate this into deeds, reverence to limit one's speaking with him, discernment to speak his word appropriately and graciously, maturity to prevent the tendency in anger to blame God for sin or to think that wrath somehow serves God's purposes — these are all possible spiritual applications of the proverb which James may have in mind as he cites it.

The proverb may be applied more specifically in a Christian context, anticipating approaching topics of concern in the epistle (E. Pfeiffer). The importance of hearing/obeying God's word could be applied to worship or teaching in the Christian community, anticipating ch. 2 (Hiebert, 125; Adamson, 78). The importance of wisdom in speaking god's word could be applied to Christian teachers, prophets, or evangelists, in anticipation of ch. 3 (Mitton, 60; Hort, 35; Adamson, 78). The importance of restricting angry speech could be applied to harmony within the Christian community, in anticipating of ch. 4 (P. Davids, 92; Ward, 183—189), as well as to teachers (Mitton, 60). Thus, it may be understood that James taps the versatility of the proverb to its fullest recognizing as many as three levels of application: popular, spiritual, and ecclesial.

---

9 Cranfield, 186; Mussner, 100; Ropes, 168.

James 1:20

James 1:20, joined to 1:19 by γάϱ, supplies the ground or reason primarily for the third member of the tripartite admonition, to be "slow to anger." However, if this third member is dependent upon the first two in order to be realised as was suggested above, then 1:20 also supplies support and motivation for the entire three-part admonition, including "quick to hear" and "slow to anger."

The verse itself expresses what makes display of anger wrong and applies to people in general despite the stylistic shift to ἀνδϱός. As P. Davids (p. 29) observes, James elsewhere uses ἀνήϱ to denote generic humanity (1:8, 12). The anarthrous ὀϱγή is tied to "a person" incorporating concrete situations rather than leaving anger in the abstract.

The distinction which sometimes can be observed between the expression of ὀϱγή as the result of a long-term, calculated indignation and θυμός as the result of a momentary, passionate irritation occasionally is raised here in the attempt to limit the kind of anger being condemned (Hiebert, 126, and Mitton, 61—62). However, since it is God's righteousness which is offered as what condemns ὀϱγὴ ἀνδϱός, the fact that ὀϱγή in the LXX is usually used to denote God's anger sets up a double standard if the peculiar sense of ὀϱγή is pressed too far. The condemnation of expressing one's anger toward another person does not exclude "flying off the handle" (θυμός). Angry display of whatever kind never (οὐκ) approaches God's standard of righteousness.

The οὐκ intimates that there may be those in view who sincerely believe that a person's anger can effect God's righteousness (Ropes, 170; Hort, 36). James counters that the person's anger and God's righteousness are opposites. The person who thinks that his angry speech is somehow a good thing through which God's righteousness works among men is mistaken.

Ropes (pp. 169—179) expounds on the importance or regarding ἐϱγάζεται in its most basic sense of "do" rather than in the less usual sense of "produce." Mitton (p. 38) is right to say that it makes little difference to the thrust of the verse that angry display is wrong. The conclusion that δικαιοσύνην θεοῦ refers in this context to the standard of righteousness as defined by God for men is virtually unanimous[10]. The verse places an

---

10 P. Davids, 93; Laws, 81; Mitton, 62; Hiebert, 127; Hort, 36; Ropes, 170; Mussner, 100.
    Discussion revolves around how to take the genitive, i.e. objective, subjective, source, etc. Impinging on this is the meaning of righteousness in this context. The view that it is the standard of righteousness set by God (as opposed to the Pauline sense of righteousness which comes entirely from God via the gospel and Christ) and an objective genitive seems plain enough in view of the ethical context of the phrase. However, the puzzlement that the phrase provides is exemplified by the fact that

absolute restriction on angry speech based on God's perspective. Anger displayed toward fellow men (5:7—9), anger against one's fellow Christian (4:1—2), anger against God (1:13), anger for whatever reason against whomever, is rejected in this verse as incompatible with God's righteousness and the demands he makes on human behaviour.

James 1:21

The use of διό to open 1:21 indicates that an inference is to be drawn from something that was said previously. Normally one would look to the immediate context. However, focusing on the ideas connected with the main verb, that the implanted word should be received, one does not find ideas which easily follow from either 1:20 or 1:19. One does find ideas which follow from 1:18 where the λόγῳ ἀληθείας appears as the means by which God ἀπεκύησεν ἡμᾶς and provides the potential for people to be ἀπαρχήν τινα τῶν αὐτοῦ κτισμάτων. If one looks to the ideas in the subordinate prepositional phrase headed by ἀποθέμενοι, an inference from 1:19—20, albeit secondary can be seen (Mussner, 100). In this case anger, as condemned in 1:20, must be taken as an instance of the wickedness which pervades the human race. Thus, no one is able to observe perfectly the proverb of 1:19 either (cf. James 3:8). A third inference may be intended by the inclusion of ἐν πραΰτητι between the subordinate prepositional phrase and the main clause. It stands as a striking contrast to the angry speech condemned in 1:20 itself[11].

The manner of gentleness or humility conveyed by ἐν πραΰτητι usually is understood to be attached to δέξασθε and the main clause. However, Laws (p. 44) rightly points out that the phrase could ably qualify either the participle ἀποθέμενοι or the verb δέξασθε. Its position between the two indicates that it should be taken with both. A humble attitude is as important to discarding old, evil ways as it is to acceptance of God's word (cf. 3:13; 4:7—10).

The second aorist form of ἀποθέμενοι[12] indicates that the action of laying aside πᾶσαν ῥυπαρίαν καὶ περισσείαν κακίας probably is viewed as antecedent to the main verb δέξασθε. Moral uncleanliness and evil interfere with proper reception of the word. Thus, they must be cast off as a filthy, old garment in anticipation of wearing a fresh, clean, new one.

---

there is some appeal in taking it as a simple possessive genitive. This would make a nice parallel to ὀργὴ ... ἀνδρός. This option would also be compatible with the view that James is writing this to straighten out those who consider man's anger to be God's tool for expressing his righteous indignation in certain situations.

11 P. Davids, 94; Ropes, 171; Dibelius, 112.

12 The verb ἀποτίθημι is often employed in texts which abrogate ethical vices. See Col. 3:18; Eph. 4:21; 1 Pet. 2:1.

Although the first is an adjective and the second a noun, the words πᾶσαν and περισσείαν comprise an alliteration and are comparable in meaning [13]. They indicate the absolute nature of the request. The word περισσείαν may also allude to the plenitude of evil in people's lives and in the world (bearing in mind 1:27; 4:1—4; 5:1—6), although it is not merely the "excess" that James wants abandoned. It is entirely possible, with ὀργή of 1:20 in mind, that by ῥυπαρίαν, as Laws (p. 81) suggests, the author conveys the idea of vulgarity, or vulgar speech, and by κακίας the author conveys the idea of malice, or malicious speech [14]. These would then be aspects of angry speech. However, attractive this may be, Laws is unable to provide an instance of either word referring specifically to speech. Taking the words in their most normal, general sense is more compatible with the absoluteness conveyed by πᾶσαν and περισσείαν as well as the tenor of repentance in the verse (cf. Zech. 3:3, LXX). It is also more likely that the author is inferring (διό) from the specific (ὀργή) to the general. He wants a general, moral cleanup for the implanted word, not just one of anger, vulgar speech, or malice.

Many discussions of δέξασθε τὸν ἔμφυτον λόγον tend to magnify the contradiction that occurs when ἔμφυτον is taken in its most usual sense of innate or inborn by noting that something already inborn can hardly be received [15]. The result of this logic is to conclude confidently that ἔμφυτον must mean implanted, planted, or even deeply-rooted [16] and, thereby, that the τὸν ἔμφυτον λόγον refers to the preaching of the gospel which initiates regeneration or even to the hearing of baptismal instruction [17].

---

13 The possibility of περισσείαν meaning "remainder" is explored by P. Davids, 94, and Mitton, 63. This meaning cannot be demonstrated for περισσεία but can be for the noun περίσσευμα. It is an attractive proposal in that it would firmly establish that James is speaking to incomplete Christians. However, without more proof, it is best to take περισσεία as "abundance."

14 Others that suggest "malice" for κακία here, although not "malicious speech," are P. Davids, 94; Mitton, 64; Hort, 36; Mayor, 68. The strength of taking it as "malice" receives support from the use of this word in the catalogues of Rom. 1:29; Eph. 4:31; Col. 3:8; Tit. 3:3; and especially 1 Pet. 2:1 (which is often regarded as being based on a similar, early catechesis as Jas. 1:21). However, outside the lists, which by their nature must accent the more distinctive meanings of words, κακία is used of evil or wickedness in general. See. 1 Cor. 5:8 (where it parallels πονηρίας); 14:20; Acts 9:29; and even 1 Pet. 2:16. It is the most prominent use of κακία in Classical Greek, LXX, and Philo.

15 P. Davids, 95; Mitton, 64; Ropes, 172; Mayor, 68.

16 P. Davids, 95; Mitton, 64; Mussner, 102; Adamson, 81; Hiebert, 131; Cranfield, 187, defend "implanted" or "planted." Mayor, 68; Dibelius, 113; Ropes, 172; Robertson, 93, defend "deeply rooted."

17 Mussner, 102. Mussner also tries to make a case for reference to baptismal teaching here and elsewhere in James in "Tauflehre," 61–67. Although the argument is ingenious and perhaps even credible especially in light of 1 Pet. 1:23–2:2, skepticism will

The approach is askew in that it all too easily dismisses the normal meaning of ἔμφυτος. First, as Laws (p. 83) suggests, the plausibility of something innate being received depends on what it is that is to be received. Secondly, and more fundamentally, it depends on what is meant by "receive."

The verb δέχομαι does mean "receive." Especially when used of people, it means "welcome." A warm, hospitable acceptance is uppermost in mind (LS—J) and is what differentiates the word from λαμβάνω. This difference is highlighted in Col. 4:10 which speaks of Mark about whom it is said that the Colossians ἐλάβετε instructions and whom they were told to δέξασθε if he came there. Further uses of δέχομαι in this way are in Jn. 4:45, Heb. 11:31, and the synoptic accounts of the sending out of the Twelve and the Seventy (Mt. 10:14, 40; Mk. 6:11; Lk. 9:5, 11, 53; 10:8, 10). Matthew 10:14, 40; 6:11; 9:5 and 10:10 indicate that receiving these messengers of Jesus refers to a warm reception of the message of the Kingdom and has nothing to do with being allowed entrance into a city. Further, Acts 8:14; 17:11; 1 Thes. 1:6; 2:13 establish that receiving the word of God has to do with acceptance of it and not just hearing it. Thus, something one already has — even innately — may yet need to be fully accepted and made welcome.

Laws (p. 83) is right, then, to claim that δέξασθε τὸν ἔμφυτον λόγον does not refer exclusively to receiving the gospel but must include, if only secondarily, knowledge of God which is imbedded in man at creation (Hort. 37—38). In terms of 1:18, part of the λόγῳ ἀληθείας by which God ἀπεκύησεν ἡμᾶς remains in man and must be welcomed and brought to fruition rather than suppressed or indeed exchanged for a lie, as Rom. 1:18—25 puts it. As in 1:18, James in 1:21 most obviously suggests Christian ideas of regeneration but does so within the equally obvious motif of creation.

The aorist tense of δέξασθε suggests that what James is demanding is something that his readers have yet to do and that they must now initiate. The word ἔμφυτον, as Ward (pp. 127—132) shows so well, carries with it a sense of inwardness and is probably to be associated with Jer. 31:33. This is so whether it is understood as innate, implanted, or deeply-rooted. The "word" is in their hearts, but it has not been fully welcomed into their lives. This is especially serious since this word is designated as having the power to save them, most likely from eschatological punishment[18]. Although the phrase τὸν δυνάμενον σῶσαι τὰς ψυχὰς ὑμῶν attaches only to

---

continue to hang over such speculation until the absence of any direct reference to baptism in the passage is satisfactorily explained.

18 P. Davids, 95; Mitton, 55; Mussner, 103.

τὸν ἔμφυτον λόγον, nevertheless the implication that its power to save is tied to its being fully accepted cannot be avoided. James' readers may have heard the word and become Christians (ἀδελφοί μου ἀγαπητοί). However, truly open and complete acceptance of the implanted word must show its effect in a person's behaviour as 1:22—25 will emphasise.

James 1:22

The particle δέ in 1:22 is again continuative[19]. It attaches the admonition γίνεσθε ... ποιηταὶ λόγου ... as yet another inference indicated by the διό of 1:21, this one relating to the first member of the tripartite admonition of 1:19. Mussner (p. 104) observes that a three-pronged progression is observable: to hear, to receive [accepted], and to do — the word.

The present imperative γίνεσθε indicates that the new condition of ποιηταὶ λόγου which James urges his readers into is to be a continuous state. Although it is possible that γίνεσθε substitutes for ἔστε, which is abandoned in the New Testament, as many suggest, this understanding is much more appropriate with respect to μὴ ... ἀκροαταὶ μόνον than to ποιηταὶ λόγου. To presume "charitable assumption" is to presume too much[20]. As with δέξασθε, the whole point is to convince people to initiate a change in their relationship to the word, to cause them to be mere hearers no longer but rather to become doers.

Dibelius points out that ποιηταὶ λόγου and ἀκροαταί (λόγου) are excellent examples of Hebrew idiom in James. In Classical Greek, the former would normally refer to an orator and the latter to a legislator[21]. James uses them together to express what is involved in a person being obedient to God's word, it being heard and then translated into corresponding action. The hearing aspect may include listening to Scripture read in worship (Ropes, 175), but primarily it must refer to hearing in a

---

19 Amphoux, "coordonnant," 98; Mussner, 104.
20 P. Davids, 96; Hiebert, 133. The use of γίνεσθε with the meaning of ἔστε in the New Testament is clear enough (Mt. 10:16; 24:44; Lk. 6:36; 12:40; Rom. 12:16; Eph. 4:32; Col. 3:5). However, a number of others instances of γίνεσθε could as easily mean "become" as "be" (1 Cor. 10:7; 11:1; 14:20; 16:4; 2 Cor. 6:14; Eph. 5:1). None of them clearly presume that those being admonished are already doing what is being commanded any more than here. In at least one instance (1 Cor. 7:23) "become" is markedly preferable. The only other instance in James is 3:1. There, γίνεσθε takes its normal meaning of "become" in referring to becoming a teacher as a Christian calling and not just teaching on the odd occasion. The participle γενόμενος in 1:25, part of a restatement of 1:22, clearly means "become."
21 Dibelius, 14; Laws, 85 and P. Davids, 96.

strictly spiritual sense. Becoming ποιηταὶ λόγου naturally follows from accepting the implanted word. The importance of hearing and then doing the law is crucial in Judaism. It is also crucial to Paul in Rom. 2:13, the only other place in the New Testament where ἀκροαταί and ποιηταί are justaposed. James probably has the idea of law in the back of his mind for in 1:25 he will bring in νόμον τέλειον τὸν τῆς ἐλευθερίας as substitute for λόγου. However, this is not the same as the Jewish law, although it may include the moral aspects. As with the implanted word, the emphasis must be put on the gospel but should not be thought to exclude the word of God in any form in which it may occur. The stress placed on doing necessarily involves the moral implications of the gospel and the ethically oriented teaching of Jesus (Schrage, 22).

Those who are ἀκροαταὶ μόνον, James says, are those παραλογιζόμενοι ἑαυτούς. Normally, a person is deceived into error by someone else who does so knowingly. The absurdity of deceiving oneself is patently obvious. The implication is that James feels those who hear the word alone should know better than to think this will be enough to result in their salvation (P. Davids, 97). Yes, the power of salvation is in the word, but it must be accepted wholeheartedly into one's life and obediently observed to be of saving value.

James 1:23—24

The opening ὅτι in 1:23 carries its usual causal sense. The author is going to expand on why a person should not be only a hearer of the word but a doer. He is going to paint an analogous picture (ἔοικεν) of the absurd self-deception involved in being ἀκροατὴς λογού . . . καὶ οὐ ποιητής. The εἴ plus indicative, identifying a first class conditional, evidences the real existence of someone (τις), probably many like this, the author knows (Hiebert, 134). The apodosis declares that such a one (οὗτος) is like a man who looks at his own face in a mirror.

With the dramatic vividness and poignancy of a parable, the aorists κατενόησεν, ἐπελάθετο, ἦν, and the perfect ἀπελήλυθεν being dramatic or gnomic, 1:24 explains (γάρ) why the author thinks the analogy fits. This man in the illustration looks at himself in the mirror, has gone away, and then immediately (εὐθέως) forgets what he looks like. The absurdity of the idea can be seen to be stressed by the otherwise unnecessary inclusion of τῆς γενέσεως, the face of his birth, and the use of κατανοέω, which accents the idea of careful, even studious observation. How could anyone after close study of his very own face in a mirror so easily and quickly forget it? Likewise, the person who says he hears the word but who does not do it raises the question of his credibility. Has he really even heard if there is no evidence of it in his behaviour?

The tendency to allegorise the illustration of vvs. 23—24 and to interpret it in light of vs. 25, which Dibelius rightly criticises[22], continues today in those who ponder the spiritual significance of γενέσεως, ἐσόπτρῳ, or κατενόησεν[23]. Even the common reaction to designate ἀπελήλυθεν a perfect of continuous state rather than gnomic (or dramatic) like the aorists with which it appears seems to come from a forward glance at παραμείνας in vs. 25[24]. Indeed, the opening δέ of vs. 25 does indicate that a contrast to the illustration is to be drawn. But it should not be forgotten that the purpose of the illustration in the first place was to portray the foolish self-deception of being a hearer of the word and not a doer. The analogy does not stand on its own as any kind of admonition or teaching, especially about the law, which has not even been introduced into the discussion yet. As Dibelius observes, interjection of too precise a logic at this point spoils the simple aptness of the analogy as an analogy.

James 1:25

The contrast in vs. 25 is that the person who hears the word (P. Davids, 98), re-specified here as νόμον τέλειον τὸν τῆς ἐλευθερίας, does what is most natural if he has really heard. He becomes a ποιητὴς ἔργου. The repetition of the near-synonymous words attempts to reproduce the Semitic way of conveying intensity. The choice of ἔργου makes an alliteration with ἐπιλησμονῆς, the adjective with which it contrasts. He becomes a deed doer rather than a forgetful hearer[25], the word ἐπιλησμονῆς being the main aspect of the illustration upon which the author wishes to draw (Mitton, 70; Hiebert, 135). Such a person (οὗτος again), he believes, will be blessed in his doing. The forward position of μακάριος exhibits the emphasis being made on the blessing. As in normal New Testament usage, the word presumes God's pleasure and resultant reward certainly in eschatological terms but not exclusive of possible contemporary blessing (Becker and Link, 217).

It is sometimes thought that ὁ παρακύψας is intended to contrast with κατενόησεν in vs. 24 and παραμείνας with ἀπελήλυθεν. At first glance these seem reasonable assumptions. However, the first contrast usually results in misconstruing κατανοέω to mean a quick glance when it actually means a thoughtful look and παρακύπτω to mean a searching

---

22 Dibelius, 115–116. P. Davids, 98–99, voices similar criticism.

23 Laws, 86; Hort, 38–40; Cranfield, 188; Mussner, 106–109; Adamson, 82; Spicq, 27–28.

24 P. Davids, 98; Hiebert, 135; Ropes, 176–177.

25 Dibelius, 120, notes that both expressions are Hebraisms, although the genitives function differently. The word ἔργου syntactically is an objective genitive whereas ἐπιλησμονῆς is a genitive of quality.

look when it actually refers to a quick glance[26]. This is done in order to place the law in a favourable light for revealing a person's true nature in contrast to a mere mirror. However, there is little reason to think the author's choice of words in this respect is anything other than stylistic. If any contrast is implied here, it must be between the possible effective results of even a quick glance at the law versus the lack of results from a long look in a mirror.

The second contrast rightly detects the emphasis on παραμείνας, but is wrong to determine this from the difference with ἀπελήλυθεν (Mussner, 109; Mayor, 74). To understand ἀπελήλυθεν as being a continuous state is to presume some significance in the mirror and the illustration which has already been suggested as inappropriate. The need for the author to add παραμείνας in vs. 25 is brought on by the use of παρακύψας. A quick look hardly exemplifies an adequate relationship to the word/law. A permanent commitment to it is required, although even a quick look into it (εἰς) if sincere should reap some observable results in obedient behaviour[27].

Precisely what James means when he introduces νόμον τέλειον τὸν τῆς ἐλευθερίας as what a person looks into and remains in raises one of the most difficult questions in the study of James, a question which has precipitated a flurry of research[28]. It is easy enough to see how the author could substitute law for word, as was noted in comments on 1:22. The change from word to law provides a much needed bridge between the implanted word, which is primarily internal, and being a doer, which is primarily external. This then grounds the implanted word in something concrete and observable. The author's desire to differentiate what he means from normal associations with νόος is clear from the addition of the two qualifiers, τέλειον and ἐλευθερίας. Jewish or Old Testament law, then, cannot be primarily in mind.

It is probable that the use of τέλειον is related to James' call for complete maturity in 1:3—4, where τέλειον occurs along with the related idea of endurance (ὑπομονή). The use of ἐλευθερίας could be intended to contrast with the presumption of man's sin and resultant death in 1:13—14 or even to the prison of self-deception raised in 1:22. But none of this

---

26 Mussner, 106; Mitton, 70; Adamson, 82; Mayor, 72.
27 P. Davids, 98, is nearest to this understanding of the contrast. He notes James' stress on endurance elsewhere, albeit with different vocabulary.
28 Most of the scholarly activity has had to do with attempts to discover the background to the description. The most complete run–down of the background is by Dibelius, 116–120. In this light, one does well to listen to the sobering comment of Laws, 87, when she says, ". . . the evidence of Jewish parallels does not decided the question of the identity or context of his law, of which he gives here no further indication."

reveals what these two words mean in connection with νόμον here. As with the implanted word, which primarily refers to the gospel, the intention here must be to specify the Christian moral teaching, most specifically that of Jesus' reformulation of Jewish moral law, into the one law of loving one's neighbor[29]. The fact that in 2:12 νόμου ἐλευθερίας again is used, this time as a redesignation of νόμον ... βασιλικόν, which is spelled out as love of neighbor, confirms this view. The moral aspect of the gospel, then, is perfect. Perhaps this is because it is inward (1:21) as well as outward. Moral demands are translated into freedom because the power to do them is supplied upon the complete acceptance (δέξασθε) of the word/law and commitment to it (παραμείνας).

James 1:26

As in 1:23, the opening εἴ τις in 1:26 is used to introduce a first class conditional. It is possible that the parallel structure is intended to signal that what follows in 1:26—27 is another reason for becoming a doer of the word and not remaining a hearer only. The recurrence of the idea of self-deception in ἀπατῶν καρδίαν αὐτοῦ and the opportunity for self-deception which δοκεῖ affords by its designation of subjective opinion-making gives added strength to the possibility[30]. If this is so, then μὴ χαλιναγωγῶν γλῶσσαν αὐτοῦ, specially noted as a primary instance of such self-deception and a re-entrance of the idea of being slow to speak from 1:19, also becomes a primary indicator of someone who is not a doer of the word, who has failed to embrace the word within, who has not cast the moral evil from his life, and who has not even heard the word properly. Unbridled speech reveals the absolute worthlessness (μάταιος) of the religion he says and even thinks he embraces[31]. So much the worse for Christianity if he claims to be a Christian.

Any publicly observable manifestation of unbecoming behaviour would probably have suited James needs here in 1:26. Most likely he chose speech because this followed naturally from its mention as the second member of the tripartite admonition in 1:19 and of course the vital part speech plays in expressing anger. James also anticipates his later discussions of this concern for control of speech in 3:1ff and 4:1ff.

---

29 On the basic point, there is little disagreement among scholars. See P. Davids, 100; Mussner, 107; Dibelius, 119–120; Hort, 41; Ropes, 179–180; Hiebert, 136. Mitton, 71–74, contains one of the more involved discussions of the possible meaning of the description.

30 Mayor, 75, notes 1:26 as being another source of self–deception. See also Corrieveau, 117.

31 This passage is the first known literary occurrence of the word θρησκός, which like its more common cognate θρησκεία refers to the observable, outward forms of religious activity like worship, prayer, etc.

The two participles χαλιναγωγῶν and ἀπατῶν supplement the main verb by providing conditions. The ἀλλά, as many note, is awkward where it is stationed between the participles[32]. The problem is that the participial phrases both denote conditions to the main clause but of different types. The first specifies a particular outward condition. The second specifies an inward condition and secondarily functions as a sort of apposition to the first participial phrase. The ἀλλά is placed before the second participle because the author's main point has to do with self-deception of which uncontrolled speech is only one instance. If he had placed it before the first participle, this emphasis on the general condition would have been lost[33].

James 1:27

After noting what falsifies a person's claim to be religious and what nullifies a religion's value in 1:26, in 1:27 James describes two essential aspects of θρησκεία καθαρὰ καὶ ἀμίαντος[34]. Both adjectives are commonly used to refer to ceremonial cleanliness. Such a meaning here would seem justifiable in view of the further qualification παρὰ τῷ θεῷ καὶ πατρὶ αὕτη which could serve to place the adherent in God's presence[35]. As the verse continues, however, it becomes apparent that what the author has done is to use a cultic motif to heighten the religious and spiritual significance of ethical purity[36]. Schrage (p. 24) calls this "die Ethisierung der Kultbegriffe." Although ceremonial deeds are not thereby rejected necessarily[37], moral behaviour is made the focus of religious deeds and is put forward as a more reliable indication of religious purity and even of true ceremonial cleanliness[38].

---

32 P. Davids, 101–102; Mussner, 111; Dibelius, 121. The difficulty has even spawned an article by Schökel which attempt to show that the ἀλλά is not adversative.

33 The proposal by Mussner, 111 (which P. Davids, 101, adopts) to understand the ἀλλά as "sondern" is compatible with the understanding related here.

34 These do not comprise a definition of religion despite the use of ἐστίν. See Mussner, 110; Ropes, 182; Hort, 43; Adamson, 88; Robertson, 103. It is partially this misunderstanding which prompts Roberts to propose unnecessarily a textual altering of 1:27 found in p. 47. He is also bothered by what he considers a non-practical aspect of religion in keeping oneself unblemished from/by (ἀπό) the world. The quick rebuttal by Johanson ably refutes Roberts' suggestions.

35 As P. Davids, 103, observes, this could well be a septuagintalism for "in God's eyes."

36 The use of θρησκεία plus θρησκός and the appearance of ἄσπιχον later, further reinforce the cultic motif.

37 Laws, 91–92; Ropes, 111; Mitton, 75.

38 The same point is made in Lk. 11:38–41. There Jesus is depicted as speaking to the Pharisees about charity (ἐλεημοσύνην) truly making a person clean (καθαρά). Corrieveau, 124, makes the point that this passage "makes the whole of Christian life a worship of God."

The two present infinitives, ἐπισκέπτεσθαι and τηρεῖν, distinguish two key purposes, or from another view, two observable results of pure and undefiled religion. They and the phrases which follow them effectively summarise and conclude this section of James, the first relating primarily to 1:21—25 and the second to 1:19—20, 26. The fact that both infinitives are in the present tense indicates that both aspects should be continually applied and/or constantly observable.

The first, to visit ὀρφανοὺς καὶ χήρας ἐν τῇ θλίψει αὐ- τῶν particularises the importance of general social concern in any religion of value. It typifies the orphans and widows as representative of the needy, under-privileged in any society (Ropes, 184; Hiebert, 142). Provision for such people is a concern of Jewish and Christian literature in general[39]. God's well-known compassion for these whose general situation is described well as being ἐν τῇ θλίψει, is presumed also in 1:9—11; 2:5; 5:1—6[40]. The author may have joined πατρί to θεῷ earlier in the verse as preparation for this statement in order to remind the readers of God's fatherhood over all men and therefore men's brotherhood with one another (P. Davids, 103; Hort, 44; Mayor, 77). The importance of this aspect of pure religion anticipates the concerns which occupy the author in 2:1—26. Visiting the widows and orphans exhibits love for them. It is faith in action. It presumes encouraging conversation, but also physical, financial, and any other assistance which will ease or remedy their plight.

The second aspect of pure religion which James mentions, to keep ἄσπιλον ἑαυτὸν . . . ἀπὸ τοῦ κόσμου, generalises a host of particular concerns. The adjective ἄσπιλον is yet another word which has cer- emonial use but which here is used in a moral sense. Its presence insures that the ἀπό is not taken as strict separation but rather as indicating the source or agent of blemishes. One is not to keep from τοῦ κόσμου but to remain unblemished by it[41]. The person whose religion is pure and undefiled will indeed be involved in the world as the first aspect demands[42], but he will protect himself from allowing the evil corruption in the world to rub off on him. This is the world which is the antithesis of God, which instills lust and desires, which disrupts social harmony, which does not accept the word of God, which never repents of sin but blames God for it, and which is the realm of abundant evil and filth, of anger, and of all uncontrolled speech. For James, κόσμος, as elsewhere in the New Testament, is all that is evil about the world. By mentioning it here,

39 Deut. 14:29; Isa. 1:17; Jer. 5:28; Ezek. 22:7; Zech. 7:10; Sir. 4:10; 29:8—9; 35:2—11; CD 6:21; Aboth 1:5; 5:12; 2 Enoch (B) 51:1—2; Mt. 25:36, 43; Acts 6:1—6; 1 Tim. 5:3—16.
40 See also Judith 9:11; Sir. 35:16—17; Ps. 58:5 (68:6); 146:9; Deut. 10:18; Job 29:12.
41 P. Davids, 103; Laws, 90; Hiebert, 143. See also Johanson versus Roberts.
42 Schrage, 24—25; Obermüller, "Contaminacion;" Spicq, 37.

the author anticipates 3:1—12; 4:1—4, assumes 1:12—15, and concludes 1:19—21. Accommodation to the world's evil influences may initially take place internally, or spiritually, but its occurrence nonetheless soon becomes observable, especially in one's speech.

Analysis

Controlled Speech

James' concern for speech to be controlled is readily apparent in 1:19—27. The central member of the tripartite admonition, "slow to speak," is given added emphasis in 1:26 where it is held that the person who does not "bridle his tongue" denigrates the religion he professes.

The idea that controlled speech is a reliable guide to the quality of a person's moral and spiritual life is made clearer in 3:2, where the view is ventured that a person who could control his tongue would be a perfect man (Genuyt, "III," 58). In terms of 1:19—27, he would be a person totally responsive in word and deed to God and his implanted word, which is intrinsic to his salvation. Controlling his tongue manifests his ability "to bridle his whole body" (χαλιναγωγῆσαι) as well. The perfect man is hypothetical, an ideal. The tongue is brought in because it is the most difficult part of the body for a person to control, as 3:4—12 goes on to show[43]. James has made control of speech the premier ethical and spiritual task of man.

Anger is one of the aspects of speech which James specifically desires to be curbed. This is affirmed in 1:20 for anger is opposed to God's righteousness. Further, anger must be presumed to be involved in the quarrels and conflicts which are denounced as disruptive to communal harmony in 4:1—2. Other kinds of speech which James desires people to avoid are exemplified in his numerous dramatic quotations (1:13; 2:3, 16, 18; 4:13, 15). One should not say he is tempted by God, nor should he speak of his plans without taking God's view into account. He should not speak in ways which express partiality toward the rich against the poor nor in ways which communicate his insensitivity to the needs of the poor. Finally, he would be wrong to say that faith and works can be separated without dire consequences. These are viewed as either harmful to human relationships or to one's relationship with God.

---

43 Laws, 145; 68; Hiebert, 208.

Jas. 1:19—27 sets forth James' view that the prerequisite for controlling speech is listening both to men and to God but especially listening to the implanted word of God. Inner responsiveness to God's will conforms a person's words to his righteous standard. Implicit is that controlled speech entails not just aborting unfit speech but also uttering positive, beneficial, appropriate words when one does speak. This positive aspect of speech receives its major support from the list of godly wisdom traits in 3:17. Involved in at least three of the traits mentioned, εἰρηνική, ἐπιεικής, εὐπειθής, is positive, beneficial, pleasant conversation. Positive, mending words are naturally a part of promoting peace in a community. Being reasonable, gentle, and considerate must include conversation. When one is compliant to another, part of this must be an eager readiness to respond to his request or ideas communicated by speech. The trait of ἀδιάκριτος, if it means "impartial" or "making no distinction" here rather than "unwavering [44]," supposes the realm of speech as well. The trait of ἀνυπόκριτος, even though it is stated negatively, implies the positive trait of sincerity, which is also relevant to oral communication.

Listening

James' concern for listening is also evident from 1:19—27. A person should be "quick to hear." He should humbly open his heart to the "implanted word" of God. The fact that he should be "not a hearer only" presumes hearing to be an important starting point.

James emphasises listening to the word of God. However, the idea of being "quick to hear" in 1:19 by its proverbial nature indicates that this is a practice which is being advocated generally. One should listen to others, whether God or man.

By incorporating so much traditional wisdom material, James exhibits his approval of — indeed, promotion of — listening to the words of past generations of sages from a variety of cultures. By incorporating so much traditional Jesus material, he manifests the value of listening to the words of Jesus. He quotes authoritatively from Old Testament Scripture which demonstrates the value for him of listening to these words of God. In that James wrote this treatise as a letter to the church-at-large, he probably expected his own words to be valuable listenting material. Finally, by

---

44 Both are possible. However, impartial is the usual meaning, especially when one brings the verb διακρίνω into the discussion. James used διακρίνω in 1:6 as wavering, or doubting, but in 2:4 as making distinctions. The scale tips slightly to "impartial" in 3:17 because none of the other traits take impartiality into account, the theme of 2:1–12, whereas the idea of doublemindedness, a theme occurring in 1:6–8 and 4:8 can be accounted for in ἁγνή or ἀνυπόκριτος.

making it so suggestive that the "implanted word" points to the gospel, James shows his advocacy of listening to those who preach it to be saved.

Listening not only has a role to play in salvation but also in simple, everyday ethics and ongoing spiritual maturity. One must know what God wants done before he can do it. Thus, hearing is vital to becoming an active doer of God's word.

The importance of listening for advancing in spiritual and ethical maturity derives not only from the communication it allows from God but also from its role in controlling speech and in preventing display of anger. For James, controlling speech is dependent upon listening, as the relationship between "quick to hear" and "slow to speak" in the tripartite admonition of 1:19 indicates. For optimum, attentive listening, the tongue must be kept still. Speaking will cause the sound of one's own voice to occupy at least in part the hearing capacity of the ear and thus impair the ability to listen to another speaker.

Good listening makes for good speaking. If a person listens more than he talks, he is less prone to say stupid, hurtful, and thoughtless things. If he listens to God — in acceptance of his implanted word — this will be true all the more. James recognizes the inability to listen as part of the evil of the world which the godly person must cast away from his life in order to develop his relationship with God. So, listening to men and to God — is the key to controlling one's speech and to the resultant positive, gracious speech. It, too, must be given a high priority in moral and spiritual development.

Words and Deeds

In 1:19—27, James stresses one of the most basic relationships between words and deeds. This is that words are to be obeyed in deeds. For James, this maxim does not pertain to just anyone's words but to words which bear the authority of God. Merely hearing God's words is not enough. They must be obeyed. The change James makes from "implanted word" to "perfect law of liberty" is at least partly done in order to make this absolutely clear. Acceptance of God's implanted word is one thing. However, being a productive doer of the perfect law of liberty forces one to think in terms of obedience. In this case, greater emphasis is given to obeying the ethical implications of the gospel as detailed by Jesus' re-constructing of Old Testament moral code (pinpointed by the love of neighbor). That it is a law of freedom in no way detracts from the importance of obeying. Rather, this accentuates the inwardness of true obedience in the acceptance of the implanted word as opposed to the outwardness of obedience required by laws as such.

Thus, the words of God/Jesus are to be translated into deeds. This is the most prominent aspect of the relationship between words and deeds in James. However, other aspects are present. Among these is the dual importance of both words and deeds in behaviour which results from true religious commitment. In 1:27, visiting widows and orphans includes both encouraging conversation and tending to physical needs. This principle is generalised in 2:12 as an initial summary/conclusion to the denouncement of practicing partiality (which occurs at the level of conversation and of action [45]). Speech and action together account for a person's outward, observable behaviour in life. As such, they are the criteria by which a person's life will be scrutinised in relation to the law of liberty. The repeated οὕτως emphasises that this fact should motivate the manner in which people speak and act on their way to ethical and spiritual maturity[46].

Both speech and deeds have their appropriate roles to play in depicting a person's life and its nearness to or distance from maximum maturity. A person's speech alone comes to the fore in revealing the inadequacy of his religion or the inadequacy of his commitment to his religion (1:26). It also emerges as an identifiable means of recognizing the evil in a person's life generally as well as the evil in society at large (1:20, 21). Deeds emerge as the more important area for ethical-spiritual evaluation in 2:16, where speech is depicted as a totally inadequate way to meet the need of the person truly desperate for food and clothing. In situations like this, even sincere words of kindness are hypocritical. The rest of the discussion in 2:13—26 goes on to stress that profession of faith without the accompanying works is useless. The trait of being non-hypocritical, not surprisingly, appears on James' list in 3:17.

Consistency of deeds to words, then, is what James seeks in people. Both a person's speech and deeds are critical in identifying his spiritual and ethical maturity. These are the basic, observable elements of his lifestyle (ἀναστροφή), which in 3:13 are seen as integral to determine whether or not a person is truly wise (P. Davids, 150).

The Power of Words

James is well aware of the negative aspects of the power of words which he so vividly depicts in 3:4—10 (See Part II). The positive aspects of

---

45 The use of the present imperative indicates habitual action, and the duplication of οὕτως supports the claim that this verse has far wider application than just the matter of impartiality. A general, life principle is being drawn. Both P. Davids, 118, and Dibelius, 147, note the catechetical qualities of the verse.

46 That both uses of οὕτως here indicate manner rather than mere consequence is confirmed by the ὡς which follows. See Bauer, 602, and the similar instances of οὕτως . . . ὡς in the New Testament (Mk. 4:26; 1 Cor. 4:1; 9:26). On the matter of emphasis in the duplication of οὕτως, see P. Davids, 118, and Laws, 116.

word-power, which James touches upon in 1:19—27, center on the
implanted word. It is specified that this word has the power to save people
from eschatological damnation. This powerful word within issues from
God and, more specifically, can be associated with the gospel of Jesus
Christ (Henderlite, 471). The acceptance of this word acquires sal-
vation-power for the individual. Because its source is in God, it is
powerful whether accepted or not. Acceptance unleashes its power to
affect the person's life in word and in deed and enable him to progress in
spiritual and ethical maturity.

James thinks that a fully mature Christian knows how and when to
deliver this powerful word for God's good purposes. In 5:19—20, he
encourages the mature Christian to make efforts to retrieve those who
have apostasised from the faith. Given the overall context and the
presence of ἐκ πλάνης ὁδοῦ, it is most likely that by πλανηθῇ, James
primarily refers to a moral wandering away (Laws, 238; Dibelius, 254). But
faith and doctrinal problems cannot be fully excluded since the person is
saved from death (σώσει . . . ἐκ θανάτου), presumably eschatological death.
The person has abandoned Christianity. In doing so, he has spurned its
moral directives as well as its doctrinal truth. In any case, the scenario
must involve the mature Christian recognising the apostate's condition,
going to him, and speaking to him about his problems until the person
re-repents and returns to the Christian community with his faith fully
restored. The power of God's word, the power of the gospel, in such a case
has been wielded in the speech of the mature. The result is the re-igniting
of faith, the covering of sin, and the cancellation of death[47].

James notes in 5:10 that the prophets were those who spoke in the
Lord's name but does not elaborate. He does recall Elijah's powerful words
of prayer in 5:17—18 stating pointedly that "Elijah was a man like us"
(ὁμοιοπαθὴς ἡμῖν). A good measure of earnestness and/or diligence is
required as προσευχῇ προσηύξατο indicates[48]. Similar requirements for

---

47 There is much confusion over whether the saint or the sinner is the object of the
last two results. The varied textual history of the verse points to the confusion of the
early church but really only adds to the problems which face us today. The majority
of the commentaries refer the first, the cancellation of death, to the sinner and the
second, the covering of sin, to both saith and sinner. See Dibelius, 259; Mussner, 233;
Laws, 240–241; Hiebert, 336–337; Mitton, 213–215. But even P. Davids, 200, and Mayor,
184, who assign both results to the sinner, are not closed to the other view. Dibelius,
258, notes the original proverb to be in Prov. 10:2 and the form given it by Christians
as ἀγάπη καλύπτει πλῆθος ἁμαρτιῶν which appears in 1 Pet. 4:8; 1 Clem. 49:5; 2
Clem. 16:14, and elsewhere.
48 The tautologous reduplication signals intensification, as is commonly noted. See Laws,
235; Mayor, 180; Hiebert, 238, although, Ropes, 312, does not think the Greek
necessarily conveys the Hebrew idea. Intensification of praying could point to earnest
utterance or to diligent utterance. Either way, it conveys an air of confidence in the
worthiness of the prayer and favour of the listening Lord.

successful prayer are in 1:6—8 and 4:2—3. Another help to successful and powerful prayer is a healthy relationship with God, as δικαίου in 5:16 indicates. This is not beyond anyone's reach. When the prayer of such a person is put into action, James 5:16 asserts that it is very powerful indeed (πολὺ ἰσχύει).

In 5:15—16, prayer is presented as being able to heal. The power in prayer is not magical, however, despite the value placed on speaking in the Lord's name (which probably refers to Christ here). Prayer power is dependent upon the Lord's power to make effective the words people utter[49]. No matter how righteous or sincere the person, it is the Lord's power which brings the results.

---

49 The notorious difficulty of the participle ἐνεργουμένη in 5:16 is recognized. Those who render it as a passive, adverbial clause include Mayor, 177–179; P. Davids, 196–197; Hiebert, 327; Mussner, 228. Laws, 234, and Dibelius, 256, favour it as adjectival, accenting the energy and conviction of the person praying. Ropes, 309, suggests that it is a middle adverbial clause, accenting the accuracy of the prayer. If James is saying anything more than that the prayer of the righteous person is very powerful, it must be that the power in prayer is not in the words, the person, or the utterance of the words, but in the one is effecting the prayer, i.e. God.

Part II
The Evil of the Tongue

Chapter 3: Background

Near Eastern Wisdom Literature

In Near Eastern Wisdom Literature, the tongue is characterised as blame-worthy for evil words that are spoken. Ahiqar (*ANET*, 429) says, "God shall twist the twister's mouth and tear out his tongue."

When the tongue is not properly controlled, it rampages for evil. Amen-em-Opet (*LAE*, 251) describes the evil of the tongue, saying:

> He is ruined and created by his tongue,
>   and yet he speaks slander
> He makes an answer deserving of a beating,
>   for its work is evil;

Ani (*ANET*, 420) says, "A man may fall to ruin because of his tongue."

Wrath from the tongue can be frightfully destructive, especially when it emanates from a king. Ahiqar (*ANET*, 428) says:

> The wrath of a king, if you should be commanded, is a burning fire. Obey it at once! Let it not be kindled against you and cover [burn] your hands!

Old Testament

The Old Testament recognizes that the power of the tongue has the potential for being used both for positive and for negative purposes. As Prov. 18:21a says, "The tongue has the power of life and death." A person's tongue has the capability of being either beneficial to society or decidedly harmful. Through it, a city may be "exalted" or "destroyed" (Prov. 11:11). These extremes are apparent at the personal, day-to-day level of communication as well (Prov. 15:4).

Yet, the Old Testament also recognizes that the tongue rarely reaches its positive potential in any individual on a regular basis (Prov. 10:20; 20:15). In fact, Ps. 116:11 is representative of Old Testament opinion when it cries out: "All men are liars."

The Old Testament, then, considers the tongue to have a decided tendency toward evil. This is further evidenced by the striking predominance with which the tongue is associated with ideas of deceit and falsehood and with images of danger and destruction. It is this basic pessimism about the tongue and man's seeming inability to harness it for positive and useful purposes (Ps. 39) which signals the Old Testament's concern for speech-ethics.

There is plenty of evidence in the Old Testament, whether simply misguided, in beautiful guise, or openly intended for harm, that words can be devastating to the individual who is unfortunate to receive them. The angry words of a king can cause an innocent man's death (Prov. 16:10). The soothing words of a prostitute can lead even a good man astray (Prov. 7:21, 23, 27). Even a prophet of God can be struck winging blows by the well-aimed words of an unrepentant people (Jer. 18:18). Speech, under these circumstances, is "like a scorching fire." as Prov. 16:27 says. It is frighteningly painful and destructive.

Circumstances which conjure up images of danger and destruction surround the mention of the tongue in the Old Testament. The tongue, the mouth, and the lips are so often cast in these negative images that they can hardly be viewed as anything but evil.

The Psalms which are attributed to David are the chief sources of reference for picturing the tongue in destructive guise. In Ps. 64:2—3, God is called upon:

> Hide me from the conspiracy of the wicked,
>> from the noisy crowd of evildoers,
> who sharpen their tongues like swords
>> and their words like pointed arrows.

The association of the tongue with these two common images of war — sword and arrow — is a favourite way of describing an enemy's speech[1]. Yet, in no way are the Psalms restricted to just these two similes. In Ps. 52:2—4, the tongue of the evil man is likened to a "sharpened razor." In Ps. 140:3, the speech of evil men is described like this:

> They sharpen their tongues as a serpent;
> Poison of a viper is under their lips[2].

The treacherous words of such men are further described in Ps. 140:4—5 in terms of traps, cords, snares, and nets. Ps. 109:3 speaks of being "surrounded" by words of hatred. The fear-evoking images of hungry lions and wild animals are used to convey the wanton evil of such men's words in Ps. 56:4 and 57:4. In Ps. 58:6, God is called upon with these words:

1　Ps. 57:4; 59:7; 64:3, speak of tongues as swords. Ps. 11:2; 57:4; 58:7; 64:3, speaks of tongues as arrows. See also Job 5:5; Jer. 9:3, 8.
2　The snake imagery is also used in Ps. 58:4.

O God, shatter their teeth in their mouth;
Break out the fangs of young lions, O Lord.

Finally, Ps. 59:7 depicts the utter disgust and baseness of the words of such men by use of a coarse image of digestion, saying, "Behold, they belch forth from their mouths."

There is awareness in the Old Testament that this destructive and evil tendency of the tongue may even turn in on the speaker. Prov. 6:2 speaks of a person "trapped by what he says, ensnared by the words of his mouth[3]."

In the Old Testament, then, the tongue is viewed as treacherous, conniving, deadly, and destructive, an evil which wantonly inflicts pain and harm of its victims. The only justifiable recompense for this evil tool is that it receives from God punishment similar to the evil it has inflicted. As Ps. 120:3—4 says:

What will he do to you,
and what more besides, O deceitful tongue:
He will punish you with a warrior's sharp arrow,
with burning coals of the broom tree[4].

Often one of the most obvious characteristics of a person who is intent on evil is the evilness of his speech. In the Old Testament, use is made of this fact by focusing much of the attack against the evil person on his evil tongue. By this method of synecdoche, the tongue is used to characterise the evil person[5]. One of the best examples of this is Ps. 52:3—4, which says:

You love evil rather than good,
falsehood rather than speaking the truth.
You love every harmful word,
O you deceitful tongue[6].

The use of the evil tongue to characterise the evil man is common in the Old Testament. Ps. 10:7 describes the wicked man by saying:

His mouth is full of curses and oppression;
Under his tongue is mischief and wickedness[7].

---

3 See also Prov. 14:3; 18:6–7; Eccl. 10:12.
4 Here it is claimed that God will deal appropriately with the owner of such a tongue, using the appropriate images of death and destruction. Weiser, 743; A. Anderson, 849; Dahood, 3:196, are unanimous in thinking that this difficult section refers to God's punitive action. The "broom tree" is noted for making excellent charcoal which gets extremely hot (Dahood, 3:196). God is called on elsewhere to deal appropriately with the evil of men in Ps. 3:7 and 7:12–13, where his speech is described in war images as well.
5 Bruggemann, 670; Banwell, "Tongue," "Mouth." and "Lip;" A. Johnson, 37.
6 See also Ps. 57:4; 58:1–11; 64:2–6; 140:1–3; Prov. 16:27; Jer. 9:1–9.
7 Briggs, 1:79, suggests that "under his tongue" is speech that is ready to be uttered. A. Anderson, 115, suggests the same but adds the thought that it could refer to the essential character of that person's speech. The expression is also found in Job 20:12. See also Ps. 10:3; 50:19; 144:11; Prov. 16:30.

In order to depict the wicked and evil state to which the Israelites had
fallen, both Isaiah and Jeremiah focus their descriptions on the evil speech
of the people (Isa. 9:20—21; 59:3—4; Jer. 9:1—9). In order to depict the
arrogance of certain evil men, Ps. 12:4 characterises them as saying, "We
will triumph with our tongues; we own our lips — who is our master[8]?"
Even when Proverbs wants to describe the prostitute/adulteress, it focuses
on her sinister and deceptive speech[9].

The fact that the evils of the tongue are used to characterise the evils
of people does not mean these sins are merely superficial. God will punish
them for what they say. Jer. 9:9 says, " 'Shall I not punish them for these
things?' declares the Lord," and Ps. 50:21 promises, "I will rebuke you and
accuse you to your face[10]."

Since in the Old Testament the evil tongue represents the whole person,
characterises him, and reaps punishment for him, it makes sense that there
should be a concerted effort in the Old Testament to motivate people to
curb the evil of their tongues. Thus, Ps. 34:12—13 says:

> Whoever of you loves life
>   and desires to see many good days,
> keep your tongue from evil
>   and your lips from speaking lies[11].

It is this very effort to control the evil of the tongue which is the
central concern of speech-ethics in the Old Testament. Its writers look
forward to the day when it will be inappropriate to characterise anyone in
this way. This day is envisaged by Zeph. 3:13, when it says:

> The remnant of Israel will do no wrong;
>   they will speak no lies,
>   nor will deceit be found in their mouth.

Speech is thought to be a product of the heart in the Old Testament[12].
Corresponding to the Old Testament view that gracious speech is the
product of a wise heart, . it is observed that an evil tongue is
unquestionable evidence of a person's evil heart. In fact, if a person's
internal nature is motivated by evil thoughts and desires, how can his
speech be anything but evil? As Proverbs observes, the mouth of the

---

8 See Dahood, 1:73, particularly, for a rendering substantially different from the one
   used here. The passage accuses Israel of other speech sins in vss. 2–3. See also Psalm,
   73:9.
9 Prov. 5:3–6; 6:24; 7:21. See J. Williams, 25, and Amsler.
10 See Ps. 10:12; 12:3; 50:21; 52:5; 58:6–9; 59:12 63:11; 64:7; 140:9–11. Job 9:20 and 2 Sam.
   1:15–16 speak of a person being condemned by their own mouth.
11 See also Eccl. 5:6; Ps. 17:3; 141:3; Prov. 10:10; 12:16; 13:3; 16:32; 17:27; 20:11; 21:23.
12 Bruggemann, 670.

wicked "gushes evil" and knows "only what is perverse[13]." Indeed, it notes that "violence completely covers the mouth of the wicked[14]." Prov. 24:1—2 warns its readers:

Do not envy wicked men;
  do not desire their company
for their hearts plot violence,
  and their lips talk about making trouble[15].

Wickedness and evil flow naturally out of a heart that is filled with evil and destructive thoughts. In a truly grotesque image, such hearts are even described as using their mouths to feed on evil that occurs around them. Prov. 19:28 (cf. Ps. 14:4) says that "the mouth of the wicked gulps down evil." Prov. 12:6 says that "the words of the wicked lie in wait for blood[16]."

Although evil flows naturally from the heart through the mouth of an evil man, he may make noble attempts to conceal the true nature of his heart by disguising his speech with what might be called counterfeit graciousness. Prov. 26:23—26 provides a brilliant description of this person:

Like a coating of glaze[17] over earthware
  are fervent lips with an evil heart.
A malicious man disguises himself with his lips,
  but in his heart he harbours deceit.
Though his speech is charming, do not believe him,

---

13 Prov. 15:28; 10:32. Similarly, Prov. 15:26; observes that the mouth of the fool cannot help but gush folly. The opposite is true of the righteous man who cannot help but spout wisdom (Prov. 15:2). See also Ps. 37:30.

14 This is one way of understanding the phrase which is repeated twice in Proverbs (10:6, 11), which is translated with "violence" (חמס) as the subject by Toy, 202, 205, and Kidner, 86. McKane, 418, and Greenstone, 102, consider "violence" to be the object of the clause. There is good evidence for the verb יְכַסֶּה (from כסה) meaning "conceal" or "cover" in similar contexts (Prov. 10:18; 11:13; and Jer. 51:51; Obad. 1:10 respectively). Even KB–H, 161, and BDB, 492, differ as to which way to view the verb in the context of 10:6 and 10:11. Under the circumstances, the suggestion of Dahood, *Proverbs* , 18, of "uncover" is even worth considering here. The evidence is so balanced on both sides that a firm stand on either would seem unwarranted. For that reason, these verses are also relevant to the discussion of the evil person's concealment of his true intentions.

15 Ps. 36:11 even depicts such evil men as plotting in their bed. See also Ps. 140:1–3. For their internal evil, see also Prov. 12:5, 12.

16 The intention of this imagery is to convey the relish with which the wicked devastate their victims with their words. Ezek. 22:9 speaks of a slanderous man being "bent on shedding blood." A similar connection is made in Isa. 33:15. McKane, 446, suggests that the intentions of ambush are in the words as well.

17 The phrase כסף סיגים occurs only here. The still popular rendering of "silver dross," although having interesting implications, is considered dubious by McKane, 603, and Kidner, 164. The idea of this simply referring to "a shiny glaze," which McKane and Kidner seem to support, is expounded by Ginsberg, 21, who suggests that the phrase be repointed based on a text from Ras Shamra. KB–H, 255, suggests that the phrase refers to lead oxide produced in the refining of silver.

for seven abominations[18] fill his heart.
His malice may be concealed by deception,
    but his wickedness will be exposed in the assembly.

Those who are not wary and who foolishly allow themselves to be
duped. Such are they who believe the words of an adulteress/prostitute
which are smoother than oil, dripping with honey, but when fully digested
are bitter as gall, sharp as a double-edged sword, and lead to death (Prov.
5:3—6). Others walk innocently into verbal ambush[19].

As already noted in Prov. 26:26b, there is confidence that sly and
conniving speech cannot forever deceive the community in which it is
spoken. Its evil will eventually be discovered. Also, Prov. 26:27 goes on to
express the added confidence that the treachery will eventually backfire on
the speaker himself[20]. It is worth noting too that Zophar (Job 20:12—16) is
confident that the evil a person bottles up "under the tongue" will
eventually sour and cause a lethally poisonous infection within him unless
God intercedes to enable him to vomit up the poison.

It is clearly dangerous, then, for anyone to use his mouth to deceive
others about true thoughts of his heart. In Isa. 29:13 (cf. Ezek. 33:30—33),
God stipulates one of the reasons why he would punish Israel is because
"[They] honour Me with lipservice, but they remove their hearts from
Me." Prov. 27:5 advises against concealing one's true feelings whether good
or bad when it says, "Better is open rebuke than hidden love[21]." Speech is
intended to be an accurate reflection of a person's true thoughts and
feelings (Vriezen, 253). Otherwise no real communication can take place
(Ps. 37:30).

The Old Testament, then, is unflinching in its conviction that an evil
tongue is an accurate reflection of an evil heart. Although a person may
attempt to cover his evil intentions with "smooth speech," this will not
necessarily be successful. In the end, his true self cannot help but be
revealed. As Prov. 27:19 (cf. Eccl. 10:2—3) says:

As water reflects a face,
    so man's heart reflects the man.

A person's only means of reversing the evil tendency of the tongue,
according to Ps. 141:3—4, is to rely on God for help. It says:

---

18 On the significance of "seven abominations," McKane, 604, suggests that "when he
    turns on his charm, he is not to be believed in or relied on, for he is hatching any
    number of villainies in his mind."
19 Ps 10:8; 62:5; 64:4—6; Prov. 10:18; 12:6; 21:19; 26:18—19; Jer. 9:8; Job 20:12.
20 See also Prov. 28:10; Ps. 7:12—16.
21 As a way of explanation, the proverb continues: "Faithful are the wounds of a friend,
    but profuse [or "deceitful"] are the kisses of an enemy." For a similar thought, see
    Prov. 14:12.

Set a guard over my mouth, O Lord;
    keep watch over the door of my lips.
Let not my heart be drawn to what is evil,
    to take part in evil deeds
with men who are evildoers;
    let me not eat of their delicacies.

Apocrypha and Pseudepigrapha

Despite the desire that its power be channelled into positive purposes for society, the Apocrypha and Pseudepigrapha like the Old Testament harbours no illusions about any mortal man completely controlling his tongue to this end. As Sir. 19:15 rhetorically asks, "Who has not sinned with his tongue[22]?" Since, as Aristeas 277 (cf. Sib.Orac. 3:36—39) suggests, "All men are by nature intemperate," it would indeed be impossible for any man to keep his tongue under absolute control. Thus, the evil tendency of the tongue is affirmed as in the Old Testament.

There are no minced words about the devastating harm that the tongue inflicts either. Sir. 28:18—21 (cf. Sir. 8:10) speaks extensively of its evil when it says:

Many have fallen by the edge of the sword,
    but not as many as by the tongue.
Happy is the man who is sheltered from it,
    and has not experienced the wrath of it,
who has not borne its yoke,
    nor been bound by its chains;
for its yoke is a yoke of iron,
    and its chains are chains of brass.
The death it causes is an evil death;
    even Hades is preferable to it.

The evil of the tongue is not confined to harming others but turns inward to harm oneself. As Sir. 5:15 says, "The tongue of a man is his downfall [23]." By depicting the devil as standing behind Job's wife and troubling her reasoning, T.Job 26:7 suggests that Satan is the power behind this evil of the tongue. It is certainly not God for neither heart nor tongue were evil when he formed them (Sir. 17:5—6; 15:20). Nevertheless, Sir. 28:22—23 contends that the righteous are protected from the tongue's evil by God, although the unrighteous certainly are not. It says:

It [the tongue] has no power over the godly;
    they will not be burned by its flame.

---

22   See also Sir. 14:1; 25:8. Sib.Orac. 3:37 observes that the entire race of man are liars.
23   See also Sir. 22:27 and Sir. 28:26.

> They that forsake the Lord will fall victim to it;
> and it will burn among them unquenchably.
> It will attack them like a lion
> and mutilate them like a leopard.

As in the Old Testament, in the Apocrypha and Pseudepigrapha the evil person is regularly characterised by his evil tongue[24]. A good example of this is found in Ps.Sol. 12:1—2, which says:

> O Lord, deliver my soul from [the] lawless and wicked man,
> from the lawless and slanderous tongue which speaks only lies and deceit.

Elaborately twisted are the words from the tongue of the wicked man[25]. For these sins of speech as well as other sins, such men are often depicted as receiving punishment (above, previous note). Wis. 4:19 suggests that God will "strike them down speechless."

Sir. 5:15—6:1 wants to make sure its readers understand that a "double-tongue" is a characteristic of an evil person and that this label must be avoided by one desiring to be righteous (cf. T.Ben. 6:5—7; Sir. 28:13). Aristeas 246 even suggests that a treacherous person can be detected by the lack of etiquette in his speech. Sir. 23:8 (cf. Sir. 22:27), though, generally agrees that "it is by his own words that a sinner is ensnared." Thus, his speech will eventually give away his evil nature to the keen observer. As Sir. 27:4—7 so picturesquely explains this:

> Shake a sieve and the dung remains[26].
> Thus the filth of a man is in his reasoning.
> A potter's work is proved by the furnace;
> and the testing of a man is in his conversation.
> The fruit of a tree makes known its cultivation.
> Thus, the reasoning of a man [makes known] the thoughts of his heart.
> Before [hearing his] reasoning, do not praise a man,
> for this is the testing of men[27].

Evil speech comes from an evil heart (T.Naph. 2:6), and this cannot be completely hidden by sugar-coated speech no matter how hard the evil

---

24 See Ps.Sol. 4:1–29; 1 Enoch 5:4–6; Sib.Orac. 3:36–39, 492–502; Sir. 27:14–15; 2 Bar. 48.

25 Ps.Sol. 12:1–2 goes on to compare the lying tongue of the wicked man with fire. However, the text becomes hopelessly corrupt at this point, and nothing more specific can be said. See *APOT*, 2:644; Ryle and James, 104–105 and Holm–Nielsen, *Salomos*, 87.

26 *APOT*, 1:405, contains the comment that "the corn which has been threshed for the first time is placed in it [the sieve] and sifted; the refuse, i.e., the dung of the oxen which has been trodden into the straw, remains behind, while the grain passes through the sieve."

27 There is a wide gulf between the contemporary German and the English translations of this passage, both of which seem to misunderstand the meaning of the key word λογισμός, which according to LS–J means "reasoning." The NEB and NAB presume too quicky that this has entirely to do with speaking, really the result of reasoning. Sauer presumes that λογισμός is entirely internal ("Gedanken"—thoughts). The truth is that the word bridges these two extremes, and in fact that is the whole point of the passage.

person may try to do so[28]. God hates such deception (Sir. 27:24), and upright men are well-advised not even to associate with these "double-hearted" men (1 Enoch 91:4). However, if such a person may be able to fool some in his community for a period of time, he will not fool all [2 Enoch (A) 46:2], and he certainly will not fool God. As Wis. 1:6—9 so forthrightly explains, this is:

> because God is a witness of his inmost being, who sees clear into his heart and hears every word he says. For the spirit of the Lord fills the whole earth, and that which holds all together is aware of what men say . . . The devices of a godless man will be brought to account, and a report of his words will come before the Lord as proof of his iniquity; no muttered syllable escapes that vigilant ear[29].

Regardless of the nature of one's heart, however, it is a general principle that a person's speech should be true to his internal feelings. Straightforward complaining is preferable to fuming inside, advises Sir. 20:2, although Sir. 8:18—19 wisely cautions against naively displaying one's heart to just anyone, especially to a stranger.

Qumranic Literature

The writers of the Qumranic literature are keenly cognisant that man is by nature evil. As 1QH 4:30 says, "He is in iniquity from his mother's womb and in guilty unfaithfulness until his old age." As a mere creature of clay, he is nothing but "a foundation of shame, a fount of defilement, a crucible of iniquity, and a fabric of sin[30]." Every candidate for admission to the community was required to confess his sin and those of his forefathers (1QS 1:25—26). However, Qumranic literature contains no diatribe on the inevitable evilness of the tongue as has been so striking in the other Jewish literature. The closest passage to this is found in the Book of Mysteries (1Q27 1:9—10), which says[31]:

---

28 Sir. 27:22–27; 2 Enoch (A) 52:14; Sir. 12:16–18. His physical demeanor will help to give him away too. See Sir. 13:24–25; 19:21–26.

29 This is taken straight from the NEB rendering of the passage. Although a bit free in places, it conveys the sense of the passage extremely well. On God's ability to see all sin, see also Sir. 15:19–20; 16:17–23; 17:20; 23:18–20; Ps.Sol. 9:6; 14:5; 1 Enoch 9:5; 2 Bar. 83:3; T.Ben. 6:7.

30 1QH 1:21–23. The Qumranic literature, especially 1QH, is extremely fond of referring to man as a creature of clay or a fabric of dust particularly when desiring to contrast the righteousness of God. See 1QH 3:23–24; 4:29–32; 7:28; 9:14; 11:21–22; 12:19–24, 31; 13:14; 17:18–19. For comment on the relationship to the righteousness of God, see Ringgren, *Qumran*, 102–112.

31 The translation is dependent on Hengel, 1:220, which is better refined than Dupont–Sommer. The Hebrew for this can be found in Barthelemy and Milik, 102.

Do not all the nations hate wickedness?
Yet it is spread abroad by every hand.
Does not the knowledge of truth emerge from the mouth of all nations?
But is there a lip or a tongue which observes it?

Despite the lack of a diatribe against the tongue, Qumranic literature does reveal its grimacing acknowledgment that the tongue can be dangerously harmful. The Teacher of Righteousness appears to have been the object of the severest of verbal torture from his enemies. He describes their volleys of words as arrows, spears, fire, and a net (1QH 2:25—29; 3:36—37). The teeth of their mouths he describes as being like a sword and a spear, containing the venom of dragons, and capable of crushing bones and drinking blood (1QH 5:7, 10—11). He describes how their efforts melted his heart like water, gripped him with fear, and eventually reduced him to tears (1QH 2:28; 5:30—33). But time and again God caused his enemies to fall in their own traps, closed the mouths of those hungry lions, and thus rescued his faithful servant (1QH 2:29—30; 5:10—11).

The teacher's enemies were the official leaders of the temple at Jerusalem. He saw in their false teaching words that had a more serious capacity for destruction that those he had endured. In 4QpNah 2:4—6 (cf. 1QpHab 10:6—12), it says that "cities and families shall perish through their counsel; honourable men and rulers shall fall through their tongue's [decisions]." It is quite likely that the wisdom poem The Seductress (4Q184) is written about these false teachers leading the people in Jerusalem[32].

Qumranic literature readily speaks of the evil of these false teachers in terms of sinful speech. It also speaks of the evil of all who align themselves with the Spirit of falseness. Such men are characterised as teachers of lies and seers of falsehood and as those who speak with derision and mockery (1QH 3:31; 4:7; 4Q184 1:2). Such things as lies, deceit, evil ill-temper, insolence, blasphemy, and words of rebellion appear to flow naturally from the mouth of such men[33] for they have willingly given their hearts over to Belial[34]. Their treacherous speech is simply the product of their treacherous hearts (1QH 4:14—15).

---

32 An English rendition of this can be found in *DSSE*, 225. The Hebrew with English translation can be found in Allegro and Anderson, 82–95. Burgmann considers the poem to be a pointed allegorical depiction of an actual, historical person, Simon Maccabeus, the high–priest of Jerusalem and arch–enemy of the Qumran community. It may or may not be Simon, but it seems highly probable that The Seductress is depicting the false teaching of the leader of Jerusalem, whoever that may have been historically.

33 Except for the last, all of the items in this list appear again as some of the "ways" of the spirit of falsehood described in 1QS 4:9–11. The notorious Man of Mockery, alias the Man of Lies and Spouter of Lies, is characterised as preaching falsehood to Israel in CD 1:14–15. See CD 12:3 for the connection between "words of rebellion" and those who are governed by "the spirit of Belial."

34 1QH 6:22. From the perspective of a person trying to preserve a semblance of

According to Qumranic literature, God's wrath is surely kindled against such wicked and deceitful men, and they eventually will reap their deserved punishment[35].

Rabbinic Literature

In LevR. 33:1, a story intended to illustrate the truth of Prov. 18:21 is recorded concerning Rabbi Simeon ben Gamaliel. One day, he asked his servant to go and buy some good food for him in the market. The servant returned with a tongue. When he then asked the servant to buy some bad food, the servant returned again with a tongue. When he asked the servant the reason for returning with a tongue both times, the servant replied, "Good comes from it and bad comes from it. When the tongue is good there is nothing better and when it is bad there is nothing worse."

Indeed, the tongue is demonstrated to be the most powerful part of the body in a story from Mid.Ps. 39:2. Here, the story is told of a man who has a dream in which the feet, the hands, the eyes, and the heart deride the tongue for boasting of its importance even though they had all just done so concerning themselves. The tongue vows that all of them would acknowledge its supremacy over the rest of them that very day. This they do when by its crudity to the king the tongue nearly causes the man to be executed.

Thus, the power as well as the positive and negative potential of the tongue are important ideas in Rabbinic literature. But is the tendency of the tongue toward good or evil? As in other Jewish literature, the rabbis consider the tongue to have a penchant for harm and evil. The literature records numerous warnings to control the tongue and also pleadings to God for aid in controlling it[36]. Also, the evil inclination in men is viewed as something which only the mightiest of men can control, as having a thirteen-year advantage in age and experience over the good inclination in men, and as being like a well-loved king leading on 248 loyal and willing troops (the limbs) to do evil, while the good inclination is like a captive in prison to whom the limbs are ever-resistant[37]. Only the words of Torah in the heart are thought to be able to resist the authority and control of the

---

righteous speech by keeping Belial out of his heart, see 1QS 10:21–23. The struggle between truth and falsehood, the forces of Belial and those of God, rages continuously in a person's heart according to 1QS 4:17,24.

35 1QH 2:24; 4:18–20; 6:29; 15:29; CD 2:5–10, 20; 8:19; 1QS 5:14, 19.
36 See GenR. 81:2; LevR. 16:2; DeutR. 1:9; EcclR. 5:5; Ber. 17a.
37 See Aboth 4:1; 2:16; ARN 16 (p. 83); ARNB 16 (p. 114); Kid. 30b; Shab. 105b.

evil inclination over men[38]. Finally, it should be noted that B. Bathra 164b lists slander among transgressions "which no man escapes for a single day[39]."

The destructive power of an evil tongue is commonly assessed in Rabbinic literature as awesome[40]. It is compared to the cruelty of an arrow that can strike and slay at a distance[41]. It is compared to a fire, but a fire that can consume stones as well as wood[42]. It is described as being set between two cheeks with a water-channel running beneath it, yet these limitations cannot restrict its ability to produce conflagrations[43]. It is said to be able to kill three men at a time. In Mid.Ps. 12:2, Rabbi Samuel is recorded as saying:

> Why is the evil tongue called a triple slaying tongue? Because it slays three persons: the person speaking, the person spoken to, and the person spoken about[44].

Indeed, it is commonly recorded haggada in Rabbinic literature that an evil tongue once killed four people[45].

Like previous literature, the rabbis typically associate speech with evil men[46]. EcclR. 3:6 recounts this saying of Rabbi Phinehas which is said in the name of Rabbi Reuben:

> . . . in the Hereafter the wicked are condemned to Gehinnom; and they grumble. . . The Holy One, blessed be He, replies to them, 'In the world in which you spent life were you not quarrelsome, slander-mongers, and evil doers?'

Balaam and Doeg specifically are viewed as evil because of their evil tongues (San. 105b; Mid.Ps. 52:6). Furthermore, DeutR. 6:14 records that

---

38 Sifre Deut. §45, 82b; GenR. 22:6; Mid.Prov. 24:3(48b).
39 In commenting on Ps. 39:2, Mid.Ps. 39:4 rhetorically asks, "Is there such a thing as a curb for the tongue?"
40 See Arak. 15a and Mid.Ps. 52:6.
41 GenR. 98:19; Mid.Ps. 12:2; Arak. 15b; DeutR. 5:10; LevR. 26:2.
42 LevR. 6:3. This idea is stated with specific reference to false swearing as a comment on Zech. 5:4.
43 LevR. 16:4. See similar descriptions about built-in safeguards against the tongue in GenR. 79:1; Arak. 15b; Mid.Ps. 52:6. In Aboth 2:15, Rabbi Eliezer warns that even the words of wise men can be like coals of fire in their capacity to injure and harm. He also compares their words to the bite of a fox and the sting of a scorpion. Herford, *Aboth*, 56, and Herts, 33, both note that he is bearing something of a grudge from being excommunicated by his Rabbinic colleagues.
44 The saying appears to be referring specifically to slander. See also NumR. 19:2; LevR. 26:2; DeutR. 5:10.
45 See Mid.Ps. 12:2; LevR. 26:2; NumR. 19:2. This is a common analysis of the deaths regarding Doeg—who spoke deceit; Saul—who heeded it; Nob, the city of priests—of which deceit was spoken, and Abner—who had the opportunity to protest but did not.
46 ARN 12 (p. 71) speaks of the wicked as talking too much, and Shab. 105b speaks of outbursts of anger in men as part of the wiles of the Tempter. Pes. 113b speaks of Canaan charging his sons not to speak in truth.

Rabbi Assi said, "One does not speak slander until he denies God[47]." Thus, Mid.Ps. 39:3 explains that the reason God gave the Torah to the people of Israel was so that they would not busy themselves with evil tongues and idle words. Aboth 1:7 advises students of the Torah not to associate with an evil person presumably because of the high probability of being on the receiving end of his evil tongue[48].

Just as a good heart is required for a person to produce good speech, so an evil heart is considered by the rabbis to be the root cause of evil speech[49]. It is in the heart that evil words are conceived and from it that they flow[50]. Some men, however, speak from a "double heart," in which case they attempt to conceal the true nature of their evil hearts with "smooth" speech (Mid.Ps. 12:1). Such deception is roundly condemned and is spoken of as something God hates[51].

Graeco-Roman Literature

Plutarch relates a story about the tongue in four slightly varied versions which is strikingly similar to the one which was just related from Rabbinic literature[52]. In essence, Plutarch says that Amasis, the king of Egypt sent a sacrificial animal to the legendary wise man Pittachus (or Bias depending on the version) and asked him to cut out the worst and the best parts of the animal. It is said that he cut out the tongue because it is the instrument of both the greatest good and the greatest evil. Likewise, in a story about Themistocles' encounter with the king of Persia, Plutarch, in *Mor*. 3:18, relates the positive and negative potential of speech to be forthrighteous and deception respectively. He says that

> speech is like rugs woven with patterns and figures; for speech, like a rug, when it is extended, displays its designs, but when it is rolled up tightly, it conceals and spoils them.

It is acknowledged within Graeco-Roman literature that despite the enormous potential of the tongue, it is difficult for people to harness it for good. Plutarch thinks that it is weak and too easily set in motion and,

---

47 Also in this passage, Rabbi Simeon suggests that slanderers will "have their tongues cut off by God."

48 ARN 9 (p. 54–56) and ARNB 16 (pp. 112–113).

49 In GenR. 73:12, it is said, "A man's heart changes his face, both for good and for ill." On the heart's effect on the whole body and on lifestyle, see Aboth 2:13–14; ARNB 32 (p. 187); GenR. 67:8; EcclR. 1:16.

50 See LevR. 16:1; Pes.Rab. 24, 125b (Braude, 1:509).

51 Pes. 113b. San. 106b speaks of Doeg as this kind of person. B.Bathra 16a says that even Job sinned in this way. See also B.Metzia 49a; 58b; Arak. 16a.

52 See Plut. *Mor*. 1:38b; 2:146f; 6:506c; 15:#89. A similar reply about the tongue is attributed to Anarchis, the sixth century B.C. Scythian prince, by Diog.L. 1:105.

therefore, naturally requires a stockade of teeth standing guard over it[53]. Similar views were current as early as Theognis, which says in 185—186, "The mind is a good thing, and so is the tongue, but few men are capable of watching over them both." Again, in 83—86, the writer sighs in dismay that in the whole world one would not be able to find "more than one ship's company of those that are modest of tongue and of eye and are not led by greed to do what is vile." Theognis is not very enthusiastic about man's basic nature anyway and says in 799 that "no man on earth is without blame." Seneca, in *De ira* (*ME*) II,32:1, concurs: "For if everyone whose nature is evil and depraved must be punished, punishment would exempt no one."

Most Graeco-Roman writers after Socrates are more likely to label a person who does or says harmful things ignorant rather than sinful[54]. Although the evils in the world come from man's own folly, greed, and ambition, and certainly not from God, according to Dio Chrysostom[55], neither are they caused by man being born evil. Theognis and those in his day thought that evil actions and words are learned from associating with bad people (Theog. 305—308, 1165—1166). The later philosophers developed other views on this. The significant thing here is that this positive view of man's initial nature and peculiar way of viewing his harmful words and deeds does not prevent the Graeco-Roman writers from labelling a person bad because of what he says nor blind them to the devastation the tongue can cause.

Concerning the latter, Plutarch in *De gar.* and elsewhere[56] goes on and on about the destruction the uncontrolled tongue can cause to others as well as to oneself. He does not hesitate to speak of habitual talkativeness as "an incorrigible evil" (Plut., *Mor.* 6:509c). He is by no means alone in this. Seneca, in *De ira*, devotes a large quantity of space to denigrate the destructiveness and evil of angry speech. Both Seneca and Plutarch employ the image of a raging fire to convey the awesome and spreading destructiveness of angry speech, although Plutarch uses it with regard to gossip as well[57]. The destructive capabilities of the tongue are skillfully and candidly articulated by the earlier poets too. Euripides, in *And.* 642, says, "From small beginnings bitter feuds the tongue brings forth." Aristophanes, in *Frogs* 813—819, splendidly describes the skilled speaker's dexterity with words, depicting him as "the tonguester . . . whetting his tusks for the

---

53 Plut., *Mor.* 15:#89 and also 6:503c. See also *Mor.* 15:87.
54 Epictetus provides exquisite examples of this view in II,26:1–7; III,20:15–16; *Ench.* 42. Adkins, 237–238, confidently links up this feature of Stoicism to Socrates, Plato, and Aristotle.
55 Dio Chrys. 32:14–16. Cic., *Fin.* 1:43–44, blames evils on man's desires.
56 Plut., *Mor.* 1:10f–11c (*De adul.*); 6:452e–464d (*De ira*).
57 Sen., *De ira* (*ME*) I,2:2; Plut., *Mor.* 6:454g, 507b.

fight," and calls his words well-capable of "dissecting, detracting, ma-
ligning." Awareness of the destructive capabilities of deceitful speech in
the realm of oratory and rhetoric is also found in Graeco-Roman
literature[58].

As has been said, the Graeco-Roman writers have no qualms about
dividing people into those who are good and those who are bad based on
what comes out of their mouths. Theog. 611—614 says, "The bad will not
hold their tongues of evil talk, but the good know to keep all things in
measure[59]. Plato, in *Laws* 792b, supplies the Athenian with this rhetorical
question: "When a man is peevish and not cheerful at all, do you regard
him as a doleful person and as a rule more full of complaints than a good
man should be?" Similarly, Theog. 365—366 observes that "it is the heart
of the viler sort which rises quicker to wrath," and Theog. 1146—1150
speaks of "crooked speech" as characteristic of the unrighteous person[60].
Seneca, in *Vit. (ME)* 20:6, appears to consider it a mark of evil that they
busy their "wretched tongues in abuse of the good."

Plutarch as well as Isocrates considers a person's speech to be foolproof
way of assessing his character[61]. In a similar vein, Epictetus believes that a
person who is overly critical, quick-tempered, boastful, always finding fault
and pinning blame on others as adequately demonstrated what kind of
person he is[62]. Seneca believes this too, as is evident from his recitation of
the following Greek proverb in *EM* 114:3: "Man's speech is just like his
life." However, he goes on in the passage to try to show not only the
character of an individual but also the general character of an entire
populace in its time can be correctly assessed as morally degenerates on
the basis of their speech. In reaching such a diagnosis, he would include,
for example, lack of concern for oratorical ability and precision of
wording as well as evil speech.

Finally, it should be noted that evil speech can be used in Graeco-
Roman literature to characterise evil in general. For example, Theog.
373—392 speaks of "Want who teaches all evil, both lies and deceits and
pernicious contentions." When Cicero, in *Fin.* 2:46, desires to depict hateful
things that are "insincere, false, and deceptive," he includes perjury among

---

58 Plato, *Gorgias* 452d, 462c–463a; Phaedrus 267b; Georgias, *Enconium on Helen* 14 (in
 Diels, 2:292–293 or Freeman, *Ancilla*, 131); Plutarch, *Mor.* 1:6b,e, 7b; 41c–42c; Sen,
 EM 108:38; Isoc. *To Nic.* 1–2; Aristoph, *Frogs*, 813–829; Thuc. III,37:3ff.
59 See also Theog. 305–308, 1167–1168, and Plut., *Mor.* 6:464d. In the latter, Plutarch
 associates man's evil words with his offensive actions.
60 Similar attitudes can be seen in Eur., fr. 156, in *NFE*. See also Dio Chrys. 32:26.
61 Plut., *Mor.* 1:10a, 33f; 6:464; Isoc., *To Nic.* 8.
62 Epict. III,2:14–15. In Epict., *Ench.* 48, he speaks of almost precisely the opposite verbal
 traits as characterising the person who, as he puts it in Stoic fashion, "is making
 progress."

his examples. When Dio Chrysostom, in 32:19, wishes to portray the harmful effects on society if philosophers were to quit thinking and teaching, "harsh cries, tongues that are mischievous and unrestrained, accuser, calumnies" come to the force. And long before, when Hesiod, in *Works* 69—84, wished to epitomise the deceitful nature of Pandora, he wrote of "her lies and crafty words."

Philonic Literature

Philo recognizes, at least in theory, that the tongue is a neutral vessel in the battle that rages in the individual between good and evil. According to *Conf.* 33—34, it can be "an ally employed by those who hate virtue and love the passions to inculcate their untenable tenets." But it can also be utilised by "men of worth for the destruction of such doctrines and to set up beyond resistance the sovereignty of those that are better."

The overwhelming tendency of the tongue is toward wicked purposes. If it is to be used for good, at least part of what is involved is for its rebellious nature to be held in check by the soul aided by the reins of conscience (*Det.* 23). The tongue's tendency toward evil is related to the tendency toward evil of people in general. In *Mut.* 49—50, Philo says:

> Infinite indeed are the defilements that soil the soul, which it is impossible to wash and scour away altogether. For there still remains evils which are bound up with the life of every mortal, which may well be abated but cannot be wholly destroyed. Should we then seek to find in the medley of life one who is perfectly just or wise or temperate or good in general? Be satisfied if you find but one who is not unjust, is not foolish, is not licentious, is not cowardly, is not altogether evil[63]

This general tendency is not congenital in Philo's view, even though it begins at birth[64]. The soul of every individual begins with both good and evil from the womb. Evil, however, dominates from birth because of the falsehood in everyone else around. Only by following a certain scheme can good eventually dominate the evil. To reach this point, a person will be in constant battle with the body which is saturated with evil and plots against the efforts of the soul of good (*L.A.* 3:69—72; 1:103). The tongue, of course, is an organ of the body.

---

63 There is a very saimilar negative assessment of man in *L.A.* 1:102–103 and a briefer one in *Abr.* 19. In *Spec.* 2:52, Philo speaks of the "terror stricken condition of our race, how charged it is with numberless evils generated by the greedy desires of the soul and also by the infirmities of the body." A much more detailed depiction of ravaging desire and its effects on the body and the soul of man is in *Spec.* 4:79–99. Elsewhere, Philo speaks of the impossibility of anyone except God being perfect throughout his life. See *Mut.* 183–185; *Virt.* 177.

64 *Spec.* 4:68 and *Praem.* 63 together inform most of the discussion which follows.

Philo depicts the tongue and its capacity to spout harmful speech as one of the most valued instruments in the war of the body and its senses on behalf of evil (*Det.* 174; *Abr.* 29). It is capable of bringing to ruin a vast multitude as well as the person speaking. With regard to the practices of the wicked, Philo says in *Som.* 2:274:

> For they ardently pursue a guilty silence and a reprehensible speech, and they work as an engine for the ruin of themselves and others. Yet it is in speech — in saying what they ought not — that they exercise themselves the most[65].

Philo considers evil speech to be one of the most prominent features of wicked men, as the above quotation indicates. This tendency to characterise evil men by their speech can also be seen in *Abr.* 20.

There are numerous other instances of this sort in Philo which go along with his tendency to depict evil in general in terms of evil speech[66]. Evil speech is the demonstrable product of evil intentions and wicked thoughts just as beneficial speech comes from thoughts guided by God[67]. The outward cannot long cover over the inward evil despite valiant attempts at deception[68]. Once his true nature has been manifested, one who wishes to cultivate good thoughts and good speech will do well to stay away from the evil person and cleave to the godly wise (*Mig.* 164).

New Testament

In the New Testament, man is presumed to be evil. When Jesus castigates "this evil generation[69]," there is no thought that other generations were not or would not be evil. Only perhaps that they might be less so. The fact that all men are sinners is a critical and often stated premise in Romans[70]. 1 Jn. 1:8 asserts that anyone who claims to be sinless lies and is talking fantasy.

The tendency for the tongue to be a prime mediator of man's evil is presumed in 1 Pet. 3:10 (Ps. 34:12) which requires the Christian as part of his ethical response to the gospel to "keep his tongue from evil and his lips from deceitful speech." Mt. 15:11 associates the mouth even more clearly with man's sinful nature when it says, "What goes into a man does not make him unclean, but what comes out of his mouth, that is what

---

65 See also *Leg.* 162; *Mut.* 240; *Spec.* 4:90.
66 See *Conf.* 48; *L.A.* 1:101–104; *Spec.* 1:235–241; 2:52–53; *Dec.* 63; *Abr.* 190; *Cher.* 94; *Leg.* 57, 199; *Mut.* 240.
67 *Prob.* 11, 99.
68 *Dec.* 49; *Mut.* 193–198; *Spec.* 2:49–50.
69 Mt. 12:45; Lk. 11:29 contain the phrase. The idea is also presumed in Mt. 12:39; 16:4; Mk. 8:12.
70 Rom. 3:9, 23; 5:12. It is also presumed in Rom. 1.

makes him unclean." However, it is clear that the mouth itself is not considered to be the direct cause of evil but rather the channel through which evil flows out from the heart. Mt. 15:18—19 says:

> But what comes out of the mouth from the heart, and these make a man unclean. For out of the heart come evil thoughts, murder, adultery, fornication, theft, false witness, and slander[71].

The passage relies upon the principle, traced out in Mt. 12:33—37, that a person's speech draws from the heart and therefore is an accurate register by which his character may be judged good or evil. Here the negative aspect of the principle is presumed. A good illustration of this is found in the description of Satan in Jn. 8:43—45 which says, "When he lies, he speaks from his own nature[72]."

A dramatic example of the principle in action is the account of Ananias and Sapphira which is relayed in Acts 5:1—11. The nature of each was judged to be evil solely on the basis of one publicly revealed lie, and absolute, immediate punishment ensued. Again, the source of the lie is viewed here as coming from the heart (5:4).

Given the view that evil speech does accurately reflect upon a person's evil nature, it is no surprise to find the tongue associated with various speech sins that are employed to characterise evil people. Ample evidence of this is supplied by the lists of vices and condemned sinners which occur in the New Testament, like Col. 3:8 which lists anger, wrath, slander, and abusive speech, and like Rom. 1:30 which lists gossips, slanderers, the insolent, the arrogant, and the boastful[73]. 2 Pet. 2:17—18 focuses on just one vice, "speaking vain boastfulness," to characterise the evil of the false teachers being denounced.

In Rom. 3:10—18, Paul quotes a catena of Psalms to verify the point that all men are sinners. Three of those quoted are about sins of the tongue and serve to epitomise the evil of men. This passage is also the strongest one in the New Testament (outside of the Epistle of James) describing the evil destructiveness of the tongue. Most other descriptions come in the form of warnings against deceivers and flatterers who entice unwary Christians away from the true gospel and sound doctrines[74].

---

71 The list in Mk. 7:21 is longer and includes coveting, wickedness, deceit, sensuality, envy, pride, and foolishness. It may be worth noting that most of the sins listed are not primarily associated with speech. They are a sampling of what is in the evil heart. How they are worked out in speech is left unexplained. Of course, the network between the heart and speech is not the primary focus of the passage anyway, which is attempting to justify criticism of Jewish dietary regulations.

72 The point, as Barrett, 349, notes, is that Satan's speech derives naturally and directly from his own character, or nature. He lies because he is a liar. See also 1 Jn. 2:20—25.

73 See also Eph. 5:4—5; 1 Tim. 1:10; 6:3—5; 2 Tim. 3:1—9; 2 Cor. 12:20.

74 See Rom. 16:17—18; Col. 2:4, 8; Eph. 4:14; 5:6; Jude 16.

Chapter 4: Epistle of James

Exegesis

James 3:1

The recurrence of the vocative ἀδελφοί μου plus the imperative μὴ . . . γίνεσθε indicates that James is initiating a new line of thought from what was undertaken in the immediately preceding context. As a section, 3:1—12 appears to be an attempt to ground and develop ideas originally introduced in 1:19—21, 26 regarding the spiritual-ethical importance of controlling the tongue and the decisive role of speech in indicating man's wickedness.

The appearance of κρίμα in this verse probably relies upon 2:12 for clarification. Since judgment involves deeds and words, those such as teachers who deal principally with words in their vocation should expect a more difficult time (μεῖζον) in eschatological judgment. They run the greater risk of condemnation in judgment that others who do not teach[1]. If judgment were merely a matter of deeds, as one might assume if it were not for 2:12, then the idea would be groundless.

The verb λημψόμεθα, being first person plural, reveals the author's inclusion of himself not only as a teacher but also as one in this precarious situation with regard to judgment — even as he writes. The participle εἰδότες enhances the fact that the notion is something James believes his readers already know (P. Davids, 137; Hiebert, 205). It introduces the notion as a cause or reason which should be sobering enough to repel unqualified people from becoming διδάσκαλοι. The present tense of the prohibition μὴ . . . γίνεσθε and its subject πολλοί disclose that from James' point of view, there are presently too many people becoming teachers (Hort, 67) and that this state of affairs needs to be halted.

---

1 The possibility of κρίμα here referring to the negative result of judgment, i.e. condemnation, as thought by Ropes, 227; Dibelius, 187; Mayor, 107, is overruled, as Laws, 144, says, by the comparison involved in μεῖζον. If 2:12 is seen to be relevant to 3:1, then the fact that κρίνεσθαι there is contemplated as a process rather than as a result adds further weight to κρίμα referring to the process of judgment in 3:1. Hiebert, 205, also agrees. Thus, what is in mind is a stricter criterion of judgment and, as a result, a greater risk of condemnation.

Presumably, James has in view teachers in the church[2], although the dictum could apply more broadly. After a generally applicable diatribe on the tongue in vss. 2—12, James will return in 3:13—18 to provide a way to distinguish between teachers whose wisdom is bona fide and those whose wisdom is not. The author may view the conflicts and quarrels described in 4:1—2 as deriving from these extraneous and falsely wise teachers.

James 3:2

James provides further basis (γάρ) for the reduction in the number of teachers by making a general assertion in 3:2. From the apt example of teachers who use their tongues so much, James moves to the universal problem of controlling the tongue. This shift of focus is brought to the fore emphatically by the otherwise unnecessary use of ἅπαντες, the strengthened form of πᾶς, to bolster the assumed first person plural subject of πταίομεν. The author's inclusion of himself in this general recognition of the prevalence of people's sinning is not so much a humble confession (Hiebert, 207) as an accounting of himself a member of the human race. It matters not so much whether the adverb πολλά refers to quantity, variety, or both. It is the bold assertion of man's sin as such that sets up the logical deduction which follows.

The double apodosis which follows the hypothesis εἴ τις ἐν λόγῳ οὐ πταίει proclaims two related ways of conceptualising the primacy of speech control for men. By definition, the person who does not stumble/sin in his speech is τέλειος ἀνήρ. By description, he is δυνατὸς χαλιναγωγῆσαι καὶ ὅλον τὸ σῶμα. The missing copula and the καί must be presumed. The ability to control speech and to do this with absolute wisdom is the key. But does the author view this ideal as ever within the reach of anyone? Looking back to the opening assertion that we all sin often, the answer must be "no," for speech must be included in making this projection. The fact is that everyone sins in his speech, which supplies μεῖζον κρίμα in 3:1 with further force. James is simply focusing attention here on the value of controlling speech at any level by projecting the optimum results if a person were to do so perfectly.

James 3:3—4

Looking ahead to the illustrations of 3:3—4, one just might think that the idea of perfectly controlled speech is attainable since the wondrously beneficial power of the controlled tongue is positively pictured. Yet, the

---

2 See Laws, 141–143, and Wanke.

illustrations do not have this purpose. Rather, they highlight only generally the power of the controlled tongue to effect a controlled body. They do not comment on whether the human tongue can be controlled as perfectly as the horse's tongue or the ship's rudder. Tugging the reins turns a horse; guiding the rudder directs a ship. When a horse's mouth is made to obey (εἰς τὸ πείθεσθαι), so does its whole body (ὅλον τὸ σῶμα again as in 3:2)[3]. The ship follows the course set by its "tongue."

The more elaborate depiction of the second illustration, comprising 3:4, adds three critical facets to the general point. First, the inclusion of ἀνέμων σκληρῶν ἐλαυνόμενα brings to notice the fact that the tongue is not powerful in itself. It is the focal point through which power is channelled into purposeful action. Secondly, the accentuation of the smallness of the rudder (ἐλαχίστου) in contrast to the great size of the ship (τηλικαῦτα) draws attention to the value, or importance, of the tongue to the body which is vastly out of proportion to its relative size. Thirdly, the addition of ὅπου ἡ ὁρμὴ τοῦ εὐθύνοντος βούλεται enhances the fact that the tongue does not control itself. It should be controlled by the person, more specifically, by his own desire, his choice of direction[4]. Thus, ultimately he is responsible if his tongue is powered into bad speech by bad influences. All three of these points are drawn upon in the next two verses, the third being already established in 1:13.

James 3:5

With οὕτως καί beginning 3:5, James indicates that he is about to draw a formal comparison with what has preceded. The accent on μικρὸν μέλος makes it apparent that he is comparing the human tongue with the rudder of a ship rather than with the tongue of a horse, although the actual size comparison is true for all three. The addition of μεγάλα αὐχεῖ makes it even clearer that human tongues are in mind. The two

---

3 It should be noted that 3:3 contains a textual difficulty consisting of whether the verse should begin with εἰ δέ or ἴδε. The textual weight is fairly even; either could have risen out of error from the other; both have stylistic parallels in the immediate context (εἴ τις in 3:2 and ἰδού in 3:4). The difficulty of making a decision here is illustrated by the "D" rating given to the UBS[3] choice of εἰ δέ and the fairly even division of the commentators on the question (summarised well by P. Davids, 138). I tend toward εἰ δέ because the precedence in 3:3 would seem to have stronger stylistic force than ἰδού in 3:4, especially since ἴδέ is not used by James elsewhere. I would have thought he would use ἰδού to maintain a stylistic pattern rather than ἴδέ. Fortunately, one's choice here hardly poses an interpretive problem. Some manuscripts have ἰδού, which is an obvious correction.

4 Both the noun ὁρμή and the verb βούλεται stress the idea of choice or desire, giving a somewhat tautologous emphasis to the idea. As Mayor, 112, indicates, the importance of deliberation in βούλομαι disallows the idea of mere whim or eratic impulse. The helsman, or pilot, has a precise destination in mind which is carefully charted.

illustrations demonstrate that such boasting has a solid basis. Nevertheless, despite views of some commentators[5], it seems impossible in view of the second portion of the verse to perceive this facility of the tongue as anything but negative. By promptly pairing the human tongue with a well-known form of uncontrolled speech like boasting, the author gently prepares the reader for the upcoming lesson of the vast differences between the human tongue and the horse's tongue or the ship's rudder. These can be perfectly controlled. The human tongue cannot be (Schrage, 40).

With his next sentence, James puts the little-large contrast to work in negative imagery. He does this by cleverly employing the adjective ἡλίκος twice, this being a word which comments on the relative size of something, either big or small. Here, it accents the smallness of πῦρ in contrast to the largeness of ὕλην, which the former can set to flames and thus destroy. Unlike the horse's tongue and the ship's rudder which are carefully monitored, the fire in the forest is totally out of control.

James 3:6

With the negative mood properly set by the third illustration, in 3:6 James launches a bold exposé on the negative, destructive capabilities of the tongue. He calls the tongue itself πῦρ and proceeds to explain in the next four phrases why this is an appropriate description and what he means by it, at times playing off the picture of the raging fire introduced in 3:5.

As all commentaries note, this is an extremely difficult verse[6]. There are serious questions regarding grammar, punctuation, syntax, and the precise meaning of certain phrases. Not without reason is the state of the text disparaged[7]. Yet, the general meaning is clear (P. Davids, 144): the human tongue by its nature is a most dangerous agency of evil.

The vast majority of scholars take the phrase with καθίσταται, finding no viable relationship between the phrase and πῦρ. It is also believed that as a predicate nominative it helps explain the article in ἡ σπιλοῦσα[8]. There is no reason to dispute this reasoning, except to say that there is an unnecessary tendency among some who argue for it to weaken the force of καθίσταται, calling it an elaborate copula and translating it "is[9]." However, the word here has more significance than that and can carry a

---

5 Laws, 147; Hort, 70–71; Mitton, 123. Those who agree with my view are: P. Davids, 140; Dibelius, 190; Ropes, 253; Hiebert, 212.
6 Dibelius, 193, rates it to be "among the most controversial in the New Testament."
7 Dibelius, 194–195, and Ropes, 233. Dibelius in fact thinks as much as ὁ κόσμος τῆς ἀδικίας ἡ γλῶσσα καθίσταται ἐν τοῖς μέλεσιν ἡμῶν a gloss.
8 See P. Davids, 142, for a convenient listing of scholar's views.
9 Mitton, 126, and Hiebert, 214.

stronger sense without being too awkward. This is so as a true reflexive, as Laws (p. 149) defends, but even as a passive.

The reflexive "appoints itself" could follow from the boasting characteristic of the human tongue raised in 3:5. However, the stipulation which occurs in the fourth phrase that the tongue is not its own agent, corresponding to the same point made at the end of 3:4, casts serious doubt on the likelihood of the tongue being considered by the author as self-appointed. The passive "is appointed" would stress that this is the divinely ordained function of the tongue within the human body (ἐν τοῖς μέλεσιν ἡμῶν). This understanding is preferred because the creational contingent corresponds with the later appearance of γενέσεως in the third phrase of the verse.

On the meaning of κόσμος, the negative inference so common to the New Testament and to James (1:27; 4:4) is hardly disputed today[10]. Being modified by such a word as ἀδικίας, leave little doubt about the matter. The somewhat surprising use of the ὁ with κόσμος must be there in order to add to the emphasis that the world of wickedness centers on the tongue unlike anywhere else in the human body. As Mussner (pp. 163—164) alertly brings out, the meaning of the phrase will be further elucidated in the second phrase.

The second phrase describes the tongue as ἡ σπιλοῦσα ὅλον τὸ σῶμα. The word σῶμα here must refer to the individual both inwardly and outwardly even as γλῶσσα in the discourse refers to speech, which has both an internal as well as an external aspect (P. Davids, 143; Mitton, 127).

This third occurrence of ὅλον τὸ σῶμα links 3:6 to 3:2, 3 and the major point of the passage that the tongue affects the whole body. Unlike the first two where the point is that the controlled tongue has a positive effect, here the point is that the uncontrolled tongue has a negative effect. The participle ἡ σπιλοῦσα is yet another word which elicits a cultic motif reminiscent of 1:27[11]. Whether the tongue is thought of as a cancerous infection (Robertson, 158) or as a fatal flaw, it is being viewed here as making the total person unacceptable before God. As touched upon in 1:21, the uncontrolled tongue gives prime evidence of a person's evil nature and need to repent. The tongue, here, is accounted blameworthy for the person's moral and spiritual imperfection.

The third phrase, φλογίζουσα τὸν τροχὸν τῆς γενέσεως, draws more explicitly from the fire metaphor. The major difficulty with this phrase is

---

10   As P. Davids, 142, records, the tendency to take κόσμος here as something morally and spiritually neutral like "instrument" (cf. Rom. 6:13) or "universe" is a factor only in older commentaries. For example, see Carr.

11   Hort, 72. See Eph. 5:27.

discovering the precise origin and thus the exact meaning and translation of the idiomatic phrase τὸν τροχὸν τῆς γενέσεως. It occurs in Orphic texts once. However, it is more common for κύκλος to replace τροχός in the effort to capture the oppressive fatalism to which humanity is subject. Similar ideas appear in other Greek texts as well as in Rabbinic and Philonic Literature, although it gradually separates from the totally pessimistic perspective of its origin[12]. According to Dibelius (p. 198), it came to mean "the ups and downs of life" but for James signifies "little more than 'life' ". No translation it seems is able to convey the impact the phrase must have made on the original readers of James. Most commentators agree that the author employs it to refer to all of human existence on the broadest possible scale — past, present, and future[13]. As the destructive evil of the tongue on the whole of an individual's life is covered in the second phrase, here it is the negative impact of the (uncontrolled) tongue on human society in general that is elucidated. In relation to the forest metaphor, a fire destroys not only trees but also the forest. So the tongue harms people but also society.

The fourth phrase, φλογιζομένη ὑπὸ τῆς γεέννης, structurally plays off of the third, adding vital information about the true agent behind the human tongue's harmfulness. It gives credence other view expressed in 3:4 that the tongue itself does not supply its own power. James calls the agent here τῆς γεέννης. The word is commonly used to designate the place of eschatological punishment in the New Testament. Appropriately for James, it originally was associated as a place of burning in relation to pagan fire sacrifices in 2 Ki. 23:10 and Jer. 7:31. It is possible that it was later used to refer to a place of constant burning outside the walls of Jerusalem where garbage was dumped. Since the word is a place and thus unsuitable as the agent required by ὑπό, it must stand ass a euphemism for Satan here[14]. Thus, what is conveyed here is tht the person who does not control his tongue makes his tongue an agent for Satan's harmful designs on the individual and on society.

James 3:7—8

With 3:7, James begins the attempt to supply incontrovertible support from common experience for his utterly negative perspective on the tongue so brazenly detailed in 3:6. The γάρ governs both the points made

---

12 The history of the phrase is more than adequately traced by Dibelius, 196–198; Ropes, 235–239; Adamson, 160–164.

13 Laws, 150; Hiebert, 217; Ropes, 235; Mayor, 117; Mitton, 128.

14 P Davids, 143; Hiebert, 218; Dibelius, 198; Mitton, 129; Mayor, 119. James 3:15 uses a euphemism for demons in connection with false wisdom.

in 3:7—8 as well as those that will be made in 3:9—12 (Hort, 74). The notion that the human tongue is evil by functional design is forefront in the author's mind.

In 3:7—8, James makes a general observation regarding man's mastery over the animal kingdom to which he contrasts his incapability to master his own tongue. James specifies that by πᾶσα . . . φύσις he means the four divisions of creatures familiar from biblical tradition (Gen. 1:26; 9:2). By expressing the verb δαμάζω in both the present and perfect tenses, he underlines his point that man's dominance over the creatures has always been true and is perpetually being proven, even as the species increase in variety and man discovers more. While δαμάζω may have a view to the taming of animals, its general meaning of "subdue" is more akin to the idea of Gen. 1:28 and better allows the universal application James makes. Man's general, God-given capability to dominate the animal kingdom includes hunting and killing as well as capturing and domesticating[15]. The subjugation of the animals to man is absolute, perpetual, and complete, in general as well as in specific cases. This is inherent in δαμάζω and is conveyed further by the first word in the verse, πᾶσα. Thus, the contrast is heightened with the point in vs. 8 that man is totally incapable of controlling his tongue. The clever use of τῇ φύσει in connection with τῇ ἀνθρωπίνῃ puts man at the same level with the creatures and further alludes to man's dependence on God for his authority over the animals.

This intended contrast of 3:8 is established by δέ and the emphatic forward position of the accusative τὴν . . . γλῶσσαν. The absolute inability of man to control his own tongue is conveyed by δαμάσαι. In light of this, the present tense of δύναται is probably gnomic. The otherwise unnecessary specification of ἀνθρώπων may, as ἀνθρωπίνῃ in 3:7, be intended to suggest man's limitations in this apart from God[16]. If so, it could be a subtle indication as to how the tongue might be controlled. As it stands, though, James' point here is that there is an incontrovertible paradox in the created world in that mankind can and does subdue the wildest and most powerful animals, but the individual cannot do anything to deter the wanton destructiveness of his own tongue, a relatively small and seemingly unpretentious part of his body[17].

---

15 On hunting and killing, see Laws, 153; Mitton, 130; Adamson, 145.
16 Cranfield, 344, and Mayor, 120.
17 Schrage, 39, accents man's weakness in his explanation that the paradox involves, "die Ohnmacht des Menschen gegenüber der Zunge." The view of DuPlessis, 239, that James imagines one person not being able to control another person's tongue takes the illustration of 3:7 too literally. By doing this, he spoils the contrast intended and causes James to observe what is only too obvious. James 3:10a gives clear indication that it is the individual's own tongue that James has in mind.

The two syntacticlly independent phrases[18] which complete 3:8 represent yet another attempt by the author to depict the tongue's evil. They both focus on aspects of its evil which make it immune to control. The first, ἀκατάστατον κακόν, accents the unsettled restlessness of its evil nature. It is hard to catch. One can never anticipate when or how it will attack. The play on the movements of a wild animal is quite apparent and in light of 3:7, masterful. This wild animal is quicker and more cunning than all the others, perhaps another indication of its demonic associations (P. Davids, 145; Mitton, 130). The second phrase, μεστὴ ἰοῦ θανατηφόρου, accents the utter potency of the tongue's evil to spread and cause death. In one sense, it may be related to the poisonous tongue of a snake which strikes at others in society (cf. Ps. 58:4; 140:3). This understanding would correspond to the third phrase of 3:6, but Satan could again be subtly referred to as well. In another sense, it could refer to the fatal effect of a poisonous tongue on the speaker. The image of self-destruction corresponds to the second phrase of 3:6 and is paralleled in Job 20:12—16[19]. The noun μεστή gives the picture of a tongue saturated with poison, conveying again its complete involvement with evil.

James 3:9

With 3:9, James begins to elaborate on the inconsistency of the tongue. Even at its best, it is unable to shed completely its evil nature. James chooses to make his point by means of the sharpest possible contrast. Man's use of the tongue to bless or praise God is contrasted with the cursing of our fellow man. The appearance and, indeed, repetition of ἐν αὐτῇ marks a shift from the personification of the tongue which has over-shadowed the discussion since 3:6 (Hort, 76; Ropes, 241). The reality of personal responsibility for the tongue is now brought back into perspective in order to prepare for the censure which will occur in 3:10.

Our most venerable use of the tongue is to praise or bless God. This capability in itself perhaps redeems the trouble the tongue causes. Our most despicable use of the tongue is to curse another person. The fact that both verbs, εὐλογοῦμεν and καταρώμεθα, are in the present tense high-

---

18   The syntax here is exceedingly unclear. Although apposition would seem to be what the author intends, this is not allowable given the nominative case of μεστή. Both μεστή and ἀκατάστατον κακόν can either be taken as independent nominatives as suggested by P. Davids, 145; Ropes, 241; Dibelius, 200; Mussner, 66, or as predicate nominatives with an assumed subject of ἡ γλῶσσα and an assumed copula as suggested by Hiebert, 221, and Mayor, 121. As elsewhere, the true sense may require rhetorical inflection which might be conveyed best by an exclamation point (Dibelius, Hiebert).

19   It may be significant in light of 1:27 but especially in light of 5:1–6 that the context of Job 20:12–19 involves the deceitful oppression of the poor by the rich.

lights the paradox involved. We do both all the time (progressive) or at least alternatively (iterative). That James envisages these polar uses of the tongue to come from all individuals is specified in 3:10a.

The addition of πατέρα to τὸν κύριον may be to make sure the reader understands that he means God here rather than Christ[20]. As in 1:27, it probably also functions as a reminder of the brotherhood of man which derives from God's creatorhood and fatherhood of all men. It then prepares for the pointed reminder τοὺς καθ' ὁμοίωσιν θεοῦ γεγονό- τας which follows τοὺς ἀνθρώπους.

This last phrase means that cursing one's fellow man amounts to cursing God. This being the case, it casts doubt on the genuineness presumed by the author of James of the praise being offered to God, especially in light of 1:26—27 (Hort, 77; Mitton, 130—131). Perhaps, James implies man's praise of God is always tainted by impure motives[21]. The tongue is not only inconsistent, speaking sometimes good, sometimes evil, but, as James has continually stressed, the tongue is evil through and through. Even in its noblest function, fails to break from evil.

James 3:10—12

As already noted, the first clause in 3:10, ἐκ τοῦ αὐτοῦ στόματος ἐξέρχεται εὐλογία καὶ κατάρα, primarily functions as clarification of the point that inconsistency of the tongue is a glaring human problem. The visual imagery evoked by ἐξέρχεται and the structure also help to elicit a smooth transition to the illustration coming up in 3:11.

The second clause in 3:10, οὐ χρή, ἀδελφοί μου, ταῦτα οὕτως γίνεσθαι, quickly handled by most commentaries, is the hub of excruciating difficulties which ramify to the end of 3:12. This is caused primarily by the contrast it seems to present to the bleak picture of the tongue painted thus far in the discourse. Its intention to be a pastoral censure of the mixture of blessing and cursing on men's tongues seems obvious. But what is its significance in the broader context? Can the author really be calling upon ἀδελφοί μου to stop allowing their tongues to speak so inconsistently when he has just been talking about how impossible this is? If so, he is asking them to keep the tongue from its apportioned task in man and to overpower this agency of Satan. The point with which he begins the discourse regarding the stricter terms of judgment for teachers requires the support of the pessimistic picture of the tongue so far established. So,

---

20 He does use ὁ κύριος to refer to Christ elsewhere in 1:1; 2:1; 5:7, 8, 14, 15.

21 In *Ebr.*, Philo says that the average person's speech at its best is only partly true and partly false.

how is this verse best understood? There are two ways to understand it which maintain consistency with the context.

First, the second clause of vs. 10 could be an attempt by the author to express his dissatisfaction with the way things are, even though there is nothing that can be done about them. He wishes the tongue were not so bent toward evil, but he realises that this is one of the facts of human existence. Understood in this way, he would not be placing blame at all on people for not controlling their tongues. The illustrations in 3:11—12 would then be emphasising, as 3:4—5 does, that the tongue defies the laws of consistency observable elsewhere in nature. The last illustration would have the point that the tongue should not attempt to become what it is incapable of becoming, thus providing an appropriate conclusion to the discourse. Just as a bitter spring cannot produce sweet water, neither can the evil human tongue speak graciously. If it tries to, it is only deceiving itself and its owner (cf. 1:26—27).

The advantage of the above interpretation is that it irons out all the inconsistency as well as making vs. 12 an appropriate conclusion. What weighs against it is that it turns on its head what appears to be the most obvious understanding of 3:10b and the verses that follow when viewed independently of the overall context. As far as vs. 10b goes, the impersonal verb χρή does appear to be able to bear the meaning required in that it can involve something the gods have spoken, as in an oracle or regarding a person's fate (LS-J, 2004). The fact that the word is not used in biblical literature gives this very Greek sense more weight than one might normally allow. It should be noted, though, that χρή came eventually to refer to an ethical "ought" in Greek literature, losing sight of its fatalistic background.

A second way to smooth out the inconsistency derives from Schrage's suggestion (p. 40) that 3:10b is intended to be a signal from the author, albeit brief, that his utterly pessimistic view of the situation regarding the tongue and man's capability to control it is not "eine Kapitulation." In this sense, his chastisement in 3:10b is to be taken as an indication of the author's belief that the tongue can be controlled, even if improvement can only be limited because of the enormity of the tongue's evil. A person, then, should try to control his tongue even though his chance of total success is nil. James does not wish to leave his readers catatonic in their combat with sin and evil. This explanation permits a slight contradiction, but it is akin to the familiar New Testament tension which is allowed to exist between man's sinful nature and God's desire that he not sin. Man cannot be morally or spiritually perfect. However, he can do better.

The distinct advantage of this approach is that it allows vs. 10b to carry its obvious overtone of censure. The illustration of vs. 11 remains a reinforcement of the censure on man's inconsistency in speech. The biggest weakness is that the approach leaves the changed emphasis of 3:12 signalled by ἀδελφοί μου to clash with 3:10b[22]. However, a tolerable explanation to remedy this might be that after the glimmer of possible improvement in controlling the tongue in 3:10b—11, the author returns to his more predominantly pessimistic point of view. Thus, the illustrations in vs. 12 refer to the fact that one cannot change the basic nature of the tongue which is evil any more than a fig tree can be changed to produce olives or a salty spring can be changed to produce sweet water. One must do what one can to make the evil tongue speak graciously even as one can cultivate an olive tree to produce the best olives it can or as one might attempt to dilute salty water. The ending of the discourse, then, would correspond to the lead of 3:1.

A more minor difficulty with this second approach is that·James does not spell out how a person is to reduce the inconsistency of his otherwise uncontrollable tongue. However, this lack can be explained by the fact that such information would digress too far from the main point of 3:1—12. The author only means to insert a note of encouragement to offset the hyperbole involved in his utterly pessimistic tone. Also, he has already touched on the issue of how to control the tongue in 1:19—27 and will do so again in 4:6—10.

Following the second approach, then, χρή states more than regret. It includes displeasure aimed at motivating ἀδελφοί μου to improve control of their tongues which waver between such extremes as praising God and cursing men. As Mayor (p. 124) rightly notes, χρή conveys a sense of ultimate urgency rather than a request, i.e. "must" rather than "should," implying that such reform perhaps bears the backing of God. The demonstrative pronoun ταῦτα points to the specific instance of blessing and cursing, while the adverb of manner οὕτως points to the general principle of inconsistency[23]. The infinitive γίνεσθαι indicates the regular occurrences of such inconsistencies.

The particle μήτι introduces 3:11 as a theoretical question expecting a strong denial. The fact that ἐκ τῆς αὐτῆς ὀπῆς is unnecessary to the sense of the question gives credence to the view that there is correspondence in terms of structure and imagery with ἐκ τοῦ αὐτοῦ στόματος and all the

---

22 Dibelius, 206, and Laws, 158, consider 3:12b to be such a poor attempt to rectify the confusing change of focus between vs. 11 and 12a that they consider it to be a gloss.

23 P. Davids, 147, follows Mayor, 123, in seeing the rebuke as concerning only cursing. By doing so, the plural of ταῦτα is ignored as is the significance of blessing–cursing as but one example of many inconsistencies of good and bad in the human tongue.

other elements of 3:10a[24]. The picturesque βρύει corresponds with ἐξέρχεται and except for the articles, τὸ γλυκὺ χαὶ τὸ πικρόν corresponds
with εὐλογία καὶ κατάρα. The point being made is clear enough. The
tongue must not be allowed to defy nature and spout good one minute
and bad the next (Laws, 157; Ropes, 242; Mitton, 132).

The recurrence of the vocative ἀδελφοί μου at the beginning of 3:12, as
already noted, probably is a signal from the author that he is making a
slight shift in focus. It is worth noting that the opening pattern of the
negative μή followed by the verb δυνάται, which can occasionally be
impersonal, plus the vocative, parallels 3:10b rather than 3:11. This
reinforces the fact that the point of the illustration is indeed different
from 3:11. In order to have corresponded to the image conceived in 3:11,
3:12 would have to say that the συκῆ produces both figs and ἐλαίας of the
ἄμπελος produce both grapes and σῦκα. However, the image here is of a
tree producing the wrong fruit. It cannot go against its own nature. This,
then, is clarified and strengthened by the next illustration which takes
similar imagery from 3:11 and turns it specifically to this point.

Water which is ἁλυκόν cannot change itself into water which is
γλυκύ and good for drinking. The use of ποιῆσαι here is unusual. Its
presence is understandable, though, as an attempt to correspond with its
use in the first illustration of the verse[25]. There is some question about the
appropriateness of a lone οὔτε, but the presumed negative in the question
which precedes it, although rough, satisfies the need for a corresponding
οὔτε[26]. As it stands, the οὔτε functions as a striking signal that this is the
concluding point of the discourse. Dibelius (p. 205) may be right about the
fact that the clause presumes ἡ πηγή, but it is not really necessary to
presume this in order for the author to make a different point from 3:11.
By making the negative attribution first the author indicates that it is
impossible for the evil tongue to make itself good (*Contra* P. Davids, 148).

This realistic final appraisal, although very nearly intolerable concise
(Mitton, 133), marks an appropriate close to the section by retaining the
negative emphasis on the tongue which has been the theme throughout. It
also supports the original point of 3:1 that teachers, by the very fact that
they deal more in words than do others, put themselves in the position of
having a more difficult time at judgment.

---

24 Hort, 78; Mussner, 168; P. Davids, 148; Dibelius, 203, pointedly discount this of inter-
    pretation as allegorical. Perhaps Hort is right to an extent, but one need not allegorise
    to see parallel structure and query its significance.
25 P. Davids, 148, and Dibelius, 205. Mayor, 125, notes appropriate references to the use
    of ποιέω with regard to trees bearing fruit in Gen. 3:11 (LXX) and Mt. 3:10.
26 Hort, 79–80; Dibelius, 205; Mayor, 125.

James 4:1—2b

The two questions which comprise 4:1 display all the marks of the kind of stress one would expect in rhetoric²⁷. Both lack finite verbs. This plus the repetition of the interrogative adverb πόθεν in the first question plus the inclusion of the adverb ἐντεῦθεν to begin the second makes the stress on origin unmistakable. The use of the plural synonyms πόλεμοι and μάχαι indicates that the conflicts whose origin is in question are serious, widespread, and probably recurring. These battles are not part of a literal war ἐν ὑμῖν but refer to verbal skirmishes among Christians²⁸. Falling in the shadow of 3:1—18, it can refer to nothing else. The negative οὐκ says that James thinks his rhetorical question in reply to the first question is correct. His specification of these verbal battles as originating ἐκ τῶν ἡδονῶν ὑμῶν does not in itself make the location of this harmful use of speech inside a person. However, τῶν στρατευομένων ἐν τοῖς μέλεσιν ὑμῶν clearly denotes the real struggle to be internal. This results in external conflict²⁹. The locative prepositional phrase recalls the negative picture of the evil tongue infecting all the members of the body with its evil in 3:6. Here, though, pleasure is pictured as compaigning within a person, presumably against whatever goodness is there to resist it³⁰. With ἐπιθυμεῖτε, James summarises the harmful activity of pleasure within and reinforces the fact that the person himself is perpetuating the internal conflict and is thus responsible for the negative effects in the Christian community. The addition of καὶ οὐκ ἔχετε expresses that the desire is insatiable and thus entirely negative.

The next verb, φονεύετε, magnifies the hideous results of this desire³¹, carrying on the war motif. The meaning is figurative just as πόλεμοι and μάχαι are. It refers to the many different kinds of speech which can demoralise and devastate another³². Some of these might occur in the heat

---

27 P. Davids, 156; Hiebert, 242; Mayor, 134.
28 P. Davids, 156; Mussner, 176; Hort, 87; Hiebert, 242; Ropes, 252; Mitton, 145.
29 Laws, 169; Hort, 89; Mitton, 146; Schrage, 43; Adamson, 166; Hiebert, 242.
30 P. Davids, 157, may well be correct to suggest that James' ideas here are founded on the well-attested Jewish concept of a good and bad *yetser*, or inclination, which vie for the individual's favour, or choice, in matters. Davids thinks James conceives of ἡδονή/ἐπιθυμία as the bad *yetser* and wisdom from above as the good *yetser*. For expansion on this, see his thesis, "Themes," 266–267. A recent article by J. Marcus traces the association of ἐπιθυμία (which first appears in James in the crucial context of 1:13-15) with evil *yetser* in Jewish literature. He concludes by showing the contexts in which evil *yetser* emerges in James.
31 Laws, 69; Ropes, 259; Mitton, 148; Mayor, 135–136; Hiebert, 245.
32 P. Davids, 158-159; Mussner, 178; Mitton, 148; Hiebert, 246. It is surprising in view of the context and the ample association of various forms of harmful speech such as slander, mockery, and anger with murder, blood, and killing that anyone seeks other interpretations. Scholars like Ropes, 255; Mayor, 137; Hort, 89, Laws, 169, take

of verbal battle like mockery, angry speech (1:20), and cursing (recall 3:9), the last of which could cause death if God chooses to honour it. Others might be employed to win a long-running dispute like the spreading of gossip or slander, or even perjury (2:6; 5:6) which could quite literally bring about the death of the opposition. The concept that a person's speech can cause death is alluded to earlier in 3:8.

The next verb, ζηλοῦτε compounds with καὶ οὐ δύνασθε ἐπιτυχεῖν to rephrase ἐπιθυμεῖτε καὶ οὐκ ἔχετε again exposing an inner problem. The next two one-word clauses, μάχεσθε καὶ πολεμεῖτε, mirror their noun cognates in 4:1, πόλεμοι καὶ . . . μάχαι. They put further stress on the fact that it is the inner conflict taking place within the individual because of insatiable desire for self-satisfying pleasures which is the true origin of verbal disputes in the Christian community. The general teaching holds for society at large as well.

A possible way of setting out the chiastic structure of 4:1—2a is as follows:

A1 πόθεν πόλεμοι καὶ πόθεν μάχαι ἐν ὑμῖν; οὐκ ἐντεῦθεν, ἐκ τῶν ἡδονῶν ὑμῶν
    τῶν στρατευομένων ἐν τοῖς μέλεσιν ὑμῶν;
    B1 ἐπιθυμεῖτε καὶ οὐκ ἔχετε
        C φονεύετε
    B2 καὶ ζηλοῦτε, καὶ οὐ δύνασθε ἐπιτυχεῖν
A2 μάχεσθε καὶ πολεμεῖτε.

Admittedly, the second line does not fit as smoothly into this arrangement as one would like. It should be seen as a necessary clarificaton of ἐπιθυμεῖτε. Other than this, the lines correspond convincingly. The result is that even more stress is given to the striking use of φονεύετε. The "A" lines, which speak of social strife, envelop the "B" lines, which denote personal, internal strife. The core, "C," should be seen, then, as an assult on the inner person as well as on the outer person, with the offending words piercing to the heart.

Analysis

The establishment of the human tongue as evil in its functional nature is one of the major objectives of James 3:1—12. This tenet is the major plank in demonstrating that the tongue cannot ever be completely controlled

---

φονεύετε to refer to physically enacted homicide. Adamson, 167–168, siding with Dib-elius, 217–218, opts to change the text to φθονεῖτε, which is unsupportable from the manuscripts. On references to speech involving killing and bloodshed, see Prov. 10:6, 11, 18; 12:6; 24:28; Ps. 14:4; Ezek. 22:9; Sir. 8:16; 26:5; 28:8–11, 19–21; 1QH 5:7, 10–11; Mid.Ps. 12:2; B. Metzia 59b; LevR. 6:3. One must also keep in mind the association made in Sir. 34:22 and Job 20:19 between oppressing and cheating the poor and murder, especially in light of Jas. 2:6 and 5:1–6.

which in turn provides support for the opening projection in 3:1 that teachers will be subject to a more rigorous judgment, presumably because they are occupied so much with words. James' logic is indisputable. If the tongue is by nature evil and thus uncontrollable, then those whose speech intertwines with their profession, like teachers, and especially teachers in the church, indeed, will have more to account for before God than others.

The evil nature of the tongue is conveyed very successfully by the fire metaphor which begins 3:6 but which stems from the forest fire illustration in 3:5. In the four phrases (three clauses) which follow in 3:6, not only is evil shown to be natural to the tongue but the devastating harmfulness of the tongue is illumined at the personal and societal level.

The first phrase, ὁ κόσμος τῆς ἀδικίας, when understood as the predicate nominative of the verb καθίσταται, which follows, establishes the tongue as the endowed location of evil in the human body. The fourth phrase asserts the tongue to be the certified agency of Satan. The tongue is evil. This is reasserted in 3:8 with the further attestation being made that it is restless and unpredictable. It is also depicted in this verse as saturated (μεστή) with poison. It is evil through and through. Even in exhibiting its capability to praise God in 3:9—10a, it is hinted that this good is overshadowed by the tongue's evil nature. Certainly the tongue's evil rules the uttering of curses. After briefly admonishing his readers from totally withdrawing from the fight to control the evil of the tongue, in indirect language 3:12 again dramatises that fact that neither the tongue itself nor man can ever change the tongue's role in the body as the agency of evil.

The power of the tongue to destroy is illuminated brilliantly by calling it a fire in 3:6, thereby associating it with the tiny spark that ignites a wasting forest fire in 3:5. Specifically, the image is applied to the tongue's ruination of a person's entire body in the second phrase of 3:6. The third phrase applies the fire image to the downfall of human society in perpetuity. In 3:8, its poison is proclaimed to be deadly (θανατηφόρου), probably with reference to others as well as to oneself.

The evil perpetuated by the human tongue is viewed by James as indicative of human sinfulness. This may be inferred from 3:2, which connects not sinning in speech to control of one's actions and to moral and spiritual perfection. The reversal of the speculation links sinfulness in speech to sinfulness in action and a less than perfect person. The presumption that James does not consider perfection possible in reality is displayed in the author's effort which follows 3:2 to demonstrate man's incapability to control his evil tongue. Earlier, in 1:20—21, uncontrolled speech epitomised by anger is presumed to reveal a wicked life in need of cleanup. Anger alone exposes a person's distance from God's righteousness.

Again, in 1:26, a person's uncontrolled tongue is said to discredit his professed religion and, thus, presumably his standing before God. In 4:16—17, boasting alone is taken as an indication of a person's sinfulness. The four dramatic quotations in 1:13; 2:3; 2:16; 4:13 refer to spoken words which demonstrate a person's sinfulness as well.

James considers a person's harmful speech to come from within him and thus indicate the evil interior of his person, whether this is designated the heart or not. This anthropological perception does not figure into 3:1—12, although it is clearly elucidated in 4:1—2b and surfaces at a few other points in the writing. One of these is at 3:14, where the effect of ζῆλον πικρόν and ἐριθείαν in the heart are considered to be boasting (κατακαυχᾶσθε) and lying (ψεύδεσθε). Another of these is at 5:5—6, where hearts that have been fattened (ἐθρέψατε) from a life of pleasure and self-indulgence are thought to provide the foundation for false condemnation and even murder (κατεδικάσατε, ἐφονεύσατε) of the righteous innocent (τὸν δίκαιον).

Neither 1:14—15 nor 4:18 bring speech into consideration, but these verses corroborate the fact that the responsibility for sin lies within the person. The first, as in 4:1—2b, elucidates ἐπιθυμία as the active agent of sin in man. In demanding ἁμαρτωλοί to purify their hearts (ἁγνίσατε), the second assumes the heart to be the seat of sin.

It should be noted that sin is not viewed entirely as coming from within a person in James. In 4:7, the author associates the influence of the devil (τῷ διαβόλῳ) with contributing to man's separation from God. As already mentioned, in 3:6 the tongue is referred to as but an agency of hell.

Part III

Speech in Inter-Human Relationships

Chapter 5: Background

Near Eastern Wisdom Literature

The hope in the Near Eastern Wisdom Literature is that speech will be used beneficially in inter-human relationships in order to foster harmony and order in society. The Counsels of Wisdom adjures people to make their speech positive when it says (*BWL*, p. 105):

> . . . speak what is of good report.
> . . . speak well of people. . . .
> [utter] what is decent.

The overriding fear in this literature is that speech will be used in ways that will be divisive and harmful. Thus, there is great concern to restrict the negative effect harmful speech can have in relationships. In this light, slander is considered to be the ultimate evil in the Counsels of Wisdom (*BWL*, 105). The slanderer engenders the wrath of God according to the Counsels of Wisdom (*BWL*, p. 106[1]). Slandering an enemy is bad enough but speaking ill about one's family is even worse, according to Ptah-Hotep (*ANET*, p. 413). Great care should also be taken not to slander a person who has a higher position in society according to Amen-em-Opet (*LAE*, p. 251).

Just as bad as initiating slander is repeating it carelessly, according to Ptah-Hotep (*LAE*, p. 163, 168). The Counsels of Wisdom (*BWL*, p. 101) says, "Speak nothing profane nor any untrue report. A talebearer is accursed."

One of the reasons why it is considered best to exercise extreme caution when talking about others is that a "talebearer" might hear what is said and repeat it all over town. Eventually, the words, by now quite distorted, could reach the subject of the conversation. Needless to say, this could cause a severe strain in the relationship, according to Ani (*ANET*, p. 420). Amen-em-Opet (*LAE*, 260) says:

---

1 Such anger of the gods at the slanderer is related to his certainty to destroy harmony and order in society. Thus, he is viewed as working against the gods who are working to promote frictionless order.

Do not circulate your words to others,
   nor fraternise with one who is too candid.
Better is a man whose knowledge is inside him
   than one who talks to disadvantage.

One of the best ways to keep from repeating ugly slander is to stay away from those who tend to utter it, as the above quotation suggests. Elsewhere, Amen-em-Opet (*LAE,* p. 251) also warns against someone prone to anger[2]. In a longer rejoinder of the quick-tempered man, Amen-em-Opet (*LAE,* p. 252) again advises to stay clear of him:

His lips are sweet, but his tongue is bitter,
   and fire burns inside him.
Do not fly up to join that man
   not fearing you will be brought to account.
Do not address your intemperate friend in your righteousness
   not destroying your own mind.
Do not say to him, 'May you be praised,' not meaning it
   when there is fear within you.

Verbal abuse of those less fortunate in society is another type of harmful speech that is condemned in this literature. As far as the Counsels of Wisdom is concerned, no god can approve of such pitiless misuse of speech (*BWL,* p. 101). Amen-em-Opet makes a list which identifies specific types of people who should not be verbally abused. It (*LAE,* pp. 262–263) says:

Do not jeer at a blind man nor tease a dwarf;
   neither interfere with the condition of a cripple.
Do not taunt a man who is in the hand of God,
   nor scowl at him if he errs. . . .
Do not reproach someone older than you,
   for he has seen the Sun before you.

Although it is more subtle, speech that reflects partiality is also considered a type of verbal abuse of the less fortunate in society. Judges in particular are charged to utter their rulings impartially in Ptah-Hotep (*LAE,* p. 170).

Finally, impolite speech is to be avoided, if only because of possible consequences. Ani (*AEL,* 2:140) says, "A rude answer brings a beating."

Old Testament

The Old Testament recognizes that speech at its optimum potential can be a vehicle for promoting harmony and good will among people, even at the

---

2 The hot–headed person, because of his lack of control, is working against order in society and therefore is to be avoided by those who would desire to work on behalf of order in society. See Frankfort, 66.

most intimate levels. The private words of lovers (S.S.) and the earnest conversation of friends[3] provide brief glimpses of this potential (Vriezen, 253). Yet, since the very beginning in the garden (Gen. 3:12), men and women have chosen to use words more often as weapons against one another and as vehicles of violence; thus promoting disharmony and conflict between each other. One of the marks of the evil man is that he "speaks continually against his brother" (Ps. 50:19) and "always stirs up dissension" (Prov. 6:14). Such distortion of the positive potential of speech is abhorred by the Old Testament writers not only because of the harm it brings to individuals but also because of the strife it interjects into society (Prov. 20:3; 17:4).

Despite the tendency of man to use his tongue for such evil purposes in society, all is not lost. There are some upright men who use their tongues for good. Their words counteract those of evil men for, according to Prov. 12:25 and 10:21, they "cheer men up" and "nourish many." In fact, the beneficial words of the righteous man and the harmful words of the evil man are pictured as being in constant conflict in a battle for men and society. As Prov. 12:6 says:

> The words of the wicked lie in wait for blood,
>   but the speech of the upright rescues them[4].

However, because of the inclination for men to use their tongues against one another to the detriment of society, the Old Testament, in particular Proverbs, exerts substantial effort to denigrate harmful speech and its users. What follows is an examination of the major types of harmful speech treated in the Old Testament.

Gossip

The Old Testament considers gossip[5] to be a particularly harmful use of speech because it strikes at the very roots of meaningful and intimate

---

3 Prov. 27:9. Although there are difficulties in determining the precise meaning of 9b which are detailed by McKane, 613, it seems quite certain that the verse has to do with the intimate communication that occurs between friends. See Toy, 485; R. Scott, 161; Thomas, 275.

4 Although the verse has some curious features, it makes good sense if "them" refers to the ambush victims of the words of the wicked. The keen speech of the upright man seeks to save such potential victims from the devastating words of the wicked. See McKane, 447, and Kidner, 126. Ps. 64:4 also pictures evil words waiting in ambush.

5 There are three main words which are in certain contexts translated "gossip." נרגן (Niphal of רגן, "whisper," "murmur") usually carries the implication of grumbling, finding fault, back-biting). רכיל (from רכל, "go about from one to another") usually emphasises the actual repetition of the information. דבה (from דבב, "move gently as an animal," "creep") usually refers to "whispering" of the information with malicious intentions. The three words are used fairly interchangeably and are sometimes used to convey the idea of slander.

communication. Prov. 11:13 (cf. Prov. 20:19) says, "A gossip betrays a confidence." Gossip cuts at the heart of friendship and can sever even the closest of friends[6]. It intensifies a quarrel like fanning a flame feeds a fire (Prov. 26:20).

The fact is that most people enjoy hearing juicy tidbits of gossip and then saving them for the nearest opportunity to share with others, as Prov. 18:8 (26:22) notes. Yet, the gossip must be careful. In spreading his gossip, he might encounter someone who disapproves and upbraids him (Prov. 25:9—10).

On the other hand, Prov. 20:19 warns against associating with the known gossip. How can one ever be sure that the gossip will not spread confidential remarks of his? In addition, he should always take care in what he says to people in confidence particularly when speaking about those in high places. His closest friend, dearest relative, or most trusted servant could turn out to be a tattle-tale and cause most serious consequences for him. Such caution is advised by Eccl. 10:20, which says:

> Do not revile the kind even in your thoughts
>   or curse the rich in your bedroom
> because a bird of the air may carry your words,
>   and a bird in the wing may report what you say[7].

Slander

Gossip may be perfectly innocent and even true. The chief fault is in the repetition of confidential information. Gossip decisively becomes slander when the repeated information is false, known to be false, or purposely twisted in such a way as to misrepresent someone or situations involving him. A certain sinister motivation is part of the make-up of the slanderer which may or may not provide the motivation for the gossip[8]. As Ezek. 22:9 describes him, the slanderous man is "bent on shedding blood." It is his intention and purpose to injure a man through defamation by secretly circulating false reports about him (cf. Prov. 10:18; 24:28—29). Indeed, such activity is like "a club or a sword or a sharp arrow," says Prov. 25:18.

Slander is pictured as an abhorrent evil from the earliest of Old Testament writings. The Decalogue decries the giving of false testimony

---

6 This is true whether the gossip is perpetrated by one of two friends (Prov. 17:9) or whether it is initiated by a third party in order to separate two friends (Prov. 16:28). Note also Prov. 25:23.

7 Although there are some difficulties in this verse, there is general agreement that the bird figure refers to unsuspected informers. See Gordis, *Koheleth*, 319, and Barucq, 172–173. The use of the bird figure with reference to words is reminiscent of the Words of Ahiqar (*ANET*, 428).

8 A clear distinction is not easily maintained since some of the Hebrew words for gossip overlap into slander. As noted by Barabas, translations differ in their rendering of these words. See also Mitchell, 340–341.

against one's neighbor[9], and Ex. 23:1 (cf. Lev. 19:16) says that "you shall not carry a false rumor." The stance against slander continues in Proverbs[10]. Ps. 15:3—4 describes the blameless man as one, "who has no slander on his tongue." Yet, as with gossip, there always seems to be plenty of ears that are open to malicious rumors (Prov. 17:4). On this the slanderer thrives.

Few are immune to slander in the Old Testament. David (Ps. 31:13; 35:15—16; 41:5—7), Jeremiah (Jer. 18:18), and even Moses (Num. 12:1; 14:35) are objects of the slanderer's scorn. Yet, even as Miriam was made leprous for her sin against Moses, the slanderer will eventually reap God's judgment[11]. Indeed, the flourishing of slander is cited by Jeremiah and Ezekiel as one of the reasons for Israel's destruction and exile (Jer. 6:28; 9:4; Ezek. 22:9). It is notable that part of Israel's punishment was to be that she herself would be the object of "malicious gossip and slander[12]."

Mockery

Hannah was ridiculed by Penninah for her barrenness (Jer. 6:28) as was Sarah by Hagar (Ezek. 22:9). The Psalmist (Ps. 35:21; 40:14—15) felt the searing pain of mockery when his enemies gaped at him saying, "Aha! Aha!" Jeremiah (6:28) and Elisha (2 Ki. 2:23) too were objects of mockery.

Unlike the gossiper and slanderer who operate behind the backs of their victim, the mocker is noted for his audacity in squarely facing his victim, taunting him with personal insults, deriding his character, and contemptuously flinging his misfortune back in his face. The astounding arrogance of the mocker is depicted in Prov. 21:24 when it says:

> The proud and arrogant man — 'Mocker' is his name;
> he behaves with overwhelming pride.

Such boastful haughtiness is abjured as sin and deserving of punishment in the Old Testament not only because of its affront to men and to God[13] but also because of its certainty to promote strife and conflict in society (Prov. 13:10). Not surprisingly, the mocker is pictured as a trouble-maker (Prov. 22:10) who can "set a city aflame" (Prov. 29:8).

The mocker is also noted for demonstrating his unabashed glee over the downfall of others. He treats the poor with contempt (Prov. 17:5; 14:31; Ps.

---

9   Ex. 20:16, although certainly most cogent when it is applied to official court proceedings, is also appropriate as a general admonition. See Cole, 161; Cassuto, 247; Childs, 424–425.

10   Prov. 19:5, 9; 21:28; 24:28–29; 25:18; 30:10.

11   Num. 12:8–10. See also Prov. 6:12–15; 19:5–9; 21:28; Ps. 57:4; 101:5.

12   Ezek. 36:3. The actual Hebrew here is עָם-ודבת לשון with לשון being the usual word for "tongue." So, Israel would be "together" and "defamed" by them.

13   See Prov. 21:4; Ps. 101:5. Concerning punishment and the offence this is to God, see Ps. 10:3–4; 12:2–5; 31:8; 52:1–5; Prov. 3:34; 14:9.

10:10), sneers at his enemies (Ps. 10:5), and gloats at their downfall (Prov. 24:17). However, this behaviour which only tends to feed his arrogance "will not go unpunished" (Prov. 17:5; cf. Eccl. 9:17). Although he can dish out devastating insults on the defenseless downtrodden, when confronted himself with the simple, deserved rebuke of an upright man, the mocker cannot take it. He can only respond by hurling further abuse and hateful remarks at his corrector (Prov. 9:7—8). Because of his inability to accept criticism, the mocker is repeatedly classified in Proverbs as a fool and associating with him sternly discouraged[14].

Cursing

The pronouncement of a curse is an acceptable use of speech in the Old Testament, especially when the recipient does something to deserve it. God himself cursed Adam, Eve, and the Serpent (Gen. 3:14—19), and curses are attached to many of the requirements of the Law (Deut. 27:1—26, for instance). Noah cursed Canaan; Jacob cursed Simeon and Levi; Joshua cursed Jericho; Jotham cursed Abimelech; Deborah cursed Meroz; Elisha cursed the children who mocked him; Nehemiah cursed the apostate Jews of Jerusalem[15]. In doing so, they were simply calling upon God to punish those they cursed, that is if he agreed the punishment was justified. They recognized that an undeserved curse is operative and that God is sovereign over such utterances. They are aware of the truth in Prov. 26:2, which says:

> Like a fluttering sparrow of a darting swallow
> an undeserved curse does not alight[16].

Proverbs also speaks approvingly of people being cursed for various reasons: for withholding grain, for calling a wicked man righteous, and for slandering a slave to his master[17].

This approval of cursing generally does not mean that it was allowable to utter a curse at any time and for any cause without due reflection. One of the marks of a wicked man is that he curses too commonly and too carelessly. As Ps. 109:17, 18 says, he "loves to curse" and "wears cursing as his garment[18]." He overindulges on God's time and demeans his gracious nature. Cursing is not to be done flippantly out of anger or spite.

---

14   Prov. 10:10; 11:9, 12–13; 14:6–7, 9; 19:25; 23:9.
15   In order, Gen. 9:25; 49:7; Josh. 6:26; Judg. 9:20, 57; 5:23; 2 Ki. 2:22; Neh. 13:25. Note also the imprecatory Psalms.
16   As McKane, 600, observes, the birds are envisaged here as remaining airborne in the sense that there is no appropriate place to land. See also Kidner, 161–162.
17   In order, Prov. 11:26; 24:24; 30:10.
18   Ps. 109:17, 18. See also Ps. 10:7; 59:12. Note the Goliath curses David without thought (1 Sam. 17:43). Apparently, it was common practice for one to curse his enemy for Job

There are certain persons, along with God (Ex. 22:28), who are not to be cursed at any time or under any circumstances. These are: parents[19], kings of Israel (Ex. 22:28), and the deaf[20]. Presumably, this is because God has chosen never to honour such curses.

Hot-Tempered Speech

People vent their anger in many ways. One of the most common is through speech. Hot-tempered speech may emerge in the form of cursing, mockery, slander, or perhaps even gossip — or a combination of these — although it certainly is not restricted to just these. The significant point is that "anger is cruel and fury overwhelming," as Prov. 27:4 puts it. Angry speech does not concern itself with who it hurts or how much. It is the epitome of speech out of control. Anger is characterised as residing "in the lap of fools[21]." Prov. 14:17, 29 notes that "A quick-tempered man does foolish things." These things are often the cause of deep remorse when calm is restored, but the damage is already done. Dissension is stirred up, perhaps the victim himself provoked to respond in anger to the harsh words of the hot-tempered man (Prov. 15:1, 18). According to Eccl. 7:9, neither should be so "quickly provoked in spirit." Both should be wise enough to heed the warning of Ps. 37:8.

Indeed, angry speech is one of the marks of wicked men, especially as used against the righteous[22]. The best thing one can do is stay away from such people (Prov. 22:24—25).

Flattery and Deceit

Flattery is considered by the Old Testament to be a self-seeking form of deceit, a dagger hidden in the cloak of a compliment. As Prov. 29:5 warns:

Whoever flatters his neighbor
is spreading a net for his feet[23].

One will do well to beware of those who kiss too profusely for the lips may belong to an enemy (Prov. 27:5) and of those who are overzealous in the overtures of friendship for their true motivations may well be for

---

claims as one of his virtues the fact that he had never cursed his enemies (Job 31:29–30).

19 Ex. 21:17; Lev. 20:9; Prov. 20:20; 30:11.
20 Lev. 29:14. It is quite possible that this verse does not refer to formal cursing but to something more like abusive language and mockery.
21 Eccl. 7:9. See also Eccl. 9:17.
22 They "gnash their teeth at them," says Ps. 37:12. See Weiser, 319; A. Anderson, 295; Dahood, 1:228; Briggs, 1:327, who all understand this as portraying anger.
23 See McKane, 636. The word usually translated "flattery" (חלק) basically means "smooth" or "slippery."

harm[24]. As far as Prov. 26:28 is concerned, just as certainly as "a lying tongue hates those it hurts, a flattering tongue works ruin." And such is its true intent. One will do better to value rebuke as a true sign of friendship rather than flattery (Prov. 28:23).

A description of Israel in Ps. 12:2 is one of the most explicit examples linking flattery with deception. It says:

> Everyone lies to his neighbor;
>   their flattering lips speak with deception.

The passage goes on to call on God to "cut off all flattering lips," among other things, to which God in effect agrees in Ps. 12:5.

Tactlessness

Some people simply do not know how to conduct themselves in delicate situations without giving offense. Whether intentionally or unintentionally, they say the wrong thing at the most inappropriate moment. For instance, an attempt to be jolly may only exacerbate a person's feeling of melancholy. As Prov. 25:20 puts it:

> Like one who takes away a garment on a cold day
>   or like vinegar poured on soda,
>   is one who sings songs to a heavy heart[25].

Indeed, Job (19:21—23) is probably not alone in his cry for sympathy from his friends in distressing times.

The boisterous "Good morning!" of an early riser will be heard as a curse by his late-rising friend (Prov. 27:5). So, some people do not know (or care) when a joke on their friend has gone far beyond the point of laughing[26].

Perjury

The courtroom adds many new facets to the comparably simple evil of slander. In the courtroom the accuser must face his victim and bring his

---

24 Prov. 27:14. There are those who take this proverb to refer simply to the inconsiderateness of a friend. See R. Scott, 162, and Kidner, 166. However, the case can be made for associating the proverb more specifically with deceitful flattery. His loud voice indicates the person's forced heartiness. This is a sign of his hollow friendship intended to disguise his malice. His early rising is a giveaway to the overzealousness of his actions. His true intentions are to curse his neighbor. See McKane, 619; Green-stone, 287; Gemser, *Salomos*, 113; Toy, 487, who all defend the latter view.

25 Unlike McKane, 588, who takes this proverb to refer to a conflict in an individual. I must side with those who see it involving two parties (25:17, 18, 21) as does R. Scott, 154; Greenstone, 269; Toy, 467; Kidner, 45, 159.

26 Prov. 26:18–19. The true intentions of a practical joker who goes too far must come under close scrutiny here. They are likened more to deceit than to playfulness. See McKane, 602.

accusation into the open as a matter of public record. The stakes have been raised in his effort to harm his victim. If he is believed, his victim will not only be defamed but will also receive punishment. If his gamble fails and his false witness revealed, he will be scorned by the public and punished as a perjurer by the judge.

For this reason, Prov. 25:8—9 warns against testifying in court too hastily. Also, one must be careful not to allow revenge to enter into his testimony (Prov. 24:28—29). The consequences of false testimony in court are simply too tragic. The innocent are deprived of deserved justice; devastating harm is done, and dissension is inevitable (Isa. 29:21; Prov. 6:19; 14:25; 25:18). Thus, Prov. 3:30 (cf. Prov. 14:18) is unflinching in its stance against perjury, saying:

> Do not accuse a man for no reason —
> when he has done you no harm.

This straightforward rejection of perjury is deeply rooted in Jewish law. Besides being stated in principle as the ninth statute of the Decalogue (Ex. 20:16), Ex. 23:1 contains a warning not to "join hands with a wicked man to be a malicious witness." Deut. 19:16—19, in discussing the specific situation when a defendant has only one accuser, stipulates that if the testimony of that person is found to be false by the judge, then they "shall do to him just as he had intended to do to his brother." Prov. 19:5 (cf. Prov. 19:1; 21:28) is also certain that in one way or another "a false witness will not go unpunished."

Partiality

Judges have an awesome responsibility in deciding between the guilty and the innocent, as indicated by the reference above to Deut. 16. In order for their verdict to be just, they must be impartial in hearing the evidence. To this end they are advised in Deut. 1:17 (cf. Deut. 16:19—20): "Do not show partiality; hear both small and great alike."

Partiality, however, is not simply a concern for the courtroom judge. A witness, even to the most trivial matter of evidence in a case, must be careful that his testimony not be partial to one side or another lest it prejudice the case. Although not exactly perjury, the effect could be just as damaging. Ex. 23:2—3 warns against this when it says:

> Do not follow the crowd in doing wrong. When you give testimony in a lawsuit, do not pervert justice by siding with the crowd, and do not show favoritism to a poor man in his lawsuit[27].

---

27 This warning astutely observes that the common man must be warned against siding with his fellow against the rich when testifying in court because of the natural feelings of pity which are easily elicited on the poor man's behalf. See Cassuto, 297; Cole, 177; Childs, 481, for further comment. Note also the similar warning in Lev. 19:15.

Of course, a person must be just as careful not to be partial against the poor in his testimony, as emphasised by Ex. 23:6. Neither should one show partiality for or against any man in or out of court for God sets a standard of impartiality for people to follow (Deut. 24:17; 10:17—19). Yet, "King Lemuel's mother" is quite concerned that partiality is usually directed against the poor rather than for them. Thus, she advises her son:

> Speak up for those who cannot speak for themselves,
>   for the rights of those who are destitute.
> Speak up and judge fairly;
>   defend the rights of the poor and needy[28].

In this way, he will be giving support to the effort of God himself who "defends the cause of the fatherless and the widow and loves the alien, giving him food and clothes" (Deut. 10:18; cf. Ps. 41:1—3).

Reproof

Reproof in the Old Testament is generally viewed as something positive, although it is readily observed that some people do not like reproof well (Prov. 9:8—9; 15:12). Such are considered the worse off, whereas those who accept reproof graciously are considered to be the better off. As Prov. 10:17 (cf. Prov. 12:1; 13:18; 15:5, 10, 32) says:

> He who heeds discipline is on the path to life
>   but whoever ignores reproof goes astray[29].

Apt reproof is thought to be healthy. As Ps. 141:5 (cf. Prov. 25:12; 27:6; Eccl. 7:5) says, "Let a righteous man . . . rebuke me — it is oil on my head. My head will not refuse it."

Reproof is viewed as a source of wisdom (Prov. 1:20—25; 5:12; 15:31; 29:15). Those who accept it are thought to be wise and discerning. As Prov. 17:10 (cf. Prov. 19:25; 21:11) says:

> A reproof impresses a man of discernment
>   more than a hundred lashes a fool.

Reproof is not only encouraged in the Old Testament because of the long-range benefit for the recipient but also because it can be a valuable aid in curtailing sinful behaviour. Reproof also relieves the reprover of the guilt of condoning sin and perhaps even prevent him from harhouring sinful attitudes toward the recipient. As Lev. 19:17 says: "You must certainly reprove your neighbor, but be sure you do not incur sin because of him."

---

28   Prov. 31:8—9. Note also Prov. 14:31; 17:5.
29   Similar statements occur in Prov. 12:1; 13:18; 15:5, 10 ,32.

Apocrypha and Pseudepigrapha

The literature of the Apocrypha and the Pseudepigrapha betrays concern
for the promotion of peace and good-will in society. As Sir. 25:1 says:

> With three things I am delighted,
>   for they are pleasing to the Lord and to men;
> harmony among the brethren, friendship among neighbors,
>   and the mutual love of husband and wife.

The tongue can be a help or a deterrent to the goal of a peaceful society
and all too often is the latter. Speech-ethics is concerned with eliminating
from a person's habits as many of the harmful ways of speaking as
possible in order to contribute toward a peaceful society. These "speech
sins" fall basically into the same categories as in the Old Testament.

Gossip is categorically condemned (Sir. 28:12[30]). In an extensive treatment of this sin, Sir. 19:5—16 admonishes, "Never repeat what you hear! . . .
Have you heard a rumor? Let it die with you!" A person who has heard
gossip is encouraged to confront the friend or neighbor who is the subject
with the rumor to find out whether or not it is true, and even if it is true
to let the person know that he is being discussed. The odds are, though, as
vs. 15 suggests, that the rumor will be found to be maliciously untrue.
There are numerous warnings, too, about betraying the confidential word
of a friend because there is no more certain a way to lose a friendship
(Sir. 22:22; 27:16—21; 6:5—17). The only circumstance in which a person is
not to be silent about something he has heard, as Sir. 19:8 suggests, is if
doing so would somehow implicate him in sin as an accomplice.

Slander receives an absolute censure (Sir. 5:14; Wis. 1:11). According to 2
Enoch (A) 52:2, one who slanders his neighbor is accursed because by his
malicious words he slanders God as well[31]. In Aristeas 252, the king is
warned not to listen to slanderers if he desires to keep from error. Slander
can be extremely damaging. It was so devastating to Tobit that he pleaded
to God for death in order to escape its torture[32]. Slander is listed in Sir.

---

30 This passage goes on to describe just how destructive a "third tongue" (γλῶσσα τρίτη)
    can be in its ability to ruin lives, destroy cities, and rob virtuous women of their
    livelihood. Sir. 21:28 says that the "whisperer" (ὁ ψιθυρίζων) not only defiles himself
    but also is hated by his neighbor. Sib.Orac. 33:377 speaks of gossip as among the sins
    which will one day flee from men. Elsewhere, Sir. 41:23 includes gossip and betraying
    of secrets in a list of practices of which one should be "ashamed." Wis. 1:10–11 also
    warns against conveying gossip.

31 Ps.Sol. 12:4 requests that "the bones of slanderers be scattered [far] away from those
    who fear the Lord." 2 Enoch (A) 10:5–6 speaks of slander as one of the sins of those
    in "Hades."

32 Tob. 3:6. T.Jos. 1:7 mentions that Joseph was slandered. T.Gad 5:1 contends that such
    slander is caused by hatred, although T.Jud. 16:3 suggests that too much wine aids in
    lubricating the mouth toward this sin.

26:5 as one of the four things Ben Sira fears. Like gossip, it can destroy friendships (Sir. 28:9). If he can, a person is well-advised to stay away from a man of such evil (Sir. 11:31).

Mockery of those in less fortunate circumstances, which can take the form of reproach or simply abusive speech, is repudiated[33]. The embittered, the old, the poor, even the repentant sinner, are mentioned as being of particular concern to Ben Sira in this regard[34]. Mockery is viewed primarily as a sin of the arrogant and rich[35]. However, even the average man is counselled so "speak no reproachful words" to his neighbor, especially when the neighbor is merrily intoxicated (Sir. 31:31), nor to do so to his friend (Sir. 22:22; 41:22). Mockery hurts, as Tobit's wife Sarah became aware (Tob. 3:13; cf. Sir. 29:25). Thus, 2 Enoch (A) 44:1—2 calls for speech to be used in a positive way toward the less fortunate in society, saying:

> Blessed is the man who does not direct his heart with malice against any man, and helps the injured and condemned, and raises the broken down and shall do charity to the needy.

Cursing is an acceptable form of speech. However, because it uses the "Holy Name," like swearing, it must not be used to excess (Sir. 23:9—11). Uncontrolled and unwarranted cursing is probably one of the features of "boorish, filthy" speech, which is condemned as sinful in Sir. 23:12—15. God is always considered to be the final arbitrator of curses (Sir. 34:24). The curse from the ungodly man will be executed on himself (Sir. 21:27). If the abused poor man utters a curse, though, it is almost certain that "his Creator will hear his prayer[36]." So too, a mother's curse is considered to be extremely damaging (Sir. 3:9). In depicting God's sovereignty, Sir. 33:12 describes him as blessing some men and cursing others. However, one is warned never to curse the day of his own birth (Sir. 23:14).

Hot-tempered speech is inexcusable and must be controlled. It promotes disharmony and quarrelling, and quarrelling promotes bloodshed (Sir. 28:8—11; 27:15). The wrathful tongue can cause death (Sir. 29:19—21). Thus, Sir. 8:16 wisely counsels:

> Do not push a dispute with a quick–tempered man
> nor ride with him through the desert.

---

33 2 Enoch (A) 52:2, 4 considers such people, along with slanderers, to be condemned by God. See also 2 Enoch (A) 44:1. Sir. 23:15 expresses the view that a person who constantly uses abusive language is unteachable and will never really "grow up" (παιδευθῇ). Such a person is very far from the ideas of wisdom (Sir. 15:8).

34 In order, Sir. 7:11; 8:6; 10:22; 13:22—23; 8:5.

35 *Arrogant*: Sir. 27:15; 22:22; 10:6—18; *Rich*: Sir. 13:19—22.

36 Sir. 4:5—6. Similarly, Sir. 34:24 implies that the curse of the one abused (vs. 22) will be heard while the pious prayer of the abuser will not be heard. See *APOT*, 1:436.

For bloodshed is nothing to him.
And when there is no one to help, he will destroy you[37].

In contrast to such a man, 2 Enoch (B) 52:5 (cf. T.Gad 6:3) says, "Blessed is he who seeks peace."

Flattery and deceit are the tools of the wicked of which all honest men must be wary. As Sir. 12:16—17 warns:

With his lips an enemy speaks sweetly,
　but in his heart he schemes to knock you into a pit.
Though he may have tears in his eyes,
　when he gets the opportunity, he will not get enough of your blood[38].
If evil comes upon you, you will find him there before you;
　feigning to help, he will trip you up[39].

According to Sir. 13:4—7, the rich are especially notorious for flattery and deceit, although God clearly hates all such evil use of speech, as does Ben Sira[40]. According to 1 Esdras 3:3, deceivers are doomed to perish. Flattery is one of the temptations T.Reub. 3:1—6 describes Joseph as having to resist from Potiphar's wife. Happily, 2 Bar. 83:19 predicts that flattery and deceit will be replaced by "proof of the truth" in the end time.

Tactless and offensive speech is the trademark of the fool[41]. As Sir. 20:20 says:

A proverb from the mouth of a fool will be rejected
　for he does not offer it at the proper time.

It is also a give-away to a person's lack of culture[42]. It is not that the actual words spoken are foolish or ill-mannered but simply that the speaker has shown either a callous or perhaps naive insensitivity to the feelings and needs of those to whom he is speaking. As Sir. 22:6 puts it: "Like music in a time of mourning is inopportune narration." The wise and gracious man, however, is concerned more about others and less about hearing himself speak, and thus, he withholds his speech, particularly rebuke, for the most receptive moment (Sir. 20:1,5).

Perjury is a treacherous evil even more grievous than death. Sir. 26:5 says:

37　Similarly, Sir. 8:10 warns not to "kindle the coals of a sinner lest you be consumed in his flaming fire."
38　See also Sir 8:11; 11:32.
39　See Sir. 19:21–26; 27:22–27.
40　Sir. 27:24. See also Sir. 25:2, in which the deceitful rich are listed as one of the three kinds of people Ben Sira hates. T.Reub. 3:5 lists flattery and deceit as one of the Seven Spirits of error.
41　Sir. 27:13. Note that the NAB, though, takes the textual reading from the Latin manuscripts ("sinners") in opposition to Rahlfs, Ziegler, *APOT*, 1:406, NEB, and Sauer, who all take the textual reading of "fools" (μωρῶν).
42　Sir. 20:19. *APOT*, 1:386, takes the first line of this verse from the Syrian manuscripts. My understanding of it follows Rahlfs and Ziegler who take the reading from the Greek manuscripts.

> There are three things which disquiet my heart,
>   and a fourth which strikes me with fear —
> a false accusation by a city, a riotous assembly of citizens,
>   and false testimony — all are more wretched than death[43].

The feelings of distress expressed by this passage probably are very near to those experienced by Susanna in the Story of Susanna before she was saved by Daniel. Onias (2 Macc. 4:1) and Joseph (T.Jos. 8:4) are also depicted as the subjects of false testimony in this literature. Perjurers, however, are confidently condemned to death by 1 Enoch 95:6.

Partiality is a major impediment to justice in society and is the enemy of truth (1 Esdras 4:38—41). Those who are entrusted to mete out justice in society, especially judges and kings, must do everything in their power to avoid being partial in reaching decisions. They must especially be careful of being intimidated by men of power in their community (Sir. 7:6) and of abusing their own power (Aristeas 192, 215—216). If they "do not have the strength to root out injustice," then they should not be judges, according to Sir. 7:6. Yet, the task of preserving justice in society goes beyond the realm of appointed officials into the entire community. There, all men are requested to exert an effort to be impartial in their speech and conduct and to resist all efforts at intimidation[44]. All should seek to imitate God,

> For he is a judge
>   who shows no favoritism.
> He is not partial with respect to the poor,
>   but hears the cries of the oppressed[45].

Finally, "filthy" speech is raised as a type of speech to be avoided in Sir. 23:13. The context does not allow much expansion on this except to say it is related to being uncultured or ignorant.

Qumranic Literature

Qumranic literature displays avid concern about the negative and harmful ways in which people can speak to or about others, especially within their own community. Penalties for gossip, slander, insult, deception, and even tactless laughter are found in their penal code (1QS 6:24—7:25). Punishments for these violations range from thirty days of separation from the community for tactless laughter to something as severe as permanent

---

43 The exact sense of this verse is difficult to convey with precision and certainty. The second item in the list is most difficult to relate to the rest. However, when ὄχλος ("a throng of people," "riot") is taken negatively, it can be seen as a logical extension of the first item in the list.
44 Sir. 4:22. The Greek is μὴ ἐντραπῇς, which literally means, "Do not turn around!"
45 Sir. 35:12–13. See also Wis. 6:7.

separation for the unredeemable crime of gossiping and slandering against the community itself[46]. In their Sabbath restrictions, a man is warned not to chide or goad his slave, maidservant, or employee (CD 11:12). 1QS 4:9—11 lists among the characteristics of the spirit of falsehood in a person: deceit, evil ill-temper, and brazen insolence. Among the pledges of the truly committed community member is one to take no part in criminal deceit (perjury) or fraud[47].

In the above survey of the rules and regulations of the Qumran community, nearly all of the "speech sins" which occur in the Old Testament can be observed. Some of these but also others can be further observed as negative attributes of the community's enemies, i.e. those wretched leaders in Jerusalem. The Teacher of Righteousness describes how he had to endure their mockery, ridicule, slander, and gossip (1QH 2:11—15; 5:23—26). These enemies are further described as deceitful, their message "smooth," and their leader a mocker[48]. It is said that they habitually show partiality to their own wickedness by declaring the wicked righteous and the righteous wicked[49]. These men and others who work for Belial, as well as Belial himself, are the objects of regular, liturgical cursing by the Qumran community[50]. So too is the insincere and hypocritical initiate into the community (1QS 2:11—18). From such evil men, the dedicated members of the Qumran community are instructed to remain totally separate[51].

---

46 Slander and gossip against the community (1QS 7:16–18) are considered such serious violations because, as Leaney, 207–208, notes, the community regarded itself as holy. The crime, then, is not just relational. It is a violation of the sanctity of the people of God, the True Israel. It should also be noted that 11QTemple 64:6–7 prescribes that one who passes on information detrimental to his people to a foreign nation should be hung. Vermes, 55, and *DSSE*, 251, speaks of this as "slander." However, his translation is misleading and conflicts with that of Maier, who translates the vital phrase, "Wenn ein Mann Nachrichten über sein Volk weitergibt und er verrät sein Volk an ein fremdes Volk und fügt seinem Volk Böses zu . . ." Unfortunately, the Hebrew text is not available yet to resolve this conflict. However, in view of the context, it seems that Maier is probably correct, even though the passage appears to be vaguely based on Lev. 19:16.
47 1QS 10:22. Two different types of deceit or fraud appear to be in mind here. The first is described as כחש עֲיוֹר, or deceit deserving punishment which could include lying in court or perjury. The other is described as מרמות and appears to refer to deceit in general. Lying is also on the list.
48 4QpNah 2:4–6; 1QpHab 10:6–12; QH 4:7; 4Q184, 1:2; CD 1:14–15. The Kittim (Romans) are also typified as mockers and ridiculers of kings and princes in 1QpHab 4:1–3. In the final battle, with the Lord on their side, the Qumran community itself is pictured as mocking and scorning the mighty (1QM 12:7–10).
49 CD 1:19. In contrast, the men of holiness (the Sons of Zadok) "declare the just man and the wicked" (CD 4:7).
50 1QS 2:6–10; 1QM 13:4–6; 4Q280–282, 286–287 (Liturgical Curses, found in *DSSE*, 253).
51 1QS 5:1, 10, 15–16; 9:17; CD 6:14–15; 13:14–15. The only exception to this ban on contact with evil men is the purchase of food and goods. E. Sanders, 312–313, suggests that the

The Qumran community took the instruction in Lev. 19:17 about reproving one's neighbor and made it a working principle in their everyday lives. Reproof was not only taken seriously as a means of maintaining positive relationships between community members — by avoiding the display of built-up anger — but also as a practical way of policing members and maintaining judicial order[52]. This appears to expand the concept of reproof beyond what the Old Testament intended. Nevertheless, it must have had considerable impact, both positive and negative, on inter-human relationships in Qumran.

Rabbinic Literature

The story is told in LevR. 33:1 of a rabbi who prepared a feast for his disciples which quite intentionally consisted of tender tongues and hard tongues. As the disciples began to eat, each one selected the tender tongues rather than the hard ones. The rabbi then said to them, "As you selected the tender and left the hard so let your tongues be tender to one another!"

The rabbi desired their pupils, and all the people of Israel, to be peaceable and loving to one another. In Aboth 1:12, Hillel says, "Be of the disciples of Aaron, loving peace and pursuing peace, loving your fellow creatures, and drawing them near to the Torah[53]."

The recommendation of gracious and loving speech is one way in which the rabbis attempted to bring about peace in their society.

---

reason for this stress on separation in Qumran is that: 1) they applied to themselves as a community the ritual purity of priests, 2) they associated ritual purity with real, internal purity.

52 See the references to "reproof" in 1QS 5:25–6:1; CD 7:2–3; 9:3–8, 18. The Qumran community appears to have viewed "reproof" as an important pre-condition for the coming of the Messiah and therefore took great pains to "fulfill" it. See CD (B) 2(20):18–20 in light of Mal. 3:16–18. Reproof functions, then, as a means to making each one in the community wholly righteous and is integral to the community fulfilling its role as the True Israel. Regarding the judicial aspect of reproof in Qumran, Schiffman, 611, says: "Whereas the Rabbinic tradition understood this reproof to be a private matter—between men—there is further evidence of its judicial character at Qumran. Indeed, it seems to be parallel to the Rabbinic *hatra'ah* ('warning')." He then goes on to point out that the two main passages about reproof are in the midst of official judicial discussions. Although I agree that there appears to be a judicial, or formal, aspect to reproof in Qumran, it does seem that the literature supports the view that reproof was also viewed as a personal matter, albeit an obligation (CD 7:2–3). Note also comments by Wernberg-Möller, 100. On policing, see comments by Talmon, 279.

53 In commenting on this statement, ARNB 24 (pp. 146–147) encourages people to follow the example of Aaron and break up quarrels in the market place, etc. See also ARN 12 (pp. 64–65). In Aboth 1:18, peace is named as one of the three by which the world is sustained.

However, far more prevalent in Rabbinic literature are proscriptions against the many and varied ways in which people speak against one another and thereby disrupt the hope of a peaceful society.

Gossip is discouraged. B. Bathra 164b says it simply: "Keep away from tale-bearing!" Abod.Zar. 3b (cf. Hag. 12b) warns that the person who neglects study of the Torah for idle gossip "will be made to eat glowing coals of juniper." Aboth narrows the focus by advising the wary: "Do not talk too much with women[54]!" In a most vivid picture of gossip, ExR. 31:9 (cf. ExR. 1:30) chides, "If one dog barks, all others gather round and bark also for no purpose, but you must not be so, for you are holy." Rabbi Abaye wisely advises to disregard gossip if the subject of the gossip has no enemies and if he has enemies to be aware that it is they who probably disseminated the rumour (Pes. 113a).

Slander attracts the unanimous condemnation of the rabbis. In Pes. 118a, it is said: "Whoever relates slander and whoever accepts slander . . . against his neighbor, deserves to be cast to the dogs[55]." Slander is said to be "more vicious — than the transgressions which are called 'great': idolatry, adultery, and murder[56]." Slander is usually what the rabbis have in mind when they speak of the evil of the tongue[57], most notably its ability to kill three people in one thrust[58]. It is described in DeutR. 6:9 as a sin rooted in arrogance that ever proliferates its evil within a person. It is viewed as a sin that is extremely offensive to God himself which he punishes in this world by inflicting perpetrators with croup and leprosy and in the next by casting offenders into Gehinnon[59]. Slanderers are thought to be the reason for the departure of the Shechinah from the earth (DeutR. 5:10), the occurrence of plagues (DeutR. 6:8—10) and leprosy (LevR. 17:3), and the withholding of rain (DeutR. 5:10). The first slanderer was the serpent (who slandered God) whose tongue was cut off and feet severed in punishment

---

54 ARN 7 (pp. 47–48) and ARNB 16 (p. 110) construe this advice to refer to the inclination of women toward gossip. The view appears to be common for in Kid. 49b a rabbi says that while ten portions of gossip descended to the world at its inception, nine of these portions wer taken by women.

55 In EcclR. 5:5, Rabbi Huna applies that statement "Do not allow your mouth to make your flesh guilty!" to slanderers. A slanderer, it is thought in Nid. 61a, should not be believed. Elsewhere, it is stated that wise men should stay away from them. See Aboth 1:7; ARNB 16 (pp. 112–113); ARN 9 (pp. 54–55).

56 Mid.Ps. 12:2. See also Arak. 15b; Mid.Prov. 6 (#12, 28a).

57 GnR. 98:9; Arak. 15b–16b; Mid.Ps. 12:2.

58 Deut.R. 5:10; LevR. 26:2; NumR. 19:2; Arak. 15b.

59 In DeutR. 6:4 and Arak. 15b, slander is associated with a person who has denied God. In EcclR. 9:12 and J. Peah 16a, a slanderer is said to sin against heaven and earth. The slanderer is considered to be one of the four classes of people who will not appear before the presence of the Shechinah (San. 103a). On croup as punishment, see Shab. 33a; Sot. 35a. On leprosy, see Arak. 16a; NumR. 16:6. On Gehinnon, see GenR. 20:1.

in order to serve as an object lesson for eternity[60]. Another much used
illustrator of slander and its punishment is Miriam, who was made leprous
for slandering Moses[61].

The rabbis were avid defenders of the dignity of every man[62]. For
example, Aboth 4:3 records Ben *'Azzai* saying, "Despise no man!" and
Aboth 1:6 (cf. Aboth 2:5) advises in the name of another rabbi: "Judge
everyone with the scale weighted in his favour." Thus, mockery, insult, or
anything that comes under the category of publicly shaming a person was
considered by them to be strictly taboo[63]. In Aboth 3:15, Ben 'Azzai says
that the person who does anything like this "has no share in the world to
come[64]." To insult a fellow human being is to insult God in whose image
all are made[65]. One rabbi in B.Metzia 59a exhorts, "Better had a man
throw himself into a fiery furnace than publicly put his neighbor to
shame." Another compares it to murder, saying, "If a man puts his
neighbor to shame in public, it is as if he shed blood[66]. On the other hand,
those who receive an insult and hold their peace are highly commended as
acting quite admirably out of love[67].

Cursing is generally thought of as a common and expedient practice in
Rabbinic literature. The rabbis involve themselves in a considerable
amount of discussion regarding legitimate forms and occasions for

60 DeutR. 5:10; LevR. 26:2; NumR. 19:22. In ExR. 3:12, the serpent is used as an object
    lesson for Moses with regard to the punishment he received for slandering God by
    not believing what he said to him (Ex. 4:1). See also Ta'an. 8a. In DeutR. 6:14, Rabbi
    Simeon suggests that like the serpent slanderers will have their tongues cut off by
    God.
61 DeutR. 6:8–10 is the most expansive on this and even quotes Rabbi Judah ben Levi as
    saying, "The pious Miriam is a warning to all slanderers." Miriam comes up other
    places in this way. For example, see ARN 9 (pp. 54–55); NumR. 16:6.
62 Reines (cited as reprinted in Coreé), 394–402.
63 This includes mocking the misfortune of one's enemy (Aboth 4:24), as well as re-
    minding a repentant person of his former sinful deeds or of his non–Jewish ancestry
    (B.Metzia 4:10; 58b).
64 See also B.Metzia 58b, in which the person who publicly shames a fellow is listed
    among those who will descend into Gehenna but not reascend, and ARNB 35 (p. 210),
    which speaks of insulters and sneerers suffering the same fate as Korah and his
    congregation.
65 GenR. 24:7. San. 58b contains the view that slapping a fellow Jew was equivalent to
    slapping the face of the Shechinah. San. 99b contains the view that a person who has
    insulted his neighbor in the presence of a scholar has insulted the Torah. See also
    San. 103a and Sot. 42a, in which the scoffer is classed among those who will not
    appear before the Shechinah.
66 B.Metzia 58b. Following this, the comment is made by another rabbi who was
    obviously an astute observer of the physical effects on someone who feels shamed,
    saying, "You say well because I have seen it, for the ruddiness departs and paleness
    comes."
67 Shab. 88b; GenR. 24:7. In ExR. 30:19, encouragement is given to those whose lives have
    been subjected to shame by assuring them that this will not carry over to the world
    to come because God is "a consuming fire."

cursing [68]. These discussions themselves imply that the rabbis wish to impose some limitations on cursing. This is definitely true with regard to cursing someone by using the Divine Name. The penalty for this is flogging [69]. For cursing one's father or mother, the prescribed penalty is stoning [70]. A woman can be divorced for cursing her husband's parents (Ket. 72a). Further caution against viewing cursing as a wholly desirable form of speaking is stated by Rab Judah in the name of Rab in San. 48b—49a: "Thus, the people say, 'Let yourself be cursed rather curse another[71].' "

The person of hot-tempered speech finds himself thoroughly chastised by the rabbis. A person should be patient in his speech and not short-tempered (ARN 1, p. 7). He should be hard to anger and easy to appease (Aboth 5:14). The hot-tempered person is considered to be forgetful, foolish, hard to get along with, quarrelsome, and arrogant[72]. His life is pictured as miserable and thoroughly undesirable (Pes. 113b).

Flattery and deceit are linked together as the scourge of mankind. The person who deceives others by a veneer of smooth talk which covers over his wicked motives[73] is considered to be a principal culprit in the decline of the moral fabric of his community which will inevitably lead to its destruction [74]. Thus, it is said in Sot. 42a that "even the embryos in their mothers' wombs curse him" and that he "will fall into Gehinnom." It is also said (Sot. 42a) that a community which tolerates flattery in its midst "is as repulsive as a menstruant woman." The flatterer is classed among those whose sins are so repulsive to God that they are not allowed into the presence of the Shechinah[75]. Deceit is a form of thievery, in the view of one rabbi[76]; another rates it as idolatry (San. 92a). The rabbis are so concerned about the evils of flattery and deceit in Jewish society that the

---

68 For instance, see Sheb. 36a; San. 48b; 52a.
69 Kid. 71a; Tos. Mak. 5:10; Sheb. 35a. See Urbach, 130–131.
70 San. 7:4. There is some discussion among the rabbis as to the usage of precisely which names for God makes one culpable. See San. 7:8; Sheb. 4:13; 35a; 36a. See also Moore, 2:134.
71 See aso Sifre Deut. #250, 120a (*RA*, 498).
72 ARN 1, p. 7 (forgetful); Hul. 89a (foolish, quarrelsome); Aboth 4:2 (hard to get along with); ARN 7, p. 47 (arrogant).
73 Mid.Ps. 12:1; Pes. 113b; San. 105b. L. Jacobs, 235, cites a relevant quotation from Maimonides, *Hilkhot Deot* 2:6, which says, "A man should be sincere and mean what he says. He should never fool others by indulging in pretense . . . A man should always have true lips, a firm spirit and a heart free of all deceit and trickery."
74 Sot. 41b speaks of justice becoming perverted and conduct deteriorating because of flattery. Tos. Sot. 7:16, in the name of Rabbi Nathan, says that the Israelites became targets for destruction because they flattered Herod Agrippa. See further, Sot. 42a.
75 San. 103a; Sot. 42a; Pes. 113.
76 Tos. B.Kamma 7:8. In B.Metzia 58b, Rabbi Judah refers to a customer who feigns interest in a purchase to the owner when he has no money as being deceitful.

question of whether or not a bride who is lame or blind should be told she is beautiful is a matter of serious debate (Ket. 17a). One rabbi even discourages people from ever praising their fellows (Arak. 16a).

Perjury manifests the powerful potential of the tongue to inflict pain and even death on an undeserving member of society (LevR. 6:3). It is viewed not just as a crime against one's fellow man or society but as an injustice to God himself. In Pes.Rab. 21, God is represented as saying to the perjurer, "I shall hold it against you as though you bore witness against Me to the effect that I did not create My world in six days and did not rest on the seventh[77]." In the Mishnah, therefore, the punishment for perjury is fair but stiff. In general, the perjurer is to suffer the same penalty for which the accused was liable, including the death penalty (Mak. 1:1—10; San. 11:6). It is hoped, then, that a person in Jewish society will be very sure of himself before giving sworn testimony in court[78].

Partiality, particularly in the courtroom, is to be judiciously guarded against. The judge receives the following advice in Aboth 1:8, from Simeon ben Shetah:

> When parties in a lawsuit are standing before you, regard them both as guilty. But when they depart from your presence regard them both as innocent, since they both have accepted the verdict.

In commenting on this, both ARN 10 (pp.58—59) and ARNB 20 (pp. 129) warn against being partial toward the poor man or the rich man. In ExR. 30:24, the impartial judge is considered to have the Shechinah by his side, but if he issues a judgment "in respect of persons," the Shechinah leaves and reports this to God who draws His sword against him in order to demonstrate to the world that he himself is a just judge (cf. Aboth 5:11). God, then, is the avenger of partiality and the model for the impartial judge, a view for which Aboth 4:29 also contends. Jewish law in the Mishnah attempts to help the judge prevent partiality by disallowing kinsmen as witnesses (San. 3:4).

Rabbinic literature gives added impetus to the idea, also found in the Old Testament, of one person reproving another (Lev. 19:17). It is an obligation to reprove a neighbor who is seen to act unseemly (Arak. 16b), but unlike Qumranic Literature, it is not at all a judicial community-wide concern. Rather, as implied in the Old Testament, it is wholly personal. Even though a person is supposed to continue to reprove until the offender's behaviour is altered [Sifra 89a (*RA*, 467)], his reproofs are to be

---

77   From Braude, 1:443. See also J. Ber. 3c. Aboth 5:11 refers to the presence of wild beasts in the world as the punishment that has been inflicted upon the world for the practice of perjury.

78   Pes.Rab. 212 (Braude, 1:44).

conducted privately and in a modest attitude in order to avoid inflicting shame[79]. It is said that proper reproof leads to love and it itself an aspect of love, that it leads to peace and is an aspect of peace[80]. A person who successfully submits to rebuke is said to merit blessing (DeutR. 1:9). The inability to give and receive reproof beneficially is considered to be a sad commentary on any community in any generation[81]. Thus, the rabbis promote loving reproof as an important practice which benefits the individuals concerned as well as society as a whole.

A close scrutiny of Rabbinic literature reveals the presence of a kind of speech taboo which has not been so explicitly expressed in previous literature. This prohibition pertains to lewd, sexual, or otherwise obscene speech. In Shab. 33a, Rabbi Hana ben Raba says:

> All know for what purpose a bride enters the bridal canopy, yet whoever speaks obscenely of it, even if a sentence of seventy years of happiness had been sealed for him, it is reversed for evil[82].

Rather than speak in this way, as the school of Rabbi Ishmael taught (Pes. 3a), "One should always discourse in decent language."

Graeco-Roman Literature

The ambitious literary efforts of the Graeco-Roman philosophers were uniformly directed toward understanding people and thereby motivating individuals to be virtuous, happy, responsible, well-adjusted, and well-integrated citizens of their communities, these communities forming segments of the ideal society. Speech-ethics is necessarily an important factor in the realisation of such a model world. The destructive power of uncontrolled tongues is a primary barrier to it, however, overshadowing the beneficial capabilities of appropriate, gracious, friendly speech which are indispensable to bring such a world about and to provide the proper climate for its functioning. This positive potential of speech, as Plutarch puts it in *Mor.* 6:504e, "which is the most pleasant and human of social

---

79 Sifra 89a–89b; Arak. 16b; Menach. 99a.
80 GenR. 64:3. In Arak. 16b and Sifra 89a–89b, Rabbi Johanan ben Nuri is cited as testifying that he reproved Akiba often for which he received Akiba's love. See also Aboth 6:6, which lists receiving reproof lovingly as one of the 48 ways of acquiring Torah.
81 Sifra 89a–89b; Arak. 16b; Shab. 49b; Sifre Deut. #1, 64a. In Shab. 119b, it is one rabbi's opinion that Jerusalem was destroyed because the people did not rebuke one another.
82 See further comment in Shab. 33a. In Meg. 25b, it is noted that when reading Scripture, indelicate expressions are to be substituted with more polite ones. ARN 28 (p. 117) and ARNB 31 (p. 184) may also have unseemliness in mind.

ties" is far too often "made inhuman and unsocial by those who use it badly and wantonly."

The vision for a peaceful society, however, cannot be held apart from the hope of society in which there are people holding pleasant and harmonious conversation with one another[83]. Quite early in Greek literature one may read Theognis, which calls upon Apollo to bring this about[84]. But later, one finds in Epictetus the following poignant specification which is a good representative of Graeco-Roman literature and which offers a fine program for speech-ethics in inter-human relationships. He says in IV,5:1—2, "The good and excellent man neither contends [μάχομαι] with anyone, nor, as far as he has the power does he allow others to contend."

Contentious and harmful speech manifests itself in a multitude of ways, and there is a wealth of material in Graeco-Roman literature to counteract as well as to warn against them. Before surveying this material, however, it would be advantageous to look separately at Aristotle's original contribution to this area of thought which is so tightly intertwined with his own peculiar perspective on ethics.

Essentially, Aristotle contends that in ethical behaviour people should choose to strive for hitting the "mean" or "middle," which alone is virtuous, and avoid the "excesses" or "extremes." The general theory is described in his *Nicomachean Ethics*, especially in II,6:1—10. In II,7:1—9:9, he sketches out how this works, defining the means and extremes for various virtues. In 7:11—13, he comes to the three which are most relevant here. These are three virtues which "have to do with intercourse in conversation and actions," he says. They are "truthfulness," "pleasantness in social amusement," and "general pleasantness in life." For the first, truthfulness is the mean, boastfulness one extreme and mock modesty the opposite extreme. For the second, the mean is to be ready-witted, the excess buffoonery, and the extreme deficiency, boorishness. For the third, the mean is friendliness. The excess is obsequiousness if of innocent motive, flattery if of harmful motive. The deficiency is quarrelsomeness or surliness. He continually emphasises that only the mean is praiseworthy but both extremes are blameworthy, or for our purposes classified as unacceptable speech. He discusses each of these in more detail in IV,6:1—8:12, where, in addition to the categories of inappropriate speech upon which he has already touched, he deals with joking, ridicule, obscene speech, tactful speech, and lying. He also puts anger into a scheme in II,7:10 and develops it in IV,5:1—15.

---

83   Plato, *Laws*, 628c; *Laws* 689d; Epict. III,13:11–13.
84   Theog. 759–764. Cic., *Fin.* 1:43, on the other hand, thinks only wisdom can enable people to live in peace.

Remarkably, in Aristotle's approach, he has managed to put into the development of just three means nearly all the categories of speech which receive disapproval from the innumerable pages of Graeco-Roman literature. To these we must now proceed.

Gossip in Graeco-Roman literature is most often discussed within the concerns about chatterers and babblers. Such people are notorious for idle speech, betrayal of secrets, and social chit-chat. As might be expected, these practices and people are summarily condemned by Plutarch in *De gar.*, but Epictetus too expresses himself frankly on this. In Ench. 33:2, he says,

> Do not talk about gladiators, or horse–races, or athletes, or things to eat or drink — topics that arise on all occasions; but above all, do not talk about people, either blaming, or praising, or comparing them[85].

He is not alone in advising people to avoid such conversation and those who relish it[86]. Although social chit-chat may begin innocently enough, Plutarch, in *Mor.* 6:503d, shrewdly describes one of the problems with it, especially if a "chatterer" is in the midst:

> For as wheat shut up in a jar is found to have increased in quantity but to have deteriorated in quality, likewise when a story finds its way to a chatterer, it generates a large addition of falsehood and thereby destroys its credit.

In *Mor.* 6:506f—507b, Plutarch (cf. Epict. IV, 1:133—134) speaks similarly of the fate of the carelessly guarded secret entrusted to someone by his friends. Once betrayed to even one other friend, "the story goes on increasing and multiplying by link after link of incontinent betrayal." In this context, Plutarch speaks of words as winged and of gossip as a spreading fire. He relates numerous stories of how gossip and betrayed secrets caused the destruction of cities, the maintenance of despots on their thrones, and even the death of a woman and her husband. In the end, he categorically labels babblers as traitors (cf. *Mor.* 6:505b—d, 508c, 510c—d). He considers barbers (*Mor.* 6:509a—c) and women (*Mor.* 507c—508c) the worst gossips and perceptively makes the diagnosis that gossips are inquisitive folk in search of stories to tell to anyone who will listen, foolishly thinking that this reveals their wisdom (Plutarch, *Mor.* 6:508c, 519d).

Gossip is bad enough in itself, but in the eyes of many Graeco-Roman writers it can degenerate into something even worse — slander. Menander 577k says, "There is nothing more distressing than slander for you yourself must take as your fault the wrong inherent in another." Isocrates, *Antid.* 18— 19, condemns slander and its concomitant evil in greater detail:

---

85 Epictetus speaks similarly in III,16:1–6. See also IV,3:2.
86 See also Hesiod, *Works* 760–764; Theog. 113–114.

I do not wonder that men . . . complain that slander [διαβολή] is the greatest evil.
What, indeed, could work more mischief? It causes liars to be looked on with respect,
innocent men to be regarded as criminals, and judges to violate their oaths. In a word,
it smothers truth, and in pouring false ideas into our ears, it leaves no man among our
citizens secure from an unjust death.

Although slander is not so vividly branded as evil by all Graeco-Roman
writers, there is a common presumption that it is inappropriate[87]. In
addition, there is advice not to listen to slander in any serious way[88], as
well as fervid condemnation of the so-called "friend" who slanders his
friend[89]. Hesiod on the topic of slander reveals some rather ignoble views.
He limits his condemnation of slander to "good men," warns against
speaking evil of another because "you yourself will soon be worse spoken
of," and advises people who have been "wronged first" in word or deed to
be sure to repay the offender "double[90]."

Despite the fact that shame and public opinion figure prominently in
moral sanctions for many Greek writers, particularly the earlier ones
(Adkins, *Merit*, 48, 154—168), this in no way is thought to open the door to
random insult, mockery, and scorn. Taunting people because disaster has
befallen them, mocking them for their unpretentious positions in society,
or ridiculing them for their unfortunate but natural bodily characteristics,
represent many such acts which receive harsh criticism from as early as
Hesiod on down to Plutarch[91]. Isocrates, *To Dem.* 29, perhaps formulates
the general principle best: "Taunt no man for his misfortune for fate is
common to all and the future is a thing unseen."

In support of Hesiod's censure of verbal abuse toward orphans or one's
own aged father (*Works* 320—324), Plutarch, *Mor.* 15:46, asserts that
fathers "are images of the universal father, Zeus; and those who do not
respect the images of the gods show their disrespect for the very gods
whose images they are[92]." People who are the objects of insult or ridicule
receive similar advice, at least from the pens of Seneca, Epictetus, and
Plutarch which can be condensed into: Bear it with gentleness, be secure in
yourself, and in effect receive no insult at all[93].

---

87   For example, Lysias 35:6; Epict. IV,5:31–32; Dio Chrys. 32:19.
88   For example, Theog. 323–324; Men. 577k.
89   For example, Theog. 93–100; Epict. II,10:12–14.
90   Hesiod, *Works*, 715–716, 719–721, 707–711. See also Theog. 363–364.
91   Hesiod, *Works* 330–334 (orphans and fathers); 717–718 (poor); Dem. 18:192; 20:16; 22:62;
     57:30; Eur. fr. 130; Epict. I,26:13–15; Plut., *Mor.* 1:35c–d; #15:88. Slaves were often the
     object of verbal as well as physical abuse for laughs in Greek poetry. Aristophanes
     criticises this practice in *Peace* 743–747 but elsewhere does it himself, in
     Birds 1323–1329 and in *Lysistrata* 1216–1224.
92   Plato, *Laws* 931a, also compares parents to gods.
93   Sen., *Const.* (*ME*) 2:1–3; 3:2; 12:3; 13:5; *De ira* (*ME*) III,43:1–5; Epict., *Ench.* 42; Plut.,
     Mor. 1:35d.

Tactless speech is related to mockery and ridicule in that regardless of how it was intended, it may be taken as mockery and ridicule. It is a joke, a song, or laughter at the most inappropriate moment[94]. Plutarch says, "There are times when we are more aroused by jokes than by insults," and "The man who cannot engage in joking at a suitable time, discreetly and skillfully, must avoid jokes altogether[95]." Perhaps for similar reasons, Epictetus (*Ench.* 33:5; cf. 33:10,15—16) recommends as a general rule, "Do not laugh much, nor at many things, nor boisterously." The basic principle receives wise scrutiny as early as Theog. 1217—1218, which says, "Never let us laugh in the joy of our good fortune, Cyrnus, when we sit beside a mourner."

To say that in Graeco-Roman literature there is opposition to using speech intentionally or unintentionally for abusive purposes is not to say that speech is considered inappropriate altogether for criticising another person's behaviour. On the contrary, such courageous use of speech is seen as one of its divine purposes by Xenophon and Menander (Xen., *EG.* 8:13; Men. 543k). However, according to Plutarch and Epictetus, this use of speech must be applied with appropriateness, great skill, and kindness[96]. Even joking can be beneficial when applied in this manner in Plutarch's view *(Mor.* 8:532d, 633e, 633f). Indeed, frankness in speech is considered the most reliable mark of true friendship, not only to Plutarch who discusses it in antithesis to flattery (*Mor.* 1:59b) but also by Isocrates (*To Antipater* 4—6).

Plutarch, in his very thorough analysis in *Quo. adul.*, says that a true friend feels free to admonish in order to eliminate error and to foster soundness and maturity in his fellow. He will of necessity use words that sting occasionally, but he will not ridicule nor publicly shame, be condescending, or arrogant. Sometimes, he may not even use words if he is really a close friend. Neither do true friends stop at just rebuke but as Plutarch concludes in *Mor.* 1:74e, "by further converse and gentle words they mollify and assuage, even as stone-cutters smooth and polish the portions of statues that have been previously hammered and chiselled." Such forthright rebuke, when combined judiciously with praise, is considered by Plutarch to be necessary for a child's education to be wholesome, by Dio Chrysostom as a blessing in a community, and by

---

94 Epict. IV,12:17, advises, "We must remember what is the proper time for song . . . for play . . . when to jest . . . when to laugh . . ."

95 Plut., *Mor.* 8:632d, 631c. In 8:631e, he compares jokes to barbed arrows. Plutarch devotes an entire section to the positive and negative benefits of joking in 8:631c—634f. Aristotle, in *EN* IV,8:1–12 (1128a1–1128b9), in his expanded discussion of wittiness and buffoonery involves himself in carefully determining what is proper and what is improper joking.

96 Plut., *Mor.* 1:66b; 2:102b; 6:461e, 464c; 7:547a; 8:632e; Epict. II,10:9; *Ench.* 45.

Diodorus Siculus as a requirement for a society desirous to grow in virtue[97].

Plutarch, as mentioned above, devotes an entire essay (*Quo. adul.*, *Mor.* 1:48e—74e) to help a person identify the true friend from the mere flatterer, and thus, to enable him to discount the flatterer's praises, his rebukes, or anything he may say in order to gain intimacy. Plutarch considers flatterers the veritable scum of the earth and flattery the worst possible abuse of the privilege of speech. This is evident in that he pens such a lengthy essay to combat this mischievous evil, but it is also manifest in his opening remarks of the essay (*Mor.* 1:49a—b), which states:

> Now if Truth is a thing divine . . . then the flatterer is in all likelihood an enemy to the gods and particularly to the Pythian god. For the flatterer always takes a position over against the maxim "Know thyself" by creating in every man deception towards himself and ignorance both of himself and of the good and evil that concerns himself; the good he renders defective and incomplete, and the evil wholly impossible to amend.

In Plutarch's essay *De educ.* (cf. *Mor.* 7:528c—533c), he displays his outrage at flatterers who prey on young men like "parasites" and turn them against their parents and all sense of virtuous living. He considers them totally dishonest, detestable, "bastard members of the human race" (*Mor.* 1:5b, 13b). But in *Quo. adul.*, he most thoroughly describes their tactics of trying to imitate friendship while hiding their true motives. This even includes attempting to feign frankness. However, the wary person should be able to spot a flatterer by his overt attempts to be agreeable to whatever his victim wishes, by his dislike and intolerance of real friends, by his use of many words, by his defensive oaths to prove his loyalty, and by his fondness for the emotional and irrational. His frankness will not be about actual faults. Plutarch warns the attentive person to be on guard against the flatterers too for they are likewise false.

Unfortunately, too many people are susceptible to the wiles of the flatterer. Aristotle, in *EN* X,3:11 (1174a,33) explains that this is,

> because they love honour, [and] seem to be more desirous of receiving than of bestowing affection. Hence, most men like flattery for a flatterer is a friend who is your inferior, or pretends to be so, and to love you more than you love him.

Isocrates, that master teacher of oratory, in his vast experience, observed that this principle is not only true of individuals but of crowds too. In *Antid.* 133 (cf. Dio Chrys. 32:7,11; 33:13), he writes:

> You observe the nature of the multitude, how susceptible they are to flattery, that they like those who cultivate their favour better than those who seek their good.

However, he is totally opposed to his pupils exploiting this feature of crowds. But many orators did exploit crowds in just this way, spurring

---

97 Plut., *Mor.* 1:9a; Dio Chrys. 32:7, 11; 33:13; Diod.S. 15:1.

Plato in *Gorgias* 462c—463a to label rhetoric "a branch of flattery." The ardent opposition to the kind of rhetoric which merely seeks to entertain and manipulate and the association of it with deceit and flattery by such men as Plato, Thucydides, Seneca, and Plutarch has been commented upon previously.   Plutarch's characterisation of flamboyant rhetoric as flattery should be compared with his depiction of poetry in *Quo. poetas* (*Mor.* 1:16a—c) as deceitful.

Plutarch's concern about the devastating harm that false friends do to individuals through their flattery and deceit certainly produces the most thorough analysis of the subject in Graeco-Roman literature, but it is by no means a new concern with him. Theognis long before evidenced concern about deceitful friends, observing in line 1220 how easy it is "for a friend to deceive a friend" and in lines 119—128 how deceit is one of "the most difficult of all things to discover." In this same light, Xenophon, *Anab.* VII,6:21, regards it as more shameful do deceive a friend than to be deceived by one. In a somewhat different but familiar vein, Hesiod, *Works* 373—375, warns against allowing "a flaunting woman to coax and cozen and deceive you: she is after your barn." Even back as far as Homer, Penelope's deception of her suitors is thought by them to be "undue" (*Od.* 2:122—125).

Partiality and perjury in court are both decried in Graeco-Roman literature. Regarding partiality, the early Athenian jurors took an oath to give "impartial hearing to prosecution and defendant alike" and to decide a verdict "strictly on the charge named in prosecution[98]." Indeed, the death penalty was prescribed for a person who accepted a bribe while acting as a juror (Aiskhines 1:87f). Plato, *Laws* 659a, speaks of judges of music contests taking oaths to fidelity, and he says that "the true judge should not take his verdict from the dictation of the audience, nor yield weakly to the uproar of the crowd . . ." Perjury is on Cicero's list (*Fin.* 2:46) of things which people who love the truth should hate. Demosthenes (48:52) regards perjury not just as a sin against the accused but as a sin "against the gods in whose name he swore[99].

Cursing another is a generally acceptable practice, especially for a good reason like deceitfully betraying a friendship, as Theog. 595—602 illustrates. Curses could also be pronounced as a formal procedure against political corruption, perjury, and treasonable activities (See Dover, 251).

---

98 Dem. (*Prosecution of Timocrates*) 24:150–151. Adkins, *Values*, 120–121, notes that the early Greek court had no professional judges or lawyers, just peers.

99 Dover, 249, in commenting on this notes that the utterance of the oath by the witness is thought to bring the gods in as witnesses to his truthfulness. Thus, the gods are thought to be offended when the oath is breached by false testimony.

Once uttered, curses were considered to be in the hands of the gods[100]. For this reason, as early as Theognis, a note of caution can be detected in Graeco-Roman literature that continues down to Plutarch. Theog. 399—400 enjoins a person to "shun [the utterance of] man-destroying oaths." Plato (*Laws* 854c, 931c), even though he thinks that a person can be absolved of a curse upon himself by going to "a curse-lifting deity," does not believe this can be done with regard to the curses of parents on their disrespectful and thereby deserving children. Thus, he wards fathers not to ask the gods to grant all their prayers or else their now-regretted, hot-tempered "prayers of passion" against their sons just might be honoured (*Laws* 687e). Likewise, the fathers should ask the gods to disregard the foolish prayers of their sons (Plato, *Laws* 688d). But children, too, ought to be aware that there is a god, Nemesis, who is on the lookout for their disrespectful words uttered against their parents which are "winged" (Plato, *Laws* 717d).

Menander, in 715k, regarded such "reviling words" against one's own father as a rehearsal for the ultimate evil of "blasphemy against divinity." In his ideal society, Plato wishes to ban imprecatory oaths in court as well as cursing in general, so much does he believe in their destructive power (Plato, *Laws* 949b, 934e). Seneca (*EM* 110:2) too wishes to eliminate cursing, not so much for the same reasons as Plato but because he believes it is totally unnecessary since the gods are already hostile toward a person so despicable as to deserve one. Again, however, he does not doubt their power, but he regards it as a regrettable evil toward future generations, especially with respect to curses of parents on their children (Sen., *EM* 60:1). Plutarch, in *Questiones Romanae* 44 (*Mor.* 4:275a) wonders whether a curse isn't "an ill-omened and gloomy thing" in order to explain why the priest of Jupiter takes no oath.

The acute censure of hot-tempered speech in Graeco-Roman literature was discussed previously. From the above survey of cursing, a connection can also now be detected between the two: anger and hot-tempered speech may lead to curses that are bitterly regretted. Although Plutarch appears to desire a complete shut-down of anger within the individual and thus labels "righteous indignation" as an attempt to rationalise misconduct (*Mor.* 6: 462e), Aristotle does not quite agree. A person is not to blame merely for being angry but for being angry in a certain way. The key to anger is to control it so that one displays his anger "to the right amount, at the right time, for the right purpose, and in the right way[101]." Seneca, *De ira* III,5:1—2, to a certain extent agrees in that he writes that "no man can consider himself safe from anger." He believes, however, that others can

---

100 Theog. 399–400, 595–602; Plato, *Laws* 687c, 931c, for example.
101 Arist., *EN* II,9:2 (1109a28–30). See also II,5:3 (1106a2); IV,5:8 (1126a14).

go a long way toward helping a person be cured from this harmful trait if they will "challenge him with kindness" when he goes on the offensive. "Animosity," he says, "if abandoned by one side, dies forthwith; it takes two to make a fight[102]."

Disapproval of vulgar and obscene speech is also present in Graeco-Roman literature. Epictetus, *Ench*. 33:15—16, warns against getting involved in raucous laughter because it can easily lead to vulgarities (Diog.L. 7:59) and obscenities. In fact, one ought to evidence his disapproval if he is nearby on such occasions by reproving the offender, or at least by blushing or frowning. Aristotle, *EN* IV,8:5—9 (1123a15—30), agrees that such talk is not in character for "a virtuous man and a gentleman." He considers it a great advance that "modern" dramatists prefer innuendo over obscenity to arouse laughter in their audiences.

Although boasting will be discussed in Part IV in conjunction with blasphemy in surveying the Jewish and Christian literature, it must be dealt with here in surveying Graeco-Roman literature. This is because the objections that are raised to it give no evidence that it was considered an offense against the gods. Boasting is simply considered bad form in personal relationships, a breach of social standards, or a blot on one's personal character. Demosthenes believes that a properly educated man will not be boastful, and Xenophon considers it a roadblock to wisdom[103]. Aristotle, even though he associates boasting with lying, considers the boaster more foolish than vicious[104]. Isocrates (*To Dem*. 30; cf. Theog. 159—160) simply advises, "Be affable in your relations with those who approach you and never haughty." Epictetus counsels against talking at great length about oneself because it is not pleasant for others. However, he also considers the person who "says nothing about himself" as displaying a principal sign of "making progress" but the reverse being true for the person who is "vain-glorious[105]." Plutarch thinks that "praise of oneself always involves dispraise from others . . . vainglory always has an inglorious end." He (*Mor*. 7:547f, 547e) also shows his abhorrence for the person who interjects self-praise when reproving another because it unduly disgraces and humiliates. Finally, there is a common feeling among Graeco-Roman writers, represented by Diodorus Siculus, that the boaster sooner or later will fall from his vain-glorious self-praise to humiliation[106].

---

102 Sen., *De ira* II,34:5. See also II,43:1–5.
103 See Dem. 18:128; 19:167; Xen., *Mem*., IV,2:1–40.
104 Arist., *EN* IV,7:10–13 (1127b10–24). See also Men. 737k, which says, "Every fool is caught by boasting and empty noise."
105 Epict., *Ench*. 33:14; 48:1–3; III,2:14–15; Frag. 21 (Loeb, 2:465; Stob. III,7:16).
106 Diod.S. 15:16. See also Theog. 159–160.

Philonic Literature

In *Dec*. 178, Philo calls God "the Prince of Peace," God's ambition being to bring "the good things of peace, all of them to all persons in every place and at every time." Philo's (*Abr*. 27) ideal man of virtue and wisdom is a man of peace who, as opposed to the worthless man, has carved out a life which is "calm, serene, tranquil and peaceful to boot." While Philo (*Abr*. 20—23) does primarily have in mind here a life of contemplation based on withdrawal from society, he does not neglect the important facet of societal relationships within his notion of peace (*Mut*. 240).

Speech is one of God's best gifts for the benefit of oneself and others in society (*Spec*. 1:342—343; *Som*. 1:102—104). However, it can only function in these positive ways if a person in sincere piety dedicates to God not only his speech but his soul and his senses as well. Such a person acknowledges that "through Him come the activities of each, the reflections of the mind, the language in which speech expresses itself, and the impressions that are made on sense[107]." Anyone who asserts personal ownership of these three faculties will find his life controlled by passions, resulting in his speech being utterly harmful and sinful. The latter is the condition in which most people in society find themselves, according to Philo (*Mut*. 49—50). Thus, he takes a considerable portion of space in his writings to describe and condemn what we have termed speech sins.

Philo's catalogue of speech sins is not remarkably distinctive from what has been encountered in previous literature, and he does not tend to say much about them when they arise in his writing. Both of these two points perhaps are illustrated best by a long section (*Sac*. 19—34) in which Philo personifies pleasure as a harlot to seduce the naive victim by her charms. At one point in the narrative, par. 22, he lists a sample of "her closest friends" who follow in her train. Among those listed are: flattery, deceit, falsehood, perjury, and injustice. The narrative continues on after this, but just before the seduction appears completed, another steps out. The other is said to have kept hidden so far, "yet within earshot[108]." But she must now speak "lest the Mind should unawares be made captive and enslaved." In antithesis to Pleasure, this woman appears free-born, "her movement quiet, her clothing plain, her adornment that of good sense and virtue." Some of those in her company are: piety, holiness, truth, justice, fidelity to oaths, sensitive social intercourse[109], a quiet temper, kindness, gentleness, and

---

107 *Her*. 108. The whole section, par. 107-110, informs the discussion which follows.

108 This occurs at *Sac*. 26. Although he does not identify Pleasure's alter-ego here as anything but "the other," Philo presumably has in mind Virtue. See *Sac*. 16.

109 The idea represented by the two words εὐσυνθεσία ("a good arrangement of words") and κοινωνία ("communion," "intercourse") is difficult to render. Colson and Whit-

meekness. She has come to warn against becoming a lover of Pleasure. She says that a lover of Pleasure will also become many other things which Pleasure has conveniently failed to mention. There follows a list of 150 items which cover pars. 32—33. Those that pertain to speech are: a babbler, untimely prating, windy-worded, slanderous, a scoffer, cross-tempered, violent tempered, quick to wrath, quarrelsome, a flatterer, deceitful, double-minded, double-tongued, a buffoon, a braggart, vain-glorious, stiff-necked, impious, profane, coarse, and impatient of rebuke.

There are some much briefer groupings of speech sins in Philo. Lying, perjury, and slander are listed in *Mut*. 240 as primary examples of "sinfulness of word." In *Flacc*. 33—34, the Alexandrian mob is charac-terised as consisting of those who are "well practiced in gossip, who devote their leisure to slander and evil speaking." He goes on to describe the jeers and insults they hurled at King Herod when he visited Alexandria. In *Leg*. 162—163, he further depicts them as "adepts at flattery." Philo (*Conf*. 48) describes the wicked man as:

> hand and glove with pretentious flattery, at open war with genuine friendship, an enemy to truth, a defender of falsehood, slow to help, quick to harm, ever forward to slander, backward to champion the accused, skilful to cozen, false to his oath, faithless to his promise, a slave to anger, a thrall to pleasure, protector of the bad and corrupter of the good.

Although Philo says very little further about any of the speech sins mentioned, he does have brief insights on some of them. With regard to gossip, he notes that rumours travel fast and are usually false (*Jos*. 246; *Leg*. 18; *Praem*. 148). He suggests that the flesh of a person's sin offering is not to be carried outside the temple because of its potential for fueling malicious gossip (*Spec*. 1:241). Philo identifies a number of people as slanderers: Flaccus and Capito against the Jews, Gaius against Macro, and the common one from Jewish tradition of Miriam slandering Moses[110]. On mockery[111], Philo himself appears to have experienced this as an envoy to Rome on behalf of the Alexandrian Jews. He seems to be keenly aware that the Jews as a people were common subjects of ridicule, and he speaks out against this. In the realm of biblical interpretation, he thinks Ham's sin was that he ridiculed the drunken Noah. He also depicts as sinful the mocking of a deaf-mute, which appears as cursing such a person in Lev. 19:14, as well as gloating against a fallen enemy. Philo's ideas about angry speech have been noted previously. Philo considers flattery diseased

---

aker use "fellow–feeling" which is not entirely satisfactory, so I have made my own attempt. It should be kept in mind that there is the possibility that the two words are meant to be taken separately which complicates things even further.

110 In order, see *Flacc*. 86; *Leg*. 199; *Leg*. 57; L.A. 3:66–67.
111 With regard to mockery, see in order: *Leg*. 368; *Dec*. 1–3; *Praem*. 169–171; *Sob*. 6; *Spec*. 4:197; *Flacc*. 121–147.

friendship and deceit utterly ignoble[112]. Flattery is a product of desire. The wise man will keep his distance from flatterers and their counterfeit adulation. He will especially beware of flattering women, even his own wife. Frank admonition[113] is the byword of statesmen and parents and should be accepted graciously. Only the arrogant take it as an insult. On the other hand, malicious joking is thought by Philo to be an aid to slander (*Leg*. 171). To potential perjurers[114], Philo utters harsh condemnation based on the commandment in the Decalogue against false witness. He describes the various nuances of their dastardly sin, which is ultimately an offence against God in whose name they took an oath as a witness in court. Further, he categorises as a lunatic the person who on the basis of comradeship would accept his friend's request to transgress the law and offend God by lying for him in court. Anyone who knows of another's perjury and does not turn him in is considered just as guilty as the perjurer himself. Philo is just as firm in pressing for impartiality, basing his advice to them on Mosaic law (*Spec*. 4:43, 59, 62, 70–72). The judge is to be the steward of God's just judgment, which is of course always fair and impartial. Finally, it should be noted that Philo bans women from the utterance or the hearing of obscenities (*Spec*. 3:174).

New Testament

One of the outstanding messages of the New Testament, recurring throughout, is that people should relate harmoniously with one another. Admonitions toward peace, love, and forgiveness abound. The direction to "live in peace with one another" occurs on Jesus' lips in Mk. 9:50 and recurs almost verbatim three times in Paul's letters[115]. Different phrasings of the same sentiment are at every turn[116]. The situation with "Love your neighbor!" and "Love one another!" is the same[117]. Jesus' memorable teaching on sincere and repeated forgiveness of one's brother, although more confined to the Gospels, is still highly significant in the New

---

112   On flattery and deceit, see in order: *L.A.* 3:182; *Prob.* 155; *Abr.* 126; *Op.* 165; *Leg.* 39.
113   On frankness and admonition, see in order: *Jos.* 42; *Spec.* 2:241,18; *Mig.* 115; *Som.* 2:81–92.
114   On perjury, see *Dec.* 86–91, 138–141, 172; *Spec.* 2:26–28; 4:40–42.
115   1 Thes. 5:13 (εἰρηνεύετε ἐν αὐτοῖς); Rom. 12:18 (μετὰ πάντων ἀνθρώπων εἰρηνεύοντες); 2 Cor. 13:11 (εἰρηνεύετε).
116   For instance, Mt. 5:9, 23–26 (Lk. 12:57–59); Rom. 14:19; 15:6; Eph. 4:2–3; Tit. 3:2; 1 Pet. 3:11.
117   Love your neighbor: Mt. 22:38–39 (Mk. 12:32; Lk. 10:26); Rom. 13:9; Phil. 2:2–4. Love one another: Jn. 13:34–35; 15:9–17; Gal. 5:13–15; 1 Thes. 4:9–10; Eph. 4:2–3; Col. 2:1–2; Heb. 10:24; 13:1; 1 Pet. 1:22; 2:17; 3:8; 4:8; 2 Pet. 1:7; 1 Jn. 2:9–11; 4:7–12. Love your enemies: Mt. 5:44 (Lk. 6:27); 1 Thes. 5:15; Rom. 12:17; 1 Pet. 3:7.

Testament [118]. One instructive passage from Paul, Col. 3:12—15 (cf. Eph. 4:1—19), bring these three themes together:

> Therefore, as those chosen by God, holy, and beloved, clothe yourselves with feelings of compassion, kindness, humility, gentleness, and patience, bearing with one another and forgiving each other if anyone might have a complaint against another. For just as the Lord forgave you, so also should you. Above all these things, put on love, which is the perfect bond of unity. And let the peace of Christ rule in your hearts, to which indeed [being] in one body you were called.

It is intended that the gospel should affect the way people relate to one another, especially those who are part of the Christian community. Disorder and disharmony do not convey the message of peace, love, or forgiveness. The unity that is desired, however, is not something that is merely external for the sake of appearances but is something genuine that comes from within each individual believer. Christ does not simply demand peace either. He brings it[119], and according to Jn. 14:27, he leaves it with his disciples (Jn. 20:19, 21, 26). Eph. 2:14 says that Christ himself is our peace[120]. Jn. 16:33 (cf. Acts 10:36) indicates that the ultimate purpose of Jesus' teaching is that "in me you may have peace."

The outright condemnation of numerous "speech sins" in the New Testament clearly indicates that a major impediment to the peace and harmony Christ seeks to effect is thought to be the tongue (fueled by evil treasure from the heart). Many of these appear in lists of vices and types of condemned sinners and include nearly all of the categories which have appeared in the previous literature surveyed, plus a few more. They are: gossip, slander, angry outbursts, shouting, disputes, dissensions, insults, deceit, perjury, boastfulness, lying, vulgarity, silly talk, and coarse jesting[121]. Some of these, and others, receive more individual attention in the New Testament and are worth inspecting. But before doing this, Jesus' stricture against judging one another should receive due regard.

---

118 Mt. 18:21–22 (Lk. 12:4); Mt. 18:23–25; Lk. 6:37; Lk. 9:51–56; Mt. 6:14 (Mk. 11:26; Lk. 6:37); Lk. 17:3–4; Eph. 4:32.

119 The message he sent out with the Twelve was that of peace (Mt. 10:13; Lk. 10:5–8). See also Jn. 16:33; Eph. 2:17 (Isa. 57:19). This is true despite Mt. 10:34 (Lk. 12:51) which speaks with short term realism of the impact of Jesus' revolutionary message. See also the comments of Beck and Brown, 780–782, which pertain to many of the ideas of this paragraph.

120 Admittedly in this instance, he primarily refers to the peace that Christ has brought in joining together Jews and Gentiles. The full context of Eph. 2:11–22, however, includes practical Christian community relationships, as well.

121 The items have been attained from Mt. 15:19 (Mk. 7:22); Rom. 1:29–30; 1 Cor. 6:10; 2 Cor. 12:20; Gal. 5:19–26; Col. 3:8–9; Eph. 4:31–32; 5:4; 1 Tim. 1:10; 2 Tim. 3:2–4; 1 Pet. 2:1. Some of them, such as slander and gossip appear on more than one list. Others, like shouting, silly talk, and coarse jesting, appear just once. Some of the items are conveyed by more than one Greek word, like slander (καταλαλία, διάβολος, βλασφημία), vulgarity (αἰσχρότης, αἰσχρολογία), and gossip (φλύαρος, ψιθυριστής).

This proverbial-like pronouncement in Mt. 7:1—2[122] presumes that God will judge a person severely if he himself severely judges others[123]. Undue criticism, drawing upon an overly harsh standard as well as being expressed in a hasty or strident manner, is in view[124]. The positive deduction to be drawn is that one ought to be merciful, compassionate, and forgiving with others if he desires the same from God[125]. Special interest in this passage comes from the fact that as a general and influential admonition of Jesus (Rom. 14:10—13; Jas. 4:11—12) it may appropriately be seen as a universal condemnation of nearly all the ways in which people speak negatively to or about one another. Gossip, slander, mockery, cursing, hot-tempered speech, perjury, and partiality all stem from undue judgment and should be seen as meriting the absolute condemnation spoken of (Hill, 146).

In the Pastorals, warnings against gossip and slander are directed specificially at women. Older women, young widows, and deacons' wives (or deaconnesses) are each cited[126]. Slander appears as the most commonly named speech sin in the New Testament, occurring at least eighteen times in contexts of censure[127]. Christians are not to associate with other "Christians" who are known slanderers (1 Cor. 5:11). When, slandered, Christian leaders display the correct example if they reply kindly to the offender (1 Cor. 4:13).

Mockery and insult are also things which Christians must expect to endure from those outside the faith who view them contemptuously[128]. Paul apparently experienced such verbal attacks commonly (Acts 13:45; 1

---

122 The parallel in Lk. 6:37 replaces ἵνα with καί and strengthens μή with οὐ. The sense is not radically different. Also, it omits the explanatory statement but quickly adds two parallel statements regarding condemnation and forgiveness to illuminate the first one on judgment.

123 The passive κριθῆτε assumes God to be the judge involved. See Allen, 66; I. Marshall, *Luke*, 266; McNeile, 90. Hill, 146, widens it to include the possibility of God's judgment operating through others. Allen, 66, notes the proverbial nature of the saying in the verse.

124 Although syntactically κρίματι is a dative of means, the criterion of manner cannot be ruled out. It is an attitude as much as anything else that is being censured here. See Hill, 146; I. Marshall, *Luke*, 266; McNeile, 90.

125 By joining the injunction with similar ones involving condemnation and forgiveness, Lk. 6:37 makes this even clearer than does Matthew.

126 Strictly speaking, only 1 Tim. 5:13, regarding younger widows, refers to gossip (φλύαρος –"chatter"). Tit. 2:3, regarding older women, and 1 Tim. 3:4, regarding deacons' wives, refer to slander (διάβολος), but the Greek word is commonly translated as abusive gossip, presumably because of the context being women.

127 Three words in the New Testament refer to "slander." They are καταλαλία and related forms [2 Cor. 12:20; 1 Pet. 2:1, 12; 3:6; Rom. 1:30; Jas. 4:11 (2)], διάβολος (1 Tim. 3:11; 2 Tim. 3:3; Tit. 2:2), and βλασφημία and related forms (Eph. 4:31; Col. 3:8; 1 Tim. 6:4; Jude 9; Rom. 14:16; Tit. 3:2).

128 Heb. 10:23; 11:36; 1 Pet. 4:4; Acts 1:13; Mt. 5:11 (Lk. 6:22).

Thes. 2:2). Christ's non-response to abuse like this should be an inspiration to his followers as to how one should deal with it[129]. They should not be "repaying insult with insult but rather imparting a blessing[130]." Similarly, Christians are to "bless those who curse you," as Christ apparently directed (Lk. 6:28; 1 Cor. 4:12; Rom. 12:4). Further with regard to cursing, a "mouth full of cursing" is taken as a sign of a sinner in the New Testament[131]. Christ is considered cursed (for our sakes) as also are those who do not believe in him (Gal. 3:10—14; 1 Cor. 16:22).

A great deal of the concern about speech sins in the New Testament, then, is generated out of a desire to encourage Christians to act graciously when they are the recipients of verbal abuse. This is rather matter-of-factly assumed to be the lot of the Christian when he is amongst those outside the Christian community. Perjury is another type of verbal abuse in which Christians of course should not engage but are expected to endure as Christ did[132].

A second grouping of speech sins evidence mainly internal concerns, i.e. maintaining harmony among diverse and sinful people who ideologically are supposed to be united in Christ. Thus, shouting, display of anger, quarrelling, strife, commotion, disputation, controversy, dissention, grumbling, and complaining[133] are blacklisted as contradicting their unique relationship before God (in Christ) and negating their call to be noticeably and positively different from the rest of the world (Phil. 2:14—15)[134].

The stance against internal strife includes anything that might contribute to friction. In this category is the matter of false teaching. Those who spread it deceitfully as well as those with an enamourment for speculative theories are in view (Rom. 16:17—18)[135].

---

129   1 Pet. 2:22–23; Mt. 20:19 (Mk. 10:34; Lk. 18:32); Lk. 22:63–65; Mt. 27:27–31, 41, 44 (Mk. 15:16–20, 31, 32; Lk. 23:11, 35–39).
130   1 Pet. 3:9. This is so that they might receive a blessing themselves. See also Mt. 5:11–12 (Lk. 6:22–23).
131   Rom. 3:14 [Ps. 10:7; Ps. 9:28 (LXX)].
132   Mt. 5:11. Jesus also was thought to have been falsely accused in his trial. See Mt. 26:59–60 (Mk. 14:55–56). Stephen's situation is similar (Acts 6:13).
133   Shouting (κραυγή — Eph. 4:31); display of anger (ὀργή–Eph. 4:31; Col. 2:8; 1 Tim. 2:8; θυμός–Rom. 2:8; 2 Cor. 12:20; Gal. 5:20; Eph. 4:31); quarrelling (μάχη–2 Tim. 2:24; Tit. 3:9; μομφή–Col. 3:13); strife (ἔρις–1 Cor. 1:11; 3:33; 2 Cor. 12:20; Rom. 13:13; Gal. 5:20; Phil. 1:15; Tit. 3:9); commotion (ἀκαταστασία–2 Cor. 12:20; 1 Cor. 14:32); disputes (ἐριθεῖαι–Rom. 2:8; Gal. 5:20; 2 Cor. 12:20; Phil. 2:3); διαλογισμός–Phil. 2:14; 1 Tim. 2:8); controversy (ζήτημα, ζήτησις–Tit. 3:10; 1 Tim. 1:4; 6:4; 2 Tim. 2:23); dissention (διχοστασία–Rom. 16:17; Gal. 5:20; 1 Cor. 3:3; αἱρετικός–Tit. 3:10; Gal. 5:20); grumbling (γογγυσμός–Phil. 2:14; 1 Pet. 4:9; Jude 19); complaining (μεμψίμοιρος–Jude 16).
134   Such internal problems fly in the face of the numerous positive injunctions in the New Testament, like "Encourage one another daily!" from Heb. 3:3. See also 1 Cor. 3:13, where strife is considered a sure indicator of being "fleshly" and "walking like mere men."
135   See also 1 Tim. 6:14; 2 Tim. 2:23; Tit. 3:9.

The concern to limit the spread of false and deceitful teaching and idle speculation in the New Testament is major and is reflected throughout[136]. It is rooted in the desire to retain moral as well as doctrinal purity. Also, the expectation is that all believers will be concerned enough for this as well as for their brothers' salvation, that they will be motivated to admonish and reprove those that err. Believers are considered "competent to admonish one another," as Rom. 15:14 says[137]. Such a delicate operation is to be done gently, patiently, and lovingly, with Scripture considered a helpful aid[138]. However, certain individuals, such as those who are persistently factious or leaders who flaunt their outrageous sins publicly, warrant more severe measures, like dissociation from the community of believers and public rebuke[139].

Another internal concern which relates to reproof within the community is the matter of impartiality. Following God's leading, there is to be no favouritism generally, nor any specifically with regard to reproving someone[140].

A third group of speech sins evidence concern for speech that is basically anti-social. Speech that is considered shameful, tasteless, and vulgar by normal societal standards is to be avoided[141]. If it is not fit for those outside the faith, certainly it is not fit for the Christian either.

---

136   Mt.24:4–24 (Mk. 13:5–6; Lk. 21:8); 1 Cor. 3:18; 6:9; 15:13; 2 Cor. 11:3; 2 Thes. 2:3; Gal. 6:7; Col. 2:4–8; Eph. 4:14; 5:6; 1 Tim. 1:4; 2:14; 6:4; 2 Tim. 2:23; 3:13; Tit. 3:9; 1 Pet. 3:10; 2 Pet. 2:13; 1 Jn. 2:26; 3:7; 2 Jn. 7; Jude 16. Paul does all he can to dissociate himself and the gospel from this kind of flattery and deceptive speaking (Gal. 1:10; 1 Thes. 2:3; 2:5–6; 1 Cor. 1:18–2:16; 2 Cor. 2:17; 4:2). Satan is thought to be the ultimate source of deceit (Acts 13:10; 2 Thes. 2:10; Rev. 12:9; 13:4; 18:23; 19:20; 20:3–8, 10.

137   See also Col. 3:16; Eph. 5:21; 1 Thes. 5:14; 2 Thes. 3:14–15; Eph. 5:11; Lk. 17:3; Tit. 1:9, 13; 2:15.

138   Gal. 6:1; Eph. 4:15; 1 Tim 5:1; 2 Tim. 2:25; 3:16; 4:2.

139   Tit. 3:10; 1 Tim. 5:19–20; Mt. 18:15–20. Dissociation is also urged by Paul for gross public immorality in 1 Cor. 5:1–13 and for persistent disregard for his instruction not to be idle in 2 Thes. 3:14–15.

140   1 Tim. 5:21; Rom. 14:10–13. Both God (Acts 10:34; Rom. 2:11) and Jesus (Mt. 22:15–16; Mk. 12:13–14; Lk. 20:20–21; Eph. 6:9; Col. 3:25) are thought to be impartial in their dealings with people.

141   Eph. 4:29; 5:4; Col. 3:8. The sense of shame that one should feel in uttering certain words comes through most clearly in words like αἰσχρότης and αἰσχρολογία. Tastelessness comes through in words like μωρολογία and σαπρός.

Chapter 6: Epistle of James

Exegesis

James 3:18

Despite Dibelius' reluctance to see a contextual relationship between 3:18 and what follows it in ch. 4, many others dauntlessly assert that the topic of "war" in 4:1—2b is quite conveniently suggested by the idea of "peace" in 3:18[1]. Two diametrically opposed situations are being exposed: one associated with fostering communal and societal peace, the other associated with causing communal and societal division.

James 3:18 represents an effort to summarise the preceding discussion about true and false wisdom and in the course of this to elevate the importance of εἰρηνική above its anonymity as one element among many in the list of traits which evidence true wisdom (ἄνωθεν σοφία) in 3:17 (Laws, 165; Hort, 87). The δέ capably conveys both of these intentions.

The precise meaning of 3:18 is enigmatic. This is at least partly due to its compressed, proverbial nature. Generally, it seems clear that a relationship between righteousness and peace is being expressed.

There are two views about how to interpret καρπὸς . . . δικαιοσύνης. However, neither of these disagree that ἐν εἰρήνῃ indicates the manner in which it is to be sown (σπείρεται). Whatever one may think the fruit of righteousness refers to, the main objective of the verse is to emphasise the importance of a peaceful manner to achieve the result.

The majority view interprets δικαιοσύνης as a genitive of definition[2]. It is righteousness itself which emerges from the context of peaceable actions by peacemakers, taking τοῖς ποιοῦσιν εἰρήνην as a dative of agency. There are problems with this approach. It is not by any means an obvious way to read the verse, even though there is precedent for taking "fruit of righteousness" in this way (Heb. 12:11; Phil. 1:11). The use of καρπός is excluded from having any real purpose or meaning in the proverb. By the introduction of the new and undefined term δικαιοσύνης into the context

---

1 Hort, 87; Mitton, 146; Schrage, 43; Adamson, 168.
2 P. Davids, 155; Mitton, 144; Hort, 87; Dibelius, 215; Adamson, 156; Tasker, 82.

and giving it such an exalted status, 3:18 becomes a very poor conclusion to 3:13—18. One cannot safely presume the Pauline sense of righteousness as a divine gift here as is often done by those who take this approach. For James, δικαιοσύνη may have eschatological implications, but it cannot be dissociated from righeous actions[3].

A second view interprets δικαιοσύνης as a genitive of possession. An unspecified reward of righteousness issues from peaceable actions for peacemakers, taking τοῖς ποιοῦσιν εἰρήνην as a dative of advantage[4]. By specifying the fruit of righteousness to be wisdom, Laws strengthens the viability of this approach considerably[5]. The primary evidence for her view is that wisdom and the fruit of righteousness are interchanged in Prov. 3:18 and 11:30 in being called the tree of life.

Joining the view of Laws to the superior understanding of τοῖς ποιοῦσιν εἰρήνην in the first approach[6] makes for the best understanding of all. In this way, 3:18 becomes a fitting summary/conclusion to 3:13—17. It then re-emphasises the point of 3:13 that a good lifestyle of behaviour performed humbly is the evidence of real wisdom. The prepositional phrase ἐν εἰρήνῃ can be seen to stand in for ἐν πραΰτητι, δικαιοσύνης for καλῆς ἀναστροφῆς τὰ ἔργα, with καρπός pointing to σοφίας. The message of 3:18 would be simple: wisdom (the fruit of righteous behaviour) is sown peacefully by peacemakers. The question about where it is sown is implicit: it is sown among men into society[7].

---

3 Hoppe, 67–71, seeks to establish the eschatological implications of δικαιοσύνης, but he is very careful to say that this does not divorce it from its ethical understanding. Indeed, the two other uses of the word in James (1:20; 2:23) are clearly associated with behaviour. See also the parallel in Isa. 32:17. It is worth noting that P. Davids, 155, is the only one of those who take this first approach to specify that righteous deeds are in view.

4 Laws, 165, and Ropes, 250–251. The matter of how to take τοῖς ποιοῦσιν εἰρήνην is not inextricably tied to the approach one takes to καρπὸς . . . δικαιοσύνης as evidenced by Ropes, 251, who does not take it as a dative of advantage whereas Dibelius, 215, and Mayor, 123, do.

5 Laws, 166. Schrage, 42, supports the association of wisdom with the fruit of righteousness, citing Sir. 1:16 and pondering the relationship of 3:18 to 3:17. See also Mussner, 175–176.

6 As P. Davids, 155, notes, the sense of tautology created by doing this is consistent with James; rhetorical way of making emphases.

7 The "where" question is the weakest aspect of most discussions of this verse with respect to either approach. Of those who take the first approach, P. Davids, 155, is the rare exception in speaking about the community. This is related to taking righteousness to refer to actions, in contrast to most others who take this approach. Of those who take the second approach, only Ropes, 251, even implies that peace is sown in the community. By taking τοῖς ποιοῦσιν εἰρήνην as a dative of advantage, Laws is unable to see the possibility of the modification I make of her approach.

James 4:1—2b

Detailed exegesis of these opening verses occurred in Part II. It will be sufficient here simply to recall that a war motif is being used to accent the harmful capabilities — indeed, actualities — of verbal assaults on others. A wide range of harmful speech could well be envisaged here, including: slander, mockery, angry speech, cursing, and perjury. The latter two come to mind particularly with respect to the charge of actual murder.

James 4:11—12

James 4:11—12 is a somewhat isolated unit of thought in the epistle. It contains no conjunction to link it formally to its immediate context. Although the fact that it begins with an imperative may seem to connect it to the series of imperatives in 4:7—10, Mussner is right to point out that 4:10 provides the conclusion to that series[8]. Besides, the imperative which opens 4:11 is modified by the negative μή, which signals a prohibition, and this is followed by the author's effort to convince the readers to comply with the imperative by reasoned entreaty. This approach is quite unlike the absolute nature of the imperatival demands in 4:7—10. Another notable difference is the shift of address from the disdain of ἁμαρτωλοί and δίψυχοι in 4:8 and μοιχαλίδες in 4:4 to the warmth of ἀδελφοί in 4:11[9]. Contextually, then, 4:11—12 does not relate to what immediately precedes. However, it does deal with a critical aspect of the concern which opens the chapter in 4:1—2b[10]. Whereas 4:4—10 dealt with the internal, spiritual aspect of the problem directed toward the worst of the disputants within the Christian community, 4:11—12 deals with the practical side of the issue for the entire church. The verbal wars which are marring the unity of the church must stop. They must quit "speaking against one another."

The present tense of the imperative καταλαλεῖτε reaffirms the emphasis in 4:1—2b that this harmful activity is presently going on. It also continues to speak of the harmful speech in general terms[11]. The word can refer specifically to slander (P. Davids, 169; Dibelius, 228), but this is more appropriate when the word occurs in a list of speech sins (Laws, 186). It certainly accents slander as one amongst a number of types of harmful speech which were also associated with φονεύετε in 4:2a, such as mockery,

---

8 Mussner, 187. Dibelius, 228, thinks that the verses are connected because of the imperative form even though he thinks they are disconnected in terms of substance.

9 Laws, 186, and Dibelius, 228.

10 P. Davids, 168; Laws, 186; Ropes, 273, all knowledge the relationship of 4:11-12 to the opening verses of the chapter. P. Davids, 168; Mitton, 162-164; Mayor, 148; Adamson, 176, point to an even broader context for 4:11-12 to include 1:19-26; 2:8; 3:1-18.

11 Laws, 186; Ropes,, 274; Mitton, 164; Mayor, 148; Hiebert, 267.

cursing, angry speech, and perjury. It is able to envelop a wider scope of speech sins, though, including other familiar types like partiality, gossip, flattery, and deceit. The word refers here to the array of disparaging things one can say to, about or which affect another.

With the reformation of the verb as the substantival participal, ὁ καταλαλῶν, the author lays out his first point of reason. The addition of a synonymous second participle, κρίνων, makes the point he is going to stress about judging the law more suitable. As far as James is concerned, to speak against a brother is also to judge him. The first emphasises the speech; the second emphasises the thought process behind the speech. Most likely, he considers κρίνων to be recognized as the more serious matter with its implication of condemnatory judgment[12]. The double repetition of ἀδελφοῦ and then τὸν ἀδελφόν and the addition of the possessive pronun αὐτοῦ to the second reinforces the inappropriateness of this action. Brothers should love one another. They should stand together against attacks upon either rather than attacking one another. Neither has any authority to take the position of judge over the other for as brothers they are of equal authority. Further, James asserts that he who criticises another, although perhaps unaware of the fact, καταλαλεῖ νόμου καὶ κρίνει νόμον simultaneously. How this can be so is explained in the first class conditional clause which follows.

In the conditional clause καταλαλέω is dropped and attention focuses on κρίνεις. This is appropriate now that it has been established in the first logical step that speaking against a brother (in Christ) makes one also guilty of judging the law. The former is part of the greater offence. The second logical step makes it clear that to judge the law is to set oneself up as superior to it. If such a person were to obey it submissively — as he should — he would be a ποιητὴς νόμου. Then, he would not presume to speak against his brother. In contrast, by choosing not to obey the law, he exalts himself as one who has enough authority over the law to pick and choose how to apply it and when to obey it. He makes himself κριτής.

James' logic only works if νόμος includes a particular tenet against one person disparaging another, or if it refers to a general, circumscribing principle of law which obviously incorporates the idea. The fact that James refrains from giving articles to his two uses of νόμος, suggests that James does not have a particular tenet of law or, indeed, a particular set of laws in mind. It is most likely, given the similar contexts between 2:1—12 and 4:11—12 (partiality/criticism), that James has kept in mind what

---

12   The word κρίνω can have the neutral meaning of "consider," but it can also refer to the punishment handed out by a judge or, in a non-legal situation, to pass judgment, criticise.

he calls in 2:8 the royal law, to love one's neighbor as oneself[13]. There, he quotes it from Lev. 19:18, but he appears to understand that its formidable position in Jesus tradition has elevated the principle to supreme importance as incorporating the essence of Jewish law. The surest indicator that it is this law which James has in mind as that which ultimately disallows the practice of speaking against one another is the appearance of τὸν πλησίον at the end of 4:12 where one would have expected τὸν ἀδελφόν again. It is difficult not to conjecture that Jesus' well-known admonition not to judge one another is not also in the back of James' thoughts here, perhaps as a negative complement to loving one's neighbor[14].

Having established by the first two logical steps (4:11) that the person who speaks against his brother disobeys the law and assumes the position of judge over it, in the third logical step commencing in 4:12, James asserts a simple but devastating truth. There is only one qualified judge of the law. He is also the origin of it. He in truth has the power to administer it for deliverance or destruction. The emphatic position of εἷς and the appearance of ἐστιν enhance the poignancy of the point. The implication of ὁ δυνάμενος σῶσαι καὶ ἀπολέσαι goes beyond the obvious ability of a judge to assess and apply the law to his authority to sentence to death the one who disparages his brother, thereby usurping the deserved place of the one, rightful judge. Whether God or Christ is in James' mind here as the judge does not affect the power of what is being said. Since νομοθέτης and κριτής refer either to God or to Christ in biblical literature, P. Davids' comment (p. 169) that James in effect is accusing the one who speaks against his brother of blasphemy is entirely appropriate[15].

The fourth step in James' logic makes the form of a rhetorical question. It accents just how out of place the one who judges his neighbor is. The question is carefully constructed to put such a person in his proper place, which is infinitely distant from the lone, qualified judge. The forward

---

13 Whether or not all agree about James' association of Jesus with the royal law, virtually all scholars recognise James to have it in mind here. See P. Davids, 170; Laws, 187; Ropes, 274; Hiebert, 268; Mitton, 166; Dibelius, 228; Mayor, 148; Mussner, 187; Schrage, 46.

14 P. Davids, 170; Laws, 187; Mitton, 165. The command is found in various forms in Mt. 7:1–5; Lk. 6:37–42; Rom. 2:1; 14:4; 1 Cor. 4:5; 5:12; Jn. 7:24; 8:15–16.

15 Ropes recognises that what tips the balance in favour of God is not the references (upon which so many other commentaries rely) which can be found for him as Judge (Gen. 17:25; Ps. 82:1, 8; Heb. 12:23; Rom. 14:11; 1 Pet. 1:17) or as Lawgiver (Ps. 9:21—LXX). Rather, it is the opening εἷς ἐστιν, reminiscent of εἷς θεός ἐστιν in 2:9 and which is the basic premise of Jewish religion. However, references to Christ judging on God's behalf are frequent in the New Testament (1 Cor. 4:3–5; 2 Cor. 5:10; Rom. 2:6; 2 Tim. 4:1,8; 1 Pet. 4:5; Jn. 5:19–29).

position — indeed, the appearance — of the personal pronoun of σύ and the expression of the copula εῖ assure this result. The present tense of εῖ and κρίνων illuminate once again the point that the practice of harmfully speaking against one another is something in which Christians are actively engaged.

James 5:9

What is said in 5:9 interrupts the smooth connection between the theme of patience which carries over from 5:8 to 10—11. The lack of an opening conjunction is significant in this respect. So too is the vocative ἀδελφοί, which James uses regularly to signal a shift of focus. Mussner, though, is right to observe that it is the theme of the nearness of eschatological judgment raised in 5:8b which leads to 5:9[16]. It appears that in light of the approaching eschaton James desires to reinforce his admonition in 4:11—12 about not disparaging one another.

The author establishes the connections to 4:11 in three ways: 1) by common subject matter, 2) by composing the opening prohibition in a similar fashion to the opening prohibition in 4:11, 3) by connecting to Jesus his reasoning for following the prohibition on the admonition against judging one another.

The use of στενάζετε as a synonym for καταλαλεῖτε stretches the normal meaning of the word. It usually refers to a sign or a groan which someone might make to himself because of the undesirable circumstances which are affecting him. Its use here to refer to making a complaint against someone else (κατ' ἀλλήλων) displays the author's creative use of words. It may well be, as Mitton suggests, that Jesus envisages the oppressive circumstances of 5:1—6 — which also require patience (5:7—8) — to be contributing to the internal bickering which he desires to cease[17].

As with καταλαλεῖτε in 4:11 and the key words of 4:1—2b, στενάζετε encompasses a wide assortment of verbal wrongs including: gossip, slander, mockery, cursing, angry speech, perjury, and probably also speech that reflects partiality. The motivational purpose clause which follows the prohibition by its employment of μὴ κριθῆτε supports the inclusion of partiality in the above list. The clause presumes to apply to complaining against one another the point made in 4:11—12 about speaking against

---

16 Mussner, 204. See also Schrage, 53, for a similar analysis. Dibelius, 244, stands alone in viewing this verse as totally isolated from its context.

17 Mitton, 187. Ropes, 297, considers the outside stress to come from the coming end of the age. However, it does not seem likely that Christians would be upset about this. Besides, the mention of the Lord's coming in 5:8 is intended as an encouragement for Christians to remain patient in the midst of oppression. The Lord's coming will mean an end to oppression and judgment for the oppressors.

another being equivalent to judging him. This, then, supplies the missing point of logic which connects the thinking to Mt. 7:1 (*contra* Dibelius, 244). The passive mood indicates that the condemning judgment of those who complain about others is to come from God or Christ.

Since James adds that ὁ κριτὴς πρὸ τῶν θυρῶν ἔστηκεν, it is most likely that he has Christ in mind as the Judge. There are those who opt for God here for the sake of consistency with their view of 4:11—12 (Laws, 213; Ropes, 297). However, the parallel with the familiar Christian slogan ἡ παρουσία τοῦ κυρίου ἤγγικεν in 5:8 mitigates this in favour of Christ[18]. No references to God being at the door can be produced, whereas there are no less than three New Testament references which are associated with Christ in this way[19]. To conjecture as Ropes does that James is teaching that God accompanies Christ at his coming is to saddle James with an eschatological notion unpronounced in Christian circles, at least in the New Testament[20]. The whole function of the eschatological date here is to motivate errant Christians to engineer an immediate change of behaviour by appealing to a fact they already know to be true. The judgment which the grumbler reaps for himself could come at any moment because all know the return of Christ, the Judge, could occur at any time.

Analysis

James 3:18 bears witness to the integral part that peace and actions which promote it play in James' hopes for the Christian community and even for society at large. His central ethical principle of loving neighbor as self (2:8) reinforces these hopes as the principle, if applied diligently by all, which would dramatically transpose the unhappy reality of inter-human relationships within and without the church.

From the grim picture he paints of the tongue in 3:1—12, there is little doubt that he recognizes the enormity of the task he set before men. From his daring in 4:1—2b to set the Christian community within the framework of war, fighting pitched battles against one another which produce fatal casualties, James exposes the serious nature of the division which impairs inter-human relationships within the church. Although he

---

18 P. Davids, 185; Mussner, 205; Hiebert, 301; Mitton, 187; Schrage, 53.

19 Mk. 13:29; Mt. 24:33; Rev. 3:20. The effort Laws, 213, makes to overturn the strength of these references is futile in light of the total lack of any reference to God being at the door.

20 Ropes, 297. His offering of Rom. 2:16 as support for the idea is hardly satisfactory since it speaks only of Jesus being the agent of God's judgment of men. It says nothing of God accompanying him.

recognizes that the root of the problem has to do with the evil, internal desires in men, he also knows that it is the abuses of uncontrolled speech which are ravaging the Christian community.

The prohibitions of 4:11—12 and 5:9 express the author's intense desire to put an end to the hurtful grumbling, unsuitably critical speech which denies those in the Christian community the peace and harmony which should be theirs as brothers and sisters in Christ. He reasons that to speak so disparagingly of a fellow Christian is the same as casting disdain upon the law of loving one's neighbor and foolishly usurping God/Christ from his proper place as originator and interpreter of the law. If this bit of reasoning does not shame a person into reform, James trusts that the imminent threat of judgment from Christ on God's behalf will effect the needed change. James has made something as seemingly minor as "harmless" gossip not only a moral crisis but a spiritual crisis of the utmost dimension.

Within these prohibitions in 4:1—2b, 11—12, and 5:9, James does not specify any particular kind of harmful speech. It appears he deliberately chooses words which can include all of the many ways speech can be used purposely to do moral and spiritual injury to another person. Gossip, slander, mockery, cursing, angry speech, flattery, deceit, perjury, partial speech, and any other description of speech which damages inter-human relationships are doubtless included. James in effect has put all of these on a par with each other in being responsible for the spiritual crisis which is affecting individuals as well as the community at large.

James' reluctance to involve himself in discussions about particular types of speech sins applies in general to the entire writing. However, references, some more obvious than others, can be detected to some specific speech sins in various places amidst sections where other, broader concerns are dominant.

The supposition that angry speech is included in the condemnation of anger in 1:19—20 is easy to see. Perhaps less obvious is the tactlessness which characterises the dramatic quotation of 2:16. Nevertheless, to speak so thoughtlessly even in genuine sympathy to those who are in such desperate need for concrete assistance surely is tactless at minimum.

Since partiality is the dominant concern of 2:1—12, no doubt the two dramatic quotations which occur in 2:3 are primarily intended to illustrate the atmosphere of partiality against the poor in favour of the rich which pervades the church. Nevertheless, the first quotation addressed to the rich man, σὺ κάθου ὧδε καλῶς, is also a form of flattery. These are words intended to impress based not on any real goodness or spiritual qualities of the rich man but rather on special consideration (ἐπιβλέψητε) of his apparel (τὴν ἐσθῆτα τὴν λαμπράν).

The dramatic quotations of 2:3 also exhibit the fact that partiality, which James wants to see eliminated from the church, is displayed in many forms which include words as well as actions. Of course, the summarising admonition of 2:12, stipulating both these forms of behaviour, makes plain the concern for partiality in the realm of speech to cease. Later, in 3:17, impartiality is listed as one of the characteristic traits of wisdom from above. The first class conditional construction of 2:9 brands all behaviour which shows partiality as sin (ἁμαρτίαν ἐργάζεσθε) and those who do them as transgressors (ὡς παραβάται) duly convicted by the law of neighbor love. In anticipation of 4:11—12, 2:4 affiliates those who make distinctions with being corrupt judges (κριταὶ διαλογισμῶν πονηρῶν[21]).

James 2:7 refers to yet another recognizable speech sin within the discussion of partiality. The verb βλασφημοῦσιν may be rightly understood as "blasphemy." However, "blasphemy" is a specific use of the word with reference to a divine being. With reference to mere mortals it refers to slanderous, reviling, and insulting speech. It may well be that James is accusing the rich of uttering blasphemies directly against τὸ καλὸν ὄνομα of "Jesus" or "Christ[22]." However, it is more likely that he pictures the rich slandering or insulting Christians, or perhaps perjuring in court against them, in light of 2:6. The Lord, thus, is indirectly discredited in this way[23].

---

21 The tendency of those like Laws, 102; Ropes, 192; Mussner, 119; Hort, 49–50, to take this verse as referring to individual subjective doubt as opposed to objective discrimination within the Christian community is hermeneutically possible. However, it unnecessarily obtrudes from the overall and the immediate context. The concern at hand is partiality directed against others. How can an assessment of the internal doubt do anything but add confusion to the understanding of the illustration in 2:2–3? James will get to the internal in 4:1–2a. Moreover, as P. Davids, 110, observes, to take διεκρίθητε to refer to minds divided between God and wickedness or the world (1:6; 4:8) is to ignore the second clause which accuses them without qualification of being driven by evil motives (διαλογισμῶν). There is no wavering implied here nor any inclination toward God. Dibelius, 136, is probably right to blame the confusion created by the author's replacement of his primary word choice for conveying the idea of partiality, προσωπολημπτέω, with διακρίνω on the irresistable attraction to play on the word κριταί.

22 There is some dispute among scholars as to whether the name "Jesus" or "Christ" is meant here. Most opt for Jesus on the reasonable logic that if Jews are included as the persecutors, then they would probably shy away from blaspheming the Messiah. Also, if baptism is in mind here, as many think is the case because of the aorist tense of the participle τὸ ἐπικληθέν, then the fact that it is the name of Jesus which predominates in the New Testament with regard to baptism also points to Jesus being in mind here.

23 Laws, 105, and Dibelius, 140, affirm that James primarily has in mind blasphemy of Jesus indirectly through verbal abuse of Christians. Laws cites Acts 5:41 as possible support. Others like P. Davids, 113, and Hort, 52, see either direct or indirect

In correspondence with 2:6, perjury may also be an aspect of James'
accusation in 5:6 that the rich condemn and kill the righteous[24]. In
correspondence with φονεύετε in 4:2, a whole range of speech sins which
are morally injurious could be included, such as slander, mockery, cursing,
partiality, etc. If the puzzling τὸν δίκαιον refers to Christ[25] rather than
collectively to the "righteous" poor (1:9; 2:5) or Christians, then slanderous
blasphemy of his name or him via Christians as in 2:7 may again be
involved. It is even possible that the charge of murder has a literal aspect
not only with regard to perjury but also as that which results from the
hoarding of provisions by the rich (5:5) and the deceptive cheating of their
hired workers out of their due pay (5:4[26]). It could well be that the
contribution such action makes to starvation, disease, and premature death
from various related causes is a very real aspect of the harsh condemnation the rich receive here.

James 5:10—11 adds another twist to the totally unwarranted treatment
Christians are receiving at the hands of the rich. He categorises it here as
suffering (κακοπαθίας) and invites the persecuted to find in Job the
model and encouragement to react to this with patience/perseverance
(ὑπομονήν). What did Job endure? Many things, including the killing of
his family, loss of wealth, shame from his appearance, but above all and
that which occupies most of the dialogue in the story: the devastating,
wrongful judgment of him by his "friends." This struck him as mockery,

---

blasphemy to be in mind, or perhaps even both. The quantity of New Testament
teaching geared toward helping Christians to respond appropriately to various forms of
verbal assault gives plenty of grounding for maintaining that it is Christians who are
primarily in mind here. Of course, there is no reason why blasphemy against the
very name of Jesus could not be part of the verbal taunting. In Dec. 63, Philo speaks
of grieving the pious as a form of blaspheming God.

24 P. Davids, 179, notes the forensic quality of κατεδικάσατε in 5:6, which is comparable
   with ἕλκουσιν ὑμᾶς εἰς κριτήρια in 2:6 as well. The judicial overtone in both verses
   is recognisable too. See also Dibelius, 239–240; Hiebert, 292; Laws, 105, who also draw
   attention to the relationship between 5:6 and 2:6.

25 This is not likely even though numerous references in the New Testament call him
   this (Acts 3:14; 7:52; 22:14; 1 Pet. 3:18; 1 Jn. 2:1, 29; 3:7, and also Isa. 53:11). It is possible,
   as Laws, 105; Mussner, 199; Ropes, 29; P. Davids, 179, suggest, that Christ is intended to
   be recognised as the penultimate "righteous one" who was killed. But the context of
   the oppressed poor is too strong to make anything but that the primary reference of
   τὸν δίκαιον.

26 Some prefer ἀπεστερημένος ("rob," "defraud") as the correct textual reading. See P.
   Davids, 177; Mussner, 196; UBS³ ("C" rating). Others perfer ἀφυστερημένος("withholding"). See Laws, 201; Ropes, 289. The merit of either is exemplified further by
   the fact that ἀφυστερημένος was preferred by UBS² without so much as a textual
   note. Laws is right to say that the sense is only minimally affected either way. The
   second reading describes the act while leaving the obvious deduction of fraud to the
   reader. The first adjudges the action as fraud while clearly implying that pay is being
   withheld.

insult, and deceit[27]. Thus, many kinds of speech sin could be in James' mind as he condemns the rich in ch. 5.

The matter of cursing appears within James' discussion of the evil of the tongue is 3:1—12. Although cursing is by no means crucial to the overall point, it appears in tandem with blessing to illustrate the unpredictable, restless inconsistency of the human tongue. However, James is unable to let the mention of this aspect of inter-human relationships pass without clearly making it as despicable. This alone is the purpose of attaching τοὺς καθ' ὁμοίωσιν θεοῦ γεγονότας to the second half of the compound sentence which details that ἐν αὐτῇ καταρώμεθα τοὺς ἀνθρώπους. By making this addition, James proclaims that it is without exception wrong to curse a fellow human being. All have value and dignity; no one has the right of place above another to verbally or otherwise deprecate him. This is because God has created each one. By implication, to do so is also to disparage the handiwork of the Creator, indeed, to blaspheme God himself (Mitton, 130—131; Gieger, 150). Although some commentators take the censure in 3:10 to refer to cursing alone, it is more likely to refer to the overall problem of inconsistency in speech[28].

James is more concerned with a person deceiving himself than with someone deceiving others (1:26). Yet, self-deception can bubble over into deception of others. This idea comes across in 3:14 where James equates boasting about being wise when one is filled with evil jealousy (ζῆλον πικρόν) and selfish ambition (ἐριθείαν) to lying against the truth (ψεύδεσθε κατὰ τῆς ἀληθείας)[29]. They consider themselves wise when they are not. They deceive themselves as well as those who believe their mis-representation of themselves and revere their "wise" teaching.

Deceptive teaching is probably also involved in the problem with the apostate believer in 5:19 who πλανηθῇ ἀπὸ τῆς ἀληθείς. The description may principally apply to moral wandering but cannot be divested from matters of faith and doctrine. The fact that the subjective verb could be middle or passive leaves open whether he was led astray or he led himself astray. Most likely, James is well aware that such matters cannot be easily separated. Usually someone else has had a hand, directly or indirectly, in causing a person to move away from gospel faith. It could as well as be a false teacher who quite deceitfully leads a believer down the path to skepticism, rejection, and moral recklessness.

---

27 This is so whether or not one understands James to have the Hebrew version of Job in view or the Testament of Job, as P. Davids, 187, poignantly suggests.

28 P. Davids, 147, and Mayor, 123. See also the earlier exegesis of 3:9—10.

29 P. Davids, 151; Mussner, 171; Ropes, 246; Mayor, 127—128. Laws, 160; Hort, 83; Dibelius, 210, take truth to apply both to ψεύδεσθε and to κατακαυχᾶσθε. While this is pos-sible, the resulting interpretation differs only marginally.

James 5:19—20 also spotlights another form of speech which is integral to mature, human relationships. Often perceived as harsh and hurtful, reproof properly administered is a strong signal of loving another and a sign of maturity in perceiving the need, in the caring manner of delivery, and even in the sober reception by the errant one. The key word here is ἐπιστρέψῃ-ἐπιστρέψας. Although reproof is not mentioned specifically, it must play a vital part in turning the wanderer around and bringing him back to faith. The reproof could have to do with immoral or improper behaviour. It could involve counterbalancing false teaching, either of a doctrinal or a moral nature. It could be a matter merely of recognizing another's sincere doubt and confusion and reviving latent faith and confidence. The Christian who does this successfully enables his brother to escape from certain eschatological doom and at the same time obtains forgiveness for his own sins as well as his brother's (especially regarding the apostasy).

Part IV

Speech in Human-Divine Relations

Chapter 7: Background

Near Eastern Wisdom Literature

In Near Eastern Wisdom Literature, the gods take on special importance because of their maintenance of order in society and because of their control over the destinies of individuals. A person would live in fear and awe of "the gods," knowing that in certain respects they all impinged on his life. However, he would attempt to develop a good relationship with the one god with whom he felt particularly akin. He would do all that might be required to cause this god to influence his life positively.

According to this literature, one of the most important aspects of a person's religious duties to his god is prayer. The Counsels of Wisdom (*BWL*, 105), includes prayer as one of the ways to retain a god's favour.

> Prayer, supplication, and prostration
> Offer him daily and you will get your reward.
> Then you will have full communion with your god.

Prayer in this sense seems to refer to the uttering of praises in tribute to the god in his temple. An example of such a prayer is found in Amen-em-Opet (*LAE*, 247) in regard for Re, the immanent sun-god. It says:

> Every temperate man in the temple says,
> 'Great is the benevolence of Re.'

Daily worshipful prayer was expected to result in rewards in daily life, as the following advice from Amen-em-Opet, (*LAE*, 250) illustrates with regard to Aten, a conception of a sun-god distinct from Re (Frankfort, 24—25):

> When he rises you shall offer to the Aten
> Saying, 'grant me prosperity and health.'
> And he will give you the necessities for life,
> And you will be safe from fear.

A person's god was believed to be capable of hearing as well as acting upon prayers of petition. Ani (*AEL*, 2:141), in the case of an unhappy wife says, "he hears her cries."

Prayer to one's god was not to be merely a matter of repeating pre-formulated words of honour. Importance was also attached to the

sincere attitude of the petitioner. A somewhat extraordinary passage from
Ani (*AEL*, 2:137) contains this idea:

> Prayer by yourself with a loving heart,
> Whose every word is hidden.
> He will grant your needs,
> He will hear your words,
> He will accept your offerings.

There is also evidence that people prayed to their god in order to make
up for wrong they might have done. In the Counsels of Wisdom (*BWL*,
105), it says, "Prayer atones for guilt."

Although the above passage may refer to confession of some type, it
should not be presumed that anything like a Hebrew concept of "sin" is in
the background. Frankfort (p. 73; cf. Morenz, 130—133) asserts, "The Egyptian viewed his misdeeds not as sins but as aberrations. They would bring
him unhappiness because they disturbed his harmonious integration with
the existing world." The last two quotations from the primary literature
must be placed within the spectrum of gods that are viewed pre-
dominately as impersonal and distant. The gods occasionally may alter a
person's life because of his petitions from what had been previously
determined, but this clearly is considered exceptional. The god's free rein
over people's lives includes the freedom to ignore petitions (McKane, 168).
The gods can be rather cantankerous. Thus, in their worship and prayer,
people are considered wise to step carefully so as to keep from riling
them. Ani (*AEL*, 2:141) issues these warnings:

> Offer to your god,
> Beware of offending him.
> Do not question his images[1].

Old Testament

There is an acute awareness in the Old Testament of the importance of
speech in man's relationship to God. Its pages are bulging with praise and
worship of him, with prayers and petitions to him. In turn, his numerous
words to men delivered through special men, through events, and through
answers to personal prayer, are on every page as well. In fact, the Old
Testament could be viewed as a monitoring of the communication lines
between God and the people of Israel. However, the Old Testament reveals
that communication between these two parties is not always congenial.

---

1   *ANET*, 420, renders this last line, "Though shouldst not inquire about his affairs."

Individuals as well as the whole nation of Israel may be overheard speaking against God. On the other hand, God's decrees of judgment and punishment are sometimes almost deafening.

What follows is an attempt to examine three basic lines of communication between the people of Israel and God in the Old Testament: praise, prayer, and blasphemy.

Praise

Praise in the Old Testament is man's verbal expression of his acknowledgment and appreciation that God is God. It ascribes greatness to God because he is great, expresses appreciation for the marvelous works he has done, gives thanks to the Lord because one owes him all, sings songs of him in order to share the joy and spread the news of his inexhaustible greatness. Ps. 96 does an extremely effective job of integrating all these aspects of praise[2].

The call to praise God in song is everywhere in the Psalms[3], and no doubt many of the Psalms themselves are meant to be sung. Such singing is rooted in a basic mood of joy about living which is mark of the people of Israel because of their confidence in God (Eichrodt, *Man* 34—35). According to Ps. 16:11, in his presence is "fullness of joy" and in his right hand "pleasure forever." Joy is a constant theme in the call to sing as is also illustrated by Ps. 95:1 and numerous other Psalms[4]. Moses, Deborah and Barak, and of course David and Solomon, sing to the Lord in the Old Testament[5]. Even the heavens and the earth are said to sing to God and are called on to do so in Ps. 96:11.

Singing is not only a result of joy but has as one of its purposes to tell others what God has done. Singing is a way of telling the wonders of God so that all may hear (Ps. 9:1, 8). One may be driven to speak of God's graciousness in answering prayer or of his power and righteousness (Ps. 66:16—20; 73:28). One might do this before friends or before kings (Ps. 22:22; 119:46). Whether one attempts to sing or speak of God's wonders on

---

2 This Psalm is essentially repeated in 1 Chron. 16:23–36, which as used there is an important part of a significant celebration of worship upon the arrival of the ark of the covenant in Jerusalem by the hand of David.

3 Among these are: Ps. 5:11; 9:1–2, 11; 13:16; 18:49; 27:6; 28:7; 30:4, 10–12; 32:11; 33:1–3; 35:28; 42:11; 43:4–5; 45:16–17; 47:1, 7; 48:1, 10; 51:15; 52:9; 56:4; 57:7–9; 59:6; 61:8; 63:3–5; 66:8; 67:1–7; 68:4; 69:30–36; 71:22–24; 75:1, 9; 79:3; 81:1–5; 89:1; 92:1–4; 95–100; 101:1; 105:1–3; 106:1–3, 47; 107:1–2; 108:1–6; 111–113; 117; 118:1–4; 135:1–4; 136; 138; 145:21; 146–150.

4 Among numerous similar references note: Ps. 32:11; 35:9; 42:4; 43:4; 47:8; 63:5; 67:4; 68:3; 71:23; 89:15; 100:1; 149:2.

5 Ex. 15:1–17; Judg. 5. David is thought to have written many of the Psalms. Solomon is spoken of in 1 Ki. 4:32 as writing 1005 songs.

a personal or on a general level, Ps. 40:5 and Ps. 106:2 suggest that they are too many to be recounted.

Songs of praise form an essential part of Israel's corporate worship, of which Ps. 149:1—4 is excellent example. Much care was taken to ensure that such singing was done well so that it might be a suitable honour to the Lord. Chronicles provides a good record of the intricacies involved in coordinating the voices and many instruments involved in Israel's worship[6].

Many Psalms contain commands to thank God or to bless him, as in Ps. 100:4, which says:

> Enter His gates with thanksgiving,
> And His courts with praise.
> Give thanks to Him; bless His name.

Both of these terms are properly regarded as synonymous with praising God (Isa. 29:13—14; Amos 5:23). The fact that many Psalms contain such imperatives should not be regarded as evidence that God desires hollow praise or meaningless thanks. He is clearly offended by lipservice (Ringgren, *Psalmists*, 77). Rather, calls to thank or bless or praise him should be seen as encouragement for all to recognize and acknowledge who God is and to express that acknowledgment forcefully and freely to him with others who also realise their debt to him[7].

According to the Old Testament, when people are surrounded by God's greatness and engulfed by his goodness, it seems the least they can do is humbly and sincerely acknowledge this by ascribing praise to him. He deserves praise because he is God. Ps. 150, in its last verse, says:

> Let everything that has breath praise the Lord.
> Praise the Lord!

Prayer

In the Old Testament, prayer and praise share an important relationship.

---

6 Note especially 1 Chron. 16; 25:1–8; 2 Chron. 5:12–13; 20:19–28; 23:13–18. Note also the use of songs in worship in 2 Chron. 29:28; 31:2; 35:15, 25; Ezra 2:64; 3:10–11; Neh. 12:27–31, 44–47.

7 Ps. 118:1–4. This is heavily stressed, too, both by Ringgren, *Psalmists* , 77–79, and Westermann, 25–30. Regarding the numerous calls and vows to bless God (Ps. 16:7; 28:6; 31:21; 34:1; 41:13; 72:18; 89:52; 103:1–2; 104:1–2; 106:48; 115–118; 144:1; 145:1), Ringgren says, "Of course, it is impossible to 'bless' in the sense that human beings can be blessed, for man cannot give blessing to God. But man can acknowledge God as the giver of all blessing, and praise him." Note also A. Anderson, 144, commenting on Ps. 16:7. Westermann further stresses that the Hebrew word usually translated "thank" as in Ps. 100:4 (הודו) is never used in the Old Testament as an expression of thanks between men. KB–H, 77 also indicates that as a noun it commonly refers to the majesty and power of God. Thus, Westermann emphasises that "I" cannot ever properly be the subject of this verb, as in "I thank you," but only God, as in "God be thanked" or "thank to God." Finally, he states (p. 27), "The expression of thanks to God is included in praise; it is a way of praising."

Essentially, all praise is prayer[8]. It is common, though, to divide prayer into the categories of praise and petition and treat them as two separate lines of communication to God. Petition generally refers to various requests to God for aid and here will include confession as well.

The recommendation of Ps. 105:4 to be in constant communication with God is representative, when it says:

Seek the Lord and his strength;
Seek his face continually.

Confidence in the value of depending on him is based on many who have experienced his goodness first-hand when they have done so (Ps. 34:8; 55:22).

God proves his reliability by the fact that he regularly hears and responds to the applications of those who seek him[9]. He is the God who hears prayers. His positive response to prayer can be illustrated time and again in the Old Testament[10]. However, he is particularly responsive to the righteous cries of those who are unjustly afflicted (Ps. 9:12; 34:15—18; 50:15). The cry of Abel's blood, of Israel in slavery, of the hired laborer who does not receive his due wages are just a few examples[11].

There are times when God does not answer prayer. The Psalmist never takes it for granted that God will hear him, almost monotonously opening his prayers with the request, "Hear my prayer, O God[12]!" He experiences more than once God's silence which he describes as "hiding himself," being "far from me," or "turning his face from me[13]." As much as God might desire to respond positively to his people's requests (Deut. 4:7), there came a time when he would not because of their compounding sins (Isa. 59:1—2). Isa. 59:7 goes on to enumerate the diabolical sins of Israel and the many ways in which "their feet ran to evil."

The prophets repeat each other in expressing God's rejection of the prayers of his special people[14]. This is not because of a few trivial sins but because they had become to corrupt of heart that they shut themselves off

---

8   Westermann, 24. However, he (pp. 30–35) still deems it important to treat the Psalms in the two broad categories of praise and petition. He (p. 156) includes confession within the category of petition as well. Ringgren, *Psalmists*, 61–91, has two separate discussions under the headings "Lament and Confession" and "Thanksgiving and Prasie."

9   Ps. 3:4; 4:2; 5:3; 6:8–9; 17:6; 18:6; 20:6; 21:2; 28:6; 30:2; 31:22; 34:4–7; 55:17; 57:2; 65:2; 77:1–2; 91:15; 116:1; 118:21; 120:1; 142:5–7.

10   Hannah (1 Sam. 1:7, 13–15), Elijah (1 Ki. 17:1; 18:1), and Jonah (Jon. 2) are just a few example.

11   Gen. 4:10; Ex. 2:23–24; Deut. 24:13–15. Note also Gen. 18:20; 19:13 (Sodom and Gomorrah), Judg. 3:15; 4:3; 6:6; 10:10 (Israel), and Neh. 9:27 (remnant of Israel).

12   Ps. 4:1; 5:1–2; 27:7–10; 28:1–2; 30:10; 35:22; 38:1–22; 39:12; 54:1–2; 55:1; 61:1; 71:2; 78:1; 83:1–2; 84:8; 86:1; 88:2; 102:1–2; 109:1–4; 141:1; 143:1.

13   Ps. 10:1; 13:1–2; 22:1; 30:7; 35:22. This happens to Saul too (1 Sam. 14:37; 28:6).

14   Besides Isa. 59, note Isa. 1:15; Jer. 11:11; 14:12; Ezek. 8:18; Mic. 3:4; Zech. 7:13.

from God's will (Zech. 7:10—12). Their punishment was that God stopped listening to their cries[15]. Thus, God does not hear the prayers of those who are so utterly corrupt in nature that they have no inclination to heed his response[16]. Prov. 14:29 captures this principle, when it says:

> The Lord is far from the wicked
>   but hears the prayer of the righteous.

When Elihu responds to Job's complaints that God is not answering his cries for help, he makes some additional insights into the situation of "unanswered prayer." He begins by asserting (Job 30:20; 33:12) that "God does speak — now one way, now another — though men may not perceive it." He speaks (Job 33:30) through visions and dreams, suffering, and angels "to bring them back from the pit." Numerous ways in which God speaks to people might be added to Elihu's list: through prophets, priests, the law, events, nature, and the accumulated wisdom of men[17]. Elihu goes on in Job 35:12—15 to emphasise that the pleas of the wicked are insincere and empty. Even more counter-productive for eliciting God's positive response to prayer is Job's doubting God's existence and righteousness. What is important, then, in praying to God is confident trust, sincerity, and careful listening for his response. Prov. 8:17 (cf. 2 Chron. 15:2) poignantly says:

> I love those who love me
>   and those who diligently seek me will find me.

The importance of sincerity in prayer cannot be overestimated. This is captured particularly well in Ps. 145:18[18]. It is foolish for people to be insincere in their communication to God, to attempt to hide sinister motives, or to cover up their evil hearts because, as Prov. 5:21 says, "a man's ways are in full view of the Lord[19]." This is helpful in shedding light on why the Lord is, as Ps. 34:18 says, so "close to the brokenhearted" and diligently "saves those who are crushed in spirit." The pain of their distress strips them of arrogance and self-righteousness, and they stand humbled before God by their circumstances and utterly dependent upon him for help. Their cry to him necessarily is absolutely sincere and of a pure heart and so, irresistible to his ear (Ps. 51:17).

---

15 Note a similar approach taken in Prov. 1:28–31. Note also 2 Chron. 15:2; Zech. 1:3; Mal. 3:7.

16 Ps. 26:1–12; 66:16–20; Prov. 21:12–13; 28:9.

17 *Prophets*: Ezek. 3:17–21; 33:7–9; *Priests*: Mal. 2:6–7; *Law*: Ex. 24:3; *Creation and Nature*: Gen. 1; Ps. 29; 33:1–9; 50:1,4; 68:34–35; 78:21–33; 105:34; Job 12:7–9; 37:1–13; Jer. 10:11–16; 51:15–16; *Accumulated wisdom of men*: Proverbs.

18 See also Ps. 17:1; 63:1; Lam. 3:25; Hos. 7:14.

19 Note also Job 34:21–22; Ps. 11:4; 33:13–18; 34:14; 94:11; 145:20; Amos 9:8.

Under these circumstances, it is common for people to be overcome by their guilt and include earnest confession of sin in their pleas for help to God[20]. Prov. 28:13 expresses confidence that true penitence will find God responsive. Confession is not strictly a matter of obeying the law (Num. 5:7) but is critical for the well-being of the guilty. Psalm 32:3—5 rehearses the importance of releasing the bottled-up guilt of sin by confession and the forgiveness of the Lord which followed.

The readiness of God to respond with forgiveness to the confession of the truly penitent is a hallmark of God's character in the Old Testament[21]. As with all prayer, God will not fail to draw near to those who sincerely seek him but hide from those who do not (2 Chron. 15:2).

The desire for sincerity in prayer in Ps. 19:14, then, is well spoken:

May the words of my mouth and the meditation of my heart
   be pleasing in your sight,
   O Lord, my Rock and my Redeemer.

Blasphemy

Broadly speaking, blasphemy in the Old Testament is regarded as any act of shameless audacity toward God by men in which his honour is purposely insulted[22]. It is the complete opposite in every way of praise and prayer but especially of confession. This line of communication to God may take many impudent forms, but essentially the blasphemer knowingly speaks against God resulting in his name being slandered. Ludicrously, he denies and makes sport of the very creator and sustainer of his own existence and well-being.

The condemnation of blasphemy is stated in various ways in the Old Testament Law. Ex. 22:28 simply says, "You shall not curse God!" Lev. 24:15—16 conveys the seriousness of this crime by articulating that the penalty for such action is death. Ex. 20:7 (Deut. 5:1) states blasphemy as a more general principle when it says, "You shall not take the name of the

---

20 Confession in the Old Testament can also refer to vows of commitment to God by an individual or group as an aspect of praise. However, both types of confession, of sin and of vows, "form an integral part of true prayer and worship," as stated by Torrance. As evidence for this, he notes Gen. 32:9–11; 1 Ki. 8:35; 2 Chron. 6:26; Neh. 1:4–11; Job 33:26–28; Ps. 22:32; 51:116; Dan. 9. He goes on to note that confession of sin will often lead to pledges of commitment to God.

21 Note Job 33:27; Ps. 57:1; 65:3; Hos. 14:2; Joel 2:32.

22 Martin and also W. White aided in constructing this definition. Blasphemy must be broadly defined because of the numerous words which are used to convey the idea in the Old Testament (גדף—revile, נאץ—scorn, חרף–taunt, קבב—despise, curse, ברך, bless) and the many different ways in which these can be applied. Note similar comments by G. Wallis. Besides this, as Währisch and Brown, 342 observe, "The concept is sometimes found in the Old Testament even where technical terms for blasphemy are lacking."

Lord your God in vain." That is, his name generally should not be misused
or uttered unnecessarily or irreverently[23]. Invoking the names of other
gods is a form of blasphemy too in that it insults God's honour by indirectly denying his power or his existence[24].

It would seem as though blasphemy would have been inconceivable to
the people of Israel (Brichto, 164). Yet, they are commonly named in the
Old Testament as perpetrators of this vilest of sins. They blasphemed God
by casting scorn on his ability to deliver them into the promised land
(Num. 14:11, 23), by deriding his ability to provide them food and water in
the desert (Ps. 78:18—19; Num. 20:10), by spitefully worshipping the idols of
other gods (Isa. 65:7; Ezek. 20:27), by rejecting his laws and despising his
words (Isa. 5:24), by speaking lies against him (Hos. 7:13—14), by questioning his love for them and his knowledge of their circumstances (Ezek.
9:9), by denying his ability to exercise justice (Ezek. 33:17; Mal. 2:17), and
by arrogantly decrying the value of being his people (Mal. 3:13—15).

Israel's enemies are noted for their blasphemy of her God too (Ps. 73:9).
Most notable of these is Sennacherib, the King of Assyria, who arrogantly
blasphemes God through his messenger, the Rabshakeh[25]. He disdainfully
assaults God and his power to rescue his people, and he mocks Hezekiah
and the foolishness of those like him who trust in God. In captivity,
Assyria again is noted for her mockery of Israel and the blasphemy of
God's name (Isa. 52:5). The Edomites too are noted for laughing at the fall
of Jerusalem, and they are branded for annihilation because of their
blasphemy (Ezek. 35:12).

The story of Job presents an intriguing dilemma with regard to the
issue of blasphemy. In the prologue, it is asserted that throughout his
suffering Job (1:22) did not sin by charging God with wrongdoing. This
would have been blasphemy. Neither does he curse God and even piously
rebukes his wife for even suggesting it (Job 2:10). Yet the charge of
Eliphaz to Job that "you vent your rage against God" seems to be valid
for Job expresses his frustration (not remorse) that he cannot find
adequate words to dispute with God (15:12—13; 9:14). Indeed, he pleads
guilty to God's charge of "contending with the Almighty" and remorse-
fully retracts his sin through repentance at the end of the book
(40:1—2, 5—6). Although it may be argued that Job's sin was something
short of blasphemy, it may also be asserted that his audacity in contending

---

23 Although this command may have originally intended to refer specifically to swearing
   a lying oath in Yahweh's name, as noted by Cole, 157, it may be applied generally to
   using the name of Yahweh "for any valueless purpose . . . any worthless practice," as
   noted by Cassuto, 243–244.
24 Ex. 20:3; 23:13; Josh. 23:7; Ps. 16:4.
25 2 Ki. 18:30–35; 19:4, 6, 22; 2 Chron. 13:13–22; 36:18–22; 37:10–29.

with God is just inside the boundaries of a general definition of blasphemy. His claim to have no wickedness on his lips (6:30) is certainly false and markedly brassy in comparison to Isaiah's keen awareness of his unclean lips before God (Isa. 6:5—7) and ignorantly self-righteous in light of the principle asserted in Prov. 20:9, which says:

> Who can say, I have kept my heart pure,
> I am clean and without sin?

Whether or not Job's sin should be thought of as blasphemy, his audacious boldness in contending with God (until God personally confronts him) bears a close resemblance to the haughty pride which characterises the blasphemer. The blasphemy of Sennacherib, for example, is viewed by God as one of the results of his overwhelming pride (2 Ki. 19:22).

Another result of Sennacherib's pride is his audacious boasting before men (Isa. 10:8—15). This, too, may be seen as a form of blasphemy. Although the boaster directs his immediate remarks to men (or to himself), God hears and is offended. This is because the boaster attributes to himself the honour and glory that are due to God alone[26]. By focusing on himself, he turns his back on God. He says in effect (Ps. 12:3), "I own my own lips — who is my master?" His presumption is usually manifest as well in his confidence that he directs his own destiny, as is the case with Sennacherib. This too offends God as Prov. 27:1 pointedly warns. What God prefers is that men boast only in their knowledge of him (Jer. 9:23—24).

Boasting, blasphemy, and pride are brought together as a triad of sins against God in Ps. 10:3—4, which says:

> For the wicked boasts of his heart's desire,
> And the greedy man[27] curses and spurns the Lord.
> The wicked, in the haughtiness of his countenance does not seek Him.
> All his thoughts are, 'There is no God.'

All of this is not to weaken the fact that the boaster commits offense against his fellow man too. Characteristically, boasting takes the form of mockery in order to humiliate others, especially those who appear to be weak[28]. Mockery, too, is seen as another manifestation of pride (Prov. 21:24) to which God is opposed (Prov. 3:34).

---

26 See Richardson and also Hahn. It is worth noting that the word commonly translated "boast" (הלל) when found in the Hithpael form means "praise" in its Qal form. "Hallelujah" also derives from this root. So, the point that boasting is the distortion of praise can be made based on the Hebrew word itself.

27 There is some difference of opinion about whether בצע is subject or object of ברך, which can mean either "bless" or "curse." There is also speculation that יהוה should go with vs. 4. Neither of these possibilities affect the value of the verse here. See NEB for a recent translation which has included both options in rendering the verse into English.

28 Note that Goliath's boasting (blasphemy) amounted to a mockery of the men in

It is apparent, then, that pride conceives many sinful children who blaspheme God in many ways. God's stand against the proud, however, is unequivocal. Prov. 16:5 (cf. Ps. 5:5) says;

> The Lord detests the proud of heart.
> Be sure of this: They will not go unpunished.

In light of the many pitfalls of pride from the perspective of the Old Testament, a person is wise to keep in mind the advice of Prov. 27:2:

> Let another praise you, and not your own mouth;
> someone else and not your own lips.

Apocrypha and Pseudepigrapha

People are exhorted to give praise to God numerous places in this literature[29]. Sirach does this in a particularly picturesque way in 39:13—15. This exhortation to praise is but a prelude to the actual offering of praise to God which follows in vss. 16—35. The words of praise, as often in this literature[30], consist primarily of reciting the innumerable reasons why God is worthy to be praised. His acts of creation, his sovereignty, his power, his justice, his mercy, and his goodness are some of the more prominent virtues regularly extolled. Regardless of God's worthiness to receive praise, praise which truly pleases and honours him must come from the hearts of people who truly love him (Ps.Sol. 3:2; 6:1; 15:3). As Sir. 15:10 obverses:

> Praise is out of place in the mouth of a sinner,
> for he is not directed by the Lord.
> Praise will be offered by the wise man,
> and the Lord will guide him in it[31].

Truly acceptable praise, like gracious speech of any kind, can only come from a heart which is continually being made gracious by its opening to God's leading. Praise of him in this sense is also inspired by him and therefore cannot be uttered by one who is closed to him (cf. Ps.Sol. 15:3).

Israel's army (1 Sam. 17), and Sennacherib's boasting was mockery of Hezekiah (2 Ki. 18:26–27).

29 Sir. 32:13; Tob. 12:6–7; 1 Enoch 47:1–2; 2 Enoch (A) 52:1, 3; Ps.Sol. 3:2; T.Gad 7:2. The Prayer of Azariah 29–68 calls on all creatures and creation to sing to God.

30 Judith 16:1–17; Tob. 8:5–7; 11:14–15; 13:1–18; Sir. 50:22–24; 51:1–30; Ps.Sol. 3:1–16; 8:29, 40; 10:6–8 (among many in this writing); 2 Bar. 54:7–11. Note especially Sir. 42:15–43:35, in which the author attempts to enumerate all the great words of God but then concludes that they are inexhaustible and that God himself is unfathomable by men. It is suggested that because of these facts, man should praise him all the more.

31 The word I have translated "guide" is from εὐοδόω meaning literally "put in the right way." The NEB translates it "inspired." The word I have translated "directed" is from διαστέλλω (in Ziegler, διεστάλη; in Rahlfs, ἀπεστάλη which means "determine," "give orders").

Praise, it is suggested by Ps.Sol. 15:5, in its relationship to man's normal speech should be seen as "the first fruits of the lips from a pious and righteous heart." The most noteworthy figures in this literature who consciously offer praise in this way are Tobit and his wife Sarah (Tob. 3:2, 11; 8:5—7; 11:14—15; 13:1—8). Judas Maccabeus, Simon Maccabeus, and Judith should be noted for their leading of the people in praise of God following victorious battles[32]. Also in Sir. 35:2 the concept of praise to God is enlarged to include acts of charity and the giving of alms (Tob. 12:8).

Prayer is a string which draws together all the varied strands of the Apocrypha and Pseudepigrapha. Instances of prayers and answered prayers are dotted throughout the literature[33]. Unflinching belief that the sovereign God of Israel does hear and respond to the prayers of the nation and of individuals continues unabated from the Old Testament[34]. If anything, the literature shows more awareness of the importance of sincerity and patience in prayer than before, these perhaps being lessons learned from previous generations of exile[35]. These traits, which exhibit themselves in one's most devotion to God, are the keys to having prayers answered[36]. The person who is devoted to God should also evidence this by his humility, another trait important in prayer (Sir. 35:16—17; cf. Aristeas 192).

As in the OT, God is especially attentive to the cries of the oppressed probably again because of the utter dependency naturally exhibited in their prayer due to their circumstances and their lack of power to fight injustices they face[37].

Sincere repentance and confession of sin are also imperative in gaining God's attention[38]. If a person desires his own sins to be forgiven, however, Sir. 28:2—7 stipulates that he must also be forgiving when his neighbor sins against him[39].

Prayer is used to petition God for many things in this literature. Some of the more prominent are for: success in battle, a safe journey, rain, health, wisdom, protection from demons, procreation, forgiveness of sins,

---

32 1 Macc. 4:24, 33, 55; 2 Macc. 15:29; 1 Macc. 13:47; Judith 16:1–17.
33 Some instances that will not be mentioned in the ensuing discussions are: 3 Macc. 2:1–20; 5:7–20; 6:2–15; Tob. 3:1–18; Sir. 46:5–6 (Joshua), 17–18 (Samuel); Wis. 7:7–12 (Solomon); T.Jos. 3:4–8:5.
34 *Nation*: Ps.Sol. 7:7; Judith 4:9–16; Sir. 48:20–21; *Individual*: Ps.Sol. 15:1; 2 Bar. 47:1–43; Add.Esther C.
35 Sir. 7:10; Ps.Sol. 2:24–29, 40; 34:18–24; Judith 9: Aristeas 17–19.
36 1 Enoch 97:5; Ps.Sol. 6:8. Judith 5:24 speaks of the importance of loyalty in order for Israel to receive God's protection.
37 Sir. 4:5; 21:5; 35:12–24; Ps.Sol. 18:3.
38 See also Sir. 17:19–21; 39:6; Ps.Sol. 9:12–13; Sib.Orac. 3:624–630; Tob. 13:6.
39 T.Gad 6:2 also urges forgiving one who sins against you. Sir. 4:6 speaks of confessing sin to others.

the nation, the temple, and justice[40]. The way in which Sir. 38:9—10 speaks of praying when one is sick is particularly noteworthy in the urgency that is conveyed and the relationship that is implied between sin and sickness. In what appears to be a later development in this literature (Wicks, 338—339), people are urged to pray specifically on behalf of others[41].

Blasphemy in the Apocrypha and Pseudepigrapha is not pictured as a sin which the people of Israel do. Perhaps as a result of the years of exile, they are now considered to be true to their God. In Bel 1—10, Daniel is accused of blasphemy by enemies, but that is with reference to the idol Bel. The one exception is in Judith 8:2, where Judith chastises the elders of Bethula for putting God to the test and "setting yourselves in the place of God." Blasphemy is primarily pictured as a sin of the gentiles (2 Macc. 10:4, 34—35; 12:14; 15:24), particularly of the numerous kings and generals who come parading through Jerusalem boasting of their greatness[42], uttering their contempt for Israel's God, and defiling the temple. These gentile blasphemers include Holofernes, Antiochus, Nicanor, Ptolemy, and Pompey[43]. Sennacherib retains the blasphemy label he merited in the Old Testament (Tob. 1:18; Sir. 48:18). It is because of these repeated "blasphemies uttered against God's name" by the gentiles that Judas Maccabeus is so confident that God will grant him victory over them and vindicate his name (2 Macc. 8:4).

The scope of blasphemy in this literature has been enlarged beyond that of insulting God directly. Despising one's own father and angering one's own mother are now called blasphemy (Sir. 3:16). So too are defrauding one's neighbor and hoarding one's wealth (T.Asher. 2:6; 1 Enoch 94:8).

As in the Old Testament, blasphemy is considered to be rooted in the sin of pride. This is most evident in the descriptions of the gentile kings and generals noted above. Pride and the boasting which usually accompanies it, although injurious to human relationships (Sir. 22:22), is

---

40 *Battle*: 1 Macc. 3:46; 4:30–33; 5:33; 7:40–42; 9:43–46; 11:71; 12:15; 2 Macc. 15:26–27; *Journey*: Tob. 4:19; 11:1; Jub. 12:21; *Rain*: Judith 8:31; *Health*: Tob. 3:2–6; 8:17; T.Gad. 5:9; T.Reub. 1:7; 4:4; T.Sim. 2:13; *Wisdom*: Aristeas 256; Sir. 4:26; *Demons-Evil*: Tob. 3:11–15; 6:17; 8:7; Aristeas 233; *Procreation*: T.Sim. 2:2; T.Jud. 1:3; T.Ben. 1:4–5; T.Jud. 19:2; T.Jos. 3:7; *Forgiveness of Sins*: 1 Bar. 1:13–2:18 (for the nation); 2 Macc. 9:11–28 (Antiochus); Tob. 3:5 (for the nation); Prayer of Manasseh; *Nation*: Sir. 36:10–11; 50:23; Jub. 22:9; Wisd. 19:22; *Temple*: 1 Esdras 4:62; 3 Macc. 1:16; 2:1–20; 3:15; 1 Macc. 4:39–40; 2 Macc. 10:4; 4 Ezra 12:48; *Justice*: Susanna 42:43; Ps.Sol. 2:24–29. See N. Johnson, 7–37, for further comments on these.
41 T.Gad. 7:1; T.Ben. 3:6. Aristeas recommends praying for relatives (242) and for one's children (248).
42 Sib.Orac. 3:202, marks the Greeks as being noted for their haughty kings. Sib.Orac. 3:732–739 warns the Greeks to cease from their arrogance.
43 *Holofernes*: Judith 6:1–9; 9:8–9; *Antiochus*: 2 Macc. 5:17–26; 7:17, 19, 31, 35–36; 9:4–28; *Nicanor*: 2 Macc. 15:6–28; *Ptolemy*: 3 Macc. 1:15–2:20; 3:11; 4:16; 6:22–29; *Pompey*: Ps.Sol. 2:1–40.

primarily a sin against God (Sir. 10:12; 5:1—6). God hates the proud and the blasphemous [2 Enoch (A) 10:5—6; 1 Enoch 96:7] and will not hesitate to punish them for their audacity[44]. Although repentance from such arrogance toward God is possible and acceptable to him[45], there will come a day when such cries for mercy will be too late (2 Bar. 85:12; Sir. 5:8). Thus, Sir. 7:17 (cf. 3:17—19) urges its readers:

Humble yourself to the utmost
   for the doom of the arrogant is fire and worms.

Qumranic Literature

Worship of God was an extremely important aspect of life in the Qumran community. An individual who became a member of this community believed that in doing so he was somehow drawing nearer to God[46]. He was becoming a part of the True Israel and joining a pure and holy community of people utterly devoted to God. In a very real sense, his life was now given over entirely to the worship of God (Dupont-Sommer, 198), albeit worship that was very much corporate, highly liturgical, and rigidly regulated. As 1QH 12:3—4 says:

I will praise your name among those who fear you
   with a song of thanksgiving and prayer
prostrating myself and making supplication continually
   from season to season.

This hymn continues on in rather lengthy fashion to describe the daily (morning and evening) and yearly cycles which regulated Qumranic worship[47]. Judging from the numbers of them that are contained in Qumranic literature, liturgical prayers were an important part of this regulated worship[48]. By this means the community member was required to do this part in the corporate community's effort to offer continual

---

44 Sir. 10:14–18; 16:8; 5:9–10; 27:28; 35:19–24; Wis. 1:6; 1 Enoch 5:4, 6; 2 Enoch (A) 10:5–6; 2 Bar. 83:16; Aristeas 263.

45 Note the repentance and conversions recorded of Antiochus (2 Macc. 9:11–28) and Ptolemy (3 Macc. 6:22–29). See also Sir. 5:8.

46 E. Sanders, 315, refers to 1QH 11:13; 12:22; 14:13–14; 16:12. He suggests that the word "draw near" in Qumranic literature refers to the act of joining the sect or being brought nearer to God within the sect.

47 Dupont–Sommer, 239, n. 2. See also Talmon, "Manual," who goes into great detail deciphering the times and cycles of prayer and worship being described in 1QH 12:4–10 in conjunction with 1QS 9:26–11:8. Within these he believes are allusions to some of the liturgical prayers which were offered by the covenanters.

48 See *DSSE*, 202–212, 250–255. Various liturgies and references to liturgy can also be seen in the main body of Qumranic literature (1QS, CD, 1QH, 1QM). The apocryphal Psalms (11QPs) may have been liturgical too. See Vermes, 58–59, and Talmon, 275, for discussion of these. An Account of David's Poems (11QPSa 27:2–11) speaks of David

worship to God[49]. He would identify with the writer of 1QH 10:14 when he says: "I must not be silent by day or by night." As an individual and truly committed member of the community, he vowed (1QS 10:13):

> Before I move my hands and feet
> 　I will bless His Name.
> I will praise Him before I go out or enter,
> 　or sit or rise,
> 　and while I lie on the couch of my bed.

The extensive efforts that went into the worship of God at Qumran did not come about as a means of seeking his favour. Rather, it was the sincere, humble response to the favour they felt he had already bestowed on them by graciously choosing them as his special people[50]. They also acknowledged God's own innate worthiness to receive praise[51]. Their words of praise and prayer were, they thought, an acceptable "offering of the lips" in which God would delight — more acceptable, indeed, than the sacrifices of the wicked ones in Jerusalem — because their offering was from a pure motive and a righteous life[52]. However, they did not consider even the words of their praise to originate in themselves but to come from God[53]. To be so specially endowed to praise God was their fortune, and it was their sincere goal always to do so.

It is not surprising, then, to find words of praise and thanksgiving to be a constant occurrence in Qumranic literature[54], nor to find an entire scroll

---

writing "3600 psalms and 364 songs to sing before the altar for the daily perpetual sacrifice, for all the days of the year; and 52 songs for the Sabbath offerings; and 30 songs for the New Moons, for the Feast days and for the Day of Atonement." In his description of the Essenes, Josephus in *BJ.* II,8:5 (#128), too, speaks of them reciting "certain ancestral prayers."

49　1QS 6:9. See also 1QH 11:4–7, 23, 25; 1QS 10:13–15, 23.
50　Vermes, 172. Their hymns highlight their own unworthiness and sinfulness before him. See 1QH 10:34–36, for example.
51　As 1QH 7:28 exults, "Who among the gods is like Thee, O Adonai?" Further passages which extol his righteousness, justice, truth, and power are: 1QS 1:26; 10:16; 11:21–22; 1QH 9:14, 39; 11:7; 12:19, 31; 14:23; 15:24; 16:9–10.
52　See 1QS 9:4, 26; 10:6, 8, 14, and especially CD 11:20:20–21, where Prov. 15:8 is quoted. It seems the prayers at Qumran were thought to be a legitimate replacement for sacrificial offers which were unable to be observed in Jerusalem. See Vermes, 176; Dupont-Sommer, 154, n. 1. Talmon, 273–274, points out that this abstention from sacrifice at Jerusalem was not only due to their severe ideological differences with the "impure" officials conducting these sacrifices but also because the Qumran community regulated their worship on a different calendar (solar) from that on which Judaism operated. The covenanters also thought that proper sacrifice could only be done in the temple at Jerusalem. Thus, they did not initiate their own. There are clear indications in their literature that in the end times they intended to restore sacrifice at Jerusalem (1QM 2:1–3). A simplified explanation of the Qumran calendar can be found in Vermes, 176–178.
53　1QH 11:4–5; 1QH 11:28, 33–36.
54　In addition to the various references already noted, see 1QM 10:8–16; 12:15 (19:16); 13; 14; 19:6.

(1QH) consisting of hymns of praise and thanksgiving to God[55]. Many of these, probably from the pen of the founder of Qumran (the Teacher of Righteousness), recount God's faithfulness in protecting and delivering him from the hands of his enemies and extol God's kindness for giving him understanding of God's truth[56]. Others praise God for his marvelous works, for his creating of the world, for forgiving sin, for working through the lives of his servants, and for not abandoning the orphans and the needy[57].

The Qumran community believed that God's very creation of speech in man was in order that (1QH 1:28—31) his "glory might be made known" and his "wonders told" so that "his name might be praised by the mouth of all men." In fact, they believed it was the eternal destiny of all men to praise and acknowledge his truth (1QH 3:22—23; 6:12; 1QM 14:6). Of course, this is because they also believed God to be all-powerful, totally sovereign, and deserving of humble praise from his creatures[58].

Among Qumranic literature are at least two liturgical pieces that are meant to represent angelic liturgy[59]. Aparently, the Qumran community believed that their earthly liturgy, as Vermes notes, "was intended to be a replica of that sung by the choirs of angels in the celestial temple[60]."

Perhaps one of the best statements illustrating the community's commitment to worship is found in a hymn which was to be sung after the final battle in which all the forces of Belial are routed (1QM 14:23). It says:

> But we, Thy holy people will praise Thy Name
> because of the works of Thy truth.
> And we shall exalt Thy magnificence
> because of Thy lofty deeds
> during the seasons and times appointed
> by the eternal testimony.

Because of the priority of the concept of corporate worship, communication to God by the individual in the form of petition is almost totally swallowed up by institutionalised prayer. As Talmon (p. 279) states:

> In order to successfully compensate the loss of the sacrificial cult, and by reason of their group-centered ideology, the Covenanters especially promoted de-individualised,

---

55 Dupont-Sommer, 199, comments on the many similarities between 1QH and the Psalms of the Old Testament.

56 *Protection and Deliverance*: 1QH 2:20–21, 31–32; 3:19–20; 5:2–3; 7:6, 34–35; *Understanding*: 1QH 4:5–6; 7:26–27; 8:4. These references represent only those passages in 1QH which speak explicitly about thanksgiving to God. The same is true for those noted in the next footnote. The idea of praise and thanksgiving to God is really implicit throughout 1QH.

57 In order, see 1QH 11:15; 16:8–9; 14:23–24; 11:3; 5:20.

58 1QH 10:9–10; 1QS 11:17–22.

59 These are "The Angelic Blessings" and "The Divine Throne-Chariot." Se *DSSE*, 212, and the comments of Vermes, 63.

60 Vermes, 175. See also 1QS 11:9–10 and comments by Dupont-Sommer, 102, n. 2.

and therefore stereotypes, forms of prayer which could be adopted without further qualification to communal devotion.

Despite the truth of this, there is no doubt that the Qumran community believed in the importance of individual, petitionary prayer. For instance, a number of the Thanksgiving Hymns appear to be reflections of God's answers to the petitions for help from the Teacher of Righteousness (cf. 1QH 2—10). The point is that there is no emphasis on this type of prayer in contrast to the immense emphasis on corporate, liturgical prayer.

There is reference to personal confession, as when 1QS 11:9 says, "As for me, I belong to wicked humanity," and when 1QH 16:6 says, "Bowing down and confessing all my transgressions, I will seek your spirit of knowledge [61]." However, much greater emphasis is put into the formal confession of initiates (1QS 1:25—26) and into the community's annual, group confession for atonement [CD(B) 2(20):28—30]. Both of these are recorded in the first person plural and contain similar wording[62]. There is no doubt in either the matter of personal or corporate confession (or petitionary prayer, for that matter) that as long as it is sincere, God will hear it[63] and "will pardon their transgressions and cast away their sins[64].

Regarding blasphemy of God, it comes as no surprise that Qumranic literature reveals the community to have been strict. Unlike Israel of old, who despicably blasphemed God by daring to speak of the precepts of his covenant with them as untrue (CD 5:12—13), this special community of God's people was determined never to do so. This "True Israel" highly revered God's law and fanatically honoured the Name[65]. According to the penal code, his name was so holy it was never to be spoken by anyone in their community for any reason, not even when it occurred in a reading from Scripture[66]. To fail to make a proper substitution resulted in permanent separation from the community. A blasphemous tongue was considered to be a product of the spirit of falsehood (1QS 4:9—11).

Josephus records with admiration the fortitude and endurance of the Essenes to withstand from the hands of the Romans "every instrument of torture to compel them to blaspheme against their Lawgiver or to eat

---

61 See also 1QH 1:21–27; 4:34. The translation of 1QH 16:6 follows *DSSE*, 196. This seems a fair approximation of a corrupt text.

62 Talmon, "Manual," 498, suggests that the initiation ceremony was actually performed on the Day of Atonement.

63 See 1QH 5:11–13, for instance, where reference is made to God hearing the Teacher's prayer for help. Also see references above, p. 463, n. 1.

64 1QH 17:15. This is said on behalf of those who have served God "faithfully" (17:4). 1QH 16:17 says that God pardons the sins of those who love him. 1QH 4:14 calls those who seek God with a double heart hypocrites.

65 See 1QS 10:13; 1Qsb 4:28; CD(B) 2(20):20; 1QH 1:30; 5:28; 2:30; 3:23; 9:38; 11:6, 25; 12:3; 17:20; 18:8; 1QM 13:7; 14:4; 8:12; 18:6, 9.

66 1QS 6:27–7:1. See Leaney, 200, and Wernberg–Möller, 113.

forbidden food[67]." What is meant by "their Lawgiver?" Dupont-Sommer is probably correct when he says that this term refers to the Teacher of Righteousness and not to Moses[68]. Although CD 15:3 says that swearing by the Law of Moses profanes the Name of God, it does not utter concern for Moses' name but only for the Law. Qumranic literature and CD 6:3—11 in particular uses the term Lawgiver to refer to the founder of the community, the Teacher of Righteousness. Unlike Moses' name, his is never mentioned in their literature, perhaps because of the honour they gave it[69].

Significant in this discussion also is CD 12:7—8, which speaks of a community member committing blasphemy by taking possessions from a Gentile unless it is the order of the Council to do so. Who has he blasphemed against: God, the Teacher of Righteousness who probably imposed this specific ban, or perhaps the Council which seems to be able to overrule it? Either of the last two possibilities would seem to be most likely in this context. It may be relevant to note here that the only other violations of the Qumran penal code other than blasphemy of God which mandated permanent separation from the community, were gossiping or slandering — not against God — but against the community itself (1QS 6:27—71; 7:16—17).

Even more significant to the discussion is 1QpHab 2:1—10 which brands the Man of Lies (the current high priest in Jerusalem and arch-enemy of the Teacher) and those who have betrayed the New Covenant as profaners of God's holy "Name" because they did not believe "the words of the Teacher of Righteousness which he received from the mouth of God." Further, it is clear that this Man of Lies and his associates in Jerusalem who arrogantly scorned and mocked the Teacher and are thought to have betrayed the people of Israel with deceitful teaching will be punished in the end[70]. Their mournful crying and howling will certainly be heard amidst the calamitous punishment of the wicked described in CD 3:29—36 (also 1QS 4:12—14). In scorning the Teacher, God's interpretive mouthpiece of the Law and the Prophets, they have rejected God's Law. In rejecting

---

67 *B.J.* II,8:10(#152, #153). Important also in this is *B.J.* II,8:9(#145), which says "Their great object of reverence next to God is the name of their Lawgiver, and if any is guilty of blasphemy against him, he is punished."

68 Dupont–Sommer, 31, 33, 87. Vermes, 155–156, appears to agree.

69 Dupont–Sommer, 87, n. 2, even thinks in light of *B.J.* II,8:9(#145), that 1QS 6:27–7:1 refers primarily to blasphemy of the Teacher rather than God. It is an intriguing possibility, yet it is difficult to believe that "the being venerated above all beings" can refer to anyone other than God.

70 1QH 2:11–15; 4:18–20; 1QH 5:23–26; CD 1:14–15; 1QpHab 2:1–10; 8:9–10; 10:6–12; 4QpNah 3:4.

God's Law they have blasphemed him. Nothing kindles his wrath more than stubborn rejection of his commandments[71].

Rabbinic Literature

Proper communication with God was a major concern to the rabbis. As it is related in their literature, attention focused on prayer and praise in both communal worship and individual piety. Rabbinic literature is filled with advice, caution, models, and examples of this concern. As in previous literature, blasphemy again arises in the discussion as a despicable aberration in human communication to God.

Praise to God is considered a responsibility that the people should fulfill with joy and gratitude, not only for the many things he has done for them but also for his personal greatness and power[72]. With singing and instruments, in worship and in prayer, praise and thanksgiving were to be continually offered to his great and holy name[73]. He was to receive blessing for providing food, for the wonders of nature and creation, for bad news as well as good (Ber. 6:1; 9:1—5). In recognition of the enormity of this task, one rabbi says (GenR. 13:15), "A thousand thousands and a million millions of benedictions and thanksgiving we are obliged to offer to thy name."

The rabbis were convinced that the massive effort exerted by the people to voice their many praises to God was worthwhile because God valued these verbal offerings more highly than any other kind of offering, including sacrifices[74]. However, they also recognized the human limitations involved in attempting to express praise for something as inexhaustibly vast and glorious as the greatness of God[75]. Thus, they cautioned against excessive and exaggerated praise because it can become monotonous and meaningless if overdone. God cannot be flattered[76]. They even recognized that sometimes pure silence before him is the best expression of praise[77]. A person's sincerity, it seems, was the key element as far as the rabbis were concerned (Mid.Ps. 88:1).

---

71 CD 2:20; 8:19; 1QH 15:18–19.
72 Ber. 59b. See also the ancient Jewish prayer called *Alenu* found in Singer, 79–80. For a critique of this prayer, see *RA*, 365–366.
73 Sot. 40a; Ber. 32a. On singing and instruments, see Suk. 3:9; 4:1; 5:1, 4; Shek. 5:1; Pes. 10:5–6; Ber. 10a; Meg. 35a.
74 Mid.Ps. 39:3; Tanchuma Wayera #1, 31b (*RA*, 357); San. 92a.
75 Mid.Ps. 88:1. In Mid.Ps. 19:2, Rabbi Abbahu compares God to a jewel without price in that "however you appraise it, you still undervalue it." See also Mid.Ps. 25:6; Meg. 18a.
76 Mid.Ps. 19:2; Meg. 18a; J. Ber. 12d.
77 Mid.Ps. 19:2; J. Ber. 18a.

Sincere intention in fact appears to be the key ingredient to qualify any personal communication to God as acceptable. This is brought out most clearly with respect to prayer. Prayer must come from the heart or it is an utterly worthless exercise in futility[78]. Such sincere, concentrated attention toward God combined with a humble submissiveness to his will is so vital to effective prayer[79] that if in coming to prayer a person cannot direct his whole heart to the task, he is advised not to pray (Ber. 30b; Tos.Ber. 2:7). This indispensable prerequisite for prayer which substantially divides answered prayer from unanswered prayer[80] is usually conveyed by the word *kawwanah*[81]. The word is used to incorporate the ideas of intention, attention, sincerity, devotion, and submission[82]. It is a requirement for all human efforts at prayer and praise to qualify as valid worship.

As long as *kawwanah* is present, the rabbis could allow wide variation in the kind of prayers which constituted acceptable worship as well as in the thing which could be considered worship. For example, both fixed and spontaneous prayer were promoted in private as well as corporate worship. Furthermore, one type of valid worship and prayer was dedicated study of the Torah[83].

A person is encouraged to pray freely whenever and wherever he is able in the field or in bed, provided the situation allows him to demonstrate *kawwanah*[84].

---

78 The importance of the heart to prayer can be seen in numerous other Rabbinic passages. For example, see Ber. 4:5; Ta'an. 2a; 8a; Tanchuma 1 (24e); 9 (111a); Sifre Deut. 41 (80a); ExR. 22:3; Yeb. 105b.

79 On the importance of submission to God's will, see Ber. 29b; Aboth 2:4; Mid.Ps. 65:2. Also see comments by Kohler, 275.

80 In Rosh Hash. 18a, one rabbi suggests that of two men suffering equally, one is healed and the other is not because "one prayed with his whole heart and was therefore answered, the other did not pray with his whole heart and was not answered." See also Mid.Ps. 108:1.

81 Meg. 20a says: "All depends on the *kawwanah* of the heart." J. Ber. 7a (*RA*, 347) says: "Prayer needs *kawwanah*."

82 The best most detailed discussion of *kawwanah* is by Kadushin, *Worship*, 185–195. L. Jacobs, 187–191, discusses the influence of medieval Rabbinic scholars in developing the concept. See also Moore, 2:223–225.

83 Sifre Deut. 11:13 (80a) says, "Just as the service of the altar is called *Abodah* [worship], so is prayer called *Abodah*. Just as the service of the altar is called *Abodah*, so is study called *Abodah*." The quotation is taken from Kadushin, 213, who gives attention to the relationship between worship and study. In addition, see the comments made on this by Moore, 2:240–241. Some rabbis considered study of Torah superior to prayer and even to action. See Shab. 10a; Sifre Deut. §41, 79a–79b (*RA*, 186), the latter of which can be found in greater length in Bonsirven, 64–65.

84 Pes.K. 158a, cited in *RA*, 343. Other passages which touch on the latitude allowed in prayer are: Tos. Ber. 3:18; Tanchuma #1 (24a). In ExR. 38:4 mere weeping is spoken of as sufficient for want of words.

As important as it was to recite the Shema[85] and the Tefillah (Amidah)[86] every day[87], it was stressed heavily that this should never become mechanistic[88]. Neither should one allow himself to be distracted while saying these prayers[89]. The really remarkable thing is that these prayers were for personal as well as public, communal use[90]. Far from becoming a rigid prayer, the Tefillah, which predates all Rabbinic literature available today[91], was encouraged to be — all still is — recited with wide variation[92]. Also, the rabbis encouraged spontaneous and private petitions at various points when it was being prayed corporately[93]. This gives evidence to the fact that even though corporate prayer became extremely important in Jewish worship, the rabbis never lost sight of the real roots of prayer life: personal, spontaneous communication to God[94]. Corporate prayer grows out of personal prayer and is never allowed to absorb the parentage which gives it meaning.

---

85 See discussion of the Shema and its significance to Jewish worship can be found in Kadushin, *Worship*, 78–96; and Moore, 1:291.

86 In the oldest schedule of synagogue worship, the corporate recitation of the Shema was followed by "the prayer" or *Tefillah* , which in its oldest form consists of Eighteen Benedictions. It is also referred to as the *Amidah* because it was said "standing." Good discussions of this prayer, its development, significance, and use can be found in Heinemann, 22–29, 218–229; Kadushin, *Worship*, 97–130; Moore, 1:291–295; Finkelstein, "Amidah." English translations of both Babylonian and Palestine versions are in Schürer, 2:455–463.

87 Ber. 1:1; 4:1–3. Daily recitation of the Shema was considered so important that one rabbi, in Shab. 119b, attributes the destruction of Jerusalem to its neglect. Apparently, the recitation of these fixed prayers, along with others, became particularly vital after the destruction of the temple and the cessation of sacrificial worship. Heinemann, 15, points out that the daily prayers were actually intended to correspond to the daily sacrifices and cites Ber. 26b as support.

88 Aboth 2:18; Ber. 1:2; 2:1; 4:3–4; 5:1; 29b; J. Ber. 38a. See Moore, 2:220–221 and *RA*, 349.

89 Ber. 2:4–5; 3:1; 4:5; Tos. Ber. 2:7 (*RA*, 347); Yoma 19b.

90 Communal use was preferred but by no means required. See Heinemann, 16. One could say them whenever and however one could as long as the requirement of *kawwanah* was met.

91 There are clear references to it by title in the Mishnah Berakoth and all throughout Rabbinic literature. Heinemann, 22, 220, is certain that in its earliest form it pre–dates the destruction of the temple (A.D. 70) by a century at least. Finkelstein, "Amidah," 2, agrees.

92 Heinemann, 24–28, 219ff, notes that not only is there wide variation in the earliest known texts of the Tefillah, there is—and always has been—a wide variation in its form and function within the various synagogal services. Note the difference in the Tefillah from its use in the morning and afternoon service in Singer, 46–55, 100–110. See also Kadushin, *Worship*, 119, where he notes that something new was to be added to it everyday in order to keep it from becoming mundane.

93 See Abod. Zar. 8a, plus Kadushin *Worship*, 120, and Heinemann, 17.

94 Heinemann, 37, 156–191. There is general agreement, as represented by Steinsaltz, 101–107, that personal and spontaneous prayer was the norm in Israel up until the Second Temple Era when "fixed prayers" began to come into use and that it was only much later that these prayers were written down, this because of their fear that the prayers would become mechanical. See Talmon, 272, for more on this.

There is not the least bit of doubt among the rabbis that God does hear
all prayers directed to him and that in some way or another he does
answer each prayer in which the person praying has *kawwanah*[95]. In their
literature, however, there is a great deal of advice and discussion regarding
how to maximise one's prayer efforts. They speak of the importance of
such things as a quiet voice, persistence, and envisaging the Shechinah in
front of oneself[96]. They discuss how long, how often, and what the proper
topics for prayer are[97]. One rabbi makes the point that prayer should not
always be petition[98]. They are aware that some people whose lives and
hearts are more devoted to God than others, who muster more *kawwanah* than others, are more effective when they pray. In this respect,
Rabbi Eleazar in Suk. 14a (cf. Yeb 64a) compares the prayers of the
righteous to a pitchfork, saying:

> Why are the prayers of the righteous likened to a pitchfork? — To teach you that just
> as the pitchfork turns the corn from place to place in the barn, so the prayers of the
> righteous turn the mind of the Holy One, blessed be He, from the attitude of harshness
> to that of mercy.

Rabbinic literature is affectionately sprinkled with stories which report the
miraculous powers of the prayers of the especially righteous. These
prayers, from people like Hanina ben Dosa, Onias the Circle-Drawer, and
Akiba, usually account for sick people who are restored to health and for
the coming of rain[99].

Something that especially stands out in Rabbinic literature is the idea
that the power of an individual's prayer is significantly boosted when it is
offered within community worship[100]. One rabbi says, "God does not reject
the prayers of the multitude[101]." Another says (Ber. 8a), "Whoever has a

---

95 ExR. 21:14; Mid.Ps. 65:2; J. Ber. 13a. God listens with equity to rich and poor alike
(ExR. 21:4; EcclR. 3:10; Aboth 4:29). Prayer has the power to annul decrees of God
(LevR. 10:5; EcclR. 7:1), and if it does not achieve its whole objective, the rabbis are
pleased to note that it at least achieves half of it, at which point Cain's request for
forgiveness is cited with the observation that God withheld half of the decrees against
him (DeutR. 8:1).
96 Ber. 24b; 31a (quiet); Sifre Deut. §29, 71b (persistent); San. 22a (Shechinah).
97 *Length*: Ber. 32b; 61a; Mekilta (Lauterbach 1:216, 2:91); *How often*: Tanchuma 9, 111a;
Tos. Ber. 3:6; J. Ber. 2b; 8a–b; 21a; *Subject Matter*: Ber. 9:3 (a man should not pray
over what is past).
98 DeutR. 2:1. Abelson, 321–339, takes this passage very seriously and makes it the
foundation for his examination of Rabbinic prayer.
99 Ber. 5:6; Ta'an. 3:8; 23a; 25b. Other accounts of people being successful in prayer for
rain can be found in J. Ta'an 64b and Mo'ed Kat. 28a.
100 Kohler, 276–277. His point is supportable as the next few quotations evidence.
However, he quotes the following line which he designates to be from Ber. 8a to
support his case: "He who prays with the community will have his prayer granted."
Although this is a valid inference, I could not locate these exact words.
101 Sifre Num. §135, 51a (*RA*, 35a).

synagogue in his town and does not go there in order to pray, is called an evil neighbor." Still another (Ber. 8a) speaks of the "acceptable time" for prayer being "whenever the community prays."

Kadushin makes a fascinating attempt to explain how important corporate prayer and worship was to the rabbis in wedding the ethical and spiritual values of the Jewish community. He explains that when ten gather in the synagogue, they represent the entire nation of Israel. When one man prays the Tefillah or any other of the statutory prayers of the community, he says, "we" and "us" when he utters his petitions because he identifies himself within the whole of Israel. He does not become dissolved into the community, however. Rather, his self-identity enlarges to include the whole community. Prayer for him is not a matter just between himself and God but requires his awareness of the relationship between himself and the others in his community[102]. As Heinemann (14—17) emphasises, this kind of worship and prayer in which the fixed prayer became such an important element requires no mediator and is rightly considered to be an authentic and original Jewish creation.

There are numerous prayers for numerous concerns included in Rabbinic literature[103]. Perhaps the most significant form the standpoint of its relative absence in previous literature is the preponderance of encouragement for intercessory prayer[104]. Rab (Ber. 12b) says, "Whoever has the power to pray on behalf of his neighbor and fails to do so, is a sinner." Further, a person is encouraged (Mo'ed Kat. 5a) to make known his need so that "many may pray for mercy on his behalf." Much of the encouragement is involved with prayer for the sick to be healed and in conjunction with that to visit them (Ned. 4a). There is dogmatic assurance that this makes a difference in the recovering of the sick person (Ned. 4a; B. Bathra 116a).

---

102 Kadushin, *Worship*, 205–220. Moore, 2:208, 219, and Abelson, 334–335, also recognize the predominant use of the first person plural pronoun to be significant.

103 An excellent sample of a wide variety of prayers is provided in *RA*, 357–368. Of course, there are numerous prayers scattered throughout the Talmud. However, they are concentrated most heavily in Berakoth. One would do well simply to consult a modern Jewish prayer book, like Singer or Birnbaum. Much of the content of these books is ancient. A few of the more significant things that are prayed for in Rabbinic literature are food (Ber. 7:1) and government (Aboth 3:2). There are also prayers in times of danger (Ber. 4:4).

104 Heinemann, 250, notes that there is not much evidence for intercessary prayer within the statutory prayers. He points out, though, that there does seem to be provision for praying on behalf of a sick person at home during a portion of the Tefillah. He concludes from this that intercessory prayer must be seen as an important aspect of communal prayer. However, because intercessory prayers are essentially personal petitions, they are not found written. It should be noted that in DeutR. 6:13, it is said that Moses prayed on behalf of his sister Miriam when she was stricken with leprosy for slandering him.

Confessional prayer is encouraged, both for the individual and for the community as a whole. Confession is an important aspect of the Tefillah and other statutory prayers (cf. Singer). It is also an important aspect of the annual Day of Atonement ceremonies[105]. Personal confession finds its importance as a necessary aspect of personal repentance[106]. Forgiveness is dependent upon forthrightness and sincerity (Mid.Ps. 51:2). Sincere confession is so highly valued by God that it is thought to be immediately effective (Hag. 5a; Ber. 12b). It is even considered possible for confession at the very end of a person's lifetime to merit forgiveness even for a life filled with wickedness[107]. Confession merits life for a person in the future world (GenR. 97). Other significant Rabbinic teachings on confessional prayer include instruction that public sins are to be confessed publicly, private sins privately (Yoma 86b; Abod. Zar. 4b); humility before God is important[108]; it is best for sin to be confessed in detail (Yoma 86b); and daily morning confession should be the custom for everyone[109].

Blasphemy in Rabbinic literature is a most heinous sin for which there is thought to be no excuse and for which punishment should be swift and absolute. In Aboth 4:5, Rabbi Yochana is recorded as saying:

> Whoever profanes the Name of Heaven in secret will suffer the penalty for it in public; ignorantly or willingly, all are the same in profaning the Name[110].

According to the Mishnah, blasphemers are to be stoned, then hung (San. 6:6; 7:4). Capital punishment for this crime was considered justified since in cursing God's name the person had "denied the fundamental principle [of faith]," this being the unity of God[111]. Such severe punishment was reserved for the person who blasphemed using the Divine Name itself[112]. Substitute names and other forms of blasphemy were considered less serious (Sheb. 36a). As in Qumran Literature, the rabbis were extremely cautious about using the Divine Name at all, to the extent that Abba Saul

---

105 See Yoma in Mishna and Talmud but especially 3:8 and 6:2. Some helpful discussion on this can be found in Moore, 1:512; Schechter, 299–305.

106 See Schechter, 335–339, and Moore, 2:513.

107 Kid. 40b; Aboth 4:22. On its value to God, see San. 43b, 44b.

108 As exemplified by Raba's prayer recorded in Ber. 17a.

109 J. Ber. 4, 7d, as cited in Heinemann, 213.

110 In commenting on this verse, Herford, *Aboth*, 99, says that profanity "includes not merely impious speech but any act or word which offends against the majesty of God." Moore, 2:108, makes a similar statement.

111 San. 45b. See also San. 50a. It is considered a great offense to God given that he has elevated man over the rest of creation (LevR. 32:2; EcclR. 10:19). Some rabbis think that blasphemy against God is unforgivable (ARN 39, p. 161; Tos. Yoma 5:6–8; Yoma 86a; Sifre Deut. §328). Pes.K 163b (*RA*, 321), however, would disagree with that view.

112 San. 7:5. There is some division among the rabbis on this. Rabbi Meir, as represented by Sheb. 4:13, thinks that cursing God with certain substitutes is just as serious as using the Divine name itself. The passage shows an awareness that his view differs from other Sages who probably have in mind San. 7:5.

say say that a person has no share in the world to come if he "pronounces the Name with its proper letters[113]." Other sins that fall into the arena of blasphemy because they give God a bad name are: erroneous teaching, putting a colleague to shame, robbing a gentile, and keeping the lost property of a Canaanite[114]. A man's blessing over his good is considered blasphemous if the food was stolen [Tos. San. 1:2 (*RA* 175)]. So is the movement of a wizard's lips and cursing by enchantment (San. 65a; 82b). The proliferation of blasphemy among men is considered to account in part as least for wild beasts and leprosy and it to preclude the coming of the Messiah[115].

As in the Old Testament, boasting in Rabbinic literature is treated as akin to blasphemy in that its sin is actually in arrogance toward God even though it generally takes place before men. The arrogant person has "thrown off the yoke of Heaven," it is said in Sot. 47b. He dares to speak in the place of God[116]. In boasting, he presumes (wrongly) God's special favour to be on him (San. 93b). Concerning punishment for such an offence against God, Rabbi Levi says in LevR. 7:6 that "a person who behaves boastfully should be punished by fire."

Some of the rabbis recognize that it is not only evil men who boast[117]. Some righteous boast as well. It is thought in such a case that God then weakens the person's power and if he is a Sage, withdraws his wisdom (NumR. 21:12; Pes. 66b).

Rather than being arrogant and boastful, a person ought to be humble[118]. Arrogant behaviour is totally out of place since both great and small are equal in God's sight (ExR. 40:4). Further, it is said (Pes.Rab. 185b, *RA*, 491) that "God loves nothing better than modesty."

---

113   San. 10:1. The name was spoken by the High Priest on the Day of Atonement (Yoma 6:2). However, priests outside of Jerusalem were not to use it (Sot. 7:6; Yoma 69b). There is some question as to what exactly this means and to what extent the Name was not pronouned by anyone except the High Priest. For discussion of this, see Urbach, 124–131, and Moore, 1:425–428.

114   In order, see Aboth 1:11; Yoma 86a; Tos. B.Kamma 10:15; B.Kamma 113b. These are cited together in Moore, 2:109.

115   Aboth 5:11; Shab. 32a (beasts); LevR. 17:3 (leprosy); S.S.R. 2:13 (Messiah).

116   LamR. 23; EcclR. 10:1; LevR. 20:2,10.

117   Like Doeg (Mid.Ps. 52:6), Egypt (NumR. 9:24), and Babylon (San. 24a). See also Aboth 5:22.

118   Aboth 4:4; 4:12; 5:22; Pes.Rab. 198a in this light.

Graeco-Roman Literature

Reverence for the gods tops Plutarch's list of standards which the study of philosophy ought to instill in the educated man[119]. This is not accidental. Such an occurrence arises out of the rich heritage of Graeco-Roman piety toward the gods from which Plutarch draws. It is also tied inextricably to the early and deep sense of the providence of the gods in Graeco-Roman literature. Hesiod, in the prologue to *Works*, 1—8, invites the Muses of Pieria to "tell of Zeus your father and chant his praise." He goes on to explain that this is appropriate because of the mighty providence of Zeus over man and his activities. Socrates, in Xen., *Mem.* IV,3:13—14, is said to have counselled that even though the gods remain unseen a person ought to be "content to praise and worship them because you see their works." When an anxious inquirer rightly perceives that "no man can ever render due thanks to the gods for their benefits," Socrates calmly replies that the pious man will simply do the best he can "to never slacken his effort."

After enumerating the natural benefits of God and his providence for which men ought to feel zealous gratitude, Epictetus, in I,16:1—14, also registers the inadequacies of praise (I,16:15) saying, "What language is adequate to praise them all or bring them home to our minds as they deserve?" Like Socrates, his reaction to men's limited abilities to give complete praise is not despair but determination to praise all the more. What truly saddens him is the neglect of praise to God by his contemporaries. He, however, will continue on in hopes of inspiring others[120].

The singing of hymns of praise is apparently an important aspect of this rich tradition[121]. But further, Theog. 943—944 volunteers that singing often accompanies prayers to the gods. Plutarch, in *Mor.* 15:#48, reveals that it was customary "to sacrifice and sing a hymn before touching food," because food was thought to come as a gift from the gods.

Prayer[122] is also a crucial part of the rich heritage of piety contained in Graeco-Roman literature. It, too, is founded upon the prevalent belief in the

---

119   Plut., *Mor.* 1:7e. See similar sentiments expressed by Plato, *Laws* 716d—e; Isoc. *To Dem.* 13; DiogL. 8:22—23 (Pythagoras). Plato considers it one of the primary duties of parents to teach children to respect and worship the gods. See *Laws* 776b, 931e.

120   Epict. I,16:20—21. Epictetus' writing is proliferated with mention of the appropriateness of people praising God for everything, even the most minute matter of nature, to which he refers in I,16:17—18. Other significant references are I,12:32; II,23:6; II,26:29—30; IV,4:18, 7:9; 10:14—17.

121   See also Theog. 1—4; DiogL. 8:23 (Pythagoras); Epict. III,26:29—30.

122   Helpful articles on this topic can be found in Greeven; *OCD*, 875; Heiler, 74—86; Dover 134—138.

providential rule of the gods. From such a view and the associated feelings of dependence on the gods, human petition for help and healing, for blessing and forgiveness, flowed naturally. Theognis represents the commonly accepted view that the gods control all the good and the bad that happens to people and duly advises in 171—172, "Pray to the gods; with the gods is power." Not surprisingly, numerous prayers are found in the pages of Theognis: to ward off bad spirits, to grant good things to happen, to protect a city, and to procure blessing in general[123]. Petition to the gods is also prescribed for the person in difficult straits (Theog. 555—556). But since the gods control both good and evil, one could also petition good for oneself and at the same time misfortune for an enemy as is done in Eur., *Electra* 807.

Even as early as Homer, there is recognition that petition to the gods could alter the course of unhappy events and affect future proceedings, especially in battle[124]. The gods could intervene in human affairs through control of nature but also by miraculous events and healing[125]. They could and would forgive offense when petitioned[126]. Xenophon (*Hipp*. 9:8) believed that the gods would give counsel and stood ready for those who asked when in need. But they had to be prepared to serve the gods obediently even when the future days of prosperity arrived.

Evidence for intercessory prayer appears as early as Herodotus who in VI,61:3—5 tells the story of how a nurse intercedes successfully to Helen, who was worshipped at Sparta, on behalf of a child "to deliver her from her ugly looks." An example is also found in Eur., *Bacc*. 360—363, in which Teiresias invites Cadmus to go with him to "make intercession both for this man [Pentheus], brute savage though he is, and for Thebes that no strange vengeance of God smite them." Plato in *Laws* 687d recommends praying on behalf of one's friend.

---

123 In order, Theog. 11–14, 341–350, 757–768, 1–4.
124 A good example of this is in *Il*. 15:525–530, where upon the prayer of Glaucus, Apollo heals his wounds to allow him to continue fighting. For the general principle, see also *Il*. 7:179; 9:496. Outside of Homer, see Men., *Perikeiromone* 49; Xen., *Cyro*. V, 1:29; Hyperides I, frag. 3; Aiskines 1:116; Lykurgus, *Leokrates* 1. All of these are cited by Dover, 134–138, who includes relevant discussion and more references.
125 On the gods' control over rain and sunshine, Dover, 133–134 cites Andokides 1:137–139; Aristoph., *Peace* 1143, 1157; Herodotus I,87:2; Xen., *Hell*. II,4:14. Concerning the control over drought, epidemics, crops, livestock, and diseases, he cites Xen., *Ath*. 2:6. He cites Lykurgus, *Leokrates* 95 concerning the miraculous diversion of a lava stream by the gods. In the light of all this, it is not surprising that Xenophon, in *Oec*. 5:20, says: "Know of a surety that the right-minded men offer prayer for fruits and crops and cattle and houses, yes, for all that they possess." Later, in 11:8, he speaks of health and strength as answered prayers.
126 Xen., *Mem*. II,2:14; Eur., *Hipp*. 117–120; Aristoph., *Clouds* 1476–1485; *Wasps* 389.

Plato (*Laws* 716d) further thinks that the pious person will "engage in sacrifice and communion with the gods continually, by prayers, offerings, and devotions of every kind." He continues on to say that the impious will not do this, but it is his view that they need not bother because their tainted gifts are in vain anyway. Whenever the gods are petitioned, he (*Laws* 801a—b) also thinks it important to take great care not to request a bad thing as though it were a good thing. With some startling perception, Plato (*Laws*, 687e) perceives that the truly wise petitioner will not want the gods to grant all his requests nor fulfill all his desires but rather, "it is the winning of wisdom that everyone of us, States and individuals alike, ought to pray for." Just as in cursing, Plato believes that a parent's prayer of blessing upon his respectful, and thereby deserving, child receives a special hearing from the gods[127].

Epictetus also admonishes people to free themselves from their desires when they approach God for counsel[128]. But he means something quite different from Plato and apparently wishes to invalidate the concept of petitionary prayer altogether in favour of a merging of a person's desires with what is really best for him. This coincides with what God desires for him. A person ought not to petition the gods to intervene in order to make life happier or better. Rather, he ought to be content with life as it occurs while at the same time maximising his own potential within God's plan for him[129]. Obviously, the peculiar concept of God held by the Stoics must be taken into account here[130]. The same is true in evaluating Seneca's even more overt antagonism toward petitionary prayer[131]. For instance, in *EM* 41:1, he says, "It is foolish to pray for this [sound understanding] when you can acquire it from yourself. We do not need to lift up our hands towards heaven . . ."

With Plutarch, the more conventional concepts of prayer prevail. Like Seneca and Epictetus, he emphasises the importance of a person's own diligent efforts to effect desired results (Plut. *Mor*. 3:239a). However,

---

127 Plato, *Laws* 931c. Xen., *Mem*. II,2:1–4, recites an instance of just such a prayer of blessing by a mother for her son.
128 Epict. II,7:10–12. Compare also Epict. I,12:4–12; III,24:95, 111, 114; Frag. 17 (Loeb, 2:461; Stob. III,4:91).
129 Epict. I,6:32–42; II,19:36; IV,6:32–38. Sharp, 108, cites as from Epictetus a passage from Codex Vaticanus 3, which encapsulates this view of Epictetus' on prayer.
130 Epict. IV,12:7–21; II,7:13; 17:22–25; IV,1:89–90, 99–100; *Ench*. 17. See also Greeven, 782; Sandbach, 26–68; Long, 107–205; Ferguson, *Heritage*; Rist; Edelstein, 71–100; Christenson, 62–73.
131 Sen. (*ME*, VII) *Vit*. 26:7–27:3; *EM* 10:4; 60:1–4; 61:1–2; 67:1–2; 117:22–24. Seneca plays a principal role in Greeven's discussion.

unlike them, this does not even tempt him to throw out petitionary prayer as pointless. Persistent prayer and diligent effort should work together in tandem, as he describes in *Mor.* 15:#67:

> What a delightful picture it is, if we imagine the man who is about to plough as laying hold of his handle before he drives his oxen forward, and calling on Zeus and Demeter to witness his work, the former as effects the growth of the seed by his rains, the latter as presiding over the fruitful powers of the earth.

Plutarch (*Mor.* 2:102d) is also supportive of prayer on the occasion of illness.

Blasphemy of the gods is something about which Plato is among the most concerned in Graeco-Roman literature. He registers his most extreme concern (*Laws* 799a—801c) in desiring to eliminate the possibility of blaspheming the gods through inappropriate words and music in public worship. In order to attain such auspiciousness, he wants the priests to regulate carefully all hymns and the poets to take great care in contriving the wording of prayers in his ideal state. He also wishes to prevent children from blaspheming the gods by shielding them from the learning of falsehoods about them through study of science on the one hand (*Laws* 821b—d) and by stopping mothers from telling untrue tales about them on the other (*Rep.* 2:381e).

Elsewhere, Menander (715k) wishes to curb those who use abusive words against their fathers because this is too often just a prelude to the more serious act of blaspheming divinity. Plutarch (*Mor.* 13:1065d—e) considers it blasphemous to attribute to the gods evil, disaster, or contention between men. Consistent with his Stoic views regarding petitionary prayer, Epictetus is insistent that people should not complain against God or blame him for anything[132]. Seneca (appropriating Socrates) perhaps explains this view best in (*ME*,VII) *Vit.* 27:1, when he says, "For when you rage against heaven I do not say, 'You are committing sacrilege,' but 'You are wasting your time.' "

Boasting, which has been considered as a branch of blasphemy in other literature, is not an offense against God in Graeco-Roman literature. Rather it is strictly an offense against men and, therefore, was examined in Part III.

Philonic Literature

Despite Philo's pessimism about man's ability to express appropriate who God is, he is decidedly enthusiastic about how important it is for men to

---

132 For example, see Epict. I,6:37–43; II,19:26.

express worship to God to the best of their ability[133]. Philo makes a strong case in *Spec.* 1:315—317 for the view that the true distinctive of the Jewish people and that which truly binds them together as one people is their reverence for the one, true God. In *Her.* 110 (cf. *Her.* 14—16), he suggests that the ideal way to accomplish this is for a person to consecrate his thoughts, speech, and senses to God: his thoughts so that they might "think of nothing else but God and his excellences," his speech so that "with unbridled mouth it should honour the Father of all with laud and hymn and benediction," and his senses so they might report faithfully the work of God in his creation.

Worship and praise of God for Philo are not a matter of man's caprice. If a person has been blessed by God — and who has not since God providentially is the cause of all good[134] — he is "duty bound to repay God his pilot . . . with hymns and benedictions and prayers and sacrifices." Collectively, these three "have obtained the single name of praise" (*Spec.* 1:224; cf. *Sob.* 58). Although he mentions sacrifices within praise above, he does not think sacrifice wholly satisfies God. Sacrifice is only meaningful if the person truly loves God and lives in holiness (*Spec.* 1:271—272).

Remarkably, Philo on the one hand can speak of God's abhorrence for counterfeit approaches to worship him (Det. 21). Yet, on the other hand he can say (*Abr.* 127) that since God "cannot suffer injury . . . he gladly invites all who set themselves to honour him under any form whatsoever." His contention in the latter passage is that those whose worship is truly God-centered will receive his blessings; those whose worship in reality is self-centered will not receive any blessing, but they will receive no punishment either. Their worship is "accepted," although possibly abhorred, despite improper motivations because this may one day lead to better, truly reverent worship.

To Philo, worship which truly honours God is a rational exercise. It is no trance-like fixation on his being (*Spec.* 2:209). God must be worshipped in all his excellences, in all his powers, in all the manifestations of his work, and in all his roles in the universe among men. The ability to articulate reverent praise and worship which covers all of this in appropriate detail requires the active participation of the mind at its sharpest.

Singing is an important means of expressing worship and praise in Philo's view. Philo clearly is impressed with groups who concentrate their efforts on praise and thanks to God in song for noteworthy manifestations

---

133 See *Sac.* 63; *Leg.* 6–7; *L.A.* 3:206; *Post.* 168; but especially *Mos.* 2:239.
134 *Mos.* 1:12; 2:5, 67, 132; 2:238; *Spec.* 1:209; *Flacc.* 102, 121, 146; *Leg.* 118, 196, 220, 336; *Mut.* 219–223; *Op.* 10,21; 172; Dec. 58; *Fug.* 79–80; *Prob.* 19–20, 41.

of his providential care. He notes that the Alexandrian Jews sang all night long upon hearing of the punishment of Flaccus (*Flacc*. 121—124). The Israelites sang hymns of praise and thanksgiving after across the Red Sea (*Mos*. 1:180; 2:256—257). Singing is mentioned as an important aspect of the Feast of Tabernacles (*Spec*. 2:209). It is a daily event for the Therapeutae and is done by them with a variety that seems to intrigue Philo (*Vita* 84—90). He also considers hymn singing a very positive trait in the individual (*Plant*. 135).

As with praise, Philo believes prayer[135] requires the fullest attention of a person's mind in order to be effective communication to God (*Her*. 14—16). Prayer also requires sincerity and purity of heart[136]. Prayer further is able to spur God's kindly nature if it comes from one whose life is given genuinely to God's service (*Mos*. 2:5; *Spec*. 1:41—42). Thus, Philo makes no apology for his unabashed view that the prayers of certain righteous men in society, such as Moses (*Mig*. 122—125), will always be more effective with God than prayer of others. One wise man coming to God sincerely is equal in worth to a complete nation (*Virt*. 185—186). As long as there are righteous men, the human race has hope, for through such men, says Philo (in *Mig*. 124), "our Saviour God holds out, we may be sure the most all-healing remedy." Philo also deems God to be especially responsive to the prayers of widows and orphans (*Mos*. 2:233—242).

Philo assumes that God does not answer every petitionary prayer (*Spec*. 1:42—43). He also acknowledges that God in his wisdom may require a long time margin in order to bring a prayer to fruition. However, he does not think such delays should inhibit a person's own efforts to prepare for or to contribute to the fulfillment of his prayers. A prime example of this is Moses who, having prayed for God to save the oppressed Israelites and to punish the Egyptians, used the time waiting for the occurrence of divine judgment to prepare himself in wisdom and virtue for his own leadership role in the event (*Mos*. 1:47—59).

There are various kinds of prayer recorded or recommended in Philo's writings. Prayers of petition, intercession, confession, and forgiveness of sin have their importance[137]. However, a distinctive emphasis in Philo is made on prayer which will bring about God's aid in internal purification. Prayer to see God, be filled, led, or guided by him is very prominent as is

---

135 Articles by Greeven, 783–784, and Larson which deal specifically with prayer in Philo have informed the following discussion.
136 *Som*. 2:149; *Spec*. 1:167; *Mos*. 2:107–108, 154.
137 On petition, see *Mos*. 1:173, 185; *Virt*. 58. On intercession, see *Spec*. 1:97; *Congr*. 109; *Flacc*. 7; *Mos*. 2:154; *Sac*. 124. On confession and forgiveness of sins, see *Deus* 135; *Spec*. 1:67, 229; 2:196; *Mos*. 2:24.

prayer to increase in virtue and in wisdom or to control the passions[138]. It should be noted that the majority of these kinds of prayer come from Moses. Prayer is not usually addressed to κύριος but rather to θεός[139]. Although at one point Moses appears to be addressed as a prayer intercessor, this instance usually is taken as involving in some way his relationship to the Divine Logos which normally functions as intercessor in Philo's view[140].

Philo maintains very strict views about blaspheming God. Based on Mosaic law, the penalty is death[141]. Blasphemy for him is not committed only be someone who launches a direct assault on God's nature or sovereignty by a curse but also by someone (*Mos.* 2:206) who "even ventures to utter His Name unseasonably." Philo encloses a number of other infractions within the sphere of blasphemy: dishonouring or cursing parents[142], perjury or any oath taken in God's name that is broken (*Spec.* 4:40; *Dec.* 86,91), augury or divination (*Spec.* 4:48), blaming God for evil that may occur (*Fug.* 81—86), boastfulness (See n. 143), and even murder (*Dec.* 133—134). He notes that some evil men blaspheme God in order to grieve pious worshippers (*Dec.* 63; *Spec.* 2:11). Such is Philo's explanation presumably of Gaius whom Philo records as having embarked upon a blasphemous tirade in front of Philo himself (*Leg.* 353—355, 368). Gaius is also depicted by Philo as committing the worst form of blasphemy by putting himself up as god to be worshipped (*Leg.* 118, 162).

Boasting is thought by Philo to be directly akin to blasphemy. These two sins are conspicuously joined together as transgressions of those responsible for the tower of Babel. The people presumptuously boasted that they could reach God (*Som.* 2:28—291). Boasting, rooted in pride, insults both God and men, regardless to whom the words are immediately directed[143]. For this reason, Philo maintains in *Virt.* 171 that "the men of windy pride whose intensified arrogance sets them beyond cure" will be dealt with by "the divine tribunal." He goes on to give two reasons for this. First, arrogance essentially is an internal problem and visible only to God. Secondly, because the very nature of the arrogant boaster's sin is that he thinks himself above all others, no mere man can suitably discipline

---

138   *Spec.* 1:41–50; 2:17; *Mig.* 171; *Post.* 13, 16; *Conf.* 39; *Congr.* 7; *Prob.* 64; *Abr.* 6; *L.A.* 3:104, 177; *Conf.* 27–31, 93; *Plant.* 52.
139   This is pointed out by Larson, 192–193. He explains that Philo understood θεός to be derived from τίθημι, and that it made reference to the good and gracious, creative power of God in contrast to κύριος which carried the concept of God's justice and judgment.
140   *Som.* 1:164. See Larson, 194–195, and Goodenough, 149–150.
141   *Mos.* 2:196–208; *Hyp.* 7:2; *Fug.* 85; *Mut.* 61.
142   *Mos.* 2:198; *Hyp.* 7:2; *Dec.* 106–120; *Spec.* 2:224–226.
143   *Dec.* 5–6, 40–42; *Fug.* 30; *Mos.* 2:240–241; *Cher.* 77.

him. Besides, he has infringed the boundaries of divinity, anyway. Philo considers the rich and the regal particularly prone to boasting, with their targets being widows, orphans, and the lowly in general and allots for them special warnings[144]. He understands (*Spec.* 1:10) circumcision among Jews to have as one of its purposes the banishing "from the soul the grevious malady of conceit." Finally, Philo (*Cher.* 107; cf. *Spec.* 1:311) asserts that "to be a slave of God is the highest boast of man."

New Testament

In the New Testament, not unlike the Old Testament, it is stressed that God should be the primary object of man's worship and numerous tributes of praise to him may be found sprinkled throughout[145]. In Satan's attempt to persuade Jesus to worship him, related in Mt. 4:10 and Lk. 4:7, Jesus' poignant response (based on Deut. 6:13) sets the staunch, monotheistic tone for the rest of the New Testament[146].

Although there is a growing realisation in the New Testament of Jesus' divinity and his worthiness to receive praise and worship, only in Revelation does one find formal, corporate praise honouring him[147]. As articulated by the Gospel of John (17:1, 4; 21:19), the goal of Jesus' earthly ministry — and even his death — was to bring glory to God the Father and not necessarily to himself. By raising him from the dead, however, God bestowed glory upon him and exalted him to a position where obeisance and profession to his Lordship are due from all men (Phil. 2:9—11; Acts 3:13).

According to Acts, praising God was a normal part of the early Christians' daily lives. It appears that praise and thanksgiving were offered to God spontaneously as well as regularly, corporately as well as individually[148]. Complementing the practice of Christians is the encouragement they receive from the New Testament epistles to rejoice continually, give thanks, and utter praise to God in all conceivable circumstances[149].

144 *Virt.* 161–174; *Spec.* 4:74; *Dec.* 40–43; *Mos.* 2:240–241.
145 For example, Rom. 11:33–36; 15:9–12; Eph. 1:3; 1 Tim. 1:17; 1 Pet. 1:3–9.
146 For instance, see Rom. 1:25. Attempts to worship individuals are sharply denounced in Acts 10:26 (Peter); Acts 14:14–15 (Paul and Barnabas); Rev. 19:10 (an angel).
147 Jesus is portrayed as accepting worship or at least reverence as divine in Mt. 2:2, 8, 11; 14:33; 15:25; 28:9, 17; Jn. 8:38. In Heb. 1:6, it is said that he should receive worship from angels. Hymns and/or praise are offered to Jesus Christ at least in Rev. 5:9–10, 12. Honours are shared with God in Rev. 5:13; 17:10.
148 *Spontaneous*: Acts 4:21; 11:18; 13:48; 21:20 (Gal. 1:24); *Regular*: Lk. 24:53; Acts 2:47; 16:25 (individual).
149 1 Thes. 5:16–18; Eph. 5:20; Phil. 4:4; 1 Pet. 4:16.

These acts could be in the form of song, again either from the individual or from a congregation, and are thought to be empowered by the Spirit (Col. 3:16).

In corporate worship, the engagement of a person's mind is thought essential to ensure that everything is understandable, especially to uncommitted enquirers who might be present (1 Cor. 14:15—25). Order, unity, and sincerity in worship and praise are also thought important[150].

Proclamation of God's goodness is viewed by 1 Pet. 2:9—10 as an essential function of Christian believers now that they are "People of God, a Holy Nation." Worship should be the natural response of gratitude for what God has done for them in Jesus Christ (Heb. 12:28; 13:15; Col. 2:8).

In the New Testament, praise is to be much more than words. As Rom. 12:1 says, a Christian is to make of his whole life "a living and holy sacrifice, pleasing to God." Doing this, it says, "is your spiritual service of worship" (cf. 1 Cor. 6:20). His life given to God in such a way becomes a pointer to doubters of God's goodness and holiness, hopefully eliciting due praise from them as well (Mt. 5:16; 1 Cor. 10:31; 1 Pet. 2:12; 4:11).

The understanding of prayer in the New Testament bears a number of similarities to the understanding of praise. Prayer is offered to God. Both personal and corporate prayer are envisaged and recorded as well as both regular and spontaneous prayer[151]. There is also an emphasis on prayer as a continual attitude of the Christian and as appropriate in all circumstances[152]. Indeed, prayer is designated an identifiable mark of a devout Christian[153]. There is also stress put upon the role of one's mind, especially in corporate prayer (1 Cor. 14:13—15). Finally, the role of the Spirit is thought integral to a good prayer life (Eph. 6:18; Rom. 8:26—27).

Christ is the principal factor in New Testament prayer. Although a new formality in a sense, the truth supporting the practice is a pillar of the Christian faith. Having obediently suffered death for the sins of men, Christ now stands as the perennial mediator between the all-righteous God and ever-sinful men (1 Tim. 2:5; Heb. 7:25—28).

A number of factors are thought to contribute to successful petitionary prayer in the New Testament. Unswerving faith, abject humility, living righteously, praying in the Spirit, and praying according to God's will are

---

150 *Order*: 1 Cor. 14:26—40; *Unity*: Rom. 14:6—12; 15:6; 1 Tim. 2:9—10; *Sincerity*: Jn. 4:24; Phil. 3:3.
151 Acts 1:14; 2:42; 4:23—31; 10:2; 20:36.
152 Phil. 4:6; 1 Thes. 5:17; 1 Tim. 2:1. If Paul is any kind of example, the openings to nearly all of this letters indicate that he prayed constantly on behalf of his readers. See Rom. 1:8—9; 1 Cor. 1:4; Phil. 1:3—4; Col. 1:3—5; 1 Thes. 1:2; 3:9—10; 2 Thes. 1:3, 11; 2:13; Phil. 1:4—6.
153 Rom. 12:12; Col. 4:2; 1 Tim. 2:11; 5:5; Acts 9:11.

chief among these[154]. In Mt. 6:7, undue length and meaningless repetition are labelled hindrances. Yet persistance is encouraged by the parable of the Unjust Judge in Lk. 18:1—8 and implied by Mt. 7:8—9 (Lk. 11:9—10). Any success that is achieved in prayer is ultimately due to God's love for his children and his desire to give good gifts to them. It is also based upon God's inherent ability to deliver faithfully whatever he desires[155]. To be forgiven of sins by God, it is required that a person readily forgive those who may sin against him[156]. Confession should be a regular part of this prayer life, as the Lord's Prayer indicates (also Lk, 18:13).

In the New Testament, confession is also related to initial repentance upon which salvation through Jesus Christ is contingent[157]. This initial confession is also thought to be one of faith in Jesus' lordship and to be a sign of allegiance to him[158].

Intercessory prayer is much in evidence in the New Testament. Jesus, it is said, intercedes for his disciples (Jn. 17:9—16; Lk. 22:31—32). The early Jerusalem church interceded for Peter when he was in jail (Acts 12:5). Paul apparently prayed regularly on behalf of the churches to whom he wrote[159]. He also prayed for Israel to be saved (Rom. 10:1). Epaphras prayed on behalf of the Colossians (Col. 4:13). There is even evidence of the church in Jerusalem praying for the church in Corinth (2 Cor. 9:14). 1 Tim. 2:1 urges that intercession be made for everyone, even kings and those in authority. Jesus urges prayer on behalf of those who might persecute (Mt. 5:44; Lk. 5:29). A distinctive feature in the New Testament is the idea of requesting intercessory prayer. Such requests come mostly from Paul, although not exclusively[160]. His requests are usually made to churches to which he is writing so that by their prayers his efforts to spread the gospel may be bolstered[161].

Blasphemy in the New Testament assumes the Old Testament ideas of slandering God. However, Christ is the one who is more in the middle of the discussion. In the Gospels, various opponents of Jesus accuse him of blasphemy for falsely claiming (in their view) to be God or doing things (like forgiving sin) over which only God has sovereignty[162]. From the per-

---

154 *Faith*: Mt. 21:22 (Mk. 11:24–25); *Humility*: Mt. 6:5–8; Lk. 18:9–14; *Righteousness* : 1 Pet. 3:12; Jn. 15:7; 1 Jn. 3:23; *In the spirit*: Eph. 6:18; Rom. 8:26–27; *God's will*: 1 Jn. 5:14.
155 Phil. 4:19; 1 Cor. 1:9; 1 Thes. 5:24; 2 Thes. 3:3.
156 Mt. 6:12–14 (Mk. 11:25–26; Lk. 11:4).
157 Acts 2:38; 3:19; 8:22; 17:30; 19:18; 26:20. Confession and repentance are associated originally with John's baptism (Mt. 3:2–6; Mk. 1:4–5).
158 1 Jn. 1:9; 4:2; Rom. 10:8–10; 14:11; Phil. 2:11; 2 Cor. 9:13; 1 Tim. 6:12; 2 Tim. 2:19.
159 2 Cor. 13:7–9; Phil. 1:10; Eph. 1:17; Col. 1:19.
160 Acts 8:24 (Simon the Sorcerer to Peter) and Heb. 13:18.
161 1 Thes. 5:25; 2 Thes. 3:1–5; Col. 4:3–4; Eph. 6:19; Rom. 15:30–33.
162 Mt. 9:1–8 (Mk. 2:1–12; Lk. 5:17–26); Mt. 26:65–66 (Mk. 14:63–64); Jn. 10:33.

spective of the Gospel writers, who believe in Jesus' divinity, those who denigrated him while he was on the cross uttered blasphemy[163]. However, blaspheming the Holy Spirit by attributing Jesus' exorcising power to Beelzebub is even more serious and is thought to bear eternal consequences[164]. Outside the Gospels, blasphemy includes not only the cursing of Christ but also the denial of Christ, rejection of his message, turning away from Christ and following false teaching, and behaviour unbecoming of a Christian[165]. All these things in one way or another lay open to disparagement of what is thought to be the basic truth of the gospel that Jesus Christ is Lord (Beyer, 623).

The New Testament has much to say about boasting. Boasting, and the attitude of arrogance which fosters it, is precisely the opposite of the humility which God desires men to have. From Jesus, comes the poignant comment upon which so many New Testament passages build: Everyone who exalts himself will be humbled, but he who humbles himself will be exalted[166]. Jesus seems to have considered the Pharisees and the wealthy to be especially prone to arrogance and boasting[167]. In 1 Jn. 2:16, boasting is associated with worldiness, and in 1 Cor. 3:1–4, it is associated with quarrelling and divisiveness within the Christian community[168]. Pauline literature, which has the most to say about boasting and the related attitudes of pride and arrogance, for the most part continues to staunchly denounce boasting as opposed to God and entirely inappropriate for Christians who have been saved only by his grace and not by any of their own achievement[169]. However, Paul does see a place for a particular kind of boasting. This is to boast in the cross of Christ[170]. He will also boast about what God has achieved through him, despite his weaknesses, to promote the gospel in Christ[171].

---

163 Mt. 27:39 (Mk. 15:29); Lk. 22:65; 23:39.
164 Mt. 12:22–32 (Mk. 3:22–30; Lk. 11:15–23; 12:10). I am aware that there are those who consider the language regarding this being an "eternal sin" to be tautologous, like McNeile, 178, and Allen, 137. However, despite their arguments, there are plenty of others who take the language literally, like Hill, 218–218, and Taylor, 243.
165 Acts 13:45; 18:6; 26:11; 1 Tim. 1:19–20; 6:1; Tit. 2:5; 2 Pet. 2:2.
166 The saying is identical in Lk. 14:11; 18:4, and nearly so in Mt. 23:12. One can see the similar notion in Mt. 11:23 (Mk. 10:15; Lk. 18:17); Lk. 16:15; Rom. 12:16; 2 Cor. 11:7; 1 Tim. 6:17; Jas. 4:10; 1 Pet. 5:6.
167 Lk. 6:24–26; 12:21; 16:5–19; Mt. 23:1–36 (Mk. 12:37–40; Lk. 20:45–47). See also 1 Tim. 6:17–19; 2 Pet. 2:10, 17.
168 See also 1 Cor. 13:4; Phil. 2:2–3; Rom. 12:16; Rev. 18:11, 15, 19.
169 Rom. 1:30 (2 Tim. 3:2); 3:27; 12:3, 16; Gal. 6:3; 1 Cor. 1:26–29; 3:21–23; 4:7; 5:6; 15:10; 2 Cor. 11:16–17; 12:4; Eph. 2:8–9; Phil. 2:3; 3:9–10; Col. 2:18; 2 Tim. 3:1–4.
170 Rom. 5:11; Gal. 6:13–14; 1 Cor. 13–14; 1 Cor. 1:31 (Jer. 9:23).
171 2 Cor. 1:12–14; 10:1–12:21; Rom. 5:11. It is in this light that Gal. 6:4 is to be understood. See a full discussion of this radical concept of boasting in Bultmann, "καυχάομαι."

Chapter 8: Epistle of James

Exegesis
James 4:2c—10

James 4:2c—3

With 4:2c—3, the author begins the attempt to provide a solution to the quagmire exposed in 4:1—2b. The frustrated desire of those who cause such grievous hurt and divisive consternation within the Christian community by various kinds of verbal assault can be traced to their stagnated prayer life. This in turn points to the collapse of any realistic relationship with God. James attempts to draw attention to two possible aspects of their "prayer" life which he believes resulted in the interruption of God's provision for the guilty parties involved.

In 4:2c, it is simply asserted that the reason they do not have what they want is because they do not ask for it. The articular infinitive διά τὸ μὴ αἰτεῖσθαι ὑμᾶς, indicates cause. Just as it is presumed that God is the benevolent recipient of prayer here, so is it also presumed, as in Jas. 1:5 and in Mt. 7:7, that he willingly provides men their requests. Most commentators agree that the assertion here shows dependence upon the traditional saying of Jesus preserved in Matthew[1]. No doubt, the οὐκ ἔχετε is intended to link with the earlier οὐκ ἔχετε and οὐ δύνασθε ἐπιτυχεῖν. However, James does not mean to imply that a functioning prayer life will obligate God to give a person every pleasure he craves. It will soon become clear that it is the desire for pleasures which is nullifying their prayer requests and obstructing their relationship with God. So, the first aspect of their problem is that at least some of the guilty ones are not praying. They are attempting to live independent of his provision for them.

The second aspect of the problem, pronounced in 4:3, is that those at fault, if and when they do make requests from God, do so with their

---

1 P. Davids, 159; Ropes, 259; Mayor, 138; Mitton, 150–151; Mussner, 168; Hiebert, 247; Adamson, 168. Both Laws, 177, and Hort, 91, raise the matter of Mt. 7:7 in discussing Jas. 4:3.

minds focused only upon having their selfish desire for pleasures satisfied[2]. They expect God to provide them with everything they want. The present tense of the verbs αἰτεῖτε, λαμβάνετε, and αἰτεῖσθε indicates that this is the normal manner of prayer for these people. The significance of the active voice form of αἰτέω in-between the two middle forms is difficult to assess. The possibility that some subtle shift in emphasis is intended, although postulated by a few, is discounted by most[3]. Current popular suggestion that the change to the active is intended to enhance the relationship with the traditional phrasing of the statement by Jesus (as in Mt. 7:7) is as good a suggestion as any[4].

The οὐ λαμβάνετε asserts that such prayers are not answered. The causal conjunction διότι followed by the adverb of manner κακῶς plus αἰτεῖσθε charges that such prayers display a bad attitude. They are motivated entirely by personal self-satisfaction. The purpose clause which follows identifies this wrong attitude more specifically. Their prayers are intended to enable them to indulge in their pleasures (ἐν ταῖς ἡδοναῖς ὑμῶν). The verb δαπανάω often means to spend or to spend freely but can also mean to expend or to be extravagant. They intend to spend their answered prayer requests entirely on their pleasure[5]. Their concentration on these things is harming the church. God can hardly honour requests of such a selfish, evil, and worldly (as he will clarify in 4:4) nature. They debase the essence of prayer which presumes an air of good-will and accommodation to God's purposes founded upon an active relationship with him.

James 4:4

With 4:4, James comes to the main point. The "Christians" whose cravings for pleasure control their lives have cut themselves off from any meaningful relationship with God they may have had or think they still have. The striking use of μοιχαλίδες in direct address to open the verse makes the point in itself, although it is followed by more detailed comment. Using imagery similar both to the prophets citing unfaithful

---

2 Some scholars, such as P. Davids, 159, and Hort, 91, understand 4:3 to be a refinement of 4:2c, and, thus, only one problem is being identified. James may be exposing two different problems which correspond to two different classes of people who could be disrupting the church, as Hiebert, 247, suggests, or which constitute the prototype of the guilty person in two different postures toward God, as Laws, 172, suggests.

3 Hort, 90; Mayor, 138; Hiebert, 248, each make different suggestions as to the significance of the shift from middle to active. Dibelius, 219, n. 63; Ropes, p. 259; P. Davids, 159; Mussner, 179, deny any shift in meaning.

4 P. Davids, 159; Mussner, 179; Adamson, 169.

5 P. Davids, 160; Ropes, 259; Mayor, 138. Hiebert, 248, suggests this is accented by the forward position of ἐν ταῖς ἡδοναῖς.

Israel for committing adultery against her God and also consistent with the New Testament imagery of the church as the bride of Christ[6], here those who seek their selfish pleasures are labelled adulteresses to their Lord. P. Davids (p. 161) is probably right in his conjecture tht the plural allows the condemning imagery to be applied to the appropriate individuals as opposed to the entire church.

What follows is a question which expresses an ideological truth the author believes his readers and the "adulteresses" already understand (οὐκ οἴδατε) but have failed to apply to their situation. It explains their inoperant prayer life, their floundering relationship to God, and his reason for calling them μοιχαλίδες. The fact is that φιλία τοῦ κόσμου and a functioning relationship with God are mutually exclusive states (Dibelius, 220; P. Davids, 161). Friendship with the world by definition is ἔχθρα τοῦ θεοῦ. Obviously, κόσμου here is totally negative, as is presumed also in 1:27, and encompasses everything evil about the world and human society (Laws, 174; Hiebert, 250). Both τοῦ κόσμου and τοῦ θεοῦ are objective genitives (Mussner, 181; Hiebert, 250; Ropes, 260).

As a matter of emphasis, practicality, and inference (οὖν), the author recasts this ideological truth into a third class conditional sentence (ἐάν plus subjunctive βουληθῇ). He sets up a hypothetical situation by which those concerned may measure the state of their relationship with God. He also clarifies that motivation or desire (βουληθῇ) is the key factor of which to take note. Mere desire φίλος εἶναι τοῦ κόσμου is equated with actually being a friend of the world, reminiscent of Jesus' equating lust after a woman with adultery in Mt. 5:28. Internally, the choice has been made. It seems clear, too, that James means friendship with the world to be equated with the desire for possessions and also the domination of pleasures within a person. If a person seeks the world, James proclaims unequivocally that he makes himself an enemy of God[7]. The forward position of the predicate nominative ἐχθρός τοῦ θεοῦ puts it into the sharpest possible contrast with τοῦ κόσμου, which is placed last in the protasis. The verb καθίσταται, being middle voice[8], emphasises one's personal responsibility for his situation of antagonism toward God. There is a presumption here that the reality of the person's situation is far removed from where he once was or from where he thinks he is in relation to God. He is in a position now to reap God's condemnation (P. Davids, 161).

---

6 P. Davids, 160, among others, provides the appropriate Old Testament and New Testament references.
7 The poignant contrast with Abraham who is called God's friend in 2:23 is unmistakable.
8 Laws, 174; Hort, 93; Hiebert, 252.

James 4:5—6

In these next two verses, the author attempts to reinforce the reality and the peril of being in such a state of tension with God. This he does by bringing the authority of Scripture to bear on the situation.

The transitional, rhetorical question which begins 4:5 pertains generally to both scriptural references. The question presumes the general principle that no part of Scripture (ἡ γραφή) is pointless or useless (κενῶς). It all has a place within the purposes of God. This is as true regarding the second reference as the first. Indeed, however one takes the notoriously difficult first reference, it is the second that has the most direct impact on the situation of antagonism toward God exposed in the preceding verses. Also, the curt introductory formula of the second reference, διὸ λέγαι, appears to assume ἡ γραφὴ λέγει from the earlier transitional question. For these reasons and because the second reference involves few exegetical difficulties, it will be examined first. Understanding the second, since it is contrasted (δέ) with the first as demonstrating a greater grace (μείζονα . . . χάριν) which God gives (δίδωσιν) to men, may prove helpful in deciphering the exegetical confusion surrounding the first reference.

The scriptural passage quoted in 4:6 is from the LXX version of Prov. 3:34, the only change being the substitution of ὁ θεός for ὁ κύριος. The focus of the quotation must be in the second line which is duplicated in the transition, with the exception of the indirect object. God gives grace ταπεινοῖς. The word originally refers to those in society of lowly estate but, in contrast to ὑπερηφάνοις which refers to insolent, personal arrogance, it must refer here to those of humble spirit generally[9]. The arrogant — whom James must identify with the malefactors in this chapter — who ally themselves with the evil world against God by their infatuation with selfish pleasures, God himself opposes (ἀντιτάσσεται). The present tense of the verb communicates the perennially active nature of God's opposition. It presumes God marshalling forces against such people in the present as well as presiding over their ultimate and future condemnation[10]. What exactly the "greater" grace consists of will yet be elaborated in vss. 7—10. For now, the simple point made from Scripture that the humble are in God's favour — in contrast to God's fundamental opposition to the arrogant — is sufficient to give solid authority to the principle of exclusivity between God and the world.

The fact that the quotation of 4:6 points to a "greater" grace indicates that the enigmatic citation of 4:5 points to a "lesser" grace, as it were. As

---

9 See Hort, 95, for detailed study of these words.
10 The common use of ἀντιτάσσω as a military word is noted by Hort, 95.

with the second, it must refer to a positive way in which God helps people beyond what they deserve[11]. This should pertain to those who vainly seek the pleasures of the world as related in 4:4.

On the basis of these criteria, one of the approaches to understanding the citation of 4:5 can confidently be eliminated from the start. This is the view that τὸ πνεῦμα refers to man's natural spirit and φθόνον, in its most usual (in the New Testament) negative sense, to envy for something someone else has. This view is championed by Adamson of modern commentaries, but it is also proffered in a considerable number of English translations[12]. Despite the contrast this understanding provides with 4:6 (required by the δέ) and the support it provides 4:4, it can hardly qualify as a "grace". Neither is there any Scripture passage that remotely matches the sentiment which results. Besides, it is generally agreed among commentators that ὃ κατῴκισεν ἐν ἡμῖν refers to the activity of God. In light of 1:12—14, it seems inconceivable that the author of James could associate with God "the sinful propensities of the spirit implanted in man," as Adamson, 172, puts it.

By far, the most popular understanding of the scriptural citation in 4:5 takes God to be the subject of the sentence, based on the relatively clear indication that God is the referent of ὅ and in 4:6 is the understood subject of δίδωσιν[13]. The reference to τὸ πνεῦμα, signifying the human spirit, becomes the direct object of ἐπιποθεῖ, with πρὸς φθόνον becoming associated with God rather than with man. One advantage of this understanding is that it is positive enough to qualify as a grace. But despite awkward attempts, it does not relate very well as support for 4:4[14]. Neither is the resultant idea an expression that can be found in Scripture. Attempts have been made and are still being made to find an appropriate reference outside canonical Scripture or to piece together various Old Testament references, yet nothing thus far is very convincing (Jeremias). For this reason, those who champion this interpretation are virtually unanimous in concluding that the precise text which James cites is unknown.

This view has the additional disadvantage of depicting God in an extremely inauspicious and unbecoming way. Laws rightly points out in

---

11 This is Mitton's, 156, definition of χάρις. It would be to wrong to project a technical Christian (Pauline) sense in James. However, the overly conscious effort of Hort, 95, to give the word no more theological significance than "acceptance" goes too far the other way.

12 Adamson, 172. The NEB, KJV, NIV, YEV, and NAB all adopt this view.

13 P. Davids, 162–164; Hort, 93–94; Ropes, 262; Dibelius, 222; Mussner, 182; Mitton, 154. This understanding is conveyed in the NASB.

14 It seems odd that the noble desire of God for his creation (man) should be cited as support for God's opposition to the person who chooses the world instead of him.

protest against this interpretation that φθόνος, which does not even appear in the LXX, is always a debased emotion. God may be jealous (ζῆλος) over people that are his, but he is not envious (φθόνος) over something that is not his[15]. Those who defend this approach (P. Davids, 164) may be right in responding that the author replaced ζῆλος with φθόνος because of the totally negative way in which he has used ζῆλος—ζηλόω up to this point (3:14, 16; 4:2). Regardless, the lack of an appropriate scripture reference still weighs heavily against this view.

Laws' fresh look at the problems of 4:5 offers intriguing possibilities, and with some amending becomes the best solution so far[16]. P Davids (p. 162) is quite right to fault her for understanding the citation as a question requiring a negative response when there is no μή to indicate this. In addition to making the quotation a question, she retains the normal negative sense of φθόνον and takes τὸ πνεῦμα, which she understands to refer to the human spirit, as the subject. By making it a rhetorical question with an assumed negative response, she transforms the citation into a positive circumstance and thus an appropriate grace. It also relates well to the previous verses.

Laws' most valuable contribution is the Old Testament references she offers as the quoted material. She finds five references in the Psalms which speak of man "longing." In Ps. 118:20, 131, 175 (LXX), the psalmist speaks of longing for the ordinances and for the salvation of the Lord. Ps. 41:1—2 (LXX) says ἐπιποθεῖ ἡ ψυχή μου πρὸς σέ, ὁ νεός, and Ps. 83:2 (LXX) remarks ἐπιποθεῖ καὶ ἐκλείπει ἡ ψυχή μου εἰς αὐλὰς τοῦ κυρίου. Ps. 83 not only speaks pointedly about coming into the presence of God but also raises the matter of prayer, the option of wickedness, the issue of God's provision for the righteous and the faithful, and most significantly, asserts in vs. 12 that the Lord God χάριν καὶ δόξαν δώσει. These are all matters which concern James in either 4:2c—4 or 7—10. Of course, the unusually phrased idea of God giving grace is most striking in relationship to the line of transition which begins 4:6. But even the idea of God giving glory (vs. 12) may relate to God's exaltation of the humble in 4:10.

Laws adeptly explains the change from ψυχή to πνεῦμα in James to be dictated by the pejorative use of the related terms ψυχική in 3:15 and also δίψυχος in 1:18 and 4:8, and also points to the relevance of Gen. 6:3. She is probably also correct in viewing Ps. 83 as the strongest candidate for being the referent of 4:5, without totally excluding the importance of the others.

---

15 Laws, 177–178. She queries the likelihood that a writer of James' familiarity with the LXX would choose such inappropriate and unprecedented language when perfectly acceptable and familiar language was available from the LXX.

16 Laws, 174–179. See also her article, "James IV. 5." The J. B. Phillips translation renders the citation as a question.

Ps. 41 has its significance in that it is a straightforward request. Ps. 118 (LXX) is significant in that vs. 20 is immediately followed by reference to God rebuking the proud (vs. 21), vs. 131 is followed by a request for mercy and help in overcoming iniquity, and vs. 134 cries out for God's salvation.

Accepting the psalms as providing the best solution to the question of the scriptural referent of 4:5, I propose some amendments. First, there is no reason to read 4:5 as a question. The group of psalms involved do not formulate the relevant words as a question.

Secondly, in retaining τὸ πνεῦμα in the sense of the human spirit as the subject of ἐπιποθεῖ, I suggest the same understanding as in the psalms. That is, God is the assumed object[17]. The human spirit longs for God. The important phrase ὃ κατῴκισεν ἐν ἡμῖν could supply this implication as well. The actual quotation would simply be ἐπιποθεῖ τὸ πνεῦμα which features in some form or another in each of the psalms in question. The attached phrase ὃ κατῴκισεν ἐν ἡμῖν is something of an aside to identify this basic human quest as a natural result of God's creative work and to clarify this as a "grace." This idea would link with the creational aspect of the implanted word in 1:21. As a reinforcement of 4:4, the point is that God in placing this drive for himself within man offers even the most wicked, worldly, pleasure-seeking person perennial, subliminal opposition to his state of antagonism toward God. In addition, this understanding of 4:5, if reference to the wider contexts of these psalms is allowed, provides a bridge to the expanded discussion of the "greater grace" which concerns 4:6—10. This "greater grace," then, details what the repentant sinner who chooses to be loyal to God can expect in the way of God's benevolence which extends to final eschatological exaltation. Two different kinds of grace can then be seen to be involved in 4:5 and 4:6. One has to do with creation, the other with regeneration (or birth and re-birth as in the implanted word in 1:21).

Thirdly, with reference to πρὸς φθόνον, I propose either of two possible understandings. The first stems directly from the above proposals. Since it has been proposed that τό πνεῦμα refers to the human spirit, albeit with a built-in predilection toward God, there is not such a big problem with attributing to this spirit φθόνος in the sense of envy. The human spirit with envy longs for God. If one keeps in mind that James is speaking to a wicked lot whose internal natures have opted for selfish pleasures and the world, it is not so difficult to conceive of this residue from creation maintaining a longing for God which is indeed envious of

---

17   The view I am espousing appears in the JB translation. Hiebert, 257, takes a similar view, although he takes τὸ πνεῦμα to refer to the Holy Spirit. The LB translates Hiebert's view.

the day when the individual's opposition to God will end and its desire for him will be fulfilled. A second possible way of understanding πρὸς φθόνον is to see it as an intensification of ἐπιποθεῖ which overrides its conventional meaning. In connection with this idea, it is worth noting that Ps. 118:131 achieves an intensification of ἐπιποθέω by rendering it as an infinitive and a verb in the standard Hebrew manner. Of these two possible ways of understanding πρὸς φθόνον, the first seems the best.

James 4:7—10

The οὖν draws special attention to the immediate clause to which it is attached, ὑπο/τάγητε ... τῷ θεῷ, as the general message that is inferred from the proverb. The fact that this call for humble submission to God is virtually repeated in 4:10 as ταπεινώθητε ἐνώπιον κυρίου confirms this. That an *inclusio* is thus formed, as Davids suggests, seems likely (P. Davids, 165; cf. Mitton, 157). If this is so, the eight imperatives which lie between the two synonymous pleas are rightly perceived as attempts to specify what the author considers to be involved in humbly submitting to God. In a secondary way, these are also inferred from 4:6. Humble submissiveness to God and the related expanded imperatives follow from the first line of the quoted proverb which refers to God's unabated opposition to those who are so arrogant as to choose the pleasures of the world over him. The three future indicatives, then, are also inferred from 4:6 (including the one 4:10). These expand on the second line of the proverb, describing the various aspects of God's "greater" grace.

All ten of the imperatives in 4:7—10 are constructed in the aorist tense and thus impress upon the reader the need for immediate response[18]. It is possible that the aorist tense also calls attention to the general relevance of the call to submission as well as the suggested manner of going about it which extends beyond the immediate situation to which James speaks. The attachment of clauses with verbs in the future indicative to three of the imperative sentences, thereby forming condition and promise sequences, reinforces this possibility.

The second imperative, presented as a contrast (δέ), is the necessary complement to submitting to God. Just as friendship with God and the world are mutually exclusive, so submission to God and resistance to Satan represent complemenatry action. Giving a middle voice emphasis to the imperatives ὑποτάγητε and ἀντίστητε, both of which are passive in form, stresses the responsibility of the individual for both actions (Ropes, 268; Hiebert, 260). It is notable that James here has made an implicit

---

18   Hiebert, 260; P. Davids, 167; Robertson, 210–211.

connection between Satan, the arrogant, the world (Mussner, 184), and self-seeking pleasures. If one is on God's side, he must oppose Satan even as God opposes the arrogant. Such opposition, with God's authority firmly entrenched by submitting to him, ensures that Satan φεύξεται ἀφ' ὑμῶν. God's grace is revealed in that he helps those who turn to depend on him.

The third imperative, ἐγγίσατε τῷ θεῷ, καὶ ἐγγιεῖ ὑμῖν, commencing 4:8, calls for another dimension of complementary action to resisting Satan (Mussner, 184; Mayor, 145). While one attempts to maintain a healthy distance from Satan he must move as close as he can to God. If he does so, God will certainly respond in kind. Contrasting 4:4, if one desires to be God's friend, he will be. The old blockade erected when one pursues the world falls away simply by a spiritual change of direction. God's forgiveness and immediate acceptance in the aftermath of rebellion against him which is followed by repentance is assumed here. It is an aspect of the next seven imperatives and the most easily recognizable depiction of God's grace.

The employment of familiar cultic language begun with ἐγγίσατε continues in the next two imperatives[19]. The first, καθαρίσατε χεῖρας, ἁμαρτωλοί, represents the external clean-up of actions. The second, ἁγνίσατε καρδίας, δίψυχοι, represents the internal clean-up required in order to approach God in a relationship. The vocatives remind the guilty parties of what they are until this clean-up is enacted. These are the dual aspects of repentance and when completed denote a person newly committed to God. The use of δίψυχοι as a synonym with ἁμαρτωλοί may be an attempt to categorise these Christians who think they can love both God and the world (Mussner, 185; Laws, 184; Hiebert, 264).

The next three imperatives, ταλαιπωρήσατε καὶ πενθήσατε καὶ κλαύσατε, comprising the first sentence of 4:9, further refine the call to repentance. True remorse over sinful rebellion against God should cause a person to feel genuinely miserable for a time. This may be manifested by an attitude of mourning and even actual weeping.

The ninth imperative, ὁ γέλως ὑμῶν εἰς πένθος μετατραπήτω καὶ ἡ χαρὰ εἰς κατήφειαν, and the only one in the third person, attempts to dramatise the drastic turnaround that takes place in sincere repentance by drawing upon the seventh imperative. The contrast with a person's former life of pursuing the pleasures of the world, typified by laughter and joy, must be replaced for a time by mourning and gloom[20].

Finally, the imperative of 4:10, ταπεινώθητε ἐνώπιον κυρίου, as mentioned above, mirrors and re-affirms the general admonition in 4:7

---

19 All commentaries agree on this. See P. Davids, 166–167.
20 Mussner, 186; Ropes, 270; Dibelius, 227; Mitton, 161.

which began this series of ten imperatives. The promise attached to it discloses what James envisages as the penultimate grace of God (Mussner, 186). Those who submit to God and who are forgiven their sins not only are permitted to relate closely to God and empowered to resist Satan successfully, but they are also assured that God ὑψώσει ὑμᾶς. The first two aspects of God's grace are ways in which God aids people in the present life. This last aspect accents grace which God gives for future life. The prospect of eschatological salvation is certainly the greatest grace of all[21].

James 4:13—17

The opening rhetorical construction, ἄγε νῦν οἱ, links the paragraph with 5:1—6 which begins identically.

Whether or not the author has Christians in view is difficult to assess. On the one hand as Laws (p. 190) rightly notes, both 4:13—17 and 5:1—6 lack ἀδελφοί, the author's characteristic indication of Christian address. On the other hand, there is no particular reason to think that he has changed his addressees just because he is chatising a wealthier class of people[22]. He does not always use ἀδελφοί. In fact, he does not use it in 4:1—10 or 5:13—18, both of which are surely addressed to Christians. The presumption in the paragraph is that those addressed know better (4:17), as Ropes, 276, notes. As is his custom, the author chooses to dramatise a specific situation which illustrates a general point that has wide application, to Christian and non-Christian alike[23]. It is wrong for anyone — but perhaps especially a Christian — to proceed in life as if God is uninvolved, unconcerned, and inactive.

James 4:13

The opening ἄγε νῦν is devised to attract the attention of the addressees, οἱ λέγοντες . . . There is a note of rejoinder in the phrase which is intensified by the νῦν[24]. The singular construction of the imperative with the plural object reveals the interjection to be a set rhetorical expression (Dibelius, 231; Hiebert, 273).

The dramatic quotation aptly identifies the addressees as travelling merchants intent upon building their businesses. It is common knowledge

---

21 Mussner, 186; Schrage, 48; Mitton, 163; Ropes, 272; cf. Jas. 1:9, 21.

22 If Christians can be called murderers (4:2), it does not seem to be certain that rich Christians who fit the description in 5:1—6 or here in 4:13—17 are necessarily excluded.

23 Those who agree that 4:13—17 pertains to Christians are: P. Davids, 172; Hiebert, 273; Ropes, 276; Dibelius, 235. Mussner, 189; Schrage, 47.

24 Hiebert, 272, and Mussner, 192.

that Jews were especially active in such endeavours within the Roman Empire[25], although James hardly means to focus on them alone in mentioning this vocation. It is the forward planning of their enterprise to which he draws attention. The future tenses of the four verbs, πορευσόμεθα, ποιήσομεν, ἐμπορευσόμεθα, κερδήσομεν, makes considerable impact in this way. It is notable that James does not depict the itinerary of these merchants with tighter precision. Instead of putting stress on the date of departure, he says σήμερον ἢ αὔριον. Instead of specifying the destination, he says εἰς τήνδε τὴν πόλιν, with the pronoun τήνδε being representative ("this or that") rather than demonstrative ("this")[26]. Finally, instead of pinpointing the length of stay more specifically, he says ἐνιαυτόν, which means "a year" but lacks the numerical adjective ἕνα or even an article to emphasise the time frame. These generalities under the guise of precision are an inevitable aspect of the hypothetical situation projected.

James 4:14

The connection of this verse with 4:13 is established firmly by οἵτινες and αὔριον. The relative pronoun relates back to οἱ λέγοντες (Mayor, 150). As an awkward anacoluthon (P. Davids, 172; Mussner, 160), it functions something like a direct address in the absence of a term to encapsulate the kind of person to which the dramatic quotation of 4:13 refers. The adverbial genitive τῆς αὔριον draws attention to the author's focus on the future, with the article τό pointing to the activities and events which fill out a day[27]. The negative οὐκ along with the present tense verb ἐπίστασθε proclaims that the future is always uncertain. Taking ποία ἡ ζωὴ ὑμῶν as a direct rhetorical question[28], the reader is reminded of the contingent nature of his own life.

---

25 Ropes, 276; Mayor, 150; Schrage, 47.

26 P. Davids, 172; Hiebert, 273; Mussner, 190; Schrage, 46; Mitton, 169; Dibelius, 232; Mussner, 190; Schrage, 46; Mitton, 169; Dibelius, 232, recognizes the movement of τήνδε here away from its normal, demonstrative use. Only Ropes, 276, and Mayor, 150, disagree.

27 Most render the phrase as "the course of the future." The textual difficulties of 4:14 are notorious and among other things have to do with whether the τό was in the original text or not. The majority of commentators think it was. See Ropes, 278; Dibelius, 233; Hiebert, 275; Mitton, 169; Metzger, 683–684. Laws, 191, prefers the τά reading which Metzger explains as an attempt to assimilate to Prov. 27:1. The omission of τό by B is thought to be in the line with the tendency of the document to omit articles. Ropes argues that such a reading allows the ideas to fit better with the thrust of 4:15, which stresses the uncertainty of life more than the uncertainty of the future. It is worth noting that in UBS², τῆς αὔριον is adopted and given a "D" rating, while in UBS³, τὸ τῆς αὔριον is adopted with a "C" rating.

28 Laws, 191; Hiebert, 275; Ropes, 277; Dibelius, 233; Mitton, 169; Schrage, 47; Adamson,

The pessimistic implication in the question is reinforced by the answer which James supplies, introduced by γάρ (Ropes, 278; Hiebert, 277). The answer is a metaphor, ἀτμὶς . . . ἐστε, which the author simultaneously explains and applies by means of two contrasting participles, φαινομένη and ἀφανιζομένη. The prepositional phrase πρὸς ὀλίγον accents the relative brevity of a person's existence, with the adverb ἔπειτα accenting the rapidity of his exit. The passive form of both participles may point to the person's lack of control even over these vital moments of his life.

James 4:15

The opening phrase of 4:15, ἀντὶ τοῦ λέγειν ὑμᾶς, presumes a great deal of the reader. It refers back to οἱ λέγοντες in 4:13. It expects the reader to understand that the subsequent dramatic quotation which follows in 4:15 is the approach to the future which is being recommended to replace what is said in 4:13.

The dramatic quotation is framed as a third class conditional with a double apodosis[29]. In this way, it reflects the uncertainty about the future which James wishes to project. James' use of the protasis, ἐὰν ὁ κύριος θέλῃ, formulates the common Christian appropriation of a sentiment which is widespread in Graeco-Roman literature but curiously absent from earlier Jewish literature[30]. It encapsulates concisely God's sovereignty and on-going involvement in the affairs of men. We are dependent upon him for our existence and for what we do.

Even though the use of the first person plural for the verbs reflects the similar construction of the verbs in 4:13, the verbs here in 4:15 function in a much broader way. This dramatic quotation characterises the approach to the future which all people should have, not just travelling merchants. The attachment of the two demonstrative pronouns to ποιήσομεν endorses the view that James has nothing against making practical plans regarding the future.

James 4:16

The opening words νῦν δέ signify that James is moving from the

---

180. The addition of a γάρ after ποία is well attested but adopted only by Dibelius, 233. See comments in Metzger, 684, and Ropes, 278–279, on this. There are numerous other textual problems of a more minor nature in 4:14. Ropes, Laws, and Metzger offer the best explanations of the generally accepted views on these.

29 It is theoretically possible for ζήσομεν to be part of a double protasis, but virtually all commentators quite rightly reject this possibility in favour of the double apodosis because of the attractiveness of projecting God as sovereign over all things, man's very life as well as his activity. For instance, consult P. Davids, 172–173, and Laws, 192.

30 P. Davids, 172–173; Laws, 192; Ropes, 280; Dibelius, 233.

highminded principle of 4:15 to an assessment of realities. The adverb brings the reader back to the attitude projected in 4:13. The evaluation that καυχᾶσθε ἐν ταῖς ἀλαζονείαις ὑμῶν is based upon how James depicts their typical approach to the future in 4:13. The label he gives applies not just to merchants but to anyone who forgets his dependency on God in planning the future. There is some difficulty in determining which of the two words, καυχᾶσθε or ἀλαζονείαις, refers to the activity of boasting typified in 4:13 and which refers to the associated attitude of arrogance[31]. Both words can refer to either. Although it matters little to the sense, it would seem most natural to view the verb as carrying the action and the participial phrase as conveying the attitude. The fact that it is καυχᾶσθε which is carried into the next sentence as an abstract noun seems to make this conclusive.

Having evaluated the activity as boasting, James unmitigatedly denounces it by remarking that πᾶσα καύχησις τοιαύτη πονηρά ἐστιν. Presumably, it is evil because man admires his achievements — or potential achievements in the case of 4:13 — as arising independently of God. The remarks of 4:15 are the basis for his firm denunciation. It is notable that the author qualifies his branding of all boasting as evil by the correlative pronoun τοιαύτη. This effectively limits his denunciation to the kind of boasting which affronts God and his sovereignty over man's future activities. Boasting in the knowledge of what God has achieved in a person, as advised in 1:9 (as in Rom. 5:2—3; 1 Thes. 2:9; Phil. 2:16), is quite another matter for which James knowingly provides.

James 4:17

There are some who completely despair of discovering in 4:17 a connection with the preceding discussion[32]. The stigma is that 4:17 appears to draw a conclusion about sins of omission but that this is not mentioned or even implied as a concern in 4:13—16.

A remedy to the problem unfolds when the conjunction οὖν, normally inferential, is not taken so strictly. Dana and Mantey suggest that οὖν can be intensive or emphatic ("indeed," "surely," "in fact")[33]. In this light, the

---

31 P. Davids, 173; Laws, 192; Dibelius, 234, read the sentence as "You boast in your arrogance." On the other hand, Hiebert, 279; Mussner, 192; Mayor, 157; Ropes, 280, switch the emphasis to "You glory in your boasting." Adamson, 181, has ". . . you boast in your braggings."

32 Dibelius, 231, and Mitton, 172. Mayor, 152, extends the context to which 4:17 applies all the way back to 1:22 which betrays a lack of confidence about finding application to the immediate context. Laws, 194, looks to Prov. 3:27–28 and James' extensive use already of Prov. 3 as the reasoning behind the inclusion of 4:17.

33 Dana and Mantey, 255. Robertson, *Grammar*, 1191, also speaks of the preponderance of non-illative uses of οὖν in the New Testament, particularly by John. Ropes, 281,

proverbial-like admonition of 4:17 can be read as a second denunciatory response to 4:13—15 of which 4:16 was the first rather than as an inference which must be drawn from the previous context. No doubt the proverb has much wider application than what concerns 4:13—15, but it can hold the ideas expressed there within this scope.

With εἰδότι . . . καλὸν ποιεῖν, the author presumes that those addressed already know the principle he shares with them in 4:15 (Ropes, 276). Anyway, if they did not know it before, they do now. He presumes with μὴ ποιοῦντι that their behaviour depicted in 4:13, whether ignorantly or defiantly, does not operate on this principle. The negative evaluation ἁμαρτία . . . ἐστιν parallels the denouncement of 4:16, πονηρά ἐστιν.

The αὐτῷ, as Mussner (p. 192) notes, is a pleonasm. It has the effect, though, of forcing the reader to personalise the proverb. It is a relative principle which varies in its application according to a person's knowledge of the good. In this case, James presumes that all know the good about how to plan for the future, but some ignore this. If they do, he maintains that they sin against God. They offend him by failing to uphold his sovereignty over their lives.

James 5:13—18

James 5:13

The verb κακοπαθεῖ, which refers to general suffering of a physical and/or emotional nature[34], was used in 5:10 in its noun form (κακοπαθείας) to describe the plight of the prophets. The subject and prepositional phrase which follows, τις ἐν ὑμῖν, indicate that James is still concerned about people within the Christian community who are experiencing hardship of various sorts. He surely has an eye on the mistreatment by the rich he has described in 5:4—6 as well as upon the physical illness which he will take up in 5:14. But he could also have in mind those who have been verbally abused by fellow Christians. Indeed, his advice could be applied by anyone who is suffering for whatever reason. The inverted word order of this first clause makes it likely it is a question[35]. The deduction is supported by the imperative, one-word

---

suggests taking οὖν here as continuative ("so then"), indicating a summation. The author likes to cap his discussions with proverbial sayings which relate somewhat enigmatically to the discussion which has preceded (as in 2:12 and 3:18).

34 P. Davids, 191; Hiebert, 316; Mitton, 197.

35 P. Davids, 191–192; Hiebert, 316; Ropes, 307; Mitton, 195; Mayor, 168. It is primarily German scholarship (Dibelius, 252; Mussner, 216; Schrage, 54) which takes κακοπαθεῖ τις ἐν ὑμῖν and εὐθυμεῖ τις as declarative sentences.

response, James' flare for rhetorical questions (22 in the epistle), and the immediate repetition of the format.

The answer, προσευχέσθω introduces the general remedy for suffering which James prescribes. The word usually refers to prayer of a general sort, but here, given the circumstances, must refer to petition by the suffering individual to God. The author will introduce other types of prayer and elaborate on how they can be made effective when he deals with the specific problem of illness, which comes under consideration in 5:14.

The second question and response, εὐθυμεῖ τις; ψαλλέτω, covers the other half of the emotional spectrum[36]. Good cheer as well as misery should be expressed to God in thanksgiving and praise. Whether the singing is within one's heart, or verbalised in personal prayer or in corporate worship is immaterial to James. His intimated point is that there is a proper response to God to fit any human mood or condition, positive or negative. The two pieces of advice may comprise a fixed set of wisdom in the early church. Regardless, it is likely that the author has in mind his own opening remarks about joy in the midst of trial from 1:2.

James 5:14

James 5:14 comprises the third question and response. The question, ἀσθενεῖ τις ἐν ὑμῖν, is identical to the first one except for the change of verb. The verb ἀσθενέω can refer to weaknesses of many sorts: physical, moral, and spiritual. However, it and its noun and adjective cognates are commonly employed, especially in the gospels, to refer to physical illness. It is the latter meaning that is primary in the context here in light of the references to oil later in the verse, the use of two other words which are associated with illness in vss. 15 and 16 (κάμνοντα and ἰαθῆτε), and the mention of the raising of the person in vs. 15[37]. The attachment of the notion of forgiving the person's sins, however, is evidence that the spiritual aspect of ἀσθενέω must retain some force here. In any case, with this third question, James appears to have narrowed quite intentionally his first general question in order to dwell on the relevance of prayer to a

---

36 Hiebert, 316, speaks of the two covering "all the varied emotional experiences of life." Mussner, 218, explains that James sees "den Menschen als eine Ganzheit."

37 P. Davids, 192; Laws, 225; Hiebert, 318; Ropes, 304; Mitton, 197; Mussner, 218; Schrage, 55; Wilkinson, 331. In contending that Jas. 5:13–18 "is not referring to physical sickness at all, but is rather giving instructions for dealing with people who are discouraged or depressed," Hayden is quite correct that neither ἀσθενέω, κάμνω, nor ἰάομαι are used exclusively to describe physical illness. In doing so, though, he ignores the weight of Mk. 6:13 and the association of oil with Jesus' healing ministry. He also misses the significance of the fact that the person is raised up (5:15), which establishes the situation in 5:14–16 to refer primarily to physical sickness.

particular kind of suffering[38]. The first portion of James' response implies that the nature of the illness he has in mind is serious, for he counsels προσκαλεσάσθω τοὺς πρεσβυτέρους τῆς ἐκκλησίας. Once sent for, James describes what the elders will do, or should do, for the Christian who has need of this aspect of their seemingly official duties as representatives of the local church[39]. That the primary advice is προσευξάσθωσαν ἐπ' αὐτόν reinforces the response given to the first question. The change to the aorist tense is consistent with the other verb (προσκαλεσάσθω) and the participle (ἀκείψαντες) in the verse and signifies the change of focus from more general ideas to a specific instance. The prepositional phrase may simply imply that the sick person is in bed. It is possible that it also refers to the common Jewish practice of laying on hands[40].

An additional duty/practice of the elders is described by the adjoining participial phrase ἀλείψαντες ἐλαίῳ ἐν τῷ ὀνόματι τοῦ κυρίου. The idea of anointing the sick with oil is easy enough to account for, as Reicke ("L'onction," 56) concludes, as "une continuation des guérisons opérées par Jésus." The practice by the Twelve is preserved in Mk. 6:13. However, the full extent of its function here in James eludes attempts at a reliably certain explanation. For this reason, numerous commentators refrain from taking a firm position on the purpose of the oil[41]. Although anointing is associated with many things in biblical and related literature, as Reicke, ("L'onction," 51—54) ably details, there is little room to dispute that ἀλείφω usually refers to a physical act and is often associated with personal grooming, cleanliness, and refreshment. The medicinal uses of oil in the ancient world are asserted with considerable confidence too. Few assert, though, that it is purely medicinal or refreshment here given the context[42]. The elders are not quasi-physicians. It is the spiritual capacity of their prayer as representatives of the church that is involved here. Division exists among scholars as to whether the application of oil is involved with exorcism of demons or is distinct from that[43]. Most do

---

38 Laws, 225; Hiebert, 318; Wilkinson, 328; Mayor, 169.
39 That this function is part of their office is generally agreed. See P. Davids, 192; Ropes, 304; Mussner, 218; Schrage, 55. Wilkinson, 336, does see the task of attending the sick as relating to the representative position of the elder.
40 That ἐπ' αὐτόν indicates the patient is bedridden is mentioned by Hiebert, 318; Mussner, 219; Mitton, 197; Wilkinson, 329. That it indicates the elders lay hands on him is mentioned by P. Davids, 193; Hiebert, 318; Mayor, 169. Both views are conjectural but possible.
41 Ropes, 305; Mayor, 172–173; Mussner, 220; Hiebert, 320; Laws, 227.
42 Wilkinson, 340, does. However, he is opposed by the view of P. Davids, 193 (who denies the oil is medicinal at all); Laws, 227; Ropes, 305; Dibelius, 252–253, who assert varying levels of spiritual significance to the application of the oil.
43 Dibelius, 252–253, maintains that the whole procedure of 5:14 is for exorcising demons. P. Davids, 193, partially agrees. Wilkinson, 332, asserts that the Mk. 6:13

agree that the attachment of "in the name of the Lord" is to guard against
any pagan, magical notions about the properties of the oil[44]. But questions
remain which cannot be answered with certainty. Is the oil part of a
sacrament? Is it a sign of something? Is it made particularly effective by
the prayers? Is it just a routine cure-all of the ancients which the church
has taken up as a matter of practical accommodation?

James 5:15

The continuative καί ensures that the comments of 5:15 are applied to 5:14,
even though they stand quite capably on their own as principles of
effectual prayer. James specifies that ἡ εὐχὴ τῆς πίστεως σώσει τὸν
κάμνοντα. In this instance, the prayer applies to the prayer which the
elders pray over the sick. That effective prayer requires faith might be
self-evident to some (and certainly should be to mature Christians).
However, the author contrasts what he says with the self-centered prayers
of those described in 4:2c—3. He also refers back to 1:5—8 where he
counsels that a person should approach God ἐν πίστει, μηδὲν διακρινόμενος. The substantival participle τὸν κάμνοντα refers to the sick,
although the verb κάμνω can mean to be weary or fatigued, physical
and/or spiritually. This may be another indication of the serious nature of
the illness envisaged (Mussner, 221).

The verb σώσει, as a future tense, in this context stands as a predictive
promise implicitly contingent upon τῆς πίστεως. That it refers here to the
restoration to health of the person who is sick is without dispute. Whether
this is intended to be taken as completely exclusive of its theological-
spiritual meaning is questionable in light of the other theologically charged
ideas which complete the verse[45]. No doubt, the complementary notion
that ἐγερεῖ αὐτὸν ὁ κύριος means to attribute to God/Christ the actual
healing of the sick person so that he is literally raised from his bed. But
this language, along with σώσει, becomes all too suggestive for mere
coincidence when the next promise that κἂν ἁμαρτίας ᾖ πεποιηκώς,

---

passage clearly distinguishes the use of oil from casting out demons. Laws, 227, agrees
with him.

44 P. Davids, 193; Laws, 227; Dibelius, 252; Adamson, 197.

45 P. Davids, 194, flatly denies any eschatological sense to σώσει. Most other commentaries assume this position. However, Mitton, 220, on the distinction between the
physical and spiritual meanings for "save," cautions: "Perhaps, however, we do less
than justice to the New Testament use of the word to make this kind of distinction.
God's forgiveness can be a factor in the restoration of physical health (Mark 2:5). This
means that a right relationship to God and what we regard as physical health are
sometimes very closely related to each other . . . In this context, too, 'save' clearly
means the restoration of physical health but not that alone. It is the restoration of the
man to total well-being, including his relationship to God."

ἀφεθήσεται αὐτῷ is viewed[46]. The third class condition does not indicate that sin necessarily figures into the illness, but the promise certainly intends to allow for that distinct possibility[47]. The author, in keeping with the age in which he lived, does not presume to be able to separate illness that is due to sin from illness that is not[48], nor does he think the elders can. Their prayer of faith for the sick will enable sin to be forgiven too, if necessary, just as in Jesus' healing ministry. James, then, allows for the possibility that the root problem is spiritual, impinging on a person's relationship with God to the point that even his salvation is in jeopardy.

James 5:16a

As in 4:17, the οὖν which connects 5:16 to 5:15 should not be read in its predominantly inferential sense. Either an emphatic or a transitional sense will suit the situation here. The author is adding another piece of advice that relates to healing and prayer. Only loosely applicable to the visitation of the elders detailed in 5:14—15.

At one level, then, when the author advises ἐξομολογεῖσθε οὖν ἀλλήλοις τὰς ἁμαρτίας καὶ εὔχεσθε ὑπὲρ ἀλλήλων he implies that the healing scenario in 5:14—15 may include confession, if the illness is due to sin. Personal responsibility for sin lies with the person who is sick and not with the elders. No one should think that the prayer of the elders will override unrepented sin. At a second level, the admonition stands on its own as a general principle. Members of the Christian community should share their burdens of sin with one another. They should intercede to God on one another's behalf. Whether James contemplates this occurring at public meetings or privately is immaterial[49]. It is spiritual intimacy and unfettered love that should come to the fore with respect to sin amongst Christians.

The purpose of this mutual confession and intercessory prayer James says is ὅπως ἰαθῆτε. The subjunctive stipulates that the healing is not automatic. God is left in control of his own decisions and actions. The healing involved here is primarily from physical illness as in 5:14—16, but internal, spiritual healing, is not excluded.

---

46 Read outside of this context, one would not hesitate to connect 5:15 to notions of salvation.
47 See P. Davids, 191; Mussner, 223; Hiebert, 323.
48 The long established connection between sin and sickness in Jewish literature is noted by virtually all commentaries. See P. Davids, 194–195; Laws, 229; Ropes, 308; Dibelius, 254; Mitton, 201.
49 P. Davids, 196, and Schrage, 56, think confession here is public, Mitton, 202, thinks it is private. Laws, 233, says there is not enough information to know anything certain.

James 5:16b—18

With 5:16b, James declares the power of prayer. This is accented by the inverted arrangement which puts πολὺ ἰσχύει at the beginning. At the same time, the author refines what is necessary for prayer to be successful by the addition of δικαίου to the subject δέησις. It is the prayer of the righteous person, not in the sense of one who is super human but in the sense of one who is obediently submissive to God and committed to his purposes. The ordinary Christian is as capable of such an attitude as an elder of the church, Elijah, or another prophet. Best understood as a passive adverbial clause, the participle ἐνεργουμένη point to God as the active agent of power in answering prayer. The subject δέησις refers to prayer of a requesting nature which has characterised the discussion throughout since vs. 14.

The author desires to prove the point regarding the prayer power of a righteous person by drawing an illustration from Elijah which fills 5:17—18. As his opening remark (Ἠλίας ἄνθρωπος ἦν ὁμοιοπαθὴς ἡμῖν) shows, he chooses Elijah not because he is super human but because he has impeccable credentials as having a close relationship with God and because his accomplishments in prayer are presumably well known. The digest of the story, as told by James, undoubtedly is based upon 1 Ki. 17:1—18:46, although he assumes details that are probably drawn from Jewish tradition[50].

The biblical story does not specifically say that Elijah prayed at the beginning (προσευχῇ προσηύξατο) or at the end of the drought (πάλιν προσηύξατο), that the drought lasted three and a half years (ἐνιαυτοὺς τρεῖς καὶ μῆνας ἕξ), or that the earth produced fruit afterward (ἡ γῆ ἐβλάστησεν τὸν καρπὸν αὐτῆς), although these are reasonable assumptions. It is possible, as many suggest, that the specification of three and a half years for the drought, half of seven years, symbolises a period of judgment[51]. There is no presumption in 1 Kings that a world-wide drought was involved, although ἐπὶ τῆς γῆς may presume to imply this[52]. However, the introduction of the phrase may be intended to prepare for

---

50 P. Davids, 197; Laws, 235; Dibelius, 256; Ropes, 311. Elijah's reputation as a powerful prayer, especially with regard to this rain episode, is enshrined in 4 Ezra 7:109. P. Davids, 197, notes other Rabbinic passages which underscore Elijah's reputation as a powerful prayer.

51 P. Davids, 197, and Laws, 237. Whatever the reason, Lk. 4:25 confirms that three and a half years was the traditional figure associated with the drought Elijah caused on God's behalf.

52 Hiebert, 329, assumes that ἐπὶ τῆς γῆς refers to Palestine alone. Whether or not the drought was limited to a particular locale in fact is not the point. The story in 1 Ki. 17:1-8 does not limit the extent and in fact makes a point about the widow who lived in Sidon (17:9) being affected. It cannot be ruled out that James is drawing upon a

ἡ γῆ . . . in 5:18. The phrase προσευχῇ προσηύξατο represents Semitic reduplication in order to supply an intensity to Elijah's prayer which signifies either sincerity or repetition.

As James relates it, the story of Elijah's prayer is a potent tribute to the power of prayer. Heaven (οὐρανός) and earth (γῆ) were affected for a significant period of time.

James 1:5—8

James 1:5

The opening particle εἰ signifies that 1:5 consists of a first class conditional sentence. In combination with the adversative δέ which follows, the impression is given that τις ὑμῶν λείπεται σοφίας is the reality as the author perceives it, while the goal for perfection (complete maturity) expressed in 1:4 is the ideal.

The second clause is curious in that it functions as the apodosis for the first clause, yet it also functions as a condition for the third clause which expresses the promise that God δοθήσεται wisdom. One cannot go from the lack of something as vital as wisdom to God's delivery of it without the advice contained in the middle clause. There he is instructed αἰτείτω παρὰ τοῦ διδόντος θεοῦ πᾶσιν ἁπλῶς καὶ μὴ ὀνειδίζοντος. He is simply to make his request to God. The preposition τοῦ διδόντος could be simply a genitive of description but here must be appositional, with πᾶσιν being a dative of advantage. The focus is not on how the request should be made but on the nature of the God to whom prayer is directed. He is a God who gives to anyone who asks. And he does so quite freely, with no negative thoughts whatsoever about the petitioner. The adverb ἁπλῶς and the negative adverbial participle μὴ ὀνειδίζοντος express positively and negatively the attitude which characterises God's compassionate manner of responding to the petitioner's request[53]. In this way, the author means to encourage his readers to offer their prayer requests to God.

James 1:6

The adversative conjunction δέ at the beginning of 1:6 forewarns of the refinement the author wishes to make to the principle of prayer petition

---

tradition of a world-wide drought, which further enhances the extent of Elijah's powerful prayer.

53 There is disagreement among commentators over whether to render ἁπλῶς as "generously" or as "freely." P. Davids, 72; Mussner, 68; Schrage, 16; Mayor, 39, understand it to mean "without mental reservation" in parallel with ὀνειδίζοντος. Ropes, 140, is alone in supporting "generously." In that it is most definitely an attitude which is being conveyed which corresponds to "not grudgingly," something which is being freely rather than generously, which emphasises quantity, seems right.

expressed in 1:5. A further condition, then, for receiving his request is
αἰτείτω . . . ἐν πίστει (cf. Mt. 21:21; Mk. 11:23). The next phrase, μηδὲν
διακρινόμενος, denotes more specifically what is meant. He must have
faith that God in his compassionate nature will deliver. He must not doubt
for a moment God's ability or his giving nature[54]. With the clause which
follows, the author attempts to explain (γάρ) with imagery (ἔοικεν) what
is so harmful and wrong about ὁ διακρινόμενος. Such a person is like
κλύδωνι θαλάσσης ἀνεμιζομένῳ καὶ ῥιπιζομένῳ. He is fickle, insecure,
easily influenced by outside forces. His faith is not firm. The imagery
about the doubter is so forceful that it gives impetus to the view that
James envisages here more than a lack of confidence in a particular
prayer request. He must have in mind a deep, internal conflict in a
person's relationship with God (P. Davids, 73). In this, he prepares for the
direct accusations of disloyalty to God in 4:2c—10.

James 1:7—8

In 1:7, James firmly denies that the prayer of the person whose faith is in
such turmoil will be answered. The γάρ is emphatic, coinciding with the
emphasis created by the demonstrative pronoun ἐκεῖνος which modifies
the already articular subject ὁ ἄνθρωπος. There is no hope whatsover ὅτι
λήμψεταί τι παρὰ τοῦ κυρίου. Thus, he is advised not even to think about
it (οἰέσθω).

The fact that the indefinite pronoun τι is used to denote σοφία, instead
of something more definite which one would expect, indicates that the
author considers doubt to circumscribe petition of God with regard to
anything which might be asked of him. It also validates the presumption
that praying "in faith" is a principle that is applicable to prayer petition
generally.

In 1:8, the author further describes ὁ διακρινόμενος (ὁ ἄνθρωπος
ἐκεῖνος) with what appear to be two independent nominatives but which
function as appositional phrases[55]. A person with such doubt is δίψυχος, a
doubleminded man. The word δίψυχος, James being the earliest known
use of it in Greek literature, masterfully depicts the internal division of a
person's allegiance and the consternation of his soul. It parallels the Jewish
concept of the double heart. The switch to the masculine ἀνήρ from the

---

54 The view expounded by Dibelius, 79–81, and carried forward by Mussner, 69, and
    Schrage, 16, that James strictly has in mind confidence that the prayer will be suc-
    cessful is too narrow. That James envisages a crisis of a person's Christian faith here,
    as P. Davids, 73, explains, does not seem to be the emphasis here, but it is certainly
    implied by the imagery of the doubter and by the later branding of his entire life as
    unstable in 1:8.
55 P. Davids, 74, and Laws, 58.

generic ἄνθρωπος is for stylistic variation and occurs regularly in James (1:12, 23; 2:2; 3:2).

A person with such doubt is also ἀκατάστατος ἐν πάσαις ταῖς ὁδοῖς αὐτοῦ. The description corresponds to the image presented in 1:6 by the tossed and driven wave. The particular point here is that the person is fickle and unreliable through and through. The reference is not to a superficial, one-time fault. The person is far — very far — from being the trusting, ready-to-mature Christian that the author desires him to be in order to receive wisdom or in order to have a successful prayer life in general.

Analysis

The type of relationship which the author James desires his readers to have with God is best categorised as that of friendship. In 4:2c—10, this is suggested by the implication that being a friend of the world and an enemy of God is undesirable. The phrase φίλος θεοῦ is also how the author chooses to express the model relationship with God of Abraham in 2:23. Friendship, among many things, demands: loyalty, respect, communication, honesty, trust, help, support, and sacrifice. It is a particularly striking way of depicting the relationship between man and God because of the mutuality that is inherent in the concept. This mutuality is spotlighted in 4:8 with the call to draw near to God followed directly by the assurance that he will likewise draw near. Mutuality plays a part in 1:12 and 2:5 in which those who love God are assured that they will receive the promise he made to them of the crown of life and of the inheritance of the Kingdom, respectively.

God's superiority in the partnership with people who are his friends is expressly denoted in 4:7 in the call to submission (also in 4:10) and in the presumption that it is God's power which frightens Satan away. The importance of acknowledging God's sovereignty over one's life, dramatised in 4:13—17, also brings his superiority to notice. God's capacity to demand repentance and to forgive sin (4:8—10; 5:15, 20), to expect unwavering and undisputed obedience (1:19—27; 2:14—26; 4:4), to judge and to condemn (4:1—12, 17), and to bestow eternal reward (1:12, 25; 2:5; 4:10) further exhibit his infinitely vast superiority over men. Yet, for James, to be a friend of God is accounted man's worthiest goal and the orientation which gives his spiritual quest vitality and meaning.

Praise

The Epistle of James does not involve itself directly in discussing corporate worship or praise of God. Neither does it contain any words of praise directed toward him. James 3:9—10 mentions blessing God, but this is in the context of illustrating the tongue's uncontrollability. Only in 5:13 is praise mentioned for its own sake. Those who are maintaining a healthy relationship with God are advised to sing their praises to him when they are happy. Presumably, this is viewed as quite a natural way for such people to express their acknowledgment that they are indebted to him for their joyful feelings. The context of the advice gives absolutely no clues whether or not James intends for it to be applied to corporate worship. Certainly, the focus at any rate is on the individual and his regular and spontaneous response to God's blessings.

Possibly, the author conceives of the other advice to pray in the face of suffering, to include praise as well as petition. James does speak in 1:2—4 of the potentially positive spiritual effects of facing life's trials and calls on his readers to contemplate such trials in a joyful frame of mind.

Prayer

The author of James presumes prayer is issued instinctively from the person who maintains a genuine relationship with God. In 4:3, the break-down of prayer is disclosed as one of the glaring deficiencies in the lives of the "adulteresses." One of the results is a highly unsatisfactory void of God's benevolent provision. In 5:13, prayer is the spontaneous response by the individual to suffering. In 1:5, request of God for wisdom comes across as only one distinctive example of the myriad of things involved in maturity which a person may lack and which God is only too happy to supply if asked. Prayer, then, is assumed to be the most natural avenue of communication between man and God.

The importance James places on a person maintaining a dynamic life of prayer with God is evidenced by the amount of attention given to it. Three solid sections (1:5—8; 4:2—10; 5:13—18) employing eighteen verses, each with a variety of direct teaching about prayer, is a substantial amount given the brevity of the writing. In addition, James concerns itself with at least three different types of prayer: prayer of petition, inter-cession, and confession. Although most of the advice given has to do with successful petitionary prayer, much of this pertains to the other kinds of prayer as well.

James 1:5—8, 4:2c—3, and 5:13, 17—18 are all primarily about petitionary prayer. James 5:13 recommends prayer to the person who is suffering. His suffering could be mental, physical, or emotional. Petition to God for help, it is assumed, will bring comfort at least and perhaps a change in the situation.

James 4:2c—4 describes the lack of prayer and improperly motivated prayer requests as contributing to the defamation and hurt taking place within the Christian communities. This denuded prayer life is also a clear signal of the turmoil taking place within the culprits themselves which they should recognize. Their lust for selfish pleasures shows them to have chosen the world over God. The audacity of those who continue to "pray" to request that God supply these selfish pleasures which will only further ally them with the world against him is incredible. Of course, God will not answer such prayers of petition.

The problem of the doubting, double-minded, unstable-in-all-his-ways person of 1:5—8 is very similar to this. Indeed, the author may well have precisely the same kind of person in mind as in 4:2c—4. The person of 1:5—8 is told that he is foolish to expect to have his prayers of petition answered by God. His doubt concerning one, individual prayer (for wisdom) is only the door to a sea of confusion within. The implication is that he is not sure what he believes or who he believes in. He is drawn to one view of God one moment and another view the next. His life corresponds to God's will one day, but he rebels against God the next. He does not trust him implicitly. But this is exactly what James says God requires in order to treat a person's petition favourably. How can God, then, grant this man of spiritual wanderlust any of his prayer requests, much less a request for something as precious as wisdom? On the other hand, James tries to encourage individuals who lack wisdom simply to ask for it. God wants to provide men with wisdom; he is capable of it, and he will do it without thinking badly of them for asking. In truth, this observation pertains to any prayer request. God will entrust it to the petitioner freely, willingly, and happily. God only expects him to ask in faith, fully trusting that God can and will supply the need.

The illustration of Elijah's prayer in 5:17—18 furnishes a similar suggestion regarding successful prayer petition. The critical importance of praying in faith is conveyed not only in the knowledge of Elijah's calling as a prophet (which is purposely de-emphasised but nevertheless present by the mere mention of his name), but also in the intensity of his prayer which is given attention by the reduplication which takes place in προσευχῇ προσηύξατο. The attitude which necessarily fuels such intense prayer is firmly dedicated faith. Here, the point is to show that prayer of this nature is successful. It is powerful enough to interfere with "natural" phenomena like rain within God's purposes. Thus, it can also cause God to effect more simple and personal requests as well. The fact that faith here is not merely momentary confidence is made evident by δέησις δικαίου, which leads to the example of Elijah in 5:16. James refers to prayer by a person who has a right relationship to God[56]. His life is a conscious attempt to conform to God's will.

A good example of a person whose confident trust in God and sincerity is virtually guaranteed by his situation in life is the person who is suffering unjustly. James 5:4 speaks of αἱ βοαί gaining immediate hearing from the Lord. The implication is that he will act on such a person's behalf with just punishment toward the offenders. On the other hand, the wailing (ὀλολύζοντες) in the midst of their punishment of the rich who unjustly treat others will go unnoticed by God. Their cries may be sincere then, but it will be too late.

Intercessory prayer is the subject of instruction in 5:14—16. The specific concern has to do with someone within the Christian community who is ill, probably in a fairly serious condition. He is advised to send for the elders of his church who will then offer prayer on his behalf with the ambition of restoring him to health. In addition to their prayer, they anoint the bedridden person with oil, although it is by no means certain what function this serves. Nevertheless, it is clearly declared that they do so in the name of the Lord. It may be that they also exercise the laying on of hands as well. Regardless of these accessories to the prayer, it is manifestly apparent that it is the intercessory prayer itself offered to the Lord which restores the person to health. The author reinforces the point made in his other teaching on prayer by characterising the prayer of the petitioners here (the elders) as ἡ εὐχὴ τῆς πίστεως. The point is stressed that even if his illness is occasioned by sin, the faithful prayer of the elders will overcome this (presuming the person is repentant), and God will heal him.

James 5:16 advises with regard to sin that Christians ought to make it a regular habit to confess their sins to one another as well as to pray for one another. This, too, will enable them to be healed when they are sick. All the help they can provide one another for spiritual growth and encouragement will positively affect their physical health and well-being. Effective intercessory prayer is not viewed as being confined to the spiritual elite but is encouraged to be employed by all in the Christian community.

It is curious that in 5:15—16, where the author directly raises the matter of confession, he does not mention prayer of confession to God. He also mentions forgiveness of sin here but without reference to personal repentance. On the other hand, in 4:7—10, which he obviously intends to be a calling of "adulteresses," "sinners," and the "doubleminded" to re-

---

56 In his M.A. thesis, Parks examines James 1:5–8; 4:1–10; 5:13–18 and concludes that "righteousness" is the concept that underlines James' teaching on prayer.

pentance, he mentions specifically neither repentance, confession, or forgiveness. These are implied, however. Repentance is inherent in submitting to God, humbling oneself, cleansing one's hands, and purifying one's heart before him. How does one draw near to God without repenting and confessing sin? Are these aspects of penitence not epitomised by misery, mourning, and weeping? The assurance of God's nearness, of the devil's fleeing, and of the person's exaltation presumes God's forgiveness, as does the fact that he gives grace to the humble. God's capacity to forgive those who have betrayed their allegiance to him in order to pursue the pleasures of the world is the greatest grace he bestows upon those who repent of their betrayal and confess their sin.

Blasphemy

The specific mention of blasphemy occurs only once in James, but the idea is suggested in a number of other contexts. In 2:7, the rich are pointedly accused of blaspheming τὸ καλὸν ὄνομα τὸ ἐπικληθέν. This refers to the blasphemy of Jesus Christ, primarily by the indirect means of scornfully abusing Christians or even by perjuring against them in court. It is implied in 3:9 that God's name is equally maligned when anyone utters a curse upon another human being who has been made καθ' ὁμοίωσιν θεοῦ. In 4:11—12, it is again intimated that verbal abuse of another constitutes an assault upon God. This time, the situation involves Christians who speak against fellow Christians. It is explained that by doing this, whether he realises it or not, the Christian usurps God from his rightful place as the only qualified νομοθέτης καὶ κριτής. Such a view of the situation is equivalent to calling it blasphemy. For James, then, blasphemy is extended beyond its basic meaning of slander aimed directly at God to the case of one person verbally assaulting another, whether this be the pagan rich slandering the Christian, the Christian reviling another Christian, or simply any human being cursed by another.

Blasphemy may also be in mind when in 1:13—15 James warns against attributing to God circumstances which lead to sin. Again, the word is not mentioned, but the action being warned against would constitute a disparagement of God's true nature which desires only good for men.

Boasting is not labelled blasphemy as such, but there is no doubt that James considers it to be the primary characteristic of rebellion against God and a major offense to God. In 3:5, boasting is raised to conjure up the negative, evil work of the tongue. In 3:14, boasting is equated with lying against the truth. Further, it is associated with ἐπίγειος, ψυχική, δαιμονιώδης, wisdom that is the antithesis of God's wisdom. In 4:6 (Prov. 3:34), arrogance is used to epitomise those who choose the pleasures of the world over God and to whom God is adamantly opposed. The opposite of arrogance, humility, characterises those who, in repentance, manifest a favourable relationship with God. Finally, in 4:13—17, it is disclosed that what appears to be such a natural and seemingly harmless thing as planning the future is equated with boasting and arrogance when it is done without thought of God's sovereignty over the future and even more particularly over whether one will even live to see another day. In that the person deems himself worthy to plan his own future, foregoing his own human frailty, he attempts to stand in a place which rightfully belongs only to God. Such boasting, as James clearly designates it, πονηρά ἐστιν, indeed, ἁμαρτία . . . ἐστιν.

Part V
The Relationship of Speech to Truth

Chapter 9: Background

Near Eastern Wisdom Literature

Near Eastern Wisdom Literature orients its concern for truthful speech around the counselor's responsibility for advising the king. How long will a king value an ill-informed or deceitful advisor? How can the principle of order in society be maintained if truth is not at the core of government?

In Meri-Ka-Re, truth is closely associated with the wise man. It is said (*LAE*, 182) that "[Falsehood] does not exist near him, but truth comes to him in full essence." Meri-Ka-Re also counsels that his truthfulness earns him the "respect" of "the magnates" he serves (*LAE*, 182).

Ani (*AEL*, 2:138) issues a general warning, saying:

Guard against the crime of fraud,
Against words that are not [true];

Amen-em-Opet (*LAE*, 252—253) frames the importance of truthful speech in religious terms, saying:

Do not converse falsely with a man,
  For it is an abomination of God . . . .
God hates one who falsifies words.
  His great abomination is duplicity[1].

Amen-em-Opet also warns of stern punishment for advisors for speaking falsely to magistrates, (*LAE*, 258, 259).

Ptah-Hotep emphasises the importance of precision and equates imprecision with distortion of the truth when he says (*LAE*, 163):

If you are a trusted man whom one magnate sends to another, be utterly exact when he sends you. Do business for him exactly as he says; beware of calumny in speech which might embroil one magnate with another, to the distortion of truth.

A person's ability to speak truthfully on a regular basis is thought to be a reliable indication of the veracity of his character as a whole. Such a

---

1 In Egyptian terms, as Frankfort, 75—76, states, "Falsehood is the opposite of Maat; it is chaos, 'the abomination of God,' that which is perennially defeated in the order of the universe. Hence it is fatal for a man to identify himself with it . . . It destroys the dishonest man, not because he acts against a divine commandment, but because he is not in harmony with Maat, the universal order."

person can be counted upon to speak the truth in every kind of circumstances and can be trusted by the king. Speaking of truth in terms of
"straightforwardness," Meri-Ka-Re (*LAE*, 183) observes, "It is the front
room of the house that inspires the back room with respect." Conversely,
lack of truthful speech indicates unreliability in character. Ahiqar (*ANET*,
429) says:

> My son, hearken not with your ears to a lying man. For a man's charm is his
> truthfulness; his repulsiveness, the lies of his lips.

Speaking the truth should not be merely a matter of expediency, but
rather it should be commitment to an ideal. Ahiqar (*ANET*, 429) says,
"Let a good mouth love the truth and speak it."

Truth is an important quality to look for in choosing one's friends (Ani,
AEL, 2:134). It is imperative in court. Personal integrity should be more
important than loyalty to a conniving employer or even a friend. As
Amen-em-Opet says (*LAE*, 258; *ANET*, 423):

> Do not overstate [through] oaths in the name of your lord,
>   [Through] pleas [in] the place of questioning.
>
> Do not bear witness false words,
>   Nor support another person [thus] with your tongue.

Amen-em-Opet is not against false or exaggerated oaths for reasons of
injustice only. It is also worried about what happens to a person internally
when he lies. "His heart," he says, (*LAE*, 253) "slips back inside him."

Even oaths made in private are warned against. In the Counsels of
Wisdom (*BWL*, 105), it says:

> Do not utter solemn oaths while alone,
> For what you say will follow you afterwards,
> But exert yourself to restrain your speech.

Apparently, the concern is that the oath-maker should not think his oath
made in secret can be broken because there are no witnesses. The power
of the spoken words themselves will hold him accountable. Thus, words
are not to be used falsely even for self-aggrandisement.

As far as Near Eastern Wisdom Literature is concerned, then, it is
critical that speech be truthful. This is the heart of speech-ethics. Respect,
integrity, avoidance of the displeasure of gods and kings, and continued
preservation of order in society are the benefits gained by people who are
reliably truthful. The ability to speak truthfully flows from an inner
quality of the heart.

Old Testament

True speech is an extremely important aspect of the concern for speech-ethics evidenced in the Old Testament. It is best viewed as one of the objectives of gracious speech, or perhaps as an extension of its meaning. It is also one of the positive ways in which one should seek to communicate with men and with God.

True speech refers to speech that is not only factually correct and free from various shades of falsehood but also to speech which is emitted by a reliable and trustworthy person[2]. Thus, honesty, sincerity, and frankness are part of its meaning. It is in this latter sense, as the subjective description of a person's character, that the concept of truth is usually found in the Old Testament. As with gracious speech, true speech is an objective reality which issues from a person with the subjective quality to produce it. True speech is produced by a true person, i.e. one who is reliable, trustworthy, and faithful in his inner man. Like gracious speech, too, true speech is related to faithfulness to God and genuine openness to his influence.

The Value of True Speech

True speech is valuable to the student who desires to mature in his wisdom. He must listen attentively to those who are able to deliver true instruction. As Prov. 23:23 says:

> Buy the truth and do not sell it;
> get wisdom, discipline, and understanding.

True speech is an essential characteristic of wisdom. In opposition to the "smooth" speech of the prostitute, Wisdom says in Prov. 8:7—8:

> My mouth speaks what is true
> for my lips detest wickedness.
> All the words of my mouth are just;
> none of them is crooked or perverse.

---

2 Most dictionary articles on "truth" make this distinction, although most tend to minimise the objective sense of truth and to dwell on אמת as conveying the personal quality of faithfulness. This is based on the fact that the root word is אמן, which means "support." See Palmer; Piper; Blackmann, "Truth;" Jepsen. Thiselton makes a significant effort to counter this tendency to overlook the factual sense of אמת in the Old Testament. Based on the earlier work of Barr, 161–205, Thiselton also attempts to discredit the overdrawn attempt by some theologians to distinguish between Greek (abstract) and Hebrew (quality) concepts of truth. In this attempt, Thiselton charges the etymology of אמת is emphasised so much that it overrides the actual, contextual meaning of the word when it refers to factual truth. He explains (p. 378) that sound methodology demands that "*emet* means 'truth' in some contexts, and 'faithfulness' in *other* [sic] contexts."

True speech is valuable to friendship. True friendship is based upon communication that is frank and honest, even when it may cause temporary hurt. As Prov. 24:26 (cf. Prov. 27:5) candidly puts it: "An honest answer is like a kiss on the lips."

True speech is valuable in relaying messages. A messenger who can dependably perceive the truth of a message and convey it accurately will soothe the anxieties of the relaying parties and help to avoid possible misunderstandings between them. Prov. 25:13 says:

> Like the coolness of snow at harvest time
>   is a trustworthy messenger to those who send him;
> he refreshes the spirit of his masters[3].

True speech is valuable to society because it is lasting. It has a permanence which extends beyond the brief moments in which it is first spoken. It can remain powerful and effective even beyond the speaker's lifetime in the hearts and minds of people who value it. Prov. 12:17 says:

> Truthful lips endure forever,
>   but a lying tongue lasts only a moment.

True speech is valuable in one's relationship to God. God wants people to speak truthfully to one another and to him (Zech. 8:16—17; Ps. 145:18). As Prov. 12:22 puts it: "He delights in men who are truthful." He knows that in order for this to take place routinely, truth must be a quality of the inner nature of men[4]. Such a person "who walks righteously and speaks what is right" will proceed unhindered by the thrones of punishment and destruction (Isa. 33:15).

God is True

The standard for true speech is set by the speech of God himself, which is pictured in Ps. 119:140 as pure and uncontaminated, like gold that has been smelted and refined[5]. As the chapter goes on to describe them, his law and his words are true (Ps. 119:142, 160). They are flawless, trustworthy, dependable, accurate, containing no falsehood as so poignantly stated in Num. 23:19 by Balaam. God's true words, though, are merely a reflection of his character not only as the true God but also as the "God of truth" (Jer.

---

3 See also Prov. 13:17 and Prov. 26:6. Prov. 22:21 implies the importance of assessing truth in messengers, according to McKane, 424. However, Toy, 424, may be right in viewing it as referring to a pupil validating his instruction to his parents.

4 Ps. 15:1–4; 51:6. Concerning the latter verse, A. Anderson, 396, and Briggs, 2:7, regard "truth" there to refer to faithfulness to God. However, the suggestion of Thiselton, 881, that the psalmist is articulating God's desire that men be "liberated from self–deception" seems right in this context. Dahood, 2:1, gives support to this view in his translation.

5 See also Prov. 30:5; Ps. 12:6; 18:30.

10:10; Ps. 31:22). As Deut. 32:4 (cf. Ex. 34:6) describes him:

> He is the Rock, his works are perfect,
> and all his ways are just.
> A faithful God who does no wrong,
> upright and just is he.

It should come as no surprise, then, that God keeps the covenant he made with Israel despite their numerous shortcomings. It is a matter of remaining true to his own character to which he swore[6]. Joshua's tribute to God in his farewell address (22:14) could well summarise God's maintenance of his character in all of his oral communication with Israel, when he says, "Not one of all the Lord's promises to the house of Israel failed: every one was fulfilled." God's speech remains true and pure even when it must be articulated by the mouth of a man. The prophet of Israel is God's official spokesman. Because he is faithful to God, open to his influence, and an attentive listener to his voice, God is able to deliver his own words via this man's mouth without taint or distortion[7]. The priest of Israel, too, was expected to be capable of preserving the truth of God's in his instruction (Mal. 2:6—7; Jer. 14:34). As one might expect, God becomes irate when those who claim the office of prophet purposely distort the truth of his message into falsehood or speak in his name when they have received no word from him[8]. Such men shall die because they have blasphemed him. They have publicly dishonoured the trueness and purity of his character[9]. They have put their own lies into the mouth of God, who in fact utters only truth.

The Lying and Deception of Men

Unlike God, men are invariably liars, says the Psalmist in Ps. 12:2 and 116:11. Instances of lying, in various shades of deception, abound in the Old Testament, especially among the most prominent characters[10]. These descriptions of deception verify the Psalmist's cry. However, the restraint in glossing over these character flaws the integrity of those who narrate

---

6   See also Gen. 22:16; Ps. 89:34–35; Ps. 105:8; 106:45; 110:4; Mic. 7:20.

7   See especially Jer. 1:9–12; 15:19; 37:2; Ezek. 3:17–21 (33:7–9).

8   See especially Jer. 14:13–16; 23:9–40; 27:9–15; 28:7–17. Overholt gives an excellent discussion of this situation. The story of Micaiah's prophecy in 1 Ki. 22:1–22 sheds some light on the political pressures put on prophets to prophesy falsely when they know they have no true word from God or to subvert their true prophecy to suit the expectations of the king. See Young, 136–152, and DeVries, *Prophet*.

9   See Deut. 18:20–22 and Ezek. 13:1–16. Prov. 30:6 speaks of a sharp rebuke to anyone who "adds to his words."

10 Eve and Adam (Gen. 3:10; 4:9), Abraham and Isaac (Gen. 12:13; 20:2; 26:7), Jacob (Gen. 27:19), Rachel (31:35), Jacob's sons (37:29–35), Jonathan (1 Sam. 20:1–20), David (1 Sam. 21:1–6; 10–15; 22:11–19; 27:1–12).

these events. These writers embody the principle expressed in Prov. 11:3, which says:

> The integrity of the upright will guide them,
> But the falseness of the treacherous will destroy them.

Just as the Old Testament recognizes the inestimable value of true speech, it also recognizes the worthlessness of false speech. Proverbs further characterises false speech as empty, hollow, "like clouds and wind without rain," and as a part of the folly of fools (Prov. 25:14; 14:8). Although it may be initially attractive, false speech contains hidden dangers that will eventually emerge. As Prov. 20:17 (cf. Prov. 21:6) puts it:

> Food gained by fraud tastes sweet to a man,
>   but he ends up with a mouthful of gravel.

This danger cannot be prevented from infecting the life of the liar and causing his destruction. Yet, the harm done by the liar is not just to himself. He does irreparable harm to those who are deceived as well. Says Prov. 26:18—19:

> Like a madman shooting firebrands arrows
>   is a man who deceives his neighbor
>   and says, 'I was only joking!'

The Psalmist likens deceit to murder (Ps. 62:3—4; 120:2), and Isaiah (37:7) contends that lies are used by the wicked to destroy the poor. In Proverbs (15:4; 6:14) it is noted that deceit "crushes the spirit" and "always stirs up dissension." It is "better to be poor than a liar," says Prov. 19:22, because an honest, poor man does more to benefit society than a rich liar who tears apart its very fabric[11]. In the Psalms, a fondness for falsehood is thought to be a basic characteristic of all evil men[12].

It is not surprising to find that God is unalterably opposed to such falsehood in men especially in light of the destructive power of lying and deceit and the truthful nature of his own speech. Perjury in court is an abomination to him, and he sets himself against the prophet who lies. But even more generally, God abhors lying in all forms in all men. "A lying tongue" appears second in the list of things the Lord hates in Prov. 6:16. Prov. 12:22 (cf. Prov. 8:12—13) says, "The Lord detests lying lips." Ps. 5:6 (cf. Ps. 120:2—4) is quite certain that God will destroy such men when it says:

> You destroy all who tell lies;
>   bloodthirsty and deceitful men
>   the Lord abhors.

---

11 Helpful comments along this line on this difficult verse are provided by McKane, 532–533; Kidner, 134; Greenstone, 208.

12 Ps. 7:14; 12:2; 35:20; 52:1–4; 58:3; 62:4; 109:2. Note also Prov. 17:4.

In the Old Testament, then, lying appears as a spiritual distortion which does extensive damage to a man's internal nature, to his fellow man, and to his standing before God (cf. DeVries).

It is for valid reason, then, that the anonymous man of Prov. 30:7—9 wisely requests that God "keep falsehood and lies far from me." Keeping with God's attitude toward falsehood, the Psalms commonly depict righteous men as being opposed to falsehood[13]. In a Psalm attributed to him (Ps. 101:6—8), David bans known liars from his household.

Israel is depicted by the prophets as a nation of liars and overflowing with those who love falsehood. Isa. 59:3b—4 says:

> Your lips have spoken falsehood,
>   and your tongue mutters wickedness.
> No one sues righteously, and no one pleads honestly.
> They trust in confusion and speak in lies[14].

Jeremiah (5:1—3, 30—31) seeks vainly for someone who speaks truth and comes to the appalling conclusion that even the prophets and priests of God speak falsely — and the people love it! Micah (6:12) states bluntly that for sins of false speech and deceit, Israel is being destroyed. After prophesying their destruction, Zeph. 3:13, however, sets the stage for a brighter day when Israel will be characterised as people of true speech.

Vows and Oaths

The making of vows and oaths is common practice among the people in the Old Testament. Although the two terms are sometimes interchangeable, differences between them can be distinguished.

A vow in the Old Testament is usually a two-party agreement involving a man and God in which the man pledges to give something in return for God's favour or blessing. It may also simply be an act of worship or commitment to God (Ellis and also Stob). Jacob vows to make Bethel a shrine and to give a tribute to God, if God will take care of him (Gen. 28:20—22). Hannah vows that if God blesses her with a son, she will dedicate the child to him (1 Sam. 1:11—28). In Psalms attributed to him, David speaks of paying his vows to the Lord daily (Ps. 61:5—8; 22:25).

An oath, on the other hand, is usually a three-party transaction to which God is called upon as a form of security to validate an agreement between two men. Depending on the situation, one or both of them swear before God that the agreement will be kept, thus giving God license to mete out the necessary punishments if either of the two break the

---

13   Ps. 31:18; 43:1; 58:6, 10; 59:12; 109:1–13; 119:163.
14   See also Hos. 11:12; 12:1; Jer. 9:1–9.

agreement. An oath might also provide a surety of the true intentions of a
person — even in the form of uttering a curse upon himself — if his
intentions are false[15]. Laban calls on God to stand as witness to the peace
agreement between himself and Jacob (Gen. 31:50). David swears to
Jonathan, on the existence of God, that Saul is trying to kill him[16]. Ruth
swears her allegiance to Naomi by saying, "Thus may the Lord do to me
and worse, if anything but death parts you and me[17]." God himself swears
on occasion in the Old Testament. Of course, when he does, it is on
himself and the integrity of his own character[18].

Vows and oaths in the Old Testament are considered to be voluntary
acts for the most part[19]. However, if a vow or an oath is sworn, it must
always be in the name of Yahweh and never any other "god." To do so
would be a blasphemous denial of his existence and an insult to the
integrity of his character (Deut. 6:13)[20].

Once a vow is pledged, it must be paid. People may lack integrity when
dealing with one another and perhaps get away with it, but they dare not
do the same when dealing with God. The God whose own words and
deeds are one, who never rescinds a pledge, will not tolerate a renege on a
pledge voluntarily committed to him. He must not be trifled with. As
Num. 30:2 says:

> When a man makes a vow to the Lord or takes an oath to obligate himself by a
> pledge, he must not break his word but must do everything he said.

Even a delay of payment is an infraction when dealing with him. He
requires the vow in full, on time.

The same obligation holds true for oaths as with vows. Once made,
they must be kept[21]. Having voluntarily sworn to be true to one's word
on the basis of God's perfect and just character, breaking that oath dishonours God. Punishment from him is demanded if he is to retain the
integrity and justice of his own name which has been blemished by the
infraction. God may tolerate occasional deceit in the patriarchs in order to
accomplish a greater purpose, but he will not allow his name to be

---

15 See Pope, "Oaths;" Gregory; Link, "Swear."
16 1 Sam. 20:3. "As the Lord lives," the most common of oath formulas is found among
    other places in Judg. 8:19; 1 Sam. 14:39, 45; 20:21; 25:26, 34; 26:10, 16; 28:10; 29:6; 1 Ki.
    17:1; 2 Ki. 5:20.
17 Ruth 1:17. This again is quite a common formula found also in 1 Sam. 3:17; 14:44; 2
    Sam. 3:35; 1 Ki. 2:23.
18 Gen. 22:16; Num. 14:21; Ps. 89:35; 95:11; Isa. 14:24; 45:23; Jer. 22:5; 49:13; 51:14; Ezek. 17:16;
    Amos 6:8; Zeph. 2:9.
19 However, an oath is required occasionally as a legal procedure. For instance, see Ex.
    22:11.
20 Ex. 22:13; Deut. 6:13; 10:20; Jer. 12:16; Isa. 65:16.
21 See Deut. 23:21–23; Ps. 22:25; 50:14; 56:12; 61:5; 65:1; 66:14; 76:11.

purposely identified with a lie. This is blasphemy as Lev. 19:12 (cf. Ex. 20:7) says. God takes such offense at those who swear falsely that Mal. 3:5 pictures him as personally testifying against such people in judgment.

Because of the sacredness of God's name and the severe consequences of tarnishing it by breaking a vow or oath, one is well-advised to take great care in making them and keeping them once they are made[22]. Jephthah's careless vow had tragic consequences because the Lord held him to it (Judg. 11:30—31). Zedekiah's rash oath in God's name to Nebechadnezzer cost him his life[23]. Israel's broken vows to God resulted in the loss of their land and in their captivity[24]. The flippancy with which her people swore falsely in God's name surely added to her punishment[25]. And so the advice of Eccl. 5:7, drawn from Deut. 23:21—23, is worth heeding:

> It is better not to vow than to make a vow and not fulfill it. Do not let your mouth lead you into sin[26].

Apocrypha and Pseudepigrapha

As in the Old Testament, there is great concern in the Apocrypha and Pseudepigrapha that a person be both truthful in character and truthful in speech. Of course, as with gracious speech, the latter is considered to be dependent on the former. As 2 Enoch (B) 42:12—13 says, "Blessed is he in whom is truth, that he may speak truth to his neighbor." Aristeas 260—261 suggests that this is a matter of maintaining a uniform lifestyle when he says that the fruit of wisdom is that a man "should live his life in truth[27]." Yet, being uniformly truthful in character and speech is not the end of the concern for speech-ethics in this literature. There is also concern that a person be a defender of truth wherever falsehood protrudes its hoary head. In doing so, he will be fighting side by side with God. Sir. 4:27—28 says:

> Fight to the death for truth
> and the Lord will fight on your side[28].

---

22 God delights in a man "who keeps his oath even when it hurts," as Pope, "Oaths," 575, says. He continues, "The security of society demands that its members speak truth in crucial situations and keep promises in matters of serious import."
23 Ezek. 17:11—15. See also 2 Chron. 36:13; Jer. 52:3; Prov. 17:7.
24 The nation pledges loyalty to God's commands in numerous places, such as Ex. 19:8; 24:3, 7; Deut. 5:27; Josh. 24:24. Their inability to keep this covenant is detailed by the prophets along with prophecy of their destruction for this.
25 Jer. 5:2; 7:9; Hos. 4:2; Zech. 5:3—4.
26 See also Prov. 6:1—5; 11:15; 20:25; 22:26—27, about the foolishness of hasty pledges.
27 T.Reub. 3:9 urges people to love the truth.
28 Sir. 4:24—25; 40:21; T.Job 42:4—5.

As in the Old Testament, God himself is the ever-reliable gauge of truth. The God of Israel is the only true God among the many gods and idols people worship[29]. He is "good and true" (Wis. 15:1), and all his ways are "mercy and truth" (Tob. 3:2 and also 3:5). Indeed, as the Song of the Three Guardsmen implies, God is the source of all truth[30]. Of course, then, when he speaks — whether through the law, the prophets, or the priest[31] — he speaks truthfully. As Sib.Orac. 3:700—701 says: "Nothing fails of its appointed end when he conceives the thought. For all over the world the Spirit of God cannot lie[32]." Thus, Sir. 37:15 directs men to depend on God as the source of truth in their lives[33], and Ps.Sol. 16:10 appeals to God: "Protect my tongue and my lips with words of truth."

In contrast to God, all men are thought to be liars[34], as in the Old Testament, and there are plenty of examples of lying and deceit in this literature to substantiate this view[35]. Lying, though, is considered to be a form of speech that has absolutely no redeemable value, and there are numerous warnings against it[36]. Thus, Sir. 7:13 advises, "Never conspire to tell a lie for its result will not be good." Indeed, lying is viewed as an extremely harmful thing, the sting of which Ben Sira himself seems to have experienced (Sir. 51:3). Ps.Sol. 12:3 laments that with his lying tongue, the wicked man is able "to burn homes to the ground[37]."

The liar is hateful to God[38]. This is probably not only because of his destructiveness but also because by his speech he opposes everything the "God of Truth" stands for. The inveterate liar, thus, is a disgrace to

---

29 Aristeas 140; Wis. 12:27. Note the long polemic against idols in Wis. 13–14.

30 See 1 Esdras 3:41. After extolling the virtues of truth as the strongest power in the world, the guardsman closes his speech with the doxology, "Blessed is the God of truth." By most accounts, this statement is considered to be an attempt to Judaise an otherwise thoroughly pagan monologue about virtuous Truth taken from sources related to the Story of Ahiqar. See R. Pfeiffer, 251–254; *APOT*, 1:32; Myers, 55–56; Zimmermann; Torrey.

31 *Law*: Sir. 33:3; *Prophets*: Sib.Orac. 3:698–701, 827; *Samuel*: Sir. 46:15; T.Levi 8:17 (priests, judges, and scribes).

32 See also Sib.Orac. 3:572–573; 2 Enoch (B) 33:4.

33 This is precisely what the wise men to, as Sir. 30:6–8 describes. N. Johnson, 74, notes that because they viewed God as "the well–spring of righteousness," this also resulted in confession of sin and a turning toward God for protection from future sin. Note that confession is also a vital part of the wise man's prayers to God in Sir. 39:6. As Wis. 3:9 states, "Those who trust in him will understand truth."

34 Sib.Orac. 3:36–39. However, in T.Iss. 7:4, Issachar tells his children he never lied in his lifetime.

35 For example, see 1 Macc. 7:10–17; 13:12–19; 16:15; the Story of Susanna, Sib.Orac. 3:492–502.

36 Wis. 1:12; 1 Enoch 96:7; 99:12; T.Sim. 3:1; T.Reub. 3:5; T.Dan. 2:1; 5:1; 6:8.

37 Note the discussion by Schüpphaus, 57, on the precise meaning of this phrase.

38 2 Enoch (A) 63:1. T.Dan. 5:1 advises men to hate lying.

mankind (Aristeas 206; Sir. 41:15). He deserves only destruction and death[39]. Sir. 20:24—26 says:

> A lie is a foul blot in a man;
>   yet it is constantly in the mouth of a habitual liar;
> It is better to be a thief than a habitual liar;
>   though both will reap destruction.
> A man who is disposed toward lies is disgraceful,
>   and his shame remains with him forever.

Not surprisingly, then, 2 Bar. 83:21 looks hopefully toward the day when the love of lying in men will be changed to the desire for truthful speech (cf. T.Jud. 25:3). It should also be noted that the name of Beliar emerges in this literature as a personage who is closely associated with lying and deceitfulness in men[40].

As in the Old Testament, the making of vows and oaths is considered to be an extremely serious matter. Simply put, once made, they must be kept. Thus, Sir. 18:22—23 advises considerable care before making them. Concerning oaths, Sir. 23:9 expresses worry that the Holy Name might become overused "out of habit." Overuse of the Holy Name in swearing, as the passage goes on to say, invites the possibility of the person reneging on one or more of his oaths and thus sinning against God. He will have heaped up so many obligations that he will not be capable of keeping them all, nor even remember them all. He will sin doubly if he consciously swears in oath in God's name that he knows from the start he cannot keep[41]. Possibly in the light of such seriousness assoicated with making oaths, Enoch, in 2 Enoch (A) 49:1, is recorded as instructing his sons not to swear by God at all. The passage reads:

> I swear to you my children, but I swear not by any oath, neither by heaven nor by earth, nor by any other creature which God created. The Lord said: "There is no oath in me, nor injustice, but truth. If there is no truth in men let them swear by the words, 'Yea, Yea,' or else 'Nay, Nay[42]' "

---

39 1 Enoch 95:6; 98:15–16; 2 Enoch (A) 10:5–6; T.Dan 2:1; the Story of Susanna, Sib.Orac. 3:492–502.

40 T.Jud. 25:3; T.Dan 5:1–2; Sib.Orac. 3:58–70.

41 Sir. 23:10–11. Breaking an oath is also on the list in Sir. 41:14–24 of things for which a person should be ashamed. The punishment for it is always severe and can be death if the oath results in or could have resulted in the death of the accused. 2 Macc. 4:34–38 makes note of Andronicus who by consciously swearing falsely to Onias caused his death. For this, Andronicus himself was punished by death. See also 1 Macc. 7:28; 9:54–56; 13:12–19; 15:10–24; the Story of Susanna.

42 *APOT*, 2:460, states that abstinence from swearing is commonplace in later Judaism and refers to Philo and Jesus. The appearance of this idea in the "A" version of 2 Enoch and not the "B" version is significant in that the "A" version, although more complete, is considered more corrupt than the "B" version. See Nickelsburg, 185, and *APOT*, 2:425. As Charlesworth, 104, says, it has been "especially re-worked by later scribes." Thus, it is extremely difficult to determine at what point before the seventeen century A.D. (the date of our earliest "A" manuscript) this idea of

Sir. 29:14—20 provides a stern warning too for those who desire to put
up security for a neighbor, for doing so "has destroyed many who once
prospered." The same goes for the borrowing and lending of money. Sir.
29:3 warns, "Keep your word and be honest with him."

Qumranic Literature

In Qumranic literature, God is the sole source, purveyor, guardian, and
standard of truth. All his words and deeds are truthful[43]. Indeed, they are
the embodiment of what truth is. Never does he — nor must he — take
anything back (1QH 13:18—19). He is the one and only being of the universe
who can accurately be described as the "God of truth[44]. This theme
permeates the writings of the Qumran community, as noted by Murphy-
O'Conner (p. 183).

The reason for Qumran's near obsession with the notion of truth as
engulfed in "God's truth[45]" is that the community envisaged the world to
be engaged in a running battle between the forces of truth and those of
falsehood. As 1QS 4:17 says, "Truth abhors the works of falsehood and
falsehood hates all the ways of truth." This conflict, which they believed to
be both moral and spiritual, was taking place not only within each person's
heart as 1QS 4:24 mentions but also between those people dominated by
falsehood and those dominated by truth. Ultimately, they believed the
conflict was between God and his forces and Belial and those aligned with
him.

The Qumran community, fully aware that Israel had in its past aligned
itself with falsehood against God[46], was absolutely resolute in its determination to be and to remain as the True Israel, foursquare on the side of
God and truth. They would be a "community of truth" (1QS 2:24—26; 8:6;

---

abstinence from swearing may have appeared. Influence from Jesus and Christian
sources, then, is just as likely as from Philo and Jewish sources. In fact, F. Anderson,
176, with some qualification agrees, saying, "Dependence on Mt. 5:34f or Jas. 5:12
appears obvious, but not certain."

43 1QS 1:12-13, 10:16; 1QH 6:10; 11:7; 13:18; 17:15. At first glance, CD 2:12-13 may appear to
    conflict with this when it speaks of God leading astray those whom he hated.
    However, the passage goes on (2:16-18) to explain what it means by this when it refers
    to the same people stumbling because of hardness of heart and their own guilty
    inclination. Further on, the idea is applied to the sons of Noah, Jacob, and all Israel
    (3:1, 4, 14; 4:1; 5:20). Qumran never fully resolves the tension of a strict dualism with
    the absolute sovereignty of God.

44 1QH 15:24. Also both 1QS 3:6 and 11:4 contain the phrase "truth of God."

45 The phrase "Thy truth" is common in Qumranic literature. For example, see 1QS 3:6;
    11:4; 1QH 6:10; 1QM 4:6; 13:12.

46 CD 2:17-3:12; 5:12-15; 6:1. The Words of Moses (1Q22) 1:10.

1QM 13:12), who "practiced truth" (1QS 1:5; 5:3, 25; 8:2) and who spoke truth and did not lie[47]. As Josephus describes the Essenes (*B.J.* II,8:7, #141), each member was committed "always to love the truth and to expose liars." He vowed never to stray at all from any of God's words (1QS 1:14—15), nor as 1QH 14:20 puts it, "barter your [God's] truth for riches or one of your precepts for bribes." In contrast to Israel of old, they would cling to the commandments of God; they would remain steadfast to his revelation (CD 3:13—16). By the hand of his anointed one, God had showed to them his truth (CD 2:12). For them, God's truth consisted of his law and its revealed interpretation, the latter of which was embodied in the instruction their Teacher of Righteousness had received from God[48].

They viewed their community as an important contrast not only to the Israel of old but also to the present Israel as well. This was especially true in light of those who were presently leading Isreal astray. The leader of this conspiracy was the high priest at Jerusalem. In Qumranic literature, he is consistently called the Spouter of Lies and his cohorts Teachers of Lies and Seers of Falsehood. It is they who are leading the people of Israel down the path toward bloodshed and destruction by their deceitful teaching[49]. They are considered to be followers of Belial and his forces of falsehood; they are not "firm in God's truth" (1QH 4:14—15). For this, God has necessarily hidden understanding from them (1QH 5:26; 14:14—15). They are leading the people away from God's law. They have scornfully rejected the community's Teacher and his inspired teaching of the law[50]. In Qumranic literature, it is they who are the leading enemies of truth. Against them and all proponents of falsehood, the community of Qumran vowed to stand firm forever.

One day, Qumranic literature acknowledges, the battle between truth and falsehood will be over. Victory will be secured by the truth of God. All lying lips shall be dumb; all men will acknowledge his truth (1QS 4:18—23).

---

47 In their penal code (1QS 7:4), lying receives a fairly stiff punishment of six months of separation. The truly committed member of the community vows that "lies will not be found in my mouth" (1QS 10:22). Lying is listed as a characteristic of the spirit of falsehood (1QS 4:9). The veracity of the community member is held in such high esteem that the testimony of a single witness (albeit of different witnesses on separate occasions) was considered valid in reporting on another community member's infringement of rules. See CD 9:17—20. See also the thorough examination of this issue in comparison with the views of the rabbis by Schiffman.

48 For the inspiration of the Teacher, see 1QH 7:13, 26; 1QpHab 2:1. For truth as a description of the Law being equated with the Old Testament, see 1QS 1:12, 15; 5:2; 6:6; CD 15:9; 16:2. For revelation outside the Law as God's truth, see 1 QS 5:8—11; CD 3:13—15; 1QS 9:18—19. For more discussion of these, see Murphy—O'Conner, 190—192.

49 1QH 2:31; 4:6, 10; CD 1:14—15; 8:13; 19:26; (B) 2(20):11; 1QpHab 2:2; 5:11; 10:6—12; 4QpNah 2:4—6; 1QpMic 10:2.

50 1QpHab 2:1—10; 1QH 2:11—15. See comments by Murphy—O'Conner, 185.

The deep concern for truth and true speech in the Qumran community carries over into their ideas about making oaths and vows. For the most part their literature advises extreme caution in making oaths and vows. Much of their thinking is based upon their understanding of Old Testament instruction. Their greatest concern, however, is about what a person names as the third-party guarantor in an oath. It must not be God (1QS 6:27) — by any of his names (Elohim or Adonai) — nor the Law of Moses. Rather, an oath should be made on the "curses of the Covenant." It is thought that if he breaks an oath based on his "he can confess and make restitution" and "will not be burdened with a capital sin" as he would be if he made his oath on God or on the Law of Moses (CD 15:1—5).

Both Philo and Josephus appear to take this strict oath practice in Qumran to mean that the people avoided making oaths completely[51]. This conclusion, however, is certainly not justified upon examination of the Qumranic literature itself. For instance, each new initiate was required to make an oath of allegiance[52], which seems to be a blend between an oath to the community and a vow to God (1QS 2:1—8). This oath was taken on the curses of the Covenant, as their rules prescribe. Married members of Qumran were required to subscribe strictly to the Old Testament ordinances concerning vows and pledges in Num. 30[53]. It should be noted that a member of Qumran was warned to make an oath of guilt only to a jugde and never to the one offended (CD 9:9—10). This was based on 1 Sam. 25:26. Based on Lev. 5:1, Qumran required that an oath of malediction be made by the owner upon an unknown thief (CD 9:11—12). Thus, it cannot be concluded that the Qumran community necessarily avoided making oaths. Rather, it should be concluded that they did make oaths but that they were very particular as to how these were formulated. They preferred to leave those who defaulted on their pledges with the punishment for a misdemeanor rather than for a capital offense.

The concern for true speech in Qumranic literature, then, is tied inextricably to the community's overwhelming concern for the whole sphere of truth. In comparing the idea of truth in Qumranic literature with that of the Old Testament, Murphy-O'Conner (p. 185) draws some perceptive conclusions that are relevant here. He observes that: 1) the whole

---

51 Philo, *Prob.* 84; Josephus, *B.J.* II,8:6(#135). In *B.J.* XV,10:4(#371). Josephus says that the Essenes were excluded from the obligation to make an oath to Herod. This may have been based on the objection of conforming to Hellenistic customs and formulations. CD 9:1, especially as translated by *DSSE*, 110, is perhaps to be seen in this light. See Braun, 2:289, who notes the same discrepancy between Philo and Josephus and the Qumranic literature itself with respect to oaths and vows.

52 1QS 5:7—11; CD 15:6—10; 16:1—9.

53 CD 7:8; 16:10—11. See comments by Dupont-Sommer, 133, 162.

theme of truth occupies a much more central place in the teaching of Qumran that it does in the Old Testament, 2) a marked evolution is perceptible in the idea of "truth" as revelation, 3) there is a marked emphasis on "truth" as a quality, or rather the quality of the community and its members, 4) because of the historical context almost every mention of "truth" has polemic overtones.

Rabbinic Literature

According to Rabbi Simeon, son of Gamaliel, (as attributed to him in Aboth 1:18) the world is sustained by three things. Named first in the triad is "truth." Such high regard for the value of truth in society is a fair representation of the views contained in Rabbinic literature. Truth in speech, truth in character, and personal honesty and integrity in thought and in action are highly regarded virtues that are promoted consistently (Moore, 2:191). A wise man should be inwardly what he is outwardly[54]. He honestly admits it when he does not know something[55]. He acknowledges the truth when he is confronted by it. Regarding integrity of the spoken work, these notable remarks are recorded in B.Metzia 4:2:

> He who exacted punishment from the generation of the Flood and the generation of the Dispersion (Gen. 11:9), will also exact punishment from him who does not abide by his spoken word.

In the discussion which is constructed in B.Metzia 49a over whether or not the above statement means that the breaking of a verbal transaction involves a legal breach of faith, Rabbi Jose, son of Rabbi Judah, raises the following objection to Rabbi Kahan's view that it does not. He says:

> What is taught by this verse, 'A just *hin* (shall you have);' surely '*hin*' is included in '*ephah*'? But it is to teach you that your 'yes' (*hen*) should be just and your 'no' should be just[56].

---

54 Ber. 28a; Pes. 113b. L. Jacobs, *Theology*, 235, cites these relevant comments by Maimonides from *Hilkhot Deot* 2:6: "Even a single false word is forbidden. A man should always have true lips, a firm spirit and a heart free of all deceit."

55 This statement and the next are drawn from Aboth 5:10. On saying "I don't know," see also Ber. 4a.

56 The quotation is from Lev. 19:36. Note that the tactical reasoning involves a play on the words "*hin*," a measure, and "*hen*," Aramaic for "yes." Similar statements concerning "yes" and "no" can be found in Sifra 91b and RuthR. 7:6. With some relevance, in Sheb. 36a, Rabbi Eleazar is recorded as saying that " 'No' is an oath; 'Yes' is an oath." This is followed by the opinion of Raba that only "No! No!" or "Yes! Yes!" constitutes an oath. Rabbi Jose ben Hanina, also in Sheb. 36a, says that even an "Amen!" implies an oath. In this light, see also Mekilta #5, 66b (Lauterbach, 2:229–239).

There is general agreement among the various opinions that are registered in the remainder of the discussion that the view of Rabbi Jose, to the effect that even a verbal transaction must not be violated, is the better understanding of B.Metzia 4:2.

As in the previous Jewish literature that has been examined, God is thought to set the standard for truly integrated speech and lifestyle. Truth is the seal and the signature of all his words and deeds[57]. In Ex.R. 38:1, David is interpreted to have said "As you are truth (Jer. 10:10) — so is your word truth (Ps. 119:89)." There simply is no point in "gainsaying the verdict of Him at whose word the world came into being, because it is wholly true and just[58]." Not surprisingly, then, there is nothing more abominable to God than when a false prophet prophesies in his name or when a prophet suppresses what God desires him to speak (San. 11:1,5). The certain punishment in either case is death. Likewise, Rabbi Eleazar of Modim speaks of a person who twists the meaning of the Torah as having no share in the world to come — regardless of his good deeds[59].

When a person lies, it is thought that he has betrayed God himself as if he had worshipped an idol (San. 92a). He has denied the Root of his own existence[60]. Although God created the world and everything in it, "falsehood he did not create," as emphasised by Rabbi Samuel ben Nahonan. Rather, "Out of their own hearts did mortals conceive false words (Isa. 59:13)[61]." Thus, lying and falsehood are foreign elements in God's world, and he rightfully despises them (LevR. 16:1). Neither does he tolerate liars in his midst (San. 103a). Despite his opposition to it, though, falsehood dominates in this world (San. 97a). Canaan is said to have charged his sons to lie (Pes. 113b). Satan is called a liar (San. 89b). Resh Lakish cogently remarks, "Falsehood is frequent, truth is rare," but he continues, "Truth can stand, falsehood cannot stand[62]." And so, as Rabbi Simeon represents him (GenR. 8:5), God cries out to men: "Let truth arise from the earth!"

As in previous literature, vows and oaths are treated in Rabbinic literature as somewhat special categories of speech which demand more

---

57 Shab. 55a; Yoma 69b; San. 111a; GenR. 8:5; 81:2; DeutR. 1:10; S.S.R. 1:9,1; Mid.Ps. 15:4.
58 S.S.R. 1:9,1. See also GenR. 55:1; EcclR. 3:9.
59 Aboth 3:15. The "right" teaching appears to be the Halachah, at least as it is explained in Aboth 5:11. See also ARN 11 (p. 63).
60 Tos. Sheb. 3:6 (*RA*, 122). Sifre Num. #2, 2a (*RA*, 397) speaks of lying as ultimately a sin against God. The rabbis include in lying many kinds of deceptive speech which they discourage. One should not promise a child something and not deliver because this teaches him to lie (Suk. 46b). One should not feign interest in a purchase when he has no money (B.Metzia 4:10, 58b). One should not subscribe to charity if he is not going to pay (EcclR. 5:5).
61 Pes.Rab. 24, 125b (Braude, 1:509).
62 Shab. 104a. These statements are made on the basis of some typically shrewd observations about the letters in אמת and שקר.

than the ordinary amount of veracity and resolution if they are to have any meaning in society. In most cases, neither vows nor oaths are obligatory and are by design verbal measures that are voluntarily undertaken to aid a person to keep his word and to insure his word, whether to God or to men (Tos. B.Metzia 3:14).

In the positive sense, vows are considered to be fences or barriers which guard a person's life of devotion to God[63]. Oaths too are thought to be helpful in controlling one's evil inclination (NumR. 15:16). Oaths are also seen to be useful to society in safeguarding true and valid testimony in court and resolving personal and business disputes[64].

When a person undertakes a vow, he must be absolutely certain he will fulfill it — and fulfill it promptly. Not to do so is recognized, at least by one rabbi, as a sure sign that a person is drifting away in his commitment to God and will soon be worshipping idols, participating in sexual immorality, bloodshed, and slander (LevR. 37:1). If he is not positive he can meet the obligation, he is better off not making the vow[65]. Rabbi Judah represents the view that it is best if a person not vow in any case (LevR. 37:1). There are vows that are considered to be non-binding: vows of incitement, vows of exaggeration, vows made in error, and vows of constraint (Ned. 3:1). There are also many restrictions, exceptions, and various ways of fulfilling vows which occupy the concern of Nedarim in the Mishnah. However, the most general of advice from Rabbinic literature is that a person ought to take great care in vowing. It is presented best in the following passage in which God is represented as saying to Israel:

> Be careful what you vow and do not become addicted to making vows for whoever is so addicted will ultimately sin by breaking his oath, and he who breaks his oath denies me without hope of pardon[66].

As established in the OT and evidenced in the above quotation, Rabbinic teaching carries on the view that the breaking of an oath is an extremely serious affront to God[67]. It is also seen to have very harmful

---

63 See Aboth 3:17, plus helpful comments by Herford, *Aboth*, 85.

64 See especially Sheb. 4:1–13 (oath of testimony); 5:1–5 (oath of deposit); and 7:1–8 (oath of restitution). See also Sheb. 47a.

65 LevR. 37:1; GenR. 81:2; Tanchuma 13a.

66 Tanchuma B, 79a, as cited in *RA*, 401. Similar advice is given in Ned. 20a. There is some question with regard to this advice as to whether "oath" is being used interchangeably with "vow," or whether it is thought that breaking a vow is a lesser fault than doing so with an oath, the one, however, leading naturally to ther other with the oath having a more certain and severe punishment. The way the advice is stated in Ned. 20a gives weight to the latter view. There appears to be an assumption in Ned. 2:2 and in comments on it in Ned. 16a, 18a, that an oath generally is more stringent than a vow, even thought there are instances when a vow is equally "more stringent."

67 See also Pes.Rab. 21, 107b (Braude, 1:443).

repercussions among men, especially if it is a court oath. As it is said in Sheb. 38b—39a (cf. Shab. 32a; LevR. 6:3), "For all other sins, the sinner only is punished, for the false oath, he and all the world." Rabbi Eleazar ben `Azariah taught that such a person "deserves to be cast to the dogs[68]." Vain oaths, rash oaths, trivial oaths, and of course blatantly false oaths — all are forbidden and discouraged by the rabbis[69]. Oaths should not be administered to a person who has a reputation for breaking them nor to a person who is always eager to give one[70]. Nor should a person goad or impel another into giving an oath, whether it be regarding a matter that is false or a matter that is true (LevR. 6:3).

NumR. 22:1 teaches that a person should meet three conditions before endeavouring to swear to the truth in God's name: 1) He must fear God (Deut. 10:20), 2) He must serve God in that he gives full attention to study of the Torah and observance of its precepts, 3) He must cleave to God. Thus, his character must be as nearly trustworthy as God's so that the community will be fully cognisant that he would never knowingly swear to falsehood nor flippantly swear even to the truth (NumR. 22:1). Unlike Qumran, Rabbinic literature betrays no particular concern about whether a person taking an oath swears by one of God's names or a legitimate substitute[71]. Swearing "by heaven and earth," however, does not appear to be considered especially binding (Sheb. 4:13). It should be noted that any oath which runs contrary to a precept of the Torah is not considered binding (B.Bathra 7:5).

---

68 Pes. 118a. As laid down in San. 11:6, false witnesses actually receive the same punishment to which the defendent was liable.
69 Sheb. 3:8–10; 3b; 20b; 'Erub. 21b, NumR. 22:1; LevR. 6:3; Pes.Rab. 23/24 (Braude, 1:494).
70 LevR. 6:3. In contrast to being eager to swear, in Derek Eretz Zuta 5:1, the wise man is characterised as keeping his "Yes, yes!" and "No, no!" to a minimum.
71 Sheb. 4:13. However, information concerning the ban on pronouncing the Divine Name with all its letters must be taken into account here. Urbach, 126–130, is not so sure how far-reaching, nor how long the ban remained in force that one reads about in Rabbinic literature. Given the little information we have, some of which conflicts, it is hard to say whether it was or was not allowed in pronouncing oaths. Its inclusion in the list of Sheb. 4:13 would cause one to presume that it was permitted. The fact that both Yahweh and Adonai are referred to by their first and last letters in the list makes one wonder if that is as much as is actually permitted in oaths. Important evidence, however, from Sheb. 35b (commenting on Sheb. 4:3, in fact) and 38b indicate that there were at least certain oaths which the rabbis thought required the Divine Name in order to be valid. The oaths under discussion there are those for testifying in court, which are imposed by a judge. In both places, there appears to be an awareness that such a position goes against some prevailing opinions, yet it is traced by the rabbis who represent it to common sense understandings of written Torah. In any case, this poses quite a contrast to the severe restrictions regarding the use of God's name in oaths pronounced in Qumran.

Graeco-Roman Literature

Truth is a highly valued entity in Graeco-Roman literature, and this is no less so with respect to speech. Truthful character, according to Plato, is the quality "which is most conducive to nobility of life[72]." He continues (*Laws* 730c; cf. *Laws* 738e):

> Of all the goods, for gods and men alike, truth stands first. Let every man partake thereof from his earliest days if he proposes to become blessed and happy so that he may live his life as a true man so long as possible.

The ideal way to be truthful "both in speech and conduct," according to Aristotle in *EN* IV,7:6—8 (1126b30—1127a8), is to develop a disposition that is habitually sincere. "The lover of truth," he says, will be truthful "even when nothing depends on it," because he has always by personal practice "avoided falsehood for its own sake." He is in fact a wholly integrated, dependably honest man, a pleasure to the gods and a most valued asset to society.

According to Plutarch (*Mor.* 1:49a), "Truth is a thing divine." Thus, it is a sacred duty in his view (*Mor.* 1:11c) to "accustom children to speak the truth." He is similarly ardent in motivating his students to get at the truth by critically questioning all speakers and also critically reading all the poets, both of whom in his opinion often play loose with the truth[73]. He (*Mor.* 6:503d) considers the fundamental purpose of all speech to be "to engender belief in the hearer." This is why he is so harsh in condemning gossips and flatterers and the like[74]. They violate the sacred purpose of speech, raping and destroying the virtuous use for which it is intended. Similarly, Isocrates in *Antid.* 18—19 condemns slander because "it smothers truth." In contrast for Plutarch, however, is the speech between genuine friends which nobly incorporates all the intended virtues of speech: truth, sincerity, honesty, and frankness[75]. In recognizing the importance of truthful speech to friendship, he builds upon a strong tradition in Graeco-Roman literature[76].

---

72 Plato, *Laws* 730b. Aristotle reiterates this in *EN* IV,7:6 (1125b30).

73 On speakers, see Plut., *De recta, Mor.* 1:37a–48d, but especially 41a. On poets, see *Quo. poetas, Mor.* 1:14e–37b, but especially 16a–c. Note also the *Philoctetes* by Sophocles, lines 108–120, in which Neoptolemus is convinced by Odysseus to tell a lie for a "greater" good.

74 See Plut., *Quo. adul., Mor.* 1:48e–74e, but especially 49a–b which contains the quotation about truth which heads the paragraph. See also *De gar., Mor.* 6:502b–515f, but especially 6:503d.

75 See his numerous remarks on frankness and friendship in *Quo. adul., Mor.* 1:48e–74e, but especially 53c, 59c, 61c, 62c–d. See also Plut., *Mor.* 15:#87.

76 For instance, see Hesiod, *Works* 370–372; Isoc., *To Antipater* 4–6.

Plato as well as Plutarch maintains that God lives up to this high
standard of truthful speech and does not himself lie or deceive[77].
Xenophon betrays similar belief when in defending Socrates from the
charge of atheism in *Mem.* I,7:2—5 he counters that Socrates was in fact
inspired by the gods, which he thinks is evidenced by the fact that he
could not be proven guilty of falsehood.

The high value placed on truth in Graeco-Roman literature is
complemented by the condemnation of falsehood and lying. As early as
Hesiod, one may read the straightforward sanction in *Works* 709, "Do not
lie to please your tongue." This very statement launches Plutarch into a
denunciation of lying and falsehood in *Mor.* 15:87[78]. In *Theog.* 607—610,
there is an attempt to sympathise with the liar in the immediate pleasure his
lie may give him, but then it is countercharged that "at the end the gain
becomes both dishonourable and bad." Similar indictments against lying
and falsehood can be found in the fifth century dramatists, Aeschylus
(*Prometheus Bound* 685—687) and Pindar (*Pythians* 1:85), and not too surprisingly, in Plato and Aristotle. Plato denounces both lies that are
voluntary as well as those that are voluntary[79]. Aristotle, in *EN* IV,7:6
(1126b30), bluntly declares, "Falsehood is base and reprehensible in itself."

Despite all the affirmations in support of truthfulness and the
denunciations of falsehood by the Graeco-Roman writers, there remains
the gnawing realisation that people do not always tell the truth. Diog.L.
1:104 perhaps expresses this best in a poignant remark attributed to
Anacharsis: " 'How is it,' he asked, 'that the Greeks prohibit falsehood and
yet obviously tell falsehoods in retail trade?' " Plato (*Phaedo* 66c) explains
this from this point of view saying, "So long as we have the body, and the
soul is contaminated by such an evil, we shall never attain completely
what we desire, that is the truth." Plutarch, in *Mor.* 1:61c, explains it this
way. He says:

> . . . our soul has its two sides: on the one side are truthfulness, love for what is
> honourable, and power to reason, and on the other side, irrationality, love of falsehood,
> and the emotions.

The Stoics, however, agree to nothing of the sort. It is every person's
nature "to assent to the true and dissent from the false," says Epictetus[80].
Therefore, it is thought that he should not produce anxiety in himself
about whether or not he has lied in an instance. Rather, he must free
himself to follow his natural instincts which will cause him always to

---

77   Plato, *Rep.* 381c–383a; Plut., *Mor.* 1:36b.
78   See also *Mor.* 1:11c and 1:21a.
79   Plato, *Laws* 730c and *Rep.* 535e but contrast *Laws* 916e, which condones lies to
      superiors.
80   Epict. III,3:2. See also I,28:1–3 and Cicero, *Fin.* 2:46.

choose the truth rather than the false[81]. The ultimate problem with this is that the "wise man" within such a system can put himself in a position in which the "truth" he tells is false by normal societal standards[82].

Curiously, Plato puts himself in a similar position to the Stoics in condoning potential lies even though it appears inconsistent with his already noted stern antagonism toward lying and falsehood. Within a long discussion in which he asserts that truth must be prized (*Rep.* 389b), he also affirms the nobility of physicians under certain conditions lying to their patients and of rulers lying to their subjects (*Rep.* 382d). However, Plato, as already noted, does assert that God does not lie and also projects God as a model for human behaviour (*Laws* 716c—d).

Regarding oaths, Plato (*Laws* 916c) staunchly proclaims:

> No man, calling the gods to witness, shall commit, either by word or deed, any falsehood, fraud or adulteration, if he does not desire to be most hateful to the gods; just such a person is he who, disregarding the gods, swears false oaths.

Plato's view on the necessity of keeping sworn oaths are typical of what resounds throughout Graeco-Roman literature[83]. Oaths usher in the gods as witnesses and thus as guarantors of a person's truthfulness. Thus, the breaking of an oath does injury to and is an offense of the worst kind against the gods. One might think he can get away with a broken oath and that it is to his advantage. However, Theog. 197—208 says, "In the end it becomes bad and the mind of the gods overcome him." With the same result in view, Theog. 1195—1196 simply dictates, "Swear no false oaths by the gods because it is impossible to conceal a debt from the Immortals." The keeping of personal vows to the gods is also naturally considered important as a necessary aspect of expressing one's devotion to them. This is something which Isocrates presses for in *To Dem.* 13. Plutarch, in *Mor.* 6:464b—c, encourages vows to be used as measures to help a person control intemperate behaviour as well as unacceptable speech.

Oaths and their reliability in particular were essential for the maintenance of Greek society. Oaths functioned as vehicles for profession of a person's loyalty to the state[84], as protectors of justice in the courts[85],

---

81 See especially Epict. IV,6:28–38, but also II,2:14; III,22:42; IV,10:2–3.
82 A statement appears in Stob. II,11^m (2:111) which deplores the idea of the occasional falsehood by wise men and may well be a reaction against the Stoics. See also Stob. I,7:9a.
83 Theog. 659–660, 823–824; Aristoph., *Clouds* 1232–1236; *Lysistrata* 915; *Wealth* 61–105; Xen., *Anab.* II,4:6; III,1:22; *Symp.* 4:49; Dem. 9:6; 11:12; 48:11, 52; Lykurgus, *Leokrates* 127; Stob. II,27:6 (Sophocles); II,27:8 (Antiphanos). See also Dover, 248–251.
84 Dover, 250, notes that Athenians took such an oath at the age of eighteen and that any action which could be called unpatriotic was considered a violation of this oath.
85 See Dem. 23:101; 24:150–151; 48:52, and the comments based on these by Dover, 249,

and as guardians of alliance and territorial treaties[86]. And of course oaths functioned as aids to enable one person to trust another person's word in business transactions and in everyday personal relations[87]. The Graeco-Roman writers themselves employ oaths quite commonly to give expression to conviction and truthfulness in what they write[88].

Oaths are not considered absolutely unbreakable. Fragment 645 from Euripides indicates that an oath involuntarily sworn under duress of impending death would be forgiven by the gods if broken. Plato, *Symp.* 183b, relates the common opinion that the gods disregarded as vows those of love given in the heat of passion. The Athenians in 410 B.C., it is said, concocted an oath to annul oaths taken against the state by certain conspirators[89]. Although a certain leniency is maintained in the unfortunate circumstances of some oath-makers, there is a firm desire to prevent any such leniency fostering an indiscriminate softening in people's determination to fulfill their oaths. A general disregard for keeping oaths, as early as Theognis, was thought to be a sure sign of a society's moral and spiritual decay[90].

Despite the important role oaths play in Greek culture as reflected in their literature, there is a significant note of reserve about the use of oaths in some corners[91]. The principal early advocate appears to have been Pythagoras to whom Diog.L. 8:22—23 attributes the advice "not to call the gods to witness, man's duty being rather to strive to make his own word carry conviction." This caution can be seen to reverberate in Isocrates who in *To Nic.* 22 counsels, "Throughout all your life show that you value truth so highly that your word is more to be trusted that other men's oaths[92]." Given their aversion to petitionary prayer and to slavery to societal norms, it is not too surprising to see the Stoics waging a campaign against oath making. Epictetus, in *Ench.* 33:6, enjoins, "Refuse if you can to take

---

309. See also Adkins, *Values*, 120–121. On the even higher value of the oath in murder trials, see Adkins, *Merit*, 216, commenting on Antiphon, *Tetralogies* Cb 8, cd 10.

86   See L. Pearson, 8, 24, 165, and Dover, 249.

87   For example, see Plut., *Mor.* #15:39, commenting on Hesiod, *Works* 282–284.

88   For example, Xen., *Cyro.* V,4:10; Plato, *Rep.* 536c; Epict. I,16:76; II,19:15, 22:6; II,19:3.

89   Dover, 252, refers to this incident from Andokides 1:98.

90   Theog. 1135–1145. See also Eur., *Medea* 492–494; Plato, *Laws* 701b.

91   Some relevant references to such reserve which will not arise in the discussion which follows appear in Stob. III,27:1–5; IV,2:25; Men. *Sententiae* 592. The latter is found in Jaekel. The so-called Delphic oracle which prescribes, "Do not use an oath!" can be found in Stob. III,1:373 as well as in Dittenberger, IV,1268:8.

92   See also Isoc., *To Dem.* 23, where he explicitly provides only two legitimate reasons for being put under oath: to clear oneself of a disgraceful charge and to save a friend from danger. In matters of money, he enjoins not to swear at all, even to the truth, because it will automatically appear suspect.

an oath at all, but if that is impossible, refuse as far as circumstances allow[93]. Cicero, in *Pro Balbo* 5:12, beams with pride when he relates the story of how the Athenians once protested at the efforts of a certain pious man to take an oath in court testimony. He concludes that "the Greeks did not wish it to be thought (that) the credibility of a man of proved honesty was more strictly secured by a ritual observance than by truthfulness of character."

The above quotation from Cicero clearly expresses the driving principle of all those in Graeco-Roman literature who desire to eliminate or at least to limit swearing. They want to protect the character of the honest man from the dishonour of needing an oath to verify his oracular honesty. They wish to project his character above the normal societal necessity which requires the swearing of oaths in order to secure the truthfulness of words which are being uttered in crucial situations[94]. The oath is really only necessary because of the dishonest character of most people and represents society's response to the fact that the simple word of the majority cannot be trusted. This perspective on oaths makes the cautioning of the honest man to be skeptical of oaths which appears in Theog. 283—292 understandable. Plutarch too, in *Mor.* 1:62d, invites skepticism over the profuse oaths which characterise the flatterer's efforts to demonstrate his genuine friendship. Plato, *Laws* 948d—949b, expresses the desire to ban the swearing of oaths by litigants in lawsuits because he says, "Well-nigh half the citizens are perjurers." They only use the oath to sanctify their false claims (cf. Isoc., *To Dem.* 23).

Philonic Literature

To Philo, there is nothing so excellent in life as truth. It is the holiest of possessions to which people ought to cling tightly. Truth is very nearly deified by Philo because of its purity and its value. In *Dec.* 138, he says:

> They [false witnesses] corrupt truth, the august, the treasure as sacred as anything that we possess in life which like the sun pours light upon facts and events and allows none of them to be kept in the shade[95].

God and truth are closely intertwined in Philo. Truth is God's attendant (*Mos.* 2:177). To turn to the truth is to turn to God (*Praem.* 58). God is the

---

93 It is worth noting that Epictetus himself does swear by the gods in his writing where it does not seem to be essential. For example, see I,16:7; II,19:15; 22:6; III,18:3.

94 From what we saw earlier of Aristotle's remark in *EN* IV, 7:6–8. (1126b30–1127a8), it would appear that he would agree with this orientation in principle.

95 Philo also compares truth to the sun in *Mos.* 2:271. Other references dealing with the value of truth are *Spec.* 4:69; *Prob.* 158. Truth is also one of those who accompanies virtue in *Sac.* 27.

true God who is also free from falsehood (*Ebr.* 45; *Mos.* 2:270). His word
is oath (*Abr.* 272). Falsehood is banished from heaven (*Spec.* 1:88—89). The
quality of immortality by its nature carries with it absolutely truthful
speech (*Prob.* 137). When Moses once was undecided about a matter, Philo
says in *Mos.* 2:237 that "he referred the difficulty to God, Who alone as
he knew can distinguish by infallible and absolutely unerring tests the
finest differences and thereby show His truth and justice."

Anyone who speaks for God as a prophet will speak in absolute
truthfulness "for prophets are the interpreters of God, Who makes full use
of their organs of speech to set forth what He wills[96]." Philo attempts to
prove that Moses was a bona fide prophet of the true God in
Mos. 2:258—287 by recording numerous instances in which he made pro-
nouncements which were realised. The clincher for Philo is when Moses
predicted the immediate destruction of some Israelites who impiously
questioned his status with God. Joseph proves himself a prophet by his
ability to interpret dreams truthfully (*Jos.* 117).

For the vast majority of people speech does not have the capacity ever
to be completely truthful. Falsity of speech is a characteristic of evil, but
according to Philo, overfamiliarity with falsehood chatacterises everyone
from birth (*Spec.* 4:68; *Conf.* 48). The situation is even worse than that.
Speech, as an aspect of the senses connected to the body, where falsity is
rampant, is an agent primarily working in opposition to truth (*Ebr.* 70—71;
Post. 101). At best the average person's speech is partly true and partly
false. The only way to improve this is for his rational, inner faculty to
become the dominant force controlling his life (*Mut.* 247; *Abr.* 20; *Spec.*
4:69). Anger, for instance, must be controlled in this way because as a
product of the passions it is no friend of truth (*L.A.* 3:123—124). As the
mind or the soul is the seat of the Divine Logos, so is it also the seat of
truth and clarity in man[97]. Truth increasingly dominant there will result in
speech that is more and more reliably truthful until perfect wisdom is
realised. In *Mos.* 2:128, Philo explains:

> For the rational principle in nature is true, and sets forth all things clearly and, in the
> wise man, being a copy of the other, has as its bounden duty to honour truth with
> absolute freedom from falsehood, and not keep dark through jealously anything the
> disclosure of which will benefit those who hear its lesson[98].

Despite his zealousness for truth to be spoken, Philo, like Plato before
him, is sympathetic toward employing the noble lie if it will benefit the

---

96   *Spec.* 1:65. The wider context of this quotation shows that Philo has in mind what
     today would be called the mechanical dictation theory of inspiration in which the
     prophet's speech is taken over totally by God. See also *Jos.* 95 and *Spec.* 4:48—52.
97   *Spec.* 1:88—90; 3:203—208; *Mos.* 2:127—130.
98   See also *L.A.* 3:127; *Congr.* 5.

hearer in the long term (*Deus* 63—69). This practice by physicians seems perfectly justified to Philo. It is also of help to Philo in his attempts to explain the necessarily false anthropomorphic language used by Moses about God.

Philo, like the Old Testament, is very strict about the fulfillment of vows or dedications made to God. This indeed is one of his bragging points about the superior rules of the Jews in *Hyp.* 7:3—4. Reneging on a vow or dedication of something to God, even if a flippant one, is compared to robbery. A life of unfulfilled vows characterizes only the evil man (*Cher.* 94). In *Spec.* 2:36—38, Philo warns against making a vow without serious reflection. He warns too about delaying too long in fulfilling it.

Philo places importance not only on prompt delivery but on high quality of offering (*Mos.* 1:251—253). The lack of those two things is what he deems as Cain's downfall in *Sac.* 52—54. God must have the best. Philo goes on to surmise the attitudes which possibly underlie such shortcomings as being: ingratitude to God, self-sufficient pride, and the feeling that one deserves the goodness that comes to him in life. On the opposite end of the scale are those who undertake the Nazarite Vow, or what Philo likes to call the Great Vow. With the greatest admiration for those who undertake it, he pictures it is the ultimate bloodless sacrificial offering to God of a person's most prized possession, himself. Philo deftly draws this comparison in *Spec.* 1:247—254 (cf. *Som.* 1:251—254).

Philo has much to say about oaths and most of his views are contained in two separate, lengthy passages: *Dec.* 84—95 and *Spec.* 2:1—28. Both are intended to be comments on the Third Commandment, not to take the name of God in vain. They are in general agreement but make different emphases in places. *Dec.* 84 presents Philo's ideal position in a nutshell:

> Swear not at all is the best course[99] and most profitable to life, well suited to a rational nature which has been taught to speak the truth so well on each occasion that its words are regarded as oaths; to swear truly is only, as people say, a 'second–best voyage,' for the mere fact of his swearing casts suspicion on the trustworthiness of the man.

Philo recognizes that life will present situations in which making an oath is unavoidable. After doing so, however, it must be kept. As he explains it, "For an oath is an appeal to God as a witness on matters in dispute, and to call Him as a witness to a lie is the height of profanity[100]. In *Dec.* 92, Philo sharply reprimands those who use oaths to fill up the

---

99 See also *Prob.* 84 where he speaks approvingly of the abstinence from oaths which he believes characterises the Essenes.

100 *Dec.* 86. See also 90–91; *Spec.* 2:9–11; *Plant.* 82; *Som.* 1:12 on the importance of keeping oaths and the relationship of this to God.

gaps in their talk and follows this with two pieces of advice for the person who is contemplating swearing an oath. First, he must carefully examine whether the matter is important enough to warrant an oath and whether he is well-enough informed in the matter to be sure of himself. Secondly, he must determine whether his life is pure enough to pronounce "the holiest of all names." Philo makes a similar emphasis, particularly on the second idea, in *Spec.* 1:1—8. However, there he advocates a person to consider first swearing by one's father or mother, the sun, earth, heavens, or even "Yes, by____[101]" for lighter matters, thus reserving God's name only for matters of utmost seriousness. In *Spec.* 2:12—25, Philo emphasises that oaths to commit illegal, immoral, or impious acts are not valid. Oaths made in anger invite repentance and confession to God. Oaths from the rich which display their arrogance and intemperance are debase. The oaths of wives and of virgins are to be overseen by husbands and fathers.

New Testament

Truth is vital to the New Testament[102]. Not only is it associated with God, but through Jesus and the Spirit of God, truth becomes a way of describing the gospel message Jesus' disciples preach, the new way of life being demanded, and even the religion being established.

First and foremost, truth in the New Testament is a quality of God. He is not only the true God but also the God who is true and who speaks truthfully, never lying[103]. Truth also characterises his Son, Jesus Christ, and indeed is identified with him, especially in Johannine literature[104]. So also, the Spirit of God "is truth" and "leads into all truth[105]. Because Jesus' teaching is from God, it is also truth.

Perhaps one of the most common uses of truth in the New Testament, especially in Pauline literature and the Pastorals, is to describe the gospel. The gospel is the gospel of truth, the word of truth, of which Paul is a herald to the Gentiles[106]. God desires all men to be saved and to come to

---

101 He speaks in admiration, *Spec.* 2:4, of people he apparently knows who are in the habit of saying "νή τόν" or "μὰ τόν" and by thus breaking off, suggest the clear sense of an oath without actually making it.
102 Informative analyses of truth in the New Testament which have aided the brief discussion that follows are: Thiselton, 883–894; Bultmann, "ἀλήθεια;" Rimbach; Murray, 123–147. The use of truth to illustrate the polymorphous character of some concepts in the New Testament by Thiselton, *Two*, 411–414, is also very illuminating.
103 Jn. 17:3, 17; 1 Jn. 5:20; 1 Thes. 1:9; Rom. 9:6; Tit. 1:2; Heb. 6:18; 2 Tim. 2:13.
104 Jn. 1:14; 3:33; 7:18; 8:26, 40, 45; 14:6; 1 Jn 5:20. See also Mt. 22:15 (Mk. 12:14); Eph. 4:24.
105 1 Jn. 5:7; Jn. 14:17; 15:26; 16:13.
106 Gal. 2:5; 2 Cor. 6:7; Col. 1:5; Eph. 1:13; 1 Tim. 2:7.

knowledge of the truth (1 Tim. 2:4; Heb. 10:26). Christians are those who know the truth, are of the truth, are established in the truth, who live by the truth, walk in it, and obey it[107]. The church is the pillar of truth (1 Tim. 3:15). Timothy is told to handle accurately the word of truth (2 Tim. 2:15). On the other hand, there are those who turn away from the truth, who oppose it, and who blaspheme the way of truth[108].

In a wider sense (but not exclusive of the gospel), truth may be invincible to opposition[109], but it is not irresistible. Not all men love the truth (2 Tim. 2:20). Some resist the knowledge of God's truth within them (Rom. 1:18). They readily exchange the truth for a lie (Rom. 1:25) and actively oppose the truth, whether it be a pre-gospel revelation of God or the gospel itself. The leading opponent of the truth is Satan, who is called a liar by nature, a hater of truth[110]. Within the church, individuals who oppose the gospel, teach false doctrine, or disobey commands implied by the gospel are considered to be akin to him[111].

In a sense, every person is a liar in his rebelliousness toward God[112]. Yet some people are especially rebellious and remain so. Lying is a trademark of the unrighteous, of those who deny that Jesus is the Christ, and of those who are bound for the Lake of Fire[113]. These have stubbornly remained outside the faith, ever-resistant to the truth of the gospel even as they fail to love truth generally (Rev. 22:5; 2 Thes. 2:10). In contrast, those who love the truth will be drawn to the gospel of truth and gain salvation. Lying and truth are mutually exclusive spiritually just as they are logically (1 Jn. 2:21—23; 4:1—3). A person will fall into one camp or the other by the measuring rod of faith in Christ.

Truth, then, is important to the Christian in many ways. Not only is it associated with his God, his Christ, and the gospel he trusts, it signifies his way of life, especially his new life in Christ. Truthful speech is now a critical sign of the change from his old life of lying rebellion toward God (Col 3:9). But truthful speech is also a vital aspect of the unity which binds together the new community of Christians (Eph. 4:25).

---

107 Rom. 10:16; Gal. 5:7; 1 Pet. 1:22; 2 Pet. 1:12; 1 Jn. 3:19; 2 Jn. 1,4; 3 Jn. 4.

108 1 Tim. 6:5; 2 Tim. 1:14; 2:18; 4:4; Tit. 1:14; 2 Pet. 2:2.

109 2 Cor. 13:8. There is controversy about how Paul intends this verse to function within the flow of his logic. But whatever it is, it is founded upon the general status of the statement as a proverb with wider implications. On the proverbial nature of the verse, see F. Bruce, *Corinthians*, 254, and M. Harris, 404.

110 Jn. 8:45. Becker and Link, 473, speaks of ψεῦδος in John conveying with it the idea of hatred for the truth.

111 2 Thes. 2:8–10; 1 Tim. 6:5; 2 Tim. 2:18; 3:3; 4:1; Tit. 1:14; 1 Jn. 2:4; 4:1–3,20.

112 Rom. 3:4. The imperative there amounts to a statement of fact. See Cranfield, *Romans*, 181–182.

113 1 Tim. 1:10; 1 Jn. 2:22; Rev. 21:8; 22:15. In direct contrast, in Rev. 14:5, the absence of lying signifies the blamelessness of the 144,000.

The concern for truthful speech among Christian adherents extends to vows and oaths. The matter of vows actually never arises as a topic of discussion in the New Testament[114]. Presumably, the Old Testament strictures about prompt fulfillment carry over[115]. On the matter of oaths, however, the demand from the mouth of Jesus in Mt. 5:33—37 is distinctive[116]. Oaths should not be made at all (ὅλως), not even to the truth[117]. The reason for making such an absolute directive seems to be twofold.

First, the majesty of God is too-often tarnished by the swearing of oaths (Gundry, 93). Whatever a person might swear by — heaven, earth, even the hairs on his own head — all ultimately involve God as guarantor because he has authority over everything. It is his reputation that is damaged, his name that is violated, every time an oath is broken. The casuistic practices of the scribes and Pharisees are to no avail, as Mt. 23:16—22 makes clear. The integrity of God's character cannot be safeguarded by skirting around the use of his name in oaths. Neither can the severity of punishment for breaking an oath be softened simply because his name was not uttered specifically.

Secondly, anything beyond a simple yes or nor is thought to be motivated by evil. As the passage concludes in 5:37: "Let your word be yes, yes or no, no for anything more than this comes from evil [or the Evil One]." Behind the attempts people make to bolster the credibility of their statements by oaths lurk sinister thoughts. Jesus' disciples, therefore, should have no part of it. Society at large should know that their statements can be taken at face value because their motives are pure. Their lives of commitment to the truth of Jesus Christ should be valid confirmation of their truthful speech and vice versa.

It is an intriguing question as to just how effective Jesus' concern to eliminate the use of oaths was among his followers[118]. The New Testament records the occasion of Peter's false swearing in Mk. 14:71 (Mt. 26:74). Paul's numerous asseverations that he is telling the truth, as those of Jesus himself, are very near to swearing[119]. In that they attempt to strengthen

---

114   The Corban vow is mentioned in Mk. 7:4 and temporary Nazirite vows are mentioned in Acts 18:18; 21:13.

115   Despite the intention of Mt. 5:33 to offer an antithesis to oaths, the Old Testament passages upon which it apparently draws include those about keeping one's vows to God.

116   Most suggest that what appears in Jas. 5:12 is closer to the original formulation. See Gundry, 91; Hill, 126–127; McNeile, 68; Allen, 54; Schneider, 18.

117   The fact that vs. 33 is intended to provide an antithesis to what follows indicates that the abolition of oath–making refers primarily to oaths even of truthful intention. See Gundry, 93; Hill, 125; McNeile, 67; Allen, 53.

118   McNeile; Schneider, 184–185; Pope, "Oaths," 577.

119   For Paul, see Rom. 9:1; 2 Cor. 1:23; 2:17; 7:14; 11:10; Gal. 1:20; Phil. 1:8; 1 Tim. 2:7. For Jesus, see Lk. 4:25; 9:27; 12:14; plus the numerous ἀμήν and ἀμὴν ἀμήν sayings.

the credibility of what is being said, it would appear that they go beyond a simple yes or no. One finds no reservations about mentioning God's oaths to David or Abraham or referring to angels swearing oaths[120]. Most baffling of all, though, is the author of Hebrews who not only presumes the conventional understanding of oaths as positive confirmation of true statements and intentions (Heb. 6:16) but also bases the crux of his argument for the complete superiority of Jesus' priesthood over the Levitical on the fact that God swore an oath regarding the priesthood of Melchizedek and did not with regard to the other (Heb. 7:20—28). It seems that Jesus' radical statement on oaths was either ignored or not taken so absolutely as the present form of it in Matthew seems to require.

---

120 Lk. 1:73; Acts 2:30 (David); 7:17; Heb. 6:3; Rev. 10:6 (angel). Heb. 3:11, 18; 4:3, also feature an oath God swore against Israel.

Chapter 10: Epistle of James

Exegesis

James 5:12

The isolation of 5:12 from its immediate context is often noted[1]. Although this is so, there is a commonly made observation which explains the location of the verse. This has to do with the motivational purpose clause which concludes the verse, ἵνα μὴ ὑπὸ κρίσιν πέσητε[2]. James raises the threat of eschatological judgment just three verses earlier in 5:9 using similar terminology, ἵνα μὴ κριθῆτε. Although the threat of judgment is not stated as specifically, it is also conveyed by ἡ παρουσία τοῦ κυρίου ἤγγικεν in 5:8 and by ἕως τῆς παρουσίας τοῦ κυρίου in 5:7. It is certainly also implied by ἀπολέσαι as far back as 4:12 and even by πονηρά and ἁμαρτία in 4:16 and 4:17. It would appear, then, that James conceives of 5:12 as the last in a series of admonitions which are tied together by their common threat of condemning judgment of God.

A closer look reveals that four out of the six admonitions are, more pointedly, prohibitions against speech sins: 4:11 — μὴ καταλεῖτε, 5:9 — μὴ στενάζετε, 5:12—μὴ ὀμνύετε, with 4:6 constituting a ban on boasting but without the same type of formulation. Both 5:7 and 5:8 call upon those who are suffering to be patient, which could include as much a censure of regrettable words born out of anger and frustration as deeds[3]. Thus, 5:12 may also be seen as the last in a series of admonitions regarding control of speech[4]. James' concern for this dimension of ethical behaviour reverberates throughout the book and should come as no surprise.

---

1 See Dibelius, 248, and P. Davids, 188, but contrast Laws, 219–220.
2 The significance of this phrase in pointing to a common judgment theme is related in various ways by P. Davids, 188–189; Ropes, 300; Schrage, 54; Mussner, 211; Minear, 7. In addition, P. Davids, 181, 189 (who depends on Francis) notes that the placement of this prohibition on making oaths probably relates to the normal practice of concluding a letter like this with an oath.
3 Both Mayor, 167, and Reicke, 56, go no further than to relate 5:12 to the concern about impatience expressed in 5:7–8.
4 Others note the general connection. See P. Davids, 188; Mitton, 191; Adamson, 194.

The opening of 5:12 with πρὸ πάντων δέ presents something of a problem for most commentators. This is because at face value it presumes a fairly close relationship with what precedes, declaring that what is now said is the most important in a series of related items. However, few see any justification for taking the phrase so literally. They prefer to take it as signifying a general emphasis unrelated to the prior context[5]. Laws (p. 220) in an unusual approach understands the phrase to be introducing the final section of admonition and not 5:12 alone. Dibelius (p. 248) despairs of finding any significance for the phrase in this context or of even knowing if it originates in this context. However, the recognition elucidated above that 5:12 is the last in a series of admonitions related to speech allows a perfectly normal reading of πρὸ πάντων δέ.

In this light, it is not so difficult to see that James considers swearing to be the pre-eminent vice within this series[6]. As to the author's reasons for conceiving of it as such, since he offers none, we can only conjecture. Even though he implies that each of the six admonitions ultimately amounts to an offense against God, perhaps he considers swearing the most serious because it most directly involves God, either by name or by association. In a broader perspective, perhaps he considers truthfulness the most important and most basic of speech for a Christian[7].

The recurrence of the by now familiar vocative ἀδελφοί μου following the introductory formula on the one hand may seem to enhance the distinctiveness of 5:12 from its surrounding context. On the other hand, it also may be seen to serve as a link between 5:12 and the series of admonitions regarding speech since three of them also begin with the vocative ἀδελφοί (4:11; 5:7, 9). The author again attempts to soften the seeming harshness of a stringent prohibition, which also presumes a tone of censure with regard to current behaviour, by affirming his solidarity with his readers.

---

5 P. Davids, 189; Mussner, 211; Mitton, 191; Hiebert, 308. Davids calls it "an emphatic epistolary introduction."
6 Adamson, 194–195. Ropes, 300, considers the "series" to consist of just 5:9 and 5:12, but he has no problem understanding 5:12 to be the more important of the two. Reicke, 56, takes πρὸ πάντων δέ literally but contrasts it with 5:7–8 with regard to impatience.
7 Minear, 8–11, masterfully brings this out in relation to 5:12. He says that the command, as enshrined in 5:12, "could not have been deleted from the catechesis without damaging the whole ethos of the new humanity." He then proceeds to list eight "basic kerygmatic and dogmatic concerns" which would be undermined if the accent on honest speech were lost. Minear also supplies evidence for the fact that Jesus himself was the initiator of this stress (Mt. 5:33–37; 12:34–37; 15:18–20) which reverberates throughout the New Testament. Although it is doubtful that James uses πρὸ πάντων δέ because 5:12 is a known command and emphasis of Jesus, this conjecture is not totally lacking in justification. Speaking truth is a radical foundation to the ethics of the Christian movement.

The present tense of the prohibition μὴ ὀμνύετε indicates that swearing is practiced by the readers and that James wants this stopped. The lack of any temporal qualifications makes it apparent that oaths are never to be made again. The brief list of items not to swear by, μήτε τὸν οὐρανὸν μήτε τὴν γῆν, especially as it ends with μήτε ἄλλον τινὰ ὅρκον, enforces the absolute nature of the command. Simply, one is not to swear, neither at any time nor upon any object. The accusative construction here is commonly noted as typical of Classical Greek. The reference to τὸν οὐρανόν and τὴν γῆν could be literal. However, it is likely that they also are representative, respectively, for God or anything associated with him and for objects one might swear by on earth. The combination of the two words is a common Hebrew way of expressing the universe.

James follows the negative injunction by a positive one. The effect is a helpful clarification of the motivation for the absolute prohibition on making oaths as well as a setting forth of an ideal for speech-ethics. The admonition is presented in a dramatic framework: ἤτω δὲ ὑμῶν τὸ Ναὶ ναὶ καὶ τὸ Ὂυ οὔ. The δέ is adversative and indicates that an alternative to making oaths is being recommended. A person's "no" should be adequate to convey his unmitigated denial or disclaimer. His "yes" should require nothing to enhance its credibility. His τὸ Ναί means ναί and his τὸ Ὂυ means οὔ, nothing less, nothing more, nothing deceptive, nothing boastful. His word is plain truth, and it is reinforced by the truthfulness in his manner of life. His character should be of such quality that no one, within or without the Christian community, has any reason to question his veracity.

The dramatic nature of the admonition is enhanced by posing the imperative in the singular in contrast to ὀμνύετε and the later subjunctive πέσητε. This also draws attention to the responsibility of each individual to speak in a direct, forthright, and honest manner. The plurality of the audience, though, is kept intact by modifying τό Ναί and τὸ Ὂυ with the plural possessive pronoun ὑμῶν.

The purpose clause, ἵνα μὴ ὑπὸ κρίσιν πέσητε, may be formally attached to the second imperative. However, it pertains to both the first and the second. Escape from eschatological judgment is the motivation for refraining from making oaths as well as for telling the truth generally. As the author perceives them, the two are intrinsically related. Some think falsehood and deception lurk beneath "yes" or "no" which is not affirmed by an oath. The common casuistic practice of ranking the affirmative value of oaths is assumed. However, from the author's standpoint, avoidance of these practices and assumptions and a move to unqualified truthfulness between people is what God requires. Failure to appropriate this standard continues to compromise not only the very concept of truth but also God himself, who is so affiliated with oaths and oath-making. This is an important matter requiring immediate change on the part of Christians. Attaching the assurance of God's eschatological condemnation upon those who fail to do so proclaims this.

Analysis

Ironically, the strongest statement in James which relates the concept of truth to speech does not use the word ἀλήθεια, although it does appear three times in the writing. Nevertheless, James 5:12, and especially the second sentence, makes as clear a call for truthful speech as one could hope to encounter. The absolute censure of oath-making presumes the practice of using oaths as cloaks to conceal degrees of truth and deception. Such practices undermine the very meaning of truth in society. By eliminating the use of oaths, James puts pressure on the very words uttered to correspond to the actual views of the speaker. This perception captures the logic of the second sentence of 5:12. Those who respond to James' pleas for the end of oath-making and the beginning of personal integrity in speech — hopefully, at least Christians — will initiate within human society a restoration of the value of integrity in personal speech. The serious nature of James' plea is conveyed by the threat of eschatological condemnation attached to it. The introduction of the plea by πρό πάντων δέ gives cause for believing that the author considers personal honesty and integrity in speech to be one of the most important principles of speech-ethics.

The fact that James associates truth with God is exhibited most clearly by two of the three explicit uses of ἀλήθεια. In 1:18, it is God's λόγῳ ἀληθείας which is specified as the means by which God "brought us forth." Here "word of truth" most likely refers to the gospel but not totally exclusive from the role of God's word in originally creating man. The most significant factor at this point is that this word which is identified with truth is clearly spoken of as originating in God. In 5:19, τῆς ἀληθείας is James' designation of what a Christian strays from when he falls into salvation-threatening error. The term could refer simply to the gospel again. However, it probably encompasses something broader than the proclamation of the gospel and with a touch of existential prejudice conceives of Christianity as a religion. In a practical sense, the designation of Christianity as "the truth" must also point to the truthfulness of its teachings, doctrinal and moral. When someone disavows by word or by practice the teachings of Christianity, they disavow Christianity, the Christ, and forfeit their salvation.

James may also be seen to be associating truth with God in 3:17, although he does not use a term which specifically means truth. However, the list of words which describe ἡ . . . ἄνωθεν σοφία contains at least three words which may include reference to the quality of truth. The words ἀγνή, meaning "pure," ἀδιάκριτος, meaning "unwavering" or "impartial," and ἀνυπόκριτος, meaning "unhypocritical," all point to a uniformity of purposes and deeds which corresponds to truthfulness of character. Although these are not said to describe God as such, they do describe qualities which God — and only he — imparts to the person who truly possesses wisdom.

The third use of ἀλήθεια in James occurs in the context of describing the person who is not wise, whose wisdom does not derive from God. In 3:14, lying κατὰ τῆς ἀληθείας is associated with people who boast, whose verbal behaviour extends from their internal jealousy and selfish ambition. Their "wisdom" is the opposite of "from above." It is "earthly," "natural," and even "demonic." The satanic influence is also conveyed in 4:7 by τῷ διαβόλῳ and in 3:6 by τῆς γεέννης.

Describing their speech as lying against the truth is a way of epitomising man's evil nature. It typifies man's antagonism toward God. It also presumes truth to be associated with God. When a person boasts, he lies against reality. He projects himself as something he is not (in this case, wise). He tries to deceive others and God, but in the end he deceives only himself. His evil cannot be hidden from God. The attitude of self-deceiving, prideful antagonism to God arises again in 4:1—10 when such people are called upon to repent. The failure to do what one knows to be right, condemned in 4:17, also typifies man's naive attempts to deceive God by disobediently ignoring the truth he provides them about how to live. In 5:6, in speaking of the rich as condemning and putting to death the righteous, James provides a generalised instance of lying against God (if perjury is understood here). Finally, it should be noted that the idea of lying against the truth applies not just to the person who is particularly rebellious against God but to all men. James 1:13—15 presumes that everyone sins, and 3:1—12 presumes the tongues of all men to be evil.

Conclusion

The first primary conclusion of this thesis is that peronsal speech-ethics is a major theme in the Epistle of James. Over eighty percent of the verses of James have been examined for their contribution to this concern anchored in 1:5—8, 19—27; 3:1—12, 18; 41—17; and 5:9, 12—18.

This thesis has found that James' concern for speech-ethics can be classified into five divisions. First, rudimentary ideas about speech-ethics demand that a person exercise control over his speech. This is a spiritual obligation directly related to growing maturity and even to salvation. Listening, both to God and to others, is crucial and aids in controlling the tongue. Listening also helps speaking to be positive and beneficial. Words and deeds need to complement one another but obedience to the words of God/Christ is vital. Finally, a person must develop an appreciation for the power that words have, especially those of God/Christ. This power can even work through him to bring back the spiritually immature to faith.

In a second division, James' concern focuses on the human tongue and its fundamentally evil nature. Of all the bodily parts, it acts most vociferously as the agency of evil, of Satan himself. The tongue reeks ruin not only upon other people but also upon the person speaking and even upon human society as a whole. James recognizes the inward, self-motivated nature of sin. However, the evil speech fostered by the evil tongue is projected as the epitome of human sinfulness.

Thirdly, James' concern for speech-ethics turns toward speech and its misuse in inter-human relationships. In this realm, speech is viewed as a major obstacle to a peaceful, loving society with respect to the Christian community as well as human society. On the other hand, speech which is truly gracious has the capability of transforming society in positive ways. James specialises in demonstrating that all the various ways by which people abuse each other verbally in the end constitute offenses against God.

Fourthly, James considers speech in human-divine relationships directly. Encouragement is given to praise God in song when joyful in acknowledgment of his sovereignty over human affairs. James probably intends to encourage praise in all circumstances, even those of great stress. Within this context arises the encouragement to pray. Advice given pertains not only to personal, petitionary prayer but also to intercessory prayer, confession, and repentance. Also, one is to avoid blaspheming God/Christ in his speech. In this concern, James' emphasis goes beyond the idea of verbally slandering God himself to include the pagan who slanders the Christian, the Christian who berates another Christian, and even the person who simply curses another. Also in this category is boasting which constitutes a major offence to God, perhaps even qualifying as the primary way of characterising man's rebellion against God.

Fifthly, James is concerned about speech and truth. Its brief counsel is that a person is to be truthful in his everyday speech, not even making an oath to his veracity. James underlines this as a primary concern of speech-ethics and indicates that it has a bearing on salvation.

As a second primary conclusion, this thesis demonstrates that the concern for personal speech-ethics which appears in the Epistle of James is a reflection of the widespread and deeply held concern for personal speech-ethics in the ancient Mediterranean world. Ample portions of primary background material provide the evidence. Numerous distinctive cultures, religions, and societies display the same basic contours of concern. Issues of controlled speech, listening, words and deeds, the power of the tongue, the evil of the tongue, speech in inter-human relationships, speech in human-divine relationships, and speech in relation to truth run through all the literature. Personal speech-ethics appears to be a basic concern of humanity.

As a third primary conclusion, this thesis demonstrates that a majority of the specific speech-ethic principles assumed or expressed in James are also advanced in background literature. These are not always found in each kind of literature but many are found in six or seven of the eight categories of literature examined and crossover into at least two cultures or societies out of the four involved, Near Eastern, Jewish, Graeco-Roman, and Christian.

The cross-cultural ideas James shares with background literature with regard to the rudiments of speech-ethics includes the idea that anger epitomises uncontrolled speech and that it is detrimental to society. Also, gracious speech is dependent upon God, listening takes place inwardly and is not merely a physical ability, and listening both to God and to other people is important as is being obedient. It is also standard to include the ideas that one's words should be consistent with one's deeds, that works and deeds together comprise ethical behaviour, and that works are a reliable gauge of a person's disposition. Finally, it is thought that the power of words is grounded in God.

Three standard ideas not found in James include: the virtue of silence, the importance of obeying parents, and the reputation of professional orators as deceivers.

Shared ideas concerning the evil of the tongue include the general tendency of the tongue toward evil, the linking of this to man's evil nature, and the importance of God's intervention to enable the tongue to be anything other than harmful. Also included is the comparability of the tongue to fire and to wild animals, and its capability to do great harm which includes causing death, personal inner destruction, and the general downfall of human society. The evil tongue is often linked to Satan. An evil tongue manifests a person's evil actions as well as the inward reality of his evil. Finally, it is generally recognized that there are those who attempt to disguise their evil intentions with their tongues.

In inter-human relationships, it is typical to view peace and harmony as general goals of society to which speech sins are a hindrance. Speech sins, often typified by anger, are thought to be an affront to God as well as to others. Some speech sins are compared to murder, and slander is often considered the worst. Partiality in speech is usually conceived of as taking place in judicial settings and as mostly affecting the poor.

With regard to speech in human-divine relationships, it is nearly universal to assert that God should receive praise because of his sovereignty and his work in creation, that singing is a valuable means of offering praise which should be spontaneous and regular, and that praise is a responsibility for the individual. Prayer petition should also be spontaneous. Often thought of as keys to effective prayer are faith in God, submission to him, and sincerity. On the other hand, the commonly mentioned interrupter of effective prayer is sinfulness. Finally, with regard to blasphemy, it is commonly thought that it can consist of verbal remarks made to other people, that boasting is akin to it, and that God should not be blamed for sin.

Standard ideas in the relationship of speech to truth include: truthful speech is of paramount importance, truthful character is intrinsic to truthful speech, God and his word are always true, and lying typifies the rebellion of men from God as well as the speech of Satan. Finally, it is commonly thought that oaths should be kept to a minimum.

With regard to the extensive lists of ideas just enumerated, it is impossible to determine the specific influence upon the Epistle of James since there are no word-for-word parallels. It must simply be said that James demonstrates itself attuned to the resounding concern for these particular facets of speech-ethics in the ancient Mediterranean world.

The evidence can be analysed from another perspective, focusing on ideas about speech-ethics in James which appear elsewhere in only one other kind of literature. Ideas of this sort indicate probable familiarity of the author with the particular kind of literature involved or at least influence from that culture or society. By this approach, the author of

James can be seen to be linked formally with Jewish, Graeco-Roman, and Christian thought. Also, his ability to digest the diverse ideas available to him in his time and place becomes unmistakable.

By far the largest number of ideas appearing in James of concern to speech-ethics but found in only one other kind of literature involves the New Testament. These specifically Christian concerns and ideas which are shared by James and the New Testament include: listening to and obeying the gospel, respecting the ethics of Jesus, understanding the occasional inadequacy of words, recognizing the power of Jesus' name, connecting the implanted word to the gospel, advocating harmony within the Christian community, viewing certain speech sins such as slander, mockery, and perjury as forms of persecution, viewing deception as false teaching, stressing intercessory prayer, conceiving of Jesus as a subject of blasphemy, seeing verbal abuse of Christians as blasphemy, viewing boasting as an aspect of worldliness, connecting truth to the gospel, and issuing a total ban on swearing.

Ideas and concerns which James shares individually with other kinds of literature are not nearly so numerous as with the New Testament. Nevertheless, they are significant. James shares with Philo the idea that of all the bodily parts the tongue is the most treacherous source of evil. With Graeco-Roman literature (also Philo), James shares concern over desires and pleasures in man, and the idea that a person should not utter curses. With Rabbinic literature, James shares the idea that the tongue is superior to the other bodily parts, that certain respected men in the community should be called upon to come and pray for the sick, that prayer should be persistent, and that the one who reproves another merits blessing from God. With the Apocrypha and Pseudepigrapha (also the Old Testament), James shares the idea that impartiality is a rule which should apply to normal human relationships as well as to formal judicial situations. With the Old Testament, James shares the idea that the implanted word is connected to salvation. With neither Near Eastern Wisdom literature nor with Qumranic literature does James share an idea that is otherwise absent from the other kinds of background literature.

Besides demonstrating the formal connection of the Epistle of James to nearly every kind of background literature surveyed in this thesis, the above analysis reveals the specially close affinity it has to the New Testament. However, its closeness to Rabbinic literature is also noteworthy.

The lack of any formal link to Near Eastern Wisdom literature and to Qumranic literature is not too surprising. With regard to Near Eastern Wisdom literature, it was stressed to begin with that the primary importance of this literature has to do with the Old Testament and perhaps to other Jewish literature but not necessarily to the Epistle of James in any direct way.

As far as Qumranic literature is concerned, it must be recognized that it represents a community possessing its own culture within a culture as does the New Testament. Thus, many of the ideas which appear in this literature having to do with community relations may be supportive of ideas in James but do not show up in this kind of analysis because they are also found in the New Testament. It should be noted too that the tendency of Philo to draw from both Jewish and Graeco-Roman ideas leaves his literature with little to offer in this kind of analysis despite its overall value as background to the Epistle of James.

In evaluating the support the background literature as a whole supplies for James' concern about personal speech-ethics, it must be said that James' ideas across the board are most consistently supported by Jewish literature. A vital link to Christian ideas found in the New Testament, although not manifested as often, is readily apparent as the singularly shared ideas noted above suggest. The connection of Jesus himself to serious warning pertaining to speech in the New Testament (Mt. 5:33—37; 7:1—2; 12:33—37; 23:16—22) can hardly be insignificant in influencing the author of James to be concerned about speech-ethics. Graeco-Roman literature does not provide support for James as often as either Jewish or Christian literature does, but it is unmistakable and significant nonetheless.

As a fourth primary conclusion, this thesis demonstrates that the Epistle of James contains ideas and emphases on the matter of personal speech-ethics that are distinct from what is found in the background literature.

With respect to the rudiments of speech-ethics, like no one else James ties a person's spiritual and ethical development to his speech-ethics. Speech is made the key to improved behaviour. Because of its link to control of speech and preparation for speech, listening too is put under the umbrella of the sacred. James also combines the general value of listening with the specific value of listening to God, Christ, or the gospel. This contributes to the author's general tendency to interlock moral and spiritual development. Viewing the whole of a Christian's life as holy is not new to James. However, the application of this concept to such routine activities as speaking and listening is startling. James places these two functions at the forefront of the spiritual battle.

With respect to the evil of the tongue, James is more completely pessimistic about the human tongue, is more clear about the role of Satan in its evil, and supplies the most compact description of its evil than any other writing. Distinctive also is James' application of the universal inability of men to control the evil of their tongues to the sinfulness of all men and their need for repentance. Finally, James' overriding concern for self-deception, as opposed to deceiving others, is noteworthy as distinctive.

With respect to speech in inter-human relationships, one of James' distinctives is that all speech sins are lumped together as offensive to God which makes them equally sinful. Refraining from them is not purely a matter of ethics but an important spiritual concern. The author is concerned generally with the deleterious effects of speech in human relationships and specifically on Christian relationships. James ingeniously interwines the love command and Jesus' words about judgment and applies this dynamic to speech in human relationships. James focuses strictly on speech that harms others. Lewd jokes or inept table manners, which do not fit into this category are not addressed. The author does not warn its readers to remain aloof from habitual slanderers or gossips. Perhaps his concern for discipleship and evangelising overrides such common advice.

As far as specific speech sins are concerned, distinctive ideas in James are: provision of a more honourable basis for not cursing another person, association of deceit with boasting, recognition that persecution from outside a community can cause division within, and unprecedented limelight given to the unacceptability of partiality.

With respect to speech in human-divine relationships, James distinctively emphasises friendship as the ideal relationship with God and the idea that making plans for the future can be considered an affront to God. The latter puts a fresh twist on God's sovereignty over the future, even going further than Prov. 27:1, upon which 4:13—17 most likely is derived. James does not have much to say about praise, but the space given over to prayer is astonishing in the light of the brevity of the writing. A large number of singular notions regarding prayer appear.

First, powerful prayer is possible from anyone. In contrast to Rabbinic literature which stresses the special qualities of the wise man who prays to heal the sick, James stresses the normalcy of Elijah. The power in the prayer of elders over the sick is tied to their role as representatives of the church, not to their individual prowess.

Secondly, confessing sin to one another is a pre-requisite for intercessory prayer. The group confession in Qumran literature is liturgical and addressed to God, and is not so personal and lucid[1]. Even the concept found in Rabbinic literature that people share their needs with one another for the purposes of prayer is not as advanced as confessing sins, as James emphasises.

Thirdly, James seems oblivious to the concepts of corporate or fixed prayer. Interest centers on the individual and his prayer life.

---

1 See Braun, 1:282, and Schmitt, 106–107, who both note the compatibility of Jas. 5:16 with 1QS 1:24–2:1 and with CD 8:28–30.

Fourthly, James connects the poor prayer life of individuals to internal division within the Christian community.

With respect to the relationship of speech to truth, few of James' ideas on speech and truth fall into the category of unique or distinctive. With his main statement paralleled so closely in Matthew, this is to be expected. What distinctives there are must be distinctives with respect to Matthew. From this vantage point it can be observed at the very least that James' phraseology most clearly presents the call for truthful speech in everyday life. This deduction made from the ban on oaths is both appropriate and insightful. Whether or not Jesus is ultimately responsible for this connection, it is James — and not Matthew — which conveys it in unmistakable language. This is not only a worthy contribution to the preservation of Jesus tradition but also makes James deserving of a distinctive ranking in its contribution to speech-ethics.

The distinctive ideas and emphases of the Epistle of James vary in nature from section to section. However, it can be observed that they tend to gravitate toward dramatising the spiritual ramifications of speech-ethics, especially for the individual but also for the Christian community. Many of James' distinctives can be identified as specifications based upon Christian ideals. The inclusion of the Epistle of James in the New Testament is not without reason. It may be concluded that James' adamant concern for speech-ethics is based upon the author's concern for the spiritual growth and well-being of his audience — which he perceives as mainly Christian — whose speech-ethics were sorely lacking.

The Introduction suggested that results of this thesis could apply to some of the inconclusive introductory problems regarding the Epistle of James. This is the case. All but the first of the items to be mentioned correlate with the demonstration of the four dimensions of the thesis which have just been discussed. The third relates as much to New Testament studies in general as to studies in James.

First, the affiliation of the Epistle of James with wisdom and wisdom literature, at least with respect to the concern for personal speech-ethics, is further substantiated by the results of this thesis.

Secondly, although no claim that the concern for personal speech-ethics in the Epistle of James predominates the thought of the writing has been made — nor would such a claim be viewed as justifiable — the results of this thesis do demonstrate that personal speech-ethics is a strong theme in James and warrants a higher profile than usually given.

Thirdly, the thorough, ideological approach that has been taken to the background literature in this thesis and the results that have been reaped may provide a spur for scholars to discover more inter-cultural concerns reflected in James or in the New Testament.

Fourthly, the multi-cultural nature of the literature which supports the ideas on personal speech-ethics in the Epistle of James points to the complexity of determining the original author of the epistle and confirms the view of many that he was a Jewish Christian who was well acquainted with the ideas of Graeco-Roman literature.

Fifthly, the results of the thesis regarding their failings at personal speech-ethic could be of some help in further identifying the original audience to whom the Epistle of James was addressed.

Sixthly, the results of this thesis should stimulate those who question the Christian nature of James' ethics to reconsider. The author most certainly is Christian as are his speech-ethics.

Lastly, the results of this thesis exhibit that it is possible to discern the author's own ideas and emphases in the Epistle of James. The methodology is exacting, but it has successfully exposed the author's distinctives with respect to personal speech-ethics.

Bibliography

Boldface indicates the shortened form in which works will appear. This will usually be simply the author's last name. Exceptions to this are when an author has more than one title in the bibliography or when authors share a last name.

Abbott, T.K. *A Critical and Exegetical Commentary on the Epistles to the Ephesians and to the Colossians*. ICC. Edinburgh: T. & T. Clark, 1897.

Abelson, J. *The Immanence of God in Rabbinical Literature*. London: Macmillan, 1912.

Abrahams, Israel. "The Talmud." In Corré, pp. 17–20. First published in *Chapters on Jewish Literature*. Philadelphia, 1899.

Adamson, James B. *The Epistle of James*. Grand Rapids: Eerdmans, 1976.

Adamson, James, B. "An **Inductive** Approach to the Epistle of James – Materials for a Fresh Study." Ph.D. thesis, Cambridge University, 1953.

Adkins, A.W.H. *From the One to the Many: A Study of Personality and Views of Human Nature in the Context of Ancient Greek Society, Values, and Beliefs*. London: Constable, 1970.

Adkins, A.W.H. *Moral Values and Political Behavior in the Ancient World*. New York: W.W. Norton, 1972.

Adkins, A.W.H. *Merit and Responsibility: A Study in Greek Values*. Oxford: Clarendon, 1960.

Agourides, S.C. "The Origin of the Epistle of St. James: Suggestions for a Fresh Approach." *GOTR* 9(1963):67-78.

Albeck, Chanoch. *Mabo le Misnah*. Jerusalem, 1959.

Albeck, Chanoch. *Einführung in die Mischna*. Berlin: de Gruyter, 1971.

Albright, W.F. "Some Canaanite-Phoenician Sources of Hebrew Wisdom." In *WIANE*, pp. 1–15.

Alexander, A.B.D. *Christianity and Ethics*. London: Duckworth, 1914.

Allegro, John M. and **Anderson**, A.A. *Discoveries in the Judean Desert of Jordan*, vol. 5. Oxford: Clarendon, 1968.

Allen, Willoughby C. *A Critical and Exegetical Commentary on the Gospel According to St. Matthew*. ICC. Edinburgh: T. & T. Clark, 1907.

Allerhand, J. "Der historische Hintergrund der Sprüche der Väter und ihre Ethik." *Kairos* 21(2–3, 1979):133–180.

Alt, Albrecht. "Solomonic Wisdom." In *SAIW*, pp. 102–112. First published in *TLZ* 76(1951): 139–144.

Alt, Albrecht. Zur literarischen **Analyse** der Weisheit des Amenemope." In *WIANE*, pp. 16–25.

Amir, Yehoshua. "Philo and the Bible." *StudPhil* 2(1973):1–8.

Ammassari, Antonio. "Towards a Law of Liberty: The Epistle of James." *SIDIC* 10(1977):23–25.

Amphoux, C.-B. "Une relecture du chapitre I de l'Épître de Jacquès." *Biblica* 59(1978):554–561.

Amphoux, C.-B. "L'emploi du **coordonnant** dans l'Épître de Jacques." *Biblica* 63(1982):90–101.

Amsler, S. "La Sagesse de la Femme." In Gilbert, pp. 112–116.

Anderson, A.A. *The Book of Psalms*. NCBC. 2 vols. London: Oliphants, 1972.

Anderson, F.I. "2 Enoch." In *OTP*, 1:91–212.

Armstrong, A.H. "Greek Philosophy and Christianity." In *The Legacy of Greece: A New Appraisal*, pp. 347–375. Edited by M.I. Finley. Oxford: Clarendon, 1981.

Austin, J.L. *How to Do Things with Words*. Oxford: Clarendon, 1962.

Austin, J.L. *Philosophical Papers*. Edited by J.O. Urmson and G.J. Warnoch. Oxford: Oxford University, 1961.

Baasland, Ernst. "Der Jakobusbrief als neutestamentliche Weisheitschrift." *ST* 36(2,1982):119–139.

Babbit, Frank Cole. *Plutarch's Moralia*. LCL. London: Heinemann, 1926.

Baldry, H.C. *The Unity of Mankind in Greek Thought*, Cambridge: Cambridge University, 1965.
Bamberger, B.J. "Philo and the Aggadah." *HUCA* 48(1977):153–185.
Banwell, B.O. "Lip." In *IIIDB*, 2:907–909.
Banwell, B.O. "Mouth." In *IIIDB*, 2:1031.
Banwell, B.O. "Tongue. In *IIIDB*, 3:1574–1575.
Barabas, S. "Gossip." In *ZPEB* 2:789.
Barclay, W.S. *Educational Ideals in the Ancient World*. London: Collins, 1959.
Barnes, Jonathan. *Aristotle*. Past Masters Series. Oxford: Oxford University, 1982.
Barone, Orlando. "James, the Brother of the Lord." *The Bible Today* 94(1978):1485–1491.
Barr, James. *The Semantics of Biblical Language*. Oxford: Oxford University, 1961.
Barr, James. "The Symbolism of Names in the Old Testament." *BJRL* 52(1969–70):11–30.
Barrett, C.K. *The Gospel According to St. John*. London: SPCK, 1978.
Barth, Marcus. *Ephesians*. 2 vols. AB. Garden City, NY: Doubleday, 1974.
Barthelemy, J.D. "Essenism and Christianity." *Scripture* 12(1961):20–24.
Barthelemy, J.D., and Milik, J.T., eds. *Discoveries in the Judean Desert*, vol. 1. Oxford: Clarendon, 1955.
Barucq, Andre. *Ecclesiaste*. Paris: Beauchesne, 1969.
Bauer, W. *A Greek-English Lexicon of the New Testament and other Early Christian Literatures*. Translated and Edited by W.F. Arndt and F.W. Gingrich. Chicago: University of Chicago, 1957.
Baumgärtel, Friedrich. "καρδία." In *TDNT*, 3:606–607.
Baumgartner, W. "The Wisdom Literature." In *The Old Testament and Modern Study*, pp. 210–237. Edited by H.H. Rowley. Oxford: Clarendon, 1951.
Beardslee, William A. *Literary Criticism of the New Testament*. Philadelphia: Fortress, 1967.
Beardslee, William A. "Uses of the Proverb in the Synoptic Gospels." *Int* 24(1970):61–73.
Beardslee, William A. "The Wisdom Tradition and the Synoptic Gospels." *JAAR* 35(1967):231–240.
Beardslee, William A. "Plutarch's Use of Proverbial Forms of Speech." *Semeia* 17(1980):101–112.
Beck, David. "The Composition of the Epistle of James." Ph.D. thesis, Princeton Theological Seminary, 1973.
Beck, F.A.G. *Greek Education 450–350 B.C.* London: Methuen, 1964.
Beck, H., and Brown, C. "Peace." In *NIDNTT* 2:776–782.
Becker, U., and Link, H.-G. "Blessing." In *NIDNTT*, 1:206–218.
Becker, U. and Link, H.-G. "Lie." In *NIDNTT*, 2:470–474.
Berger, Peter, and Luckmann, Thomas. *The Social Construction of Reality*. Garden City, NY: Doubleday, 1966.
Best, Ernest. *1 Peter*. NCBC. London: Marshall, Morgan, & Scott, 1971.
Best, Ernest. *A Commentary on the First and Second Epistles to the Thessalonians*. London: Adam & Charles Black, 1972.
Beyer, Hermann. "βλασφημία." In *TDNT*, 1:621–625
Birnbaum, Philip. *Daily Prayer Book*. New York: Hebrew Publishing, 1969.
Black, Matthew. *The Scrolls and Christian Origins*. London: Nelson, 1961.
Black, Matthew. ed. *The Scrolls and Christianity*. London: SPCK, 1969.
Black, Matthew. *Romans*. NCBC. London: Marshall, Morgan, & Scott, 1973.
Blackman, E.C. "Mind, Heart." In *TWBB*, pp. 144–146.
Blackman, E.C. "Truth." *TWBB*, p. 269.
Blank, Sheldon H. "The Curse, Blasphemy, the Spell and the Oath." *HUCA* 23(1950–51):73–95.
Blenker, Alfred. "Jakobs brevs sammenhaeng." *DTT* 30(1967):193–202.
Blenkinsopp, Joseph. *Wisdom and Law in the Old Testament*. Oxford: Oxford University, 1983.
Blocher, Henri. "The Fear of the Lord as the 'Principle' of Wisdom." *TB* 28(1977):3–28.
Blondel, J.-L. "Le fondement théologique de la parénèse dans l'épître de Jacques." *RTP* 29(1979):141–152.
Boggan, Charlie William. "Wealth in the Epistle of James." Ph.D. thesis, Southern Baptist Theological Seminary, 1982.
Boismard, M.-E. "Une liturgie baptismale dans la Prima Petri: (II) Son influence sur L'Épître de Jacques. *RevB* 64(1957):161–183.
Bok, Sissela. *Lying*. London: Quartet Books, 1980.

Boling, Robert. *Judges*. AB. Garden City, NY: Doubleday, 1975.

Bonhöhher, Adolf. *Die Ethik des stoikers Epiktet*. Stuttgart: Enke, 1894.

Bonhöffer, Adolf. *Epiktet und das Neue Testament*. In Religionsgeschichtliche Versuche und Vorarbeiten, vol. 10. Giessen, 1911.

Bonsirven, J., ed. *Textes rabbiniques des deux premiers siècles Chretiens pour servir a l'intelligence die Nouveau Testament*. Rome: Pontifical Biblical Institute, 1955.

Boussett, Wilhelm. *Kyrios Christos: A History of the Belief in Christ from the Beginnings of Christianity to Irenaeus*. Translated by John T. Steely. New York: Abingdon, 1970.

Bowker, John. *The Targums and Rabbinic Literature*. Cambridge, Cambridge University, 1969.

Box, G.H. *The Apocalypse of Abraham*. London: SPCK, 1919.

Braaten, Carl E. *Eschatology and Ethics*. Minneapolis: Augsburg, 1974.

Bratcher, Robert G. "Exegetical Themes in James 3–5." *RevExp* 66(1969):403–413.

Braude, William G., trans. *Pesikta Rabbati*. 2 vols. London: Yale University, 1968.

Braude, William G., trans. *The Midrash on the Psalms*. 2 vols. New Haven, CT: Yale University, 1959.

Braumann, Georg. "Der theologische Hintergrund des Jakobusbriefes." *Theologische Zeitschrift* 18(1962):401–418.

Braun, Herbert. *Qumran und das Neue Testament*. 2 vols. Tübingen: J.C.B. Mohr, 1966.

Breasted, J.H. *Development of Religion and Thought in Ancient Egypt*. New York, 1912.

Brichto, H.C. *The Problem of the Curse in the Hebrew Bible*. SBL Monograph, no. 13, Philadelphia, 1963.

Briggs, Charles. *The Book of Psalms*. ICC. 2 vols. Edinburgh: T. & T. Clark, 1906.

Bright, John. *Jeremiah*. AB. Garden City, NY: Doubleday, 1965.

Brockington, L.H. "Speak." *TWBB*, p. 233.

Brooks, James A. "The Place of James in the New Testament Canon." *SWJT* 12(1969):41–56.

Brown, Raymond E. *The Gospel According to John*. 2 vols. London: Geoffrey Chapman, 1966.

Bruce, F.F. *New Testament History*. Garden City, NY: Doubleday, 1972.

Bruce, F.F. *I & II Corinthians*. NCBC. London: Marshall, Morgan, & Scott, 1971.

Bruce, F.F. *The Book of Acts*. NICNT. Grand Rapids: Eerdmans, 1954.

Bruce, F.F. *The Epistle to the Galatians*. NIGTC. Grand Rapids: Eerdmans, 1982.

Bruce, F.F. *Second Thoughts on the Dead Sea Scrolls*. London: Paternoster, 1956.

Bruce, W.S. *The Ethics of the Old Testament*. Edinburgh: T. & T. Clark, 1909.

Bruggemann, W. "Tongue." In *IntDB*, 4:670.

Bryce, Glendon E. *A Legacy of Wisdom: the Egyptian Contribution to the Wisdom of Israel*. London: Associated University Presses, 1979.

Bullock, C. Hassell. *An Introduction to the Old Testament Poetic Books: the Wisdom and Songs of Israel*. Chicago: Moody, 1979.

Bultmann, Rudolf. *History of the Synoptic Tradition*. Translated by John Marsh. New York: Harper & Row, 1963.

Bultmann, Rudolf. *Primitive Christianity in its Contemporary Settings*. Translated by R.H. Fuller. New York: Thames and Hudson, 1956.

Bultmann, Rudolf. "ἀλήθεια." In *TDNT*, 1:241–247.

Bultmann, Rudolf. "καυχάομαι." In *TDNT*, 3:648–652.

Bultmann, Rudolf. *Theology of the New Testament*. 2 vols. Translated by Kendrick Grobel. New York: Charles Scribner's Sons, 1955.

Burgmann, Hans. " 'The Wicked Woman': Der Makkabäer Simon?" *RQ* 8(1972–75):323–359.

Burney, C.F. *Notes on the Hebrew Text of the Books of Kings*. Oxford: Clarendon, 1943.

Burney, C.F. *The Book of Judges*. London: Rivingtons, 1918.

Burrows, Millar. *The Dead Sea Scrolls*. London: Secker & Warburg, 1956.

Burrows, Millar. *More Light on the Dead Sea Scrolls*. London: Secker & Warbrug, 1958.

Burrows, Millar. "Old Testament Ethics and the Ethics of Jesus." In *Essays in Old Testament Ethics*, pp. 225–243. Edited by James J. Crenshaw and John T. Willis. New York: KTAV, 1974.

Cadoux, Arthur T. *The Thought of St. James*. London: Clarke, 1944.

Calhoun, George. "The Art of Formula in Homer-ΕΠΕΑ ΠΤΕΡΟΕΝΤΑ." *Classical Philology* 30(1935):215–227.

Calmet, Augustin. "Vraie et fausse sagesse: Jacques 1,19–27. 3,13–18." *BVC* 58(1964):19–28.

Cantinat, Jean. "Sagesse, justice, plaisirs: Jc. 3,16 – 4,3." *AsSeign* 56(1974):36–40.

Carlston, C.E. "Proverbs, Maxims, and the Historical Jesus." *JBL* 99(1980):87–105.

Carr, Arthur. "The Meaning of 'Ο ΚΟΣΜΟΣ' in James III,6." *Exp* ser. 7, 8(1909):318–325.

Carrington, Philip. *The Primitive Christian Catechism: A Study of the Epistle.* Cambridge: Cambridge University, 1940.

Carson, D.A. "Divine Sovereignty and Human Responsibility in Philo: Analysis of Method." *NovT* 23(1981):148–164.

Cassuto, U. *A Commentary on the Book of Exodus.* Translated by Israel Abrahams. Jerusalem: Magnes, 1967.

Castle, E.B. *Ancient Education and Today.* Harmondsworth, Middlesex: Penguin, 1961.

Chadwick, Henry. "Philo and the Beginnings of Christian Thought." In *The Cambridge History of Later Greek and Early Medieval Philosophy*, pp. 137–192. Edited by A.H. Armstrong. London: Cambridge University, 1967.

Charlesworth, James. *The Pseudepigrapha and Modern research.* Missoula: Scholars, 1976.

Cheyne, T.K. *Jewish Religious Life After the Exile.* London: G.P. Putnam's Sons, 1898.

Childs, Brevard S. *Exodus.* OTL. London: SCM, 1974.

Christ, Felix. *Jesus Sophia: Die Sophia-Christologie bei den Synoptikern.* Abhandlungen zur Theologie des Alten und Neuen Testaments, no. 57. Zurich: Zwingli, 1970.

Christensen, Johnny. *An Essay on the Unity of Stoic Philosophy.* Copenhagen, Munksgaard, 1962.

Cladder, H.J. "Die Anlage des Jakobusbriefes." *ZKT* 28(1904):37–57.

Cohen, A., ed. *The Minor Tractates of the Talmud: Massekboth Ketannoth.* 2 vols. London: Soncino, 1965.

Cole, R. Alan. *Exodus.* TOTC. London: Tyndale, 1973.

Collins, John J. *The Sibylline Oracles of Egyptian Judaism.* SBL Dissertation, no. 13. Missoula: Scholars, 1974.

Colson, F.H., and **Whitaker**, G.H. *Philo.* 10 vols. LCL. London: Heinemann, 1929–62.

Corré, Alan, ed. *Understanding the Talmud.* New York: KTAV, 1975.

Corrieveau, R. "Genuine Religion — James 1:26." *Studia Moralia ... Academiae Alfonsiannae.* 5(1967):113–125.

Cowley, A. *Aramaic Papyri of the Fifth Century B.C.* Oxford: Clarendon, 1923.

Cranfield, C.E.B. "The Message of James." *SJT* 18(1965):182–193, 338–345.

Cranfield, C.E.B. *The Epistle to the Romans.* ICC. Edinburgh: T. &. T Clark, vol. 1:1975, vol. 2:1979.

Crenshaw, James L. *Old Testament Wisdom: An Introduction.* Atlanta: John Knox, 1981.

Crenshaw, James L. "Impossible **Questions**, Sayings, and Tasks." *Semeia* 17(1980):19–34.

Crenshaw, James L., ed. "**Prolegomenon**." In *SAIW*, pp. 1–45.

Crenshaw, James L. "The Problem of **Theodicy** in Sirach: On Human Bondage." *JBL* 94(1975):47–64.

Cross, Frank Moore, Jr. *The Ancient Library of Qumran and Modern Biblical Studies.* Garden City, NY: Doubleday, 1958.

Crouch, James E. *The Origin and Intention of the Colossian Haustafel.* Forschungen zur Religion und Literatur des Alten und Neuen Testaments, no. 109. Göttingen: Vandenhoeck & Ruprecht, 1972.

Cundall, Arthur, *Judges.* TOTC. London: Tyndale, 1968.

Dahood, Mitchell. *Psalms.* 3 vols. AB. Garden City, NY: Doubleday, 1966.

Dahood, Mitchell. *Proverbs and Northwest Semitic Philology.* Rome: Pontifical Biblical Institute, 1963.

Dana, H.E. and **Mantey**, Julius R. *A Manual Grammar of the Greek New Testament.* Toronto: Macmillan, 1927.

Danby, Herbert. *The Mishnah.* Oxford: Clarendon, 1933.

Daube, David. "Rabbinic Methods of Interpretation and Hellenistic Rhetoric." In *Corré*, pp. 275–289. First published in *HUCA* 22(1949):239–264.

Davids, Peter. *Commentary on James.* NIGTC. Grand Rapids: Eerdmans, 1982.

Davids, Peter. *Themes in the Epistle of James that are Judaistic in Character.* Ph.D. thesis, University of Manchester, 1974.

Davids, Peter. "Theological **Perspectives** on the Epistle of James." *JETS* 23(1980):97–103.

Davids, Peter. "Tradition Citation in the Epistle of James." In *Scripture, Tradition, and Interpretation* (Fest. for E.F. Harrison). Edited by W.W. Gasque and W.S. LaSor. Grand Rapids: Eerdmans, 1978.

Davids, Peter. "James and Jesus." In *Gospel Perspectives V: The Jesus Tradition Outside the Gospels*, pp. 63–85. Edited by David Wenham. Sheffield: JSOT Press, 1985.

Davids, T.W. Rhys. "Wisdom." In *Encyclopedia of Religion and Ethics*, 12:742–747. Edited by James Hastings. 12 vols. Edinburgh: T. &. T. Clark, 1921.

Davidson, Robert. "Some Aspects of the Old Testament Contribution to the Pattern of Christian Ethics." *SJT* 12(1959):373–387.

Davies, W.D. "The Moral Teaching of the Early Church." In *The use of the Old Testament in the New and other Essays*, pp. 310–332. Edited by James M. Efird. Durham, NC: Duke University, 1972.

Davies, W.D. "The Relevance of the Moral Teaching of the Early Church." In *Neotestamentica et Semitica*, pp. 30–49. Edited by E. Earle Ellis and Max Wilcox. Edinburgh: T. &. T. Clark, 1969.

Davies, W.D. *The Setting of the Sermon on the Mount*. Cambridge: Cambridge University, 1964.

Davis, James A. "Wisdom and Spirit: An Investigation of 1 Cor. 1:18–3:20 against the Background of Jewish Sapiential Traditions of the Hellenistic-Roman Period." Ph.D. thesis, University of Nottingham, 1982.

Deasley, A.R.G. "The Idea of Perfection in the Qumran Texts." Ph.D. thesis, University of Manchester, 1972.

De Jonge, M. *The Testaments of the Twelve Patriarchs*. Assen, Netherlands: Van Gorcum, 1953.

De Jonge, M. "Christian Influence in the Testaments of the Twelve Patriarchs." In *Studies in the Testaments of the Twelve Patriarchs*, pp. 193–246. Edited by M. De Jonge. Leiden: E.J. Brill, 1975.

De Jonge, M. *The Testaments of the Twelve Patriarchs: A Critical Edition of the Greek Text*. Leiden: E. J. Brill, 1978.

Delcor, M. *Qumrân: Sa piété, sa théologie et son milieu*. BEThL, no. 46. Gembloux, Belgium: Louvain University, 1978.

Delling, Gerhard. "τέλος." *TDNT*, 8:49–87.

Denis, Albert M. *Introduction aux pseudépigraphes greco d'Ancien Testament*. Studia in Veteris Testamenti pseudépigrapha, no. 1. Leiden, E.J. Brill, 1970.

Deppe, Dean. "The Sayings of Jesus in the Epistle of James." Ph.D. thesis, Free University of Amsterdam, forthcoming.

De Vries, S.J. "Lying." In *IntDB*, 3:192.

De Vries, S.J. *Prophet against Prophet*. Grand Rapids: Eerdmans, 1978.

Dewey, Kim. "*Paroimai* in the Gospel of John." *Semeia* 17(1980):81–99.

Dibelius, Martin. *A Commentary on the Epistle of James*. Hermeneia. Edited by Heinrich Greeven. Translated by Michael A. Williams. Philadelphia: Fortress, 1976; Reprint from 1921.

Debelius, Martin. *A Fresh Approach to the New Testament and Early Christian Literature*. London: Nicholson and Watson, 1936.

Diehl, Ernst. *Anthologia Lyrica Graeca*. Aedibus: Teubner, 1936.

Diels, Hermann. *Die Fragmente der Vorsokratiker: Griechisch und Deutsch*. Revised by Walther Kranz. 3 vols. Berlin: Weidmannsche, 1935.

Di Lella, A.A. "Conservative and Progressive Theology: Sirach and Wisdom." *CBQ* 28(1966):139–146.

Dillistone, F.W. "Wisdom, Word, and Spirit: Revelation in the Wisdom Literature." *Int* 2(1948):275–287.

Dillman, Charles N. "A Study of Some Theological and Literary Comparisons of the Gospel of Matthew and the Epistle of James." Ph.D. thesis, University of Edinburgh, 1979.

Dillon, John. *The Middle Platonists*. London: Duckworth, 1977.

Dinur, B.Z. "The Tractate Aboth as a Historical Source" [Hebrew]. *Zion* 35(1970):1–34.

Dittenberger, Wilhelm. *Sylloge Inscriptionum Graecarum*. 4 vols. Lipsiae: S. Hirzelium, 1915–24.

Dodd, C.H. *Gospel and Law: The Relation of Faith and Ethics in Early Christianity*. Cambridge: Cambridge University, 1951.

Dodd, C.H. "The Ethics of the New Testament." In *Moral Principles of Action*, pp. 543–555. Edited by Ruth Nanda Anshen. New York: Harper & Row, 1952.

Dörrie, Heinrich. "Sophia." In *Der Kleine Pauly*. Edited by K. Ziegler and W. Sontheimer. Stuttgart: Alfred Druchenmüller, 1964–75.

Dover, K.J. *Greek Popular Morality in the Time of Plato and Aristotle*. Los Angeles: University of California, 1974.

Bibliography

Drioton, E. "Sur la Sagesse, d' Aménémopé." In *Mélanges bibliques rédiges en l'honneur de André Robert*, pp. 254–280. Edited by H. Cazelles. Paris, 1957.

Driver, S.R. *Deuteronomy*. ICC. Edinburgh: T. &. T. Clark, 1895.

Driver, S.R., and **Gray**, George B. *The Book of Job*. ICC. Edinburgh: T. &. T. Clark, 1921.

Dunn, James D.G. *Christology in the Making*. London: SCM, 1980.

Du Plessis, P.J. τέλειος. *The Idea of Perfection in the New Testament*. Kampen: J.H. Kok, 1959.

Dupont-Sommer, A. *The Essene Writings from Qumran*. Translated by G. Vermes. Oxford: Blackwell, 1961.

Earp, F.R. *The Way of the Greeks*. Oxford: Clarendon, 1929.

Easton, B.S. "New Testament Ethical Lists." *JBL* 51(1932):1–12.

Ebner, Eliezer. *Elementary Education in Ancient Israel During the Tannaitic Period*. New York: Bloch, 1956.

Eckert, Karl-Gottfried. "Zur Terminologie des Jakobusbriefes." *TLZ* 89(1964):521–526.

Edelstein, Ludwig. *The Meaning of Stoicism*. Cambridge, MA: Harvard University, 1966.

Efros, Israel I. *Ancient Jewish Philosophy*. Detroit: Wayne State University, 1964.

Eichrodt, Walther. *The Theology of the Old Testament*. 2 vols. Translated by J.A. Baker. London: SCM, 1967.

Eichrodt, Walther. *Man in the Old Testament*. Studies in Biblical Theology, no. 4, Translated by K. and R. Gregor Smith. Chicago: Alec Allenson, 1951.

Ellis, E.E. "Vow." *IllDB*, 3:1627.

Elmslie, W.A.L. "Ethics." In *Record and Revelation*, pp. 275–302. Edited by H. Wheeler Robinson. Oxford: Clarendon, 1962.

Epstein, I. ed. *Baba Metzia*. London: Soncino, 1962.

Erman, Adolph. *The Literature of the Ancient Egyptians*. Translated by Aylward M. Blackman. London: Methuen, 1927.

Erman, Adolph. "Eine ägyptische *Quelle* der 'Spruche Salomos' " *SPAW* 15(1924):86–93.

Farandos, Georgios. *Kosmos und Logos nach Philon von Alexandria*. Amsterdam: Rodopi, 1976.

Farrar, Frederick. *The Early Days of Christianity*. 2 vols. London: Cassell, Petter, Galpin & Co., 1882.

Feine, Paul. *Der Jakobusbrief nach Lehranschauungen und Enstehungsverhältnissen*. Eisenach: Wilckens, 1893.

Felder, Cain Hope. "Wisdom, Law, and Social Concern in the Epistle of James." Ph.D. thesis, Columbia University, 1982.

Felder, Cain Hope. "**Partiality** and God's Law: An Exegesis of James 2:1–13." *Journal of Religious Thought* 39(1982–83):51–69.

Ferguson, John. *Greek and Roman Religion: A Source Book*. Park Ridge, NJ: Noyes, 1980.

Ferguson, John. *Heritage of Hellenism*. London: Thames & Hudson, 1973.

Feuillet, A. "Jesus et la sagesse divine d'après les evangeles synoptiques: Le 'Logion Johannique' et l'Ancien Testament." *RB* 62(1955):161–196.

Feuillet, A. *Le Christ Sagesse de Dieu d'après les épîtres pauliniennes*. Paris: J. Gabalda, 1966.

Fichtner, Johannes. "Isaiah among the Wise." In *SAIW*, pp. 429–438. Translated by Brian W. Kovacs. First published as "Jesaja unter den Weisen," *TLZ* 74(1949):75–80.

Filson, Floyd. "The Christian Teacher in the First Century." *JBL* 60(1941):317–328.

Findlay, J.A. "James iv. 5, 6." *ET* 37(1926):381–382.

Finkelstein, Louis. *The Pharisees*. 2 vols. Philadelphia: Jewish Publication Society of America, 1962.

Finkelstein, Louis. "Introductory Study to Pirke Aboth." *JBL* 57(1938):13–50.

Finkelstein, Louis. "The Development of the **Amidah**." *JQR* N.S. 16(1925–26):1–43, 127–170.

Fischel, Henry. "The Transformation of Wisdom in the World of Midrash." In Wilken, pp. 67–101.

Fischel, Henry. *Rabbinic Literature* and Greco-Roman Philosophy: A Study of Epicurea and Rhetorica in Early Midrashic Writings. Studia Post-biblica, no. 21. Leiden: E.J. Brill, 1973.

Fischel, Henry. "*Story and History: Observations on Greco-Roman Rhetoric and Pharisaism*." In *AOS Middle West Branch Semi-Centennial Volume*, pp. 59–88. Edited by D. Sinor. Oriental Series, no. 3. Bloomington, IN: Asia Studies Research Institute, 1969.

Fischel, Henry. "**Epicureanism**." In *Encyclopedia Judaica* 6(1971):817.

Flavelle, A. "Lie, Lying." *IllDB* 2:900–901.

Flusser, David. "Qumran an the Jewish 'Apotropaie Prayers.' " *Israel Exploration Journal* 16(1966):194–205.

Forbes, P.B.R. "The Structure of the Epistle of James." *EQ* 44(1972):147–153.

Francis, Fred O. "The Form and Function of the Opening and Closing Paragraphs of James and I John." *ZNW* 61(1970):110–126.

Frankfort, Henri. *Ancient Egyptian Religion*. New York: Harper & Row, 1948.

Freeman, Kathleen. *The Pre-Socratic Philosophers: A Companion to Diels, "Fragmente der Vorsokratiker."* Oxford: Blackwell, 1949.

Freeman, Kathleen. *Ancilla to the Pre-Socratic Philosophers*. Oxford: Blackwell, 1956.

Fry, Euan. "The Testing of Faith: A Study of the Structure of the Book of James." *BTr* 29(1978):427–435.

Furnish, Victor Paul. *Theology and Ethics in Paul*. New York: Abingdon Press, 1968.

Furnish, Victor Paul. *The Love Command in the New Testament*. New York: Abingdon Press, 1972.

Gemser, Berend. "The Instruction of 'Onchsheshongy and Biblical Wisdom Literature." In *SAIW*, pp. 134–160. First published in *Supplements to Vetus Testamentum* 7(1960):102–128.

Gemser, Berend. "The Spiritual **Structure** of the Biblical Aphoristic Wisdom." In *SAIW*, pp. 208–219. First published in *Adhuc loquitur: Collected Essays of Dr. B. Gemser*. Edited by A. van Selms and A.S. van der Woude. Leiden: E.J. Brill, 1968.

Gemser, Berend. *Sprüche Salomos*. Handbuch zum Alten Testament, no. 16. Tübingen: J.C.B. Mohr, 1963.

Genuyt, F. "Épître de Saint Jacques. Chapitre II." *SemBib* 19(1980):25–31.

Genuyt, F. "Épître de Saint Jacques. Chapitre III." *SemBib* 22(1981):55–59.

Genuyt, F. "Épître de Saint Jacques. (4,1–5,6)." *SemBib* 23(1981):44–56.

Genuyt, F. "Épître de Saint Jacques. (5,6–20)." *SemBib* 24(1981):28–36.

Gertner, M. "Midrashim in the New Testament." *JSS* 7(1962):267–292.

Geyser, A.S. "The Letter of James and the Social Condition of His Addressees." *Neotestamentica* 9(1975):25–33.

Gieger, Loren G. "Figures of Speech in the Epistle of James: A Rhetorical and Exegetical Analysis." Ph.D. thesis, Southwest Baptist Theological Seminary, 1981.

Gilbert, Maurice, ed. *La sagesse de l'Ancien Testament*. BEThL, no. 51. Gembloux, Belgium: Louvain University, 1979.

Ginsberg, H.L. "The North-Canaanite Myth of Anath and Aghat." *BASOR* 98(1945):15–23.

Ginsberg, Louis. "The Religion of the Jews at the Time of Jesus." In Corré, pp. 347–359. First published in *HUCA* 1(1924):307–321.

Glanville, S.R.K. "The Instructions of Onchsheshongy." In *The Catalogue of Demotic Papyri in the British Museum,* vol. 2. London: Trustees of the Britis Museum, 1955.

Glatzer, Nahum, H. "Hillel the Elder in the Light of the Dead Sea Scrolls." In *The Scrolls and the New Testament*, pp. 232–244. Edited by Krister Stendahl. London: SCM, 1957.

Goetzmann, J. "Wisdom." In *NIDNTT*, 3:1030–1033.

Goldin, Judah, trans. *The Fathers According to Rabbi Nathan*. Yale Judaica Series. New Haven, CT: Yale University, 1955.

Goldin, Judah. *The Living Talmud*. New York: Mentor, 1957.

Goodenough, E.R. *An Introduction to Philo Judaeus*. Oxford: Blackwell, 1962.

Goodenough, E.R. *By Light, Light*. London: Oxford University, 1935.

Goodenough, E.R. *Jewish Symbols in the Greco-Roman Period*. 13 vols. New York: Pantheon, 1959–69.

Goodenough, E.R. "Problems of Method in Studying Philo Judeaus." *JBL* 58(1939):51–58.

Goppelt, Leonhard. *Theory of the New Testament*. 2 vols. Edited by Jürggen Roloff. Translated by John E. Alsup. Grand Rapids: Eerdmans; Vol. 1:1981; Vol. 2:1982.

Gordis, Robert. "The Social Background of Wisdom Literature." *HUCA* 18(1943–44):77–118.

Gordis, Robert. *Koheleth — The Man and His World*. New York: Jewish Theological Seminary of America, 1955.

Gordis, Robert. *The Book of Job*. New York: Jewish Theological Seminary of America, 1978.

298 *Bibliography*

Gordis, Robert. "A Dynamic Halakhah: Principles and Procedures of Jewish Law." *Judaism* 28(1979):263–282.
Gosling, J.C.B. *Plato.* London: Routledge & Kegan Paul, 1973.
Grant, Michael. *Greek and Latin Authors 800 B.C. — A.D. 100.* New York: H.W. Wilson, 1980.
Graves, Allen Willis. "The Judaism of James." Th.D. thesis, Southern Baptist Theological Seminary, 1942.
Gray, John. *Joshua, Judges and Ruth.* NCBC. London: Nelson: 1967.
Gray, John. *I & II Kings.* OTL. London: SCM, 1970.
Green, Gene. "Theology and Ethics in 1 Peter." Ph.D. thesis, University of Aberdeen, 1979.
Greenberg, Simon. "Jewish Educational Institutions." In *The Jews: Their Religion, History, and Culture,* pp. 380–417. Edited by Louis Finkelstein. New York: Schocken, 1971.
Greenstone, Julius. *Proverbs.* Philadelphia Jewish Publication Society of America, 1950.
Greeven, Heinrich. "εὔχομαι." in *TDNT,* 2:775–784.
Greeven, Heinrich. "Jedes Gabe ist Gut, Jak. 1,17." *Theologische Zeitschrift* 14(1958):1–13.
Gregory, Thomas M. "Oath." In *ZPEB,* 4:476–479.
Gressman, H. "Die neugefundene Lehre des Amen-em-ope und die vorexilische Spruchdichtung." *ZAW* 42(1924):272–296.
Gressman, H. *Israel's Spruchweisheit im Zusammenhang der Weltliteratur.* Berlin: Karl Curtius, 1925.
Griffith, F. "The Instruction of Amen-em-opet." *Journal of Egyptian Archaeology* 12(1926):191–231.
Grumach, I. *Untersuchungen zur Lebenslehre des Amenope.* Munich, 1972.
Gundry, Robert H. *Matthew: A Commentary on His Literary and Theological Art.* Grand Rapids: Eerdsman, 1982.
Guthrie, D. *New Testament Theory.* Leicester: Inter-Varsity Press, 1981.
Guthrie, W.K.C. *A History of Greek Philosophy.* 6 vols. completed. Cambridge: Cambridge University, 1962ff.
Guttman, Julius. "The Religious Ideas of Talmudic Judaism." In Neusner, *Rabbinic,* pp. 39–52. First published in *Philosophers of Judaism,* pp. 30–43. New York: Holt, Rinehart, and Winston, 1964.
Guttman, Alexander. *Rabbinic Judaism in the Making.* Detroit: Wayne State University, 1970.
Guttman, Alexander. "Tractate Abot — Its Place in Rabbinic Literature." *JQR* N.S. 41(1950–51):181–193.
Gywnn, A. *Roman Education from Cicero to Quintilian.* Oxford: Clarendon, 1926.
Haarbeck, Hermann. "Tongue." In *NIDNTT,* 3:1078–1081.
Hasse, W., ed. *Philon und Josephus.* ANRW, II.21,1. New York: de Gruyter, 1984.
Habel, Norman C. *The Book of Job.* Cambridge: Cambridge University, 1975.
Hackforth, R. "Moral Evil and Ignorance in Plato's ethics." *Classical Quarterly* 40(1946):118–120.
Hadas, Moses. *Aristeas to Philocrates.* New York: Harper, 1951.
Hadidian, D.Y. "Palestinian Pictures in the Epistle of James." *ET* 63(1952):227–228.
Hahn, H.C. "Boast." In *NIDNTT,* 1:227–229.
Hahn, H.C. "Anger." *NIDNTT,* 1:107–113.
Halson, B.R. "The Epistle of James; 'Christian Wisdom?' " *Studia Evangelica* 4(1,1968):308–314 = TU 102.
Hardie, W.F.R. *Aristotle's Ethical Theory.* Oxford: Clarendon, 1968.
Hare, R.M. *Plato.* Oxford: Oxford University, 1982.
Harrelson, W.J. "Blessings and Cursings." In *IntDB,* 1:447.
Harris, J.G. "Aspects of the Ethical Thinking of the Qumran Covenanters." *EQ* 37(1965):142–146.
Harris, Murray J. "2 Corinthians." In *Expositor's Bible Commentary,* vol. 10. Edited by Frank Gaebelein. Grand Rapids: Zondervan, 1976.
Harrison, R.K. *Jeremiah and Lamentations.* TOTC. London: Oliphants, 1979.
Hayden, D.R. "Calling the Elders to Pray." *BSac* 138(1981):258–266.
Hayes, A.D.H. *Deuteronomy.* NCBC. London: Tyndale, 1973.
Hayes, William C. "The Middle Kingdom in Egypt." In *The Cambridge Ancient History,* vol. 1, part 2. Edited by I.E.S. Edwards, C.J. Gadd, and N.G.L. Hammond. Cambridge: Cambridge University, 1971.
Heiler, F. *Prayer.* Translated by Samuel McComb. London: Oxford University, 1933.

Heinemann, J. *Prayer in the Talmud — Forms and Patterns*. Studia Judaica, no. 9. Berlin: de Gruyter, 1977.
Henderlite, Rachel. "The Epistle of James." *Int* 3(1949):460–476.
Hendrickson, William. *The Gospel of Matthew*. Edinburgh: Banner of Truth Trust, 1973.
Hengel, Martin. *Judaism and Hellenism*. 2 vols. Translated by John Bowden. London: SCM, 1974.
Hengel, Martin. "Qumran und der Hellenismus." In Delcor, pp. 333–372.
Henson, Herbert H. *Christian Morality*. Oxford: Clarendon, 1936.
Herford, R. Travers. *Talmud and Apocrypha*. London: Soncino, 1933.
Herford, R. Travers. *Pirke Aboth*. New York: Bloch, 1925.
Herford, R.T. "Pirke Aboth: Its Purpose and Significance." In *Occident and Orient* (Fest. for M. Gaster's 80th Birthday), pp. 244–252. Edited by B. Schindler. London: Taylor's Foreign Press, 1936.
Herford, R.T. *Christianity in Talmud and Midrash*. Clifton, NJ: Reference Book Publishers, 1903.
Herrmann, Siegried. "Steuerruder, Waage, Herz und Zunge in ägytischen Bilderen." *Zeitschrift für ägyptische Sprache und Altertumskunde* 79(1954):106–115.
Hertz, J.H. *Sayings of the Fathers*. London: Horovitz, 1952.
Hertzberg, Hans Wilhelm. *I & II Samuel*. OTL. London: SCM, 1964.
Heschel, Abraham. "The Meaning of Observance." In Neusner, *Theology*, pp. 92–103. First published in *The Jewish Frontier* (April, 1954):22–28.
Hiebert, D. Edmond. *The Epistle of James*. Chicago: Moody, 1979.
Hiebert, D. Edmond. "The Unifying Theme of the Epistle of James." *BibSac* 135(1978):221–231.
Hiebert, D. Edmond. "The Worldliness of Self-Serving Oaths." *Direction* 6(1977):39–43.
Hilgert, Earle. "Central Issues in Contemporary Philo Studies." *Biblical Research* 23(1978):15–25.
Hillars, Delbert. *Lamentations*. AB. Garden City, NY: Doubleday, 1972.
Hill, David. *The Gospel of Matthew*. NCBC. London: Marshall, Morgan, and Scott, 1972.
Hollander, H.W. "The Ethical Character of the Patriarch Joseph." *Studies in the Testament of Joseph*, pp. 47–104. Edited by George W.E. Nickelsburg. Missoula: Scholars, 1975.
Holm-Nielsen, Svend. *Hodayot: Psalms from Qumran*. Aarhus: Universitetsforlerget, 1960.
Holm-Nielsen, Svend. *Die Psalmen Salomos*. JSHRZ, Band 4, Lieferung 2. Gütersloh: Gerd Mohn, 1977.
Hoppe, Rudolf. *Der theologische Hintergrund des Jakobusbriefes*. Forschung zur Bibel, no. 28. Würzburg: Echter, 1977.
Horsley, R.A. "Paul and the Pneumatikoi." Ph.D. thesis, Harvard University, 1970.
Horsley, R.A. "Wisdom of Words and Words of Wisdom in Corinth." *CBQ* 39(1977):224–239.
Horsley, R.A. "The Law of Nature in Philo and Cicero." *HTR* 71(1978):35–59.
Hort, F.J.A. *The Epistle of St. James*. London: Macmillan, 1909.
Houlden, J.L. *Ethics and the New Testament*. Harmondsworth, Middlesex: Penguin, 1973.
Huby, Pamela. *Greek Ethics*. London: Macmillan, 1967.
Irwin, Terence. *Plato's Moral Theory: The Early and Middle Dialogues*. Oxford: Clarendon, 1977.
Jacob, E. *Theology of the Old Testament*. London: Hodder & Stoughton, 1958.
Jacobs, Irving. "Elements of Near-Eastern Mythology in Rabbinic Aggadah." *Journal of Jewish Studies* 28(1977):1–11.
Jacobs, Louis. *A Jewish Theology*. London: Darton, Longman & Todd, 1973.
Jacobs, Louis. *The Principles of the Jewish Faith*. London: Vallentine, Mitchell, & Co., 1964.
Jacobsen, Thorkild. *The Treasures of Darkness: A History of Mesopotamian Religion*. London: Yale University Press, 1976.
Jaeger, H. "The Patristic Conception of Wisdom in the Light Biblical and Rabbinical Research." TU 79(1961):90–106 = *Studia Patristica* 4.
Jaeger, Werner Wilhelm. *Paideia: The Ideals of Greek Culture*. 3 vols. Translated by Gilbert Highet. New York: Oxford University, 1945.
Jaeger, Werner Wilhelm. *The Theology of Early Greek Philosophers*. Translated by Edward S. Robinson. Oxford: Clarendon, 1947.
Jaekel, Siegfried, ed. *Menandri Sententiae*. Aedibus: Teubner, 1964.
Jastrow, Marcus. *A Dictionary of the Targumim, the Talmud Babli and Yerushalmi, and the Midrashic Literature*. London: W.C. Luzae, 1903.

Jepsen, Alfred. "אָמַן." *TDOT*, 1:292–323.
Jeremias, Joachim. "Jac. 4:5: ἐπιποθεῖ." *ZNW* 50(1959):137–138.
Johanson, Bruce C. "The Definition of 'Pure Religion' in James 1:27." *ET* 84(1973):118–119.
Johnson, Aubrey R. *The Vitality of the Individual in the Thought of Ancient Israel.* Cardiff: University of Wales, 1949.
Johnson, L. T. "The Use of Leviticus 19 in the Letter of James." *JBL* 101(1982):391–401.
Johnson, Norman B. *Prayer in the Apocrypha and Pseudepigrapha: A Study in the Jewish Concept of God. JBL* Monograph, no. 2. Philadelphia: SBL, 1948.
Johnson, S.L. "Paul's Final Words to the Colossians." *BibSac* 121(1964):311–320.
Jurkowitz, Paul. "The Epistle of James: A New Testament Wallflower." *Bible Today* 94(1978):1478–1484.
Kadushin, Max. *The Rabbinic Mind.* New York: Bloch, 1952.
Kadushin, Max. *Worship and Ethics: A Study in Rabbinic Judaism.* Evanston: Northwestern University, 1964.
Kaiser, Otto. *Isaiah.* OTL. Translated by R.A. Wilson. 2 vols. London: SCM, 1974.
Kaplan, Mordecai. "Rabbinic Judaism." In Neusner, *Rabbinic*, pp. 29–37. First published in *The Greater Judaism in the Making*, pp. 5–13. New York: Reconstructionist Press, 1960.
Kaye, Bruce, and Wenham, Gordon, eds. *Laws, Morality, and the Bible.* Leicester: Inter-Varsity Press, 1978.
Kelly, Francis Xavier. "Poor and Rich in the Epistle of James." Ph.D. thesis, Temple University, 1973.
Kelly, J.N.D. *The Epistles of Peter and of Jude.* BNTC. London: Adam & Charles Black, 1969.
Kennedy, A.R.S. "Education." In *Dictionary of the Bible*, 1:646–652. Edited by J. Hastings. Edinburgh: T. & T. Clark, 1906.
Kennedy, George. *The Art of Persuasion in Greece.* London: Routledge, & Kegan Paul, 1963.
Kennedy, H.A.A. "The Hellenistic Atmosphere of the Epistle of James." *Exp*, ser. 8, 2(1911):37–52.
Kent, Charles Foster. *The Wise Men of Ancient Israel and their Proverbs.* New York: Silver, Burdett & Co., 1899.
Kent, Charles Foster, and Burrows, Millar. *Proverbs and Didactic Poems.* London: Hodder & Stoughton, 1927.
Kevin, Robert Oliver. "The Wisdom of Amen-em-opt and its Possible Dependence upon the Hebrew Book of Proverbs." *Journal of the Society of Oriental Research* 14(1930):115–157.
Kidner, Derek. *Proverbs.* TOTC. London: Tyndale, 1964.
Kim, Seyoon. *The Origin of Paul's Gospel.* J.C.B. Mohr: Tübingen, 1981.
Kimbrough, S.T., Jr. "The Ethic of the Qumran Community." *RQ* 6(1969):483–498.
Kirk, J.A. "The Meaning of Wisdom in James: Examination of a Hypothesis." *NTS* 16(1969):24–38.
Kissane, Edward J. *The Book of Job.* Dublin: Browne and Nolan, 1939.
Kitchen, K.A. "Proverbs and Wisdom of the Ancient Near East: The Factual History of a Literary From." *TB* 28(1977):69–144.
Kittel, Gerhard. "Der geschichtliche Ort des Jakobusbriefes." *ZNW* 41(1942):71–105.
Koester, Helmut. "One Jesus and Four Primitive Gospels." *HTR* 61(1968):203–227.
Kohler, K. *Jewish Theology.* New York: Macmillan, 1918.
Kraft, Robert A. *The Testament of Job.* SBL Texts and Translations, Pseudepigrapha Series, no. 4. Missoula: Scholars, 1974.
Küchler, Max. *Frühjüdische Weisheit.* Göttingen: Vandenhoeck & Ruprecht, 1979.
Kuhn, K.G. *Kondordanz zu den Qumrantexten.* Göttingen: Vandenhoeck & Ruprecht, 1960.
Kürzdörfer, K. "Der Character des Jakobusbriefes." Inaugural dissertation, University of Tübingen, 1966.
Kustas, George L. *Diatribe in Ancient Rhetorical Theory.* Twenty-Second Colloquy of the Center for Hermeneutical Studies. Berkeley, CA: Graduate Theological Union and University of California, 1976.
Kutsch, Ernst. "Eure Rede aber sei ja ja, nein nein." *Evangelische Theologie* 20(1960):206–218.
Ladd, George Eldon. *A Theology of the New Testament.* Grand Rapids: Eerdmans, 1974.
Lang, Bernhard. "Schule und Unterricht im alten Israel." In Gilbert, pp. 186–201.
Larson, C.W. "Prayer of Petition in Philo." *JBL* 65(1946):185–203.
Laporte, Jean. "Philo in the Tradition of Biblical Wisdom Literature." In Wilken, pp. 103–135.

Lauterbach, J.Z. *Mekilta de Rabbi Ishmael.* 3 vols. Philadelphia: Jewish Publication Society of America, 1933.

Laws, Sophie. *A Commentary on the Epistle of James.* BNTC. London: Adam & Charles Black, 1980.

Laws, Sophie. "The Doctrinal Basis for the Ethics of James." *Studia Evangelica* 7(1982):299–305.

Laws, Sophie. "Does Scripture Speak in Vain? A Reconsideration of James IV. 5." *NTS* 20(1973–74):210–215.

Leaney, A.R.C. *The Rule of Qumran and Its Meaning.* London: SCM, 1966.

Lehman, M.R. "Ben Sira and the Qumran Literature." *RQ* 3(1961):103–116.

Leisegang, H. "Sophia." In *Paulys Realencycopädie der classischen Altertumswissenschaft*, pp. 1019–1039. Edited by G. Wissowa. Stuttgart, J.B. Metzlersche, 1894ff.

Lewis, J.J. "The Table-Talk Section in the Letter of Aristeas. *NTS* 13(1966):53–56.

Lillie, William. "The Pauline House-Tables." *ET* 86(1974–75):179–183.

Lillie, William. *Studies in New Testament Ethics.* Edinburgh: Oliver & Boyd, 1961.

Lindars, Barnabas. *The Gospel of John.* NCBC. London: Marshall, Morgan & Scott, 1972.

Lindblom, Johannes. "Wisdom in the Old Testament Prophets." In *WIANE*, pp. 192–204.

Link, H.-G. "Blessing." In *NIDNTT*, 1:206–215.

Link, H.-G. "Swear." *NIDNTT*, 3:740–743.

Lohse, Eduard. "Glaube und Werke: Zur Theologie des Jakobusbriefes." *ZNW* 48(1957):1–22.

Lohse, Eduard. *Colossians and Philemon.* Translated by William R. Poehlmann and Robert J. Karris. Philadelphia: Fortress, 1971.

Lohse, Eduard. *Die Texte aus Qumran.* Darmstadt: Wissenchaftliche Buchgesellschaft, 1971.

Long, A.A. *Hellenistic Philosophy: Stoics, Epicureans, Sceptics.* London: Duckworth, 1974.

Luck, Ulrich. "Die Theologie des Jakobusbriefes." *Zeitschrift für Theologie und Kirche.* 81(1984):1–30.

Luck, Ulrich. "Der Jakobusbrief und die Theologie des Paulus." *Theologie und Glaube* 61(1971):161–179.

Luck, Ulrich. "Weisheit und Leiden: Zum Problem Paulus und Jakobus." 92(1967):254–258.

McGlinchy, James M. *The Teaching of Amen-em-ope and the Book of Proverbs.* Washington, D.C.: Catholic University of America, 1939.

MacGorman, John W. "Comparison of the Book of James with the Jewish Wisdom Literature." Ph.D. thesis, Southwestern Baptist Theological Seminary, 1956.

MacGorman, J.W. "Introducing the Book of James." *SWJT* 12(1969):9–22.

McKane, William, *Proverbs: A New Approach.* OTL. London: SCM, 1971.

McKane, William. *Prophets and Wise Men.* Studies in Biblical Theology. London: SCM, 1965.

McKane, William. "Functions of Language and Objectives of Discourse according to Proverbs, 10–30." In Gilbert, pp. 166–185.

McNeile, A.H. *The Gospel according to St. Matthew.* London: Macmillan, 1928.

Maier, Johann. *Die Tempelrolle vom Toten Meer.* Ernst Reinhardt, 1978.

Malherbe, Abraham. "Hellenistic Moralists and the New Testament." ANRW, forthcoming.

Mandelbaum, B. "Two Principles of Character Education in the Aggadah." *Judaism* 21(1972):84–92.

Mangan, C. "Christ the Power and the Wisdom of God: The Semetic Background to 1 Cor. 1:24." *Proceedings of the Irish Biblical Association* 4(1980):21–34.

Mansoor, Menaham. *The Thanksgiving Hymns.* Leiden: E.J. Brill, 1961.

Marböck, J. "Sir. 38,24–39, 11: Der schriftgelehrte Weise. Ein Beitrag zu Gestalt und Werk Ben Siras." In Gilbert, pp. 293–316.

Marcus, J. "The Evil Inclination in the Epistle of James." *CBQ* 44(1982):606–621.

Marcus, Ralph, trans. *Josephus: Jewish Antiquities*, Books XV–XVII. LCL. London: Heinemann, 1963.

Marcus, Ralph, trans. *Philo: Supplement.* 2 vols. LCL. London: Heinemann, 1953.

Marcus, Robert. "The Pharisees in the Light of Modern Scholarship." In Corré, pp. 178–192. First published in *JR* 32(1952):153–163.

Marmorstein, Arthur. *The Old Rabbinic Doctrine of God.* London: Oxford University, 1927.

Marmorstein, Arthur. *Studies in Jewish Theology.* Edited by J. Rabbinowitz and M.S. Lew. London: Oxford University, 1950.

Marrou, H.I. "Education and Rhetoric." In *Legacy of Greece: A New Appraisal*, pp. 185–201. Edited by M.I. Finley. Oxford: Clarendon, 1981.

Marrou, H.I. *A History of Education in Antiquity.* Translated by George Lamb. London: Sheed and Ward, 1956.

Marrow, S.B. "*Parrhesia* and the New Testament." *CBQ* 44(1982):431–446.

Marshall, I. Howard. *1 and 2 Thessalonians.* NCBC. London: Marshall, Morgan & Scott, 1983.

Marshall, I. Howard. *Commentary on Luke.* NIGTC. Grand Rapids: Eerdmans, 1978.

Marshall, I. Howard. *Acts.* TNTC. Leicester: Inter-Varsity, 1980.

Marshall, S.S.C. "Διψυχος: A Local Term? *Studia Evangelica* 6(1969):348–351 = TU 112(1973).

Marshall, S.S.C. "The Character, Setting, and Purpose of the Epistle of St. James." B.Litt. thesis, Oxford University, 1968.

Martin, R.P. "Blasphemy." In *IllDB*, 1:201.

Massiebieau, "L'Épître de Jacques est-elle l'oeuvre d'un chretien?" *RHR* 32(1895):249–283.

Maston, T.B. "Ethical Dimensions of James." *SWJT* 12(1969):23–40.

Mattuck, Israel. *Jewish Ethics.* London: Hutchinson's University Library, 1953.

Mauchline, John. *1 and 2 Samuel.* NCBC. London: Oliphants, 1971.

Mayer, Gunter. *Index Philoneus.* Berlin: de Gruyter, 1974.

Maynard-Reid, Pedrito Uriah. "Poor and Rich in the Epistle of James: A Socio-Historical and Exegetical Study." Th.D. thesis, Andrews University, 1981.

Mayor, J.B. *The Epistle of St. James.* New York: Macmillan, 1913.

Meecham, H.G. "The Epistle of St. James." *ET* 49(1937–38):181–183.

Meecham, H.G. *The Letter of Aristeas.* Aberdeen: Aberdeen University, 1935.

Melnick, R. "On the Philonic Conception of the Whole Man." *JSJ* 11(1980):1–32.

Menander, *The Bad-Tempered Man.* Translated by Philip Vellacott. London: Oxford University, 1960.

Metzger, Bruce, ed. *A Textual Commentary on the Greek New Testament.* London: United Bible Societies, 1971.

Metzger, Bruce. *An Introduction to the Apocrypha.* New York: Oxford University, 1957.

Meyer, Arnold. *Das Rätsel des Jakobusbriefes.* Giessen: A. Topelmann, 1930.

Middendorp, Th. *Die Stellung Jesus ben Siras zwischen Judentum und Hellenismus.* Leiden: E.J. Brill, 1973.

Milgrom, J. "On the Origins of Philo's Doctrine of Conscience." *StudPhil* 3(1974–75):41–45.

Minear, Paul. "Yes or No: The Demand for Honesty in the Early Church." *NovT* 13(1971):1–13.

Mitchell, Hinckley G. *The Ethics of the Old Testament.* Chicago: University of Chicago, 1913.

Mitton, C. Leslie. *The Epistle of James.* Edinburgh, Marshall, Morgan & Scott, 1966.

Mitton, C. Leslie. *Ephesians.* London: Marshall, Morgan, & Scott, 1976.

Moeller, Henry R. "Wisdom Motifs and John's Gospel." *BETS* (1963):92–100.

Momigliano, A.D. *Alien Wisdom: The Limits of Hellenization.* Cambridge: Cambridge University, 1975.

Montgomery, James A. *The Books of Kings.* Edited by Henry S. Gehman. ICC. Edinburgh: T. & T. Clark, 1951.

Moore, George Foot. *Judaism.* Cambridge, MA: Harvard University, vols. 1–2, 1927; vol. 3, 1930.

Moore, George Foot. *Judges.* ICC. Edinburgh: T. &. T. Clark, 1895.

Moore, George Foot. "The Idea of Torah in Judaism." In *Corré*, pp. 160–175. First published in *Menorah Judaism* 8(1922):1–14.

Morenz, Siegfried. *Egyptian Religion.* Translated by Ann E. Keep. London: Methuen, 1973.

Morris, Kenneth F. "An Investigation of Several Linguistic Affinities between the Epistle of James and the Book of Isaiah." Th.D. thesis, Union Theological Seminary (Richmond, VA), 1964.

Morris, Leon. *The Gospel according to John.* NICNT. Grand Rapids: Eerdmans, 1971.

Motyer, J.A. "Curse." *IllDB*, 1:319.

Moule, C.F.D. "Important Moral Issues: Prolegomena: The New Testament and Moral Decisions." *ET* 74(1963):370–373.

Mounce, William. "The Origin of the New Testament Metaphor of Rebirth." Ph.D. thesis, University of Aberdeen, 1981.

Mowinckel, Sigmund. *The Psalms in Israel's Worship.* Translated by D.R. Ap-Thomas. Oxford: Basil Blackwell, 1962.

Mowinckel, Sigmund. "Psalms and Wisdom." In *WIANE*, pp. 205–224.

Mowvley, Harry. "The Concept and Content of 'Blessing' in the Old Testament." *BTr* 16(1965):74–80.

Muilenburg, James. *The Way of Israel: Biblical Faith and Ethics.* Religious Perspectives, no. 5. London: Routledge & Kegan Paul, 1962.

Muilenburg, James. "The Ethics of the Prophet." In *Moral Principles in Action,* pp. 527–542. Edited by Ruth Nanda Anshen. New York: Harper & Row, 1952.

Müller, H.P. "חכם." *TDOT,* 4:364–385.

Mundle, Wilhelm. "Hear, Obey." In *NIDNTT,* 2:172–180.

Mundle, Wilhelm. "Curse." In *NIDNTT,* 4:364–385.

Murphy-O'Conner, Jerome. "Truth: Paul and Qumran." In *Paul and Qumran,* pp. 179–230. Edited by Jerome Murphy-O'Conner. London: Geoffrey Chapman, 1968.

Murray, John. *Principles of Conduct.* London: Tyndale, 1967.

Murtonen, A. "The Use and Meaning of the Words *lebarek* and *berakah* in the Old Testament." *VT* 9(1959):158–177.

Mussner, Franz. *Der Jakobusbrief.* 4th ed. Freiberg: Herder, 1981.

Mussner, Franz. " 'Direkte' und 'Indirekt' **Christologie** im Jakobusbrief." *Catholica* 24(1970):111–117.

Mussner, Franz. "Die **Tauflehre** des Jakobusbriefes." In *Zeichen des Glaubens* (Fest. for B. Fischer), pp. 61–67. Edited by H. auf der Maur and B. Kleinheyer. Zurich, 1972.

Myers, Jacob. *I & II Esdras.* AB. Garden City, NY: Doubleday, 1974.

Nauck, Augustus, ed. *Tragicorum Graecorum Fragmenta.* Aedibus: Teubner, 1889.

Nauck, Wolfgang. "Salt as a Metaphor in Instruction for Discipleship." *ST* 6(1952):165–178.

Nel, Philip Johannes. *The Structure and Ethos of the Wisdom Admonitions in Proverbs.* New York: de Gruyter, 1982.

Neusner, Jacob. *Invitation to the Talmud.* London: Harper & Row, 1973.

Neusner, Jacob. *Form-Analysis and Exegesis: A Fresh Approach to the Interpretation of Mishnah.* Minneapolis: University of Minnesota, 1980.

Neusner, Jacob. *Judaism: The Evidence of the Mishnah.* London: University of Chicago, 1981.

Neusner, Jacob, ed. *The Modern Study of the Mishnah.* Leiden: E.J. Brill, 1973.

Neusner, Jacob. *Rabbinic Traditions about the Pharisees before 70.* 3 vols. Leiden: E.J. Brill, 1971.

Neusner, Jacob, ed. *The Study of Ancient Judaism.* New York: KTAV, 1981.

Neusner, Jacob, ed. *The Study of Judaism: Bibliographic Essays.* New York: KTAV, 1972.

Neusner, Jacob, ed. *Understanding Jewish Theology.* New York: KTAV, 1973.

Neusner, Jacob, ed. *Understanding Rabbinic Judaism.* New York: KTAV, 1974.

Nichelson, Ernest W. *Jeremiah: Chapters 26–52.* Cambridge: Cambridge University, 1975.

Nickelsburg, George W.E. *Jewish Literature between the Bible and the Mishnah.* London: SCM, 1981.

Nickelsburg, George W.E. "Riches, the Rich, and God's Judgment in 1 Enoch 92–105 and the Gospel according to Luke." *NTS* 25(1979):324–344.

Noack, Bent. "Jakobsbrevet som kanonisk skrift." *DTT* 27(1964):163–173.

North, Helen. *Sophrosyne. Self-Knowledge and Self-Restraint in Greek Literature.* Cornell Studies in Classical Philology, no. 35. Ithaca, NY: Cornell University, 1966.

Noth, Martin. *Leviticus.* OTL. London: SCM, 1965.

Nötscher, Friedrich. *Zur theologischen Terminologie der Qumran-Texte.* Bonn: Hanstein, 1956.

Nötscher, Friedrich. " 'Gesetz der Freiheit' im NT und in der Mönchsgemeinde am Toten Meer." *Biblica* 34(1953):193–194.

Obermüller, Rudolf. "Hermeneutische Themen im Jakobusbrief." *Biblica* 53(1972):234–244.

Obermüller, Rudolf. "Contaminacion? En torno a una defenicion de la religion (Sant., 1:27)." *Rivista Biblica* 34(1972):13–19.

Oesterley, W.O.E. *The Wisdom of Egypt and the Old Testament.* London: Society for the Propagation of the Gospel, 1927.

Oesterley, W.O.E. *An Introduction to the Books of the Apocrypha.* London: Society for Promoting Christian Knowledge, 1935.

Oldfather, W.A. *Epictetus.* 2 vols. LCL. London: Heinemann, 1926.

Ong, Walter. *The Presence of the Word.* New Haven, CT: Yale University, 1967.

Osborn, Eric. *Ethical Patterns in Early Christian Thought.* Cambridge: Cambridge University, 1976.

Otzen, Benedikt. "Die neugefunden hebräischen Sektenschriften und die Testamente der zwölf Patriarcher." *ST* 7(1953):125–157.

Overholt, T.W. *The Threat of Falsehood: A Study in the Theology of the Book of Jeremiah.* London: SCM, 1970.

Packer, J.I. "Obedience." In *IllDB*, 2:1107.

Palmer, F.H. "Truth." In *IllDB*, 3:1601.

Parks, Ronald William. "The Distinctives of Petitionary Prayer in the Epistle of James." M.A. thesis, Regent College, 1981.

Payne, D.F. "Education." In *IllDB*, 1:414–415.

Pearson, Birger A. "Hellenistic-Jewish Wisdom Speculation and Paul." In Wilken, pp. 43–66.

Pearson, Birger A. "The Pneumatikos — Psychikos Terminology in 1 Cor." Missoula: Scholars, 1973.

Pearson, Lionel. *Popular Ethics in Ancient Greece.* Stanford: Stanford University, 1962.

Perdue, Leo G. "Paraenesis and the Epistle of James." *ZNW* 72(1981):241–256.

Pfeiffer, Ernst. "Der Zusammenhang des Jakobusbriefes." *Theologische Studien und Kritiken* 23(1850):163–180.

Pfeiffer, Robert H. *History of New Testament Times, with an Introduction to the Apocrypha.* New York: Harper, 1949.

Phillips, Anthony. *Deuteronomy.* Cambridge: Cambridge University, 1973.

Piper, O.A. "Truth." In *IntDB*, 4:713.

Polhill, John B. "The Life-Situation of the Book of James." *RevExp* 66(1969):369–378.

Pope, Marvin H. *Job.* AB. Garden City, NY: Doubleday, 1965.

Pope, Marvin H. "Oaths." In *IntDB* 3:575–577.

Porter, J.R. *Leviticus.* London: Cambridge University, 1976.

Porteus, N.W. "The Basis of the Ethical Teaching of the Prophets." In *Studies in Old Testament Prophecy*, pp. 143–156. Edited by H.H. Rowley. Edinburgh: T. & T. Clark, 1950.

Porteus, N.W. "Royal Wisdom." In *WIANE*, pp. 247–261.

Procksch, O. "λέγω." In *TDNT*, 4:93.

Rabin, Chaim. *Qumran Studies.* London: Oxford University, 1957.

Rahlfs, Alfred, ed. *Septuaginta.* 2 vols. Stuttgart: Deutsche Bibelgesellschaft, 1935, 1979.

Rankin, O.S. *Israel's Wisdom Literature: Its Bearing on Theology and the History of Religion.* Edinburgh: T. &. T. Clark, 1936.

Ranston, Harry. *The Old Testament Wisdom Books and Their Teaching.* London: Epworth, 1930.

Reese, J.M. "The Exegete as Sage: Hearing the Message of James." *BTB* 12(1982):82–85.

Reese, J.M. "Christ as Wisdom Incarnate: Wiser Than Solomon, Loftier Than Lady Wisdom." *BTB* 11(1981):44–47.

Reese, J.M. *Hellenistic Influence on the Book of Wisdom and Its Consequences.* Anelecta Biblica, no. 41. Rome: Pontifical Biblical Institute, 1970.

Reicke, Bo. *The Epistles of James, Peter, and Jude.* AB. Garden City, NY: Doubleday, 1964.

Reicke, Bo. "The New Testament Concept of Reward." In *Aux sourcés de la tradition*, pp. 195–206. Edited by Oscar Cullman and Philippe Menoud. Paris: Delachaux & Niestle, 1950.

Reicke, Bo. "L'onction des malades d'après Saint Jacques." *La Maison-Dieu* 113(1973):50–56.

Reines, Chaim W. "Honor in Rabbinic Law and Ethics." In Corré, pp. 394–402. First published in *Judaism* 8(1959):59–67.

Rendall, Gerald H. *The Epistle of St. James and Judaic Christianity.* Cambridge: Cambridge University, 1927.

Rendtorff, Heinrich. *Hörer und Täter.* Hamburg: Furche, 1953.

Richardson, Allan. "Pride." In *TWBB*, p. 176.

Rickenbacher, Otto. *Weisheits Perikopen bei Ben Sira.* Orbis Biblicus et Orientalis, no. 1, Göttingen: Vandenhoeck & Ruprecht, 1973.

Riesner, Rainer. *Jesus als Lehrer.* Tübingen: J.C.B. Mohr, 1981.

Rimbach, J.A. "Truth: A Biblical Word Study." *CurTM* 7(1980):171–175.

Ringgren, Helmer. *Religions of the Ancient Neat East.* Translated by John Sturdy. London: SPCK, 1973.

Ringgren, Helmer. *The Faith of Qumran.* Translated by Emile T. Sander. Philadelphia: Fortress, 1963.

Ringgren, Helmer. *The Faith of the Psalmists.* London: SCM, 1963.

Rist, John. *Stoic Philosophy.* Cambridge: Cambridge University, 1969.

Rist, John, ed. *The Stoics.* London: University of California 1978.

Roberts, D.J. III. "The Definition of 'Pure Religion' in James 1:27." *ET* 83(1972):215–216.
Robertson, A.T. *Practical and Social Aspects of Christianity: The Wisdom of James.* New York: Hodder & Stoughton, 1915.
Robertson, A.T. *A Grammar of the Greek New Testament in Light of the Historical Research.* Nashville: Broadman, 1934.
Robinson, H. Wheeler. *Inspiration and Revelation in the Old Testament.* Oxford: Clarendon, 1946.
Robinson, J. Armitage. *St. Paul's Epistle to the Ephesians.* London: James Clark, n.d.
Robinson, James M. "Jesus as Sophos and Sophia: Wisdom Tradition and the Gospels." In Wilken, pp. 1–7.
Robinson, James M. "LOGOI SOPHON: On the Gattung of Q." In *Trajectories through Early Christianity*, pp. 71–113. Edited by James M. Robinson and Helmut Koester. Philadelphia: Fortress, 1971.
Romaniuk, C. "Le thème de la sagesse dans les documents de Qumran." *RQ* 9(1977–78):429–435.
Ropes, James H. *A Critical and Exegetical Commentary on the Epistle of St. James.* ICC. Edinburgh: T. &. T. Clark, 1916.
Roth, Wolfgang. "On the Gnomic-Discursive Wisdom of Jesus Ben Sirach." *Semeia* 17(1980):59–79.
Rowley, H.H. *Job.* NCBC. London: Nelson, 1970.
Royce, J.R. "Philo and the Immortality of the Race." *JSJ* 11(1980):33–37.
Ruffle, John. "The Teaching of Amenemope and Its Connection with the Book of Proverbs." *TB* 28(1977):29–68.
Runia, D.T. "Philo's *De aeternitate mundi:* The Problem of Its Interpretation." *Vigilae Christianae* 35(1981):105–151.
Russell, R.S. *Between the Testaments.* London: SCM, 1965.
Rustler, M. "Thema und Disposition des Jakobusbriefes: Eine formkritische Studie." Unpublished dissertation, Wien, 1952.
Rylaarsdam, J. Coert. *Revelation in Jewish Wisdom Literature.* Chicago: University of Chicago, 1946.
Ryle, H.E., and James, M.R. *Psalms of the Pharisees.* Cambridge: University Press, 1891.
Saldarini, Anthony J. *The Fathers according to Rabbi Nathan (Version B).* Studies in Judaism in Late Antiquity, no. 11. Leiden: E.J. Brill, 1975.
Sandbach, F.H. *The Stoics.* London: Chalto & Windus, 1975.
Sanders, E. P. *Paul and Palestinian Judaism.* London: SCM, 1977.
Sanders, Jack T. "Ben Sira's Ethics of Caution." *HUCA* 50(1979):73–106.
Sanders, Jack T. *Ethics in the New Testament.* London: SCM, 1975.
Sandmel, Samuel. *Philo Judaeus: An Introduction.* Oxford: Oxford University, 1979.
Sandmel, Samuel. *Philo's Place in Judaism.* New York: KTAV, 1971.
Sandmel, Samuel. "Virtue and Reward in Philo." In *Essays in Old Testament Ethics* (Fest. for J. Philip Hyatt), pp. 215–223. Edited by James L. Crenshaw and John T. Willis. New York: KTAV, 1974.
Sandmel, Samuel. "The Confrontation of Greek and Jewish Ethics: Philo, De Decalogue." *Central Conference of American Rabbis Journal* 15(1968): 54–63, 96.
Santos, Gerasimos Xenophon. *Socrates: Philosophy in Plato's Early Dialogues.* London: Routledge & Kegan Paul, 1979.
Sauer, George. *Jesus Sirach (Ben Sira).* JSHRZ, Band 3, Lieferung 5. Gütersloh: Gerd Mohn, 1981.
Scarborough, William J. "The Influence of James in the Galatian Churches prior to Paul's Letter to the Galatians." Ph.D. thesis, Boston University, 1940.
Scharbert, Josef. "אלה." *TDOT*, 1:265.
Schawe, E. "Die Ethik des Jakobusbriefes." *Wort und Antwort* (Salzburg) 20(1979):132–138.
Schechter, Solomon. *Some Aspects of Rabbinic Theology.* London: Black, 1909.
Schiffman, Lawrence H. "The Qumran Law of Testimony." *RQ* 8(1972–75):603–612.
Schmidt, W.H. "דבר." *TDOT* 3:94–96.
Schmitt, J. "Contribution à l'étude de la discipline penitentielle dans l'église primitive á la lumiere des textes de Qumran." In *Les manuscript de la Mer Morte*, pp. 93–109. Paris: Colloque de Strasbourg, 1957.
Schnabel, Eckart. *Law and Wisdom from Ben Sira to Paul.* Ph.D. thesis, University of Aberdeen, 1983.
Schnackenburg, Rudolf. *The Moral Teaching of the New Testament.* Translated by J. Holland-Smith and W.J. O'Hara. London: Burnes & Oates, 1975.

306   Bibliography

Schneider, Johannes. "ὀμνύω." In *TDNT*, 5:176–185.
Schökel, L. Alonso. "Culto y justicia en Sant. 1,26–27." *Biblica* 56(1975):537–544.
Scholem, Gershom. "Tradition and Commentary as Religious Categories in Judaism." In Neusner, *Theology*, pp. 45–51. First published in *Judaism* 15(1966):23–39.
Schrage, W. "Der Jakobusbrief." In *Die Katholischen Briefe*. Edited by H. Balz and W. Schrage. Göttingen: Vandenhoeck & Ruprecht, 1973.
Schrage, W. *Ethik des Neuen Testaments*. Göttingen: Vandenhoeck & Ruprecht, 1982.
Schultz, H. and Esser, H.-H. "Thanks." In *NIDNTT*, 3:816–820.
Schüpphaus, Joachim, *Die Psalmen Salomos*. Leiden: E.J. Brill, 1977.
Schürer, Emil. *The History of the Jewish People in the Age of Jesus Christ*. Revised and edited by Geza Vermes, Fergus Millar, and Matthew Black. Edinburgh: T. & T. Clark, Vol. 1, 1973; Vol. 2, 1979.
Schwartz, E. *Die Ethik der Griechen*. Stuttgart: K.F. Koehler, 1951.
Schweizer, Eduard. *The Good News according to Matthew*. Translated by David Green. London: SPCK, 1976.
Schweizer, Eduard. "Traditional Ethical Patterns in the Pauline and Post-Pauline Letters and Their Development (Lists of Vices and House-Tables)." In *Text and Interpretation*, pp. 195–201. Edited by Ernest Best and R. McL. Wilson, 1979.
Scott, E. F. *The Ethical Teaching of Jesus*. New York: Macmillan, 1924.
Scott, E. F. *The Varieties of New Testament Religion*. New York: Charles Scribner's Sons, 1946.
Scott R.B.Y. *Proverbs, Ecclesiastes*. AB. New York: Charles Scribner's Sons, 1974.
Scott, R.B.Y. *The Way of Wisdom in the Old Testament*. London: Macmillan, 1971.
Scott, R.B.Y. "The Study of Wisdom Literature." *Int* 24(1970):20–45.
Scott, R.B.Y. "Wisdom in Creation: The 'AMON of Proverbs VIII 30." *VT* 10(1960):213–223.
Scott, R.B.Y. "Solomon and the Beginnings of Wisdom." In *WIANE*, pp, 262–279.
Scroggs, R. "Paul: *Sophos* and *Pneumatikos*." *NTS* 14(1967–68):33–55.
Seitz, Oscar J.F. "James and the Laws." *Studia Evangelica* 2 = TU 87(1964):472–486.
Seitz, Oscar J.F. "Antecedents and Signification of the Term '*Dipsychos*.' " *JBL* 66(1947):211–219.
Seitz, Oscar J.F. "Afterthoughts on the Term '*Dipsychos*.' " *NTS* 4(1957–58):327–334.
Selwyn, E.G. *The First Epistle of St. Peter*. London: Macmillan, 1946.
Shapiro, David. "The Idealogical Foundations of Halakhah." In Neusner, *Theology*, pp. 107–120. First published in *Tradition* 9(1967):100–122.
Sharp, Douglas S. *Epictetus and the New Testament*. London: Charles H. Kelly, 1914.
Shepherd, Massey H. "The Epistle of James and the Gospel of Matthew." *JBL* 75(1956):40–51.
Sheppard, G.T. *Wisdom as a Hermeneutical Construct: A Study in the Sapientializing of the Old Testament*. Berlin: de Gruyter, 1980.
Simpson, D.C. "The Hebrew Book of Proverbs and the Teaching of Amenophis." *Journal of Egyptian Archaeology* 12(1926):232–239.
Singer, S. *The Authorised Daily Prayer Book*. London: H.M. Printers, 1962.
Skehan, Patrick. "A Single Editor for the Whole Book of Proverbs." In *SAIW*, pp. 329–340. First published in *Studies in Israelite Poetry and Wisdom*, pp. 15–26. CBQ Monograph Series 1. Catholic Biblical Association of America, 1971.
Sleeper, C. Freeman. "Ethics as a Context for Biblical Interpretation." *Int* 22(1968):443–460.
Sleeper, C. Freeman. "Rudolf Bultmann and the Task of New Testament Ethics." *Hartford Seminary Quarterly* 6(1966):46–57.
Slingerland, H. Dixon. *The Testaments of the Twelve Patriarchs: A Critical History of Research*. SBL Monograph, no. 21. Missoula: Scholars, 1977.
Smith, John. M.P. *The Moral Life of the Hebrews*. Chicago: University of Chicago, 1923.
Smith, W. Stevenson. "The Old Kingdom in Egypt and the Beginning of the First Intermediate Period." In *Cambridge Ancient History*, vol. 1, part 2. Edited by I.E.S. Edwards, C.J. Gadd, and N.G.L. Hammond. Cambridge: Cambridge University, 1971.
Snaith, John G. *Ecclesisticus or The Wisdom of Jesus Son of Sirach*. Cambridge: Cambridge University, 1974.
Snaith, N. H. *Leviticus and Numbers*. NCBC. London: Nelson, 1967.
Solmsen, Friedrich. *Plato's Theology*. Ithaca, NY: Cornell University, 1942.
Songer, Harold S. "The Literary Character of the Book of James." *RevExp* 66(1969):379–389.

Sorg, Theo. "Heart." In *NIDNTT*, 2:181.

Speiser, E.A. *Genesis*. AB. Garden City, NY: Doubleday, 1964.

Spicq, C. "L'Epitre (Jac. 1,22–27): La vraie vie Chretienne." *AsSeign* 48(1965):21–38.

Spitta, F. *Der Jakobus untersucht*. Göttingen: Vandenhoeck & Ruprecht, 1896.

Stählin, G. "Zum Gebrauch von Beteuerungsformeln im Neuen Testament." *NovT* 5(1962):115–143.

Stauffer, Ethelbert. "Das 'Gesetz der Freiheit' in Ordensregel von Jericho." *TLZ* 77(1952):527–532.

Stein, Robert. *The Method and Message of Jesus' Teachings*. Philadelphia: Westminster, 1978.

Steinsaltz, Adin. *The Essential Talmud*. Translated by Chaya Galai. New York: Basic Books, 1976.

Stevens, George Barker. *The Theology of the New Testament*. International Theological Library. Edinburgh: T. & T. Clark, 1899.

Stob, Henry. "Vow." In *ZPEB*, 5:890.

Strack, H.L. *Introduction to the Talmud and Midrash*. Philadelphia: Jewish Publication Society, 1931.

Strack, H.L., and Billerbeck, Paul. *Komentar zum Neuen Testament erläutert aus Talmud und Midrash*. 5 vols. Münich: Beck, 1922–56.

Suggs, M. Jack. *Wisdom, Christology, and Law in Matthew's Gospel*. Cambridge, MA: Harvard University, 1970.

Talmon, Shemaryahu. "The Emergence of Institutionalized Prayer in Israel in the Light of Qumran Literature." In Delcor, pp. 267–284. BEThL, no. 46. Gembloux: Louvain University, 1978.

Talmon, Shemaryahu. "The 'Manual of Benedictions' of the Sect of the Judean Desert." *RQ* 8(1959–60):475–500.

Tarn, W.W. *Hellenistic Civilization*. Edited by G.T. Griffith. London: E. Arnold, 1930.

Tasker, R.V.G. *The General Epistle of James*. TNTC. London: Tyndale, 1956.

Tasker, R.V.G. *The Gospel according to St. Matthew*. London: Tyndale, 1961.

Taylor, Vincent. *The Gospel according to St. Mark*. London: Macmillan, 1966.

Tcherikover, Victor A. "The Ideology of the Letter of Aristeas." *HTR* 51(1958):59–85.

Teicher, J.L. "The Pre-Pauline Church in the Dead Sea Scrolls." *Journal of Jewish Studies* 3(1952):111–118, 139–150.

Terrien, Samuel. "Amos and Wisdom." In *SAIW*, pp. 448–455. First published in *Israel's Prophetic Heritage*, pp. 108–115. Edited by Bernhard W. Anderson and Walter Harrelson. New York: Harper & Row, 1962.

Thackeray, H. St. J., trans. *Josephus: The Jewish War*, Books I–III. LCL. London: Heinemann, 1927.

Theodorides, Aristide. "The Concept of Law in Ancient Egypt." In *The Legacy of Egypt*, pp. 291–322. Edited by J.R. Harris. Oxford: Clarendon, 1971.

Thiselton, Anthony C. "Truth." In *NIDNTT*, 3:877–883.

Thiselton, Anthony C. *The Two Horizons*. Grand Rapids: Eerdmans, 1980.

Thiselton, Anthony C. "The Supposed Power of Words in Biblical Writings." *JTS* N.S. 25(1974):283–299.

Thomas, D. Winton. "Notes on Some Passages in the Book of Proverbs." *VT* 15(1965):270–278.

Thompson, J.A. *Deuteronomy*. TOTC. Leicester: Inter-Varsity, 1976.

Thompson, J.A. *Jeremiah*. NICOT. Grand Rapids: Eerdmans, 1981.

Thompson, John Mark. *The Form and Function of Proverbs in Ancient Israel*. The Hague: Mouton, 1974.

Thomson, George. *The First Philosophers: Studies in Ancient Greek Society*. London: Lawrence & Wishart, 1955.

Thomson, J.A.K. "Winged Words." *Classical Quarterly* 30(1936):1–3.

Torrance, J.B. "Confession." *IIIDB* 1:310.

Torrey, C.C. *Ezra Studies*. Chicago: University of Chicago, 1910.

Torrey, C.C. *The Apocryphal Literature*. New Haven, CT: Yale University, 1945.

Torrey, C.C. "The Story of the Three Youths." *American Journal of Semitic Languages* 23(1907):177–201.

Townsend, Michael J. "Christ, Community, and Salvation in the Epistle of James." *EQ* 53(1981):115–123.

Toy, Crawford H. *The Book of Proverbs*. ICC. Edinburgh: T. & T. Clark, 1904.

Turner, Nigel. *Syntax*. Vol. 3 in *A Grammar of New Testament Greek*. Edited by James Hope Moulton. Edinburgh: T. & T. Clark, 1963.

Untersteiner, M. *The Sophists.* Translated by Kathleen Freeman. Oxford: Blackwell, 1954.

Urbach, E.E. *The Sages: Their Concepts and Beliefs.* 2 vols. Translated by Israel Abrahams. Jerusalem: Magnes, 1975.

van Roon, A. "The Relation between Christ and the Wisdom of God according to St. Paul." *NovT* 16(1974):207–239.

van Unnik, W.C. "The Christian's Freedom of Speech in the New Testament." *BJRL* 44(1962):466–488.

Vattioni, Francesco. *Ecclesiastico.* Napoli: Instituto Orientale di Napoli, 1968.

Vermes, Geza and Pamela. *The Dead Sea Scrolls: Qumran in Perspective.* London: Collins, 1977.

Vermes, Geza. *Scripture and Tradition in Judaism.* Studia Post-Biblica, no. 4. Leiden: E.J. Brill, 1961.

Via, Dan Otto. "The Right Strawy Epistle reconsidered: A Study in Biblical Ethics and Hermeneutic." *JR* 49(1969):253–267.

Viviano, B.T. *Study as Worship: Aboth and the New Testament.* Leiden: E.J. Brill, 1978.

Vlachos, C. "ΕΠΙΣΤΟΛΗ ΤΗΣ ΔΙΨΥΧΙΑΣ." *Deltion Biblikon Meleton* 3(1975):61–73, 134–145.

Volker, Walther. *Fortschritt und Vollendung bei Philo von Alexandria.* Leipzig, 1939.

von Arnim, H. *Stoicorum Veterum Fragmenta.* 4 vols. Stuttgart: Teubner, 1905.

von Dobschütz, E. "The Most Important Motives for Behavior in the Life of the Early Christians." *American Journal of Theology.* 15(1911):505–524.

von Rad, Gerhard. *Wisdom in Israel.* Translated by John D. Martin. London: SCM, 1972.

von Rad, Gerhard. *Old Testament Theology.* 2 vols. Translated by D.M.G. Stalker. Edinburgh: Oliver & Boyd, 1965.

Vouga, F. "Parole pour les riches (Jc. 5:1–6)." *Bulletin du Centre Protestant d'Etudes.* 31(1979):5–12.

Vriezen, Th.C. *An Outline of Old Testament Theology.* Oxford: Basil Blackwell, 1958.

Währisch, H. and Brown, C. "Revile." In *NIDNTT,* 3:340–345.

Walbank, F.W. *The Hellenistic World.* Glasgow: William Collins Sons, 1981.

Wallace, R.S. "Praise." In *IllDB,* 3:1256.

Wallis, Gerhard. "גדה." In *TDOT,* 2:417.

Wallis, R.T. "The Idea of Conscience in Philo of Alexandria." *StudPhil* 3(1974–75):27–40.

Wanke, J. "Die urchristlicher Lehrer nach dem Zeugnis des Jakobusbriefes." *ErfTS* 38(1977):489–511.

Ward, R.B. "The Communal Concern of the Epistle of James." Ph.D. thesis, Harvard University, 1966.

Ward, R.B. "**Partiality** in the Assembly: James 2:2–4." *HTR* 62(1969):87–97.

Ward, R.B. "The Works of **Abraham**: James 2:14–26." *HTR* 61(1968):283–290.

Ward, R.B. "James and Paul: Critical **Review**." *Restoration Quarterly* 7(1963):159–164.

Weiser, Arthur. *The Psalms.* OTL. London: SCM, 1959.

Weiss, I. H., ed. *Sifra.* Vienna: Jacob Scholssberg, 1862.

Weiss, Johannes. *Earliest Christianity: A History of the Period A.D. 30–150.* Translated by F.C. Grant. 2 vols. New York: Harper, 1959.

Weiss, K. "'Motiv und Ziel des Jacobusbriefes." *ThV* 7(1976):107–114.

Wendland, Heinz-Dietrich. *Ethik des Neuen Testaments.* Göttingen: Vandenhoeck & Ruprecht, 1975.

Wernberg-Möller, P. *The Manual of Discipline.* Leiden: E.J. Brill, 1957.

Wessell, W.W. "An Inquiry into the Origin, Literary Character, Historical and Religious Significance of the Epistle of James." Ph.D. thesis, University of Edinburgh, 1953.

Westermann, Claus. *The Praise of God in the Psalms.* Translated by Keith R. Crim. London: Epworth, 1966.

Wettstein, Johan Jakob. *Novum Testamentum Graecum.* 2 vols. Amsterdam: Ex Officina Dommeriana, 1752.

White, R.E.O. *Biblical Ethics,* vol. 1 Exeter: Paternoster, 1979.

White, William, Jr. "Blasphemy." In *ZPEB,* 1:624.

Whitehouse, W.A. "Obey." In *TWBB,* pp. 160–161.

Whybray, R.N. *The Intellectual Tradition in the Old Testament.* New York: de Gruyter, 1974.

Whybray, R.N. *Wisdom in Proverbs.* Studies in Biblical Theology, no. 45. London: SCM, 1965.

Whybray, R.N. "Yahweh-Sayings and Their Contexts in **Proverbs**, 10,1–22,16." In Gilbert, pp. 153–165.

Wicks, Henry. *The Doctrine of God in Jewish Apocryphal and Apocalyptic Literature.* London: Hunter & Longhurst, 1915.

Wifstrand, Albert. "Stylistic Problems in the Epistle of James and Peter." *ST* 1(1948):170–182.

Wilckens, Ulrich. "σοφία." In *TDNT*, 7:465–476.

Wilder, Amos N. *Eschatology and Ethics in the Teaching of Jesus*. New York: Harper, 1950.

Wilken, Robert L., ed. *Aspects of Wisdom in Judaism and Early Christianity*. London: University of Notre Dame, 1975.

Wilkinson, J. "Healing in the Epistle of James." *SJT* 24(1971):326–345.

Williams, A. Lukyn. "The Epistle of St. James and the Jewish-Christians of His Time." *ChQR* 123(1936):24–32.

Williams, James G. *Those Who Ponder Proverbs: Aphoristic Thinking and Biblical Literature*. Sheffield: Almond, 1981.

Williams, James G. "The Power of Form: A Study of Biblical Proverbs." *Semeia* 17(1980):35–58.

Williams, R.J. " 'A People Come out of Egypt': An Egyptologist Looks at the Old Testament." *Supplements to VT* 28(1974):231–252.

Williams, R.J. "Scribal Training in Ancient Egypt." *JAOS* 92(1972):214–221.

Williams, R.J. "Egypt and Israel." In *The Legacy of Egypt*, pp. 257–290. Edited by J.R. Harris. Oxford: Clarendon, 1971.

Williams, R.J. "The Alleged Semitic Original of the Wisdom of Amenope." *Journal of Egyptian Archaeology* 47(1961):100–106.

Winston, David. *Philo of Alexandria: The Contemplative Life, the Giants, and Selections*. Classical of Western Spirituality. New York: Paulist, 1981.

Winston, David. *Wisdom of Solomon*. AB. Garden City, NY: Doubleday, 1979.

Winston, David. "Philo's Theory of Cosmogony." In *Religious Syncretism in Antiquity*, pp. 157–171. Edited by B.A. Pearson. Missoula: Scholars, 1975.

Winston, David. "Freedom and Determinism in Philo of Alexandria." *StudPhil* 3(1974–75):47–70.

Winter, Dennis. "Motivation in Christian Behaviour." In *Law, Morality, and the Bible*, pp. 193–215. Edited by Bruce Kaye and Gordon Wenham. Leicester: Inter-Varsity, 1978.

Winter, J. *Sifra: Halachisches Midrash zu Leviticus*. Schriften der Gesellschaft des Judentum, no. 24. Breslau: Munz, 1938.

Wolff, Hans Walter. *Hosea*. Hermeneia. Translated by Gary Steinsell. Philadelphia: Fortress, 1974.

Wolfson, H.A. *Philo*. 2 vols. Cambridge, MA: Harvard University, 1948.

Wolfson, H.A. "The Philosophy That Faith Inspired: Greek Philosophy in Philo and the Church Fathers." In *The Crucible of Christianity*, pp. 309–316. Edited by Arnold Toynbee. London: Thames and Hudson, 1969.

Wolfson, H.A. "Philo Judaeus." In *The Encyclopedia of Philosophy*, 6:151–155. Edited by Paul Edwards. New York: Macmillan, 1967.

Wolverton, Wallace J. "The Double-Minded Man in the Light of Essene Psychology." *ATR* 38(1956):166–175.

Wood, James. *Wisdom Literature: An Introduction*. London: Gerald Duckworth, 1967.

Worrell, John Edward. "Concepts of Wisdom in the Dead Sea Scrolls." Ph.D. thesis, Claremont Graduate School, 1962.

Wuellner, Wilhelm. "Der Jakobusbrief im Licht der Rhetorik und Textpragmatik." *LingBib* 44(1978–79):5–66.

Wurthwein, Ernst. "Egyptian Wisdom and the Old Testament." In *SAIW*, pp. 113–133. First published in *Wort und Existenz*, pp. 197–216. Göttingen; Vandenhoeck & Ruprecht, 1970.

York, Anthony D. "The Targum in the Synagogue and in the School." *JSJ* 10(1979):74–86.

Young, Edward J. *My Servants the Prophets*. Grand Rapids: Eerdmans, 1952.

Young, Edward J. *The Book of Isaiah*. NICOT. 3 vols. Grand Rapids: Eerdmans, 1969.

Young, Franklin. "The Relation of 1 Clement to the Epistle of James." *JBL* 67(1948):339–345.

Zaimon, Joel H. "The Traditional Study of the Mishnah." In Neusner, *Modern*, pp. 1–12.

Ziegler, Joseph. *Sapientia Jesu Filii Sirach*. Septuaginta, Vetus Testamentum Graecum, no. 2. Göttingen: Vandenhoeck & Ruprecht, 1965.

Zimmerli, Walther. *Ezekiel 1*. Hermeneia. Translated by Ronald E. Clements. Philadelphia: Fortress, 1979.

Zimmerli, Walther. "Zur Struktur der alttestamentlichen Weisheit." *ZAW* 61(1933):177–204.

Zimmerman, Frank. "The Story of the Three Guardsmen." *JQR* 54(1963–64):179–200.
Zmijewski, Joseph. "Christliche 'Vollkommenheit': Erwägungen zur Theologie des Jakobusbriefes." *SNTU* 5(1980):50–78.

Index of Passages

I. Near Eastern Wisdom Literature

Egyptian

Instruction of Amen-em-Opet

ANET

p. 423	250

LAE

p. 174	24
p. 244	26
p. 245-246	23
p. 247	24, 187
p. 250	25, 187
p. 251	105, 139, 140
p. 252	25, 140
p. 252-253	249
p. 253	250
p. 258	25, 250
p. 258-259	249
p. 260	139
p. 262-263	140

Instruction of Ani

ANET

p. 420	24, 25, 105, 139, 188

AEL

2:134	250
2:137	188
2:138	249
2:140	140
2:141	187, 188
2:143	25

Instruction for Vizier Kagemni

LAE

p. 177	24

Instruction for King Meri-Ka-Re

LAE

p. 182	249
p. 183	249

Instruction for Vizier Ptah-Hotep

ANET

p. 412	23
p. 413	139
p. 414	25, 26

LAE

p. 161	25
p. 163	24, 139, 249
p. 164	24
p. 165	26
p. 168	23, 24, 139
p. 170	140
p. 173	26
p. 175	23, 25, 26

Babylonian

Words of Ahiqar

ANET

p. 428	23, 27, 105, 142
p. 429	27, 105, 250

Counsels of Wisdom

BWL

p. 101	23, 139, 140
p. 105	25, 139, 187, 188, 250
p. 106	139

II. Old Testament

Genesis

1	192
1:26	129
1:28	129

3:10	253
3:11 (LXX)	134
3:12	141
3:14-19	144

4:9	253
4:10	191
6:3	227
6:5	32
9:2	129
9:25	144
11:9	263
12:13	253
15:6 (LXX)	85
17:25	179
18:20	191
19:13	191
20:2	253
22:16	253
26:7	253
27:19	253
27:33-37	41
28:20-22	253
31:35	253
31:50	256
32:9-11	193
37:29-35	253
41:33	33
48:14	41
49:7	144

Exodus

2:23-24	191
4:1	156
4:10-17	29, 33
8:15	34
9:4	39
15:1-17	189
18:24	34, 37
19:8	37
20:3	194
20:7	193, 257
20:16	143, 147
21:17	145
22:11	256
22:13	256
22:28	40, 145, 193
23:1	143, 147
23:2-3	147
23:6	148
23:13	194
24:3	37, 192, 257
24:7	37, 257
34:6	252

Leviticus

5:1	262
10:16	56
19:12	18, 257
19:13	18
19:14	40

19:15	18, 147
19:16	18, 51, 148, 154, 158
19:18	18, 179
19:36	263
20:9	145
24:15-16	193
29:14	145

Numbers

5:7	193
5:16-28	41
12:1	143
12:8-10	143
14:11	194
14:21	256
14:23	194
14:35	143
20:10	56, 194
23-24	36
23:19	252
30:2	256
31:14	56

Deuteronomy

1:17	147
4:7	191
4:39	32
5:1	36, 193
5:27	37, 257
6:3-4	36
6:6	36
6:13	218, 250
9:1	36
10:17-19	149
10:18	98, 148
10:20	256, 266
11:8	36
11:13	36
14:29	98
15:5	36
16	147
16:19-20	147
18:20-22	36, 253
19:16-19	147
20:3	36
21	215
23:21-23	256, 257
24:13-15	191
24:17	148
30:8	35
30:14	19, 29, 36
32:2	36
32:2-3	31
32:4	252
32:7	35
33:16	31

Joshua

6:26	144
9:3-15	40
22:14	253
23:7	194
24:24	37, 257

Judges

3:15	191
4:3	191
5	189
5:23	144
6:6	191
8:19	256
9:20	144
9:57	144
10:10	191
11:30-31	257
14:14	33
14:18	33
15:16	33
17:1-4	40
17:2-3	40
17:6	40
21:1	40

Ruth

1:17	256

1 Samuel

1:7	191
1:11-28	255
1:13-15	191
3	36
3:17	256
12:14-15	36
14:6-15	41
14:24-28	41
14:37	191
14:39	256
14:44	256
14:45	256
17	196
17:43	144
20:1-20	253
20:3	256
20:21	256
21:1-6	253
21:10-15	253
22:11-19	253
25:25	39
25:26	256, 262
25:34	256
26:10	256
26:16	256
27:1-12	253

28:6	191
28:10	256
29:6	256

2 Samuel

1:15-16	108
3:35	256
16:7-8	40
16:10	40
19:16-23	40
21:1-6	40

1 Kings

2:2-4	37
2:8	40
2:23	256
3:12	33
4:32	189
8:35	193
17:1	191, 256
17:1-8	240
17:1-18:46	240
17:9	240
18:1	191
22:1-22	253

2 Kings

2:22	144
5:20	256
18:26-27	196
18:30-35	194
19:4	194
19:6	194
19:22	194, 195
19:28	38
22:11	37
23:10	128

4 Kings (LXX)

19:28	86

2 Chronicles

5:12-13	190
6:26	193
13:13-22	194
15:2	192, 193
20:19-28	190
23:13-18	190
29:28	190
31:2	190
35:15	190
35:25	190
36:13	256
36:18-22	194
37:10-29	194

Erza
2:64	190
3:10-11	190

Nehemiah
1:4-11	193
8:9	37
9:27	191
12:27-31	190
12:44-47	190
13:25	144

Job
1:22	194
2:10	194
4:3	38
5:5	106
5:27	37
6:11	30
6:30	195
7:11	30
8:8-10	35
9:4	32, 33
9:14	194
9:20	108
11:8	29
12:7-9	192
13:5	31
15:2	28
15:12-13	194
16:3	28
18:2	28
19:1	38
19:2	28
19:21-23	146
20:12	107, 110
20:12-16	110, 130
20:12-19	130
20:19	136
21:2	37
29:8-10	29
29:12	98
29:21	29
29:31	34
30:20	192
31:29-30	145
32:4-10	30
32:7-8	30
32:18	30
33:2	37
33:3	32
33:4	30
33:12	192
33:26-28	193
33:27	193

33:30	192
33:33	37
34:2	37
34:16	37
34:21-22	192
34:37	30
35:12-15	192
35:16	30
37:1-13	192
37:24	32
38:2	30
40:1-2	194
40:4-5	31
40:5-6	194
42:3-6	31

Psalms
3:4	191
3:7	107
4:1	191
4:2	191
5:1-2	191
5:3	191
5:6	254
5:11	189
6:8-9	191
7:12-13	107
7:12-16	110
7:14	254
8:11-13	37
9:1	189
9:1-2	189
9:8	189
9:11	189
9:12	191
9:21 (LXX)	179
9:28 (LXX)	173
10:1	191
10:3	107
10:3-4	143, 195
10:5	144
10:7	107, 144, 173
10:8	110
10:10	144
10:12	108
11:2	106
11:4	192
12:1-5	14
12:2	146, 253, 254
12:2-3	108
12:2-5	143
12:3	108, 195
12:4	108
12:5	146
12:6	253

13:1-2	191		35:9	189
13:3	27		35:15-16	143
13:16	189		35:20	254
14:4	109, 136		35:21	143
15:1-4	252		35:22	191
15:3-4	143		35:28	189
16:4	194		36:11	109
16:7	190		37:7	30
16:11	189		37:7-9	28
17:1	192		37:8	145
17:3	27, 32, 108		37:12	145
17:6	191		37:30	109, 110
18:6	191		37:30-31	31
18:30	253		37:34	30
18:49	189		38:1-22	191
19:14	193		38:12	30
20:6	191		39	106
21:2	191		39:1	27
22:1	191		39:2	116
22:22	189		39:12	191
22:25	255, 256		40:1	30
22:32	193		40:5	190
26:1-12	192		40:8	36
27:6	189		40:14-15	143
27:7-10	191		41	228
28:1-2	191		41:1-2 (LXX)	227
28:6	190, 191		41:1-3 (LXX)	148
28:7	189		41:5-7	143
29	192		41:13	190
30:2	191		42:11	189
30:4	189		42:4	189
30:7	191		43:1	255
30:10	191		43:4	189
30:10-12	189		43:4-5	189
31:8	143		44:1-4	35
31:13	143		45:16-17	189
31:18	255		47:1	189
31:21	190		47:7	189
31:22	191, 252		47:8	189
32:3-5	193		48:1	189
32:9	37		48:10	189
32:11	189		50:1	192
33:1-3	189		50:4	192
33:1-9	192		50:14	256
33:13-18	192		50:15	191
34:1	190		50:16-19	36
34:4-7	191		50:19	27, 107, 141
34:8	191		50:21	108
34:12	121		51:6	252
34:12-13	108		51:15	189
34:12-13 (LXX)	76		51:17	192
34:13	56		51:116	252
34:14	192		52:1-4	254
34:15-18	191		52:1-5	143
34:18	192		52:2-3	106

52:5	108	71:2	191
52:7	29	71:22-24	189
52:9	189	71:23	189
54:1-2	191	72:18	190
55:1	191	73:9	108, 194
55:17	191	73:28	189
55:22	191	75:1	189
56:4	106, 189	75:9	189
56:12	256	76:11	256
57:1	193	77:1-2	191
57:2	191	78:1	191
57:4	106, 107, 143	78:4	35
57:7-9	189	78:18-19	194
58:1-11	107	78:21-33	192
58:3	254	79:3	189
58:4	106, 130	81:1-5	189
58:5	38	82:1	179
58:6	106, 255	82:8	179
58:6-9	108	83	227
58:7	106	83:1-2	191
58:10	255	83:2 (LXX)	227
59:6	189	84:8	191
59:7	27, 106, 107	86:1	191
59:12	108, 144, 255	86:11	36
61:1	191	88:2	191
61:5	256	89:1	189
61:5-8	255	89:15	189
61:8	189	89:34-35	253
62:1	30	89:35	256
62:3-4	254	89:52	190
62:4	254	91:15	191
62:5	110	92:1-4	189
63:1	192	92:6	29
63:3-5	189	94:11	192
63:5	189	95-100	189
63:11	108	95:1	189
64:2-3	106	95:11	256
64:2-6	106	96	189
64:3	106	96:11	189
64:4	141	100:1	189
64:4-6	110	100:4	190
64:7	29, 108	101:1	189
65:1	256	101:5	143
65:2	191	101:6-8	255
65:3	193	102:1-2	191
66:8	189	103:1-2	190
66:14	256	104:1-2	190
66:16-20	189, 192	105:1-3	189
67:1-7	189	105:4	191
67:4	189	105:8	253
68:3	189	105:34	192
68:4	189	106:1-3	189
68:34-35	192	106:2	190
69:4	30	106:13	31
69:30-36	189	106:45	253

106:47	189
106:48	190
107:1-2	189
108:1-6	189
109:1-4	191
109:1-13	255
109:2	254
109:3	106
109:17	144
109:18	144
110:4	253
111-113	189
115-118	190
116:1	191
116:11	105, 253
117	189
118 (LXX)	228
118:1-4	189, 190
118:20 (LXX)	228
118:21	191
118:21 (LXX)	228
118:131	228, 229
118:134	228
118:175 (LXX)	20, 131, 227
119:11	36
119:89	264
119:114	30, 36
119:130	35
119:140	252
119:142	252
119:146	189
119:147-148	36
119:160	252
119:163	255
124:3	86
130:5	30, 36
131:1	29
135:1-4	189
136	189
138	189
140:1-3	106, 109
140:3	106, 130
140:4-5	106
140:9-11	108
141:1	191
141:3	27, 108
141:3-4	110
141:4	148
142:5-7	191
143:1	191
144:1	190
144:11	107
145:1	140
145:8	28
145:18	192, 252
145:20	192
145:21	189
146-150	189
146:9	98
149:1-4	190
149:2	189
150:6	190
Proverbs	
1:8	33, 35
1:20-25	148
1:28-31	192
1:33	34
2:1-2	33
2:1-6	35
3:18	176
3:27-28	234
3:30	147
3:34	143, 195, 247
3:34 (LXX)	225
4:1	33
4:10	33
4:20	35
4:23	32, 34
5:1	33
5:1-2	33
5:3-6	108, 110
5:6	32
5:7	33
5:12	148
5:21	192
6:1-5	257
6:2	107
6:12-15	143
6:14	141, 254
6:16	254
6:19	147
6:20	33
6:20-22	46
6:20-24	34
6:24	108
6:27	58
7:1-3	33, 34
7:21	106, 108
7:23	106
7:24	33, 34
7:27	106
8:6	33
8:7-8	251
8:12-13	254
8:17	192
8:33	33, 34
9:7-8	143
9:8-9	148
10:2	103

10:6	109, 136	15:23	31
10:8	28, 32, 34	15:26	109
10:10	28, 42, 108, 144	15:28	32, 109
10:11	31, 109, 136	15:31	34, 148
10:17	148	15:32	148
10:18	109, 119, 136, 142	16:1	32, 42
10:20	105	16:5	196
10:21	141	16:10	42, 106
10:32	31, 109	16:15-16	32
11:3	254	16:20	33, 34, 35, 36
11:9	144	16:21	31, 32
11:11	38, 105	16:23	32
11:12-13	144	16:24	31, 38
11:13	109, 142	16:27	106, 107
11:15	257	16:28	142
11:26	144	16:30	107
11:30	176	16:32	28, 108
12:1	148	17:1	28
12:5	109	17:4	141, 143, 254
12:6	109, 110, 136, 141	17:5	143, 144, 148
12:12	109	17:7	42, 257
12:14	30	17:9	142
12:15	34	17:10	148
12:16	28, 108	17:27	27, 28, 108
12:17	252	17:28	29
12:22	252, 254	18:6-7	107
12:23	29	18:8	142
12:25	141	18:21a	105
13:3	108	18:21	115
13:10	143	19:5	143, 147
13:17	252	19:5-9	143
13:18	148	19:9	143
14:3	107	19:20	33, 34
14:6-7	144	19:22	254
14:8	32, 254	19:25	144, 148
14:9	143, 144	19:27	33, 34
14:12	110	19:28	109
14:14	42	20:3	28, 141
14:15	32	20:5	29
14:17	28, 145	20:9	194
14:18	147	20:11	28, 108
14:23	42	20:15	105
14:25	147	20:17	254
14:29	28, 145, 192	20:19	142
14:31	143, 148	20:20	145
14:35	31	20:25	257
15:1	28, 31, 145	21:4	143
15:1-4	38	21:6	254
15:2	109	21:11	148
15:4	105, 254	21:12-13	192
15:5	148	21:17-18	33
15:8	200	21:19	110
15:10	148	21:23	108
15:12	148	21:24	143, 195
15:18	28, 145	21:28	143, 147

21:29	32	29:8	143
21:30	42	29:11	28
22:10	31, 32	29:15	148
22:11	31, 32	29:19	42
22:12	42	29:20	28, 29
22:17-18	34	29:21	28
22:21	252	29:22-23	31
22:24-25	145	30:5	253
22:26-27	257	30:6	253
23:9	144	30:7-9	255
23:12	33, 34	30:10	143, 144
23:22	33, 35, 251	30:11	145
23:23	42	30:18	29
23:26	42	31:8-9	148
24:1-2	109		
24:17	144	*Ecclesiastes*	
24:24	144	3:7	29
24:26	252	5:6	108
24:28	136	5:7	257
24:28-29	142, 143, 147	6:11	28
25:8-19	147	7:5	148
25:9-10	142	7:9	28, 145
25:11	31	8:2	42
25:12	34, 148	8:4	42
25:13	252	9:17	144, 145
25:14	254	10:2-3	110
25:15	31, 38	10:12	107
25:17	146	10:20	142
25:18	142, 143, 146, 147		
25:20	146	*Isaiah*	
25:21	146	1:15	191
25:23	142	1:17	98
26:2	41, 144	5:24	194
26:6	252	6:5-7	195
26:18-19	110, 146, 254	9:20-21	108
26:20	142	10:7	32
26:22	142	10:8-15	195
26:23-26	109	14:24	256
26:26	110	29:1	32
26:27	110	29:3-4	31
26:28	146	29:13	110
27:1	195, 232, 288	29:13-14	190
27:2	196	29:14	32, 37
27:4	145	29:21	147
27:5	110, 145, 146, 252	32:17	176
27:6	148	33:15	109, 252
27:9	141	33:19	29
27:10	42	37:7	254
27:14	146	40:6	83
27:19	110	42:1-4	76
28:9	192	45:23	256
28:10	110	51:7	36
28:13	193	52:5	194
28:23	148	53:11	184
29:5	143	57:19	171
		59	191

59:1-2	191	8:18	191
59:3-4	108, 255	9:9	194
59:7	191	13:1-16	253
59:13	264	17:11-15	257
61:1	78	17:16	256
65:7	194	20:8	37
65:16	256	20:27	194
		22:9	109, 136, 142, 143
Jeremiah		33:7-9	192
1:9-12	253	33:17	194
5:1-3	254	33:30-33	110
5:2	257	35:12	194
5:28	98		
5:30-31	254	*Daniel*	
6:28	143	1:4	33
7:9	257	1:30	33
7:24-27	36	9	193
7:28	37		
7:31	128	*Hosea*	
9:1-9	107, 108, 255	4:2	257
9:3	106	7:13-14	194
9:4	143	7:14	192
9:8	106, 110	10	14
9:9	108	10:13	38
9:23	221	11:12	255
9:23-24	195	12:1	255
10:10	252, 264	14:2	193
10:11-16	192	14:9	32
11:8	37		
11:11	191	*Joel*	
12:16	256	2:32	193
14:12	191		
14:13-16	253	*Amos*	
14:34	253	3:1	36
18:18	37, 106, 143	4:1	36
22:5	256	5:1	36
23:9-40	253	5:23	190
27:9-15	253	6:8	256
28:7-17	253	9:8	192
31:31-34	37		
31:33	36, 91	*Obadiah*	
37:2	253	1:10	109
44:17	37		
49:13	256	*Jonah*	
51:14	256	2	191
51:15-16	192		
51:51	109	*Micah*	
52:3	257	1:2	36
		3:1	36
Lamentations		3:4	191
3:25-26	30	6:12	254
3:25	192	7	36
		7:20	253
Ezekiel			
3:5	29	*Zephaniah*	
3:17-21	192	2:9	256
		3:13	254

Zechariah

1:3	192
3:3 (LXX)	90
5:3-4	257
5:4	116
7:10	98
7:10-12	191
7:11-12	36, 37
7:13	192

Malachi

8:16-17	252
2:2	36, 37
2:6-7	192, 253
3:5	257
3:7	192
3:13-15	194
3:16-18	154

III. Apocrypha and Pseudepigrapha

Letter of Aristeas

17-19	197
18	49
139	46
140	258
192	152, 197
200	46
201	48
206	258
215	43
215-216	152
233	198
239	47
242	47
248	198
252	149
253	43, 48
255	45, 198
256	45, 198
260-261	257
263	199
266	45
294	46

1 Baruch

1:13-2:18	198

2 Baruch

46:5	48
47:1-43	197
48	112
54:2-11	196
83:3	113
83:16	199
83:19	151
83:21	259
85:12	199

3 Baruch

1:6-7	47

Bel and the Dragon

1-10	198

1 Enoch

3:3	151
5:4-6	112, 199
9:5	113
47:1-2	196
51:3	46
91:4	48, 113
94:5	46
94:8	198
95:6	152, 258
96:7	198, 258
97:5	197
98:15-16	258
99:12	258

2 Enoch (A)

10:5-6	149, 199, 258
44:1-2	150
44:3	43
46:2	113
49:1	259
52:1	196
52:2	149, 150
52:3	196
52:4	150
52:14	113
63:1	258

2 Enoch (B)

33:4	47, 258
42:12-13	257
42:13	45
43:2	44
51:1-2	98
52:5	151

1 Esdras

3:41	258
4:38-41	152
4:62	198

Additions to Esther

C:24	46

4 Ezra

3:20-28	48
7:109	240
12:48	198

Judith

1-2	48
4:9-16	197
5:24	197
6:1-9	198
8:2	198
8:28-29	46
8:31	198
9	197
9:8-9	198
9:11	98
11:20-23	46
16:1-17	196, 197

Jubilees

12:21	198
22:9	198

1 Maccabees

2:62	49
2:65	49
2:66	46
3:46	198
4:24	197
4:30-33	198
4:33	197
4:39-40	198
4:55	197
5:33	198
7:10-17	258
7:28	259
7:40-42	198
9:43-46	198
9:54-56	259
11:71	198
12:15	198
13:12-19	258, 259
13:47	197
15:10-24	259
16:15	258

2 Maccabees

4:1	152
4:32-38	259
5:17-26	198
7:17	198
7:19	198
7:31	198
7:35-36	198
8:4	198
9:4-28	198

9:11-28	198, 199
10:4	198
10:34-35	198
12:14	198
15:6-28	198
15:12	46
15:17	48
15:24	198
15:26-27	198
15:29	197

3 Maccabees

1:15-2:20	198
1:16	198
2:1-20	197, 198
3:4	198
4:16	198
5:7-20	197
6:2-15	197
6:22-29	198

4 Maccabees

2:11-23	43
5:35-6:1	46

Prayer of Azariah

29-68	196

Psalms of Solomon

2:1-40	198
2:24-29	197, 198
2:40	197
3:1-16	196
3:2	196
4:1-29	112
6:1	196
6:8	197
7:7	197
8:29	196
8:40	196
9:6	113
10:6-8	196
12:1	112
12:3	258
12:1-2	112
12:4	149
14:5	113
15:1	197
15:3	196
15:5	197
16:10	258
18:3	197
34:18-24	197

Sibylline Oracles

3:20-27	49

3:36-39	111, 112, 258
3:37	111
3:58-70	259
3:202	198
3:492-502	112, 258
3:572-573	49, 258
3:584-586	47
3:624-630	197
3:698-701	49, 258
3:700-701	258
3:732-739	198
3:827	258
33:377	149

Sirach

1:16	176
1:22-23	43
1:25	48
2:15-17	45
2:24-26	45
3:1-2	48
3:1-15	46
3:8	47
3:9	48, 150
3:10	98
3:16	198
3:17-19	199
3:28	46
4:5	197
4:5-6	150
4:6	197
4:8	45
4:11-17	45
4:23	44, 45
4:24-25	257
4:26	198
4:27-28	45, 257
4:29	47
5:1-6	199
5:8	199
5:9-10	199
5:10	46
5:11	85
5:11-13	44
5:12	85
5:14	149
5:15	111
5:15-6:1	112
6:2-4	43
6:5	45
6:5-17	149
6:34-35	46
6:36-37	46
7:6	152
7:10	197

7:11	150
7:13	258
7:17	199
7:27-28	46
8:5	150
8:6	150
8:8-9	46, 47
8:10	111, 151
8:11	151
8:16	136, 150
8:18-19	113
9:14-16	46
9:15	46
10:6-18	150
10:12	199
10:14-18	199
10:22	150
11:7	45
11:8	44
11:31	150
11:32	151
12:16-17	151
12:16-18	113
13:4-7	151
13:19-22	150
13:22-23	150
13:24-25	113
14:1	111
14:20-15:10	46
15:8	150
15:10	196
15:12-20	113
15:20	111
16:8	199
16:17-23	113
16:22-23	46
17:5-6	47
17:19-21	197
17:20	113
18:14-16	45
18:19	44
18:22-23	259
19:5-16	149
19:8	149
19:15	111, 149
19:21-26	113, 151
20:1	44, 151
20:2	113
20:4	44
20:5	151
20:5-6	44
20:7	44
20:12	44
20:18-19	44

20:19	15	29:25	150
20:20	151	30:1-3	46
20:21	43	30:6-8	258
20:24-26	258	30:24	43
20:26	48	31:13	44
21:5	197	31:31	150
21:14-15	44	32:7-8	44
21:16-17	43	32:13	196
21:17	45	34:22	136
21:20	44	34:24	150
21:24	44	35:2	197
21:25	43, 46	35:2-11	98
21:26	45	35:12-13	152
21:27	48,150	35:12-24	197
21:28	149	35:16-17	98, 197
22:6	151	35:19-24	199
22:12	44	36:10-11	190
22:22	149, 150, 198	36:16	47
22:27	111, 112	36:22-23	45
23:2	46	37:8	46
23:8	112	37:11	44
23:9	259	37:12	46
23:9-11	150	37:15	47,258
23:12-15	150	37:17-18	48
23:13	152	37:22	45
23:14	150	37:25	45
23:15	44, 150	39:6	197, 258
23:18-20	113	39:6-8	47
25:1	149	39:13-15	196
25:2	151	39:16-35	196
25:8	111	40:21	45, 257
26:5	136, 150, 151	41:14-24	259
26:14	44	41:15	258
27:4-7	112	41:22	150
27:13	151	41:23	149
27:14-15	112	42:15	49
27:15	150	42:15-43:35	196
27:16-21	149	46:4-5	49
27:22-27	113, 151	46:5-6	197
27:28	199	46:13-15	47
28:2-7	197	46:13-24	47
28:8-11	136, 150	46:15	258
28:9	150	46:17-18	197
28:12	149	46:27-29	46
28:13	48, 112	48:3-6	49
28:14-18	48	48:12-16	49
28:18-21	111	48:18	198
28:19-21	136	48:20-21	197
28:22-23	111	50:22-23	196
28:24-25	43	50:23	198
28:26	111	51:1-30	196
29:3	260	51:3	258
29:8-9	98		
29:14-20	260	*Song of Susanna*	
29:19-21	150	42:43	198

Testament of Job	
26:7	111
42:4-5	257

Testament of the Twelve Patriarchs

Testament of Asher	
2:6	198
Testament of Benjamin	
1:4-5	198
3:6	198
6:5-7	48, 112
6:7	113
Testament of Dan	
1:8	43
2:1	258
2:1-4:7	43
5:1	258
5:1-2	259
6:8	43, 258
Testament of Gad	
5:1	149
5:9	198
6:2	197
6:3	150
7:1	198
7:2	196
Testament of Issachar	
4:1	48
7:4	258
Testament of Joseph	
1:7	149
3:4-8:5	197
3:7	198
8:4	152
10:6-11:4	44
14:2	44

15:1-7	44
17:1-8	44
Testament of Judah	
1:3	198
16:3	43, 149
19:2	198
25:3	259
Testament of Levi	
8:17	258
Testament of Naphtali	
2:6	112
3:1	44
Testament of Reuben	
1:7	198
3:1-6	151
3:5	151, 258
3:9	257
4:4	198
Tobit	
1:18	198
3:1-18	197
3:2	197, 258
3:2-6	198
3:6	149
3:11	197
3:11-15	198
3:13	150
4:19	198
6:17	198
8:5-7	196, 199
8:7	198
8:17	198
11:1	198
11:14-15	196, 197
12:8	197
13:1-19	196
13:6	197

IV. Qumranic Literature

CD	
2:5-10	115
(B) 2 (20):11	261
2:12	261
2:12-13	260
2:16-18	260
2:17-3:12	260
(B) 2 (20):18-20	154
(B) 2 (20):20	115, 202, 204
(B) 2 (20):28	52

(B) 2 (20):28-30	202
(B) 2 (20):33	52
3:1	260
3:4	260
3:7-12	52
3:13-15	261
3:13-16	261
3:13-20	53
3:14	260
3:29-36	203

4:1	260
4:7	153
5:12-13	202
5:12-15	260
5:20	260
6:1	260
6:3-11	203
6:14-15	153
6:21	98
7:2-3	154
8:8	262
8:13	261
8:19	115, 204
8:28-30	288
9:1	262
9:3-8	154
9:6-8	50, 51
9:9-10	262
9:11-12	262
9:17-20	261
9:18	154
10:18	50
10:18-20	50
11:12	153
11:20-21	200
12:3	114
12:7-8	203
13:14-15	153
15:1-5	262
15:3	203
15:6-10	262
15:9	261
16:1-9	262
16:2	261
16:10-11	262
19:26	261

1Q22
1:10	55, 260

1Q27
1:9-10	113

1QH
1:7	52
1:14	52
1:21-23	113
1:21-27	202
1:23	53
1:27-29	53
1:28-31	201
1:29	52
1:30	202
2:8	54
2:11-15	153, 203, 261
2:17-19	52

2:20-21	201
2:23	53
2:24	115
2:25-29	114
2:28	114
2:29-30	114
2:30	202
2:31	261
3:19-20	201
3:22-23	201
3:23	202
3:23-24	202
3:31	114
3:36	114
4:5-6	201
4:6	261
4:7	114, 153
4:10	52, 261
4:14	52, 202
4:14-15	261
4:16-17	53
4:18-20	115, 203
4:25	54
4:27	52, 54
4:29-32	113
4:30	113
4:31-32	53
4:34	202
4:39	53
5:2-3	153
5:7	114, 136
5:10-11	114, 136
5:11-13	202
5:18-19	204
5:20	201
5:23-26	153
5:26	53, 261
5:30-33	114
6:10	260
6:12	201
6:22	114
6:29	115
7:6	201
7:6-12	53
7:10-12	54
7:13	261
7:26	52, 261
7:26-27	201
7:28	113, 200
7:29	54
7:34-35	201
8:4	201
8:16	54
8:35-36	54
8:36	54

9:14	113
9:17	52
9:23	52
9:38	202
9:39	200
10:4	52
10:7	51, 53
10:9-10	201
10:14	200
10:20	52
10:34-36	200
11:3	201
11:4-5	200
11:4-7	200
11:6	202
11:7	200
11:13	199
11:15	201
11:21-22	113
11:23	200
11:25	200, 202
11:28	200
11:33-36	200
12:3	202
12:3-4	199
12:11-13	52
12:9	200
12:19-24	113
12:22	199
12:31	54, 113, 200
12:34	53
13:14	113
13:18	260
13:18-19	55, 260
14:8	52
14:13-14	199
14:14-15	53, 199, 261
14:20	261
14:23	200
14:23-24	201
15:11	53
15:12	53
15:14	55
15:18-19	52
15:24	200, 260
15:29	115
16:6	202
16:7	53
16:8-9	201
16:9-10	200
16:12	199
16:17	202
17:4	202
17:15	202, 260
17:18-19	113

17:20	202
17:26	53
17:26-28	52
18:8	202
18:9	53
1QM	
2:1-3	153
4:6	260
8:12	202
10:8-16	200
12:7-10	153
12:15	200
13:4-6	153
13:7	202
13:12	53, 260, 361
14:4	202
14:6	201
14:23	201
18:6	202
18:9	202
19:6	200
19:16	200
1QHab	
2:1	52
2:1-10	203, 261
2:2	261
4:1-3	153
5:9-12	51
5:11	261
8:9-10	203
8:106-112	203
10:6-12	114, 153, 203, 261
1QHos	
2:5	52
1QMic	
10:2	261
1QS	
1:5	53, 261
1:9	50
1:12	261
1:12-13	260
1:14	54
1:14-15	53, 261
1:15	261
1:16-17	53
1:21	52
1:24-2:1	288
1:25-26	113
1:26	200
2:2	52
2:2-4	52
2:6-10	153

2:11-18	153	10:12	52
2:24	53	10:13	200, 202
2:24-26	260	10:13-15	200
2:26	53	10:14	200
3:6	260	10:16	200, 260
3:6-12	53	10:19-20	51
4:3	52	10:21-22	50
4:9	261	10:21-23	115
4:9-11	114, 153, 202	10:22	51, 153, 261
4:12-14	203	10:23	200
4:17	260	10:24	50, 51
4:18	52	10:25	50, 51
4:18-22	261	10:26	50
4:24	115, 260	10:30-31	52
5:1	53, 153	11:1	50
5:2	261	11:2-9	53
5:3	53, 261	11:3	52
5:7-11	262	11:4	260
5:8-11	261	11:6	52
5:10	153	11:9	202
5:14	54, 115	11:9-10	201
5:15-16	153	11:15	52
5:19	115	11:17	53
5:25	50, 261	11:17-22	201
5:25-6:1	50, 51, 154	11:18	52
6:6	52, 261	11:21-22	240
6:9	200		
6:24-7:25	49, 152	*1QSb*	
6:27	262	1:2	53
6:27-7:1	202, 203	3:27	54
7:4	261	4:28	202
7:9	50	5:23-25	54
7:16-17	203		
7:16-18	153	*4Q184*	
8:2	53, 261	1:2	114, 153
8:6	53, 260		
8:9	52	*4Q280-282*	153
8:21	54		
9:4	200	*4Q286-287*	153
9:17	153		
9:18-19	261	*4QpNah*	
9:25	53	2:4-6	114, 153, 261
9:26	200	3:4	203
9:26-11:8	199		
10:1-8	54	*4QpSa*	
10:6	200	27:2-11	199
10:8	200		
		11QTemple	
		64:2-6	52
		64:6-7	153

V. Rabbinic Writings

Mishnah		1:5	55, 98
		1:6	156
Aboth		1:7	117, 155
1:1	57	1:8	158
1:4	55		

1:11	55, 210	2:1	206
1:12	154	2:4-5	206
1:15	57, 58	3:1	206
1:17	56, 57, 58	4:3-4	206
1:18	154, 263	4:4	208
2:1	58	4:5	206
2:4	58, 205	5:1	206
2:4-5	57	5:6	208
2:5	57, 156		
2:6	56	*Mak..*	
2:8	59	1:1-10	158
2:13	57, 59		
2:13-14	117	*Ned.*	
2:15	56, 58, 116	2:2	265
2:16	115	3:1	265
2:18	206		
3:2	208	*Pes.*	
3:3-4:7	59	10:5-6	204
3:6	57		
3:9	58	*San.*	
3:10	57, 59	3:4	158
3:12	58	4:5	57
3:14	58	6:6	209
3:15	156, 264	7:4	157, 209
3:17	56, 265	7:5	209
3:19	58	7:8	157
4:1	56, 115	10:1	60, 210
4:2	157	11:1	264
4:3	156	11:5	264
4:4	210	11:6	158, 266
4:5	209		
4:6	56	*Sheb.*	
4:12	210	4:1-13	265
4:18	58	4:3	59, 266
4:22	209	4:4	208
4:24	156	4:13	157, 209, 266
4:29	158, 207	5:1	206
5:10	57, 263	5:6	207
5:11	158, 210, 264	7:1	208
5:12	98		
5:14	56, 86, 157	*Shek.*	
5:15	86	5:1	204
5:17	58		
5:22	210	*Sot.*	
6:1	59	7:6	210
6:6	55, 57, 58, 159		
6:7	59	*Suk.*	
6:9	58	3:9	204
		4:1	204
B. Metzia		5:1	204
4:2	263, 264	5:4	204
4:10	156, 264		
		Ta'an.	
Ber.		3:8	207
1:1	206		
1:2	206	*Yoma*	
		3:8	209
		6:2	209, 210

Talmud

Abod.Zar.
3b	155
4b	209
8a	206

Arak.
15a	116
15b	116, 155
15b-16b	155
16a	117, 155, 158
16b	158, 159

B.Bathra
16a	117
73a	60
116a	208
164b	116, 155

B.Kamma
113b	210

B.Ketzia
49a	59
58b	117, 156, 157, 264
59a	156
59b	136

Ber.
2b (J.)	207
4 (J.)	209
7a (J.)	205
7d (J.)	209
8a-b (J.)	207
10a	204
12d (J.)	204
13a (J.)	207
17a	56
18a (J.)	204
21a (J.)	207
24b	57
29b	205, 206
30b	205
32a	204
38a (J.)	207
59b	204

Erub.
21b	266

Hag.
5a	209
12b	155

Hul.
89a	56, 157

Ket.
17a	57, 158
56a	60
72a	59

Kid.
30b	115
40b	209
49b	155
71a	157

Meg.
15a	60, 204
18a	56, 57
20a	205
25b	159
28a	60
35a	204

Menach.
99a	159

Mo'ed Kat.
5a	208
28a	207

Ned.
4a	208
16a	265
18a	265
20a	265
61a	155

Peah
16a (J.)	155

Per.
3a	159
66b	210
113	157
113a	155
113b	116, 117, 157, 264
118a	155, 266

Rosh Hash.
18a	205

San.
22a	207
24a	210
43b	209
44b	209
45b	209
48b	157
48b-49a	157
50a	209
52a	157

58b	156	72b	59
65a	210	86a	57, 58, 209, 210
82b	60, 210		
89b	264	**Tosephta**	
92a	157, 264		
93b	210	*B.Kamma*	
97a	264	7:8	157
99b	156	10:15	210
103a	155, 156, 157, 264		
105b	116, 157	*B.Metzia*	
106b	117	3:14	265
111a	264		
		Ber.	
Shab.		2:7	205, 206
10a	205	3:6	207
30b	57	3:18	205
32a	210, 266	*Mak.*	
33a	144, 149	5:10	60
49b	159		
55a	264	*San.*	
88a	58	1:2	210
88b	59, 156		
104a	264	*Sheb.*	
105b	56, 115, 116	3:6	264
119b	159, 206		
		Sot.	
Sheb.		7:16	157
36a	59, 157, 209, 263		
		Yoma	
Sot.		5:6-8	209
35a	155		
40a	204		
41b	157	**Midrash**	
42a	156, 157		
47b	210	*Mekilta* (Lauterbach)	
		1:216	207
Suk.		2:91	207
14a	207	2:182	58
46b	264	2:229-239	263
		Midrash Psalms	
Ta'an.		12:1	59, 117, 157
2a	205	12:2	57, 116, 136, 155
4a	57	15:4	264
8a	156, 205	19:1	57
20a	57	19:2	204
23a	207	25:6	204
25b	207	30:2	59
64b	207	30:4	59
		39:2	115
Yeb.		39:3	117, 204
64a	207	39:4	116
105b	205	51:2	209
		52:6	116, 210
Yoma		65:2	205, 207
19b	206	86:1	56
49d (J.)	60	88:1	204
69b	210, 264	108:1	205

Midrash Proverbs
6:12 (28a)   155
24:3 (48b)   116
24:31 (48b)   59

Pesikta Rab Kahana
21   158, 265
23/24   266
24 (125b)   117, 264
185b   211
198a   210
212   158

Pesikta Rabbati
66b   56
99a   56
113b   56, 57, 59
158a   205
163b   209

Genesis Rabbah
8:5   264
13:15   204
19:1   56
20:1   155
22:6   116
24:7   156
44:22   59
55:1   264
67:3   57
67:8   59, 117
73:12   57, 117
79:1   116
81:2   56, 115, 264, 265
97   209
98:9   155
98:19   116

Exodus Rabbah
1:30   60, 155
3:12   156
4:3   59, 60
21:14   207
22:3   205
30:19   156
30:24   158
31:9   155
38:1   264
38:4   205
40:4   211

Leviticus Rabbah
1:11   59
6:3   11, 136, 158, 266
7:6   210
10:5   207
16:1   117, 264

16:2   115
16:4   116
16:5   56
17:3   155, 210
20:2   210
20:10   210
26:2   57, 116, 155, 156
32:2   209
32:4   60
33:1   57, 115, 154
35:7   58
37:1   265

Numbers Rabbah
9:24   210
14:10   58
15:16   265
16:6   155, 156
19:2   57, 116, 155
19:22   156
20:19   60
21:12   210
22:1   266

Deuteronomy Rabbah
1:9   56, 115, 159
1:10   264
2:1   207
3:8   60
5:10   116. 155. 156
6:4   155
6:8-10   155, 156
6:9   155
6:13   208
6:14   116, 156
8:1   207
11:6   58
12:1   59, 11, 157
12:2   57, 116, 136, 155
15:4   264
19:1   57
19:2   204
25:6   204
30:2   59
30:4   59
39:2   115
39:3   117, 204
39:4   116
51:2   209
52:6   116, 210
65:2   205, 207
86:1   56
88:1   56
108:1   205

Ruth Rabbah
1:13   60
7:6   263

Esther Rabbah
6;12   56

Ecclesiastes Rabbah
1:16   57, 117
3:6   116
3:7   57
3:9   264
3:10   207
3:11   60
5:5   56, 115, 155, 264
7:1   207
9:12   155
10:1   210
10:19   209

Song of Solomon Rabbah
1:9   264
2:13   210
4:11   57

Lamentations Rabbah
23   210

Sifra
89a   57, 158
89a-89b 159
91b   263
110c   58
111b   58

Sifre Deut.
1,64a   159
29,71b   207
32,73a-73b 59
41,79a-79b 58, 205
41,80a   205
45,82b   59, 116
79,91a   58
117,98b   59
250,120a   159
328   209

Sifre Num.
2,2a   264
135,51a   207
60a   56

Tanchuma
13a   265
1,24a   205

1,24e   205
9,111a   205, 207
B,79a   265

Other Rabbinic Works

Aboth de Rabbi Nathan
(Version A: Goldin)
1 (p. 7)   55, 157
6 (p. 40)   58
7 (p. 47)   57
7 (pp. 47-48)   155
7 (p. 48)   55
9 (p. 54-56)   117, 155, 156
10 (p. 55)   57
10 (pp. 58-59) 158
11 (p. 63)   264
12 (p. 64-65)   154
12 (p. 71)   57, 58, 60, 116
15 (p. 78)   56
16 (p. 83)   115
21 (p. 98)   58
24 (pp. 103-105) 58
24 (p. 104)   58
28 (p. 117)   58, 159
32 (p. 187)   57
39 (p. 161)   209

Aboth de Rabbi Nathan
(Version B: Saldarini)
15 (p. 110)   55
16 (p. 110)   155
16 (pp. 112-113) 117, 155
16 (p. 114)   115
20 (p. 129)   158
22 (p. 140)   55
24 (pp. 146-147) 154
31 (p. 184)   58, 59, 159
32 (p. 184)   59, 117
32 (p. 191)   58
35 (p. 210)   156
44 (p. 275)   58

Derek Eretz Zuta
5:1   266

Maimonides

Hilkhot Deot
2:6   157, 263

Tamma de Be Eliyyahre
Friedman, p. 31   58

VI. Graeco-Roman Literature

Aeschylus

Prometheus Bound
685-687   268

Aiskhines
   1:24   65
   1:87F   165
   1:116   212

Andokides
1:137-139   212

Antiphones
Frag. 262   65

Aristotle

EN
   II,5:3   64, 166
   II,6:1-10   160
   II,7:1-9:9   160
   iI,7:10   160
   II,7:11-13   160
   II,9:2   64, 166
   IV,5:8   64, 166
   IV,6:1-8:12   160
   IV,7:6   267, 268
   IV,7:6-8   267
   IV,7:10-13   167
   IV,8:1-12   163
   IV,8:5-9   167
   X,3:11   164

Aristophanes

Birds
1323-1329   162

Clouds
1232-1236   269
1476-1485   212

Frogs
813-819   118
813-829   67, 119
   2:373   62

Lysistrata
915   269
1216-1224   162

Peace
743-747   162
1143   212

1157   212

Wasps
389   212

Wealth
61-105   269

Cicero

Fin.
   1:43   160
   1:43-44   118
   2:46   119, 165, 268
   2:46-47   61, 63, 66

Quint.Frat.
   I,1:37   64

Demosthenes
   18:128   167
   18:192   162
   19:167   167
   20:16   162
   22:62   162
   24:60,102   65
   24:150-151   165
   48:52   165
   57:30   162

Dio Chrysostum

Orationes
   32:2   64, 86
   32:7,11   164
   32:12-16   63
   32:14-16   118
   32:19   120, 162
   32:26   119
   33:1   68
   33:13   164
   33:45   68

Diodorus Siculus
   15:1   164
   15:16   167

Diogenes Laertius
   1:88   62
   1:104   268
   1:105   61, 117
   5:40   63
   7:59   63, 167
   8:20   61, 64

8:22-23	64, 211, 270
8:23	211

Epictetus

Discourses

I,6:32-42	213
I,6:37-43	214
I,12:4-12	213
I,12:19-35	65
I,12:32	211
I,16:1-14	211
I,16:7	271
I,16:15	211
I,16:17-18	211
I,16:20-21	211
I,16:76	270
I,18:1-23	64
I,26:7	64
I,26:13-15	162
I,28:1-3	268
I,28:1-33	64
II,2:14	269
II,7:10-12	213
II,7:13	213
II,8:11-14	63
II,10:9	63, 163
II,17:22-25	63, 213
II,19:3	270
II,19:15	270, 271
II,19:26	214
II,19:36	213
II,22:6	270, 271
II,23:1-47	63
II,23:6	211
II,23:15	63
II,26:1-7	118
II,26:29-30	211
III,2:14-15	119, 167
III,3:2	268
III,13:11-13	160
III,16:1-6	161
III,16:7-10	68
III,18:3	271
III,20:15-16	118
III,22:42	269
III,24:95	63, 65, 213
III,24:111	65, 213
III,24:114	65, 213
III,26:29-30	211
IV,1:89-90	213
IV,1:99-100	213
IV,1:133-134	161
IV,1:146-155	66
IV,3:2	161

IV,4:18	211
IV,5:1-2	160
IV,5:31-32	162
IV,6:32-38	213
IV,6:28-38	269
IV,7:9	211
IV,7:20	63
IV,10:2-3	269
IV,10:14-17	211
IV,12:7-18	63, 67
IV,12:7-21	213
IV,12:17	63, 163

Enchiridion

17	213
33:2	63, 161
33:5	163
33:6	270
33:10	163
33:14	167
33:15-16	163, 167
42	63, 66, 118, 162
45	63, 163
48	119
48:1-3	167

Euripedes

And.

642	118

Bacc.

360-363	212
383-389	61

Electra

807	212

Hipp.

117-120	212

Medea

492-494	270

Pheonissae

469	63

Frag.

17	213
21	167
130	162
156	119
645	270

Gorgias

Enconium on Helen

14	68

Herodotus

I,87:2	212
VI,61:3-5	212

Hesiod

Works and Days

1-8	211
69-84	120
282-284	270
320-324	162
330-334	162
370-372	267
373-375	165
707-711	162
709	268
715-716	162
717-718	162
719-721	162
760-764	69, 162

Homer

Il.

7:179	212
9:435-443	66
9:496	212
15:525-530	212

Od.

2:122-125	165

Hyperides

I,frag. 3	212

Isocrates

Antid.

18-19	161, 267
133	164

To Antip.

4-6	163-267

To. Dem.

13	211, 269
14	65
20	63
23	63, 270
29	162
30	167
31	63
41	61, 63

To Nic.

1-2	67, 119
1-10	68
8	67, 119
9	67
22	270
33	63
34	63, 66
38	66
39	65
42-43	65

To Philip

104	69

Lykurgus

Leokrates

1	212
127	269

Lucian

Demonax

51	64

Menander

543k	163
560k	68
577k	161, 162
frag. 600	65
662k	66
682k	62
715k	166, 214
737k	167
767k	67
821k	67

Perikeis

49	212

Sentientiae

592	270

Ovid

Ex Ponto

I,2:113-123	68, 86

Plato

Gorgias

452d	68, 119
462c-463a	119,165

Laws

628c	160
659a	165
687c	166
687d	213
687e	166, 213

688d	65, 166	Plutarch	
689d	160		
701b	65, 270	*Lives*	
701c	61	1:5	61, 65
716c-g	264		
716d	213	*Moralia*	
716d-e	211	Vol. 1	
717d	66, 69, 169	5b	164
730b	267	6b-e	119
730c	267, 268	7b	119
738e	267	7e	64, 65, 211
776b	211	9a	164
792b	119	10a	63, 67
799a-801c	214	10b	86
801a-b	213	10f	62, 67
821b-d	214	10f-11c	118
854c	166	11a-c	67
916c	269	13b	164
916e	268	14a	66
931a	162	14e-37b	65, 267
931c	166, 213	16a-c	165, 267
931e	211	21a	268
934e	166	31f	65
948d-949b	166, 271	33f	67, 69
		35c-d	162
		35d	162
Lysias		36b	268
35:6	162	37a-48d	267
		38b	117
Phaedo		38c	65
66c	268	39b	64, 85
		39c	65
Phaedrus		40b	65
261b	68	41a	267
267b	119	41a-42c	65
		41c-42c	67, 199
Prot.		41d	62
326b	66	48d	65
		48e-74e	164, 267
Rep.		49a	267
381c-383a	268	49a-b	164, 276
381e	214	53c	267
382d	269	59b	263
383a	66	59c	267
389b	269	61c	267, 268
534e	65	62c-d	267
535e	268	62d	271
536c	270	66b	163
		73	68
Symp.		74e	163
183b	269		
		Vol. 2	
Pindar		102b	163
		102d	214
Pythians		145e	65
1:85	268	146f	117

Vol. 3
18	117
208c	62
237d	65
239a	213
239d	62

Vol. 4
275a	166

Vol. 6
452e-464d	118
454f	64
454g	118
455b	64
461e	63, 163
462e	67
464	119
464b-c	269
464c	63, 163
464d	67, 119
502b	68
502b-515f	267
502c	64
502d	64
503a	64
503c	118
503d	161, 267
504c	63
504c-f	61
504e	159
505b-d	67, 161
505d	61
505f	62
506c	62, 117
506e	67
506f-507b	161
507a-b	69
507b	118
507c-508c	161
508c	161
509c	118
510a	62, 63
510c-d	161
510d-514c	62
510e	62
514e	61
515a	62
519d	161

Vol. 7
528c-533c	163
547a	163
547e	167
547f	167

Vol. 8
532d	163
631c	163
631c-634f	163
631e	163
632d	163
632e	163
633e	163
633f	163

Vol. 12
967b	62

Vol. 13
1065d-e	214

Vol. 15
39	270
46	162
48	211
67	214
87	118, 267, 268
88	162
89	61, 63, 117, 118

Seneca

Const.
2:1-3	162
3:2	162
12:3	162
13:5	162

EM
10:4	213
38:1-2	67
41:1	213
60:1	166
60:1-4	213
61:1-2	213
67:1-2	213
108:7-11	65
108:35	65
108:36-37	66
108:38	119
108:38-39	66, 67
110:2	166
114:3	119
117:22-24	213

ME (De Ira)
I,2:2	118
II,32:1	118
II,34:5	167
III,1:1	64
III,5:1-2	64,166
III,6:3	64

III,43:1-5	162	943-944	211
VII,15:7	65	979-982	66
VII,17-30	66	1135-1145	270
VII,20:5	66	1146-1150	119
VII,27:7-8	65, 66	1165-1166	118
		1167-1168	62, 119
Vit.		1179-1180	66
20:6	119	1195-1196	269
26:7-27:3	213	1217-1218	163
27:1	214	1220	165

Sophocles

Xenophon

Philoctetes
108-120   267

Anab.
II,4:6   269
III,1:22   269
VII,6:21   165

Thycydides
III,37:3   119
III,38   65

Ath.
2:6   212

Cyro.
V,1:29   212

Theognis
1-4	211, 212
11-14	212
83-86	118
93-100	162
95-298	63
113-114	161
119-128	165
159-160	167
171-172	212
185-186	118
197-208	269
283-292	271
295-298	61
305-308	118, 119
323-324	162
341-350	212
363-364	162
365-366	61, 63, 64, 119
373-392	119
399-400	166
480-496	64
555-556	212
595-602	165
607-610	268
611-614	62, 119
625-626	63
659-660	269
757-768	212
759	61
759-764	160
799	118
823-824	269

V,4:10   270

Eq.
8:13   163

Hell.
II,4:14   212

Hipp.
9:8   212

Dec.
5:20   212
11:8   212

Dem.
9:6   269
11:12   269
23:101   269
24:150-151   269
48:11   269
48:52   269

Mem.
I,1:19   66
I,7:2-5   268
II,2:1-4   65, 212, 213
III,11:10   63
IV,2:1-4   213
IV,2:1-40   167

Symp
4:49   269

VII. Hellenistic-Jewish Literature

Josephus

B.J.
II,8:5 (128)   49, 200
II,8:6 (135)   49, 262
II,8:7 (141)   261
II,8:9 (145)   203
II,8:10 (152,153)   203
II,10:4 (371)   262

Philo

Abr.
  6   217
 19   120
 20   121, 172
 20-23   73, 168
 21   70, 71
 29   70, 121
 37   73
 60-61   72
126   170
127   215
190   121
208   70
245   71
272   272

Agr.
 17   71
 60-67   72

Cher.
 77   72, 217
 94   121, 273
107   218

Conf.
 27-31   217
 33-34   120
 37   70
 39   70, 217
 48   73, 121, 169, 272
 93   217

Congr.
  5   272
  7   217
 33   70
 46   73
 51-53   71
 53   71, 73
 80   69
109   216

Dec.
  1-3   169
  5-6   217
 13   74
 37-39   72
 40-42   217
 40-43   218
 47   72
 49   121
 58   215
 63   121, 184, 217
 84   273
 84-85   273
 86   217, 273
 86-91   170
 90-91   273
 91   217
 92   273
106-120   217
119-120   72
133-134   217
138   271
138-141   170
172   170
178   168

Det.
 23   70, 120
 40   70
 43-44   73
102   70
126-129   70, 73
131   74
174   74, 125
175-176   70

Deus
 63-69   273
135   216

Ebr.
 45   272
 70-71   272

Flacc.
  2   70
 27   216
 33-34   169
 40   73
 51   70
 86   169
102   215
121   215
121-124   216

121-147	169	196	215
146	215	199	212, 169
		220	215
Fug.		336	215
30	217	353-355	217
79-80	215	368	169, 217
81-86	217		
85	217	*Mig.*	
122	72	51	72
		79-80	74
Her.		80-81	70, 71, 74
11-12	72	115	170
14	70, 71	122-125	216
14-16	215, 216	124	216
14-17	74	128	72
15-16	71	129	72
108	168	164	121
110	215	171	217
127	70	210	71
Hyp.		*Mos.*	
7:2	217	1:12	215
7:3-4	273	1:47-49	216
		1:173	216
Jos.		1:180	216
42	74, 170	1:185	216
95	272	1:251	253, 273
117	74, 272	2:5	215, 216
173	71	2:24	216
246	169	2:66	73
268	74	2:67	215
299	74	2:107-108	216
		2:127-129	70, 73
L.A.		2:127-130	272
1:101-104	121	2:128	272
1:102-103	120	2:132	215
1:103	120	2:138-141	73
3:54	72	2:154	216
3:66-67	169	2:196-208	217
3:69	72, 120	2:198	70
3:104	217	2:206	217
3:123-124	71, 272	2:212	73
3:127	272	2:233-242	216
3:131	17	2:237	272
3:177	217	2:238	215
3:182	170	2:239	215
3:206	215	2:240-241	218
		2:256-257	216
Leg.		2:258-287	272
6-7	215	2:270	272
18	169	2:271	271
39	170		
57	121, 169	*Mut.*	
118	215, 217	39	70
162	70, 121, 217	49-50	120, 168
162-163	169	61	217
171	170		

183-185	120	52-54	273
193	73	63	215
193-198	121	65-66	72
195-199	73	124	216
219-223	215		
240	121, 168, 169	*Sob.*	
240-242	70	6	169
240-244	73	52	70
247	74, 272	58	215
Op.		*Som.*	
10	215	1:12	273
21	215	1:102-104	74, 168
165	170	1:105-108	71, 73
172	215	1:164	217
		1:251-254	273
Plant.		2:28-291	217
52	217	2:62	72
82	273	2:81-92	170
135	216	2:83	73
		2:149	216
Post.		2:165	71
13	217	2:192-193	71
16	217	2:260	70
55	73	2:261-167	71
101	71, 73, 272	2:262	70
108	73	2:264	71
108-111	70	2:267-273	70
168	215	2:274	121
Praem.		*Spec.*	
58	272	1:1-8	274
63	120	1:10	218
81	73	1:41-42	216
82	73	1:41-50	217
107	73	1:42-43	216
148	169	1:65	272
169-171	169	1:67	216
		1:88-89	272
Prob.		1:88-90	272
2	73	1:97	216
11	73, 121	1:167	216
19-20	215	1:209	215
41	215	1:224	215
64	217	1:229	216
84	262, 273	1:247-254	273
99	73, 121	1:259	70
108	70	1:271-272	215
137	272	1:311	218
155	73, 170	1:315-317	215
158	271	1:317	72
		1:342-343	168
Sac.		1:343	74
16	168	2:1-28	273
19-34	168	2:4	274
26	168	2:7	20
27	271		

2:9-11	273	4:48	217
2:11	217	4:48-52	272
2:12-25	274	4:68	272
2:17	217	4:69	73, 271, 272
2:26-28	170	4:70-72	170
2:36-38	273	4:77-99	120
2:49-50	121	4:90	70, 121
2:52	120	4:197	169
2:52-53	72, 121	4:474	218
2:62	72		
2:195	69	*Virt.*	
2:196	216	58	216
2:198	217	161-174	218
2:209	216	171	217
2:224-226	217	177	120
2:235-241	121	184	73
2:241	169, 170	185-186	216
2:261-267	72		
2:343-344	168	*Vita*	
3:174	170	31	71
3:203-208	272	75-82	71
4:40	217	84-90	216
4:40-42	170	190	73

VIII. New Testament

Matthew		7:1	181
1:25	76	7:1-2	171, 287
1:34	76	7:1-5	179
2:2	218	7:7	222, 223
2:8	218	7:8-9	220
2:11	218	8:3	82
3:2-6	220	8:16-17	82
3:10	134	8:23-27	82
4:4	76, 80	8:29	82
4:10	218	8:32	82
5:9	170	9:1-8	82, 220
5:10	81	9:5	91
5:11	172, 173	9:9	82
5:11-12	173	9:18-26	82
5:16	219	10:10	91
5:18	80	10:13	171
5:19	80	10:14	91
5:28	223	10:15	79
5:33	276	10:16	82, 92
5:34	260	10:17-21	78
5:33-37	276, 279, 287	10:21-23	79
5:37	276	10:24	79
6:5-8	220	10:32	76
6:7	220	10:40	91
6:11	91	11:15	79
6:12-14	220	11:19	81
6:14	171	11:23	221

12:16-21	76		27:27-31	173
12:22-32	221		27:39	221
12:32-33	75		27:41	173
12:33	81		27:44	173
12:33-35	75		28:9	218
12:33-37	122, 287		28:17	218
12:34	78			
12:34-37	279		*Mark*	
12:36-37	75		1:4-5	220
12:39	121		1:16-20	82
12:45	121		1:21-22	82
12:50	80		1:23-28	82
13:18-23	80		1:24	82
13:43	79		1:41	82
14:33	218		1:44-45	82
15:1-9	80		2:1-12	82, 220
15:3-9	80		2:5	238
15:11	121		2:13-14	76
15:18-19	122		3:11-12	76
15:18-20	279		3:13	82
15:19	171		3:22-30	221
15:25	218		3:35	80
16:4	121		4:13-40	80
16:17	78		4:23	79
16:20	76		4:26	102
17:9	76		4:35-41	82
17:14-21	82		5:7	82
18:15-21	174		5:13	82
18:21-22	171		5:28-34	82
18:23-25	171		6:7	82
20:3	75		6:11	91
20:6	75		6:13	236, 237
20:19	173		7:1-13	80
20:29-34	82		7:4	276
21:20-22	82		7:9-13	80
21:21	242		7:16	79
21:22	220		7:21	122, 171
22:15	274		7:34	82
22:15-16	174		8:12	121
22:38-39	170		8:30	76
23:1-36	221		9:9-10	76
23:3	81		9:14-29	82
23:12	221		9:50	170
23:16-22	276, 287		10:15	221
24:2-24	174		10:34	171, 173
24:19-20	82		10:46-52	82
24:33	181		11:11	78, 82
24:36	82		11:20-25	82
24:44	92		11:23	242
25:29	79		11:24-26	220
25:36	98		11:25-26	220
25:43	98		11:26	171
26:59-60	173		12:13-14	174
26:65-66	220		12:14	274
26:74	276		12:32	170

12:33	82
12:37-40	221
12:40	81
13:5-6	174
13:29	181
14:55-56	173
14:63-64	220
14:71	276
15:16-20	173
15:29	221
15:31	173
15:32	173
16:15	82

Luke

1:73	277
4:7	218
4:22	78
4:25	240, 276
4:31-32	82
4:33-37	82
4:34	82
4:35	76
4:41	76
5:13	82
5:14	76
5:17-26	220
5:27-28	82
5:29	220
6:22	172
6:22-23	173
6:24-26	221
6:27	170
6:28	173
6:35	81
6:37	171, 172
6:43-45	75, 81
6:45	78
6:47	80
7:14	82
8:8	79
8:11-15	80
8:21	80
8:23-25	82
8:28	82
8:32	82
9:1	82
9:5	91
9:11	91
9:21	76
9:27	276
9:31	76
9:37-43	82
9:51-56	171
9:53	91

10:5-8	171
10:8	91
10:10	91
10:12	79
10:13-14	79
10:16	79
10:17-20	82
10:26	170
10:38-42	79
11:4	220
11:9-10	220
11:15-23	221
11:28	82
11:29	121
11:38-41	97
12:4	171
12:8-9	76
12:10	221
12:14	276
12:21	221
12:40	92
12:51	171
12:57-59	170
14:11	221
14:35	79
16:5-19	221
16:14-15	79
16:15	221
16:17	80
17:3	174
17:3-4	171
17:26	82
18:1-8	220
18:4	221
18:9-14	220
18:13	220
18:17	221
18:32	173
18:35-42	82
20:20-21	174
20:45-47	221
20:47	81
21:8	174
21:14-15	78, 82
21:23	82
22:31-32	220
22:63-65	173
22:65	221
23:11	173
23:35-39	173
23:39	221
24:44	80
24:53	218

John

1:14	274
3:33	274
4:24	219
5:1-14	82
5:19-29	179
5:23	79
5:24	79, 80
7:16-18	79
7:18	274
7:24	179
8:15-16	179
8:26	79, 274
8:38	218
8:40	274
8:43-45	79, 122
8:45	274, 275
8:47	79
8:51-52	79
10:27-28	79
10:33	220
12:38-43	82
13:34-35	170
14:6	274
14:10	79
14:15	80
14:17	274
14:21	80
14:23-24	80
14:27	171
14:31	79
15:5	80
15:7	220
15:9-17	80, 170
15:26	274
16:13	274
16:33	171
17:1	218, 274
17:3	274
17:4	218
17:6-8	79
17:9-16	220
20:19	171
20:21	171
20:26	171
21:19	218

Acts

1:1	81
1:8	82
1:13	172
1:14	219
2:1-37	82
2:30	277
2:38	220
2:42	219
2:47	218
3:13	218
3:14	218
3:19	220
4:5-12	82
4:8	78
4:12	79
4:21	218
4:23-31	219
4:31-35	82
5:1-11	122
5:4	122
5:41	183
6:1-6	98
6:3	82
6:6	82
6:13	173
7:17	277
7:23	81
7:52	184
7:55-56	78
8:6	82
8:14	91
8:22	220
8:24	220
9:11	219
9:17-28	78
9:27	76
10:2	219
10:26	218
10:34	174
10:36	171
11:18	218
12:5	220
13:10	174
13:45	172, 221
13:46	76
13:48	218
13:52	82
14:3	76, 78, 82
14:14-15	218
16:25	218
17:11	91
17:30	220
18:6	221
18:9	76
18:18	276
19:8	76
19:18	220
20:24	78
20:32	78
20:36	219
21:13	276
21:20	218

22:14	184	14:5-12	219
26:11	221	14:10-13	172, 174
26:20	220	14:11	179, 220
26:26	76	14:16	172
28:3	76	14:19	78, 120
28:26-28	79	15:2	78
		15:6	219
Romans		15:9-12	218
1	121	15:14	174
1:8-9	219	15:16	170
1:18	275	15:30-33	220
1:18-25	91	16:17	173
1:25	218, 275	16:17-18	82, 122, 173
1:29	90		
1:29-30	171	*1 Corinthians*	
1:30	80, 122, 172, 221	1:4	219
2:1	179	1:5	78
2:6	181	1:9	220
2:8	173	1:11	173
2:11	174	1:18-2:16	174
2:12	81	1:19	220
2:13	92	1:26-29	221
2:16	181	1:31	221
3:4	275	1:32	79
3:9	121	2:12-13	78
3:10-18	122	3:1-4	221
3:14	173	3:3	174
3:23	121	3:13	174
3:27	221	3:18	174
5:2-3	234	3:21-23	221
5:11	221	3:18	174
5:12	121	3:33	173
6:13	127	4:1	102
6:16	92	4:3-5	179
8:26-27	219, 220	4:5	179
9:1	276	4:7	221
9:6	274	4:12	173
9:29	90	4:13	172
10:1	220	5:1-13	174
10:8-10	220	5:6	221
10:10	78	5:11	172
10:14-18	76	5:12	179
10:16	275	6:9	174
10:18-21	79	6:10	171
11:33-36	218	6:20	219
12:1	219	9:26	102
12:3	221	10:7	92
12:4	173	10:31	81, 219
12:12	219	11:1	92
12:16	219	12:3	78
12:17	170	13:4	221
12:18	170	13:5	74
13:9	170	13-14	221
13:13	173	14:12	78
14:4	179	14:13-15	219

14:15-25	219
14:20	90, 92
14:20-25	76
14:26	78
14:26-40	219
14:30-37	76
14:32	173
14:34-35	76
15:10	221
15:13	174
16:4	92
16:22	173

2 Corinthians

1:12-14	221
1:23	276
2:9	81
2:17	81, 174, 276
4:2	174
5:10	179
6:7	274
6:14	92
7:14	276
9:13	220
9:14	220
10:1-12:21	221
10:5	81
11:3	174
22:7	221
11:10	276
11:16-17	221
12:4	221
12:19	78
12:20	74, 122, 171, 172, 173
13:7-9	220
13:8	275
13:10	78
13:11	170

Galatians

1:10	174
1:20	276
1:24	218
2:5	274
3:10-14	173
5:7	275
5:13-15	170
5:19-26	171
5:20	75, 173
6:1	174
6:3	221
6:4	221
6:7	174
6:13-14	221

Ephesians

1:3	218
1:13	79, 274
1:17	220
2:8-9	221
2:11-22	171
2:14	171
2:17	171
4:1-19	92, 171
4:2-3	170
4:14	82, 122, 174
4:16	174
4:21	89
4:24	174
4:25	275
4:25-32	77, 78
4:29	174
4:29-31	78
4:31	74, 90, 172, 173
4:31-32	171
4:32	171
5:1	92
5:4	171, 174
5:4-5	122
5:5	84
5:6	82, 122, 174
5:11	174
5:20	218
5:21	174
5:27	127
6:1-2	81
6:9	174
6:18	219, 220
6:19	220

Philippians

1:3-4	219
1:4-6	219
1:8	276
1:10	220
1:11	175
1:14-18	76
1:15	173
2:2-3	221
2:2-4	170
2:3	173, 221
2:9-11	218
2:11	220
2:14	173
2:14-15	173
2:16	234
3:3	219
3:9-10	221
4:4	218
4:5	77

4:6	219
4:8-9	81
4:19	220

Colossians

1:3-5	219
1:5	274
1:28-29	83
2:1-2	170
2:3	79
2:4	82, 122
2:4-8	174
2:8	82, 122, 173, 219
2:18	221
3:5	92
3:8	74, 90, 122, 172, 174
3:8-9	171
3:9	275
3:12-15	171
3:13	173
3:16	174, 219
3:18	89
3:20	81
3:25	174
4:2	219
4:3-4	220
4:5-6	77
4:10	91
4:13	220

1 Thessalonians

1:2	219
1:5	83
1:6	91
1:9	274
2:2	173
2:3	174
2:3-5	82
2:5-6	174
2:9	234
2:13	91
3:9-10	219
3:14	81
4:9-10	170
4:11	76
5:13	170
5:14	174
5:15	170
5:16-18	218
5:17	219
5:24	220
5:25	220

2 Thessalonians

1:3	219
1:7-9	81

1:11	219
2:3	174
2:8-10	275
2:10	174, 275
2:13	219
3:1-5	220
3:3	220
3:14-15	174

1 Timothy

2:1	219, 220
2:2	76
2:3-4	76
2:4	275
2:5	219
2:7	274, 276
2:8	173
2:9-10	219
2:11	219
2:12-15	76
2:14	174
3:3	77
3:4	81, 172
3:11	172
3:15	275
5:1	174
5:2	174
5:3-16	98
5:5	219
5:13	75, 172
5:19-20	179
5:21	174
6:1	221
6:3-5	122
6:4	172, 173
6:5	275
6:12	220
6:14	173, 174
6:17	221
6:17-19	221

2 Timothy

1:14	275
2:13	274
2:15	275
2:18	275
2:19	220
2:20	275
2:23	173, 174
2:24	173
2:25	174
3:1-4	221
3:1-9	122
3:2	221
3:2-4	171

3:3	172, 275
3:8	275
3:13	174
3:15-16	80
3:16	174
4:1	179, 275
4:2	174
4:4	275
4:8	179

Titus

1:2	274
1:6	81
1:7	74
1:9	174
1:13	174
1:14	275
1:16	81
2:2	172
2:3	172
2:5	221
2:9	76
2:15	174
3:2	77, 170, 172
3:3	90
3:9	173, 174
3:10	173, 174

Hebrews

1:6	218
3:3	173
3:11	277
3:18	277
4:3	277
4:8-9	79
5:7-9	80
5:12	84
6:3	277
6:16	277
6:18	274
7:20-28	277
7:25-28	218
10:23	172
10:24	170
10:26	275
11:36	172
12:11	175
12:23	179
12:28	219
13:1	170
13:15	219
13:18	220

James

1:1	17, 131
1:1-18	7

1:2	84, 236
1:2-3	16
1:2-4	244
1:2-8	9
1:2-11	14
1:3-4	95
1:4	7, 10, 11, 12, 16, 20, 241
1:5	6, 9, 20, 22, 26, 29, 30, 222, 241, 242
1:5-6	17
1:5-8	2, 3, 11, 238, 241, 244, 245, 246, 283
1:6	6, 16, 100, 183, 241
1:6-8	100, 104
1:7	7, 16, 242
1:7-8	242
1:8	20, 88, 242
1:9	6, 17, 184, 231, 234
1:9-12	1, 2, 12, 16
1:11	17
1:12	22, 88, 226, 243
1:12-13	16
1:12-15	99
1:13	6, 85, 89, 99, 125, 138
1:13-14	95
1:13-15	135, 216, 247, 282
1:14-15	138
1:15	85
1:16	6, 84
1:17	11, 12, 16, 20
1:17-18	3, 16
1:17-21	22
1:18	11, 16, 17, 19, 21, 84, 89, 91, 227, 281
1:19	6, 7, 84, 88, 92, 96, 100
1:19-20	16, 89, 98, 182
1:19-27	2, 3, 7, 9, 16, 99, 100, 101, 103, 133, 177, 243, 283
1:19-21	14, 99, 123
1:20	89, 99, 102, 136, 176
1:20-21	86, 137
1:20-2:28	7
1:21	6, 11, 17, 19, 21, 89, 90, 91, 92, 96, 102, 127, 228, 231
1:21-25	98
1:22	9, 85, 92, 95, 234
1:22-25	14, 86, 92
1:22-27	16
1:23	96, 243
1:23-34	94
1:24	93, 94
1:25	12, 19, 20, 92, 93, 94, 243
1:26	6, 86, 96, 97, 98, 102, 123, 128, 185
1:26-27	22, 96, 131, 132

1:27	6, 17, 21, 86, 90, 97, 102, 127, 130, 131, 224
2:1	6, 17, 18, 84, 131
2:1-9	1
2:1-11	16
2:1-12	178, 182
2:1-13	1, 2, 12, 13
2:2	85, 243
2:2-3	183
2:3	6, 85, 99, 138, 182, 183
2:4	100, 183
2:5	6, 17, 84, 98, 184, 243
2:6	12, 136, 183, 184
2:7	17, 183, 184, 247
2:8	6, 18, 21, 177, 179, 181
2:9	18, 183
2:10-11	18
2:11	18
2:12	6, 9, 19, 96, 102, 123, 183, 235
2:12-13	16
2:13	9, 85
2:14	84
2:14-16	13
2:14-26	6, 10, 12, 13, 17, 18, 243
2:16	85, 99, 102, 138, 182
2:18	99
2:19	2, 16
2:22	17, 20
2:23	12, 85, 176, 224, 243
2:24	6
2:25	85
3:1	6, 84, 96, 123, 133, 134
3:1-12	3, 6, 7, 13, 14, 16, 99, 123, 133, 136, 138, 181, 185, 282, 283
3:1-18	177
3:2	12, 20, 99, 124, 125, 127, 137, 243
3:2-12	124
3:2-18	14
3:3	125, 127
3:3-4	124
3:4	6, 125, 127, 128
3:4-5	132
3:4-10	102
3:4-12	99
3:5	125, 126, 128, 137, 247
3:6	126, 127, 128, 130, 135, 137, 138, 282
3:7	129, 130
3:7-8	128, 129
3:8	89, 129, 130, 136, 137
3:9	130, 136, 247
3:9-10a	137
3:9-10	185, 244
3:9-12	129, 185
3:10	84, 130, 131, 132, 185
3:10-12	131
3:10a	129, 134
3:10b	122, 134
3:10b-11	133
3:11	131, 132, 133, 134
3:11-12	132
3:12	9, 131, 132, 133, 134, 137
3:12a	133
3:12b	133
3:13	7, 10, 19, 89, 176
3:13-17	176
3:13-18	2, 9, 11, 17, 124, 176
3:13-4:13	7
3:14	6, 10, 138, 185, 227, 247, 282
3:15	10, 11, 128, 227
3:16	10, 227
3:17	10, 11, 19, 100, 102, 175, 176, 183, 282
3:18	3, 6, 9, 11, 85, 175, 176, 181, 235, 283
4:1	96, 135, 136
4:1-2	3, 10, 89, 99, 124
4:1-2a	136, 183
4:1-2b	135, 138, 175, 177, 180, 181, 182, 222
4:1-4	90, 99
4:1-10	2, 231, 246, 282
4:1-12	243
4:1-17	2, 283
4:1-18	135
4:2	184, 227, 231
4:2a	177
4:2c	222, 223
4:2c-3	222, 238, 244
4:2c-4	227, 245
4:2c-10	3, 222, 242, 243
4:2-10	234
4:2-3	17, 104
4:3	222, 244
4:4	17, 127, 177, 223, 226, 228, 230, 243
4:4-10	17, 177
4:5	225, 226, 227, 228
4:5-6	225
4:5-7	21
4:6	225, 226, 227, 228, 229, 247, 278
4:6-10	22, 133, 220
4:7	138, 230, 243, 282
4:7-10	7, 89, 177, 225, 227, 229, 246

4:8	20, 21, 100, 177, 183, 227, 230, 243
4:8-10	243
4:9	6, 230
4:10	177, 221, 224, 229, 230, 243
4:11	6, 9, 18, 84, 172, 177, 179, 180, 278, 279
4:11-12	2, 9, 16, 18, 172, 177, 178, 180, 181, 182, 183, 247
4:12	17, 179, 227, 278
4:13	99, 138, 231, 232, 233, 234
4:13-15	235
4:13-17	2, 3, 231, 243, 248, 288
4:13-5:12	1
4:14	232, 233
4:14-5:20	7
4:15	6, 99, 232, 233, 234, 235
4:16	6, 233, 235, 278
4:16-17	138
4:17	9, 85, 138, 231, 234, 235, 239, 243, 278, 282
5:1	6
5:1-6	1, 12, 16, 17, 90, 98, 130, 136, 180, 231
5:1-18	14
5:2	9
5:4	6, 18, 184, 246
5:4-6	235
5:5	184
5:6	136, 184, 282
5:7	6, 17, 18, 131, 180, 181, 278
5:1-8	180, 278, 279
5:7-9	89
5:7-20	14
5:8	6, 16, 17, 131, 180, 181, 278
5:8b	180
5:9	2, 3, 6, 16, 17, 18, 180, 182, 278, 279, 283
5:10	103, 235
5:10-11	84, 180
5:11	6
5:12	9, 18, 84, 260, 276, 278, 279, 281
5:12-18	2, 3, 283
5:13	235, 244
5:13-15	16
5:13-18	231, 235, 236, 244, 246
5:14	6, 17, 131, 235, 236, 238, 240
5:14-16	236, 246
5:14-15	239
5:15	17, 131, 236, 238, 239, 243
5:15-16	104, 246
5:16	6, 104, 236, 239, 245, 246, 288

5:16a	239
5:16b	240
5:16b-18	240
5:17	6
5:17-18	17, 103, 240, 244, 245
5:18	241
5:19	185, 281
5:19-20	20, 103, 186
5:20	6, 18, 243

1 Peter

1:3-9	218
1:17	179
1:22	170, 275
1:22-23	173
1:23	83
1:23-2:2	90
2:1	89, 90, 171, 172
2:9-10	219
2:12	172, 219
2:16	90
2:17	170
2:18-25	75
3:1-6	76
3:6	172
3:7	170
3:8	170
3:10	75, 121, 174
3:11	170
3:12	220
3:16	27
3:18	184
3:19	173
4:4	172
4:5	179
4:8	103, 170
4:9	173
4:11	79, 219
4:16	218
4:17	81
5:6	221

2 Peter

1:7	170
1:12	275
2:2	221, 275
2:10	221
2:13	174
2:17	221
2:17-18	122

1 John

1:9	220
1:18	121
2:1	184
2:3-5	80

2:4	275	*Jude*	
2:9-11	170	9	172
2:16	221	16	122, 173, 174
2:17	80	19	173
2:20-25	79, 122		
2:21-23	275	*Revelation*	
2:22	275	2:8	79
2:26	174	2:11	79
2:29	221	2:17	79
3:7	174, 184	2:28	79
3:17-18	81	3:6	79
3:19	275	3:13	79
3:21-24	80	3:20	181
3:22	80	3:22	79
3:23	220	5:9-10	218
4:1-3	275	5:12	218
4:2	220	5:13	218
4:6	79	10:6	277
4:7-12	170	12:9	79, 174
4:20	275	13:4	174
5:2-4	80	14:5	275
5:7	274	17:10	218
5:14	274	18:11	221
5:20	274	18:15	221
		18:19	221
		18:23	174
2 John		19:10	218
1	275	19:20	174
4	275	20:2-8	174
7	174	20:10	174
		21:8	275
3 John		22:5	275
4	275	22:15	275

Index of Authors

Abelson, J. 207, 208
Adamson, James B. 14, 84, 87, 90, 94, 95, 97,
  128, 129, 135, 136, 175, 177, 222, 223, 226,
  232, 234, 238, 278, 279
Adkins, A.W.H. 118, 162, 270
Agourides, S.C. 14, 16
Albeck, Chanoch 55
Allegro, John M. 114
Allen, Willoughby C. 75, 172, 221, 276
Ammassari, Antonio 19
Amphoux, C.-B. 14, 85, 92
Amsler, S. 108
Anderson, A.A. 27, 107, 104, 114, 190, 252
Anderson, F.I. 260
Austin, J.L. 42

Baasland, Ernst 8
Banwell, B.O. 107
Barclay, W.S. 34
Barr, James 39, 256
Barrett, C.K. 82, 122
Barth, Marcus 78
Barthelemy, J.D. 113
Barucq, Andre 142
Bauer, W. 102
Baumgärtel, Friedrich 32, 33
Beardslee, William A. 8
Beck, David 14
Beck, F.A.G. 66
Beck, H. 171
Becker, U. 94, 275
Berger, Peter 3
Best, Ernest 76, 79, 83
Beyer, Hermann 221
Birnbaum, Phillip 208
Blackman, E.C. 32, 251
Blank, Sheldon H. 40, 41
Blenker, Alfred 14
Blocher, Henri 32
Blondel, J.-L. 12, 13, 14, 20
Boggan, Charlie William 2
Boismard, M.-E. 21, 22
Bok, Sissela 3
Bonsirven, J. 205

Braude, William G. 158, 204, 265, 266
Braumann, Georg 16, 17, 21
Braun, Herbert 262, 288
Brichto, H.C. 41, 194
Briggs, Charles 27, 107, 145, 252
Brockington, L.H. 35, 39
Brown, C. 171, 193
Brown, Raymond E. 82
Bruce, F.F. 275
Bruggemann, W. 107, 108
Bultmann, Ruadolf 221, 274
Burrows, Millar 9

Cadoux, Arthur T. 6
Calhoun, George 69
Calmet, Augustin 10
Cantinat, Jean 10, 14
Carrington, Philip 21
Cassuto, U. 143, 147, 194
Charlesworth, James 259
Childs, Brevard S. 143, 147
Christ, Felix 8
Christensen, Johnny 213
Cladder, H.J. 7
Cole, R. Alan 143, 147, 194
Colson, F.H. 168, 169
Corrieveau, R. 96, 97
Cranfield, C.E.B. 1, 17, 18, 19, 20, 87, 90, 94,
  129, 275
Crenshaw, James J. 7

Dahood, Mitchell 38, 107, 108, 109, 145, 252
Dana, H.E. 234
Davids, Peter 1, 2, 4, 5, 7, 8, 9, 10, 11, 14, 15, 16,
  17, 18, 20, 21, 84, 85, 87, 88, 90, 91, 92, 93, 94,
  95, 96, 97, 98, 102, 103, 104, 123, 125, 126,
  127, 128, 130, 133, 134, 135, 175, 176, 177,
  179, 181, 183, 184, 185, 222, 223, 224, 226,
  227, 229, 230, 231, 232, 233, 234, 235, 236,
  237, 238, 239, 240, 242, 278, 279
Davies, W.D. 9, 18, 20
Deppe, Dean 9
De Vries, S.J. 253, 254

Dibelius, Martin 1, 4, 9, 12, 13, 14, 15, 16, 18, 20,
   21, 85, 86, 89, 90, 92, 94, 95, 96, 97, 102, 103,
   104, 123, 126, 128, 130, 133, 134, 136, 175,
   176, 177, 179, 180, 181, 183, 184, 185, 223,
   224, 226, 230, 231, 232, 233, 234, 235, 237,
   238, 239, 240, 242, 278, 279
Diels, Hermann 68
Dillistone, F.W. 8
Dillman, Charles N. 9, 11, 12
Dillon, John 8
Dittenberger, Wilhelm 270
Dover, K.J. 212, 269, 270
Driver, S. R. 31
Dunn, James D.G. 8
Du Plessis, P.J. 10, 12, 129
Dupont-Sommer, A. 54, 55, 113, 199, 200, 201,
   203, 262

Eckert, Karl-Gottfried 19
Edelstein, Ludwig 213
Eichrodt, Walther 38, 40, 41, 42, 189
Ellis, E.E. 255

Farrar, Frederick 14
Felder, Cain Hope 2, 9, 10, 18
Ferguson, John 213
Feuillet, A. 8
Finkelstein, Louis 206
Forbes, P.B.R. 14
Francis, Fred O. 7, 278
Frankfort, Henri 140, 187, 188, 249
Freeman, Kathleen 68
Fry, Euan 14, 20
Furnish, Victor Paul 15

Gemser, Berend 9, 29, 146
Genuyt, F. 99
Gertner, M. 14
Geyser, A.S. 1
Gieger, Loren G. 185
Goldin, Judah 57
Goodenough, E.R. 217
Goppelt, Leonhard 19
Gordis, Robert 142
Gray, John 31, 40
Green, Gene 16
Greenstone, Julius 109, 146, 254
Greeven, Heinrich 212, 213, 216
Gregory, Thomas M. 256
Gressman, H. 8
Gundry, Robert H. 276
Guthrie, D. 6, 12

Hahn, H.C. 195

Halson, B.R. 8, 22
Harris, Murray J. 275
Harrison, R.K. 37
Hayden, D.R. 236
Heiler, F. 212
Heinemann, J. 206, 208, 209
Henderlite, Rachel 16, 19, 20
Hendrickson, William 75
Hengel, Martin 8, 113
Herford, R.T. 116, 209, 265
Hertzberg, Hans Wilhelm 40
Hiebert, D. Edmond 14, 20, 84, 85, 87, 88, 90,
   92, 94, 96, 98, 99, 103, 104, 123, 124, 126,
   128, 130, 135, 177, 179, 181, 184, 223, 224,
   226, 229, 230, 231, 232, 233, 234, 235, 236,
   237, 239, 240
Hill, David 75, 80, 82, 172, 221, 222, 276
Hollander, H.W. 44
Holm-Nielsen, Svend 112
Hoppe, Rudolf 8, 9, 10, 11, 12, 13, 15, 16, 18, 19,
   20, 176
Horsley, R.A. 8, 71
Hort, F.J.A. 20, 84, 87, 88, 91, 94, 96, 97, 123,
   126, 127, 130, 131, 134, 135, 175, 183, 185,
   222, 223, 224, 225, 226
Houlden, J.L. 16

Jacob, E. 39
Jacobs, Louis 60, 157, 205, 263
Jacobsen, Thorkild 26
Jaekel, Siegfried 270
Jepsen, Alfred 251
Jeremias, Joachim 226
Johanson, Bruce C. 97, 98
Johnson, Aubrey R. 107
Johnson, Norman B. 198, 258

Kadushin, Max 205, 206, 208
Kelly, Francis Xavier 1
Kelly, J.N.D. 76, 79, 83
Kent, Charles Foster 9
Kevin, Robert Oliver 8
Kidner, Derek 42, 109, 141, 144, 146, 254
Kim, Seyoon 8
Kirk, J.A. 10, 11
Kissane, Edward J. 31
Koester, Helmut 8
Kohler, K. 60, 205, 207
Küchler, Max 81

Ladd, George Eldon 1
Larson, C.W. 216, 217
Lauterbach, J.Z. 58, 263

Laws, Sophie 6, 18, 20, 84, 88, 89, 90, 91, 92, 94,
    95, 97, 98, 99, 102, 103, 104, 123, 124, 127,
    128, 129, 133, 134, 135, 175, 176, 177, 179,
    181, 183, 184, 185, 222, 223, 224, 226, 227,
    230, 231, 232, 233, 234, 236, 237, 238, 239,
    240, 242, 278, 279
Leaney, A.R.C. 153, 202
Lillie, William 12
Lindars, Barnabas 82
Lindblom, Johannes 9
Link, H.-G. 256
Lohse, Eduard 9, 12, 18, 20, 76
Long, A.A. 213
Luck, Ulrich 8, 10, 13
Luckmann, Thomas 3

MacGorman, John W. 8
McKane, William 15, 29, 32, 34, 35, 38, 109, 110,
    141, 144, 145, 146, 188, 252, 254
McNeile, A.H. 75, 172, 221, 276
Maier, Johann 52
Mansoor, Menahem 54
Mantey, Julius R. 234
Marrow, S.B. 77, 82
Marshall, I. Howard 78, 79, 80, 172
Marshall, S.S.C. 20
Martin, R.P. 173
Massiebieau, L. 16
Maston, T.B. 6, 20
Mauchline, John 40
Maynard-Reid, Pedrito Uriah 2
Mayor, J.B. 9, 21, 22, 84, 90, 95, 96, 98, 103, 104,
    123, 125, 128, 129, 130, 133, 134, 135, 176,
    177, 179, 185, 222, 223, 230, 234, 235, 237,
    241, 278
Milik, J.T. 113
Menander 161, 163, 166
Metzger, Bruce 232, 233
Meyer, Arnold 14, 16, 258
Minear, Paul 278, 279
Mitchell, Hinckley G. 142
Mitton, C. Leslie 18, 78, 87, 88, 90, 91, 94, 95, 96,
    97, 103, 126, 127, 128, 129, 130, 131, 134,
    135, 175, 177, 179, 180, 181, 185, 222, 226,
    229, 230, 231, 232, 234, 235, 236, 237, 238,
    239, 278, 279
Montgomery, James A. 40
Moore, George Foot 41, 56, 57, 60, 157, 205, 206,
    208, 209, 210
Morenz, Siegfried 188
Motyer, J.A. 41
Mounce, William 22
Mowinckel, Sigmund 41
Mowvley, Harry 41
Muilenburg, James 7, 35, 36, 37, 39, 42

Mundle, Wilhelm 69
Murphey-O'Conner, Jerome 260, 261, 262
Murray, John 274
Murtonen, A. 41
Mussner, Franz 9, 12, 15, 16, 17, 18, 20, 21, 84,
    85, 87, 88, 89, 90, 91, 92, 94, 95, 96, 97, 103,
    104, 127, 130, 134, 135, 176, 177, 178, 180,
    181, 183, 184, 185, 222, 223, 224, 226, 230,
    231, 232, 234, 235, 236, 237, 238, 239, 241,
    242, 278, 279
Nichelson, Ernest W. 37
Nickelsburg, George W.E. 259
Noack, Bent 16
Noth, Martin 41
Nötscher, Friedrich 19

Obermüller, Rudolf 8, 9, 12, 16, 17, 98
Ong, Walter 3
Overholt, T.W. 253

Palmer, F.H. 251
Parks, Ronald William 246
Pearson, Birger A. 8
Pearson, Lionel 270
Perdue, Leo G. 4, 13, 15, 22
Pfeiffer, Ernst 7, 86, 87
Pfeiffer, Robert H. 258
Piper, O.A. 251
Polhill, John B. 16
Pope, Marvin H. 31, 256, 257, 276
Porter, J.R. 41
Porteus, N.W. 8
Procksch, O. 39

Rahlfs, Alfred, ed. 43, 45, 196
Rankin, O.S. 8, 9
Ranston, Harry 9
Reese, J.M. 8, 14
Reicke, Bo 18, 19, 85, 237, 278, 279
Reines, Chaim W. 156
Rendall, Gerald H. 6
Richardson, Allan 195
Rimbach, J.A. 274
Ringgren, Helmer 113, 190, 191
Roberts, D.J. III. 97, 98
Robertson, A.T. 87, 90, 97, 127, 229, 234
Robinson, H. Wheeler 8
Robinson, J. Armitage 78
Robinson, James M. 8
Ropes, James H. 9, 14, 16, 18, 85, 87, 88, 89, 90,
    92, 94, 96, 97, 98, 103, 104, 123, 126, 128,
    130, 134, 135, 176, 177, 179, 180, 181, 183,
    184, 185, 222, 223, 224, 226, 229, 230, 231,
    232, 233, 234, 235, 236, 237, 239, 240, 241,
    278, 279

Rylaarsdam, J. Coert 8, 9
Ryle, H.E. 112

Saldarini, Anthony J. 55
Sandbach, F.H. 213
Sanders, E.P. 153, 199
Sanders, Jack T. 16
Sandmel, Samuel 8
Sauer, George 43, 45, 112
Scharbert, Josef 40, 41
Schawe, E. 6, 9, 17, 18
Schechter, Solomon 209
Schiffman, Lawrence H. 154, 209
Schmidt, W.H. 39
Schmitt, J. 288
Schnabel, Eckart 9
Schnackenburg, Rudolf 6, 9, 11, 18, 19
Schneider, Johannes 276
Schrage, W. 6, 12, 14, 17, 18, 19, 20, 93, 97, 98,
    126, 129, 132, 135, 175, 176, 179, 180, 181,
    231, 232, 235, 236, 237, 239, 241, 242, 278
Schüpphaus, Joachim 258
Schürer, Emil 206
Scott, R.B.Y. 7, 9, 29, 33, 141, 146
Seitz, Oscar J.F. 18, 20
Selwyn, E.G. 21, 76, 79, 83
Sharp, Doublas S. 213
Shepherd, Massey H. 9
Singer, S. 56, 204, 206, 208, 209
Sleeper, C. Freeman 3, 5
Snaith, N.H. 41
Songer, Harold S. 14
Sorg, Theo. 32
Spicq, C. 94, 98
Stauffer, Ethelbert 19
Steinsaltz, Adin 206
Stevens, George Barker 17, 20
Stob, Henry 255
Suggs, M. Jack 8

Talmon, Shemaryahu 154, 199, 200, 201, 202
Tasker, R.V.G. 175
Taylor, Vincent 221
Thackeray, H.St.J. 49

Thiselton, Anthony C. 39, 42, 251, 252, 274
Thomas, D. Winton 141
Torrance, J.B. 193
Torrey, C.C. 258
Toy, Crawford H. 29, 33, 35, 87, 109, 141, 146,
    252

Urbach, E.E. 58, 60, 157, 210, 266

van Roon, A. 8
van Unnik, W.C. 77, 82
Vermes Geza 153, 199, 200, 201, 203
Via, Dan Otto 16, 19, 20, 86
Vlachos, C. 20
von Rad, Gerhard 8, 9, 32, 39
Vriezen, Th. C. 32, 38, 110, 141

Währisch, H. 193
Wallis, Gerhard 193
Wanke, J. 9
Ward, R.B. 1, 10, 19, 85, 87, 91
Weiser, Artur 27, 38, 107, 145
Weiss, K. 20
Wernberg-Möller, P. 154, 202
Wessell, W.W. 1, 14, 21
Westermann, Claus 190, 191
White, R.E.O. 16, 20
White, William, Jr. 193
Whitaker, G.H. 168, 169
Whybray, R.N. 15
Wicks, Henry 198
Wilkinson, J. 236, 237
Williams, James G. 14, 38, 108
Winston, David 8, 43, 47, 79
Wolverton, Wallace J. 20
Worrell, John Edward 8
Wuellner, Wilhelm 14
Wurthwein, Ernst 9

Young, Franklin 253

Ziegler, Joseph 43, 45, 196
Zimmerli, Walther 9
Zimmerman, Frank 258
Zmijewski, Joseph 12, 13, 19, 20

Index of Names and Subjects

Aaron 29, 33, 34, 154
Abraham 21, 72, 224, 253, 277
Adam and Eve 144, 253
Adultery against God 224, 244, 246
Ananias and Sapphiara 122
Anger 28, 43, 49, 50, 51, 56, 64, 71, 75, 86, 88, 89,
    98, 99, 116, 118, 136, 137, 140, 144, 145, 153,
    157, 160, 166, 168, 169, 171, 177, 178, 180,
    182, 198, 278, 285
— appropriate 166
— as fire 105, 118
— meaning of Greek words 88
Arrogance 50, 108, 122, 143, 150, 155, 157, 199,
    210, 217, 225, 229, 247
Athenians 119, 165, 269, 270, 271

Balaam 36, 41, 116
baptism 17, 21, 183
Beelzebub 221
Belial 50, 53, 114, 153, 201, 260-261
Beliar 259
birth 17, 228
blasphemy 114, 184-185, 193-196, 198-199, 202-
    203, 209-210, 214, 217, 220-221, 247-248,
    256, 284, 285
— capital punishment 209
— of Christ 183-184, 284
— definition 193
— denial of Christ 221
— examples 194-195, 247
— gentiles 198
— of the Holy Spirit 221
— indirect 198, 203, 210, 214, 217, 221, 247,
    256, 284, 285
— insulting the Teacher of Righteousness 203
— Israel's enemies 194, 198
— laughter 194
— Jesus accused of 220
— meaning of word 183
— speaking God's name 202, 209-210, 217
Blessing 40, 41, 48, 55, 94, 131, 159, 173, 185
Blood 109, 114, 135, 136, 142, 150, 156
Boasting 122, 126, 138, 160, 167, 198, 221, 234,
    247-248, 278, 282

— as blasphemy 195, 210, 217, 247, 285
— in Christ 221
Boorish 44, 57, 150, 160
Bridle 61, 125

Catechetical instruction 21, 22, 90
Ceremonial 97, 127
Chatter See Speech, mindless
Christian community See Christianity
Christianity 10, 17, 21, 22, 76, 78, 87, 96, 103,
    121, 135, 171
— defense of faith 77
Christians See Christianity
— verbal fighting 135-136, 235
Christology 17
Commandments
— of Christ 80
— of God 35, 53, 80, 204
Confession See Prayer, confession
Confession
— mutual 239, 246
Conflict See Dissension
Congenial 57
Counselor 42, 249
Court 143, 146-147, 158, 166, 170
Curse 30, 40, 41, 48, 56, 59, 60, 107, 130, 131,
    133, 142, 144-145, 150, 156-157, 164, 172,
    177, 178, 180, 182, 184
— appropriate 144, 156-157, 165
— careless 144, 150, 165
— examples 144
— God sovereign over 144, 150, 166
— inappropriate 144, 150, 157, 165
— repay with blessing 173

Daniel 33, 34, 36, 152, 198
David 30, 32, 33, 34, 36, 37, 40, 106, 143, 144,
    189, 253, 256, 277
Deaf 40
Deceit See Flattery and Lying
— as thievery 157
Demons 76, 82, 130, 237
Dissension 24, 145, 147, 150, 154, 157, 160, 171,
    173, 180-181, 182, 247, 289

Disobedience 36
— to the gospel 81
Divine Logos 116
Doeg 116
Doer 66, 93, 94, 95, 96, 101
Double tongue 112, 169
Doubleheartedness See Doublemindedness
Doublemindedness 20, 100, 113, 117, 169, 177,
    242, 245, 246
Drunk 61, 71
Dualism 260-261

Ears 33, 35, 46, 52, 57, 64, 71, 79, 101, 143
Eli 36
Eleazar 46
Elihu 30, 32, 192
Elijah 21, 29, 103, 191, 240-241, 288
Elisha 49, 143, 144
Envy 122, 227, 228
Esau 41
Eschatology 9, 12, 16, 17, 18, 76, 91, 94, 103,
    108, 128, 176, 180, 181, 186, 231, 278
Etiquette 44, 57, 66, 73, 112, 140, 151, 174
Eusebius 1
Evil 50, 53, 56, 59, 75, 89
— desires 182
— discovered 110
— of mankind 89, 98, 118, 120, 121, 124
— of mouth 109
— of tongue remedy 110-111, 115, 133
— words 105
— world 98-99, 102, 127, 183, 224

Faith 10, 16, 17, 20, 51, 77, 103, 185, 275
— profession of 102
False speech See Lying
Flattery 81, 122, 145-146, 151, 153, 157, 164,
    165, 168, 169, 170, 171, 178, 182, 267
— definition 145
— worst use of speech 164
Fool 28, 29, 32, 34, 43, 44, 45, 63, 109, 144, 145,
    151
Forgiveness 40, 170-172, 186, 209
Frankness 163
Freedom 19
Friendship 110, 141, 146, 149, 162, 243
— betrayed by cursing 165
— beware 145, 150, 161, 170
— false 164-165, 169, 170, 184
— with God 229, 230, 243, 288
— hurt by gossip 142
— with world 224, 229, 230, 243

Gloat 144

Gluttony 61
God
— creator 16, 35, 49, 84, 91, 127, 131, 150, 158,
    185, 193, 196, 201, 215, 228, 264, 281
— enemy of 224
— fear of 35, 149, 187
— gracious speech 33
— image of 156
— jealous 227
— as judge 179, 181, 182
— judgment of 107, 108, 112, 115, 123, 137, 143,
    172, 179, 181, 182, 189, 224, 243, 254, 257,
    278, 281
— justice of 31, 51, 196
— knowledge of 91
— nature of 28
— not deceived 113
— not envious 226-227
— obedience to 35, 45, 47, 52, 243
— one 215
— punishment of See judgment of
— relationship with 99, 101, 104, 187, 223, 224,
    230, 239, 243, 244, 248
— Shechinah 207
— sovereignty 16, 25, 31, 41, 42, 48, 53, 57, 70,
    127, 196, 201, 220, 233, 234, 235, 243, 260,
    283, 288
— true speech 252-253, 258, 263, 271-272, 274,
    281-282, 285
— unity See one
— wise 20, 25, 29, 30, 35, 45, 47, 52, 57, 247
Gospel 19, 76, 77, 81, 83, 90, 93, 96, 101, 103,
    171, 221
— true 122
Gossip 55, 69, 71, 136, 139-140, 141-142, 149,
    153, 155, 161, 169, 171, 172, 178, 180, 182,
    267
Gossiper
— stay away from 142, 150, 161
— as traitor 161
Grace 225-227, 230, 231, 247
— greater 223, 228, 229, 231, 247
— lesser 225

Hagar 143
Hannah 143, 191
Harmony 28, 72, 73, 87, 99, 139, 140, 141, 154,
    160, 168, 170, 171, 173, 175, 181, 283, 285,
    286
Healing 17, 31
Heart 32, 33, 34, 35, 36, 37, 42, 45, 46, 48, 50, 52,
    53, 57, 59, 78, 91, 236
— good 75, 108
— evil speech 75, 108, 109, 112, 117, 119, 122,
    138, 171

Hebrew 92, 94, 229
Hillel 56
Holy Spirit 11, 78, 82, 83, 219, 221, 228
— blasphemy of 221
Honesty 57, 260, 267
Hot-tempered speech See Anger
Humility 29, 89, 167, 176, 192, 199, 210, 225, 229, 248

Idolatry 157, 198, 258, 264
Impartiality
— judges 140, 147, 152, 158, 165, 170, 285, 286
— God 148, 152, 158, 170, 174, 282
Instruction
-- catechetical See Catechetical instruction
— children 64, 65, 163
— good 31, 33, 34, 53, 62, 65
— from parents 35, 46, 47, 58, 65, 72
— unqualified 56
Insult See Mockery
Internalization 26, 48, 72
Isaac 41
Israel 36, 37, 41, 53, 146, 208, 255
— as blasphemer 194
— no deceit 108
— evil 108
— as object of slander 143

Jacob 41, 253, 256
James, Epistle of
-- audience 290
— author 4, 9, 84, 123, 290
— catchwords 15, 21
— Christian nature 290
— Christology 16
— date 4
— ethical character 6
— ethical themes 20
— ethics 13, 15, 16, 18, 19, 21
— imperatives 6
— importance of speech-ethics 6, 7, 290
— multiple themes 15
— outlines 14, 15
— persuasive 14
— prophetic 12
— research 1, 2
— purpose 100
— style 125
— sub-Christian 15,16
— as wisdom literature 8, 289
Jeremiah 37, 143
jealousy 10
Jerusalem 31, 53, 114, 159, 194, 198
Jesus
— divine 220-221

— imitating 21, 173
— as peace 171
— teachings 9, 17, 18, 93, 96, 162, 172
— wisdom 8, 72
Jethro 34
Job 21, 29, 34, 37, 111, 184, 194
Joke 163, 170, 253
Joseph 33, 34, 36, 44, 71, 74, 149, 151, 152, 272
Joshua 49, 144
Josiah 37
Judas Maccabeus 48, 197, 198
Judging one another 171, 172, 178
Judith 46, 197, 198
Justice 53
Justification 17, 20

Kawwanah 205, 207
King 27, 31, 42, 43, 47, 48, 105, 106, 149, 189, 198, 220, 249
Kingdom of God 18, 79, 91

Laughter 61, 146, 153, 162, 263, 167, 230
— as blasphemy 194
Law 9, 36, 45, 46, 50, 51, 52, 53, 81, 92, 93, 95, 178-179, 202, 261
— Decalogue 18, 142, 170
— of freedom 19, 96, 101
— judging 178
— of love 18, 96, 179, 182, 183, 288
— royal 18, 19, 20, 179
Liar
— high priest 261
Liars
— everyone 253, 258, 268, 275, 282
— examples 253, 261, 264
Lie
— noble 269, 272-273
Lips 23, 27, 31, 32, 33, 38, 45, 46, 50, 53, 56, 67, 70, 106, 107, 108, 109, 111, 114, 121, 195, 196, 197, 200, 210, 250, 252, 254, 255, 258
Listening
— to others 25-26, 33-37, 46, 52, 53, 58, 64-66, 71, 79-80, 87, 88, 100, 283
— to Jesus 79, 100, 283
— to the Epistle of James 100
— to God 35-39, 47, 52-53, 58, 65, 72, 80, 87, 100, 283
— to parent 65
— to Scripture 71, 87, 92, 100
— to the wise 46, 58, 65-66, 100
Love See also Law, of love
— neighbor 18, 19, 20, 101, 170, 181
Luther 1
Lying 3, 50, 105, 107, 108, 109, 112, 119, 120, 122, 138, 160, 162, 167, 185, 247, 252, 253-

255, 258, 264, 268, 272-273, 275, 282
— spiritual damage 250, 255
— God hates 254, 258
— rebellion against God 275

Man
— inability to control tongue 129
— inner 32, 45, 73, 75, 91, 95, 96, 97, 99, 100, 101, 108, 113, 127, 136, 138, 177, 230, 242
— mastery over animals 129
— righteous 31, 109, 111
— wicked 27, 36, 113, 115, 123, 132, 145
— wise 29, 32, 33, 43, 44, 55, 56, 57, 63, 188
Mary (sister of Martha) 79
Maturity 20, 38, 71, 87, 101, 102, 163, 186, 243, 251, 283
— complete See Perfection
Meditate 46, 52
Memorization 34
Men
— wickedness demonstrated by speech 107, 112, 119, 120, 137, 141
— wicked See Man, wicked
— as liars 245, 268, 275, 282, 285
Merchant 231, 234
Micah 40
Mind 24, 25, 61, 64, 70, 72, 73, 168
— of Christ 78
Miriam
— slander of Moses 143, 156, 169
Mockery 61, 136, 143-144, 150, 153, 156, 160, 162, 169, 171, 172, 177, 180, 182, 184, 194
— Christian expect 127-173, 183, 286
— definition 143
Moses 29, 31, 33, 34, 35, 37, 46, 56, 60, 71, 74, 143, 169, 189, 203, 216, 272, 273
Mourn 230
Mouth 23, 27, 28, 29, 30, 38, 43, 45, 46, 50, 51, 53, 57, 58, 61, 65, 70, 78, 106, 107, 108, 149, 196

Nebuchadnezzer 48, 257
New Testament 3, 5, 8, 16, 18, 94, 128, 132

Oaths 165, 250, 253, 255, 257, 259, 264-266, 269, 273, 274, 275, 278-280
— absolute ban 275, 278-280, 281, 286
— casuistry 276, 280
— conditions for swearing 266, 274
— definition 255-256
— dishonest intentions 271, 276, 281
— examples 256, 259, 262, 269, 277
— forbidden types 266, 270, 274
— God keeps 253
— God sovereign over 170, 265, 281

— imprecatory 166
— keeping 256, 259, 265, 269, 273-274
— in the name of God only 256, 259
— not in God's name 259, 262, 269
— useful in society 265, 269-270
Oaths and vows
— breaking 257, 265, 273
— caution 262, 265-266, 269, 270-271, 273, 285
Obedience 16, 17, 26, 35, 37, 47, 53, 58, 66, 72, 92, 95, 101, 283
Old Testament 3, 12, 18, 27-43, 80, 100, 154, 158, 226
Onias 46
Orator 65, 67, 68, 71, 73, 119, 164
Order 139, 140, 187, 249

Paraenesis 12.-13, 22
Partiality 18, 102, 140, 147-148, 152, 158, 164, 168, 172, 180, 182, 184, 285
Patience 20, 25, 28, 32, 56, 57, 77, 180, 184, 278
Paul 8, 16
Peace 10, 25, 100, 149, 151, 154, 168, 170-171, 175-176, 181, 283, 285
Perfection 20, 21
Perjury 136, 146-147, 151, 152, 158, 165, 168, 170, 171, 173, 177, 178, 180, 182-184
— against God 159
Personal speech-ethics
— basic concern of humanity 284
— definition 2
— disclaimers of book 4
— distinctive ideas in James 287-289
— fivefold division in James 2-3, 4, 283-284
— Judaism 5
— Mediterranean world 3, 284
— objectives of background literature 4
— organization of book 4
— primary theme in the Epistle of James 2, 283, 289
— purpose of book 5
— spiritual crisis 182, 287
— standard ideas missing from James 284
Planning 232-233, 235, 248, 288
Pleasures
— evil 135
— harmful to prayer 223, 245, 247
— personified as lover 168-169
— selfish 223, 228, 229, 247-248
Pharisees 79, 81, 97
Pharaoh 33, 34
Poor 100, 143, 147, 152, 158
Praise of children 163
Praise of God 70, 130, 133, 188-190, 196-198, 199, 201, 204, 211, 214-216, 218-219, 243-244, 283, 285

— all senses 215
— continual 199-200, 204, 211, 218, 244, 285
— daily See continual
— empowered by Spirit 219
— examples 197
— impure 131, 215
— rational 219
— reason for 196, 200, 201, 204, 205, 215, 218, 219, 244, 285
— silence 204
— sincere 190, 196-197, 200, 204, 215, 216, 244
— singing 189-190, 201, 211, 215-216, 219, 236, 244, 283, 285
— thanksgiving 190, 204, 211, 218, 244
— words inadequate 204, 211, 214
Praise of man discouraged 158
Prayer 27, 46, 49, 56-57, 96, 103, 187, 190-193, 197-198, 201-202, 205-209, 212-214, 216-217, 219-200, 222, 227, 235-243, 244-247, 283-284, 285
— answer delayed 216
— confession 188, 192, 197, 202, 209, 216, 220, 230, 239, 284
— continual 187, 191, 208, 219
-- through Christ 219
— daily See continual
— corporate 201-202, 207, 219
— doubt 242-243, 245
— of Elijah 240-241, 245-246
— with effort 213-214, 216, 240, 246
— faith 238, 242
— family 187
— favor of gods 187, 212
— fixed 206, 208
— forgiveness of God 193, 197, 212, 220, 230, 231, 236, 238-239
— heard by God 191, 197, 207, 213, 236, 238, 241
— intercessory 198, 208, 212, 216, 220, 239, 246-247, 284, 286
— — examples 220
— — requesting 220
— kawwanah 205, 207
— mark of devout Christian 246
— merging with God's desires 213, 219, 223, 245
— not answered 191-192, 213, 216, 220, 222, 242-243, 244, 245, 246
— persistence 214
— petitionary 191, 197-198, 201, 202, 207, 212, 216, 219-220, 222, 236, 240, 242-246, 283, 285
— examples 197-190, 212, 216-217, 245
— relationship to praise 191
— request for wisdom 243, 245

— righteous more effective 216, 239-241, 246, 286
— purification 216
— Shema 206
— for sickness 208, 212-213, 214, 236, 246, 286
— sin and sickness 198, 236, 238-239, 246
— sincere 187, 192, 205, 209, 216, 246, 285
— spontaneous 205, 219, 244
— successful 104, 150, 192, 197, 205, 207, 213-214, 223, 238-242, 245-246, 285
— Tefillah 206, 208, 209
— use of oil 236-237, 246
— for wisdom 213, 245
Preaching 76, 83, 90, 101
Pride
— root of blasphemy 195-196, 198-199, 217
Prophetic writing 9, 12
Prophets 52, 87, 103, 106, 253
— false 253, 264
Proverb 85, 175, 229, 235, 275
— tripartite See Tripartite proverb

Q 8
quarreling See Dissensions

Rahab 21
Rebekah 41
Receive
— meaning of word 91
Religion 96, 97, 98, 99, 102, 138, 274, 281
Repent 230, 243, 247, 248
Reproof 51, 148, 154, 158-159, 163, 169, 174, 186
Respect 29, 30
Rich 12, 99, 130, 142, 150, 158, 182, 184, 185, 218, 235, 246, 247
— as liars 254
Riddles 33
Righteousness 53, 175-176
— of God 88, 89, 100, 113, 137
Rudder 125, 126

Salvation 99, 101, 220, 228, 231, 239, 275
Samson 33
Samuel 36, 47
Sarah 143, 197
Satan 111, 128, 218, 229, 230, 285
— as liar 122, 174, 264, 275
Saul 32, 40, 41, 57, 191
Scripture 72, 79, 85, 100, 225, 226
— as wisdom 80
Secrecy 51, 161
Self-control 60-61, 69
Self-deception 93, 95, 96, 185, 282
Self-righteousness 30
Sennacherib 194, 195, 198
the Seventy 91

Shame 162, 163, 165, 182, 184, 259
Shammai 56
Shimei 40
Silence
— bad 51, 57, 70, 121, 200
— evangelist 76
— good 24-25, 29-31, 44-45, 49, 51, 56-57, 62, 67, 70, 72, 76, 149
— Jesus' 76
— powerful 70, 74
Simon Maccabeus 52, 114, 197
Sin 28, 40, 44, 49, 57, 59, 98, 103, 118, 121
— confess 113
— of omission 234-235
— with tongue 111
Sincerity 100
Slander 55, 116, 122, 136, 142-144, 149-150, 153, 155-156, 162, 169, 171, 172, 177, 180, 182, 183, 267, 285, 286
— definition 142
— of family 139
— prominent in New Testament 172
— punished by God 155
— repayed with slander 162
— repeating 140
— by serpent 155-156
— worst evil 139, 142, 155, 161, 285
Slanderer
— examples 169
— stay away from 149
— Solomon 33, 34, 37, 40, 47, 49, 189
Speech See also Tongue and Words
— beneficial to others 139
— careless See mindless
— coarse 152, 159, 160, 167, 169, 170, 171, 174
— contentious See Discussion
— control 23-25, 27-33, 43-46, 49-51, 55-58, 60-64, 69-71, 75-79, 87, 99-100, 124-125, 127, 278, 283
— dedicated to God 168
— eloquent 45
— filthy See coarse
— hot-tempered See Anger
— idle See mindless
— impartial 100
— gracious 28, 31, 32, 33, 35, 36, 45-46, 50, 57, 63, 77, 87, 100, 108, 132, 154, 173, 283
— judge of character 122
— means and extremes 160
— mindless 23, 24, 47, 50, 61, 63, 75, 96, 101, 117, 118, 139, 169
— obscene See coarse
— penalties for 152
— positive potential 141, 159
— quick 33, 56, 169

— successful 23
— tactless See Tactlessness
— timely 31, 70, 87
— true thoughts 100
— of women 55, 76, 155, 165, 170, 172
Spirit, human 226, 227, 228
Spirit, Holy See Holy Spirit
Suffering 235, 246, 278

Tactlessness 146, 151, 152, 160, 163, 182
Teacher of Righteousness 51, 53, 153, 201, 202, 203, 261
— blasphemy of See Blasphemy, insulting the Teacher of Righteousness
Teachers
— Christian 87, 92, 124
— evaluation of speech 124
— false 53, 114, 124, 173, 174, 185, 186, 210, 275
— judgment of 123, 134, 137
— wise 22, 23, 25, 185, See also Counselor
Teaching See Instruction
Teeth 61, 107, 114, 118
— as guards over tongue 118
Temptation 99
Theraputae 71, 216
Tongue 25, 29, 30, 38, 42, 53, 56, 61, 64, 65, 70, 101, 125, 181, 247
— as agent of Satan 128, 131, 137, 138, 283, 285
— as cancerous infection 127, 135
— destructive power 105-106, 111, 115, 116, 117, 118, 121, 127, 128, 129, 137, 283, 285, 286
— evil personified 105-107, 111, 115, 120, 126, 127, 130, 285
— inconsistent 131, 185
— as murderer 116, 135, 150, 151, 155, 156, 177, 254, 285
— as poison See like serpent
— potential for good 115, 117
— like serpent 106, 110, 130, 137
— tendency toward evil 132, 133, 136-137, 247, 283, 285
— as weapon 106, 110, 111, 112, 114, 116, 141, 142, 145, 254
Torah 57, 58, 60, 115, 266
— drawing near to 154
— helps control evil tongue 117
— study of 155
Tripartite proverb 85-87, 89, 92, 96, 99, 101
— origin 85-87
True speech See also Truth
— basic to Christianity 279, 280, 282
— defined 251
— eternal 252

— from God 258, 263, 272, 274
— God as standard 252, 253, 258, 260, 264, 268, 274
— natural 268, 272
— objective and subjective 251
Truth 17, 19, 51, 52, 70, 160, 168, 249-252, 257, 260-263, 284, 285
— anger as enemy 272
— characteristic of wise man 249, 252, 257, 263, 282
— divine 267, 271
— doing 53, 257, 260, 263
— fight for 257, 260-261
— gauge of good character 249, 280, 282
— the gospel 274-275, 281, 286
— importance 250, 251-252, 263, 267, 274, 279, 285
— importance to speech 249, 257, 263, 267, 285
— internal 250, 272
— Jesus 274
— precision 249, 252
— prophets 253, 272
— quality for friendship 250, 252, 267
— Spirit 274

Verbosity 28, 44, 57, 61, 62, 169
Vices 89, 171
Vow, Great 273
Vows See also Oaths, 40, 50, 200, 255-257, 259, 264-266, 269, 273
— definition 255
— keeping 256, 259, 265, 269, 273
Vulgarity 61, 73, 90, 171

Waiting 30, 32
Widows and orphans 98, 102, 148, 162, 201, 216, 218
Wisdom
— a gift from God 11
— horizontal 35
— Epistle of James 19
— relationship with Spirit 11
— traits 100
Wisdom Literature
— Babylonian 3, 7, 31
— characteristics 8-9
— Egyptian 3, 7, 31
— Graeco-Roman 3, 5, 8, 9, 132
— Jewish 9
— Near Eastern 5, 23-27, 31, 38
— Rabbinic 3, 8, 128
— Origin 7-8
Words
— of God 17, 36, 83, 91
— implanted 17, 19, 89, 90, 92, 93, 96, 99, 100, 101, 103, 228, 286

— oral, superior 3
— of truth 18, 19
— written, inferior 3
Words
— abusive 40, 122, 140, 150, 162, 173, 247, 283
— as animals 106-107, 114, 116, 130
— basis of God's judgment 113
— dangerous 61, 70, 74, 106, 110, 114
— destructive 38, 48, 101, 106, 114, 159, 254
— disrespectful 56, 63, 90
— as drugs 68, 74
— eternal 26-27, 38-42, 48, 67, 69, 82
— like fire 24, 105, 111, 114, 116, 126, 127, 137, 143, 161, 254
— poignant 32, 57
— foolish 50
— gauge of character 30, 75
— healing 31, 104
— inspiring 48
— insufficient 204, 286
— insulting See disrespectful
— irretrievable 74
— judgment of 75
— of kindness 31, 63, 70, 71
— limitations 42
— magical 41, 60, 104
— malicious See disrespectful
— many See Verbosity
— power of 26-27, 38-42, 48-49, 54-55, 59-60, 62, 67-69, 74, 81-83, 102-104, 283
— beneficial 124-125, 159
— — convictions 68, 83
— — God's 59, 74, 79
— — God's grace 77
— — gospel 103, 283
— — Jesus' 81-82, 286
— — names 39
— — salvation 93
— — Torah 59
— — understanding 74
— of prostitute 74
— reviling See disrespectful
— silly 50, 171
— simple See succinct
— smooth 67, 106, 110, 117, 145, 153, 157, 251
— succinct 28, 29, 33, 44, 57, 58, 63
— as things 39
— as traps 106, 114
— travel of 24, 142, 162, 169
— vulgar See Vulgarity
Worship 76, 87, 92, 96, 97, 199-201, 215, 218-219
— corporate 190, 199, 218
— of Jesus 218
— rational 215

Wissenschaftliche Untersuchungen zum Neuen Testament

Alphabetical Index
of the first and second series

Appold, Mark L.: The Oneness Motif in the Fourth Gospel. 1976. *Volume II/1.*
Bachmann, Michael: Sünder oder Übertreter. 1991. *Volume 59.*
Baker, William R.: Personal Speech-Ethics. 1995. *Volume II/68.*
Bammel, Ernst: Judaica. 1986. *Volume 37.*
Bauernfeind, Otto: Kommentar und Studien zur Apostelgeschichte. 1980. *Volume 22.*
Bayer, Hans Friedrich: Jesus' Predictions of Vindication and Resurrection. 1986. *Volume II/20.*
Betz, Otto: Jesus, der Messias Israels. 1987. *Volume 42.*
– Jesus, der Herr der Kirche. 1990. *Volume 52.*
Beyschlag, Karlmann: Simon Magnus und die christliche Gnosis. 1974. *Volume 16.*
Bittner, Wolfgang J.: Jesu Zeichen im Johannesevangelium. 1987. *Volume II/26.*
Bjerkelund, Carl J.: Tauta Egeneto. 1987. *Volume 40.*
Blackburn, Barry Lee: 'Theios Anēr' and the Markan Miracle Traditions. 1991. *Volume II/40.*
Bockmuehl, Markus N. A.: Revelation and Mystery in Ancient Judaism and Pauline Christianity. 1990. *Volume II/36.*
Böhlig, Alexander: Gnosis und Synkretismus. Part 1. 1989. *Volume 47* – Part 2. 1989. *Volume 48.*
Böttrich, Christfried: Weltweisheit – Menschheitsethik – Urkult. 1992. *Volume II/50.*
Büchli, Jörg: Der Poimandres – ein paganisiertes Evangelium. 1987. *Volume II/27.*
Bühner, Jan A.: Der Gesandte und sein Weg im 4. Evangelium. 1977. *Volume II/2.*
Burchard, Christoph: Untersuchungen zu Joseph und Aseneth. 1965. *Volume 8.*
Cancik, Hubert (Ed.): Markus-Philologie. 1984. *Volume 33.*
Capes, David B.: Old Testament Yaweh Texts in Paul's Christology. 1992. *Volume II/47.*
Caragounis, Chrys C.: The Son of Man. 1986. *Volume 38.*
– see *Fridrichsen.*
Carleton Paget, James: The Epistle of Barnabas. 1994. *Volume II/64.*
Crump, David: Jesus the Intercessor. 1992. *Volume II/49.*
Deines, Roland: Jüdische Steingefäße und pharisäische Frömmigkeit. 1993. *Volume II/52.*
Dobbeler, Axel von: Glaube als Teilhabe. 1987. *Volume II/22.*
Dunn, James D. G. (Ed.): Jews and Christians. 1992. *Volume 66.*
Ebertz, Michael N.: Das Charisma des Gekreuzigten. 1987. *Volume 45.*
Eckstein, Hans-Joachim: Der Begriff der Syneidesis bei Paulus. 1983. *Volume II/10.*
Ego, Beate: Im Himmel wie auf Erden. 1989. *Volume II/34.*
Ellis, E. Earle: Prophecy and Hermeneutic in Early Christianity. 1978. *Volume 18.*
– The Old Testament in Early Christianity. 1991. *Volume 54.*
Ennulat, Andreas: Die ›Minor Agreements‹. 1994. *Volume II/62.*
Feldmeier, Reinhard: Die Krisis des Gottessohnes. 1987. *Volume II/21.*
– Die Christen als Fremde. 1992. *Volume 64.*
Feldmeier, Reinhard and *Ulrich Heckel* (Ed.): Die Heiden. 1994. *Volume 70.*
Fornberg, Tord: see *Fridrichsen.*
Fossum, Jarl E.: The Name of God and the Angel of the Lord. 1985. *Volume 36.*
Fridrichsen, Anton: Exegetical Writings. Ed. by C. C. Caragounis and T. Fornberg. 1994. *Volume 76.*
Garlington, Don B.: The Obedience of Faith. 1991. *Volume II/38.*
– Faith, Obedience and Perseverance. 1994. *Volume 79.*
Garnet, Paul: Salvation and Atonement in the Qumran Scrolls. 1977. *Volume II/3.*
Grässer, Erich: Der Alte Bund im Neuen. 1985. *Volume 35.*
Green, Joel B.: The Death of Jesus. 1988. *Volume II/33.*
Gundry Volf, Judith M.: Paul and Perseverance. 1990. *Volume II/37.*
Hafemann, Scott J.: Suffering and the Spirit. 1986. *Volume II/19.*
Heckel, Theo K.: Der Innere Mensch. 1993. *Volume II/53.*
Heckel, Ulrich: Kraft in Schwachheit. 1993. *Volume II/56.*
– see *Feldmeier.*
– see *Hengel.*

Heiligenthal, Roman: Werke als Zeichen. 1983. *Volume II/9.*
Hemer, Colin J.: The Book of Acts in the Setting of Hellenistic History. 1989. *Volume 49.*
Hengel, Martin: Judentum und Hellenismus. 1969, ³1988. *Volume 10.*
– Die johanneische Frage. 1993. *Volume 67.*
Hengel, Martin and *Ulrich Heckel* (Ed.): Paulus und das antike Judentum. 1991. *Volume 58.*
Hengel, Martin and *Hermut Löhr* (Ed.): Schriftauslegung. 1994. *Volume 73.*
Hengel, Martin and *Anna Maria Schwemer* (Ed.): Königsherrschaft Gottes und himmlischer Kult.
    1991. *Volume 55.*
– Die Septuaginta. 1994. *Volume 72.*
Herrenbrück, Fritz: Jesus und die Zöllner. 1990. *Volume II/41.*
Hofius, Otfried: Katapausis. 1970. *Volume 11.*
– Der Vorhang vor dem Thron Gottes. 1972. *Volume 14.*
– Der Christushymnus Philipper 2,6 – 11. 1976, ²1991. *Volume 17.*
– Paulusstudien. 1989, ²1994. *Volume 51.*
Holtz, Traugott: Geschichte und Theologie des Urchristentums. Ed. by Eckart Reinmuth
    and Christian Wolff. 1991. *Volume 57.*
Hommel, Hildebrecht: Sebasmata. Volume 1. 1983. *Volume 31.* – Volume 2. 1984. *Volume 32.*
Kähler, Christoph: Jesu Gleichnisse als Poesie und Therapie. 1995. *Volume 78.*
Kamlah, Ehrhard: Die Form der katalogischen Paränese im Neuen Testament. 1964. *Volume 7.*
Kim, Seyoon: The Origin of Paul's Gospel. 1981, ²1984. *Volume II/4.*
– »The ›Son of Man‹« as the Son of God. 1983. *Volume 30.*
Kleinknecht, Karl Th.: Der leidende Gerechtfertigte. 1984, ²1988. *Volume II/13.*
Klinghardt, Matthias: Gesetz und Volk Gottes. 1988. *Volume II/32.*
Köhler, Wolf-Dietrich: Rezeption des Matthäusevangeliums in der Zeit vor Irenäus. 1987.
    Volume II/24.
Korn, Manfred: Die Geschichte Jesu in veränderter Zeit. 1993. *Volume II/51.*
Koskenniemi, Erkki: Apollonios von Tyana in der neutestamentlichen Exegese. 1994. *Volume II/61.*
Kuhn, Karl G.: Achtzehngebet und Vaterunser und der Reim. 1950. *Volume 1.*
Lampe, Peter: Die stadtrömischen Christen in den ersten beiden Jahrhunderten. 1987, ²1989.
    Volume II/18.
Lieu, Samuel N. C.: Manichaeism in the Later Roman Empire and Medieval China. 1992. *Volume 63.*
Löhr, Hermut: see *Hengel.*
Maier, Gerhard: Mensch und freier Wille. 1971. *Volume 12.*
– Die Johannesoffenbarung und die Kirche. 1981. *Volume 25.*
Markschies, Christoph: Valentinus Gnosticus? 1992. *Volume 65.*
Marshall, Peter: Enmity in Corinth: Social Conventions in Paul's Relations with the Corinthians. 1987.
    Volume II/23.
Meade, David G.: Pseudonymity and Canon. 1986. *Volume 39.*
Mell, Ulrich: Die »anderen« Winzer. 1994. *Volume 77.*
Mengel, Berthold: Studien zum Philipperbrief. 1982. *Volume II/8.*
Merkel, Helmut: Die Widersprüche zwischen den Evangelien. 1971. *Volume 13.*
Merklein, Helmut: Studien zu Jesus und Paulus. 1987. *Volume 43.*
Metzler, Karin: Der griechische Begriff des Verzeihens. 1991. *Volume II/44.*
Niebuhr, Karl-Wilhelm: Gesetz und Paränese. 1987. *Volume II/28.*
– Heidenapostel aus Israel. 1992. *Volume 62.*
Nissen, Andreas: Gott und der Nächste im antiken Judentum. 1974. *Volume 15.*
Noormann, Rolf: Irenäus als Paulusinterpret. 1994. *Volume II/66.*
Okure, Teresa: The Johannine Approach to Mission. 1988. *Volume II/31.*
Philonenko, Marc (Ed.): Le Trône de Dieu. 1993. *Volume 69.*
Pilhofer, Peter: Presbyteron Kreitton. 1990. *Volume II/39.*
Pöhlmann, Wolfgang: Der Verlorene Sohn und das Haus. 1993. *Volume 68.*
Probst, Hermann: Paulus und der Brief. 1991. *Volume II/45.*
Räisänen, Heikki: Paul and the Law. 1983, ²1987. *Volume 29.*
Rehkopf, Friedrich: Die lukanische Sonderquelle. 1959. *Volume 5.*
Reinmuth, Eckart: Pseudo-Philo und Lukas. 1994. *Volume 74.*
– see *Holtz.*
Reiser, Marius: Syntax und Stil des Markusevangeliums. 1984. *Volume II/11.*
Richards, E. Randolph: The Secretary in the Letters of Paul. 1991. *Volume II/42.*

Wissenschaftliche Untersuchungen zum Neuen Testament

Riesner, Rainer: Jesus als Lehrer. 1981, [3]1988. *Volume II/7.*
– Die Frühzeit des Apostels Paulus. 1994. *Volume 71.*
Rissi, Mathias: Die Theologie des Hebräerbriefs. 1987. *Volume 41.*
Röhser, Günter: Metaphorik und Personifikation der Sünde. 1987. *Volume II/25.*
Rose, Christian: Die Wolke der Zeugen. 1994. *Volume II/60.*
Rüger, Hans Peter: Die Weisheitsschrift aus der Kairoer Geniza. 1991. *Volume 53.*
Salzmann, Jorg Christian: Lehren und Ermahnen. 1994. *Volume II/59.*
Sänger, Dieter: Antikes Judentum und die Mysterien. 1980. *Volume II/5.*
– Die Verkündigung des Gekreuzigten und Israel. 1994. *Volume 75.*
Sandnes, Karl Olav: Paul – One of the Prophets? 1991. *Volume II/43.*
Sato, Migaku: Q und Prophetie. 1988. *Volume II/29.*
Schimanowski, Gottfried: Weisheit und Messias. 1985. *Volume II/17.*
Schlichting, Günter: Ein jüdisches Leben Jesu. 1982. *Volume 24.*
Schnabel, Eckhard J.: Law and Wisdom from Ben Sira to Paul. 1985. *Volume II/16.*
Schutter, William L.: Hermeneutic and Composition in I Peter. 1989. *Volume II/30.*
Schwartz, Daniel R.: Studies in the Jewish Background of Christianity. 1992. *Volume 60.*
Schwemer, A. M.: see *Hengel.*
Scott, James M.: Adoption as Sons of God. 1992. *Volume II/48.*
Siegert, Folker: Drei hellenistisch-jüdische Predigten. Part 1. 1980. *Volume 20.* – Part 2. 1992.
    Volume 61.
– Nag-Hammadi-Register. 1982. *Volume 26.*
– Argumentation bei Paulus. 1985. *Volume 34.*
– Philon von Alexandrien. 1988. *Volume 46.*
Simon, Marcel: Le christianisme antique et son contexte religieux I/II. 1981. *Volume 23.*
Snodgrass, Klyne: The Parable of the Wicked Tenants. 1983. *Volume 27.*
Sommer, Urs: Die Passionsgeschichte des Markusevangeliums. 1993. *Volume II/58.*
Spangenberg, Volker: Herrlichkeit des Neuen Bundes. 1993. *Volume II/55.*
Speyer, Wolfgang: Frühes Christentum im antiken Strahlungsfeld. 1989. *Volume 50.*
Stadelmann, Helge: Ben Sira als Schriftgelehrter. 1980. *Volume II/6.*
Strobel, August: Die Stunde der Wahrheit. 1980. *Volume 21.*
Stuckenbruck, Loren: Angel Veneration and Christology. 1995. *Volume II/70.*
Stuhlmacher, Peter (Ed.): Das Evangelium und die Evangelien. 1983. *Volume 28.*
Sung, Chong-Hyon: Vergebung der Sünden. 1993. *Volume II/57.*
Tajra, Harry W.: The Trial of St. Paul. 1989. *Volume II/35.*
– The Martyrdom of St. Paul. 1994. *Volume II/67.*
Theissen, Gerd: Studien zur Soziologie des Urchristentums. 1979, [3]1989. *Volume 19.*
Thornton, Claus-Jürgen: Der Zeuge des Zeugen. 1991. *Volume 56.*
Twelftree, Graham: Jesus the Exorcist. 1993. *Volume II/54.*
Visotzky, Burton L.: Fathers of the World. 1995. *Volume 80.*
Wagener, Ulrike: Die Ordnung des ›Hauses Gottes‹. 1994. *Volume II/65.*
Wedderburn, A. J. M.: Baptism and Resurrection. 1987. *Volume 44.*
Wegner, Uwe: Der Hauptmann von Kafarnaum. 1985. *Volume II/14.*
Welck, Christian: Erzählte ›Zeichen‹. 1994. *Volume II/69.*
Wilson, Walter T.: Love without Pretense. 1991. *Volume II/46.*
Wolff, Christian: see *Holtz.*
Zimmermann, Alfred E.: Die urchristlichen Lehrer. 1984, [2]1988. *Volume II/12.*

For a complete catalogue please write to the publisher
J. C. B. Mohr (Paul Siebeck), P. O. Box 2040, D-72010 Tübingen.